John Cooke

The Preacher's Assistant

Containing a series of the texts of sermons and discourses published either singly or in volumes, by divines of the Church of England. Vol. 2

John Cooke

The Preacher's Assistant
Containing a series of the texts of sermons and discourses published either singly or in volumes, by divines of the Church of England. Vol. 2

ISBN/EAN: 9783337114039

Printed in Europe, USA, Canada, Australia, Japan

Cover: Foto ©Lupo / pixelio.de

More available books at **www.hansebooks.com**

AN HISTORICAL REGISTER OF ALL THE AUTHORS

In the SERIES alphabetically difposed,
WITH
Their TITLES, DEGREES, and PREFERMENTS,

EXHIBITING IN
Chronological Order a fuccinct View of their feveral Works,
As alfo a Reference, for the Ufe of
YOUNG STUDENTS IN DIVINITY,
To moft Public LIBRARIES where they are to be found.

TO WHICH ARE ADDED
An APPENDIX to each VOLUME,
An INDEX of OCCASIONAL Sermons mentioned in the SERIES,
AND
Two LISTS of the ARCH-BISHOPS and BISHOPS of ENGLAND and IRELAND from the Year 1660 to the prefent Time,

BY JOHN COOKE, M.A.
LATE CHAPLAIN OF CHRIST-CHURCH, OXFORD,
AND RECTOR OF WENTNOR, SALOP.

Σπούδασον σεαυτὸν δόκιμον παρατῆσαι τῷ Θιῷ, ἐργάτlw ἀνεπαίχωτον, ὀρθοτομοῦντα τὸν λόγον τῆς ἀληθείας. St. Pauli II. Epift. ad Tim.

VOL. II.

OXFORD:
Printed for the EDITOR, at the Clarendon-Prefs — and Sold by Meff. FLETCHERS, DANIEL PRINCE and J. COOKE, R. BLISS, and S. ARNOLD, *Oxford* — Meff. MERRILLS and DEIGHTON, *Cambridge* — and by moft of the Bookfellers in *London*.
M DCC LXXXIII.

AN
HISTORICAL REGISTER
OF
AUTHORS, &c. in the SERIES.

N.B. The AUTHORS, having this additional Mark ‡ prefixed, came too late to be inserted in the *first*, and are only to be found in the *second* Volume.

ABBOT Henry, B.A. Lecturer of St. John Baptist, Bristol.
 Pf. cxxxiii. 1. 8° 1713. *Bristol.* County-Feast.
ABBOT Henry,^a M.A. Chaplain to Lord Bathurst.
 Pf. lxxxi. 1,2. 8° 1724. Muf. f. *Gloucester.* The Use and Benefit of Church-musick towards quickening our Devotion.
ABBOT Robert, V. of Cranbrook, Kent.
 * Prov. iv. 19. 12° 1662. A Vol. entitled the Young man's warning-Piece.
ABDY Stothard, M.A. Arch-Deacon of Essex.
 * Lam. iv. 9. 4° 1759. Before the Sons of the Clergy.
 * Ecclef. ix. 16. 4° 1763. School-Feast. At *Felsted.*
 * Exod. xviii. 19. 4° 1773. Assize.
ABERNETHY *John*, M.A.
 Pf. xx. 6. 8° 1715. Accession.
 Dan. xii. 4. 8° 172 Before Synod.
 1 Cor. iii. 3. 4° 1724. *Belfast.* Fast on account of Divisions.
 Difc. in 2 Vol. 8° 1743. Concerning the Being and natural Perfections of God. *Fed. Bal. Wadb. Worc.* Oxon. *Pub. L.* Camb.

a *Q.* The same.

Sermons

Sermons in 2 Vol. 8° 1748. and Vol. 3. 4. 8° 1751. On various Subjects. *Bod. Bal.* Oxon. *Pub. L. Queen's.* Camb. *Dr. W's. L.* London.

Tracts and Sermons in 8° 1751. *Queen's.* Camb.

ACRES Joseph,   V. of Blewberry, Berks.
     Pſ. lxxviii. 4. 8° 1715. The true Method of propagating Religion and Loyalty. *Bod. Sion.*
     Pſ. cxxvi. 5, 6. 8° 1715. Th. for Acceſſ. Glad Tidings to G. Britain.
     Pſ. cxi. 4. 8° 1715. Acceſſ. G. Brit. Jubilee; or the joyful Day.
     Prov. xiv. 34. 8° 1715. 2 ſ.
     Prov. xxxi. 13. 8° 1715. Ch. ſ.
     * Matt. xxv. 35, 36. 8° 1728. Open. a Work-houſe.

ACTON *Samuel*.
     * Jer. viii. 8. 8° 1714. Folly of wiſe Scepticks.
     * Luke xiv. 23. 8° 1714. Goſpel-Compulſion.
     * Epheſ. iv. 5. 8° 1714. Salvation by Grace.
     * John xix. 3. 8° 1717. Sacrament.

ADAM *Dean*.
     * - - - - 1766. Fun. ſ.

ADAM Thomas,   R. of Wintringham, Lincolnſ.
     * Rev. iii. 18. 8° 1772. Chriſt's Riches. *Queen's.* Camb.
     * Matt. xvi. 6. 8° 1776. Peter's Confeſſion.
     * Evangelical Sermons in 8° 1781.

ADAMS George, M. A.
     * Sermons and Diſſertations in 8° 1752. An Expoſition of some Articles in Religion.

ADAMS John, DD. R. of St. Alban Woodſtreet, then of St. Bartholomew, Chap. in Ord. and Prov. of King's Coll. Camb.
     Iſai. xxxii. 17. 4° 1695. *Brit. M.*
     Pſ. xxxiii. 1. 4° 1695. Th. *All S. Magd.* Oxon. *Trin.* Camb. *Sion.*
     Dan. iii. 28. 4° 1696. Nov. 5. *Jeſ. Magd.* Oxon. *Sion.*
     Pſ. lxvi. 16. 4° 1700. On a Quaker's Recantation. *Sion.*
     Matt. xxv. 30. 4° 1702. Eton Sch Feaſt. *St. John's.* Crmb.
     Acts xxviii. 5, 6. 4° 1705. *Jeſ. Worc.* Oxon. *Trin. Queen's.* Cam. *Sion.*
     Hoſea xi. 9. 4° 1707. Bef. Queen. *Univ. Or. Magd.* Oxon. *Trin. St. John's. Queen's.* Camb.
     John vi 67, 68. 4° 1707. Lent. *Univ. Magd. Oriel.* Oxon. *Trin. St. John's. Queen's.* Camb.
     Rev. ii. 10. 4° 1708. Fun. of Rev. Mr. Staynoe. *Oriel. Worc. Magd.* Oxon. *Trin. St. John's. Queen's.* Camb. *Sion.*
     Jer. iii. 15. 4° 1708. Conſ. Bp.   *Univ. Magd. Worc.* Oxon. *Trin. St. John's,* Camb. *Sion.*
     Pſ. v. 11. 4° 1709. Th. *Linc. Ox. Trin. St. John's.* Camb. *Eton.*
     Iſai xlix. 23. 4° 1710. Acceſſ. b. Com. *Bod. Linc.* Oxon. *Sion.*
     John xxi. 17. 4° 1710. Conſ. Bp.   *Magd. Jeſ.* Oxon.
     Iſai. lvii. 15. 4° 1712. *Linc.* Oxon.
     Job xiii. 6. 4° 17

ADAMS Rice, M.A. R. of Donhead St. Mary, Wilts, and Preb. of Sarum.
　　Prov. x. 9. 8° 1708. V. ſ. The Excellency of Wiſdom &c. *Univ. Linc.* Oxon. *Sion.*
　　* Sermons in 8° 1736.
ADAMS Richard, M.A. Fell. of Braze-noſe Coll. Oxon.
　　* Matt. xxv. 41. 4° 1676. m. e. G. p. 454. Hell.
　　Col. iii. 20, 21. 4° 1676. ſ. m. e. C. p. 390. The Duties of Parents and Child. *Bod.*
　　1 Tim. ii. 15. 4° 1683. c. m. e. p. 633. How child-bearing Women ought to be encouraged.
　　Luke xvi. 31. 4° 1690. c. m. e. p. 214.
　　2 Cor. v. 1. 4° 1690. The earthly and Heavenly Building opened.
ADAMS Samuel, D.D. R. of Alveſcot, Oxon.
　　Rom. 13. 1. } 8° 1716. on Rebellion.
　　1 Cor 13. 1. }
ADAMS Thomas
　　* Rev. xxii. 12. fo. 1660.
ADAMS William, M.A. late Stud. of Ch. Ch. Oxon. and R. of Staunton upon Wye, Herefordſ.
　　15 Occaſ. Sermons in 8° 1716. *Magd. Mert. Linc. Worc.* Oxon.
ADAMS William, D.D. Maſter of Pemb. Coll. Oxon. and Chancellor of Landaff.
　　Luke ix. 55, 56. 4° 1741. Nov. 5. Falſe Zeal reproved.
　　Pſ. cxxxii. 6, 7. 4° 1742. Faſt. Nov. 10. The Love of our Country explained.
　　Gal. vi. 9. 4° 1749. *Salop.* Infirm. Perſeverance in well-doing.
　　* Sermons in 8° 1777. *Pemb.* Oxon.
ADAMSON John, M.A. Preb. of Linc. and R. of Burton Coggles, Linc.
　　Matt. xxi. 13. 4° 1698. Conſ. Ch. The Duty of daily frequenting the publick Service of the Church.
　　Rev. xiv. 13. 8° 1707. Fun. *Linc.* Oxon.
ADAMTHWAITE John, M.A. late of Queen's Coll. Oxon.
　　* 1 Cor. xiii. 13. 4° 1771. Ch. ſ. *Birmingham.*
　　* John xv. 17. 4° 1778. Soc. ſ. *Birmingham.* Nature and Principles of Society conſidered.
ADDERLEY Thomas, A.B. of St. John's Coll. Oxon. Chaplain to Sir Edw. Boughton, Warwickſhire.
　　Pſ. 122. 6. 4° 1676. The Care of the Peace of the Church, the Duty of every Chriſtian. *Trin.* Camb.
ADDINTON Stephen, of Harborough.
　　* - - - - - - - -
ADDISON Anthony, V. of St. Helen's, Abingdon, Berks.
　　Pſ. lxviii. 28. 4° 1704. Oxon. Th. *Bod.*
ADEE Herbert, V. of Friſton and Snape, Suffolk.
　　1 Cor. ii. 14. 8° 1712.
ADEE Nicholas, V. of Rodborne Cheny, Wilts.
　　Luke xx. 14. 4° 1685. V. ſ. A Plot for a Crown. *Sion.*

ADEY William, Cur. of Lanchaster, Durham.
  * Sermons in 2 Vol. 8° 1760.
  * 16 in 8° 1755. on pract. Subjects.
ADIS Henry, (a Free Willer)
  * 2 Chron. xxxii. 25. 4° 1660. Fanatack's Mite cast in the King's Treasury. *Brit. M.*
ADKIN Lancaster, M.A. at Belaugh and Scotto, Norf.
  * Judges xx. 26. 8° 1782. Fast. s.
AGAR William, Chaplain to the 20th Reg. of Foot, and R. of South Kelsey &c. Linc.
  * 14 Sermons in 8° 1759. Military Devotion &c. *Bod. Sion.*
AGATE William, Lect. of St. Lawrence Jewry, Lond.
  Jer. v. 3. 4° 1750. A Persuasive to Repentance.
  * 11 Chron. xx. 3, 4. 8° 1758. Fast.
AICKIN Joseph, Clerk.
  Act. ix. 6. 12° 1705. *Dublin.* Conformity of the human Will to the divine.
AIRES Joseph, V. of Blewbery, Berks.
  * Prov. xiv. 34. 8° 1715. 2 s. Nation. Sins, and the Causes of them.
AITKEN William, one of the Ministers of South-Leith.
  * 10 Sermons. in   17
ALANSON. Edward, M.A. R. of Clifton-Reyns & Hardmead, Bucks.
  Heb. vi. 10. 4° 1723. *Liverpool.* Cl. s.
  Job. xxvii. 5, 6. 4° 1734. V. s. The man of Integrity's Character with the Advantageousness of it.
ALCHORNE William, B.D. R. of High Ongar, Essex.
  Col. iii. 4. 4° 1674. Fun.
ALCOCK Thomas, M.A. late of Braz-nose Coll. Oxon.
  * Heb. vi. 16. The Nature and Obligation of Oaths. *Exon. Oxon.*
  * 1 Tim. i. 8, 9. Ass. s.
  * Luke xiii. 2–5. 8° 1756. Fast. Earthquake at Lisbon. *Bod. Exon.*
ALDRED Jeremiah
  Ps. xviii. 48, 49. 8° 1716. Th. s.
ALDRICH Charles, DD.
  Exod. xxxiii. 19. 4½ 1723. Th. After the Plague. *Worc. Oxon.*
ALDRIDGE William
  * John. v. 7. 8° 1777. Doctrine of the Trinity.
ALEXANDER John
  * Eccles. ix. 10. 4° 1766. Fun. s. composed by the Author the Day preceeding his Death.
ALGOOD Major, R. of Symonbourn, Northumb.
  ------ 4° 1684. Fun. of Rev. Geo. Ritchbell.
ALLAN James, Minister at Eymouth.
  * ———————— Synod.
ALLANSON
  * John xiii. 34 8° 1770. Ass. *York.*
ALLASON John, DD. Fell. of Queen's Coll. Oxon. & Chaplain to Lord Barnard
  2 Sam. xviii. 3. 4° 1713. Ass. s.   *ALLEINE*

ALLEINE Joseph
   * Remains in 8°. 1764.
ALLEINE Richard
   Prov. xxviii. 14. 8° 1674. *Bod.*
   1 John v. 4. 8° 1676. Sev. f. The world conquered. *Bod.*
ALLEN Fifield, D.D. (late Student of Ch. Ch. Oxon.) Arch-Deacon of Middlesex.
   Pf. xxxii. 9 4° 1739. Aff. f. *Queen's.* Camb.
   2 Kings viii. 11, 12. 4° 1751. Jan. 30. *All S.* Ox. *Queen's.* Cam.
ALLEN John, M.A. Fell. of Trin. Coll. Camb. and Chapl. to the Bishop of Chester.
   Levit. xix. 12. 4° 1682. Aff. f. Of Perjury. *Magd.* Oxon. *Queen's.* Camb.
ALLEN John, M.A. (late Fell. of Mert. Coll. Oxon.) R. of Eastwick, Herts.
   Pf. cxxxiii. 1. 8° 1725. Aff. f.
   Tit. ii. 15. 4° 1740. Conf. Bp. Gilbert. *Queen's.* Camb.
ALLEN John, M.D.
   2 Cor. v. 1. 8° 1740. Fun. f.
   John xii. 3-8. 8° 1741. Ch. Sch. The Ends of Providence in appointing the poor &c.
   Acts xiii. 36. 8° 1744. Fun. of John Nicholas, Esq.
   * Pf. ciii. 13-18. 8° 1746. Fun.
   * Prov. xxix. 1. 8° 1750. Faft. On Earthquake.
   * 2 Cor. i. 6. 8° 1752. Fun. *Rev. Obad. Hughes,* DD.
   * Gen. xix. 14. 8° 1756. Faft. On Earthquake.
ALLEN John, M. A. Vice Principal of St. Mary Magd. Hall, Oxon.
   * Rom. viii. 16. 8° 1758. Mond. W. week. The twofold Evidence of Adoption.
   * Ecclef. vii. 16. 8° 1759. 2 f. The Weakness & Wickedness of being righteous over much—the Folly of affected Wisdom, and the Ruin confiquent upon both.
   * James ii. 14. 8° 1761. No Acceptance with God by Faith only. *Queen's.* Camb.
   * 1 Cor. ix. 27. 8° 1769. The Enthusiast's Notion of Election to eternal Life disproved.
   * Isai. viii. 9, 10. 8° 1773. Associations ag. the established Church indefensible. *Queen's.* Camb.
ALLEN Joseph, M.A. Master of the Grammar Sch. Chester.
   * 1 Cor. xv. 33. 8° 1712. 2. f. Danger of evil Communications.
ALLEN Joshua, R. of St. Bride's, Pembrokes. & late Chaplain to Sir Tho. Robinson.
   Jam. ii. 10. 1° 1730. Uniform & Sincere Obedience our indispenfable Duty.
   26 Sermons in 8° 1751. On the most important Subjects of the Xn. Religion.
ALLEN Richard, Pastor of the Church at Henfield, Suffex.
   Ezra. vii. 27. 4° 1675.
   Phil. i. 21. 4° 16   Fun. f.
   * Deut. xxxiv. 5-8. 4° 1702. Royal Fun.

ALLEN Robert
 * Difcourfes in 8° 1662.
ALLEN Thomas
 * 1 Pet. v. 1–4. 8° 1719. An Expedient to make the Church of England the moſt flouriſhing Church in the world.
ALLEN Thomas, ª R. of Kettering, Northampton.
 Rom. x. 9, 10. 8° 1744. Bef. Criminals in Newgate.
ALLEN William, DD. V. of Bridgewater. Somerſetſ.
 Aƈts ii. 27. 4° 1697. Eaſter. A praƈtical Improvement of the Articles of Xt's Defcent into Hell, and rifing again from the dead.
ALLEN William, Cur. of Lambeth.
 * Exod xx. 16. 8° 1743 Aſſ. at Kingſton.
ALLESTREE Charles, M. A. V. of Daventry, Northamptonſ.
 Judges v. 31. 4° 1685. Oxon. *Sion.*
 Num. xxiii. 10. 4° 1695. Royal Fun. The Defire of all men. *Cb. Cb. Oriel.* Oxon.
ALLESTREE Richard, S. T. P. R. Oxon. Prov. of Eton Coll. and Chaplain in Ord.
 * Luke xi 34. 4° 1666. Oxon.
 40 Sermons in 2 vol. fo. 1684. Oxon. *Bod. Cb. Cb. All S. New. C. Univ. Queen's, Pemb. King's, Queen's.* Camb. *Brit. M.*
ALLESTREE Thomas, M. A. R. of Aſhaw, Warwickſ.
 A Funeral Hankerchief, to which are added 3 f. in 8° 1691. *Trin.* Camb.
ALLET Thomas
 2 Sam. xii. 23. 8° 1720. Fun. of Hen. Clements, Bookfeller London. The Xtian's Support under Lofs of Friends, *Worc.* Oxon. *Sion.*
ALLEYNE John, B. D. (late of Eman. Coll. Camb.) R. of Loughborough, Leiceſterſ. and Preb. of Lincoln.
 Epheſ. iv. 11, 12, 13. 4° 1701. *Camb.* V. f. Epifcopacy the great Bond of Union. *Jeſ.* Camb. *Eton.*
 Rom. xv. 5, 6. 4° 1707. *Camb.* Aſſize. Unanimity in the Truth a neceſſary Duty, with the means of obtaining it. *All S.* Oxon. *Trin.* Camb.
ALLEYNE Richard
 Col. ii. 8. - - - - -
ALLINGTON John, R. of Uppingham, and V. of Leamington Haſtang. Warwickſ.
 * 2 Sam. xix. 9, 10. 12° 1660. Faſt. f. } *Trin.* Camb.
 * Pſ. cxviii. 22, 23. 12° 1660. Th. f. }
 Aƈts viii. 1. 4° 1672. Jan. 30. *Trin. St. John's.* Camb.
 John iv. 23. 4° 1676. Vifit. The reformed Samaritan ; or the Worſhip of Godly the Meafures of Spirit and Truth. *Bod. Pub. L.* and *Trin.* Camb.
ALLISON Francis, DD. Vice Prov. of the Coll. at Philadelphia.
 * Epheſ. iv. 1–7. 12° 1758. Bef. Synod.
ALSOP
   1661. Jan. 30. b. C.
    a ℞ The fame.

ALSOP George, M. A. Chapl. to Sir Robert Robinson.
    Matt. xxii. 11. 4° 1679. b. the Admin. of the H. Sac. *Bod.*
ALSOP Nathaniel, B. D. R. of Church-Langton, Leicesterſ.
    Exod. xx. 12. 4° 1682. Aſſize. *Worc.* Oxon. *Brit. M.*
ALSOP Nathaniel
    Zeph. i. 8. 4° 1683. c. m. e. p. 589. The Sinfulneſs of ſtrange Apparel.
    Epheſ. iii. 19. 4° 1690. c m. e. p. 200. The Fulneſs of God. *Bod.*
ALSOP Vincent, Miniſter of the Goſpel.
    * Pſ. cxxi. 4. 4° 1696. On his Majeſty's wonderful Deliverance from Aſſaſſination &c. *Clare-Hall.* Camb.
    * Iſai. i. 6. 12° 1698. Ref. Manners.
    * Gen. xviii. 32. 4° 1701. Faſt. ſ.
ALTHAM Roger, DD. R. of St. Botolph, Preb. of St. Paul's, and Arch-Deacon of Middleſex.
    Amos v. 24. 4° 1702. Elect. Lord Mayor. The pious and juſt Magiſtrate. *Jeſ.* Camb.
    Dan. ix. 7. 4° 1703. Jan. 30. *Ch. Ch. St. John's.* Oxon. *Jeſ.* Camb.
    2 Tim. ii. 15. 4° 1705. C. ad Coll. *Sion. Ch. Ch.* Oxon. *Trin.* Camb. *Sion.*
    Gal. vi. 10. 4° 1706. Before the Sons of the Clergy. Xtian Charity. *Ch. Ch. All S. Wadh.* Oxon.
    1 Pet. iii. 10, 11. 4° 1712. Faſt. b. Commons. *Bod. Linc.* Oxon. *Trin. St. John's.* Camb. *Sion.*
    Pſ. xcvi. 9. 4° 1728. Opening a Church. Relative & inherent Holineſs both required to the true Worſhip of God.
    Sermons in 2 vol. 8° 1732. On ſeveral Occaſions. *Wadh.* Oxon.
ALTON
    * Mark iv. 9. 8° 1767. On beautifying a Church.
AMBROSE Iſaac
    Epheſ. vi. 12. 4° 1662. War with Devils, Miniſtration of, and Communion with Angels.
AMORY Thomas, DD.
    * John viii. 12. 8° 1735. Aſſociation ſ.
    Phil. i. 20. 1° 1738. Fun ſ.
    * Tit. ii. 1. 8° 1741. Ord. ſ.
    * 2 Cor. iv. 5. 8° 1742. 2 ſ. Self-dedication to God.
    2 Chron. x. 5–13. 8° 1745. Faſt. ſ.
    * 4 Sermons in 8° 1747. On Daily Devotion.
    8 Sermons in 8° 1748. On a general ſut. Judgm. *Queen's.* Camb.
    * 8 Sermons in 8° 1753. On Contentment, the Reaſonableneſs of Religion and the Advantages of Prayer. *Queen's.* Camb. *Br. M.*
    * Heb. x. 24. ⎱ 8° 1765. Ord. ſ.
    * 2 Tim. ii. 15. ⎰
    * Heb. xi. 13. 8° 1766. Fun. of Dr. *Samuel Chandler. Queen's.* Camb.
    * 22 Sermons in 8° 1766. On various Subjects. ⎱ *Queens.* Camb.
    * 20 Sermons in 8° 1775. ⎰ *Dr. W's. L.* Lon.

B   * John

* John i. 47. 8° 1768. N. B. This Sermon was publifhed by him, but written by his Uncle.

ANDERSON Henry, M. A. V. of Kingfumbowrn, Hants.
  Pf. lxxiii. 25. 4° 1685. May 29. *Sion.*

ANDERSON *James*, M. A.
  Ezra. iv. 15. 8° 1714. Jan. 30. *Sion. Brit. M.*
* Jude iii. 8° 1720.
  Pf. cxlvi. 7. 8° 1737. b. Prifoners for Debts.

ANDERSON William, Chapl. to the Hon. united Company trading to the Eaft Indies.
  4 Sermons in 8° 1708. preached at Fort-Will. Bengal. *Brit. M.*

ANDREW Tho, V. of Burbage, Wilts.
  Prov. iv. 10–14. 8° 1712.
  John i. 14. 8° 1731. Xtmas-day. *Queen's.* Camb.

ANDREWES Thomas[a], M. A. Of Trin. Coll. Camb.
  1 Pet. ii. 17. 4° 1717. Acceffion.
  Rom. xiv. 19. 8° 1717. Election Lord Mayor. The things which make for Peace.

ANDREWS John, M. A. V. of Farningham.
  1 Pet. iv. 11. 8° 1744. V. f. Of fpeaking as the Oracles of God:

ANDREWS Thomas[a], M. A. Fell. of Trin. Coll. Camb.
  Matt. v. 20. 8° 1717. *Trin.* Camb.

ANGIER *John*
  * Sermons in 8° 1662. Help to better Hearts.

ANGUISH Thomas, M. A. V. of St. Nicholas, Deptford. Kent.
  Tit. iii. 1. 8° 1732. Acceffion.
  Acts xxiv. 2, 3. 4° 1745. Rebellion. Allegiance and Support, a Debt of Gratitude to his Majefty.
  Luke xiii. 4, 5. 8° 1756. Faft. On the Earthquake.

ANNAND William, DD. Of Univ. Coll. Oxon. Dean of Edinburgh.
  Hofea xiv. 2. 4° 1661. 2 f. In defence of the Liturgy.

ANNESLEY *Samuel*, DD.
  Acts xxiv. 16. 4° 1667. m. e. C. p. 1. How we may be confcientious. *Ch. Ch.* Oxon. *Trin.* Camb.
  Zech. i. 5, 6. 4° 1673. Fun. *St. John's.* Camb.
  Suppliment to the morning Exercife at Cripplegate. 4° 1674. *Bod. Ch. Ch. N. Coll. Madg.* Oxon. *Trin.* Camb.
  Matt. xxii. 37, 38. 4° 1674. f. m. e. C. p. 1. How we may love God. *Bod.*
  Heb. x. 14. 4° 1675. m. e. P. p. 677. Of Indulgences.
  * Heb. viii. 6. 4° 1676. m. e. G. p. 1. 68. The Covenant of Grace. Continuation of the Morn. Exercife. 4° 1683. *Bod.*
  Ecclef. vi. 11, 12. 4° 1683. c. m. e. p. 1. How Vanity is abated &c.
  Matt. xi. 9. 4° 1690. Cafuiftical morning Exercife. p. 1.

A N O N Y M O U S.

* Houfe of Mourning, or funeral Difcourfes in fo. 1660.
* Collection of Farwell-Sermons in 4° 1663.

a R. The fame.

Several Difcourfes tending to promote Peace and Holinefs among Chriftians. To which are added 3 other diftinct Sermons 8° 1685

Sermons at Boyle's Lecture from 1691, to 1732, in 3 Vol. fo. 1739. *New Coll. J.f. St. John's, Queen's, Magd.* Oxon. *Cl. Hall. Trin. King's.* Camb.

* 4 Plain Difcourfes in 12° 1700 by a Prefbyter of the Ch. of Eng.

* Mercurius Theologicus, containing Mr. Harris's 8 S. & Dr. Blackall's 8 S. at Boyle's Lecture 4° 1701. *Ch. Ch.* Oxon.

* 3 Difcourfes in 12° 1710. An infallable way to Contentment.

A Treatife of the three Evils of the laft Times 8° 1711. [John Hildrop, DD.]

4 Sermons upon moft important Subjects, or Catechetical Lectures on Matt. xxviii. 19. p. 1. 21,39. and on Luke xviii. 15,16,17. p. 59. 8° 1715

* Eaftcheap Lectures in 2 Vol. 12° 1724.

* 12 Sermmons in 8° 1729. preaced at Coward's Lecture.

* Limeftreet Sermons (26) in 2 Vol. 8° 1732. Entitled a Defence of fome important Doctrines by feveral eminent Diffenters.

* Sermons againfts Popery in 2 Vol. 1735. *Braz. N.* Oxon. *Queen's.* Camb.

* Difcourfes on Conjugal Duty in 2 Vol. 12° 1740.

* 7 Sermons in 8° 1743. Entitled the fhameful Sin, or Cautions againft Whoring, & Directions about Marrying.

Three Difcourfes on Ifai. liii. 9. p. 11. Ifai. xi. 6-9. p. 29. Heb. ii. 4. p. 41. in 8° 1750.

* Berryftreet Sermons (52) in 2 Vol. 8° 1757. A Collection of Difcourfes on the principal Heads of the Chriftian Religion.

* 4 Sermons in 8° 1768. On Humanity and Beneficence. [*Kippis Andrew*, DD.]

* Family Difcourfes in 12° 1768, by a Country-Gentleman.

* 7 Sermons in 12° 1770, by a Lady.

* 2 Difcourfes in 8° 1771. On the Sufficiency of the Scriptures, and the Right of private Judgment, and on the Doctrine of the Trinity, by a Friend to Truth.

* Sermons in 12° 1772. To the Rich and Studious by a Phyfician, [Dr. Fothergill.]

* Sentimental Sermons in 8° 1777.

* The Scotch-Preacher. A Collection of Sermons by fome of the moft eminent Clergymen of Scotland in 12° 3 Vol. 1. Vol. 1775. 2 Vol. 1776. 3 Vol. 1779.

*Gen. ii. 1. 8° 1750. Diff. on the Trinity. *Bod.* Oxon. *Queen's.* Camb.

—— xxii. 1-12. 1735.

*—— xxxv. 2, 3. 12° 1693. The Worfhip of God in private Houfes. *Bod.*

*—— xxxviii. 23. 12° 1773. Leap Year-Lectures.

*—— xlix. 10 &c. 1758. Diff.

‡* —— 14-18. 8° 16. Afs or the Serpent. *Brit. M.*

*—— 18. 4° 1688. [C. T.]

*Exod.

*Exod. ix. 3. 8° 1747. Diftemper among the Cattle.
* ——— 3, 6. 8° 1747.
* ——— xii. 26, 27. 8° 1672. (and 1 Pet. iii. 21.) 2 f. *Bod.*
* ——— 51. 8° 1672. Acc. f.
* ——— xv. 9, 10. 4° 1759. Faft.
* ——— xx. 15. 8° 1779. Evafion of Payments due to the State on account of Cuftoms and Excife.
Numb. xi. 4-6. 4° 1690. *Ch. Ch.* Oxon. [T. G. DD.]
* ——— xvi. 1-4. 8° 1683 On the Death of Algernon Sidney, Efq; beheaded on Tower-Hill.
* ——— xxiii. 23. 4° 1694. Nov. 5. [W. R.]
Deut xvii. 15. 8° 1515. Th. Camb.
* ——— xxiii. 1. 12° 1773. Faft.
*Joshua i. 8. 8° 1780. The Excellency of the Sacred Writers. For the Benefit of a Society for diftributing Bibles among his Majefty's Forces by Sea and Land. [Clericus.]
* ——— xxiv. 15. 12° 1722. The regular Method of governing a Family. (and Eccl. iii. 1.
* ——————— 15. 8° 1735. Family Religion. *Brit. M.*
* Judges v. 23. 4° 1680. [J. L.]
——— xix. 30. 8° 1708. Jan. 30. *Worc.* Oxon. *Eton.*
* 1 Sam. ii. 3. 8° 1760. Ref. Manners.
* ——— xi. 14, 15. 8° 1708. [J. C.]
* ——— xii. 23, 24, 40. *Ch. Ch.* Oxon.
* ——— xxiv. 5. 4° 1675. Mofes and Aaron. *Ch. Ch.* Oxon.
* 2 Sam. i. 5-18. 8° 1708. [Loyal Layman]
* ——— iii. 38. 8° 1660. Fun. f.
——— xii. 5. 4° 1689. Fun. f.
* ——— xviii. 33. 8° 1660. Abfalom's unnatural Rebellion.
* ——— xx. 19. 4° 1767. At a Quaker's Yearly-meeting.
——— xxi. 15-17. 4° 1691. Monthly Faft. *Bod.*
* ——— xxiv. 12-15. 8° 1753. Royal Folly, or David's Sin in numbering the People, by a Fell. of St. John's Coll. Oxon. *St. John's, All S.* Oxon.
1 Kings i. 5. 8° 169 *Bod.*
* ——— xvi. 30. 8° 1714. Fun. Ahab's Evil. *Ch. Ch.*. Oxon.
——— xxi. 12, 13. 4° 1700. or Works. 8° 1716. 1. p. 270. Jan. 30. [Edm. Hickeringill.]
* 2 Kings iv 38. 8° 1759. Commemor. of Founder at All Soul's Coll. Oxon. *All S. Worc. Bal.* Oxon. *Queen's.* Camb. [Benjamin Buckler, DD.]
* ——— vii. 2. 8° 1732. On the wilful Murders of R. Smith on the Bodies of his Wife and Child through a Diftruft of Providence.
* ——— xi. xiv. 8° 1660. Athaliahs Treafon.
* 2 Chron. vii. 14. 8° 1779. Faft.
* ——— xx. 4. 8° 1781. Faft.
*Ruth iii. 14. 12° 1773. Leap-Year Lecture.
Ezra vi. 10. 4° 1674. Godlinefs no Friend to Rebellion. *Brit. M.*

*Job.

* Job ii. 1. 4° 1685.
—— ii. 10. 12° 1736. Againſt Self-murder. [Bp. Z Pearce.]
*—— v. 6. 12° 1677. On the Period of human Life.
*—— xiv. 1, 2. 8° 1772. Univerſal Funeral Sermon.
———— 8. 8° 1708. Fun. ſ. by a Preſbyter of the Ch. of England.
*—— xix. 25, 26. 8° 1761 An Eſſay. [J. W.]
*—— xxxi. 1. 12° 1773. Leap-Year Lecture.
*—— xxxiv. 30. 8° 1732. Preached at Lincoln's-Inn. by a Layman. [Gordon.]
* Pſalm. xvi. 3. 8° 1758. 2 Diſc. Demonſtrations of Religion and Virtue.
—— xxiii. 4. 4° 1691. [Shadrach Cooke.]
—— xxxvii. 12. 4° 1680. The Plotter's Doom. *Eton. Trin.* Camb.
*———— 37. 8° 1703. Fun. ſ. [S. S.]
—— xlii. 11. 4° 1683. c m. e. p. 925.
—— lvii. 9. 8° 1723. Muſick. *All S.* Oxon.
—— lxii. 1–4. 8° 1690. Faſt. June 18.
———— 12. 8° 1740. Eternal Miſery &c.
*—— lxviii. 30. 8° 1712. By a divine of the Church of England. *Ch. Ch. Wadh.* Oxon.
*—— lxxiii. 15. 8° 1711. Providence vindicated. *Ch. Ch.* Oxon.
*—— lxxvii. 14. 4° 1689. Th. ſ. [T. P.] *Ch. Ch.* Oxon
*—— lxxix. 8. 4° 1686. Murder King Charles 1ſt. *Ch. Ch.* Oxon.
—— lxxxiii. 3, 4. 4° 1678. Nov. 5. [Bp. John Williams] *Bod.*
—— lxxxv. 1. 4° 1689. Th. ſ. [B. Jenk.] *Cl. Hall.* Camb.
*—— xc. 9. 8° 1745. A ſeaſonable Conſideration on the Year's end.
*—— xci. 5, 6. 8° 1712. On a general Sickneſs in England.
*—— xciv. 20. 4° 1664 Aſſ. ſ.
—— cxviii. 1. 8° 1723. On the late Conſpiracy.
*———— 22, 23. 4° 1660. A Parrallel between David, Chriſt and King Charles 1ſt. in their Humiliation and Exaltation.
———— 24. 4° 1670. *Bod.*
—— cxxxvi. 23. 8° 1715. Auguſt 1. [Sam. Bolde.]
*—— cxlviii. 8. 8° 1703. Faſt. After a Storm. [D. P.]
—— cxcv. 5. 4° 1752. On Painting. *In Æd. Walpolian.* p. 99.
* Prov. iii. 3, 4. 8° 1664. Whoredom unmaſked.
*—— xii. 10. 12° 1760. Compaſſion to Animals.
*———— 4° 1761. 2 ſ. Compaſſion to Animals.
*—— xiv. 34. 8° 1779. A Diſcourſe.
*—— xviii. 22. 8° 1752.
*—— xxiv. 21. 8° 1780. Faſt. ſ.
*—— xxi. 21, 22. 8° 1732. Nov. 5.
*—— xxx. 7–10. 4° 1768. Fun. Diſcourſe. By a Quaker. *Briſtol.*
———— 31. 4° 1684. Jan. 30. 3 ſ. Againſt Non-reſiſtance. *Bod.*
*—— xxxi. 10. V. Diſc. on Conj. Duty. v. 2. 309. [W. L.]
‡*———— 14. 8° 1716. *Brit. M.*
Eccleſ. iii. 1. 12° 1732. The Way of Living. [and Joſh. 24. 25.]
*———— 4. 4° 1716. On Ridicule.
* Eccleſ.

*—— iii. 4. 12°1720. The Reasonableness of Observing. Jan. 30. In Scotland as well as in England.

—— vii. 1. 4° 1695. By a Non-juror.

—— 14. 4° 1695. A Persuasive to Consideration. *Ch. Ch. All S.* Oxon. [Jeremy Collier.]

—— viii. 4. 8° 1713. Jan. 30. Whigs no Christians.

—— x. 20. 8° 1729. Nov. 5. *Eton.*

‡*—— 27. 8° 1707. *Brit. M.*

*—— xii. 7. 4° 1677. Fun. f. [R. J.]

Isai. i. 26. 4° 1662. Oxford Assize.

—— v. 25. 4° 1678. F. Angliæ Speculum. [Bp. Patrick.] *Ch. Ch. C. C. C.* Oxon.

—— vi. 13. 4° 1683. c. m. c. p. 959.

*—— vii. 13–16. 8° 1667. Critical Dissertation.

—— xi. 6–9. 8° 1750. 3 Disc. [and Isai. liii. 9. and Heb. ii. 4.] by a Protestant Divine.

*—— xlvi. 8. 8" 1764. The Use of Reason and Reflection in Religious Matters.

—— liii. 8. 4° 1688. [F. D. or John Higgins.] *Bod.*

—— —— 9. 8° 1750. V. 3. Disc. above.

*—— lviii. 6. 4° 1778. Fast.

—— lix. 1, 2. 8° 1708. Fast. The Sins which withhold good things from us, by a Minister of the Church of England. *Eton.*

*—— lxv. 16. 8° 1667. Rebukes for Sin.

*—— lxvi. 15. 8° 1667. [T. D.]

* Jerem v. 9. 12°1782. Fast.

*—— vi. 30. 4° 1697. On restoring the Coin. By a Minister of the Church of England.

*—— xviii. 7, 8. 4° 1692. On the late Earthquakes &c. by a Rev. Divine. *Bod.*

*Lament. iii. 22. 8° 1756. Fast. On the Earthquake.

*Ezek. viii. 14. 8° 1716. Antient and modern Idolatry parallelled. [by a Lady]

*—— ix 5, 6. 4° 1686. 2 Sund. after Easter. [by H. H. S. J.] *Ch.Ch. Bal.* Oxon.

*—— xxxiii 11. 12°1756. 4 f. New Call to Unconverted.

*Dan. iv. 17. 8°1726. On August 1.

‡*—— xi. 31. 8° 1716. *Brit. M.*

* Hosea x. 2. 4° 1683. On Discovery of the Plot. By a Presbyter of the Church of England. *Worc. Oriel.* Oxon.

* Joel ii. 12. 8°1742. Fast. A warning concerning the War.

*—— xii. 13. 4° 1778. Fast. Dedicated to the Duke of Richmond.

*—— —— 12, 13. 4° 1680. Fast. December 22.

*Amos iii. 3. 8° 1712. Farewell. [John Swynfen.]

*—— iv. 12. 8° 1666. A Welcome to the Plague. [S. S.]

*Jonah iii. 9. 4° 1777. Fast.

Micah vi. 5. 4° 1689. Nov. 5. Advice to the English. Protestans.

Nahum iii 1. 8° 1720. Against Gaming and Stock-jobbing. *Brit. M.*

Ecclesiaf. viii. 10. 8° 1709. Labour in vain. *Univ. Linc.* Oxon.

*Ecclesiaf.

*Ecclesiaſ. x. 27. 8° 1706. On the Union.
* Matth. iv. 3. 4° 1663. On a person offering to cut his Throat. [R. J.]
*—— 21. 8° 1664.
*—— v. 5. 8° 1733. Beauty and Blessedness of a calm and quiet Disposition.
—— vi. 16. 1704. Faſt.
—— 22, 23. 8° 1734. Christian Liberty set forth in 2 Diſc. [and Luke xi. 52.]
—— vii. 1. 1674. A Treatiſe.
*—— x. 16. 4° 1752. A Caution to Free-Masons.
—— xi. 1, 2. 1670. Bcd.
—— xvi. 18. 4° 1687. On St. Peter's-day. [Bp. Patrick.] *Ch.Ch. All S. Magd. Jeſ.* Oxon. *Brit. M.*
*—— xix. 8. 4° 1663. Catholic way. *Jeſ.* Oxon.
—— 29. 8° 1749. A Diſſertation.
*—— xx. 30. 8° 1666. [S. S.]
*—— xxi. 33. 12° 1703. The Duty of Husbandmen.
*—— xxii. 37. 4° 1686. [P. E. a Benedictine Monk.] before their Majeſties at Windſor. *All S.* Oxon.
*—— xxiii. 8. 8° 1774. 2 Diſc. Human Authority in matters of Faith.
—— xxiv. 44. *Eton.*
‡*—— xxvi. 39. 8° :737. *Brit. M.*
*—— xxvii. 21–23. 8° 1753. The candid Determination of the Jews in preferring a Thief and a Robber before Chriſt.
*—— xxviii. 19. 8° 1715. 3 Serm. on Water-baptiſm and the baptiſmal Covenant. [and Luke xviii. 15, 16, 17.]
—— 19. } 8° 1740. 3 Diſc. { pt. 1.
Mark iii. 28, 29. } { pt. 21. Sin againſt the Holy Ghoſt.
—— x. 14. 12° 1737. Infant Baptiſm. [Joſ. Trapp, DD]
—— xii. 41, 42. 8° 1742. 2 ſ. A Perſuaſion to Charity. [Doughty]
* Luke vii. 41. 42. 8° 1734. 3 Diſcourſes.
*———— 41, 42. 8° 1743. Relative Duty of Debtors and Creditors.
—— 7, 47. 8° 1712. Lent. The thankful Penitent. [Edm. Brome.] *Linc.* Oxon. *St. John's.* Camb.
—— ix. 55, 56. 8° 1715. Nov. 5. By a Shropſhire Clergyman.
———— 8° 1722. Farewel. [Sir Rich. Cocks.]
*—— 56. 8° 1778. 2 Faſt. ſ. Laſt War.
' *—— x. 36, 37. 12° 1698. Fun of Tho Firmin. *Jeſ.* Oxon.
*—— 42. 8° 1752.
—— 52. 8° 1734. See above Matt. vi. 22, 23.
—— xii. 1. 4° 1683. Eſſay on Hypocriſy and Phariſaiſm.
—— 57. 8° 1714. (or 8° 1720. p. 1. Reaſon &c.) [Dan. Whitby. DD.] *Queen's,* Camb.
—— xiii. 3–5. or xxiii. 3, 5. 8° 1670. On one found dead in a Pit. *Bod.*
*—— 5. 8° 1756. Faſt. Earthquake.

* Luke

* Luke xvi. 2. 8° 1753. The falſe Accuſers. A Sermon lately preached in a Chapel near St. James, Weſtminſter.
* —— xvi. 5. 8° 1767. At a Quakers Annual Meeting at Briſtol.
—— xviii. 15–17. 8° 1715. p. 59. Of Infant-baptiſm. [and Matt. xxviii. 19.]
* —— xxi. 19. 1732. 3. Diſc. 1 Poſſeſſion of our own Souls. 2 Chriſtian Patience. 3 Directions to attain Happineſs.
‡* —— 26. 8° 1716. *Brit. M.*
—— xxii. 19. 4° 1680. The great Idol of the Maſs overthrow, by a Proteſtant.
John i. 19. 8° 1708. On Predominant Paſſion. 2 ſ. (and 1 Tim. i. 12.)
—— iii. 3. 8° 1719. The Nature and Neceſſity of the New-birth, By a Country Clergyman.
* —— iv. 14. 8° 1666. [S. S.]
—— xi. 25. 8° 1732. Eaſter.
—— 26. 8° 1712. Fun. of a Day-labourer. [Bryars.]
—— 49, 50. 8° 1716. Jan. 30. *Eton.*
—— xiii. 34, 35. 8° 1679. *Bod.*
—— xv. 8. 1712. Charity ſ.
* —— xviii. 40. 4° 1771. Releaſe of Barabbas—or Cauſes of popular Clamour. By a Quaker.
* —— xx. 21, 22. 8° 1718. A Vindication of the Chriſtian Prieſthood.
—— xxi. 15. 4° 1706. Charity ſ. *York.* [John Bradley.]
—— 21, 22. 8° 1708. June 10. *Trin.* Camb.
Acts ii. 24, 32, 36. 8° 1710. Againſt Quakeriſm. Of the Reſurrection, and Aſcenſion of the Body of Holy Jeſus. *Univ. Linc.* Ox. *Queen's,* Camb.
—— 41, 42. 12° 1688. The true Mother Church.
* —— vii. 26. 4° 1778. Faſt.
‡ * —— xiii. 2, 3. 4° 1697. *Brit. M.*
—— 22. 8° 1715. Acceſſion. By a Clergyman in the Country.
—— xvi. 30, 31. 8° 1700. and 12° 1726. Xns way to Heaven. *Bod.*
—— xvi. 30, 31. 8° 1707. *Eton.*
—— xx. 28. 8° 1684. *Oxon. Bod.*
* —— xxvi. 23. 8° 1770. Looking-glaſs of the Almoſt-Chriſtian.
*Rom. i. 16. 8° 1771. 2 ſ. Sufficiency of the Scriptures, and the Right of private Judgment.
* —— iv. 8. 4° 1699. Fun. for an Infant.
* —— viii. 6. 8° 1739. By a Methodiſt.
—— xii. 1. 4° 1670. [Joſeph Glanvill.]
—— xii. 12. 4° 1693. Rejoicing in Hope. *Bod. Pub. L.* Camb.
—— xii. 18. 4° 1678. The peaceable Chriſtian.
—— xii. 21. 4° 1683. c. m. c. p. 553. How we ought to do our Duty towards others, when they do not theirs towards us.
* —— xii. 12. 8° 1780. On the Pomp and Vanities of the World, by a Lady.
* —— xiii. 2. 4° 1667. Anniverſary Sermon. A loyal Fear dropt on the Vault of our late martyred Sovereign. *Queen's,* Oxon.
Rom.

OF AUTHORS, &c.

*Rom. xiii. 4. 8° 1779. To Magistrates.
* ——— xiv. 15. 4° 1679. Ministers obliged to preach the Gospel. *Cb. Cb.* Oxon.
——— 19. 4°   May 29.
* ——— 19. 1675. Conc. ad Cl. [S. T.]
1 Cor. i. 20. 8° 1725. The Jewish Philosophers encountred and confuted. *Worc.* Oxon. [Tho. Collins.]
* ——— ii. 9. 8° 1688. b. Sons of the Clergy. Necessity of Heresies.
* ——— iii. 15. 12° 1673. *Cb. Cb. Or.* Oxon.
* ——— 22. 8° 1693.
* ——— iv. 1. 8° 1693. *Bod. Pub. L.* Camb. [G. T.]
——— x. 13. 8° 1692. Serm. or Treatise. *Bod.*
——— xii. 3. 8° 1718. [Will. Law.]
* ——— xv. 33. 8° 1773. *Lancaster.* To two Soldiers condemned.
*2 Cor. ii. 16. 8° 1731.
* ——— iii. 17. 8° 1667. A Glympse of Eternity. [A. C.]
* ——— 1739. New year's-day. Translated from Monsieur Superville.
——— v. 1. 8° 1678. Fun. of Lady Mary Armyne. [T. D. M. A.]
* ——— 6. 8° 1667. Farewell to Life. [S. S.]
* ——— 17. 12° 1711. Nature of Grace. *Eton.*
‡* ——— 8° 1739. Resurrection. *Brit. M.*
* ——— vi. 3. 4° 1691. Officium Cleri Desiderium Populi.
* ——— vii. 9. 12° 1720. *Norwich.* Before the Execution of J. Marketman.
——— xiii. 11. 4° 1704. Farewell. [Rawson.]
* ——— 14. 4° 1771. Love and Unity.
Gal. ii. 5. 8° 1716. Comprehension and Toleration considered. *Linc. Worc.* Oxon. *Jes.* Camb.
——— iv. 4, 5. 1739.
——— vi. 10. 12° 1712. Doing good to all men &c. [*John Billingsley.*]
* ——— 15. 8° 1753. *Norwich.* 2 Discourses.
*Ephes. v. 15. 8° 1664. [R. A.]
* ——— 16. 8° 1690. *Bod.*
* ——— 33. 8° 1709. Norfolk. Wedding S. *Linc.* Oxon. [C. H.]
——— vi. 4. 4° 1742 On Education.
* ——— 11. 4° 1685. Christian's Spiritual Armour.
*Phil. ii. 2. 12° 1753. On the New Style.
*Col. i. 12. 4° 1681. [W. W]
* ——— iii. 19. 4° 1698. V. Disc. on Conjugal Duty. v. 1. p. 140.
1 Tim. i. 5. 8° 1719. The Law of Laws, or the golden Rule of the Gospel, by a corresponding Member of the Society for propagating Xn. Knowledge.
——— 12. 8° 1708. On Xtian. Patience. (and John i. 19. 2 f.)
——— ii. 1, 2. 4° 1679. Jan. 30. [John Cave.]
——— 1, 2, 3. 12° 1713. Access. By a Presbyter of the Church of England.

* 1 Tim. ii. 9. 4° 1747. Dangerous Confequences of Luxury, Excefs of Apparel &c.
———— iv. 6. 8° 1701. [Conc. ad Cl.] *Eton.*
———— 7. 8° 1673. Nonconformift. *Bod.*
Tit. ii. 15. 8° 1728. 2 Difc. Duties between Paftor and People. [John Howard.]
——— iii. 1. 4° 1684 Th. Sep. 9. 1683. [J. Clapham.]
————— 8° 1710. Jan. 30. [Bp. Fleetwood.]
*———— 4–7. 12° 1708. Baptifmal and fpiritual Regeneration.
Heb. ii. 4. 8° 1753. p. 41. See 3 Difc. above Ifai. xi. 6–9.
*——— ix. 27. 8° 1668. The Sinner's Arraignment. *Ch. Ch.* Oxon.
*James iii. 17. 4° 1781. Preached at St. Clement's, Lombard-ftreet.
*—— v. 11. 12° 1710. Happinefs of Afflictions. [John Howard.]
1 Pet. iii. 15. 4° 1683. c. m. e. p. 33.
———— 21. 8° 1672. (and Exod. xii. 26, 27.) 2 f. *Bod.*
*—— iv. 12–19. 8° 1723.
*—— v. 6. 4° 1778. Faft. Dedicated to the Duke of Richmond.
———— 8. 8° 1731. The Xtian cautioned againft his fpiritual Adverfary. *Queen's.* Camb.
2 Pet. i. 16–19. 8° 1751. A Critical Differtation.
——— iii. 3. 8° 1716. Ag. Scoffing at Religion.
* 1 John v. 7. 8° 1711. before the Univerfity of Oxford. *Bal.* Oxon. *Queen's.* Camb.
———— v. 14. 4° 1670. *Bod.*
*Rev. iii. 19, 20. 8° 1779. Faft. *Eton.*
——— xi. 3–14. 8° 1667. On the two Witneffes. [K. H.]
*——— 13. 4° 1692. 2 Serm. On the Witneffes and Earthquake. [C. W.]
*———— 15. 8° 1667. On the feven Dials.
*—— xvi. 1 &c. 8° 1667. Kingdom of Chrift and Antichrift.
*—— xvii. 5 8° 1768. Mafonry way to Hell.
*—— xviii. 13. 8° 1732. Effay on the Merchandize of Slaves and Souls of Men.
ARCHER Andrew, M. A. Preacher at the Chap. Tunbridge-Wells, Kent.
Pf. lxviii. 1–4. 4° 1704. Th. for the Victory at Blenheim.
ARCHER Edmond, B. D. Fell. of St. John's Coll. Oxon.
Zech. vii. 4, 5. 8° 1710. Jan. 30. *Bod. Univ. Magd. Linc. Hertf.* Oxon. *Sion. Queen's.* Camb.
ARCHER Edmund, DD. Arch-Deacon of Taunton and Canon-refidentiary of Wells.
2 Cor. viii. 9. 8° 1712. Oxon. Ch. f. *Jef.* Camb. *Sion.*
ARCHER *John*
1 Kings ii. 15. 8° 1714. Acceff. The Kingdom turned about.
ARDERNE James, DD. Dean of Chefter, and Chapl. in Ord.
Rev. i. 10. 4° 1671.
2 Tim. iv. 5. 4° 1677. Vif. f. *Bod. Ch. Ch. Queen's.* Oxon.
ARMAND *James*, Minifter at Hanau.

* Cant.

* Cant. ii. 4. 8° 1762. On the Peace. Tranſlated by Tho. Davey of Norwich. *Queen's*. Camb.

ARMSTRONG John, B.D. (of St. John's Coll. Camb.) R. of Aſtwick, Bedfordſ. and Cur. of Cartmall. Lancaſh.
    Matt. xvi 26. 12° 1704. The Soul's Worth and Danger.

ARNALD Richard, B.D. (Fell. of Eman. Coll. Camb.) R. of Thurcaſton, Leiceſterſ.
    Col. ii. 8. 4° 1726. Leiceſter School-feaſt.
    Deut. xxxiii. 8. 4° 1737 *Leiceſt*. Viſit. ſ.
    2 Kings xiv 8, 9. Th. after Reb. 4° 1746. The Parable of the Cedar and Thiſtle exemplified in the great Victory of Culloden.

ARNOLD Edmond, LL.B. Fell. of New Coll. Oxon.
    1 Kings viii. 44, 45. 4° 1740. Faſt. National Humiliation the beſt Atonement for Sins.
    Prov. xxiv. 21. 8° 1745. Rebellion. The Folly and Danger of a Revolution in Religion and Government.

ARNOLD Thomas
    Dan. vi. 10. 4° 1660. Th. June 28.

ARROWSMITH Edward, M.A. R. of St. Olave, Hart-ſtreet, Lond.
    Pſ. cxxvi. 3. 4° 1724. May 29. *Queen's*. Camb.
    Rom xiii. 1. 4° 1735. Acceſſion. The Reaſonableneſs and Origin of Government, and what ought to be the Behaviour of every Chriſtian under it. *Brit. M.*
    Rom. xiv. 19. 4° 1737. Jan. 30. The Duty of following after the Things that make for Peace. *Queen's*. Camb.
    2 Sam. x. 12. 4° 1744. Faſt. April 11. for the Spaniſh and French War.
    Iſai. xxvi. 9. 8° 1745. Faſt. Dec. 18.

ARROWSMITH John, DD. Maſter of Trin. Coll. Camb.
    * John i. 1-18. 4° 1660.
    3 Serm. in 8° 1668. *Bod.*

ARWAKER Edmund, R. of Drumglaſs in Ireland, and Chaplain to the Duke of Ormond.
    2 Chron. ix. 8. 4° 1698. *Dublin*. Trinity ſ.

ASH St. George, Biſhop of Derry.
    Matt. xxvi. 13. 4° 1694. *Dublin*. Commemoration. *Magd. Ox.*
    Iſai. xxiv. 16. 8° 1712. Th. b. Iriſh Proteſtants. *Magd. Bal. Worc.* Oxon. *Queen's*. Camb. *Brit. M.*
    2 Pet. iii. 11. 4° 1714. 2 ſ. At Tunbridge. *Brit. M.*
    Pſ. lxvii. 2. 4° 1715. Prop. Goſpel. *Ch. Ch.* Oxon.
    Pſ. v. 6. 8° 1716. Jan. 30.
    Pſ. xc. 16. 4° 1716. Ref. Manners. *Ch. Ch.* Oxon.

ASHBURNHAM Sir William, Biſhop of Chicheſter.
    Matt. vii. 15. 4° 1745. Nov. 5. b. Commons.
    Job xxix. 14-16. 4° 1749. Aſſize for Smugglers.
    * 1 Sam. xii. 24. 4° 1759. May 29. b. Lords.
    * Rom. 1. 16. 4° 1760. Prop. Goſpel.
    * Pſ. ciii 7. 4° 1764. b. Govern. of the Lond. Hoſpital.

ASHE
    ‡ * Sermons in 8° 1741.
ASHENDEN Thomas, R. of Dingley, Northamptonſ.
    Judges vii. 6. 4° 1682. Aſſize. No Penalty, no Peace.
ASHETON William, DD. R. of Beckenham, Kent, and Chaplain to the Duke of Ormond.
    Matt. vii. 21, 4° 1673. *Bod. Ch. Ch.* Oxon. *Trin.* Camb.
    1 Cor. x. 31. 4° 1700. County-feaſt. *Bod. Queen's, St. John's.* Camb.
    Eccleſ. ix. 10. 8° 1700. b. Sons of the Clergy. *Wadh.* Oxon.
ASHTON John, M. A. (Fell. of Trin. Coll. Camb.) and R. of Aldingham, Lancaſh.
    Tit. ii. 15. 4° 1749. Viſit. ſ.
ASHTON Thomas, DD. Fell. of Eton-College.
    Tit. iii. 1. 4° 1745. Rebellion.
    2 Pet. i. 19. 8° 1750. Differtation. *Braz. N.* Oxon.
    * Luke vii. 4, 5. 4° 1754. On opening a Church.
    * Pſal. lxxviii. 34. 4° 1758. Faſt. ſ.
    * Sermons in 8° 1770. *Wadh.* Oxon.
ASHWOOD John
    * Difcourſes in 8° 1707.
ASHWORTH Caleb, DD. Daventry, Northamptonſ.
    * 2 Sam iii. 38. 8° 1749. Fun. of the Rev. *Iſaac Watts*, DD.
    * 1 Theſſ. iv. 13. 8° 1759. Fun. of *James Floyd. Queen's.* Camb.
    - - - - - 1769. Fun. of the Rev.
    * Heb. xiii. 7. 8° 1770. Fun. of the Rev. Mr. *Clark. Queen's.* Camb.
ASPIN William, DD. R. of Emberton, Bucks.
    Eccleſ. iv. 4. 4° 1684. *Camb.* Of Envy.
ASPLIN Samuel, M. A. R. of Burthrop, Gloceſterſhire, and Cur. of Woolwich in Kent.
    2 Cor. iv. 5. 8° 1711. Farewell. *Brit. M.*
    2 Sam. xix. 11. 8° 1715. May 29.
    - - - - - - The Divine Rights and Duties of Chriſtian Prieſthood.
ASTON Henry Hervey, Hon. M. A. R. of Shottley, Suffolk.
    Heb. xiii. xvi. 4° 1745. b. the Sons of the Clergy.
ASTON Thomas, M. A.
    Iſai. lvii. 21. 4° 1685. b. the loving Society. *St. John's.* Camb.
    - - - - - 4° 1685. July 5. The Day before the Battle and Victory over the Rebels.
    Pſ. li. vi. 4° 1691. *Magd.* Oxon.
ASTRY Francis, DD. Treaſurer of St. Paul's, and R. of St. Martin's Ludgate, Lond.
    1 Cor. iv 7. 4° 1716. Humility recommended. *Trin.* Camb.
    Prov. iii. 27. 4° 1733. Spitt. W. *Sion.*
ATKEY Anthony
    Jerem. xii. 1. 8° 1732. Fun. of *S. Browne.* The Rectitude of Providence under the ſevereſt Difpenſations. *Queen's.* Camb.

ATKINS Robert, M.A. (Fell. of Wadh. Coll. Oxon.) V. of St. John's. Exon.
    6 Sermons in 12º 1712. *Exon.* The Sin and Danger of Popery.
    2 Cor. xiii. 11. 8º 1715. *Exon.* Farewel.
ATKINS Samuel
    *Pf. xxvii. 13. 8º 1703. Fun. f.
ATKINSON B Andrew, Minifter of the Gofpel.
    * 1 Cor. x. 15. 8º 1734.
    * 2 Tim. iii. 15. 8º 1734.
    * Ifai. xlix. 23. 8º 1736. On the Marriage of the Prince of Wales.
    * 4 Difcourfes in 8º 1737. On the Decay of Practical Religion.
ATKINSON Chriftopher, R. of Yelden, Bedfordf.
    * Pf. cxix. 71. 4º 1766. A Poetical f. Benefit of Affliction.
    * 2 Sermons in 8º 1767. Faith, Hope, and Charity.
    * 20 Difcourfes in 8º 1775. On the moft interefting and important Subjects.
ATKINSON Miles, B.A. of Leeds, Yorkf.
    * 2 Chron. xii. 7. 8º 1779. Faft. The Neceffity of National Reformation.
ATTERBURY Francis, Bp. of Rochefter.
    Sermons and Difcourfes in 2 Vol. 8º 1730. On feveral Subjects and Occafions. *Bod. Cb. Ch. All S. Univ. Magd. New Coll. Oriel, Worc. Linc. Pemb. Bal.* Oxon. *Trin. Cl. H.* Camb.
ATTERBURY Lewis, DD. R. of Milton, Bucks, and formerly Chaplain to the Duke of Glocefter.
    Prov. xxiv. 21, 22. 4º 1684. Affize. A good Subject—or the Teft of Religion and Loyalty. *Ch. Ch.* Oxon.
    1 Cor. v. 8. 4º 1686. County-feaft. *Ch. Ch.* Oxon.
    Rev. xviii. 2. 4º 1691. Babylon's Downfall—or England's happy Deliverance from Popery and Slavery.
ATTERBURY Lewis, L.L.D. and Chapl. to his Majefty at Whitehall.
    Pf. xc. 12. 4º 1687. Fun. of Lady Compton. *Ch. Ch.* Oxon.
    10 Serm. in 8º 1699. Preached b. her Royal Highnefs Princefs Ann of Denmark. *Bod. Ch. Ch.* Oxon.
    Another Vol. in 8º 1703. *Ch. Ch.* Oxon.
    1 Sam. xii. 23, 24. 4º 1705. Th. Aug. 23. *Ch. Ch.* Oxon.
    Pf. xxxvii. 37. 4º 1713. Fun. of Lady Gould. The perfect and upright man's Character and Encouragement.
    Rom. xiii. 1. 4º 1716. Th. after Rebellion.
    Sermons in 2 Vol. 8º 1743. On felect Subjects.
ATTON   V. of Welton with Sutton, Leicefterf.
    * Mark iv. 9. 8º 1767. On Beautifying a Church.
ATWOOD [a]   B.D. Preb. of Wells.
    Matt. vii. 12. 8º 1723. Affize.
ATWOOD George [a], B.D. Arch-D. of Taunton.
    Pf. cxlvi. 2, 3. O.T. 4º 1751. On the Death of the Pr. of Wales. The Mortality of Princes, the great Difappointment of Hum. Confidence.

    [a] Q. The fame?

AVERY Benjamin
 *Micah vi. 5. 8° 1773.
AUDLEY Matthew, M. A. Cur. of St. Mary Abb. Church, and St. Lawrence Pountney, Lond.
 Rom. xii. 18. 4° 1705. Of Christian Moderation and Peace. *Worc.* Oxon.
AUDLEY Matthew, Cur. and Lect. of St. Mary Rotherhithe and Chapl. to the Lond. Hospital.
 1 Sam. xx. 19. 4° 1739. The Duties and Offices of Friendship.
 * Matt. iv. 24, 25. 4° 1742. The Duty of Benevolence and Charity. *Wadh.* Oxon.
 Isai. xxxi. 1. 4° 1750. b. Antigallicans.
 * Luke xiv. 14. 4° 1752. On the Death of the Duke of Richmond.
 * Luke xvi. 27, 28. 4° 1757. b. the Governors of the London Hospital. *Wadh.* Oxon.
 * 2 Cor. ix. 12. 4° 1775. b. the Gov. of the Lond. Hosp.
AWBREY Timothy, DD
 Isai xxviii. 29. 4° 1715. May 29. b. C. *Queen's.* Camb.
 Matt. xxii 21. 8° 1713. Vil. f. Advice to the Clergy.
AYCRIGG Benjamin, S. S. T. M.
 * 1 Cor. vii. 23. 8° 1715. Wedding f.
AYERST William, (M. A. of Univ. Coll. Oxon.) DD. and Preb. of Canterbury.
 Ps. 122. 6–9. 8° 1712. The Duty and Motives of praying for Peace. *Trin. Queen's.* Camb.
AYLEWORTH William.
 2 Kings ii 12. 8° 1662. Coron. f. *Bod.*
AYLMER Justin, B. D. Fell. of St. John's Coll. Camb. and R. of St. Clement's Ipswich, Suff.
 1 Pet. ii. 7. 4° 1704. Assize.
AYLMER William, A Convert from Popery.
 2 Pet. ii. 1. 8° 1713. *Oxon.* Recantation. *Bod. Sion. Ch. Ch. Magd. Linc.* Oxon.
AYRAY James
 ‡ * John i. 19. 8° 1689. At the Spanish Ambassador's Chappel. *Brit M.*
AYSCOUGH Francis, DD. Fell. C. C. C. Oxon. and R. of North Church, Herts. and Chap. to the Prince of Wales.
 Rom. xii. 3. 4° 1736. Jan. 30. b. C. *Worc.* Oxon.
 * Rev. iii. 17. 4° 1752. Visit. f. *Eton.*
 * Job xiv. 14. 4° 1755. Against Self-murder.
AYSCOUGH Philip, M. A. R. of St. Olave's, Southw.
 Rom. i. 19. 8° 1729. Lent.
 1 Pet. iv. 4. 17.
B.   A.
 Gen. xlviii. 21. 4° 1665. Fun.
B.   R.
 Ps. xxxvii. 37. 4° 1677. *Bod.*

BABINGTON

BABINGTON Humfrey, DD. R. of Boothby-Painell, Lincolnſ.
Pſ. ci. 1. 4° 1678. Aſſ. *Trin. St. John's.* Camb.
BACKHOUSE James, M. A. Fell. of Trin. Coll. Camb.
* 2 Cor iv. 5. 4°1758. Conſecr. of Bp. Yonge. *Queen's.* Camb.
BACKHOUSE William, M. A. Fell. of Chriſt's Coll. and V. of Meldreth, Camb.
* 1 Kings xiii. 1. 4° 1763. Viſit. ſ. Caution againſt religious Deluſion. *Queen's.* Camb.
BACON James
* Exod. xxiii. ii. 8° 1660. The Sinfulneſs of Compliance with a Multitude in ſinning.
BACON Thomas, R. of St. Peter's in Talbot Country, Maryland.
Epheſ. vi. 8. 12°1749. 2 ſ. A Chriſtian ſlave's Duty.
Col. iv. 1. 12°1750. 4 ſ. The Duties of Maſters.
Gal. vi. 10. 4°1751. Opening of a Charity ſchool.
BADDELLEY George, DD. R. of Markfield, Leiceſterſ. and Cur. of St. James's, Weſtminſter.
12 Sermons in 12°1752. On ſeveral Subjects.
* 12 Diſcourſes in 8° 1766.
BADLAND Thomas
2 Cor. iv. 18. 12°1676.
BAGNAL Thomas, B. A.
* Heb. iii. 4. 8° 1767. b. Free-Maſons. The Excellency and Uſefulneſs of Maſonry.
BAGNALL Gibbons, M. A. Preb. of Hereford Cathedral.
* Exod xv. 20. 8° 1762. At the Meeting of the three Choirs.
BAGNOLD Joſeph, M. A. R. of Creton, Lincolnſ.
Matt. x. 16. 8° 1709. Wiſdom and Innocency, *Linc.* Oxon.
BAGOTT Lewis, Bp. of Briſtol and Dean of Ch. Ch. Oxon.
* Matt. ix 4, 5. 4°1776. *Oxon.* b. the Governors of the Radcliffe Infirmary, Oxon.
* 12 Diſcourſes in 8°1780. On the Prophecies, preached in Lincoln's Inn Chapel at the Lecture of the late Bp. of Gloceſter (Warburton.) *Ch. Ch.* Oxon. *Trin.* Camb.
BAGSHAW Edward, Student of Ch. Ch. Oxon.
* 1 Cor. xi. 19. 4° 1661. *Pub. L.* Camb.
. Matt. xvi. 3. 4° 1662.
John iv. 24. 4° 1662. The ſpiritual Nature of God, and his Worſhip.
Zech. xiv. 5, 9. 4° 1669. The Doctrine of the Kingdom, and perſonal Right of Chriſt.
BAGSHAW Henry, DD. Student of Ch. Ch. Oxon. and R. of St. Botolph's Biſhopgate-ſtreet, Lond. and afterwards Preb. of Durham.
Heb. xii. 11. 4° 1667. Fun. The Excellency of primitive Government. *Ch. Ch.* Oxon. *Pub. L. St. John's.* Camb. *Sinn.*
Iſai. i. 26. 4° 1673. Elect. of Lord Mayor. *Ch. Ch.* Oxon, *Sion.*
Pſ. xxxvii. 37. 4° 1676. Jan. 30. *Bod.*
4 Sermons in 8° 1680, Againſt Papiſts and Socinians. *Sion. Trin.* Camb.

BAGSHAW Henry, M.A.
   Matt. xxi. 13. 4° 1698.
BAGSHAW John, DD.
   2 Sam. xix. 14. } 4° 1660. Th.
   ――――― 15.
BAINE James
   * Rom. iv. 6. 8° 1758. At an Evening Lecture.
   * Disc. in 8° 1778.
BAKER Aaron, M. A. late of Wadh. Coll. Oxon.
   2 Sam. xv. 31. 4° 1678. Nov. 5. *Bod.*
BAKER George, M. A. Arch-D. of Totnes, Devon. and Preb. of
      St. Peter's, Exon.
   1 Cor. xi. 22. 8° 1733. Conf. Ch. The Respect due to a Church
      of God.
BAKER Richard, M. A. R. of Cawston-Norf. and lately Fellow of
      Pemb.-Hall, Camb.
   * John vii. 17. 4° 1782. Visit. s. How the Knowledge of Salva-
      tion is attainable.
BAKER Samuel
   * Deut. xxviii. 7. 8° 1710. Th. for Victory.
   Prov. xiv. 34. 8° 1729. Assize.
BAKER Samuel, DD. Chancellor and Residentiary of the Church of
   York.
   Mark vii. 13. 8° 1745. Reb. s.
BAKER William, Bp. of Norwich.
   1 Cor. xv. 16. 4° 1709. The Misery of Christians without a fu-
      ture state, and their Happiness with it. *Wadh.* Oxon.
BAKER William, DD. Fell. of St. John's Coll. Camb.
   Acts i. 8. 8° 1716. The Authority of the Church in Controver-
      sies of Faith. *Magd.* Oxon. *St. John's.* Camb.
   Jude xi. 4° 1726. Jan. 30. b. C. *All S. Worc.* Oxon. *Queen's.*
      Camb.
   Exod. xxxiii. 21–23. 8° 1728. *Camb.* The Credibility of Mys-
      teries &c.
BALDWIN James, M. A. R. of Icklingham St. James's, Suff.
   * Rom. xii. 1. 8° 1718. *Norwich.* Cor. s. The present Govern-
      ment, the Ordinance of God.
BALDWIN William, M. A. R. of St. Mary, Rotherhithe.
   Eccles. iii. 12. 4° 1701. b. Corp. of Trinity-house.
BALGUY John, M. A. V. of North-Allerton, Yorks. and Preb. of
      Sarum.
   A Collection of Practical Discourses with 6 others before printed
      in 8° 1748.
   20 Sermons in 8° 1750. Vol. 2. Posth. *Queen's.* Camb.
   5 Sermons in 8° 1739. (2d. Edit.) to which is added one on
      Rom. xii. 10. Assize. *All S.* Oxon.
BALGUY Thomas, DD. Arch-D. of Winchester.
   * Heb. xiii. 7. 4° 1769. Conf. of Bp. Shipley. *Queen's.* Camb.
   * 1 Pet. ii. 13. 8° 1775. Consecration of Bp. North.

BALL

BALL Nathaniel, M.A. Paftor of Barley, Herts.
   John viii. 36. 8° 1683. The fubject of fev. Sermons.
   *Col. 1. 27. 8° 1692. Sev. Sermons. At the Hope of Glory.
BALL Nathaniel, (late Mafter of the Free-School, Chelmsford, Effex.) R. of Wifley, and. affiftant Preacher at Berwick, and King's Street Chapel, St. James's
   8 Sermons in 8° 1745. On feveral important Subjects.
   Jofhua xxiv. 15. 8° 1745. Reb. Jofhuah's Refolution to ferve the Lord applied to the prefent times.
   Pf. cvii. 1, 2. 8° 1746. Th. after Rebellion.
   Pf. xlvi. 9. 8° 1749. Th. for Peace. The evil Effects of War, and the Bleffings of Peace.
   *2 Tim. iii. 16, 17. 8° 1755. Vif. f.
   *13 Serm. in 8° 1756. 8 republ. with the Addition of 5 *viz.*
   *1 Theff. 5. 17. 8° 1756. Rational account of Prayer.
   *Matt. vi. 9 &c. 8° 1756. Brief Expofition of the L's Prayer.
   *Rom. viii. 28. 8° 1756. Perfeverance in the Love of God, the beft Comfort under Afflictions.
   *Prov. xxiii. 23. 8° 1756. The Nature and Importance of Truth.
   *1 Cor. xi. 29. 8° 1756. The true Nature of the Lord's Supper, and the Danger of receiving it unworthily.
   *Pf. xliv. 4, 5. 8° 1756. Faft. True Religion, Loyalty, and Union &c.
   *Pf. xcvi. 8. 12° 1759. Th. f.
   *Job. v. 12. 8° 1763. Nov. 5.
BALL Richard, DD. Chap. in Ord. Mafter of the Temple, and Preb. of Linc.
   Matt. xxii. 21. 4° 1682. The true Chriftian Man's Duty both to God and King. *Pub. L.* Camb.
BALLARD Edward, DD. (Fell. of Trin. Coll. Oxon.) V. of Old Windfor, Berks.
   1 Cor. xi. 19. 8° 1734. There muft be Herefies. *Were.* Ox. *Brit. M.*
   1 Pet. ii. 16. 8° 1734.
   Matt. x. 16. 4° 1746. Confec. of Bp Beauclerk. *Eton. Queen's.* Cam.
BALLARD Reave, M.A. (of Ch. Ch. Oxon.) V. of Great Bloxham, Surry.
   Ezra vii. 25, 26. 4° 1745. Affize.
   Tit. iii. 1. 4° 1746. Affize. The Rule of Obedience.
BALLWARD John, R. of Burgh-Caftle, Suff.
   *Prov. xxiv. 21. 8° 1774. Vifit. f.
BAMPTON John, LL. B. of New Coll. Oxon.
   Mark x. 14.   16
BANKS Robert
   Pf. cxix. 136. 8° 1700. Ref. Manners.
BANDINELL James, DD. (late Fell. of Jef. Coll. Oxon.) R. of Wiggington, Oxon. and Pub. Orator of the Univ. of Oxon.
   *8 Sermons in 8° 1780. Preached b. the Univ. at the Lect. founded by the late Rev. and pious J. Bampton, M.A Canon of Sarum. To which is added a Sermon on Rom. ix. 3. A Vindication of

St. Paul from the Charge of wishing himself accursed. *Bod. Trin.* Camb.

BANNER Richard, DD. of Univ. Coll. Oxon.
    James v. 13. 8° 1737. Musick at Worcester. *Worc.* Oxon.

BANSON John, M. A. V. of St. Bartholomew the less, and Chapl. to the Lord Mayor.
    Isai. ix. 12, 13. 4° 1730. Fast. Sept. 2. The Design of God's Visitations.

BANYER Edward, DD. Afternoon-Preacher at Gray's Inn.
    Numb. xi. 29. 4° 1739. bef. the Sons of the Clergy. *Queen's.* Cam.
    Amos iii. 2. 4° 1747. Jan. 30.

BANYER Josiah
    Heb. xi. 29. 8° 1666.

BARBER James, M. A. of Ch. Ch. Oxon.
    Ps. cvii. 23, 24. 8° 1735. The Navy, the sole Def. of the Nation.

BARBER Joseph
    * 6 Sermons in 12° 1770. On Regeneration.

BARCLAY James, Cur. of Edmonton, and Master of the Academy at Tottenham, H. Cross Road.
    * Heb. vii. 25. 8° 1763. Coming unto Christ &c. Reasons of mens' refusing considered.
    * 20 Sermons in 8° 1777. on divers interesting Subjects.

BARFORD William, M. A. Chapl. to the Hon. House of Commons, and V. of Fordenbridge, Hants.
    * Ps. lxxvi. 10. 4° 1770. Jan. 30. before Commons.

BARKER Edmund, R. of Buriton, Hants.
    Luke xix. 27. 4° 1660. Plea for Cæsar. *Sion. Trin.* Camb.
    Ps. xc. 12. 4° 1661. Fun. of Lady Eliz. Capel. *Trin.* Camb.

BARKER George, B. D. R. of Danby upon Wisk, Yorks.
    Mal. ii. 7. 8° 1697. *York.* Visit. s.
    Sermons in 8° 1697. *York.*

BARKER James
    Col. iii. 12. 4° 1661.

BARKER John
    * John xvii. 20, 21. 4° 1683. Casuist. m. Ex. p. 965.

BARKER John
    * Amos iv. 12. 8° 1720. Fast. for Plague.
    * Job xxii. 10. 8° 1721. Ref. Manners.
    * Num. xxiii. 23. 8° 1722. Nov. 5.
    * John xv. 16. 8° 1723. Conversion the Act of Christ, an Obligation to S. &c.
    Rom. vi. 4. 8° 1735. Ch. School. To walk in Newness of life, the great Duty of Christians.
    Ps. cix. 96. 8° 1735. Fun. of *Sam. Newman.*
    2 Cor. xi. 3. 8° 1735. Popery the Corruption of Christianity. V. Vol. 1. ag. Popery. *Braz. N.* Oxon.
    †* Job vii. 1. 8° 1738. Fun. of Rev. *J. Newman.*
    * Matt. xxv. 40. 8° 1739. Ch. School.
    *John xviii. 11. 8° 1741. Fun.   *Queen's.* Cam.
                                                      * Isai.

*Iſai. xlvii. 8. 8° 17   V. Prot. Syſtem, vol. 2.
13 Serm. in 8° 1748. on ſeveral Subjects. *Brit. M.*
*Pſ. xxiii. 4. 8° 1758. Fun. of *B. Groſvenor*, DD.
* Sermons in 2 vol. 8° 1764.

BARKER *Matthew*
  Mark ii. 10. 4° 1676. ſ. m. e. C. p. 247. A religious Faſt. *Bod.*
  Magd. Camb.
  Matt. xi. 24. 4° 1690. Caſ. m. e. v. 4. p. 33. *Bod.*
BARKER Ralph, DD. Fell of Gonvil and Caius Coll. Camb. R.
  of Braſted, Kent, and Chaplain to Abp. Tillotſon.
  John xxi. 17. 4° 1691. Conſ. Abp. Tillotſon. *Bod. Magd.* Oxon.
  Trin. Camb. *Sion.*
BARKER Richard, M. A. Fell. of Wincheſter Coll. and R. of St.
  Maurice Wincheſter.
  Gal. i. 10. 4° 1707. The Danger of pleaſing Men. *Queen's.* Ox.
  St John's. Camb.
BARKER Samuel, M. A. V. of Chippenham, Camb.
  1 Theſſ. iv. 13. 4° 1702. Fun. of the Counteſs of Orford. *Trin.* C.
BARKER *Thomas*
  * 1 Pet, iii. 4. 8° 1712. Fun. ſ.
BARKSDALE Clement, M. A. R. of Naunton, Gloceſterſ.
  2 Sam. xv. 25. 4° 1660. May 24.
  James v. 7. 8° 1667. *Bod.*
  Pſ. cxxii. 6. 4° 1679. Nov. 5. *Sion.*
BARLOW William, R. of Chalgrave, Oxon.
  John viii. 11. 8° 1690. Penitentiary Sermon. *Bod.*
  1 Cor. vi. 11. 8° 1690. A Treatiſe of Fornication. *Bod.*
BARNARD Francis, DD. R. of St. Bartholomew near the Royal
  Exchange and Preb. of Norwich.
  Pſ. xc. 12. 4° 1735. Fun. of Mrs. Fullerton.
BARNARD *Jonathan*
  * Sermons in 8° 1727.
  2 Tim. ii. 14. 8° 1742.
BARNARD Jonathan, M. A. V. of Oſpringe, Kent.
  Pſ. cxxvii. 1. 4° 1707. Aſſize.
BARNARD Nicholas, Dean of Ardagh, Ireland.
  Acts xxvi. 17, 18. 8° 1709. Fun. of Bp. Atherton.
BARNARD Tho. M.A. Maſter of the Gram. ſchool at Leeds, Yorkſ.
  Prov. xiv. 3, 4. 4° 1710. Aſſize.
  Pſ xxxv. 14. 8° 1718. *York.* Fun. A ſorrowful Reſpect paid to
    the dead vindicated, and proper Limits ſet to it. *St. John's.* C.
BARNARD William, Bp. of Derry.
  * Matt iii. 9. 4° 1752. *Dublin.* Ir. Prot. ſchools.
BARNARDISTON J. DD. Maſter of Corp. Chriſti Coll. Camb.
  * Matt. xxii. 21. 4° 1766. Jan. 30. b. Commons.
BARNE Miles, DD. Maſter of Peterhouſe, Cam. and Chapl. in Ord.
  1 John. v. 4. 4° 1670. *Camb.* Faith's Victory. *Univ.* Ox. *Trin.* C.
  2 Pet. iii. 16. 4° 1675. Th. Oct. 17. *Bod. Ch. Ch. Univ. Queen's,*
  Magd. Oxon. *Pub. L.* Camb. *Sion.*

John xviii. 36. 4° 1682. *Camb.* 2 f. A Discourse concerning the Nature of Christ's Kingdom. *Ch. Ch.* Oxon. *Trin. St. John's.* Camb. *Sion.*

Luke xix. 14. 4° 1683. *Camb.* Th. Sept. 9. *Univ. Queen's, Linc. Worc.* Oxon. *Trin. Queen's, St. John's.* Camb.

2 Cor. vii. 2. 4° 1684. Assize *Trin. St. John's.* Camb.

BARNES Joshua, B. D. King's Professor of Greek in Camb.
Matt. ix 9. 4° 1703. St. Matthew's-day b. Gov. Lond. Hospital. *Bod. St. John's.* Camb.

BARNES Ralph, B. A.
* Rom. xiii. 3. 8° 1759. Assize.

BARNES William George, M. A. Lect. of St. Bride's, London.
A Select Number of Sermons and Discourses in 2 Vol. 8° 1752. On moral, theological and practical Subjects.

BARNET A.
Pf ii. 3, 4. 8° 1694. Fun.

BARNOUIN Francis James, Cl.
*Job xix. 23–27. 8° 1767. Essay.

BARON John, DD. Master of Baliol Coll. Oxon.
Gal. vi. 10. 4° 1699. *Oxon. Ch. f. Bod. Bal.* Oxon.

BARON William, Chapl. in Ord. and R. of Hamltead-Marshal and Enborne, Berks.
Acts xix 38. 4° 1683. Assize at Abingdon, Berks. *Ch. Ch.* Ox.

BARR John, R. of Oumby near Lincoln.
Exod xv 6. 8° 1746. *Linc.* Th. f. after Rebellion.

BARRET John
* Phil. ii. 12. 12° 169. Farw. f.
* 1 Kings xviii. 21. 12° 169   Farw. f.
* Amos v. 25. 12° 1699. Ref. Manners.

BARRET John, at Ashfield, Nottingham.
*- - - - - 8° 1777. Fun. f.

BARRETT Serenus, Cur. of New-Fishbourne, Sussex.
*Eccles. ix. 10. 4° 1715. Fun. f.
1 Thess. v. 21. 4° 1722.

BARRINGTON Lord
Miscellanea Sacra, in which are the following Dissertations in v. 3.
* Gen. iii. &c.   Fall of Man.
* —— iv. 16. God's Presence.
* Gal. iii. 16.   } 8° 1770. *All S. Worc. O. Trin. C.*
* Heb xii. 22–25.
* 1 Pet. iii 17–22.

BARRINGTON Shute, Hon. Bp. of Salisbury.
*Prov. i. 32. 4° 1772 Jan. 30. b. Lords.
*Pf ii. 8. 8° 1775. Prop. Gosp. in foreign parts.

BARROW John, Can. of Windsor and V. of New-Windsor, Berks.
Phil. i. 15–18. 4° 1683. Vis. f. *Ch. Ch.* Ox. *St. John's.* Cam. *Sion.*

BARROW Isaac, DD. Master of Trin. Coll. Camb.
His Works in 3 Vol. fo. 1716. *Bod. Ch. Ch. All S. Univ. New C. St. John's, Mert. Worc. Wadh. Or. Trin.* Oxon. *Pub. L. King's, Trin. Cl. H. Queen's.* Camb. *Sion. Dr. W's. L.* Lond.

OF AUTHORS, &c.

* Matt. xvi 19. fo. 1687. Conc. Lat. De Potef. Clav. V. 4 vol. *Bod.*
* Joel ii 12. fo 1687. Conc. ad Cl. V. 4 Vol. *Bod.*
BARTHOLOMEW William, M. A. V. of Campden, Gloucefterf.
  Luke xi. 21, 22. 4° 1660. On proclaiming K. Charles 2. *Or. Ox.*
BARTLET *William*
  * Ecclef xi. 9. 8° 1714. Fun. f.
  * Matt xi 23. 8° 1714. Barnabas's Character and Succefs.
  * Pf. cxxxii. 18. 8° 1718. Acceflion.
BARTON Cutts, DD. R. of St. Andrew's, Holborn, Lond.
  * Pf. civ. 24. 4° 1754. b. Coll. Phyficians.
  * Matt xxv. 35, 36. 4° 1758. b. Gov. of the Sm. Pox Hofp. Lond.
BARTON David, M.A. R. of St. Margaret's, New-fifh-ftreet, Lond.
  Hag. 1. 9. 4° 1670. Mercy in the midft of Judgm. *Univ.* Oxon.
BARTON Henry, DD. Warden of Mert. Coll. Oxon.
  * Ifai. v. 3, 4. 4° 1762. Faft. f. b. C. *Worc.* Ox. *Queen's.* Camb.
BARTON Philip, L.L D. Canon of Ch. Ch. Oxon. and Fell. of Winch. Coll.
  1 Cor. xiii. 13. 4° 1735. b. the Sons of the Clergy. The fuperior Excellency of Charity. *Worc.* Oxon. *Queen's.* Camb.
  2 Chron. xx 3. 4° 1740. Faft. f. b. C. The Nature and Advantages of a religious Faft. *Worc* Oxon. *Queen's.* Camb.
  1 Cor. xiv. 12. 4° 1750. The Edification of the Ch. of Chrift. *Worc.* Oxon. *Queen's.* Camb.
BARTON Philip, L.L.D. V. of Portfea and Chapl. in Ord.
  * Luke vii. 5. 8° 1754. Conf. Chapel. *Bod. Worc.* Oxon.
  * 2 Pet. i. 19. 8° 1757. Conc. Lat. Firmitas Prophetici Sermonis, *Bod.*
BARTON Phi. B.D. Can. Refid. of Exon. and R. of Buriton, Hants.
  * 1 Tim. iii. 7. 4° 1766. Confec. of Bp. Lowth. *Worc.* Oxon. *Queen's.* Camb.
BARTON Richard, B. D.
  3 Difcourfes in 8° 1737. On the Analogy of Divine Wifdom.
BARTON Samuel, DD. Preb. of Weftminfter.
  Phil. ii. 2. 8° 1689.
  Amos iv. 12. 4° 1690. Faft.
  Pf. cxliv. 10. 4° 1692. Th. *Bod. Magd.* Oxon.
  Pf. lxxv. 1. 4° 1696. Th. b. C. *C.C.C.* Ox. *Trin. Queen's.* Camb.
  Prov. 21. 15. 4° 1698. El. Lord Mayor. *C.C.C.* Oxon.
  Ephef. v. 11. 12° 1699. Ref. Manners.
  John v. 14. 4° 1701. Faft. Fire at Lond. *C.C.C.* Oxon.
  Luke xvi. 9. 4° 1705 Spittal W.
BARWICK John, DD. Dean of St. Paul's and Chapl. in Ord.
  2 Tim iv. 7, 8. 4° 1660. Fun. of Bp. Morton. *Bod. Ch. Ch. Queen's, St. John's.* Ox. *Pub. L. Trin. St. John's.* Ca. *Brit. M.*
  Prov. xiv. 8. 4° 1661.
BASIRE Ifaac, DD. Arch-D. of Northumb. and Chapl. in Ord.
  Rom. ii. 22. 8° 1668. Sacrilege arraigned and condem. *Bod. Sion.*
  Heb. xi. 4. 8° 1673. Fun. of Bp Cofin. *Bod.*
BASSET *J.*
  Luke vi. 22, 23. 8° 1734.   BASSET

BASSET Will. R. of Brinklow, Warw. and of St. Swithin, Lond.
  1 Cor. vi. 19, 20. 4° 1670. *Bod. Trin.* Camb.
  Rom. xii. 1. 4° 1679. County-feaſt. *Pub. L. Trin.* Camb. *Brit. M.*
  Pſ. cxxxiii. 1. 4° 1683. Comp. Feaſt. Of Unity. *Sion.*
  1 Pet. ii. 13. 4° 1684. On Catechiſing. *Magd.* Oxon.
BATE Edward, V. of Leighford and Cur. of Ellenhall, Staffordſ.
  Rom. i. 20.   } 8° 1748. 2. ſ. The Speculative and practical
  ——— 20, 21. }   Atheiſt.
BATE James, M. A. R of St. Paul's Deptford, Kent.
  Deut. iv. 6. 4° 1734. Aſſize. The Advantages of a national Obſervance of Divine and human Laws. *Queen's.* Camb.
  2 Kings x. 15. 4° 1738. b. Ubiquarians. The practice of Religion and Virtue the only ſure Foundation of Friendſhip.
  Pſ. cxii. 3, 4. 4° 1742 2 ſ.
  John viii. 36. 4° 1740. b. Ubiquarians. The Faith and Practice of a Chriſtian the only True foundation of rational Liberty.
  Acts vii. 2. 4° 1740. b. Ubiquarians. Human Learning uſeful to true Religion.
  Prov. ii. 3–5. 4° 1753. Sch. Feaſt. Canterbury.
BATEMAN Edmund, DD. Arch-Deacon of Lewes, and R. of St. Dunſtan's in the Eaſt Lond.
  1 John iv. 7. 4° 1738. Spitt. W. *Queen's.* Camb. *Brit. M.*
  2 Kings iv. 1, 2. 4° 1740. b. the Sons of the Clergy. *Queen's.* Camb. *Sion.*
  Deut. xxxiii. 18, 19. 4° 1741. Col. of Georgia. *All S.* Oxon.
  Eccleſ. vii. 16. 4° 1743. May 29. Trin. Sund. *Queen's.* Camb.
BATEMAN Richard Tho. R. of St. Bartholomew the Great, Lond.
  John iii. 5. 8° 1747. The Nature and Neceſſity of Regeneration.
BATEMAN Thomas, M. A. Chapl. to his Grace the Duke of Gordon, and V. of Whaplode, Linc.
  * 2 Chron. xv. 1, 2. 4° 1778. Military ſ.
  * 1 Cor. xv. 35. 8° 1780. The Reſurrection of the Body.
  * Luke xxiii. 42, 43. 8° 1780. The Intermediate State of the Soul.
BATEMAN Wynne, M. A. Fell. of St. John's. Camb.
  Rom. i. 20, 21. 4° 1746. Conc. ad Clerum. *Queen's.* Camb.
[BATES J.]
  * Eccleſ. iv. 9–12. 8° 1707.
BATES John, M. A.
  Jonah iv. 11. 8° 1714. On the Mortality of the Cattle. *Sion.*
  * John xiv. 28. 8° 1714. Fun. of *Matt. Henry. Queen's.* Camb.
  * Heb. xiii. 7. 8° 1714. Fun.
BATES J.
  * - - - - - - 1756.
BATES William, DD.
  His Works fo. 1700. *Ch. Ch. Jeſ. St. John's, Queen's.* Oxon. *Trin. Magd.* Camb.
  ‡* 1 Theſſ. iv. 17. 8° 1678. Fun. of *T. Manton*, DD.
  ‡* Rev. xxii. 12. 8° 1678. Fun. of *Benj. Aſhurſt.*
  Sermons in 8° 1693. on ſeveral Occaſions. *Pemb.* Oxon.

BATT

BATT Michael, M. A. Preacher at St. James's, Edm. Bury. Suff.
    1 Cor. iv. 21. 4° 1686. Vif. f.
BATT William, M. A. R. of Wraxhall, Somerfetf.
    * Mat. xii. 25. 4° 1754. Elect. Mayor. Union and Loyalty.
BATTELY John, DD. Arch-D. of Canterbury.
    1 John v. 4. 4° 1694. *Bod. C. C. C. Magd. Or.* Oxon.
BATTELL Ralph, M A. Sub-Dean of the Royal Chapl. and R. of Edwath, Bedfordf.
    Matt. vii. 12. 4° 1684. Affize. The civil Magift. coercive Power.
    Pf. c 1, 2. 4° 1694. The Lawfulnefs and Expediency of Church-mufick. *Pub. L.* Camb. *Sion.*
BATTIE William, Chapl. in Ord.
    1 Pet ii. 15. 4° 1678. b Lord Mayor. *Bod. All S.* Oxon. *Sion.*
    Gal. iii. 1. 4° 1680. Ag. Popery. *All S.* Oxon. *Sion.*
BATTY Adam, M. A. R. of Clerkenwell, Lond.
    Prov. i. 9. 4° 1728. *Brit. M.*
    26 Sermons in 2 Vol. 8° 1739. *All S.* Oxon.
[BATTY Jofeph]
    ‡* Gal. i. 1.
BAXTER *Benjamin*
    * Ecclef. viii. 12. 8° 1662. A pofing Queftion.
BAXTER *Richard*, Chapl. in Ord.
    * Ezek. xxxiii. 11. 12° 1660.
    Ezek. xxxvi. 31. 4° 1660. Faft. *Trin.* Camb. *Brit. M.*
    Luke x. 20. 4° 1660.
    Heb. xi. 1. 4° 1660. b. King. *Ch. Ch.* Oxon. *Pub. L. Trin; Queen's.* Camb.
    * Ifai. i. 10. 8° 1662.
    * Luke x. 41, 42. 4° 1662. Saint or Brute.
    * Cor. xiii. 5. 8° 1662.
    * John iii. 17. 4° 1663.
    * 2 Cor. xii. 1. 4° 16 Fun. of *J. Corbert. Worc.* Oxon. *Brit. M.*
    Hab. iii. 17, 18. 12° 1666.
    1 Cor. xii. 27, 28. 4° 1675. m. e. P. p. 25. Chrift, and not the Pope, the univerfal Head of the Church.
    Matt. v. 16. 4° 1676. f. m. e. C. p. 545. What Light muft fhine in our Works. *Bod.*
    ‡* Pf. cxix. 111. 12° 1680. Fun. of *Mary Coxe.*
    * John xii. 26. 4° 1680. Fun. of Henry Afhhurft, Efq. Faithful Souls fhall be with Xt. *Ch. Ch.* Oxon. *Pub. L.* Camb.
    2 Cor. ii. 7. 4° 1683. c. m. e. p. 263. The Cure of Melancholy and over-much Sorrow by Faith and Phyfick.
    * Difcourfes in 4 Vol. fo. 1707. *Dr. Wt's. L.* Lond.
BAYES *Jofhua*
    1 Cor. xiv. 9. 8° 1735. Of the Worfhip of God in an unknown Tongue. V. 2 Vol. ag. Popery. *Braz. N.* Oxon.
BAYLEY Francis, Chapl. to Sir William Button.
    1 Theff iv. 14. 4° 1660. Fun. f.
BAYLY Anfelm, L.L.D Sub-Dean of his Majefty's Chapl. Royal.

3 Dif-

  3 Difcourfes in 8° 1751. The Antiquity, Evidence and Certainty of Chriftianity.
  * 2 Difc. Pf cxix. 48. 8° 1778. On the Commandments of God.
BAYLY Benjamin, M. A. R. of St. James's, Briftol.
  Sermons in 2 Vol. 8° 1721. On various Subjects. *Sion.*
BAYLY Edward, R.
  * Luke xvi. 9. 8° 1749. Bath-Infirmary.
  * Dan. iv. 35. 4° 1756. Faft.
BAYLY Thomas, Bp. of Killala.
  Gal. v. 12. 8° 1709. *Bod.*
BAYLYE Thomas, B. A. of Braz. N. Coll. Oxon.
  1 Cor. ii. 9. 8° 1710. A Glympfe of Paradife.
BAYNE James, M. A. Minifter of the Gofpel, Edinburgh.
  * Difcourfes in 8° 1778. On various Subjects.
BEACH John, M A. Miffionary at Connecticut.
  * John iii. 9. 8° 1760. Annual Conv. of the Clergy at Newhaven.
BEAN Charles, M. A. Fell. of Mert. Coll. Oxon. V. of Lidd, and Proctor of the Clergy of Cant.
  Acts vii. 26, 27, 28. 4° 1707. Th. for the Union. *Bod. Magd.* Ox.
  Num. xiv. 4. 8° 1716. Th. June 7.
  Tit. iii. 1, 2. 8° 1716. Vif. f.
BEAR John, B.D. R. of Shermanbury in the Diocefe of Chicheſter.
  2 Tim. ii. 2. 8° 1748. *Ox.* De primævorum Patrum Auctoritate.
BEARCROFT Philip, DD. Chapl. in Ord.
  Pf. xxxiii. 1. 8° 1726. Sch. Feaſt. *Worc.*
  Ifai. xli. 17–20. 4° 1738. Col. of Georgia. *Queen's.* Camb.
  Matt. xxviii. 20. 4° 1743. Conf. Bp.   *Queen's.* Camb.
  Tit. iii. 1. 4° 1744. Faſt. *Eton.*
  Gal vi 2. 4° 1745. Prop. Gofpel. *All S.* Ox. *Queen's.* Cam. *Sion.*
  Pf. xxxiv. 14. 4° 1748. An. meet. Char. Schools. The Wife and ufef. Inftitut. of our Char. fchools. *All S. Worc.* Ox. *Trin.* Cam.
BEARCKOFT William, M. A. Chapl. to the Lord Mayor.
  * Luke xii. 4, 5. 8° 1756. Faft. for Earthquake. b. Lord Mayor.
BEARE Nicholas, M. A. V. of St. Botolph, Alderfgate, Lond.
  Gal. vi. 15. 4° 1679. Metamorphofis Chriftiana. *Bod.*
  Pf. cxviii. 24. 4° 1707. Th. f.
  Pf. xcix. 1. 8° 1710. God's Government of the world, beft Comfort in bad times. *Linc.* Oxon.
BEARNE Edward
  1 Tim. ii. 1, 2. 4° 1726. Jan. 30. 2 f. at Hammerfmith.
[BEASTON John]
  * - - - - - 1778. Faft.
BEAUCLERE James, Right Honourable Bp of Hereford.
  1 Sam. xv. 23. 4° 1752. Jan. 30. b. Lords. *Worc* Oxon.
BEAULIEU Luke, B.D. Chapl. to Ld Jefferies, and Preb. of Gloc.
  Rom. xii. 18. 4° 1784. Affize. *Cb. Ch.* Oxon. *St. John's.* Camb.
  Jude iii. 4° 1686. b. Lord Mayor. *Ch. Ch. Magd.* Oxon.
  Ifai. xlix. 23. 4° 1702. Coron. f.
  Rom. xiii. 1. 4° 1706. Affize. The reciprocal Duty between Kings and Subjects. *Ch. Ch.* Oxon.

BEAUMAN William.
　Mal. ii. 7. - - - - -
BEAUZVILLE Samuel, B. A. Minister of the French Church, Bethnal-Green.
　* Deut. x. 8. 8° 1778. Charity f.
BECHER Henry, M. A. Fell. of St. John's Coll. Oxon, and R. of St. James's, Duke's Place.
　Isai. i. 26. 4° 1728.
BECONSALL Thomas, M. A. Fell. of Braz. N. Coll. Oxon.
　John v. 28, 29. 4° 1697. *Oxon.* Easter. *Ch. Ch. Univ. Magd. Jes,* Oxon. *Trin.* Camb.
BEDFORD Arthur, M. A. Chapl. to the Prince of Wales, and to the Haberdasher's Chapel at Hoxton near London.
　2 Tim. ii. 16. } 12° 1705. The Abuse and Effects of the Stage.
　　　　　　　 } 8° 1730. Ag. the Playhouse.
　1 Pet. ii. 13. 4° 1717. Assize. The Doctrine of Obedience and Non-Resistance to Higher Powers.
　Isai. ii. 2. 8° 1717.
　Isai. lx. 10. 8° 1717.
　Prov. iv. 34. 8° 1717. Assize.
　Matt. xxii. 21. 8° 1717. Coron. f. *Eton.*
　Luke 19. 42. 8° 1717.
　1 Cor. xiv. 15. 8° 1733. The Excellency of Divine Musick.
　Lev. v. 1. 4° 1734. Ref. Manners.
　Rom. xiv. 1. 8° 1738. The Doctrine of Assurance — or the Case of a weak and doubting Conscience. *Queen's.* Camb. *Sion.*
　1 John v. 7. 8° 1741. Lady Moyer's Lect. *Bod. New C. C. C. C.* Oxon. *Sion.*
BEDFORD Arthur, M. A. V. of Sharpbrooke, Bedford.
　1 Sam. xii. 24. 4° 1746. Th. af. Rebellion.
BEDFORD Thomas, M. A. R. of Wike St. Mary, Cornwal.
　* 2 Sam. xviii. 33. 4° 1667. Fun. of Marquess of Tavistock.
　* James iv. 1. 4° 1770. Origin of our Grievances.
　* ———— 4° 1778. Fast.
BEDFORD William, DD. R. of St. George's, Botolph-Lane &c.
　Gen. or Exod. xviii. 25. 4° 1698. 2 f. Assize.
　2 Tim. i. 13. 4° 1698. Conc. ad Cl. *Lond. Ch. Ch.* Oxon.
　Zech. vii. 9, 10. 4° 16　　Assize.
BEDLE Joseph, V. of Great Bursted, Essex, and Chap. in Ord.
　Ps. vii. 15. 4° 1679. Nov. 5. *Bod.*
BEESTON Edmund, M. A. R. of Sproughton and Whatfield, and Lect. of St. Mary Tower, Ipswich.
　Practical Serm. and Disc. in 8° 1739. on several Subjects.
BEILBY Samuel, M. A. R. of Folkton, Yorkshire.
　* Tit. iii. 2. 4° 1781. *York.* Assize.
BELBIN Peter,　of St. Mary's, Reading, Berks.
　* - - - - 8° 1732. Fun. of Mr. Benj. Tomkins.
　* Heb. x. 23. 8° 1738. Farw. f.
　* Acts xiv. 15-17. 8° 1741. Confirmation.
　Vol. II.　　　　　　　E　　　　　　　　BELCHIER

BELCHIER John, M. A. V. of Barton, Camb.
 * Exod. xviii. 21. 4° 1754. Elect. Memb. Parliament.
BELISARIO Mendes Isaac, one of the Chief Teachers.
 * 1 Chr. xxix. 27, 28. 4° 1761. Roy. Fun. Transl. from the Span.
BELL George, M. A. Chapl. to the Bp. of London.
   Rom. i. 16. 4° 1713. b. the Sons of the Clergy. *Queen's. Wad.* Ox.
   1 Pet. i. 22. 8° 1713. Elect. Ld May. *Ch. Ch.* Ox. *St. John's.* C.
   Pf. xci. or xcvii. 1. 4° 1718. May 29.
BELL George, M. A. R. of Croft, and Preb. of York.
   Matt. vii. 12. 8° 1722. *York.* Assize.
 * Zech. xi. 7. 8° 17
BELL John, a B. A. of Queen's Coll. Oxon.
 * 1 Cor. xv. 58. 8° 1744. Farw. f.
BELL John, a V. of Bridekirk.
 * - - - - 1761. Assize.
BELL Thomas, M. A. V. of Liverpool.
   Ezek. xxxvi. 34, 35. 8° 1719. Char. f. The Advantages of an early and religious Education.
BELL William, DD. V. of St. Sepulchre's, London.
   Pf. cxxvii. 1. 4° 1661.
   Josh. xxiv. 15. 4° 1672. Of Family Religion. *Sion.*
   Acts xxiv. 16. 4° 1678. Fun. *Sion.*
   Ephef. v. 15, 16. 4° 1678. Fun. f.
BELL William, DD. Preb. of Westminster, and Chapl. to her Royal Highness Princefs Amelia.
 * Tit. i. 15. 4° 1774. Conf. of Bp. Thomas.
BELLAMY Daniel, Minister of Petersham and Kew, and V. of St. Stephen's near St. Alban's.
   12 Difcourfes in 8° 1744. on the Truth of the Christian Religion. *Bod. Trin.* Camb.
 * Pf. cxii. 6. 4° 1756. Sch. Feast.
 * Family Preacher (in 8° 1754. 1st Edit.) in 2 Vol. 4° 1776. confifting of practical Difcourfes for every Sunday throughout the Year, as also for Xtmas-day, Good-friday, and other particular Occafions. *Bod. Pub. L.* Camb.
BELLAS George, DD. R. of Yattendon, and V. of Basilden, Berks.
 * 2 Sam. xxiv. 11–13. 4° 1779. Before the Univ. of Oxon.
BELLINGER Charles, M. A. Lect. of Trin. in the Minories, Lond.
   Pf. lxxv. 1. 8° 1746. Th. af. Rebel. The Duty of Thankfgiving.
BELLINGTON Thomas
 * Matt. iii. 9. 8° 1718. Vifit. f.
BELSHAM Thomas
 * Rom. x. 2. 12° 1775. Bef. Diff. Clergy. The Evil, Nature, and pernicious Tendency of intemperate and mifguided Zeal.
BELWARD John, B. A. R. of Burgh-Castle, Suffolk.
 * Prov. xxiv. 21. 8° 1774. Vifit. f.
BENET Gilbert, M. A. R. of St. Peter's at the Arches in the City of Linc.

Judg.

a Q. The fame.

Judg. ix. 14,15. 8° 1746. *Linc.* Th. af. Rebellion. 2 f. Jotham's Parable—or a Contraſt betw. a Proteſt. Prince and a Pop. one.
* Tit. ii. 11–13. 8° 1754.

BENN *William*
* Diſcourſes in 8° 1683. on the Soul's Proſperity.

BENNET *Benjamin*, M. A.
* 6 Diſcourſes in 8° 1714. Ag. Popery. *Ch. Ch.* Oxon.
* Diſcourſes in 2 Vol. 8° 1728. Chriſtian Oratory.
14 Diſcourſes in 8° 1730. On the Truth, Inſpiration, and Uſefulneſs of the Scripture.

BENNET *Philip*, M. A. Fell. of Magd. Coll. Camb.
Pſ. cxxii. 6. 8° 1745. Rebel. The Duty of national Prayer to avert God's Judgments.
Pſ. lxxxv. 10. 8° 1749. Aſſize. The Harm. betw. Juſtice & Peace.
2 Theſſ iii. 16. 8° 1749. Th. The Means of enjoying and perpetuating Peace.

BENNET *R.*
*Matt xviii. 20. ⎱ 8° 1769. 2 Diſc. On opening a new Meeting-
*Acts v. 45.   ⎰ houſe at Hampſtead.
* Epheſ. v. 31–33 8° 1776. Wedding ſ.

BENNET *Thomas*, DD. V. of Cripplegate, Lond.
Rom. xii. 13. 8° 1710. Charity-Schools recommended. *Linc.* Ox. Sion. *Trin. St. John's.* Camb.
1 John iv. 11. 8° 1716. Char. ſ. The Caſe of the reformed Epiſcopal Churches in great Poland, and Poliſh Pruſſia, conſidered. *Worc. Linc.* Oxon. *Sion.*
Matt. xxv. 40. 4° 1717. Spittal W. Beneficence to our Saviour. Chriſt. *Ch. Ch.* Oxon.

BENNETT *Thomas*, M. A. of Trin. Coll. Camb. and Lect. of St. John the Evangeliſt, Weſtminſter.
* 12 Lectures in 8° 1775. (Purſuant to the Will of Dr. Buſby) on the Apoſtles Creed.

[BENNETT *William*]
* — — — — — 1780. Faſt. Profeſſors admoniſhed in the Day of Calamity—or the Lord's Controverſy with Iſrael.

BENNION *John*, M. A. V. of Malmeſbury, Wilts.
Deut. i. 16, 17. 4° 1681. *Oxon.* Aſſize. *Bod. Queen's.* Oxon.

BENSON *George*, DD
* Job xiv. 10. 8° 1725.
*Eccleſ. xii. 1. 8° 1735. 3 Diſc. Delays dangerous to young or old.
* Matt. xii. 7. 8° 1734. The Excellence of moral Duties above poſitive Inſtitutions. *Queen's.* Camb.
2 Theſſ. ii. 1–12. 8° 17   Diſſertation, that the Bp. of Rome is the Man of Sin.
* Acts xiii. 38, 39. 8° 1748. Goſp-method of Juſtif. *Queen's.* Cam.
17 Sermons in 8° 1748. *Queen's.* Camb.
* 2 Cor. v. 4. 8° 1755. Fun. of Rev. Mr. *Reed. Queen's.* Camb.
Pſ. xliv. 1–8. 8° 1758. The glorious firſt of Auguſt—The Bleſſings of the Revolution. *Queen's.* Camb.

BENSON Martin, Bp. of Glocester.
  Eccles. vii 2. 4° 1736. Spittal M. *Queen's*. Camb.
  Ps. lxxviii. 5-8. 4° 1738. Jan. 30. b. Lords. *Queen's*. Camb.
  Mal. i. 11. 4° 1740. Prop. Gospel. *All S*. Oxon. *Queen's*. Camb.
BENTHAM Edward, DD. Regius Professor of Divinity, and Canon of Ch. Ch. Oxford.
  Rom. i. 28. 8° 1744. *Oxon*. Assize. The Connection between Irreligion and Immorality. *Worc*. Oxon. *Queen's*. Camb. *Eton*.
  1 Tim ii. 1, 2. 8° 1750. Jan. 30. b. Commons. *Worc*. Oxon. *Queen's*. Camb. *Eton*.
  * Prov. xxii. ii. 4° 1722. An. meet. Char. Sch. *Magd. Worc.* Ox.
BENTHAM Joseph
  * James i. 10. 4° 1669. 2 s. Dissuasive from Error.
  * 1 Cor. xiv. 40. 4° 1669. 2 s. Vis. Persuasive to Order.
BENTLEY Richard, DD. Master of Trin. Coll. Camb.
  8 Serm. at Boyle's Lect. in 4° 1692. A Confutation of Atheism —or so. 1739. V. 1. *Ch. Ch. All S. New C. C. C. C. Worc. Wadh. Univ. Bal.* Oxon. *Pub. L. Trin. St. John's, Cl. H. C. Sion.*
  1 Pet. iii. 15. 4° 1696. Of Revelation, and the Messias. *Ch. Ch. All S. Magd. Or.* Oxon. *Trin.* Camb.
  2 Cor. ii. 17. 8° 1715. *Camb*. On Popery. *Ch. Ch. Magd. Bal.* Oxon. *Trin. St. John's, Cl. H.* Camb. *Sion*.
  Rom. xiv. 7. 4° 1717. bef. King. *Ch. Ch. Magd.* Oxon. *Queen's, Cl. H.* Camb. *Eton*.
BENTLEY William, DD.
  Ps. xlii. 11. 8° 1702. Royal Fun. *Brit. M.*
  * Rev. xxi. 9. 8° 1735.
  * - - - 8° 1738.
BERAULT Peter, Chapl. in his Majesty's Ships, the Kent & Victory.
  Luke xiii. 3. 8° 1698.
  Ephes. v. 16. 8° 1698.
  James v. 12. 8° 1698.
BERDMORE   M. A. V. of St. Mary's Notting. and Preb. of Southwell.
  Rom. xiv. 19. 4° 1710. Assize. *Bod. Sion.*
  1 Cor. x. 10. 8° 1715. Assize. Ag. murmuring.
  Gal. iv. 8. 8° 1716. On the King's Birth-day.
  Ps. cxxii. 8, 9. 8° 1717. Assize.
BERIDGE John, M. A. R. of Massingham-magna, Norfolk.
  Judg. xvii. 6. 4° 1662. May 29. *Univ.* Oxon.
BERJEW John
  * Deut vii. 13. 4° 1775. Assize.
BERKELEY George, Honourable, M. A.
  Matt. vii. 12. 4° 1686. Assize.
BERKELEY George, Bp of Cloyne.
  Rom. xiii. 2. 8° 1713. Of passive Obed. *St. John's.* Camb. *Eton*.
  John xviii. 3. 4° 1732. Prop. Gospel. *Worc.* Ox. *Queen's. C. Sion.*
BERKELEY Joshua, DD. Stud. of Ch. Ch. Ox. & Dean of Tuam.
  * 2 Tim. ii. 15. 4° 1780. V. s. The Difficulties attending a just
                                                            Explanation

Explanation of the Scrip. confidered, as they have arifen from the gradual Progrefs of revealed Relig. thro' a length of Time.

BERNARD Nicholas, DD. R. of Whitchurch, Salop.
    Rom. xiii. 2. 4° 1661. On regal Power. *Bod. C.C.C.* Oxon.

BERNARD Thomas, M. A.
    Prov. xiv. 34. 4° 1710. Affize, at Chelmsford.

BERNARD Thomas, M. A. V. of Earls Coln, Effex.
    Prov. i. 5. 8° 1736. Sch. Feaft. The Advantages of Learning.

BERRIMAN John, M. A. Cur. of St. Swithin, and Lecturer of St. Mary Aldermany.
    1 Kings xxi. 12, 13. 8° 1721. Jan. 30. The Cafe of Naboth confidered, and compared with that of the royal Martyr. *Sion. Eton.*
    8 Sermons in 8° 1741. At Lady Moyer's Lecture. *Sion.*

BERRIMAN William, DD. R. of St. Andrew's Underfhaft, and Fell. of Eton. Coll.
    2 John x. 11. 8° 1733. Append. to Boyle's Lect. V. 2. p. 339. The Duty of fhunning the Conver. of Infidels and Hereticks.
    Numb. xxiii. 23. 4° 1721. Nov. 5. *Bod. Sion.*
    Pf. cii. 19, 20, 21. 4° 1721. b. redeemed Captives. *Bod. Sion.*
    Matt. vii. 6. 4° 1722. *Ox. n.* Act. The Brutifhnefs of defpifing Religion, and the Treatment due to it. *Bod. Worc. Ox. Sion.*
    Job. xxxi. 28. 4° 1722. Elect. Lord Mayor. The Authority of the civil Powers in matters of Religion afferted and vindicated. *Bod. Queen's. Camb. Sion. Eton.*
    8 Sermons in 8° 1725. At Lady Moyer's Lect. *Bod. Trin.* Oxon. *Queen's.* Camb. *Sion.*
    Pf. cxii. 9, 10. 4° 1725. An. meet. Ch. Schools. *Bod. Sion.*
    Acts vii. 22. 4° 1726. Sch. Feaft. Human Learning recommended from the Example of Mofes. *Bod. Queen's.* Camb. *Sion.*
    Ecclef. xi. 2. 8° 1730. Spittal W. The Obligation and Proportion of Charity. *Sion.*
    Ecclef. v. 8. 4° 1733. Jan. 30. b. Lord Mayor. The Regard had by Providence to profperous Iniquities. *Sion.*
    Boyle's Lect. 2 Vol. 8° 1733. *Sion.* or fo 1739. Vol. 3. p. 581 &c. *St. John's.* Oxon.
    Deut. xiv. 29. 8° 1737. b. Sons of the Clergy. The tything of the third year. *Queen's.* Camb. *Sion.*
    Mark ix. 50 4° 1739. b. relig Societies. *Queen's.* Camb. *Sion.*
    Lam. iii. 27. 4° 1742. Prot. Irifh Sch. Youth the proper Seafon of Difcipline. *Worc.* Oxon. *Queen's.* Camb. *Sion.*
    1 Tim iv. 16. 4° 1742. Conc. ad Cler. *Lond. Queen's.* Camb.
    * 1 Tim. iii. 16. 8° 1741. Diff. Critical being the Subftance of 8 Sermons preached at Moyer's Lect. *Trin. St. John's, Bal.* Oxon. *Queen's* Camb.
    * 1 Cor. xi. 19. 8° 17 Act f.
    Chriftian Doctrines and Duties explained and recommended in 3 Vol. 8° 1751. *Bod. Ch. Ch. All S. New. C. Trin. Jef. Magd. Pemb.* Oxon. *Pub. L.. Cl. H. Trin.* Camb. *Sion.*

                                                         * 3 Vol.

* 3 Vol. in 8° 1763. *Bod. Braz. N. Oriel.* Oxon. *Eton.*
BERROW Capel, Lect. of St. Bennet's Paul's Warf, Lond.
  2 Chron. xxxii. 8. 4° 1746. Rebell.
  2 Chron. xvi. 9. 4° 1746. Th. after Reb. The Providence of God over Xtian Kingdoms and States confidered and applied.
BERRY Richard, M. A.
  Matt. ii. 10, 11. 4° 1672. *Dublin.* Epiphany. *Bod. Queen's.* Ox.
BERWICK John, DD. Dean of St. Paul's, London.
  Prov. xiv. 8. 4° 1661. Oct. 20. Deceivers deceived, or the Miftakes of Wickednefs.
BESOMBE Robert, Chapl. to Lord Baltimore.
  Judg. i. 19. 8° 1734.
BEST William, DD. Minifter of St. Lawrence-Jewry, and St. Mary Magdalen, Milk-ftreet, Lond.
  Acts xi. 29, 30. 8° 1734. Char. f. for the Relief of the Saltzburgers. *Worc.* Oxon.
  2 Cor. viii. 12. 4° 1742. Col. of Georgia. *All S. Worc.* Oxon. *Queen's.* Camb.
  Phil. ii. 25. 8° 1746. The royal Soldier. *Bal.* Ox. *Queen's.* Cam.
BETHAM John
  * Luke i. 31. 4° 1686. Annunciation. *Trin. St. John's.* Camb.
BETHAM Rob. M. A. of Queen's Coll. Ox. Cur. of Ware, Herts.
  Rev. ii. 5. 4° 1744. Faft. National Vices the Bane of Society.
[BETHUNE Angus,] M. A.
  * - - - - - 1774. Chriftian Fortitude.
BETTESWORTH Charles, M. A. R. of Kingfton-Bowfey, Suffex.
  Acts viii. 17. 8° 1712. Conf.
BETTY Joseph, M. A. Fell. of Exeter Coll. Oxon.
  Gal. i. 1. 8° 1729. *Oxon.* The divine Inftitution of the Miniftry, and the Abfolute Neceffity of Ch-Government. *Worc.* Oxon. *Queen's.* Camb.
BEVAN Thomas, M. A.
  * An Expofition of the Lord's Prayer in 12° 1673.
BEVERIDGE William, Bp. of St. Afaph.
  1 Cor. xi. 16. 4° 1689. Conc. ad Syn. *Bod. Ch. Ch. Magd. St. John's.* Oxon. *Sion.*
  2 Cor. ix. 2. 4° 1707. Prop. Gofpel.
  Acts iii. 1. 8° 1708. The great Neceffity and Advantage of pub. Prayer. *Pub L.* Camb.
  1 Cor. xi. 26. 8° 1708. Of frequent Communion. *Pub. L.* Cam.
  Matt. viii. 34. 8° 17
  Thefaurus Theologicus, 8° 1711. 4 V. *Bod. Univ. Dr. W's. L. L.*
  His whole Works containing all his Sermons in 2 Vol. fo. 1720. *Bod. Ch. Ch. Magd. Mert. Worc. Pub. L.* Camb.
BEVERLEY *Thomas*
  Luke xxiii. 39–43. 4° 1670. Of a death-bed Repentance. *Sion.*
  Matt. xxvi. 26. 4° 1687. Of the true Spiritual Tranfubftantiation. *Bal.* Oxon. *Sion.*
  Deut. xxxiii. 25. 4° 1693. The Bleffing of Mofes on the Tribe of Afher, *Sion.* Matt.

Matt. xvi. 26. 4° 1694. Of the loss of the Soul. *Sion.*
Heb. ii. 4, 5. 4° 1694. On Miracles. *Bod. Pub. L.* Camb.
Hab. iii. 2. 4° 1695. Roy. Fun.   A Persuasion to Prayer.
 Trin. Camb. *Sion.*
John xvii. 7, 8. 4° 1695. Of the great Gosp. Grace of Faith. *Sion.*
* 1 Cor. xv. 24–28. 4° 1698. Kingdom of God all in all. *Pub. L.*
 Trin. Camb.

BEVERLEY Thomas, R. of Lully, Harts.
 * Discourses in 4° 1683. On the Principles of Protestant Truth and Peace.

[BEVERTON Simon,] Minister of Pershore, Worcest.
 Matt. v. 4. 8° 1717. Jan. 30.

BILLINGSLEY John
 * Jude xxii. 23. 8° 1700. Ref. Manners.
 Gal. vi. 10. 12° 1712. Doing Good to all Men.
 * 1 Kings x. 9. 8° 1714.
 * 2 Cor. v. 1, 2. 8° 1717. Ordin. S.
 * Phil. i. xviii. 8° 1717. Char. S.
 24 Sermons in 8° 1723. Against Popery.
 Isai. xlii. 3. 8° 1727.

BILLINGSLEY S. M.A. V. of Horley, and R. of Newdigate, Surry.
 Ps. xviii. 49, 50. 8° 1716. Th.
 * 2 Cor. iv. 5. 8° 1741. Ord. S.

BILSTONE John, M.A. Chapl. of All Soul's Coll. Oxon. and V. of Hannington, Wilts.
 13 Sermons in 8° 1749. preached before the University of Oxon. *Bod. All S.* Oxon.
 * 1 Cor. xv. 10. 8° 1756. Operation of Grace.
 * Joel ii. 12, 13. 8° 1758. Fast. Solemn and sincere Repentance the best Expedient for Success in time of War. *Exon.* Oxon.
 * 1 Chron. xxix. 15. 8° 1759. Fun. of Thomas Rowney, Esq; *Worc.* Oxon.
 * Gal. iv. 18. 8° 1761. Christian Zeal.
 * John x. 22, 23. 8° 1763. Cons. of a Church.
 * Gal. iv. 3–5. 8° 1763. Ignorance of Jewish Church to the Intent of their Institutions. *Exon.* Oxon.

BINCKES William, DD. Dean of Litchfield.
 Luke xxiii. 34. 4° 1702. Jan. 30. (censured by the House of Lords.) *Ch. Ch. Magd.* Oxon. *Pub. L.* Camb.
 Ps. cxxiv. 6, 7. 4° 1704. Nov. 5. b. Commons. *Ch. Ch. C. C. C. Magd. Worc. Jes.* Oxon. *St. John's.* Camb.
 Luke vii. 4, 5. 8° 1710. Cons. Ch. Of Parochial Churches. *Ch. Ch. Magd. Bal. Linc.* Ox. *Pub. L. Trin. Queen's.* Camb. *Sion.*

BINGHAM Joseph, M.A. R. of Havant, Hants.
 Ps. ciii. 13. 8° 1714. Of the Mercy of God to penitent Sinners, or fo. 1725. V. 1. p. 835. *Bod. St. John's.* Oxon.
 John xx. 23. fo. 1726. V. 2. p. 257. 2. s. On Absolution. *Bod. St. John's.* Oxon. *Sion.*

BINGLEY

BINNELL Robert, M. A. Minister of Newport, Salop.
 Heb. x 24. 8° 1751. Salop-Infirmary. The Christian Strife—or Emulation in good Works recommended.
BIRCH Peter, DD. Preb. of Westminster and Chapl. in Ord.
 John xvi. 3. 4° 1689. Nov. 5. b. Commons. *Ch. Ch. Magd. Worc. Oxon. Trin. Camb.*
 2 Sam. i. 21. 4° 1694. Jan. 30. b. Commons. *Ch. Ch. Magd. Jes. Oxon. Trin. Cl. H. St. John's. Camb.*
 Rev. xiv. 13. 4° 1700. Fun. of Lady Gething, *Bod.*
BIRCH Tho. B. A. Cur. of Redgrave, and R. of Billingford, Norf.
 Rom. xii. 21. 8° 1720. 2 f. The Unreasonableness of Revenge, and the great Duty of Christian Charity.
 Rom. v. 1. 8° 1729. Faith the Condition of Justification.
BIRCH Thomas, M. A. F. R. S. R. of St. Margaret's Patten's, and St. Gabriel, Fenchurch, Lond.
 Pf. cxxxix. 14. 4° 1749. b. Physicians. The Wisdom and Goodness of God proved from the Frame and Constitution of Man. *Queen's. Oxon. Brit. M.*
BIRD John, B. D. (Stud. of Ch. Ch. Ox.) R. of Cheddington, Bucks.
 2 Cor. v. 20. 4° 1663. Vis. f. The Divine Ambassador.
BIRKITT Edward, Clerk, Cur. of Greenwich.
 * 1 Tim. iii. 16. 4° 1770. Christmas-day.
 * 2 Kings xix. 19. 4° 1780. Fast.
BISBIE Nathaniel, DD. R. of Long Melford, Suff.
 Phil. i. 29. 4° 1682. Assize. *Bod. Pub. L. Trin. St. John's. Camb.*
 Matt. xxiii. 15. 4° 1683. The modern Pharisee. *All S. Oxon. Brit. M.*
 Judges xvii. 6. 4° 1684. Assize. Anarchy. *Pub. L. Camb.*
 Numb. xxvi. 9. 4° 1684. Assize. Sedition.
[BISCOE John]
 * Discourses in 8° 1665.
BISCOE Rich, M. A. Chapl. in Ord. R. of St. Martin Outwich, L.
 1 Pet. i. 8. Boyle's Lect. 2 Vol. 8° 1742. *New C. Ox. Brit. M.*
BISHOP Hawley, DD. (Fell. of St. John's Coll. Oxon.) R. of Creek, Northamptonf.
 Isai. xxix. 19. 8° 1747. *Northamp.* Infirmary. *Queen's. Camb.*
BISHOP Charles, M. A. R. of Rudford, and Under Master of the Coll. School at Glocester.
 * Pf. lxviii. 4, 5. 4° 1769. An. meet. 3 Choirs.
BISHOP Thomas, DD. Minister of St. Mary at Tower-Church in Ipswich, Suff.
 8 Serm. at Lady Moyer's Lect. and   } *Bod. Ch. Ch. New C. Ox.*
 1 Cor. xv. 28. 8° 1726. Conc. ad Cler. } *Queen's. Camb. Sion.*
BISSE   A Nonjuror.
 Ezek. xxi. 25—27.
BISSE Philip, Bp. of Hereford.
 Nehem. xiii. 13, 14. 4° 1701. b. Sons of the Clergy. *Ch. Ch. C. C. C. Magd. Wadh. Oxon. Trin. Queen's. Camb. Sion.*
                Isai.

OF AUTHORS, &c. 41

Ifai. lxii. 6,7. 4° 1710. Faſt. *C.C.C. Linc.* Oxon. *Pab. L. Trin. St. John's.* Camb.
Zech. viii. 10,11. 4° 1711. May 29. *Ch.Ch. C.C.C. Worc. Linc.* Oxon. *Pub. L.* Camb.
Matt. v. 16. 4° 1717. Prop. Goſpel. *Ch. Ch. C.C.C. Magd. Worc.* Oxon. *Pub. L. Queen's.* Camb.

BISSE Thomas, DD. Fell. of C.C.C. Oxon. and Chancellor of Hereford.
Heb. v. 4. 4° 1708. Trin. f. A Defence of Epiſcopacy. *Bod. Ch. Ch. Magd. Or.* Oxon. *Trin. Queen's. St. John's.* Camb.
2 Chron. xix. 6. 8° 1711. *Oxon.* Aſſize. Jehoſaphat's Charge. *Bod. C.C.C. Magd.* Oxon. *St. John's.* Camb. *Sion.*
* Pſal. cxliv. 14. 8° 1711. Acceſſion. *Sion.*
1 Kings viii. 18. 8° 1712. Open. Church. The Merit and Uſefulneſs of building Churches. *Bod. C.C.C. Magd.* Oxon.
1 Theſſ. v. 19. 4° 1712. *Oxon.* Whitſunday. *Bod. C.C.C. Magd. Bal. Linc.* Oxon. *St. John's.* Camb. *Sion.*
1 Cor. iii. 10,11. 8° 1713. *Oxon.* Act. *Ch. Ch. C.C.C. Magd. Or. Bal. Worc.* Oxon.
Pſ. lxxi. 20. 4° 1714. May 29. b. Commons. *Magd. Linc.* Oxon. *Pub. L.* Camb. *Sion.*
1 Tim. vi. 3,4. 8° 1716. Viſ. f. Pride and Ignorance the Ground of Errors in Religion. *C.C.C.* Oxon. *Pub L.* Camb.
Iſai. li. 1,2. 8° 1716. b. Sons of Clergy. *All S. Wadh.* Oxon. *St. John's.* Camb. *Sion.*
1 Cor. vii. 31. 8° 1717. The Xtian Uſe of the World. *C.C.C.* Oxon. *St. John's.* Camb.
1 Chron. xvi. 29. 8° 1717. 4 f. The Beauty of Holineſs in the Common Prayer. *Bod. Univ. Magd. Ch. Ch C.C.C. Linc.* Ox. *Pub. L. St. John's.* Camb.
1 Chron. xvi. 4, 5, 6. 8° 1720. A Rationale on Cathedral Worſhip or Choir Service. *Bod.*
1 Cor. xiv. 40. 8° 1723. 3 f. Decency and Order in public Worſh.
Pſ. cxliv. 12. 8° 1725. Open. Char. Sch. *All S.* Ox. *Queen's.* C.
Rom. xiii. 3,4. 8° 1726. The Ord. and Office of the Magiſtrate.
Eccleſ. ii. 8. 8° 1726. Muſick the Delight of the Sons of Men. *Bal.* Oxon.
Pſ. cxxxiii. 1,2. 8° 1727. County Feaſt. Society recommended. *All S.* Oxon. *Queen's.* Camb.
Zech. iv. 10. 8° 1729 Muſick. *All S.* Oxon. *Queen's.* Camb.
A Courſe of Sermons in 8° 1740. *Oxon.* On the Lord's Prayer. *All S. Worc. Linc.* Oxon.

BISSET Will. one of the Miniſters of St. Catherine's by the Tower.
Pſ. xciv. 15. 8° 1704. Ref. Manners. Plain Engliſh. *Or.* Oxon. *Queen's.* Camb. *Brit. M.*
Prov. xxix. 24. 8° 1704. Ref. Manners. } more Plain Engliſh.
Prov. xiv. 9. 8° 1704. Ref. Manners.
Rev. xiv. 13. 8° 1727. Fun. *Queen's.* Camb. *Eton.*

VOL. II.   F   BLACKALL

BLACKALL Anthony, M A. V. of Elvaſton, Nottingham.
*Prov. xxiv. 21. 4° 1704. Aſſize. Duty to God and the Queen.
St. John's Camb.
BLACKALL Offspring, Bp. of Exon.
His Works in 2 Vol. fo. 1723. Ch. Ch. C.C.C. All S. New. C. St.
John's, Trin. Worc. Pemb. Oxon. Pub. L. Trin. Camb.
His Serm. on the Lord's Prayer. 8° 1727. Wadb. Oxon.
Serm. at Boyle's Lectures 8° 1708. Cl. H. Camb.
BLACKALL Theophilus, M. A. R. of Monkhampton, Devonſ.
John xii. 37. 4° 1730. `Exon. Viſ. ſ.
BLACKBURN J.
*Pſ. xxxiii. 10–12. 8° 1749. Th. ſ.
BLACKBURNE Francis, M. A. Arch-Deacon of Cleveland.
* 1 Tim. i. 5–9. 8° 1742. Aſſize. York.
* Gal. iv. 9, 11. 8° 1753. On old Xmas-day. Queen's. Camb.
* 2 Tim. iii. 16, 17. 8° 1753. Ordination. Queen's. Camb.
BLACKBURNE Lancelot. Abp. of York.
Epheſ. iv. 31, 32. 4° 1694. The Unreaſonableneſs of Anger.
John iii. 16. 4° 1697. Advent. b. Lord Mayor.
1 Tim. iii. 16. 4° 1705. The Myſtery of Godlineſs. Ch. C. Ox.
Trin. Camb.
Matt. v. 10, 11. 12. 4° 1708. On St. Stephens-day. The Bleſ-
ſedneſs of ſuffering Perſecution for Righteouſneſs Sake. Ch. Ch.
Univ. Oxon. Trin. Camb.
Tit. i. 5. 4° 1714. Conc ad Synod. Bod. Ch. Ch. Ox. Queen's. C.
Matt v. 3. 4° 1715. Spitt. ſ. Ch. Ch. Oxon.
Iſai. l. 10, 11. 4° 1716. Jan. 30. Sion.
BLACKETT Bridges Edward, LLD. R. of Stoke Damerel, Devon.
* 2 Kings viii. 11–13. 4° 1753. Jan. 30. b Commons.
* John xiii. 34, 35. 4° 1760. b. Gov. of Exon, and Devon, Hoſp.
* John iv. 21. 4° 1771. Conf. St. Aubyn's Chap. Plymouth, Dev.
BLACKWELL Samuel, B. D. R. of Brompton, Yorkſhire.
2 Sam. xx. 19. 4° 1705. Aſſize.
John ix. 4. 8° 1705. Fun. of Lady Annabella Norwich.
Acts xvi. 30. 8° 1719.
BLACKWELL Thomas, M. A. R. of St. Clement Danes, Lond.
Pſ. cxxix. 5. 4° 1746. Th. after Reb. The Dangers of the late
Rebellion, and our happy Deliverance conſidered ; and a ſuit-
able conſequent Behaviour recommended.
BLADEN Thomas, DD. Dean of Ardfert.
2 Cor. v. 1.   ⎫   ⎧ p. 1. for the Sick.
Rev. xv. 3.   ⎬ 4° 1695. Bo. l. Of Divin. ⎨ 11 Th. ſ. many Del.
Ezek. xxxiii. 8.   ⎭   ⎩ 17 a troubled Conſ.
BLAGRAVE Jonathan, DD. Sub-Almoner, Chaplain in Ord. and
R. of Longworth Berks.
Luke xii. 4, 5. 4° 1691. b. Queen. All S. Ox. Trin Queen's. C.
Prov. xxvii. 4. 4° 1693. The Nature and Miſchief of Envy.
Pub. L. Camb.

BLAIR

BLAIR Hugh, DD. Minister of High Church, and Professor of Rhe-
torick and Belles Letters in the University of Edinburgh.
* 1 Vol. of Sermons, 8° 1777. *Bod. Sion.*
* 2 Vol. of Sermons, 8° 1780. *Bod.*
* Isai. xi. 9. 8° 1750. Prop. Xn. Know. V. Scotch Preacher v. 1.
p. 73. The Importance of religious Knowledge to mankind.
BLAIR James, M. A. Commissary of Virginia, President of William
and Mary Coll. and R. of Williamsburg.
Our Saviours divine Sermon on the Mount explained in 4 Vol.
8° 1720. *Bod Ch Ch.* Oxon. *Sion.*
5 Vol. 8° 1723. On the whole Chapter. *Bod.*
BLAKE Malachi
* - - - - 1735. On the Fire at Blanford, Dorsets.
BLAKE Martin, B. D
Ps. cxxii. 8, 9. 4° 1661.
BLAKE Edward, DD. late Fell. of Oriel Coll. Oxon.
* Matt. vi. xxxiii. 8° 1756. Act. s. Religion and it's temporal
Promises connected, *All S. Wadh.* Oxon.
BLAKES   jun. of Leeds, Yorkshire.
* - - - - 8° 1769.
BLAKEWAY Rob. Chap to Ld Herbert, and R. of Little Ilford, Ess.
Rom. xiii. 1, 2. 8° 1716. 21. An Exhortation to Obedience and
faithful Adherence to King George.
BLAMFORD Samuel
* Discourses in 8° 1660.
BLANE John, Preacher in the French Churches.
Gal. i. 7-9. 8° 1708. The Anathema of the false Prophets.
BLAYNEY Benjamin, B. D. late of Hertford Coll. Oxon.
* Dan. ix. 20. to end. 4° 1775. 2 Dissertations on Daniel's 70
Weeks. *Queen's.* Camb.
BLENNERHAYSETT Thomas, R. of Patching, Sussex.
Ps. xxi. 3. 8° 1715. Th. Jan. 30. *Queen's,* Camb.
Eccles. viii. 2. 4° 1716. Jan. 30. *Sion.*
BLIGH Michael
* Deut. xxxii. 9. 8° 1765. Church of God his peculiar Portion &c.
BLISS Anthony, M. A. V. of Portsmouth.
Zech. vii. 5. 8° 1725. Jan. 30.
BLISS Thomas, B. A. late Student of Ch. Ch. Oxon. V. of Ashford
and Yarnescombe, Devon.
* Gen. xlv. 4, 5. 8° 1769. Joseph a Type of Christ.
BLOMER Ralph, DD. Can. of Cant. and R. of All-hallows, Lom-
bard-street, Lond.
Tit. iii. 1. 8° 1710. Acc. b. Conv. *Linc.* Ox. *Trin. St. John's.* C.
John ix. 41. 4° 1712. Cor. Acad. *Cant.* June 28. *Brit. M.*
Ephes. iv. 3. 4° 1712.
Acts ix. 15. 16. 4° 1716. At the Enthronement of Abp. Wake. *Eton.*
1 John iii. 20, 21. 8° 1730. Fun. of Dr. Grandorge.
BLOMFIELD Barrington, DD. R. of Bedingham, Suff.
Jude 3. 8° 1728. *Camb. St. John's.* Camb.

BLOWER John, M. A. R. of St. Martin and Preb. of York.
　Heb. xiii. 7. ⎫ 8° 1714. 2 Fun. f. ⎧ of Abp Sharp ⎫ St. John's. C.
　Pf. xcvii. 1. ⎭　　　　　　　　⎩ of Queen Ann ⎭
BLOWER Samuel, Paftor of the Church at Abingdon.
　* Pf. xviii. 46. 8° 1697. Fun. f.
BLYTH S.
　* 2 Tim. iv. 7, 8. 8° 1754. Fun. of Rev. Mr. Bourn. Queen's. C.
BODINGTON John, M. A. of Sidney Coll. Camb. and R. of Blof-
　　fomvile, Bucks.
　Cant. iii. 11. 12° 1662.
BOEHM Anthony William, Chapl. to Prince George of Denmark.
　Several Difc. &c. 8° 1717. Pemb. Oxon.
　* Rev. xviii. 4. 8° 1718. Duty of Reformation.
　2 Cor. vii. 9–11. 8° 1721. Faft. The Doctrine of godly Sorrow.
BOLDE Samuel, R. of Steeple, and V. of Shapwick, Dorfetf.
　1 Pet. i. 15. 4° 1675. Man's great Duty. Bod.
　Gal. iv. 29. 4° 1682. Ch. for French Refugees. ag. Perfecution.
　　Bod. Queen's. Camb.
　* Rev. iii. 20. 12° 1687. Bod. Oxon. Trin. Camb.
　Rom. viii. 18. 4° 1689. An Exhortation to Charity &c. Brit. M.
　* Phil. iii. 8. 8° 1697. On the true Knowledge of Jef. Chrift.
　　Queen's. Camb.
　Pf. cxxxvi. 23. 8° 1715. Acceffion.
　Deut. xxxiii. 29. 8° 1716. Acceffion.
BOLDERO John, R. of Clipfum and Dingley, Northamptonf.
　Deut. i. 16, 17. 8° 1722. Affize. Northampton.
BOLTON Robert, LLD. Dean of Carlifle.
　* Gen. vi. 8, 9. 8° 17　　Walking with God.
　Gal. vi. 10. 4° 1739. Spitt. T. St. John's. Camb. Brit. M.
　Luke vi. 26. 8° 1741. Vif. The Woe denounced by Xt to them,
　　of whom all men fpeak well confidered. All S. Oxon.
[BOLTON Samuel]
　* Lev. x. 3. 8° 1660. A facramental Difc. on the Tree of life.
BOLTON Theophilus, Arch-Bp. of Cafhel.
　Tit. iii. 1. 8° 1721. Anniv. of Irifh. Reb.
BOLTON William, one of the School-mafters at the Charter-houfe.
　Numb. xvi. 26. 4° 1683. Th. Sep. 9. Core redivivus. St. John's.
　　Camb. Sion.
　Gen. xliii. 34. 4° 1684. Co. Feaft. Worc. Oxon. St. John's. Cam.
BONAR John, M. A.
　* Pf. cxxii. 9. 12° 1779. Nature and Tendency of the Ecclefiaf-
　　tical Conftit. in Scotland. V. Scot's Pr. v. 1. p. 1. Queen's. C.
BONAR John, B. A. Chapl. of his Majefty's Ship the Cerberus.
　* Neh. iii. 8. 4° 1773. The Advantages of the infular Situation
　　of Great Britain.
BOND Daniel, B. A. V. of Lye, Gloucefterf.
　1 Chron. v. 6, 7. 8° 1729. Affize.
　2 Chron. xix. 5–7. 8° 1729. Affize.

BOND

OF AUTHORS, &c.   45

BOND Henry, LLB. V. of Cowley, Glouceſt.
  * 3 Diſc. in 8° 1711. *Hertf.* Oxon.
  Eccleſ. xi. 10. 12° 17   2 Sermons.
BONHOME Joſhua, R. of Suddington, Leiceſt. and Chapl. in Ord.
  Rev. i. 16. 4° 1675. Viſ. ſ A new Conſtellation. *Ch. Ch.* Ox.
  Trin. Camb. *Sion.*
BONNEY Thomas, M. A. R. of St. Andrew, Underſhaft, Lond.
  * Pſ. xxix. 10. 4° 1763. Th. ſ.
BOOKER More, M. A. V. of Delvin, Ireland.
  * Pſ. xix. 11. 8° 1756. Fun. of the Counteſs of Droghede.
BOOKEY Sacheverell, LLB. V. of Wickingham, Norf.
  1 Theſſ. iv. 13,14. 4° 1739. *Norwich.* Ag. the Fear of Death.
BOOTH *ABRAHAM*
  * Gal. ii. 19. 8° 1770. Eſſay. The Death of legal Hope, the Life of evangelical Obedience.
  * - - - - - 8° 1772. Fun.
  * 1 Cor xv. 55–57. 8° 1773. Fun.
BOOTH Peniſton, DD. Dean of Windſor.
  Gal. iii. 27. 8° 1718. Of Baptiſm.
BORASTON George, M. A. R. of Hever, Kent.
  Matt. vii. 12. 4° 1684. Co. Feaſt. The royal Law. *St. John's.* C.
BOREMAN Rich. DD. R. of St. Giles's in the Fields, Lond.
  Matt. v. 34. 8° 1662. Antidote ag. Swearing. *Bod. Sion.*
  Phil. ii. 5. 4° 1663. Viſ. The Pattern of Xnity. *Queen's.* Ox.
  Phil. iii. 20. 4° 1669. Fun. of the Dutcheſs of Dudley, *Ch. Ch.*
  C.C.C. Oxon. *Trin.* Camb.
  Phil. iii. 15. 4° 1669.
BORFET Abiel, Miniſter of Richmond, Surry.
  Pſ. xx. 5. 4° 1696. Th. April 16. *Ch. Ch. Worc.* Oxon.
BOSSUET Benigne James, Bp. of Meaux.
  * Rev. xiv. 5. 4° 1686. Fun. *Magd.* Oxon.
BOSTON *Thomas*
  ‡ * 1 Theſſ. 5. 20,21. 8° 1694. *Edinburgh, Brit. M.*
BOSTON *Thomas,* Miniſter of the Goſpel at Ettrick.
  * Diſcourſes in 2 Vol. 8° 1753. Four fold State. *Pub. L.* Camb.
  * Sermons in 3 Vol. 8° 1773. An Illuſtration of the Doctrines of the Xtian Religion with reſpect to Faith and Practice. *Bod.*
  * 17 Diſcourſes in 8° 1773. On the diſtinguiſhing Characters of true Believers, *Bod.*
  * 10 Faſt Sermons in 8° 1773. *Bod.*
  * 4 Sermons in 8° 1773. On ſacramental Occaſions. *Bod.*
  * 2 Diſcourſes in 8° 1775. The Xtian Life delineated. *Bod.*
  * 8 Diſc. in 8° 1775. A View of this and the other World. *Bod.*
  * 10 Sermons in   Chiefly relating to the Grounds of the Lord's Controverſy with this Generation.
  * Sermons in   The Method of Recovery from the Ruins of the Fall of Jeſus Chriſt &c.
BOSTWICK *David,* M. A. late Miniſter of the Preſbyterian Church, New York.
                 * 2 Cor.

  *2 Cor. iv. 5. 8° 1759. b. Synod. *New York.* Self-disclaimed and Christ exalted.
  * Acts ii. 39. 8° 1765. A fair and rational Vindication of the Right of Infants to Baptism.
BOSWELL John, B. A. V. of St. Mary Magdalen, Taunton.
  * Pf. xvi. 7. 8° 1730. May 29.
BOTELER Edward, M. A. Chapl. in Ord. and R. of Wintringham, *Lincolnf.*
  Pf. lxxii. 4. 12° 1661. Affize.
  Pf. xxi. 3. 8° 1662
  Matt. xxv. 21. 8° 1662. Fun.
  Jer. xxxi. 33. 8° 1664.
  Heb. xiii. 14. 8° 1664. Fun.
  Luke xix. 42. 12° 1666. Open. gen. Affize. *Trin.* Camb.
BOTT Thomas, M. A. R. of Spixworth near Norwich.
  Luke ix. 56. 8° 1724. A Discourse. The Peace and Happiness of this World the immediate Design of Xy. *Queen's.* C. *Brit. M.*
  Phil. i. 10. 8° 1730. Vif. Morality founded in the Reason of things, and the Ground of Revelation. *Queen's.* Camb.
  Matt. vii. 12. 8° 1738. Jan. 30. At *Norwich.*
BOUGHEN Edward, Parson of Wood Church, Kent.
  1 Cor. i. 10. 8° 1714. Vif. April 18.
BOULTER Hugh, Abp. of Armagh.
  Luke xii. 42–44. 4° 1714. *Dublin.* Vif. *Wadh.* Oxon. *Pub. L.* Camb. *Eton.*
  1 Pet. ii. 13, 14. 8° 1715. Affize. The Foundation of Submission to our Governors. *Eton.*
  2 Tim. i. 6, 7. 8° 1716. Conf. of Bp. Gibson.
  Prov. xxi. 11. 8° 1716. Ref Manners. *Ch. Ch.* Oxon. *Eton.*
  Heb. x. 24. 8° 1716. Spitt. W. *Ch. Ch.* Oxon.
  Eccles. viii. 2. 4° 1716. Affize. The Obligation of Oaths to the Government, and the Pretences of breaking them considered. *Ch. Ch.* Oxon.
  2 Pet. ii. 10. 8° 1719. Affize. The Character and evil Consequences of Seditiousness. *Trin.* Camb.
  Isai. lv. 6, 7. 4° 1720. Faft b. Lords for the Plague. *Ch. Ch. Linc. Worc* Oxon. *Brit. M.*
  Luke xxiv. 47. 4° 1721. Prop. Gofpel. *Ch. Ch.* Oxon. *Sion.*
  Gen. xviii. 19. 8° 1722. An. meet Char. Schools.
  2 Cor. xiii. 11. 4° 1722. Farewell. *Ch. Ch.* Oxon.
BOUNCHER Samuel, M. A. R. of East-Horfely, Surry.
  2 Sam. xxii. 4. 4° 1693. Faft.
BOURDALOUE
  * Sermons in 4 Vol. 12° 1776. Tranfl. from the French by A. C.
BOURKE Dean Joseph, Abp. of Tuam.
  * 2 Theff. i. 3. 4° 1776. Ir. Prot. Schools.
BOURN *Samuel,* of Bolton, Lancaf.
  * 1 John iii. 2. 8° 1722. The transforming Vision of Christ in the future State.

* 1 John

* 1 John iii. 3. 8° 1722. The Believers Hope of the same.
N. B. At the end his Fun. Serm. by his Son S. *Bourn.*
* Kings ii. 3. 8° 1722.

BOURN Samuel, of Birmingham.
* Acts xix. 25. 8° 1735. Nov. 5.
* Phil. i. 27, 28. 8° 1738. b. Diffent. Ministers. *Wadh.* Oxon.
* Ezek. xxxiii. 2. 12° 1754. 4 f. A new Call to the unconverted.
* 20 Sermons in 8° 1755. On the most serious and practical Subjects of the Christian Religion.

BOURN Samuel, of Norwich.
* Mark iv. 30. 4° 1752. b. Diff. Ministers. The Rise, Progress &c. of the Christian Religion.
* Disc. in 2 Vol. 8° 1760. On the Principles and Evidences of Nat. Religion and Xtian Revelation. *Queen's.* Camb.
* Disc. in 2 Vol. 8° 1763. and 1764. On select Parables. *Bod.* *Queen's.* Camb.
* Disc. in 2 Vol. 8° 1777. On various Subjects Critical, Philosophical and Moral. *Bod.*.

[BOWATER John]
John i. 12. 8° 1694. *Bod.*

BOWBER Thomas, M. A. formerly of Wadh. Coll. Oxon.
2 Chron. xxxv. 24. 4° 1705. Royal Fun. *Pub L. St. John's.* Cam.

BOWCHIER Richard, B. D. Fell. of St. John's Coll. Camb. and Chapl. to the Bishop of Chichester.
Gal. v. 25. 4° 1692. b. Lord Mayor. *Bod. Univ. Linc.* Oxon.

BOWDEN *John*
* 1 Tim. iv. 16. 8° 1704.

BOWEN Samuel
Pf. xviii. 46. 8°   Fun.

BOWERS Thomas, Bp of Chichester.
Prov. xxiv. 21. 8° 1722. Jan. 30. b. Lords. *Queen's.* Camb.

BOWICK William, B. A.
Phil. i. 1, 2. 8° 1716.

BOWLES Thomas, DD. (late Fell. of Magd. Coll. Oxon.) and V. of Brackley, Northamptonshire.
Heb. i. 1, 2. 8° 1728. Christmas.
* Rom. xiii. 1. 4° 1741. Affize. *Northamp.*. The End and Design of civil Government.

BOWMAN Thomas, M. A. V. of Martham, Norfolk.
* Rom. x. 3. 8° 1762.
* 7 Discourses in 12° 1766. on the Principles of Xnity.

BOWMAN William, M. A. V. of Dewsbury, Yorkshire.
Matt. xv. 6. 8° 1731. Vif. Traditions of the Clergy destructive of Religion. *Wadh. Worc.* Oxon. *Queen's.* Camb. *Brit. M.*

BOWTELL John, DD. Fell. of St. John's Coll. Camb.
Rom xvi. 17. 8° 1711. Dissenters imposed on by their Teachers. *Ch. Ch. Linc.* Oxon. *St. John's, Queen's.* Camb.

BOWYER Thomas, M. A. V. of Martock, Somersetshire.
Neh. xiii. 14. 4° 1734. Augment. of a Chapelry.

1 Cor. xvi. 2. 4° 1735. Ch. f. The meafure of Xn. Beneficence, and Ufefulnefs and Neceffity of charitable Ufes.

BOYDELL John
*Pf.cl.4. 8° 1727. Erect. an Org. in St. Ofwald's Ch. Derb. *Brit. M.*

BOYS Edward, DD. R. of Mautby, Norf. and fometime Fell. of C. C. C. Camb.
16 Serm. in 8° 1672. preached on fev. Occafions. *Sion Pub. L. C.*

BOYS James, M. A. V. of Coggefhall, Effex.
A practical Expofition on the 39 Art. &c. to which is added a Serm. on 1 John v. 7. fo. 1716. p. 271. *Bod. Sion.*

[BOYSE Chriftopher]
* Acts ii. 24. 4° 1707. Eafter.

BOYSE Joseph, of Dublin.
‡ * 1 Theff v. 19. 4° 1691. 2 f. The Sin and Danger of quenching the Spirit.
* - - - - 4° 1695. Royal Fun.
* - - - - 4° 1698. Ref. Manners.
* - - - - 4° 1705. Fun. of Rev. *Mr. Travers.*
* Pf. cxxii. 7, 8. 8° 1714. Acceffion.
38 Serm. on particular Occ. V. 1 Vol. of his Works in fo. 1728.

BRACKENRIDGE William, DD. R. of St. Michael-Boffifhaw, Librarian of Sion. Coll. and F. R. S. and A. S.
* 17 Serm. in 8° 1764. On feveral Subjects. *Sion.*

BRADBURY Thomas
* Ezra vi. 14. 8° 1708. Ref. Manners.
* Phil. iv. 6. 12° 1711. On Prayer.
* 4 Serm. in 12° 1713. Chriftian's Joy.
* Nehem. v. 13. 8° 1715. Th. f.
* 1 Kings ii. 46. 8° 1716. Nov. 5. *Wadh.* Oxon.
‡ * Jude 2. 8° 1717. Jan. 30. *Brit. M.*
Jude 5. 8° 1719. Jan. 30. *Brit. M.*
* Sermons in 8° 1723. Concerning offences. *Ch. Ch.* Oxon.
Heb. i. 3. 8° 1729. *Eton.*
* Sermons in 2 Vol. 8° 1726. Myftery of Godlinefs.
* 1 Cor. xi. 24. 8° 1737. Lord's fupper.
* Phil. iii. 8, 9. 8° 1738. 2 f. Fun. of Rev. *Mr. Bragge.*
* 3 Sermons in 8° 1732. on Exod. xx. 7. The Sin and Danger of profane Swearing.
* Rom. viii. 32. 8° 1732. Xt's Suff. V. Lime-ftreet. S. v. 2. p. 3.
* 6 Sermons in 8° 1737. on Heb. vi. 12.
* 3 Sermons in 8° 1749 On the Duty and Doctrine of Baptifm. *Braz. N.* Oxon.
* Sermons in 8° 1749. Revilings and Confeffion of a Faith.
* 10 Sermons in 8° 1752. The Power of Chriftians over Plagues and Health, and his Name as the God of Ifrael confidered as Arguments of his fupreme Deity.
* 54 Sermons in 3 Vol. 8° 1772.

BRADFORD John, M. A.
Pf. cvii. 4° 1746. Th. f. Oct. 9.

BRADFORD Samuel, Bp. of Rochester.
  Rom. iii. 8. 4° 1696. 4° 1696. Nov. 5. b. Lord Mayor. *Sion.*
  Ezra x. 3, 4. 8° 1697. Ref. Manners. *Ch. Ch.* Oxon.
  Ephes. iv. 3. 4°|1698. b. L .May. Persuasive to Peace and Unity.
  Prov. xxiv. 21. 4° 1692. Jan. 30. b. K. *All S.* Ox. *Trin.* Camb.
  2 Tim. iii. 14, 15. 4° 1700. School Feast.
  Isai. i. 26. 4° 1700. El. Lord Mayor.
  Ps. xi. 3, 4. 4° 1700. Nov. 5. b. Lord Mayor. *Eton.*
  John vi. 45. — 1 Tim. i. 15. — John iii. 16, 17. At Boyle's Lect. 4° 1700 or so. 1739. Vol. 1. *Bod. Ch. Ch. St. John's.* Oxon. *Trin. Queen's.* Camb.
  Esther ix. 20–22. 4° 1704. Nov. 5. b. Ld Mayor. *Pub. L.* Cam.
  Ephes. iv. 11–13. 4° 1708. Cons. of Bps Trimnel and Blackall. *Ch. Ch.* Oxon. *Trin. St. John's, Queen's.* Camb.
  Tit. iii. 4–7. 12° 1709. 2 s. on baptismal and spir. Regeneration.
  Acts iv. 32. 8° 1709. Ann. Meet. *Ch. Sch. Trin.* Camb.
  James iii. 17. 8° 1710. An Exhortation to Purity and Peace. *Linc.* Oxon. *Trin. St. John's, Queen's.* Camb. *Sion.*
  Prov. iv. 25–27. 4° 1710. Jan. 30. b. Ld Mayor. *Ch. Ch. Linc.* Oxon. *Sion.*
  Gal. v. 1. 4° 1713. Nov. 5. b. Lord Mayor. The Reasonableness of standing fast in English and Xtian Liberty. *Wadh.* Ox. *Queen's.* Camb. *Sion.*
  1 Cor. x. 10. 8° 1715. The Sin and Danger of murmuring ag. God and our Governors.
  Rom. ii 28, 29. 4° 1716. The Unprofitableness of external without internal Religion. *Trin. Queen's.* Camb.
  Luke xii. 51. 8° 1716. Christian Religion the Occasion, not the Cause of Division. *Eton.*
  John xvii. 20, 21. 8° 1718. The Nature of Xtian Union, and the Method of restoring it. *Ch. Ch.* Oxon. *Trin. Queen's. Cl. H.* C.
  Matt. xii. 25. 4° 1719. Jan. 30. b. Lords. *Queen's. Cl. H.* Cam.
  Matt. xxviii. 19, 20. 4° 1719. Prop. Gospel. *Ch. Ch. Worc.* Ox. *Queen's.* Camb. *Sion.*
  Prov. xiii. 11. 4° 1720. The honest and dishonest Ways of getting Wealth. *Ch. Ch.* Oxon. *Queen's.* Camb.
  Heb. vi. 1, 2. 8° 1724. The Design and Use of Confirmation. *Queen's.* Camb.

BRADLEY Christopher, M. A. of Peter-house, Camb. and R. of Thornton, York.
  2 Cor. iv. 17, 18. 4° 1666. *York.* The Eye of Faith looking at Eternity.

BRADLEY John, M. A. R. of St. Mary Bishop the Elder. York.
  John xxi. 15. 4° 1706. *York.* Ch. s. b. Lord Mayor of York, on St. Stephen's-day.
  Isai. xlv. 7. 4° 1713. Th. for Peace.

BRADLEY Thomas, DD. Chapl. in Ord. and Preb. of York.
  Numb. xxiii. 21. 4° 1661. *York.* The Day of the King's Coronat.
  Job xxix. 14–17. 4° 1663. *York.* Assize.

Matt. xxii. 21. 4° 1663. *York*. Affize.
Rev. ii. 1. 4° 1663. *York*. Conc. ad Cler. *Univ*. Oxon.
Acts xv. 28. 4° 1663. *York*. Vif.
Rom. v. 19. 4° 1667. Aff. 2 f. Of the firft and fecond Adam. *Univ*. Oxon. *Sion*.

BRADLEY Thomas
* 1 Kings xix. 4. 4° 1670. Elijah's Epitaph. The Author's own Fun. f. *Univ*. Oxon.

BRADSHAIGH Thomas, M.A. Chapl. in Ord. and R. of Stratford, Suff. and of Langham, Effex.
Pf. lxxiii. 13, 14. 8° 1715. Vif.
Luke x. 25. 8° 1720. Vif.
1 Cor. xi. 1. 8° 1747. Jan 30.

BRADSHAW William, Bp. of Briftol.
2 Cor. i. 9, 10. 8° 1714. Nov. 5. b. Lord Mayor. *Bod*.
Rom. xiii. 5. 4° 1730. Jan. 30. b. Lords. *Bod*. *All S*. Oxon.

BRADSHAW William, Fell. of Sidney Coll. Camb.
* John ii. 1–12. V. Difc. on Conj. Duty. Vol. 2. p. 395.

BRADY Nich. DD. Chap. in Ord. and Minif. of Richmond, Surry.
‡ * Matt. xvi. 26. 4° 1693. Nov. 26. b. King. *Brit. M*.
Rev. xiv. 13. 4° 1693. Fun. of Shadwell. *Bod*. *Pub. L*. Camb.
‡ * Pf. cxxxiii. 1, 2. 4° 1695. b. Apothecaries. *Brit. M*.
Acts xx. 32. 4° 1696. Farewel. *Eton*.
‡ * 2 Chron. v. 13, 14. 4° 1697. On St. Cecilia's day. *Brit. M*.
14 Serm. in 8° 1704. V. 1. preached on fev. Occafions. *Trin*. C.
15 Sermons in 8° 1706. V. 2. preached on fev. Occafions *Worc*. Oxon. *Trin*. Camb.
Luke x. 41, 42. 8° 1707. b. Queen. *Univ*. *Hert*. Oxon. *Trin*. Camb. *Eton*. *Sion*.
John x. 16. 8° 1707. Th. Union. *Sion*.
Acts viii. 14–17. 8° 1708. Confirmation.
Heb. xiii. 14. 4° 1708. Fun. f.
Acts xv. 41. 4° 1705. The End of Confirmation, and the due Effects of it.
2 Sam. xix. 14. 4° 1715. May 29. At Richmond.
Rom. vi. 21. 4° 1724. Affize.
14 Select Serm. in 8° 1730. Vol. 3. On practical Subjects. *New C*. *St. John's*. Oxon. *Pub. L*. *Queen's*. Camb.
Serm. in 3 Vol. 8° 1730. *Bod*. *St. John's*. Oxon. *Sion*.

BRADY Nich. LLB. R. of Footing, and Lect. of Clapham. Middl.
Pf. cxviii. 23, 24. 4° 1738. May 29. b. Lord Mayor.

BRAGGE Francis, B. D. V. of Hitchin and Preb. of Linc.
Practical Difcourfes in 2 Vol. 8° On the Parables.
V. 1. 1702. V. 2. 1704. *Bod*. *Ch. Ch*. *All S*. *Univ*. *Pemb*. Oxon. *Pub. L*. *Trin*. *Queen's*. Camb. *Sion*.
Practical Obfervations in 2 Vol. 8° On the Miracles.
V. 1. 1702. V. 2. 1726. *Univ*. *Ch.Ch*. *All S*. *Pemb*. Ox. *Queen's*. Camb.
13 Sermons in 8° 1713. Of Undiffembled and perfevering Religion, *All S*. Oxon. *BRAGGE*

BRAGGE Robert
   Matt. ix. 31. 4° 1674. Fun. A Cry for Labourers in God's Vineyard. *Bod.*
   * Ifai. lix. 19. V. Lime-f. S. Vol. I. p. 1. Holy Spirit's Standard againft Error.
   * Gal. ii. 16. V. Lime-f. S. V. II. p. 87. 4 f. Sinn. |uftif. by G.
BRAILSFORD J. M. A. V. of North-Wheatley, Nottingham, and Chaplain to the Right Hon. Lord Middleton.
   * Rom. iii. 18. 4° 1761. Affize. The Nature and efficacy of the Fear of God in fpiritual and public Life &c.
   * 13 Serm. in 8° 1776. *All S.* Oxon.
BRALESFORD Humphry, M. A. R. of Hawkfworth, and Preb. of Southwell, Nottingham.
   Rom. x 15. 8° 1724. *Nottingham.* Vif. f.
BRAMHALL John, Abp. of Armagh.
   His Works fo. 1677. *Dublin. Bod. Univ. Mert. St. John's. Trin. Or. Bal.* Oxon. *Trin. Queen's.* Camb. *Sion.*
BRAMSTON
   Rom. x. 2. 8°   Nov. 5.
BRAMSTON John, M. A. R. of Theydon Garnon, Effex.
   Ecclef. vii. 10. 8° 1724. Affize. *Queen's.* Camb. *Eton.*
   Pf. i. 2. 4° 1724. Affize.
BRAMSTON William, DD. Chap. in Ord. R. of St. Chriftopher's, and Preb. of Worc.
   Prov. xxvii. 1. 4° 1695. b. Lord Mayor. The Neceffity of a prefent Repentance. *Pub. L.* Camb.
   Acts xxiv. 14. 4° 1697. Open. Lect. at Maldon. *Pub. L. Trin. C. Sion.*
   1 Tim. vi. 6. 4° 1702. Acceffion.
   Pf. xx. 7. 4° 1706. Th. *Queen's.* Camb.
   John vii. 15. 4° 1708. Sch. F. Hu. Learning not prejud. to Xnity.
   Rev. iii. 15, 16. 4° 1713. 2 f. The great Sin of Lukewarmnefs in Religion. *Bod. Linc.* Oxon. *Queen's. St. John's.* Camb.
   1 Tim. ii. 1, 2. 4° 1714. At the Temple. *Trin. Queen's. St. John's.* Camb. *Sion.*
BRANDON John. R. of Finchamfted, Berks.
   1 Theff. iv. 7.   169, A practical Difcourfe.
BRAY Thomas, DD. Minifter of St. Botolph, Aldgate, London.
   Dan. xii. 3. 4° 1699. Ord. of Miffionaries. *Ch. Ch. C. C. C. Magd.* Oxon. *Trin. Queen's.* Camb.
   * Ecclef. xii. 1. 8° 1704. Early Religion.
   1 John iii. S. 8° 1708. Ref. M. For God or for Satan. *Ch. Ch.* Oxon. *Pub. L. Queen's.* Camb.
   1 Tim. vi. 12. 4° 1709. Fun. of Mr. Dent. The good fight of faith in the Caufe of God &c. *Ch. Ch. Univ.* Ox. *Trin. Queen's.* Cam.
   * Prov. xxxi. 10-28. V. Bellamy's Fam. Pr. 8° 1754. (1ft Edit.) Vol. II. p. 266. The virtuous Wife defcribed.
BRAY Tho. DD. R. of Ex. Coll. Oxon. and Canon of Windfor &c.
   * 2 Pet. i. 19. 8° 1761. The more fure word of prophecy. *Wor.* Ox.
   * 1 Pet. ii. 16. 4° 1763. Jan. 30. b. Com. *Braz. N. Were.* Oxon.

BREKELL John, Liverpool.
  * - - - 8° 1744. The Dangers of the Sea.
  * John iii. 3–5. 8° 1761. Regeneration.
  * 20 Difcourfes in 8° 1765. On the Grounds and Principles of the Chriftian Religion. *Bod. Pub. L.* Camb. *Sion.*
  * Job xxi. 12. 8° 1766. Open. an Organ at St. Peter's, Liverp.
  * Jer. xxxi. 29. 8° 1767. Differtation. *Queen's.* Camb.
  * Phil. i. 11. 8° 1769. Liverpool-Infirmary.
BRENT Charles, M.A. R. of Ch.Ch. Briftol, and Can. of St. David's.
  1 Cor. x. 24. 4° 1704. Ch. Perfuafions to a public Spirit.
  Prov. iii. 9. 4° 1708. b. Comp. of Merchants.
  1 Cor. xv. 41. 8° 1721. Fun. of Mr. Colfton.
  Eccles. x. 19. 8° 1728. b. Comp. of Merchants. Money effayed.
BRETON John
  Ephes. iv. 3. 8° 1714.
BRETT Joseph, M.A. R. of St. Clement's, and St. Auftin's, Norw.
  Prov. xvi. 12. 4° 1704. *Norwich.* Acceffion. *St. John's,* Camb.
  6 Serm. in 8° 1715. *Bod. All S. Ch. Ch. Linc. Worc.* Oxon. *Pab. L. Queen's. St. John's.* Camb. *Sion. Eton.*
BRETT Thomas, LL.D. R. of Betteshanger, Kent.
  6 Difc. in 8° 1712, 13, and 14. On various Subjects. *Bod. All S. Ch. Ch. Linc. Worc. Jef. O. Pub. L. Queen's. St. John's.* C. *Sion. Eton.*
  Difc. in 8° 1720. Concerning the ever-bleffed Trinity.
BREVAL Frank Durant de, DD. Preb. of Weftminfter.
  1 John v 4. 4° 1670. French, and tranflated into Englifh by Dr. Peter du Moulin. *Bod. Queen's. Magd.* Oxon.
  Rev. ii. 10. 4° 1670. Faith in the juft victorious over the world. *Bod. Queen's.* Oxon.
BRIDEOAKE Ralph, B.D. Arch-Deacon of Winchefter.
  2 Kings iv. 7. 4° 1730. b. Sons of the Clergy. *Wadh.* Oxon.
BRIDGE Francis, DD. R. of St. Mildred, Bread-ftreet, London.
  Pf. lviii. 10, 11. 4° 1684. Nov. 5. b Lord Mayor. *Ch. Ch. All S. Magd.* Oxon. *Trin. St. John's.* Camb.
BRIDGEN Will. DD R. of Folkington and Weft-Dean, Suffex.
  1 Tim. ii. 1. 8° 1712. Affize. *St. John's.* Camb.
BRIDGES Ralph, DD. V. of South Weald, Effex.
  2 Cor. v. 7. 4° 1724. Act. f.
  1 Kings iii. 9 4° 1727. b. Lord Mayor. The Wife King's Concern for his People. *Bod.*
  * 1 Kings i. 9. 4° 17
  Rom. v. 13. 4° 1738. Affize.
BRIDGES William
  ‡ * Ifai. ix. 1. 8° 1667. Fulnefs of Chrift.
  * John xiv. 18. 8° 1667.
  * Rom. vii. 33. 8° 1667.
  James i. 24. 4° 1667. p. 51.
BRIGGS Jofeph, M.A. V. of Kirkburton, Yorkfhire.
  Sound Confiderations in 8° 1675. For tender Confciences.
  1 Cor. i. 10. 8° 1675. p. 1. The Obligation of Confcience to Union and Communion with Fellow-Chriftians.

Heb. x. 25. 8° 1675. The Obligation of Confcience not to for-
sake publick Affemblies.
BRIGHT George, DD. Dean of St. Afaph and Chapl. in Ord.
6 Serm. in 8° 1695. *Magd.* Oxon. *Pub. L.* Camb. *Brit. M.*
* Several Difc. in 8° 1699.
BRINGHURST J. M. A. R. of St. Peter All St's in Stamford, Berks.
1 Cor. x. xxxi. 4° 1749. Nov. 5. b. Lord Mayor. The Glory of
God, the beft Principle of Action in Man, *Queen's.* Camb.
BRINGHURST Ifaac, DD. R. of Toddington, Herts.
Matt. xi 30. 4° 1689. b. Lord Mayor. The Eafinefs and Diffi-
culty of the Chriftian Religion. *Bod. Sion.*
BRINSLEY John, Minifter of the Gofpel at Yarmouth.
* John xviii. 11. 8° 1660. Drinking the bitter Cup.
Pf. lxxii. 15. 4° 1661. 2 f.
Heb. ii. 1. 8° 1662.
1 Tim. i. 15. 8° 1662.
2 Cor. xii. 9. 8° 1663.
Pf. xxxix. 1. 8° 1664.
BRINSLEY William
* Difc. in 12° 1667.
BRISTED Ezekiel, R. of Meeching, alias Newhaven, Suffex.
Ifai. lx. 10. 8° 1715.
BRISTED John, M. A. R. of St. Peter's and St. Mary Weftcut in
Lewes, Suffex.
* - - - - - 1743. Nature and Ufe of Prophecy.
Pf. cvi. 17. 4° 1750. On the Earthq. Admonitions to Repentance.
BROAD Thomas
Pf. ix. 16. 1696. On the Affociation.
BRODHURST Edward
* Sermons in 8° 1733.
BROGRAVE Robert, M. A. R. of Gatefide, Durh. & Chapl. in Ord.
Matt. v. 16. 4° 1689. b. King and Queen. Of Example. *Ch. Ch.*
Oxon. *Eton.*
BROME Edmond, B. D. Fell. of St. John's Coll. Camb.
6 Serm. in { John xvi. 7. The glo. Defc. of the H. G. p. 1. 15. 35.
8° 1709. { John xx. 20. On Eafter. p. 73. 83. } *All S.* Oxon.
{ John i. 14. On the Nativity. p. 95. } *Pub. L.* Camb.
Mark ii. 20. } p. 1.
Matt. 6. 16. } 2 Dif. 8° 1711. *Camb.* The Ufe and Meafures, and
} p. 39. Man. of Xtian Fafting. To which is added
A Serm. on Acts xvii. 34. Rarenefs, but Bleffings of Faith. p. 211.
Luke vii. 47. 8° 1712. The thankful Penitent.
BROME James, M. A. R. of Chariton, Kent.
Amos viii. 11, 12. 4° 1678. Faft. The Famine of the Word
threatened to Ifrael. *Sion.*
Ifai. 22. 12–14. 4° 1679. Faft. God's Call to weeping and mourn-
ing. *Sion.*
Prov. xxix. 2. 4° 1694.
* Joel iii. 19. 8° 17   Faft

2 Cor.

2 Cor. v. 11. 8° 1702.
Gal vi. 7. 8° 1702.
Cant. v. 1. 8° 1707.
BROMESGROVE Samuel, M. A. Preacher at the Tabernacle in Spittal Fields.
Judges v. 21. 4° 1704. Th. f.
BROMLEY Robert Anthony, Preacher at the Foundling-Hospital and Lect. of St. John's, Hackney.
* Job xxix. 13. 4° 1770. At the Foundling Hosp.
* Pf. cxxii. 1. 4° 1771. On open. Ch. and Organ.
*   8° 1772. Latter End.
* Eccles^{us}. iv. 10. 4° 1774. At the Foundling Hosp.
‡ * Luke viii. 52. 8° 1782. Humane Society.
BROMWICH
* Luke xi. 24. 8° 1770. *Birmingham*. On Charity.
BROOKBANK Joseph, B. A.
Rom xiii. 2. 12° 1661. 3 f. Rebels tried and cast.
BROOKE Henry, M. A. Fell. of Christ's Coll. in Manchester.
- - - - - *Manchester*, 2 f. Th. f. Oct. 9. 1746.
1 Pet. ii. 13. 8° 1747. Aff. Respect and Submission due to the Constitution both in Church and State.
BROOKE James, M. A. R. of Hill Croome and V. of Hanley Castle, Worcestf.
Prov. x. 7. 4° 1706. Fun. of Sir Francis Russel, Bart.
Col. iii. 16. 8° 1723. Musick. The Duty and Advantage of singing to the Lord. *Worc*. Oxon.
BROOKE John, M. A. R. of Great Yeldham, Essex.
Rev. xiv. 13. 4° 1693. Fun of John Symmons, Esq;
BROOKE Thomas, LLD. R. of Nantwich, and Dean of Chester.
Pf. cxlv. 10. 8° 1732. Florists-meeting. *Queen's*. Camb.
Acts xxiv. 25. 4° 1732. Assize.
Pf. cxxxiii. 1. 4° 1746. Aff. The Pleasure and Advan. of Unity.
BROOKE Z. DD. Fell. of St. John's Camb, and Chapl. in Ord.
* 11 Discourses in 8° 1764. *Pub. L.* Camb.
BROOKER Daniel, V. of St. Peters, and Minor Can. of Worc.
Pf. xxxiii. 1-3. 4° 1743. Music at Worcester.
John xviii. 38. 4° 1745. Jan. 30.
* Pf. xxi. 11-13. 4° 1746. Th. for Victory.
BROOKES Henry
Deut. xxiii. 9. 8° 1707. Fast.
BROOKS Hen. M. A. R. of Camerton, and Henton Blewet, Somerf.
Pf. xlvi. 1. 8° 1732. Fun. God a good mans present Help and Comfort &c.
* Luke vii. 13-15 8° 1734. Raising the Widow's Son of Nain.
BROOKS *Thomas*, Preacher at Fish-street-Hill. London.
Pf. xxxix. 9. 8° 1660. Fun. The Mute Xtian under the smarting Rod. *Bod. Sion.*
2 Cor. ii. 11. 8° 1661. Remedies ag. Satan's Devices. *Bod. Sion.*
Lam. iii 24. 8° 1662. *Sion.*

Heb.

Heb. xii. 14. 8° 1662. Holiness the only way to Happiness. *Sion*.
Rom. viii. 32-34. 8° 1664.
Matt. vi. 6. 8° 1665. Two arguments for closet-prayer. *Bod*.
1 Pet. i. 4. 8° 1668. Fun. *Bod*.
Isai. xlii. 24, 25. 4° 1670. Fire of London. *Bod*.

BROOME William, LLD. R. of Patham, and V. of Eye, Norfolk.
  1 Tim. ii. 1, 2. 8° 17   Cor. *Brit. M*.
  Pf. cxxii. 6. 4° 1737. Assize. *Brit. M*.

[BROUGH William, DD.]
  *Disc. in 8° 1660.

BROUGHTON John, DD. V. of Kingston upon Thames.
  Judges v. 3. 4° 1705. Th. Sep. 7. 1704 *Cl. H*. Camb.
  Ecclef. viii. 11. 4° 1707. b. Queen. *Bod. Ch. Ch. Magd*. Oxon.
    Pub. L. Trin. Camb. *Sion*.
  2 Sam. xii. 5. 8° 1713. On the Execution of Mr. Noble. *Sion*.
  Mark xi. 17. 4° 1714. Conf. of Kew Chapel. Of the House of
    Prayer.
  1 Tim. ii. 2. 4° 1722. Assize.

BROUGHTON Thomas, B. A. Fell. of Ex. Coll. Oxon, and Cur.
  of the Tower.
  Acts x. 1, 2. 8° 1737. The Christian Soldier.

BROUGHTON Thomas, M. A. V. of St. Mary Redcliffe, Bristol,
  and Preb. of Sarum.
  1 Sam xii. 23-25. 4° 1745. Jan. 30.
  Col. iii. 14. 4° 1752. *Bristol* Infirmary.. The Perfection of the
    Christian Morality asserted. *Queen's*. Camb.
  * 15 (Posth.) Sermons in 8° 1779. On select Subjects.

BROUGHTON Will. M. A. R. of   Worcesters.
  * Matt. xx. 6, 7. 8° 1726. Idleness in spiritual affairs considered.

BROUSTON. M. [a]
  Isai. xli. 14. 4° 1699. Believer's Support under Persecution *Cl.*
  Hall. Camb.

BROWN Edward, M A. R. of Langley, Kent.
  2 Pet. i. 7. 4° 1699. Co. Feast.

BROWN James, M. A. V. of Kingston near Taunton, Somersets.
  * Pf. xxiii. 4. 8° 1756. Fun. f.

BROWN John, DD. (of St. John's Coll. Camb.) V. of Newcastle.
  John viii. 32. 4° 1746. 2 Ass f.
  Ephef. iv. 3.   17   Visit.
  Prov. iii. 17. 8° 1750. *Bath* Hosp. On the Pursuit of false Pleasure and the Mischief of immoderate Gaming.
  * 12 Sermons in 8° 1764. On various Subjects.
  * Pf. cxliv. 12. 4° 1765. b. Gov. of Asylum.

BROWN John
  * Rom. viii. 28, 39. 8° 1758. Fun. f.
  * Acts viii. 36-38. 8° 1764. Baptism.

BROWN Richard, DD. Can. of Ch. Ch. and Reg. Prof. of Heb. &c.
  Oxford.

    [a] This Person was broke upon the Wheel at Montpellier, Nov. 6. 1698.

Job xix. 25, 26. 8° 1747. *Oxon.* 3 f. Job's Expectation of a Resurrection. *Worc.* Oxon..
    2 Kings v. 18, 19. 8° 1750. *Oxon.* The Case of Naaman considered. *Worc.* Oxon.

BROWN Simon
    * Jer. vii. 10. 8° 1710. *Univ.* Oxon.
    * Disc. in 2 Vol. 8° 1722. *Brit. M.*

BROWNE Charles, M. A.
    * 1 Pet. ii. 16. 4° 1740. 2 f. Assize at Hertford.

BROWNE Francis, DD. Chapl. in Ord. and Can. of Windsor.
    Prov. xxix. 25. 4° 1712. Jan. 30. b. Lord Mayor. *Ch. Ch.* Oxon. *St. John's.* Camb. *Brit. M.*
    2 Cor. v. 10. 4° 1724. Spitt. W.

BROWNE John, M. A. R. of Beeby, Leicestershire, and Chaplain to the Prince of Wales.
    6 Serm. in 8° 1721. The Necessity and Benefits of duly observing the holy season of Lent. *Wandsworth. Ch. Ch.* Oxon. *Brit. M.*
    Acts xxiv. 14. 4° 1725. The Reasons for adhering stedfastly to the established Religion, though the Papists call it Heresy.
    Prov xiv. 34. 4° 1729. Ass. Advantages of Righteousness to a Nation.
    8 Serm. in 8° 1730, 1731, and 1732. At L. Moyer's Lec. *NewC.* O.
    John ix. 41, 4° 1735. 2 f. The Obligation to believe the divine Mission of Jesus Christ.

BROWNE Moses, V. of Olney, Bucks.
    * Luke ii 7. 8° 1754. Xtmas. The Nativity and Humility of Jesus Christ particularly considered.
    * 1 Pet. v. 1. 8° 1761. Vis. f. The Xn's glorious Coronation-day.
    * Nehem. iv. 10. 8° 1765. Ref. Manners. The Causes that obstruct the Progress of Reformation, &c.

BROWNE Peter, Bp. of Corke and Ross.
    Num xxv. 21. 8° 1698. *Dublin.* Ref. Manners.
    Sermons in 2 Vol. 8° 1749. On various Subjects.

BROWNE Philip, V. of Halstead, Essex, and Chaplain to the Duke of Albermarle.
    Rom. xiii 1. 4° 1682. Vis. f. Sovereign's Authority and the Subject's, Duty
    Acts xx. 16. 4° 1684. On the observation of Holy-days. *C. C. C.* Oxon. *Sion.*

BROWNE Theophilus, M. A. R. of Thwaite, Norf.
    Exod. xxiii. 16. 4° 1708. *Norwich.* Harvest-sermon.

BROWNE Thomas, DD. Fell of St. John's Coll. Camb.
    Rom. x. 15. 4° 1688. Conc. Lat. *Cant.* Pro. Grad. Bacc. Cant. *Bod. Bal.* Oxon. *Pub. L. St. John's. Queen's.* Camb. *Eton. Sion.*
    Rom. x. 15. 4° 1688. Latin serm. *Cant.* Cor Acad. Cant. De Ordinatione. *Bod. Bal. C. C. C. Or. Pub. L. St. John's. Queen's.* Camb. *Eton. Sion.*

BROWNE W. M. A. V. of Wing, and Minis. of Burton upon Trent.
    Rom. xiv. 19. 8° 1716. *York.* Th.

BROWNRIG

BROWNRIG Ralph, Bp. of Exeter.
  40 Serm. Vol. 1. fo. 1661. *Univ. Ch. Ch. Queen's.* **Oxon.** *Queen's.* Camb. *Sion.*
  25 Serm. Vol. 2. fo. 1664. *Bod. C. C. C. Magd. Mert. Wadh.* Ox. *Pub. L. Trin.* Camb. *Sion.*
BROWNSWORD John, B. A. Cur. of Nuthurſt, Suſſex.
  Matt. xix. 20, 21. 4° 1739. Ag. the Methodiſts.
BROWNSWORD William, Cur. of Steyning, Suſſex.
  Col. iii. 2. 4° 1704. b. Candidates in Suſſex.
BRUCE Lew. DD. Preac. of his Majeſty's Chap. Somerſethouſe, Lond.
  1 Cor. x. 31. 4° 1743. Col. Georgia. The Happineſs of Man the Glory of God. *All S.* Oxon. *Brit. M.*
  Matt. vii. 20. 4° 1745. Reb. The Fruits of Popery.
  Luke x. 37. 4° 1752. b. Gov. Weſtm. Inf. good Samar. *Brit. M.*
  *Rom. xiii. 8. 4° 1762. b. Gov. Lond. Hoſp.
BRUCE Michael
  Rom. xv. 7. 8° 1725. *Belfaſt.* b. Sub-Synod. Rel. Communion.
BRUCE Titus, Preſbyter of the Church of England
  Rom. xiii. 2. 4° 1682. Monarchy maintained. *Trin.* Camb. *Sion.*
BRUMHALL
  Luke xii. 1. 4° 1677. m. e. C. p. 520. How is Hypocriſy diſcoverable and curable.
BRUNNING Benjamin
  James iii. 17. 4° 1660. The beſt Wiſdom.
BRUNSELL Samuel, DD. R. of Bingham, and Preb. of Southwell, Notting.
  Eccleſ. x. 17. 4° 1660. May 29. Solomon's bleſſed Land. *Bod. Worc.* Oxon.
BRYAN Auguſtine
  Exod. xviii. 21. 8° 1718. Elect. Lord. Mayor. *Sion.*
BRYAN John, DD. late Paſtor in Coventry.
  Pſ. xci. 9, 10. 8° 1670. 8 ſ. Dwelling with God the Intereſt and Duty of Believers. *Trin.* Camb. *Sion.*
BRYAN Matt. LLD. Lect. of St. Michael's, Crooked-Lane, Lond.
  2 Cor. v. 11. 4° 1684. Certainty of a fut. Judgm. *Queens.. C. Sion.*
  Exod. xx. 8. 4° 1686. On the Lord's-day. *C. C. C.* Oxon.
  Epheſ. iv. 1. 4° 1692.
BRYANT Henry, M. A.
  * Joſhua vii. 8. 4° 1758. Faſt.
BRYARS John, M. A. R. of Billingford, Norfolk.
  Phil. iv. 17. 8° 1711. Ch. ſ.
  John ii. 26. 8° 1712. Fun. of a Day-labourer.
BRYDEN Will. DD. Miniſter at Dolton, County of Dumfries.
  *Prov. xxiv. 21. 8° 1778. Faſt. Piety and Loyalty.
BRYDGES Henry, Hon. M. A. R. of Broadwell, Gloceſt.
  Matt. xiii. 45, 46. 4° 1701. b. Lev. Co. *Ch. Ch.* Ox. *St. John's.* C.
  Acts vii. 60. 8° 1709. Jan. 30. b. Queen. *Ch. Ch. Univ. Worc. Hert.* Oxon. *Trin.* Camb. *Sion.*
  Eccleſ. viii. 14. 8° 171 Jan. 30. b. Commons.

BRYSON James, M.A.
* 13 Sermons in 8° 1778. On several important Subjects, *Belfast*.
BUCHANAN Charles, R. of Ditchingham, Norfolk.
  1 Cor. i. 10. 4° 1710. *Norwich*. Vis. s.
  1 Cor. xi. 27–29. 8° 1712. *Norwich*. On the Sacrament.
BUCK James, DD. V. of Stradbrook, Suffolk, and Chaplain to the Earl of Lincoln.
  Rom. vii. 25. 4° 1660. Th. b. L. St. Paul's Thanksg. *Worc*. Ox.
BUCK Maximilian, M.A. V. of Kemping and Seale, Cant.
  Ps. li. 17. 8° 1703. Jan. 30. *Univ*. Oxon. *Trin. Queen's*. Camb.
  1 Kings xviii. 12. 8° 1704.
  2 Pet. ii. 6. 8° 1718.
BUCK Robert
  Matt. vi. 13. 8°
BUCKLER Benjamin, DD. Fell. of All Soul's Coll. and Custos Archivorum, Oxon. V. of Cumner, and R. of Inckpen, Berks.
  * Ephes. ii. 21. 4° 1759. Act s. The Alliance of Religion and Learning considered. *Bal. Worc*. Oxon. *Queen's*. Camb.
  * Kings iv. 38. 8° 1759. Commem. of Founder. *All S*. Oxon.
BUCKRIDGE Thomas, M.A. Fell. of King's Coll. Camb. Chapl. to Lord Onflow, V. of Send. and R. of Merrow, Surry.
  * 6 Sermons in 8° 1767.
BUDGELL Gilbert, M.A. R. of Simonsbury, Dorsets.
  James iv. 3. 4° 1690. On Prayer. *Bod. Ch. Ch*. Oxon.
BUDWORTH William, M.A. (Fell. of Wadh. Coll. Oxon.) Minister of St. Michael's, Southampton.
  Matt. xii. 25. 8° 1752. *Winton*. Jan. 30.
  Ps. xxxv. 20. 8° 1745. Reb. s. The Consequences of the pres. Rebellion recommended to the Consider. of all Protestants.
BUERDSELL James, M.A. Fell. of Braz. Nose. Coll. Oxon.
  6 Disc. and Essays in 12° 1700. On several Subjects. *Oxford*.
BULKELEY Benj. DD. (of Pemb. Coll. Ox.) R. of Chinkford, Ess.
  1 Tim. ii. 1, 2. 4° 1722. At the Mayor's Entr. into his Office.
  Josh. v. xiii. 8° 1731. *Oxon*. Act. Insufficiency of human Reason in matters of Religion. *Linc*. Oxon.
BULKELEY *Charles*, Minister of the Gospel, London.
  * 15 Disc. in 8° 1752. *Queen's*. Camb.
  * John v. 35. 8° 1753. On the Death of Dr. *James Foster. Queen's*. Camb.
  * John iii. 5. 8° 1754. 2 Disc. On catholic Communion.
  * Ezek. xxvi. 17, 18. 8° 1756. On the Earthquake at Lisbon. *Queen's*. Camb.
  * Zech. viii. 16, 17. 8° 1756. Fast The Nature and Necessity of national Repentance, *Queen's*. Camb.
  * Ps. cii 13–15. 8° 1759. The Surren. of Quebeck. *Queen's*. C.
  * Disc. in 2 Vol. 8° 1761. On public Occasions.
  * Esther ii. 17. 8° 1761. Royal Marriage.
  * 2 Tim. i. 12. 8° 1766. On the Death of the Rev. Mr. *B. Treacher*.
  * Discourses in 2 Vol. 8° 1771. On the Parables and Miracles of our Saviour. * Isai.

OF AUTHORS, &c. 59

* Ifai. ii. 22. 4° 1778. On the Death of the Earl of Chatham. The Vanity of human dependencies ſtated and explained.

BULKELEY Richard, M. A. Preb. of Hereford.
 Pſ. cxxxvi. 3. 4° 1685. May 29. *Pub. L.* Camb.

BULKLY John
 Exod. xx. 8. 4° 1697. *Dublin.* On the Lord's day.

BULL
 * John xiv. 16. 4° 1663. V. Coll. Farew ſ.

BULL Digby, M. A. R. or Sheldon, Warwickſ.
 Pſ. cxxii. 6. 4° 1695. Churche's requeſt to her faithful Sons.
 Joel ii. 1. 4° 1695. The Watchman's Voice. *Jeſ.* Ox. *Trin.* C.
 * Iſai. xxvi. 4. 4° 1695. An Exhortation to truſt in G. &c. *Jeſ.* Ox.

BULL George, Bp. of St. David's.
 Some important Points of primitive Chriſtianity maintained and defended in ſev. Serm. and other Diſc. in 3 Vol. 8° 1713. *Bod. Univ. Ch. Ch. C. C. C. Mert. New C. Bal. Pemb.* Oxon. *Pub. L. Trin. Queen's.* Camb. *Sion.*

BULL Michael, M. A. R. of Bradſtead, Kent.
 Eſther x. 3. 8° 1715. Aſſize. Of the Love of one's Country. *Queen's.* Camb.

BULL Rob. R. of Tortworth, and Preb. of Glouceſter.
 Pſ. cxii. 7. 8° 1714. Aſſize. *Eton.*
 Pſ. cxxii. 6. 8° 1715.
 Pſ. v. 7. 8° 1723. Conf. Ch. *Queen's.* Camb. *Eton.*

BULLOCK Richard, M. A.
 * Prov. iv. 13. 4° 1754. Sch. Feaſt. Biſhop's Stockford.

BULLOCK Thomas, Dean of Norwich.
 Matt. 5. 33, 34. 4° 1723. The Nature of Oaths. *Queen's.* Camb. *Brit. M.*
 Acts ii. 22, 23. 8° 1724. Chriſt the Prophet foretold by Moſes. *Queen's.* Camb. *Brit. M.*
 7 Serm. in 8° 1726. The reaſoning of Chriſt and his Apoſtles in their Defenſe of Chriſtianity conſidered. *Univ. Ch. Ch. New C. Or. Worc.* Oxon. *Cl. H.* Camb. *Sion.*
 Acts ii. 46. 4° 1726. County Feaſt. *Univ.* Oxon. *Sion.*
 Matt. xxi. 33, 34. 8° 1728. The Goſpel, a Reinforcement of the Law of Nature. *All S.* Oxon. *Cl. H. Queen's.* Camb. *Brit. M.*

BUNCOMBE Samuel
 * Eccleſ. vii. 14. 8° 1767. On a Fire.

BUNDY Richard, DD. Chapl. in Ord. and Preb. of Weſtminſter.
 Serm. in 2 V. 8° 1740. On ſev. Occaſ. *All S.* Ox. *Queen's.* Cam.
 16 Sermons in 8° 1750. V. 3. On ſome of the moſt important points of the Chriſtian Religion. *Queen's.* Camb.

BUNYAN John
 * Rev. xxi. 10. to Ch. xxii. 5. 12° 1665.

BURD Richard, DD. Lect. of St. Mary, Aldermanbury, and R. of Over-wallop, Hants.
 Matt. xxi. 41. 4° 1684. May 29. Annual meet. of the Natives of St. Martin's.

        2 Chron.

2 Chron. vi. 41. 4° 1702. 2 f. Open. Church. An Exhortation to frequent the Church. *St. John's*, Camb.

Dan. xii 13. 4° 1704. Vif. Degrees of Glory.

BURDETT Char.^a M. A, Chapl. to the Eng. Factory at Smyrna.
Prov. iii. 17. 4° 1724. b. Levant Co.

BURDETT Charles,^a M. A. R. of Guildford, Surry.
* 1 Cor. x. 11. 4° 1760. Jan. 30. b. Commons.

BURFORD Samuel
* 2 Theff. iii. 1. 4° 1765. Ord. f.

BURGES Samuel, R. of Initow, Devonshire.
John ix. 4. 8^u 1707. Fun. f.

BURGESS Anthony
* 147 Sermons in fo. 1661.

BURGESS Cornelius
* Amos v 13. 8° 1660. *Pub. L.* Camb.

BURGESS Daniel
Ecclef. xii. 1. 4° 1690. c. m. e. p. 410. Converfion of young Perfons. *Bod.*
Exod. xxxvii. 23. 12° 1697. Ref. Manners.

BURGESS J. Lancashire.
Mark v. 12, 13. 8° 1770. Beelzebub driv. and drowning his Hogs.

BURGH Sydenham, M. A.
Micah. vi. 8. 8° 1723. Open. new Fair.

BURGHOPE George, R. of Gaddefden, Herts.
1 Sam. xxvi. 11. 4° 1704. Jan. 30. *St. John's.* Camb.

BURGHOPE M. M. A. R. of St. James's Clerkenwell, Lond.
Gal. v. 24. 4° 1701. Govern. of the Paffions. *Ch. Ch.* Oxon.

BURKITT Will. M. A. (of Pemb. Hall Camb.) R. of Milden, Suff.
Heb. xiii. 7. 4° 1680. Fun.

BURLEIGH Richard, Cur. of Beaulieu.
* Prov. xvi. 16. 4° 1777. Affize. *Winchefter*.

BURN Richard, LLD. Chancellor of Carlifle.
* Difcourfes in 4 Vol. 8° 1774. On practical Subjects chiefly extracted from Divines of the laft Century. In this Collection are 5 Serm. by the Editor on the following Subjects, *viz.*
* Matt. xvii. 15. 1 Vol. p. 431. On Drunkennefs.
* Pf. xlvii. 1. 1 Vol. p 456. On Pfalmody.
* Pf. cxxxix. 2. 2 Vol. p. 97. On God's Knowledge.
* Prov. xiv. 24. 2 Vol. p. 442. The folly of Sin.
* 1 Sam. xii. 3. 4 Vol. p. 372. On Reftitution.

BURNABY Andrew, DD. V. of Greenwich.
* 6 Occaf. Serm. in 8° 1777.
* Gal. iv. 18. 8° 1780. Religious Zeal. Ag. Riots.
‡ * Acts xxvii. 31. 4° 1781. Faft. b. Commons.

BURNET   DD.
Matt. xii. 32.

BURNET Alexander, Abp. of Glafgow.
Rev. xiv. 13. 4° 1673. *Glafgow.* Fun. of Marquifs of Montrofe.
a 2. The fame.

BURNET Gilbert, Abp. of York.
* Exod. xx. 14.
Rom. xiii. 5. 4° 1675. The dutiful Subject. *Bod. Ch. Ch. Magd. Trin.* Oxon. *Pub. L.* Camb.
* Daniel xii. 3. 4° 1668. b. Prince of Orange. *Queen's.* Camb.
2 Sam. ii. 12. 4° 1675. Jan. 30. The royal Martyr lamented. *Bod. Univ. Worc. Magd. Trin. Linc.* Oxon. *Pub. L.* Camb. *Sion.*
* Dan. iv. 11, 12. 8° 16
Ephef. v. 15, 16. 4° 1678. Fun. *Magd.* Oxon.
Amos iv. 11, 12. 4° 1680. Fast. for Fire of Lond. *Magd. Jef. Wadh. Or.* Oxon. *Brit. M.*
* Joel iii. 19. 8° 16   Jan. 30.
Rev. iii. 2, 3. 4° 1680. Fast. *Bod. Ch. Ch. Queen's. Wadh. Oriel,* Oxon. *Trin. St. John's,* Camb.
Zech. viii. 19. 4° 1681. Jan. 30. *Worc. Magd. Wadh. Or.* Oxon. *Trin. St. John's.* Camb. *Sion.*
Matt. xii. 25. 4° 1681. Elect. Lord Mayor. *Bod. Ch. Ch. Magd. Or.* Oxon. *Pub. L. Trin. St. John's.* Camb.
Pf. xxxvii. 37. 4° 1682. Fun of Mr. Houblon. *Magd. Or. Wadh.* Oxon. *Brit. M.*
Pf. xxii. 21. 4° 1685. Nov. 5. *Bod. All S. Wadh. Ch. Ch. Or.* Ox. *St. John's.* Camb. *Brit. M.*
Pf. cxviii. 23. 8° 1688. Dec. 23. b. Prince of Orange. *Bod. Ch. Ch. All S. Magd. Or. Worc. Wadh.* Oxon. *St. John's. Cl. H.* Camb. *Sion.*
Pf. cxliv. 15. 4° 1689. Coron. *Bod. Ch. Ch. All S. Wadh. Oriel, C. C. C. Linc.* Oxon. *Pub. L. Trin. St. John's, Queen's. Cl. H. C.*
* 2 Sam. i. 14. 4° 1689.
2 Sam. xxiii. 3, 4. 4° 1689 Fun,
Mich. vi. 5. 4° 1689. Nov. 5. *Bod. All S. Magd. Wadh.* Oxon. *Pub. L.* Camb.
Acts vii. xxvi. 4° 1689. An Exhortation to Peace and Union. *Bod. Magd. Jef.* Oxon. *Pub. L. Trin.* Camb.
1 Tim. iii. 16. 4° 1689. Xtmas. *Bod. All S. Ch. Ch. Magd. Wadh.* Oxon. *Pub. L. Trin. St. John's.* Camb.
Acts xvii. 26. 8° 1690. *Bod. Wadh.* Oxon.
Luke xix. 41, 42. 4° 1690. Fast. *Bod. Ch. Ch. All S. Magd. Oriel,* Oxon. *Trin. Queen's, St. John's, Cl. H.* Camb.
Pf. lxxxv. 8. 4° 1690. Fast. July 16. *All S. Magd. Or. Jef. Wadh.* Oxon. *Pub. L. Trin. St. John's.* Camb. *Sion.*
Pf. cxliv. 10, 11. 4° 1690. Th. Oct. 19. b. King and Queen. *Bod. All S. Or. Wadh.* Oxon. *Cl. H. St. John's.* Camb.
Prov. xxxi. 30, 31. 4° 1691. Fun. of Lady Brook. *Magd. Or. Jef. Wadh.* Oxon. *Pub. L. Trin. St. John's.* Camb. *Brit. M.*
Pf. xii. 1. 4° 1691. Fast. April 29. *Bod. Or. Wadh.* Oxon. *Pub. L. Trin. St. John's.* Camb. *Sion.*
Prov. xx. 28. 4° 1691. Th. Nov. 26. *Bod. Magd. Oriel, Wadh.* Oxon. *Pub L. Trin.* Camb.

Eccles.

Eccles. ii. 26. 4° 1692. Fun. of Mr. Boyle. *Bod. Ch. Ch. Univ. All S. Magd. Or. Wadh.* Oxon. *Pub. L. Trin. St. John's.* Camb.
1 Cor. i. 26. 4° 1694. Lent. b. Queen. *Bod. All S. Oriel, Wadh.* Oxon. *Pub. L. Trin. St John's* Camb.
Pf. cv. 5. 4° 1694. May 29. b Queen. *Bod. Magd. Oriel, Wadh.* Oxon. *Trin* Camb.
2 Tim. iv. 7. 4° 1694. Fun. Abp. Tillotson. *Ch. Ch. Univ. All S. Magd. Or. Wadh.* Ox. *Pub. L. Trin. Queen's, St. John's.* Cam.
2 Cor. vi. 1. 4° 1695. Lent. b. King. *Magd. Or, Wadh.* Oxon. *Pub. L. St. John's, Queen's.* Camb *Brit. M.*
2 Chron. ix. 8. 4° 1697. Th. for the Peace. *Magd. Bal. Or. Wadh.* Oxon. *Pub. L. Trin.* Camb. *Brit. M.*
Gal. iv. 4. 4° 1697. Christmas. The time when Christianity was made known. *Univ. Magd. Or. Wadh.* Oxon. *Pub. L. St. John's.* Camb. *Brit. M.*
Ephes. v. 2. 4° 1697. Lent. *Magd. Or. Wadh.* Ox. *Trin.* C. *Eton.*
Gal. vi. 10. 4° 1698. Spitt. M. *Magd. Or. Wadh.* Ox. *Trin.* C.
Prov. xxvii. 5,6. 4° 1700. Ref. Manners. Charitable Reproof. *Or. Wadh.* Oxon. *St. John's.* Camb.
Mal. i. 11. 4° 1704. Prop. Gospel. *Bod. Ch. Ch. Or. Wadh.* Ox. *Pub. L. St. John's, Queen's.* Camb. *Sion.*
1 Cor. xii. 26, 27. 4° 1704. Char. On a Brief for the Exiles of Orange. *Or. Wadh.* Oxon. *Queen's, St. John's.* Camb. *Brit. M.*
Phil. ii. 1,2. 4° 1704. Vis. *Ch. Ch.* Oxon. *Pub. L.* Camb.
Pf. xlix. 20. 4° 1706. Lent.
Matt. xxiv, 12. 4° 1706. Spittal M.
Deut. iv. 6,7,8. 4° 1706. Th. June 27. *Ch. Ch Linc.* Ox. *Queen's.* Camb. *Sion.*
Pf. lxxii. 4. 4° 1706. Th. Dec. 31. *Ch. Ch. Magd. Wore. Oriel, Hert.* Oxon. *Pub. L. Trin. Queen's.* Camb. *Sion.*
Mat. xxii. 21. 8° 1710. May 29. *Magd. Bal. Worc. Oriel, Linc.* Oxon. *Trin. St. John's.* Camb.
Pf. cxliv. 15. 8° 1710. Th. 2 s. *Or. Worc.* Ox. *Pub. L.* C. *Sion.*
Pf. cxxii. 6-9. 4° 1711. Spitt. M. *Or. Linc.* Oxon.
14 Sermons preached on several Occasions—and an Essay towards a new Book of Homilies in 7 s. 8° 1713. *Bod. Ch. Ch. New C. St. John's. Wadh.* Oxon. *Pub. L.* Camb. *Sion.*
Dan. iv. 27. 8° 1714. Spittal M. *Bod. Worc. Wadh.* Ox. *Pub. L. Trin. Queen's.* Camb.
Acts xx. 32. 4° 1714. Vis. *Ch. Ch. Or. Worc. Wadh.* Ox. *Pub. L. St. John's. Queen's. Cl. H.* Camb. *Brit. M.*
Pf. ii 10,11. 4° 1714. b. King. *Bod. Wadh.* Oxon. *Trin. Queen's.* Camb. *Sion.*

BURNET Gilbert,[a] M.A.
  Heb. i. vi. 8° 171 . Trinity.

BURNET Gilbert,[a] V. of Coggeshal, Essex, and Minister of Clerkenwell, London.
  Deut. iv. 6-8. 8° 1725. Accession. *Queen's.* Camb.

[a] The same.   48 Practical

48 Practical Serm. in 2 Vol. 8° 1747. On various Subjects. *Wadh. Hert.* Oxon. *Brit. M.*
BURNETT John, of Hull, Yorkshire.
 * 1 Sam. xxx. vi. 8° 1774. 2 s. The goodman's Duty and Pract.
BURNETT Tho. DD. R. of Westkington Wilts, and Preb. of Sarum.
 * 16 Sermons at Boyle's Lect V. p. 401.
 Ephes. v. 2. 8° 1722. *Bristol.*
 Rom. xiii 5. 8° 1726. Nov. 5. *Queen's.* Camb.
BURNEY Richard, M. A. R. of St. Peter's, Canterbury.
 Prov. viii. 15. 4° 1660. 8 s. *Eton.*
BURRELL Alexander, M. A. R. of Addestock, Bucks.
 Micah vi. 8. 8° 1725. Assize.
BURRELL John, R. of Euston, Suffolk.
 Rev. ii. 9. 4° 1683. Jan. 30. *Camb.* The divine Right of Kings. *St. John's.* Camb.
BURRELL William, M. A. R. of Brightling, Sussex.
 2 Pet. ii. 10. 8° 1712. Assize.
 Acts xxiv. 16. 8° 1712. Assize.
BURROUGH Henry, LLD. Preb. of Peterborough.
 * Lectures in 8° 1773. On the Church Catechism, Confirmation, and the Nat. and Obligation of relig. Vows. *Queen's.* Camb.
BURROUGH John, R. of Gittisham, Devonshire.
 Gal. iv. 18. 8° 1718. Vis. *Eton.*
BURROUGHS James
 * Discourses in 8° 1733. *Queen's.* Camb.
BURROUGHS Jeremy
 * Discourses in 4° 1660.
 * Ps. xxxii. 1. 4° 1668. Gospel-Remission.
 * Rev. xviii. 4. 8° 1715. Nov. 5.
BURROUGHS John, R. of Tresham, Devonshire.
 Ps. xlvii. 7. 12° 1712. 2 s. The devout Psalmodist.
BURROUGHS Joseph, Pastor in London.
 * Ps. xxxvii. 7. 4° 1713. Th. for Victory.
 * Jerem. x. 2. 8° 1715. Total Eclipse of the Sun.
 1 Tim. iii. 13. 8° 1730. Ordination of Deacons. *Brit. M.*
 * Prov. xiv. 34. 8° 1731. Ref. Manners. *Queen's.* Camb.
 John xx. 21-23. 8° 1735. Of Auricular Confession and Absolution. V. Vol. 2. Ag. Popery. *Braz. N.* Oxon. *Brit. M.*
 * - - - - 1737. New Year's-day.
 * Sermons in 8° 1741.
 ‡ * 1 Cor. xv. 57. 8° 1752. Fun. of Rev. *Mr. Weatherly. Brit. M.*
 * - - - 1754. Fun. of Rev. *Mr. Isaac Kimber.*
 * 1 Thess. iv. 13-18. 8° 1755. Fun. of Rev. *Mr. Morris. Queen's.* C.
[BURROUGHS Thomas]
 * Ps. xxxix. 9. 4° 1662. A Remedy for Griefs.
BURROW Robert, LLD. V. of Darrington, Yorkshire.
 2 Chron. xix. 5. 8° 1723. Elect. Lord. Mayor. Civil Government and Society vindicated from the Charge of being founded on, and preserved by dishonest Arts. *Brit. M.*

Pf. lxxxv. 10. 8° 1729. Affize. *Brit. M.*
BURSCOUGH William, Bp. of Limerick &c.
 1 Theff. iv. 18. 8° 1711. Fun. of the Dutchefs of Rutland. *Bod. Bal. Linc. Hert.* Oxon. *Pub. L.* Camb.
 1 Cor. iv. 1. 8° 1715. Conf. of Bp.   *St. John's.* Camb.
 Pf. cxlvii. 1. 4° 1715. May 29. The Duty of Praife and Thankf-giving. *Ch. Ch.* Oxon.
 * Pf. lxxvi. 10. 4° 17   Nov. 5.
 Pf. lxxviii. 42. 4° 1715. Nov. 5. The Revolution recommended to our Memories. *Queen's.* Camb. *Brit. M.*
 Ephef. v. 20. 4° 1716. May 29. b. Commons. *Ch. Ch. Magd. Bal. Linc.* Oxon.
 1 Pet. ii. 16. 4° 1722. Nov. 5. The Abufe of Liberty, *Wadh.* Oxon. *Queen's.* Camb. *Brit. M.*
BURTON B. V. of Ravenftone,
 * Phil. ii. 6, 7. 8° 1756. Vif. Jefus Chrift God and Man.
 * Jerem. xxiii. 6. 12° 1763. 3 f. Active and paffive Righteoufnefs of Chrift &c.
BURTON Henry, B.D. Minifter of Friday-ftreet, London.
 Jofh. vii. 16. 4° 1665. Faft.
BURTON Hezekiah, DD. R. of Barnes near Lond. and Preb. of Norwich.
 Several Difc. in 8° 1684. *Ch. Ch. All S. C. C. C. Univ. Queen's. Pemb.* Oxon. *Queen's.* Camb. *Dr. W's. L.* Lond. *Sion*
 A fecond Vol. of Difc. 8° 1685. *Ch. Ch. All S. C. C. C. Univ. Queen's. Pemb.* Oxon. *Queen's.* Camb. *Dr. W's L.* Lond. *Sion.*
BURTON John, DD. Fell. of C. C. C. Ox. and Fell. of Eton-Coll.
 1 Sam. ii. 17. 4° 1729. *Oxon.* Hophni et Phinees—five Impietas Sacerdotum publicæ Impietatis Caufa. *Worc.* Oxon.
 1 Sam. iii. 12, 13. 4° 1729. *Oxon.* Heli—five Exemplum Magif-tratus intempeftivâ Lenitate peccantis. *Worc* Oxon.
 Gen. xviii. 19. 4° 1733. Col. of Georgia. *Worc.* Oxon. *Eton.*
 Prov. xxiv. 21. 8° 1734. *Oxon.* Jan. 30. The Principles of Xtian Loyalty. *Worc.* Oxon.
 Deut. xxiii. 8. 8° 1741. *Oxon.* Faft. *Worc.* Oxon.
 Jer. ix. 23, 24. 8° 1744. *Oxon.* Faft. The Folly and Wickednefs of mifplacing our Truft and Confidence. *Worc.* Ox. *Brit. M.*
 Gen. xxxix. 9. 8° 1746. *Oxon.* Affize. Principles of Religion the only fufficient Reftraint from Wickednefs. *Worc.* Oxon.
 1 Sam. xii. 7. 8° 1746. *Oxon.* Th. after Reb. The Expoftulation and Advice of Samuel to the Men of Ifrael applied. *Worc.* Ox.
 * 1 Cor. xiii. 10, 11. 8° 1756. Conc. ad Cler. De Fundamentalibus.
 * 1 Kings xii. 2, 3. ⎫ 8° 1759. *Oxon.* Duæ Conciones coram Bacc.
 * 1 Kings xix. 20. ⎭ Determ. *Braz. N.* Oxon. *Queen's.* Camb.
 * 1 Cor. iii. 12–15. 8° 1760. *Oxon.* Conc. Acad.
 * Matt. xv. 1–6. 8° 1766. Papifts and Pharifees compared. *Queen's.* Camb. *Eton.*
 * Sermons public and occafional bef. the Univerfity of Oxon. in 2 Vol. 8°. 1 Vol. 1764. 2 Vol. 1766. *Bod. C. C. C. Braz. N. Wadh.* Oxon. *Queen's.* Camb. *Eton.*

BURTON Thomas, M.A. V. of Hallifax, Yorkſhire.
    Pſ. xlvi. 10. 8° 1713. Th. for the Peace.
BURY Arthur, DD. R. of Exeter Coll. Oxon. and Preb. of St.
    Peter's, Exon.
    James iii. 15, 16. 4° 1660.
    2 Sam. i. 18. 4° 1662. Jan; 30. The Uſe of the Bow. *Bal. Or.* Ox.
    Rom. x. 15. 8° 1682. b. Sons of Clergy. *Wadh.* Oxon.
    Exod. iv. 24–26. 4° 1692. Danger of delay. Repentance. *Bod.*
BURY Samuel
    * Matt. xxv. 21. 8° 1707. Fun.
BUSH William
    1 Cor. ix. 24. 8° 1692. The celeſtial Race. *Bod.*
BUSH William, at Enfield, Middleſex.
    * 1 Tim. v. 22. 8° 1746. Faſt The Inadventencies and Indiſ-
    cretions of good Men, a great Cauſe of general Corruption in
    Society.
BUSHEL Seth, DD. V. of Lancaſter.
    1 Theſſ. v. 14. 4° 1673. 2 Viſ. ſ. *St. John's*. Camb.
    2 Cor. v. ii. 4° 1678. Fun. of Sir H. Houghton. *Brit. M.*
    Luke xvi. 25. 12° 1682. Subſtance of ſev. Sermons.
BUTLER D.   A miniſter of the Church of England.
    2 Cor. x. 17. 8° 1707. Fun. of Sir Cloud. Shovel.
BUTLER James,   of Royſton, Herts.
    * Rom. xiii. 1. 8° 1747. Jan. 30. Extent and Limits of Subjec-
    tion due to Princes.
BUTLER John, DD. Canon of Windſor and Chapl. in Ord.
    Gal. v. 1. 4° 1678. Chriſtian Liberty aſſerted in oppoſition to
    the Roman Yoke. *Bod. Ch. Ch. Magd. Queen's.* Oxon. *Pub. L.*
    St. John's. Camb.
    Luke xxi. 25, 26. 4° 1684. Jan. 30. *Ch. Ch.* Oxon.
BUTLER John, Bp. of Oxon.
    Luke xvii. 17, 18. 8° 1746. Th. after Rebellion. *Brit. M.*
    * John 1. 47. 4° 1753. Fun. of Dr. Kenrick. *Queen's.* C. *Brit. M.*
    * 1 Cor. ix. 11. 4° 1754. b. Sons of the Clergy.
    * Matt. xi. 4, 5. 4° 1754. b. Gov. Weſtmin. Infirmary.
    * Luke xix. 41. 4° 1758. Faſt. b. Commons.
    * Pſ. xxix. 2. 4° 1763. Hutchin's Lect. Liturgy. *Queen's.* Cam.
    * 1 Kings viii. 59. 4° 1776. Faſt. b. Commons.
    * Deut. 15, 11. 4° 1778. b. Gov. of Radcliffe Inf. *Oxon.*
    * Eccleſ. vii. 14. 4° 1778. Faſt. b. Lords.
BUTLER Joſeph, Bp. of Durham.
    15 Serm. &c. in 8° 1749. to which are added 6 preached on pub.
    Occaſions. *Bod. All S. Univ. New C. Or. Worc.* Oxon. *Queen's.*
    Camb. *Brit. M.*
    * 8 Sermons at Boyle's Lect. V. p. 409.
BUTLER Lilly, DD. Miniſter of St. Mary Aldermanbury, Preb. of
    Cant. and Chaplain in Ord.
    Iſai. lvii. 21. 4° 1691. *Ch. Ch.* Oxon.
    Rev. xiv. 13. 4° 1694. Fun.
Vol. II.   I   Neh.

Neh. ix. 26, 27. 4° 1696. Faſt. June 26. *Ch. Ch.* Oxon.
Prov. xxix. 2. 4° 1696. Elect. Lord. Mayor. *Ch. Ch.* Oxon.
Gal. iv. 18. 8° 1697. Ref. Manners. *Bod. Ch. Ch.* Oxon. *Eton.*
James iv. 9, 10. 4° 1697. Faſt.
Jer. v. 29. 4° 1698. Jan. 30. *Ch. Ch.* Oxon.
Hoſ. x. 12. 4° 1701. Faſt. *Ch. Ch.* Oxon.
Phil. i. 21. 4° 1702. Fun. of Clopton Havers, M. D. *Ch. Ch.* Oxon. *Pub. L.* Camb. *Brit. M.*
James i. 27. 4° 1704. b. Sons of Clergy. *Ch. Ch. All S. Wadh.* Oxon. *Trin. Queen's.* Camb.
Rom. x. 11. 8° 1709. Boyle's Lect. or fo. 1739. Vol. 2. p. 433. Religion no matter of Shame.
1 Sam. xii. 23, 24. 4° 1710. Nov. 5. b. Ld May. *Linc.* Ox. *Sion.*
Pſ. cxxii. 3. 4° 1714. Elect. Lord Mayor. *Eton.*
Phil. ii. 21. 4° 1716. Ag. Self-love.

BUTLER William, LLB. R. of St. Ann's within Alderſgate, and Preb. of St. Paul's, London.
Eſther iv. 14. 4° 1704. Th. for Victory.
Prov. xxi. 30. 4° 1712. Faſt.
Tit. iii. 1. 4° 1715. Aſſize.
Matt. viii. 22. 4° 1719. Vice the Deſtruction of the Soul. *Brit. M.*
Epheſ. v. 11. 8° 1722. Ref. Manners.
Exod xx. 7. 4° 1723. Viſ. *Eton.*
Neh. v. 19. 4° 1724. Elect. Lord Mayor.
Exod. xviii. 21. 4° 1729. Elect. Lord Mayor.

BUTLEY John, B. A. Student of Ch. Ch. Oxon.
Pſ. cvii 2. 4° 1746. Th. after Rebellion.
Heb. xiii. 1. 4° 1748. b. Antigallicans, at Greenwich.
* 2 Maccab. iv. 8. 8° 1754. b. Antigallicans.

BUTT George, M. A. (late Student of Ch Ch. Oxon.) R. of Stanford, V. of Clifton upon Tame Worceſterſhire, and Chapl. to the Earl of Finlater and Seafield.
* Phil. iv. 5. 8° 1775. Viſ.
* 2 Tim. i. 10. 4° 1776. Fun. of Bp. Johnſon.

BUTTS Robert, Bp. of Ely.
Rom. xiii. 4. 4° 1712. *Norwich.* Acceſſion.
Pſ. cxxii. 6. 4° 1737. Acceſſ. b. Lords. *Brit. M.*

BYAM Henry, DD. Chapl. in Ord. Can. of Exon, and R. of Luckham, Somerſetſ.
13 Sermons in 8° 1675. *Bod.*

BYLES Mather, M. A. Paſtor of a Church in Boſton, New England.
* 1 Sam. xvii. 45. 8° 1740. The Glories of the Lord of Hoſts, and the Fortitude of the religious Hero.

BYNNS Richard, DD. Fell. of Trin. Coll. Camb. Chapl. to the Duke of Somerſet, and R. of Cheadle, and Preb. of Litchfield.
Iſai. lvii. 1. 4° 1693. Jan. 30. b. Commons. *Bod.*
1 Cor. iv. 1, 2. 4° 1701. Viſ. The Office of the Miniſtry accounted for. *Eton.*
Acts xxiv. 16. 8ᵇ 1710. Aſſize. *Trin.* Camb.

1 Cor.

1 Cor. xv. 33, 8° 1712. Affize. Evil Communication. *Linc*. Ox. Trin. Camb.

BYRCH William, M. A. Minifter of St. Mary's in Dover, Kent.
  * Pf. lxxxii. 6–8. 8° 1737. Death of Queen Caroline.

BYRCHE William, DD. Chapl. to the Abp. of Canterbury and Chanc. of Worcefter.
  1 Tim. iii. 7. 8° 1717. Conf of Bp. Chandler. *St. John's*. C. Sion.

BYRDALL Thomas
  Luke xiii. 6–8 12° 1666. 7 f. The Parable of the barren Fig-tree. *Bod*.
  1 Tim. iv. 8. 12° 1666. 5 f. The Profit of Godlinefs. *Bod*.
  Mark. viii. 36, 37. 12° 1666. 4 f. The Unprofitablenefs of worldly Gain. *Bod*.
  Matt. xi. 12. 12° 1666. 2 f. Victorious Violence. *Bod*.

BYROM John, M. A. R. of Stanton Quintin, Wilts.
  Rom. xiii. 1. 4° 1681. Affize. The Neceffity of Subjection.

C. G. M. A.
  John xviii. 36. 8° 1717.

C. N.
  Tit. i. 5. 4° 1681. *Bod. Sion*.

C. T.
  ‡ * 2 Sam. xxiv. 14. 4° 1704. Faft. for Storm at York.

CADE Anthony, B. D.
  Rom. ii. 15. 4° 1661. On Confcience. *Bod*.

CADE William, M. A. and Prieft of the Church of England.
  Matt. xvi. 18, 19. 4° 1678. Ag. the Pope's Supremacy. *Bod. Trin. St. John's*. Camb. *Sion*.

CADOGAN Bromley Will. M. A. R. of St. Luke's Chelfea, and St. Giles's Reading, Berks, and Chapl. to the Rt Hon. Ld Cadogan.
  * 2 Chron. xx. 20. 8° 1780. The Power of Faith. Preached for the Benefit of a Society inftituted for the purpofe of diftributing Bibles amongft his Majefty's Forces by Sea and Land.

CÆSAR J. James, DD. Chapl. to the King of Pruffia, and Minifter of the Pruffian Church, London.
  Acts xiii. 36. 4° 1702. Royal Fun.
  Pf. lxxvi. 11, 12. 4° 1702. Th. f.
  * Ezek. xvii. 19. 4° 1704. Th. f.
  John xi. 25, 26. 4° 1705. Fun. of the Queen of Pruffia, *Brit. M*.
  Pf. lxxi. 5, 6. 4° 1713. Fun. of King of Pruffia.
  1 Kings i. 39. 8° 1714. Th. f.
  1 Tim. ii. 15. 4° 1716.
  Pf. cxxvii. 3. 4° 1717. On the Birth of a Prince. *Ch. Ch*. Oxon.

CÆSAR John, V. of Croydon, in Surry.
  Jer. xxiii. 10. 4° 1708. Affize.
  Acts xxiv. 16. 4° 1708. Affize.

CALAMY Benjamin, DD. V. of St. Lawrence-Jewry, Preb. of St. Paul's, and Chapl. in Ord.
  * 2 Sam. xxiv. 14. 4° 1663. V. Coll. Far. f. *Magd*. Camb.
  Tit. iii. 8, 9. 4° 1673. *Sion. Cl. H*. Camb.

John

John v. 14. 4° 1682. May 29. Cb. Cb. Magd. Oxon. Pub. L.
Queen's, St. John's, Cl. H. Camb.
Luke xi. 41. 4° 1683. Of a scrupulous Conscience. Bod. Worc.
Oxon. Pub. L. Cl. H. Trin. Camb. Sion.
Eccles. x. 20. 4° 1683. Th. Sept. 9. Magd. Oxon. Pub. L. St.
John's. Cl. H. Camb.
Rom. iii. 8. 4° 1683. Sept. 30. Of passive Obedience. Cb. Cb.
Magd. Bal. Or. Linc. Oxon. Trin. Cl. H. Queen's. Camb.
Isai. lvii. 21. 4° 1684. Sept. 3. b. Lord Mayor. Cb. Cb. Magd.
Oxon. St. John's, Cl. H. Camb.
Matt. xxvi. 52. 4° 1684. Artillery Co. Cb. Cb. Worc. Or. Oxon.
Pub. L. Queen's, Cl. H. Camb.
13 Serm. in 8° 1726. Preached upon Several Occasions. Cb. Cb.
C. C. C. Bod. Univ. Bal. Mert. St. John's, Worc. Oxon. Pub. L.
Queen's. Trin. Camb. Brit. M.

CALAMY Edmund, Pastor of Aldermanbury Church, London.
* Ps. cxxii. 6. 4° 1660.
* Ps. cxix. 92. 8° 1661. Fun.
1 Sam. iv. 13. 4° 1662. Oxon. The godly Man's ark in the day
of Distress. Cb. Cb. Bal. Oxon. Pub. L. Camb.
*. 1 Thess. iv. 14. 4° 1662.
* Gal. v. 13. - - - - Doubtful Conscience.
* Isai. lvii. 1. 4° 1663. V. Coll. Farew. f.
*Rom. xii. 1. 4° 1670. Reason in matters of Religion. Bal. Ox.
* Acts xxvi. 8. 4° 1676. m. c. G. p. 423. Resurrection.

CALAMY Edmund, DD, Pastor in Westminster.
John ix. 4. 4° 1694. Fun. of Mr. Stephens. Bod. Pub. L. Camb.
Gen. iv. ix. 8° 1699. Ref. Manners. Eton.
* Rom. ix. 16. 8° 1702. Divine Mercy exalted.
‡ * Ps. xxxvii. 37. 8° 1708. Fun. of Mich. Watts. Brit. M.
‡ * Matt xxiv. 44. 8° 1708. Fun. of Rev. Mr. Sylvester. Brit. M.
‡ * Prov. xix. 8. 8° 1708. Fun. of Francis Lewis. Brit. M.
* Jer. xiv. 4. 8° 1708. 2 s. Caveat ag. New Prophets. St. John's. C.
* 1 Tim. vi. 9 8° 1709. On frequent Bankrupcies.
* Isai. lxvi. 5. 8° 1712. 2 s.
* Matt. x. 16. 8° 1713. b. Diss. Ministers. Exon. Queen's. Camb.
Mal. iii. 16. 8° 1714. Seasonableness of rel. Societies, Queen's. C.
* Matt. xvi. 18. 8° 1715.
* Isai. lxvi. 19. 8° 1715. 3 s.
* Tit. ii. 6. 8° 1717. Sobermindedness.
Acts xx. 28. 8° 1716. Ord.   Eton, St. John's. Camb.
Eccles. vii. 10. 8° 1720. Coronat. Eton, St. John's. Camb.
13 Serm. in 8° 1722. On the Doctrine of the Trinity. Cb. Cb.
Trin. Dr. W's. L. Lond. Brit. M.
Rom. x. 15. 8° 1724. Ord.
Job v. 26. 8° 1726. Fun.

CALDER John, DD.
* Gal. vi. 10. 8° 1772. Ch. School.

CALDER

CALDER R.
 ⸹ * Pſ. xc. 12. 8° 1701. *Aberdeen.* Schola Sepulchri. *Brit. M.*
CALDWELL J.
 1 John iv. 1. 1741.
CALTHROP John, M. A. V. of Boſton, Lincolnſhire.
 * Luke xii. 4, 5. 8° 1759. b. Linc. Militia. A religious Fear, the Principle of true Fortitude.
CALVERT *Thomas*
 Matt. xiii. 45, 46. 12° 1660. *Brit. M.*
CAMELL Robert, LLD. R. of Bradwell, Suffolk.
 3 Serm. } Pſ. cxxxvii. p. 15. The Benefit of Affliction.
 8° 1726. } Jer. vi. 8. Sept. 29. p. 41.
 } Gal. iv. 16. April 8. p. 67.
CAMFIELD Benjamin, R. of Aileſton near Leiceſter.
 Matt. vii. 12. 4° 1671. A practical Diſcourſe on the Rule of Righteouſneſs.
 Pſ. xviii. 2. 4° 1678. Faſt. Nov. 13. *Bod. Queen's.* Oxon.
 Heb. i. 14. 8° 1678. A theological Diſcourſe of Angels and their Miniſtries. *Bod.*
 Deut. xxvii. 15. 4° 1680. Commination-office vindicated. *Pub. L.* Camb. *Sion.*
 Heb. vi. 2. } 4° 1682. p. 1. Of Epiſcopal Confirmation. *Bod.*
 Acts xi. 23. } 2 Diſc. p. 72. *Pemb.* Oxon. *Sion.*
 Pſ. cxlvi. 15–18. 4° 1684. On the Great Froſt. *Bod. Ch. Ch. Ox. Queen's.* Camb. *Sion.*
 2 Chron. xiii. 5. 4° 1685. On proclaiming King James. *Pub. L.* Camb.
CAMPBELL George, DD. Principal of Mariſhal Coll. Aberdeen.
 * Matt. v. 13, 14. 8° 1752. The Character of a Miniſter of the Goſpel as a Teacher and Pattern.
 * 2 Tim. i. 7. 8° 1771. b. Synod. The Spirit of the Goſpel, neither a Spirit of Superſtition nor of Enthuſiaſm. *Queen's.* C.
 * Prov. xxiv. 21. 8° 1776. Faſt. The Nature, Extent and Importance of Allegiance.
 * - - - - 1777. Prop. Chriſtian Knowledge.
 * 1 Cor. i. 25. 12° 1779. 2 ſ. The Succeſs of the firſt Publiſhers of the Goſpel, a Proof of its Truth. V. Scotch Preacher. v. 3. p. 156.
CAMPBELL Thomas, LLD.
 * Matt. v. 48. 4° 1780. *Dublin.* Ch. School.
CAMPBELL *William*, of Armagh.
 * Matt. xxviii. 20. 8° 1774. b. Synod. Chriſt's preſence with his Church &c.
CAMPION Abraham, DD. Dean of Lincoln, and Chapl. in Ord.
 Pſ. cxxvii. 1. 4° 1694. *Oxon.* Aſſize. Of National Providence. *Bod. Ch. Ch. Magd.* Oxon. *Sion.*
 Col. i. 12. 4° 1700. The Inheritance of the Saints in Light. *All S.* Oxon.

CAMPLIN John, M. A. Precentor of Briſtol.
* Matt. xiv. 7. 4° 1766. b. Governors of Briſtol Infirmary.
* 2 Cor. iv. 7. 8° 1777. The Evidence of Chriſtianity not weakened by it's Miniſter's Frailty.

CANARIES James, DD. Miniſter of the Goſp. at Selkirk in Scotland
Gal. v 6. 4° 1686. Ag. Popery.

[CANER Henry,] M. A. Miniſter of King's Chapel, Boſton.
* Nehem. ii. 20. 8° 1749. Rebuilding a Chapel.

CANHAM P. LLB.
Heb. xi. 4. 8° 1711. Fun.   Eton.

CANNELL Joſeph, M. A. of Linc. Coll. Oxon. Lect. of St Nicholas Coleably and St Nicholas Olave, London.
1 Kings i. 5. 4° 1708. On the French Invaſion. Univ. Oxon. Queen's. Camb. Sion.

CANNING Richard, M. A. Miniſter of St. Lawrence, Ipſwich, R. of Harkſtead, Suffolk.
1 Cor. x 9. 8° 1746. Ipſwich. Faſt. for Rebellion.
Rom. x. 17. 8° 1747. Ipſwich. Viſ.

CANNON Robert, DD. Dean of Lincoln.
Acts xi. 18. 4° 1707. Camb. b. Queen at Newmarket. Cl. H. Camb. Brit. M.

CAPPE Newcome
* Pſ. cxviii. 15. 4° 1758. After a Victory by the King of Pruſſia.
* - - - - 1770. Fun.
* Prov. xxviii. 9. 8° 1776. Faſt.
* Deut. xxiii. 9. 8° 1780. York. Faſt.

CARDALE George, M. A. R. of Wanlip, Leiceſter.
* Epheſ. iv. 31, 32. 4° 1755. Aſſ. Peace, Good-will, and Forgiveneſs of Injuries recommended.

CARDALE Paul, Miniſter at Eveſham, Worceſterſ.
* Diſcourſes in 8° 1740.
* Matt. xiii. 43. 8° 1761. Fun.

CARDEW Cornelius, M. A. V. of Ewny near Lalant &c. and Maſter of the Grammar School at Truro, Cornwal.
* Rom. viii. 10. 8° 1779. b. Free-maſons.

CARELESS Thomas, M. A. V. of Cirenceſter, Glouceſterſ.
Pſ. xxi. 3. 4° 1661. Coron.

CARKEET Samuel
* Matt. x. 11. 8° 1719. Goſpel worthineſs.

CARLETON George, M. A. Sub-Dean of the Royal Chapel.
15 Serm. in 8° 1736. Preached at the Royal Chapel at Whitehall. Bod.

CARLOS James, M. A. R. of Blofield, Norfolk.
* Rom. xiv. 1. 4° 1773. Viſ.

CARLYLE Alexander, DD. Miniſter of Inverneſs and Almoner to his Majeſty.
* Pſ. xlviii. 12, 13. 12° 1779. The Tendency of the Conſtitution of the Church of Scotland to form the Temper, Spirit and Character of her Miniſter's. V. Scotch Preach. v. 2. p. 1.

CARMICHAEL

CARMICHAEL Frederick
* Sermons in 8° 1757. On important Subjects.
CARPENDER John, M.A. late Fell. of Linc. Coll. Oxon.
Acts x. 33. 8° 1708. Comparifon between Prayer and Preaching.
CARPENTER Benjamin
* John xv. 12. 8° 1780. b. Diff. Clergy. Difference of Sentiments, no Objection to the Exercife of mutual Love.
[CARPENTER Jofeph]
* 1742. Faft.
CARPENTER Richard
Matt. vii. 16. 4° 1663. Nov. 5. Bod.
CARPENTER Will. DD. V. of Treneglos cum Warbftow, Cornwal.
* 2 Sam. xxiv. 14. 4° 1776. Faft.
CARR George, fen. Clergyman of the Englifh Epifcopal Church at Edinburgh, Scotland.
* Sermons in 3 Vol. 12° 1777.
CARR R. V. of Sutton.
Col. iii. 5. 169 A practical Difcourfe.
CARRE Thomas, Confeffour of Sion.
* Pf. ii. 10. 12° 1670. Fun. of King Charles 1ft.
CARRINGTON James, fen. M.A. Chancellor of the Diocefe of Exeter.
The Theory of Chriftianity &c. on the Creed. 8° 1750.

V. 1. Exod. xx. 8. ⎫ The Duty of keep. holy the Sabb. Day. ⎫
Pf. cxix. 71. ⎪ Temporal Afflictions advantageous. ⎪
Pf. cxii. 6. ⎪ Duty, Meafures & Rew. of Benevolence. ⎪
James iv. 3. ⎨ Abufe of Prayer. ⎬ V. B. F. Pr. 4° 1776. V. 1, 2.
Prov. xxvii. 4. ⎪ Ag. Envy. ⎪
Ephef. vi. 4. ⎪ Parents Duty to Children. ⎪
Ephef. vi. 2, 3. ⎪ Children Duty to Parents. ⎪
V. 2. Prov. xviii. 21. ⎪ Sin and Folly of prophane Swearing. ⎪
Ecclef. xi. 3. ⎪ A Leffon on Death. ⎪
1 Cor. xv. 22. ⎭ The Refurrection of univerfal mankind. ⎭

CARRINGTON James, jun. LL.B. Preb. of Exeter and R. of Doddefcombleigh and St. Martin's, Devon.
* Ifai. ii. lxxviii. ⎱ A Strict. on the Land of Luxury. ⎱ V.B.F.Pr.
* Ephef. v. 15. ⎰ The Apoftolical Caution. ⎰
CARSWELL Francis, DD. V. of Bray, Berks, and Chapl. in Ord.
2 Sam. xv. 3, 4. 4° 1684. Affize.
Ifai. i. 26, 27. 4° 1689. Affize. England's Reftoration parallelled in Judah's. Ch. Ch. Magd. Oxon. Trin. Camb. Sion.
CARTE Sam. M.A. V. of St. Mary's in Leicef. & Preb. of Litchfield.
1 Cor. x. 10. 4° 1694.
Prov. iii. 7. 4° 1705. El. M. of Parl. Self-conceit. Ch. Ch. Ox.
CARTER Benjamin, M. A. R. of St. Martin's Outwich, Lond. and V. of Weftham, Effex, and Chapl. in Ord.
Pf. xxxiii. 12. 8° 17
Tit. iii. 1. 8° 1712. Affize.

Col. iii. 14. 4° 1712. El. Lord Mayor.
Prov. 24. 21. 8° 1715. Jan. 30.
Deut. xi. 26. 8° 1716. Th. June 7.
1 Tim. ii. 2. 4° 1717. Assize. *Eton.*
Gal. v. 13. 8° 1717. Assize. The Use and Abuse of Xn. Liberty.
Prov. xviii. 24. 4° 1718. Sch. Feast. The Excellency of Friend-
 ship. *Brit. M.*
Prov. xxix. 2. 4° 1721. *Eton.*
Pf. cxxix. 1, 2. 4° 1722. Nov. 5. *Brit. M.*
Rom. ii. 14, 15. 8° 1726. Assize.
-16 Disc. in 8° 1729. on pract. Subjects. *Ch. Ch.* Ox. *Queen's.* C.
CARTER Edmund, M. A. R. of Goadby, Leicester.
 Eccles. iii. 7. 8° 1712. Assize.
CARTER John, R. of Easton, Suff. and Chapl. to the E. of Rochford.
 Sermons in 8° 1722. On several texts of Scripture, with an Ap-
 pendix of 4 Sermons.
CARTER Nicholas, M. A. Minister of Dorchester, Dorsetshire.
 Pf. cxviii. 6. 8° 1715. On Rebellion. *Queen's.* Camb.
 Matt. xii. 25. 8° 1716. Jan. 30. *Brit. M.*
 Eccles. viii. 2. 8° 1716. Assize. *Brit. M.*
CARTER Nicholas, DD. Cur. of St. George's Chap. in Deal; and
 V. of Tilmaniton, Kent.
 17 Serm. in 8° 1738. on divers Subjects. *Queen's.* Camb.
 Pf. xxxiii. 20-22. 8° 1740. Fast. *Brit. M.*
 *Matt. xxiii. 8-10. 8° 1752. On St. Athanasius's Creed.
 *Nehem. ix. 28. 4° 1757. Fast.
CARTWRIGHT Thomas, Bp. of Chester.
 2 Chron. vii. 8, 9. 4° 16
 Rev. xiv. 13. 4° 16
 Matt. xix. 24. 4° 1662. b. Ld. Mayor. The Danger of Riches.
 Jude 22. 23. 4° 1676. Assize. *Bod. Ch. Ch. Univ.* Oxon. *Sion.*
 Judges xvii. 6. 4° 1676. Assize. *Queen's.* Oxon. *Trin.* Camb.
 Acts vii. 60. 4° 1682. *Edinb.* Jan. 30. *Brit. M.*
 Prov. xxiv. 21, 22. 4° 1684. County Feast. *Ch. Ch.* Oxon. *St.*
  John's Camb.
 1 Kings viii. 66. 4° 1686. Accession. *Bod. Ch. Ch. Magd. Oriel,*
  Jef. Oxon. *Sion.*
CARVER Marmaduke, R. of Harthill, Yorkshire.
 Isai. i. 26. 8° 1662. Assize.
CARY Mordecai, Bp. of Killala.
 James i. 27. 4° 1744. *Dublin.* Ir. Prot. School. *Ch. Ch. All S.*
  Worc. Oxon. *Brit. M.*
CARY Thomas, M. A. V. of St. Philip and Jude, and Preb. of Bristol.
 Ezra ix. 13, 14. 4° 1691. Monthly Feast.
 * Luke xii, 15. 4° 1691.
CARYL *Joseph*
 * Rev. iii. 4. 4° 1662. *Magd.* Camb.
CASAUBON Merick, DD. Can. of Cant. and R. of Ickham, Kent.
 Hosea iii. 4, 5. 4° 1660.

CASE

CASE Charles, M.A.
* 13 Serm. in 12° 1774. On primitive Xnity and Ch. Fellowship.
CASE Thomas
　Rev. ii. 5. 8° 1662. Farwel.
　Isai. lviii 13, 14. 4° 1674. s. m. e. C. p. 132. Of Sabbath Sanctification. Bod.
　2 Tim. i. 13. 4° 1676. m. e. G. p. 1. 2 Disc. Religion useful and profitable for Ministers and People.
CASTELL Abraham, B.A. L. A.P.
　Mal. iii. 1. 4° 1731. Advent.
CASTLE Abraham
　Mark iv. 24. 8° 17　　Vis. Ag. false Swearing. Worc. Oxon.
CASTLEMAN John, M.A. Preb. of Bristol, and V. of South-Petherton, Somerset.
　Luke xvi. 9. 4° 1744. Charity s. Bristol Infirmary.
CATCOTT Alex. Stopford, M.A. (sometime Fell. of St. John's, Coll. Oxon.) and R. of St. Stephens, Bristol.
　Ps. lxxxii. 6. 4° 1736. Assize. The supreme and inferior Elohim. Brit. M.
　Isai. xxiii. 8. 4° 1745. Bristol. b. Merchants. The Honourableness and Antiquity of Merchandize.
　* 18 Serm. in 8° 1752. St. John's. Oxon. Dr. W's. L. London.
CATHERALL Samuel, M.A. Chapl. to Lord Cholmondeley.
　Num. xxiii. 10. 4° 1692. Fun. of Lady Cholmondeley. Bod. Pub. L. Camb.
CATTELL Joseph, M.A. V. of Rothwell, Yorks.
　Exod. xiv. 15. 8° 1711.
　* 2 Sam. xxiv. 15. 8° 1715.
CATTELL Thomas, M.A. Chapl. of Christ's Coll. Manchester.
　Rom. xiii. 5. 4° 1734. Ass. Hum. Laws oblig. on the Consciences.
CAVE John, R. of Cold Orton, Leicestershire.
　1 Tim. ii. 12. 4° 1678. Jan. 30. Bod. St. John's. Camb. Sion.
　Mic. iv. 5. 4° 1679. Assize.
　Rom. i. 15. 8° 1681. 4 s. Nov 5. and Jan. 30. The Gospel preached to the Romans. Bal. Oxon. St. John's. Camb. Sion.
　Heb. xii. 9. 4° 1682. 2 s. Submission to the Will of G. Bod. Sion.
　Ps. xviii. 48. ⎫ 4° 1683. Sept. 2. David's Deliverance. ⎫ Sion.
　――― 49. ⎭　Th. Sept. 9 and Thanksgiving. ⎭
　1 Cor. vii. 30. 4° 1685. Fun. of F. Wollaston. C.C.C. Ox. Trin. Camb. Sion.
CAVE Will. DD. Can. of Windsor, and V. of Islington, Middlesex.
　2 Cor. ii. 11. 4° 1676. b. King. Bod. Ch. Ch. Univ. Queen's. Oxon. Sion.
　Acts xvii. 6. 4° 1680. b. Lord Mayor. Christianity and Popery compared. Magd. Jes. Oxon. Sion.
　Ps. iv. 7. 4° 1684. b. King. Ch. Ch. All S. C.C.C. Magd. Oxon.
CAWDREY Zachary, R. of Bathumley, Cheshire.
　Rev. xiv. 13. 4° 1684. Fun. of Lord Delamere.
Vol. II.　　　　K　　　　CAWTHORN

CAWTHORN James, M. A. Mafter of the Grammar School at Tunbridge, Kent.
  Job. xxix. 14–17. 8° 1735. Elect. of Burgeffes.
  Ifai. lviii. 12. 4° 1748. b. Co. of Skinners. Benevolence, the Source and Ornament of civil Diftinction.
CAWTON Thomas, Minifter of the Gofpel at St. Bartholomew's behind the Royal Exchange, London.
  Phil. i 27. 8° 1662. God's Rule for a Godly life. *Bod.*
  Num. xxiii. 10. 8° 1675. Balaam's Wifh—or the Vanity of defiring without endeavouring to obtain the Death of the upright.
CENNICK John, late of Reading, Berks.
  * Sermons in 2 Vol. 12° 1762.
CHADWICK Daniel, V. of Arnall, Nottinghamf.
  Pf. cxliv. 15. 8° 1698. Ref. Manners.
CHAFY John, M. A. V. of Broad Chalk, Wilts.
  * Jon. iii. 4, 5. 8° 1757. Faft.
CHALMERS James, DD. V. of Fingringho, Effex.
  John xx. 21. 4° 1714. Vif. The divine Inftitution, and Model of the chriftian Priefthood.
CHAMBERLAIN Thomas, DD. Dean of Briftol.
  Prov. xxix. 2. 8° 1730. Affize.
CHAMBRE Richard, M. A.
  1 Sam xii. 24. 8° 1710. Th. b. Lord Mayor.
  1 Cor. x. 24. 4° 1710. Sch. Feaft.
  Phil. i. 27. 4° 1711. b. Lord Mayor. On St Simon and Jude. The Duty and Neceffity of Xn Converfation. *Pub. L.* Camb.
CHAMBRE Rowland, M. A.
  * Ephef. vi. 10, 4° 1759. b. a Reg. of Volunteers on receiving their Colours.
CHAMBRES Charles, M. A. V. of Dartford, Kent.
  Prov. iii. 4. 4° 1715. Sch. Feaft. Religion and Virtue, the fure way to human Favor and Efteem.
  Acts xii. 5. 8° 1722. On Bp. Atterbury's Imprifonment. The facred Authority of Bps, and the Piety of praying for them in Prifon. *Bod.*
  Pf. xc. 17. 8° 1729. On opening a Workhoufe.
  1 Sam. xii. 22–24. 8° 1733. May 29. b. Lord Mayor.
CHANDLER Edward, Bp. of Durham.
  Pf. cxxxiii. 1. 4° 1707. Th. for Union. *Ch. Ch. Magd.* Oxon.
  Pf. cvii. 42, 43. 8° 1710. Th. Nov. 22. *Magd.* Oxon. *Pub. L.* C.
  John xviii. 36. 8° 1714. Nov. 5. *Ch. Ch.* Oxon.
  Pf. lv. 19–21. 4° 1716. Th. after Reb. *Trin. Queen's.* Cam. *Sion.*
  John i. 14. 8° 1718. Chriftmas. b. King. *Bod. Ch. Ch.* Oxon. *St. John's, Queen's.* Camb.
  Judges xvii. 6. 4° 1718. Jan. 30. b. Lords. *Bod. Ch. Ch.* Oxon. *Pub. L. Trin. St. John's, Queen's.* Camb.
  Matt. xiii. 31, 32. 4° 1719. Prop. Gofpel. *Ch. Ch.* Oxon. *Sion.*
  Gen. iv. 9. 4° 1724. Ref. Manners. *Queen's.* Camb. *Eton.*

[CHANDLER

[CHANDLER Henry]
    * Rom. xiv. 17. 8° 1699. Bigotry.
    * Heb. xi. 1. 8° 1718.
CHANDLER Samuel
    1 Theff. v. 13. ⎫ 8° 1691. 2 Difc. The Nature and Advan. of a
    John. xiii. 34. ⎭ general Union among Proteftants. *Bod. Trin.* C.
CHANDLER Samuel, DD. Minifter in the Old Jewry, London.
    Acts ix. 38. 8° 1727. Charity f.
    * John xiii. 17. 8° 1728. Knowledge and Practice. *Brit. M.*
    * Ephef. ii. 20. 8° 1735. Scripture and Tradition confidered.
    1 Tim. iii. 14,15. 8° 1735. 2 Difc. The Notes of the Church.
    V. Vol. 1. ag. Popery. *Braz. N.* Oxon.
    Ifai. v. 20. 8° 1738. Ref. Manners. *Queen's.* Camb. *Brit. M.*
    * Rom. vi. 23. 8° 1741.
    Ifai. viii. 12–14. 8° 1745. On the Invafion.
    Ifai. xxv. 9. 8° 1746. Th. for fuppreffing the Invafion.
    * Phil. iii. 21. 8° 1746. Fun of George Smith. *Brit. M.*
    * 2 Cor. ix. 12. 4° 1748. Acceffion. St. Paul's rules of Charity
    and his Incurablenefs of Superftition. *Queen's.* Camb.
    * Job ix. 5,6. 8° 1749. On the Earthquake. *Queen's.* Camb.
    * 1 Pet. v. 4. 8° 1752. Fun. of - - - - *Queen's.* Camb.
    * Phil. iii. 7.8. 8° 1753. Ch. School. Excellency of the Know-
    ledge of Chrift. *Queen's.* Camb.
    * Matt. xvi. 3. 8° 1759. Faft. Signs of the Times, the manner
    of recommending it enforced. *Queen's.* Camb.
    * 1 Cor. i. 21. 8° 1759. Ord. of - - - - - Preaching the
    Gofpel a more effectual method of Salvation than Human
    Wifdom, and Philofophy. *Queen's.* Camb.
    * Gen. ii. 2,3. 8° 1760. 2 Difc The Origin and Reafon of the
    Inftitution of the Sabbath. *Queen's.* Camb.
    * 1 Chron. xxix. 28. 8° 1760. Death of K. George 2d. *Queen's.* C.
    * Sermons in 4 Vol. 8° 1769. On various Subjects. Publifhed
    by *Thomas Amory,* DD. *Queen's.* Camb.
CHAPMAN John, M.A. Minifter of Barnard Caftle, Durham.
    2 Sam. xxii. 24. 4° 1683. Th. Sept. 9. *Worc.* Oxon.
CHAPMAN John, DD. Arch-D. of Sudbury, Gloc. and R. of Mer-
    fham, Kent.
    1 Tim. iii. 15. 4° 1739. Conf. of Bp. Mawfon. *Queen's.* Camb.
    Brit. M.
    1 Pet. ii. 16. 4° 1743. b. Commons.
    1 Theff. v. 21. 4° 1748. Conc. ad Synod. *Queen's.* Camb. *Eton.*
    Matt. x. 42. 4° 1752. Ann. meeting of Char. School. *Braz. N.*
    Oxon. *Brit. M.*
CHAPMAN Richard, M.A. Stud. of Ch. Church. Oxon. and V.
    of Chefhhunt, Herts, and Preb. of Linc.
    Pf. cxv. 1. 4° 1703. Th. Dec. 3. *Bod. Ch. Ch.* Oxon.
    Jer. xviii. 7,8. 4° 1703. *Bod.*
    Pf. cxliv. 15. 4° 1704. Th.

Prov.

Prov. xvi. 7. 4° 1709. Th. Nov. 22. *Ch. Ch. Linc.* Oxon. *St. John's.* Camb.
Pf. xviii. 50. 4° 1716. Th. June 7. Good Kings, Care of Heaven.
CHAPMAN Stephen
Heb. xiii. 16. 4° 1703. *Oxon Bod.*
CHARLTON Samuel, DD. Chaplain in Ord.
Matt. v. 8. 8° 1714. On the Death of Queen Anne.
CHARNOCK Stephen, B. D. fometime Fell. of New Coll. Oxon.
His Works, being fev. Difcourfes in 2 Vol. fo. 1684. On the Exiftence, Attributes and Providence of God, and various other Subjects. *Bod. New C. Trin.* Oxon. *Pub. L. Trin.* Cam.
* N. B. Difc. in 8° 1699.
CHAUNCY Angel, DD. R. of St. Andrew underfhaft, Lond. and Preb. of Sarum.
* 1 Cor. x. 11. 4° 1747. Fire at London, *All S.* Oxon.
* Acts x. 38. 4° 1758. Spittal f. b. Lord Mayor.
CHAUNCY Charles, DD.
* Prov. xxv. 26. 8° 1767. On the Repeal of the Stampt-Act.
[CHEESMAN Abraham]
Ephef. ii. 4. 4° 1663.
* Difcourfes in 8° 1668.
CHEESMAN M.
Matt. v. 8. 4° 1663.
CHEESMAN Thomas, M. A. formerly of Pemb. Coll. Oxon. and Minifter of the Gofpel at Eaft-Ilfly, Berks.
Luke viii. 52. 4° 1695. Fun.
Rom. vi. 23. 8° 1707. Fun.
CHETWOOD Knightly, DD. Dean of Gloucefter.
2 Chron. i. 11, 12. 7° 1700. *Eton* Sch. Feaft. Solomon's Choice. *St. John's.* Camb. *Sion.*
Luke x. 28. 4° 1708. Spittal T. Practical Goodnefs on Chriftian Principles. *Worc.* Oxon. *St. John's.* Camb. *Sion.*
1 Kings x. 9. 4° 1715. Th. Jan. 30.
CHELSUM James, DD. (late Stud. of Ch. Ch. Oxon.) R. of Drokinsford, Hants, and V. of Lathbury, Bucks.
* 1 Tim. i. 8. 4° 1777. *Oxon.* Aff. The Excellency of our Laws.
CHETWYND John, M. A. V. of Temple, and Preb. of Briftol.
Ecclef. xii. 13, 14. 4° 1682. Affize. A memorial for Magiftrates. *Pub. L.* Camb.
1 Sam. vii. 12. 4° 1682. Nov. 5. Ebenezer.
CHEYNEY John, of Warrington, Lancafterf.
* Job xxvii. 8. 12° 1677. 2 f. Rel. and Hypocrify, *Queen's.* Ox.
CHILCOT William, M. A.
Acts xvii. 31. 8° 1697.
Matt. xv. 19. 12° 1734. Sev. Sermons on evil Thoughts.
CHILLINGWORTH William
* Sermons in fo. 1664. *Bod. Queen's, Trin.* Camb.
CHISHUL John
Heb. iii. 8–9. 8° 1668. A word to Ifrael, *Bod.*

OF AUTHORS, &c.   77

CHISHULL Edmund, B.D. Fell. of C.C.C. Oxon. Chapl. in Ord'
and V. of Walthamstowe, Essex.
   Pf. cvii. 23, 24. 4° 1698. Levant Co. C.C.C. Oxon. *Trin. St.*
John's. Camb.
   James v. 8. 4° 1707. The great Danger and Mistake of all new
uninspired Prophecies relating to the End of the World. *Univ.*
C.C.C. Worc. Oxon. *Cl. H. Queen's.* Camb. *Sion.*
   1 Tim. iv. 16. 4° 1711. Vis. The orthodoxy of an English Clergyman. *Bal. Linc.* Oxon. *Pub. L. Queen's.* Camb.
   Phil. iv. 5. 8° 1712. Assize. Modesty and Moderation. *C.C.C.*
Bal. Linc. Oxon. *Queen's, St. John's.* Camb. *Sion.*
   Pf. xxix. 10. 8° 1712. Assize. The Duty of good Subjects in
respect to public Peace. *St. John's.* Camb. *Brit. M.*
   Rom xii. 19. 1° 1712. Ag. Duelling. *C.C.C.* Oxon. *Queen's.*
St. John's. Camb. *Sion.*
   2 Kings iv. 1, 2. 4° 1714. b. Sons of the Clergy. The Excellency
of a proper charitable Relief. *C.C.C. Worc. Wadh.* Oxon. *St.*
John's, Queen's. Sion.
   Tit. iii. 1. 8° 1716. The Subject minded of his Duty.
   1 John v. 20. 8° 1718. } 2 Assize f. *C.C.C.* Oxon.
   Acts xvii. 31. 8° 1718. }
   * Rom. vi. 8. 8° 1719. Fun.
CHOPPIN R. Minister at Dublin.
   Luke xii. 42, 43 Fun. of *Joseph Boyse,* V. the End of his 2 Vol.
fo. 1728. *Queen's.* Camb.
CHURCH Tho. DD. V. of Battersea, and Preb. of St. Paul's, Lond.
   Pf. xxxvii. 37. 4° 1748. Fun. of Rev. Mr. Cawley.
   Prov. xxx. 9. 4° 1751. An. meet. Ch. Sch. *Queen's.* Cam. *Brit. M.*
   * Luke x. 37. 4° 1750. Fun. of Dr. Pelling. Published by Mr.
William Scott, 1778.
   * Pf. ciii. 2–5. 4° 1752. b. Coll. of Physicians. *Braz. N.* Oxon.
Brit. M.
   * 2 Kings xix. 3. 4° 1753. b. Gov. of Ly. Hosp. *Braz. N.* Ox.
   * Gal. vi. 9. 4° 1754. b. Gov. of Middl. Hosp. *Braz. N.* Oxon.
   * James i. 27. 4° 1756. b. Sons of the Clergy.
CHURCHILL Charles
   * Serm. in 8° 1765. On the Lord's Prayer. *Dr. W's. L.* Lond.
CHURCHILL F. F. DD. late Fell. of Clare Hall. Camb.
   * 2 Sam. i. 19. 4° 1773. Conc. ad Cl. *Camb.* pro Grad. Doctor.
CHURCHILL John, B.D. Fell. of *C.C.C.* Oxon. and R. of Eggesford and Chawley, Devonf.
   * Prov. xxii. 2. 8° 1781. b. Gov. of Dev. and Exon, Hosp.
CLAGETT Nich. M.A. Preacher of St. Mary's, Edmonsbury.
   1 Thess. iv. 11. 4° 1683. Aff. A Persuasive to Peaceableness and
Obedience. *Magd.* Oxon. *Pub. L.* Camb. *Sion.*
   1 Tim. iv 15. 4° 1686. Vis.
CLAGETT Nicholas, Bp. of Exeter.
   ‡ * Eccles. v. 1. 4° 1694. b. King and Queen.
   2 Cor. i. 12. 4° 1704. Xn. Simplicity. *Ch. Ch.* Ox. *Pub. L.* Cam.

Luke

Luke xii. 48. 4° 1714. Sch. F. Duties and Obligat. arising from the Advantages of Life. *Ch.Ch.* Ox. *Trin. Queen's, Cl. H.* Cam.
1 Thess. v. 12, 13. 4° 1718, Conf. of Bp. White. *Ch. Ch.* Oxon. *Trin. Queen's, Cl. H.* Camb.
1 Cor. xiv. 26. 4° 1726. Vis. Of Edifying. *Cl. H.* Camb.
Matt. xxv. 23 4° 1720. Spitt. T. *Eton.*
1 Cor. x. 24. 4° 1733. Spittal M.
1 Tim. ii. 1, 2. 4° 1736. Jan. 30. b. Lords. *Queen's.* Camb.
Acts xi. 18. 4° 1736. Prop. Gospel. *All S.* Ox. *Queen's.* C. *Sion.*
Heb. xiii. 16. 4° 1739. Ann. meeting Charity School. *Queen's.* Camb. *Brit. M.*
Ps. xcii. 1. 4° 1742. Accession. *Queen's.* Camb.

CLAGETT William, DD. Preacher to the Hon. Soc. of Gray's-Inn, London, and Chaplain in Ord.
‡ * Gal. vi. 10. 4° 1687. b. Gov. Lying-Hosp. *Brit. M.*
17 Sermons in 8° 1704. V. 1. preached upon several occasions. *Bod. Ch. Ch. All S. C.C.C. Mert. Queen's, Pemb.* Oxon. *Pub. L. Queen's.* Camb.
11 Sermons in 8° 1704. V. 2. *Bod. Or. Ch. Ch. All S. C.C.C. Mert. Queen's. Pemb.* Oxon. *Pub. L. Queen's.* Camb.
34 Serm. in 2V. 8° 1720. *Ch. Ch. New C. St. John's. C.C.C.* Ox.

CLAPHAM Jonathan, R. of Wramplingham, Norfolk.
Tit. iii. 1. 4° 1684. Th. Christian Obedience recommended.

CLARIDGE Richard, M. A. R. of Peopleton, Worcester.
Rom. viii. 31. 4° 1689.
2 Kings xxiii. 25. 4° 1692. A looking-glass for relig. Princes. *Bod.*

CLARK John
Phil. i. 23. 4° 1676. Fun. of Rev. Mr. Aske.

CLARK John, M. A. Minister of St. George's Tombland in Norwich, and R. of Norwold, Norfolk.
Rev. xiv. 13. 8° 1716. *Norwich.* Fun. of Mr. Hall.

CLARK Joshua, M. A. R. of Somerby, Lincoln.
2 Cor. iv. 7. 4° 1698. Vis. *Pub L.* Camb.
* Heb. xiii. 7. 4° 1691. Conf. of an Abp and 3 Bps. *Pub. L.* C.

CLARK N. R. of St. James's Shafton, Dorsets.
Ps l. 16, 17 } Body of Divinity 293. } *Bod. Ch. Ch.* Ox.
1 Kings xviii 21. } 8° 1717-182. V. 2.309. }

CLARK Samuel, sen. of St. Alban's.
* Acts xxvi. 28. 8° 1742. 3 s. The Nature and Causes of Irresolution in Religion.

CLARK Samuel, jun. of Birmingham.
* Isai. xxvi. 9. 8° 1755. Fast. Earthq. at Lisbon.

CLARK Wilfrid, M. A.
* 1 Pet. ii. 16. 4° 1754. Jan. 30. b. Lord Mayor.

CLARKE Alured, DD. Dean of Exeter.
Gal. vi. 10. 4° 1726. St. Paul's Sch. Feast *Brit. M.*
Ps. lxxviii. 8. 4° 1731. Jan. 30. b. Commons. *Worc.* Ox. *Queen's* Camb. *Brit. M.*
Luke ix. 2. 4° 1736. Opening an Hosp. at *Winchester.* *Queen's.* Camb. *Brit. M.* Rom.

Rom. xiii. 10. 4° 1741. *Exon.* b. Truſtees for Charity Sch. *Exon,*
Queen's. Camb. *Eton.*
[CLARKE Auguſtus]
 * Pſ. l. 15. 12° 1781. Th. ſ. for Lord Gordon's Releaſe from
 the Tower.
CLARKE Edward, M. A. V. of St. Mary's, Nottingham.
 2 Sam. i. 27. 4° 1702. Roy. Fun. and Aſſize.
 Pſ. lxiv. 9, 10. 4° 1703. Thankſgiving. *St. John's.* Camb.
CLARKE Edward, M. A. Fell. of St. John's Coll. Camb. and R. of
 Pepperharrowe, Surry.
 * Pſ. l. 23. 4° 1759. Th. ſ.
CLARKE James, LLB.
 * 2 Chron. xix. 6. 7. 4° 1779. Aſſize.
CLARKE John, DD. Dean. of Sarum.
 * 8 Serm. at Boyle's Lecture. V. p. 153. *St. John's. Jeſ.* Oxon.
 Prov. xi. 11. 8° 1732. The Xrter of a good Magiſtrate.
CLARKE John, R. of Collingtree, Northampton.
 * Luke ii. 10. 8° 1762. Chriſtmas-day.
CLARKE Joſeph, DD. R. of Long-ditton, Surry.
 Gal. iv. 18. 4° 1721. Viſ. *St. John's.* Camb.
CLARKE Joſeph, M. A. Fell. of Magd. Coll. Camb.
 John v. 14. 4° 1746. Th. after Rebellion.
CLARKE Joſhua, Chaplain to the Bp. of Norwich.
 Heb xiii. 17. 4° 1691. Conſ. of 4 Bps. *Bod. Ch. Ch.* Ox. *Sion.*
CL*A*RKE *Matthew,* Miniſter of St. Michael's Alley, London.
 ‡ * John xix. 30. 8° 1723. Fun. of *J. Foxon. Brit. M.*
 Zech. iii. 8, 9. 8° 17 Ref. Manners.
 1 Pet. v 4. 8° 1723. Fun. of *Jer. Smith. Brit. M.*
 Gen. xii. 2. 8° 1724. Char. School. On New year's day.
 * Sermons in 8° 1727.
CLARKE REUBEN, DD. Chaplain in Ord. and Arch-D. of Eſſex.
 1 Kings viii. 44, 45. 4° 1741. Faſt. b. Commons. *Queens..* Cam.
CL*A*RKE *Richard,* late Miniſter of St. Philip's Ch. Charles Town.
 * Gen. ii. 2, 3. 4° 1759. Eſſay on the Number 7.
 * Levit. xxv. 3, 4. 8° 1760. Explanation of the ſabbatical Year
 of Moſes by the Goſpel of Jeſus Chriſt.
CLARKE Samuel
 1 Theſſ. v. 12, 13. 4° 1661.
CLARKE Samuel, DD. R. of St. James's, Weſtminſter.
 18 Sermons 8° 1734. *Univ. Mert. Ch. Ch.* Oxon. *Pub. L. Trin.*
 Cl. H. King's. Camb. *Dr. W's. L.* London.
 Sermons in 10 Vol. 8° 1730. *Bod. Univ. Ch. Ch. All S. Queen's.*
 New C. St. John's. Worc Waah. Hert. Pemb. Jeſ. Oxon. *Pub. L.*
 Trin. Camb.
CLARKE Stephen, M. A. late of Mert. Coll. Oxon. and R of
 Burythorne, Yorkſhire.
 15 Diſc. &c. in 8° 1727.
 Eccleſ. ii. 1. 8° 1730. *York.* Charity School.

CLARKE Thomas, M. A. R. of Eserick and Chapl. to the Duke of Devonshire.
Prov. xiv. 34. 8° 1724. York. Affize.
- - - - 1731. Aff. The Divine Inflitution of Government.
CLARKE William
1 Sam. xxiv. 20. 8° 1745.
CLARKSON Christopher, DD. R. of Strathern, Leicestershire.
Ephes. ii. 12. 4° 1733. Vis. The Insufficiency of Reason, and the Necessity of Revelation to assure men of the Pardon of Sin.
Col. iii. 1–3. 4° 1737. Fun.
CLARKSON David, B. D. sometime Fell. of Cl. Hall, Camb.
Rom iii. 24. 4° 1675. m. e P. p. 441. Justification.
1 Chron. xxix. 18 4° 1677. m. e. C. p. 538. What must Xtians do, that the Influence of the Ordinances may abide upon them.
* 31 Sermons and Discourses in fo. 1696. On several divine Subjects. Queen's. Camb.
CLAUDE Francis
* 2 Sam. iii. 32, 33, 38. 4° 1677. Fun. of Marshal Turenne. Translated. Bod. Pub L. Camb.
CLAUDE Isaac, Minister of the Walloon Church.
Acts ix. 36, 37. 8° 1695. Royal Fun.
CLAVERING Robert, Bp. of Peterborough.
Heb. xiii. 16. 4° 1708. Ch. s. for a Fire at Lisburn, Ireland. The Excellency of Charity. Bod.
1 John iv. 21. 4° 1729. Spittal M. Universal Love.
1 Sam. xii. 25. 4° 1730. Jan. 30.
Ecclef. x. 18. 4° 1733. Ann. meeting Charity Schools.
CLAVERING Robert, M. A. R. of St. Peter's, Malborough, and V. of Preshut, Wilts.
1 Thess iv. 11. 4° 1730. Assize. Duty of living peaceably &c.
CLAYTON John, M. A. Preb. of St. Michan's belonging to Ch. Ch. Dublin.
* 1 Cor. i. 23, 24. } 4° 1706. Christ crucif. the Power of God and
* ——— 21–25. } the Wisdom of God.
CLAYTON John, M. A. late Fell. of Braz. N. Coll. Oxon.
Rom. xiii. 4. 8° 1736. Assize. The Necessity of duly executing the Laws ag. Immorality and Profaneness.
CLAYTON N.
* John iv. 19–23. 8° 1776. The Importance of Sincerity in public Worship &c.
* 1 Cor. x. 33. 8° 1776. Minister of the Gospel represented.
CLAYTON Robert, Bp. of Corke.
Rev. xiv. 13. 4° 1727. Dublin. Royal Fun.
2 Thess. iii. 10. 4° 1740. Dublin. Irish Prot. Sch. The Religion of Labour. Ware. Oxon. Queen's, Cl. H. Brit M
CLAYTON Thomas, R. of St. Michael's at the Pleas, Norwich.
Ecclef. v. 1. 8° 1727. Serious Attention at Divine Worship. Ch. Ch. Magd. Linc. Oxon.
Rom. xii. 4, 5. 4° 1713. Unity of Worship. Trin. Queen's. Cam.

CLEAVER

CLEAVER John, M. A.
  Tit iii. 1. 4° 1676. Of the Subject's Duty. *Sion.*
CLEAVER Will. M. A. late of Linc. Coll. Oxon.
  Luke xii. 5. 8° 1739. *Oxon.* Affize. The Doctrine of a future State necessary to the Welfare and Support of civil Government. *Worc.* Oxon.
  Gal. iv. 4. 8° 1743. *Oxon.* The Fitness and Propriety of the time of our Saviour's coming. *Worc.* Oxon *Brit M.*
  2 Tim. iii. 15. 8° 1750. *Oxon.* The Expediences and Advantages of an early Education in Piety and Virtue. *Worc.* Oxon
  * 1 Sam. xiii. 14. 8° 1762. Enquiry into the true Xrter of King David. *Braz N. Worc.* Oxon.
CLEEVE Alexander, B. A. V. of Strckton upon Tees, Durham.
  * Matt. x. 8. 4° 1773. b. Gov. Lying-in Hosp. London.
CLEGG *James,* M D.
  * Matt. xvi. 18. 8° 1731. Ord.   *Queen's.* Camb.
  * - - - - 1736. Fun.
  * Rom. xiv. 19. 8° 1738. The things that make for Peace and Edification among Christians.
CLELAND Benjamin
  * John xiv. 1-3. 8° 1667.
CLELAND Thomas
  Rom. x 11. 4° 1660. The Xn's Encouragement to believe. *Sion.*
CLEMENT Benjamin, B. A. late Preb of the Collegiate Church of St. John's, Wolvehampton, Staff and V. of Baunton. Devon.
  * Serm. in 2 Vol 8° 1774. On several Subjects and Occasions.
CLERKE Francis, LLD Commissary of Lewes, Sussex, and Chancellor of Chichester.
  Amos iii. 2. 8° 1722. *Ex n.*
CLERKE John, Fell of All Soul's Coll. Oxon. and R. of Ulcomb and Harisham, Kent
  1 Cor. x 10. 4 1654 May 29.
CLERKE Samuel, B. D. Minister of Archesdem, Essex.
  Ps cxliv. 9, 10. 4° 1693. Th. *Brit. M.*
  2 Sam. xxii. 38-41. 4° 1696. Th. April 16.
  Matt. iii. 8. 4° 1700. Lent.
CLIFFORD James. M. A. Chaplain to the Society, Serjeant's Inn, Fleetstreet, London.
  * 1 Cor. xi 27-29. 12° 1694. Sev. Serm. on the Xtian Religion.
CLIFFORD Will. M. A.
  Ps. ii. 4. 4° 1682. The Power of Kings &c. *Bod.*
CLIFTON Jo. Chaplain to the Lord Mayor.
  Luke ix. 55, 56. 4° 1703. Jan. 30. A modest Revival of a primitive Christian Doctrine. *St. John's.* Camb.
CLIVE Robert, M. A. Arch-Deacon of Salop.
  * John vi 44 8° 1770. Viz. The Christian Religion agreeable to the Nature, Powers, and Principles of Mankind.
CLOGIE Alex. Minister of Wigmore &c. Herefordshire.
  Col iii. 5. 12° 1694. Vox. Corvi. *Bod.*

Vol. II.   L   CLUBB

CLUBB John, R. of Whatfield and V. of Debenham, Suffolk.
  Deut. xii. 12. 4° 1751. *Ipswich.* b. Sons of Clergy.
CLUTTERBUCK Tho. DD. Arc-D. of Winton, and V. of South Stoneham, Hants.
  Rom. xii. 13. 4° 1687. Spittal W. *Bod. Pub. L.* Camb.
COATES James, V. of Galmpton, Yorkshire.
  Heb. xiii. 7. 8° 1717. *York.* Vif.
COBDEN Edward, DD Arch-D. of Lond. and Chapl. in Ord.
  * 28 Disc. in 4° 1757. On various Subjects and Occasions. *Bod.*
COCHRANE James, Hon.
  * Matt. x. 16. 4° 1777. *Reading.* At a monthly Meeting.
  * Rom. i. 20. 4° 1780. *Reading.* On the Existence of a Deity.
COCK John, M.A. of Chrift's Coll. Camb. and V. of St. Oswald's, Durham.
  Luke xiii. 28. 8° 1704. *St. John's.* Camb.
  James i. 27. 8° 1707. b. Bp. Cofin, (1669.)
  Rom. xvi. 17, 18. 8° 1707. A serious Exhortation to avoid such as cause Divisions in Chrift's Church. *Linc. Oxon. Trin.* Cam.
  6 Serm. &c. in 12° 1705. Advice to the Clergy. *Ch. Ch.* Oxon.
  12 Sermons in 12° 1710.
COCKBURN John, DD. R. of Northaw, Middlefex.
  15 Serm. in 8° 1697. On several Occasions and on various Subjects. *C. C. C.* Oxon. *Trin.* Camb. *Sion. Dr. W's. L.* Lond.
  Pf. clxvii. 12–14. 4° 1703. *Amsterdam.* Th. Dec. 5. *Ch. Ch.* Ox.
  Pf. cxlviii. 8. 4° 1703. *Amst.* On the Storm Dec. 9. *Ch. Ch.* Ox.
  Pf. xc. 12. 4° 1706. Human Life displayed.
  Heb. xiii. 4. 8° 1708. The Dignity and Duty of a married State. *Magd. Linc.* Oxon. *Trin.* Camb. *Brit. M.*
  Heb. xii. 12, 13. } 8° 1708. 2 Disc. at the End of his, " Right
  ———— 15.   } " Notions of God and Religion."
  2 Sam. vi. 12. 8° 1711 Accession.
  Acts ii. 47. 4° 1712. Salvation in the Church only.
  Rev. xiv. 13. 4° 1713. Fun. of Bp. Compton. The Blessedness of Christians after Death. *Ch. Ch. C. C. C.* Oxon.
COCKBURN Patrick, M. A.
  1 Tim. ii. 1–4. 8° 1728. *Edinburgh.* Coron.
COCKBURN William
  Gen xlix. 5–7. 4° 1713. Jan. 30.
COCKMAN Thomas, DD. Master of Univ. Coll. Oxon.
  Rom. xii. 2. 8° 1733. *Oxon.* Act. The Duty of nonconforming to the World. *Worc. Linc.* Oxon. *Queen's.* Camb. *Sion. Brit. M.*
  Select theological Disc. in 2V. 8° 1750. *All S. New C. Wadh.* Ox,
COCKS Sir Robert, DD. R. of great Rolwright, Oxon.
  * Luke vi. 36. 8° 1714. The great Importance of a meek and merciful Spirit. *Worc.* Oxon.
  * Isai. lvii. 20, 21. 8° 1715. Assize. Nothing but Religion can secure our Peace and Happiness in this life, and that which is to come. *Worc.* Oxon.

Pf.

Pf. xxxiii. 1. 8° 1716. Th.
COCKS Sir Richard
  * Matt. v. 48. 8° 17   Againſt Popery.
COCKS Philip, M. A. R. of Acton, Middlesex.
  * 1 Tim. iv. 16. 8° 1774. Conf. of Bp. - - - -
CODRINGTON Thomas
  Luke xviii 35–38.
[COHEN Moſes]
  * Prov. xx 01. 4° 1761. Acceſſion.
COKAYNE Will. B. D. (late Fell. of St. John's Oxon.) Profeſſor of Aſtronomy Greſham Coll. and R. of Kilkhampton, Devonſ.
  Acts xvii. 22. 4° 1750.- Nov. 5. b. Lord Mayor. *Worc*. Oxon.
  * Iſai. xxvi. 9. 4° 1753. Faſt. b. L. Mayor.
COKE Thomas, M. A.
  * Prov. xxii. 6. 8° 1773. Sch. Feaſt at *Crewkerne*, Somerſet.
COKER Thomas, M. A. Canon of Sarum.
  2 Pet. ii. 1. 8° 1721. *Braz. N.* Oxon.
COLBATCH John, DD. Fell. of Trin. Coll. and Caſuiſt-Profeſſor of Divinity. Camb.
  Prov x. 7. 4° 1718. *Camb.* Commem. *Ch. Ch.* Oxon. *St. John's*. *Queen's.* Camb. *Eton*.
COLBY John
  * Prov. xxxi. 10. 12° 1732. Wedd. f. V. Sermons on Conj. D. Vol. 1. p. 51.
COLBY Samuel, M A.
  Prov. xxviii. 2. 8° 1708. Jan. 30.
  ——— xxxi 8. 8° 1708.
  Matt. xi 28. 8° 1709. Sacrament. *Univ.* Oxon.
  1 Cor. xi. 29. 8° 1708. Sacrament. *Univ.* Oxon.
COLE *Thomas*
  Luke iii. 4, 5. 4° 1676. f. m. e. C. p. 593. How we may ſteer an even Courſe between Preſumption and Despair *Bod*.
  1 Sam. xvii. 34–37. ⎱ 4° 1683. C. m. e. p. 572. How may the well
  Pf. xxvii. 14.   ⎰ Diſcharge of our preſent Duty give us Aſ-
  Prov. x. 29.   ⎱ ſurance of Help from God for the well Diſ-
  2 Chron xv. 2.   ⎰ charge of all future Duties. *Bod*.
  Epheſ. i 19, 20. 4° 1690. C. m. e. p. 223. *Bod*.
  * Sermons in 12° 1692.
COLE Thomas, LL.B. Aſſiſtant-Preacher at St. Paul's Covent-Garden, London.
  * Rom ix. 32, 33   2 ſ. Imputed Righteouſneſs.
  * 6 Diſc. in 8° 1761. Ag Luxury, Infidelity, and Enthuſiaſm.
COLEIRE Richard, M. A. Fell. of All Souls Coll. Oxon. V. of Iſleworth, and Miniſter of Richmond &c.
  Pf. xx. 6. 8° 1708. Th. On the Scotch Defeat.
  Luke xxiii. 28. 4° 1713. Jan. 30. At the Temple. *Worc*. Oxon. *Queen's*. Camb.
  Jerem. xxviii. 16. 8° 1715. On the Rebellion. *Ch. Ch.* Oxon.

L 2   2 Sam.

2 Sam. xxii. 44. 4° 1716. Th. for fuppreffing the Rebellion. *Cb. Cb.* Oxon.
Ruth ii. 19. 4° 1719. Ch. f. At Ifleworth.
1 Cor. xiii. 4–7. 4° 1721. b. Corporation at Kingfton.
—— xii 4–7. 4° 1721. Vif. f.
Judg. xix 30. 8° 1723. On the Rape and Murder of a Woman at Ifleworth. *Queen's.* Camb.
2 Sam. xxiii. 3. 4° 1726. b. Corporation at Kingfton. The Magiftrates Character and Charge.
2 Cor. xiii. 11. 4° 1727. Farewel f. At Kinfton.
Pf. lxxxii 1. 4° 1729. Affize. Kings and Judges, the Vicegerents of God.
Prov. xxii. 6. 4° 1729. Ch. f. At Ifleworth.
Pf. cl. 3–6. 4° 1738. On erecting of an Organ at Ifleworth.
– – – – 1739. Faft. Jan. 9.
Rom. xiii. 6. 4° 1742. Inauguration. b. Univ. of Oxon.
2 Pet. iii 3, 4. 4° 17 Vifit.
Joel ii. 16–18. 4° 1745. Fult.

COLEMAN *Benjamin*, M. A. late Preacher at Bath.
Job x. 20.
‡ * John ix. 4. 8° 1717. *Bofton.* Fun. of Rev. Mr. *Brattle* and *Eben. Pemberton. Brit. M.*
20 Sacram. Difc. in 8° 1728. *Bod. Sion.*
* Difcourfes in 2 Vol. 8° 1728. Chriftian Oratory.
* Numb. x. 3. 12° 1735. } 2 f. V. *J. Turrell's* Life.
* 2 Sam xi 23. 12° 1735

COLERIDGE John, V. of Ottery St. Mary, Devon.
* Rom. xiii. 1. 4° 1777. Faft. Government of divine Inftitution.

COLES Thomas, DD.
2 Kings x 15. 4° 1664.

COLET John, DD Dean of St. Paul's, London.
Rom. xii. 2 (preached 1511.) printed 4° 1661. and 1701. *Bod. Cb. Cb Bal* Oxon. *Sion.*

COLLET *Jofeph*
* John xiv. 1. 8° 1713. Fun.
* – – – – 1742. Divine Providence.

COLLETT J. R. of Cublington, Bucks.
* 3 Difcourfes in 8° 1774. *Bath* On the feveral Eftates of Man — on Earth—in Heaven—and Hell, deduced from Reafon and Revelation.

COLLIER Arthur, M. A. R. of Langford Magna near Sarum.
Rom xiii. 1. 8° 1713. May 29. Xn Principles of Obedience. *Sion.*
Rom. i. 17. 8° 1716.
* Sermons in 8° 1730.

COLLIER Giles, M. A. V. of Blockley, Worcefterf.
Ifai. lvii. 1. 4° 1661. Fun.

COLLIER Jeremy, M. A.
1 Cor. xv. 29. 4° 1686. The Difference between the prefent and future State of our Bodies. *Ma_gd.* Oxon. *Sion.*
Ecclef.

Eccles. vii. 14. 4° 1695. A Persuasive to Consideration &c. *Bod.*
Rom. vi. 18. 8° 1704. Prop. Gospel.
12 Discourses in 8° 1725 On practical Subjects. *Bod. Worc. Bal.*
St. John's. Oxon. *Pub. L.* Camb. *Lion.*
James i. 13, 14. 8° 1726. *Brit. M.*
COLLIER Nathaniel,[a] M. A. V. of Croydon, Surry.
    Ps. lxxxii. 6, 7. 4° 1714. Death of Queen Anne.
COLLIER Nathaniel,[a] M. A. v. of Croydon, Surry.
    Ps. xliv. 4–6. 4° 1739. Fast. Jan. 9. The divine Aid, the best Support against our Enemies
    Rom. xi. 33. 4° 1743. Access. b. Lord Mayor.
    Prov. xxviii. 27. 4° 1752. Commem. Ch. Sch.
COLLIER Philip
    Ps. cxxii. 6–9. 4° 1712. Visit.
COLLIER William, M A.
    Isai. xxxiii 15. 16. 8° 17   Assize.
    Ps. lxxxi. 13, 14. 8° 1744. Fast.
COLLINGES John, DD. Minister of St. Stephen's, Norwich, before the Ejection.
    Disc. in 4° 1678 About the actual Providence of God. *Bod.*
    Rom. vi. 3, 4. 4° 1680. On Water-baptism. *Bod.*
    Cantic. i.   4° 1683. Several Sermons. *Sion.*
    * Sermons in 8° 1684. On useful Subjects.
    Ps cxxxiii. 1. 4° 1689. Th. The Happiness of Brethrens dwelling together in Peace and Unity.
COLLINS
    * Jude 3. 4° 1663. V. Coll. Farw. S.
COLLINS   V. of Burham, Kent.
    * Ezek. xxxvii. 22. 4° 1707. Union of the two antient Kingdoms.
    * Ps. i, and ii. 8° 1709. Several Sermons.
COLLINS Edward, LL. B. V. of Breaze, Cornwall.
    1 Pet ii. 13. 8° 1723. Assize.
[COLLINS Hercules]
    ‡ * Job iii. 17–19. 4° 1684. Fun. of F. Bamfield and R. Ralphson *Brit M.*
    ‡ * 2 Tim. ii. 15. 8° 1702. Temple Repaired. *Brit. M.*
COLLINS Richard,   R. of Crayford, Kent.
    2 Cor. vi. 3. 4° 1705. Visit. The Danger of ungoverned Zeal.
    Rom. xiv 19. 8° 1715. Assize The Paths that lead to Peace.
    Ps. xciv. 16 8° 1716.
COLLINS Richard, M. A. V. of Mempham, Kent, and Chapl. to the Royal Navy at Chatham.
    Jerem. vii. 23. 8° 1710. Fast. b. Ld Mayor. *Trin. St. John's.* C.
COLLINS S. M. A.
    Prov xvi. 20. 4° 1698. Th. for Peace. *Trin* Camb.
COLLINS Thomas, B. D. Fell. of Magd. Coll. Oxon.
    1 Cor. i. 20. 8° 1725.

a Q. The same.

COLLINS Thomas, M. A. V. of Knaresborough, Yorkſhire.
  Iſai. lvi. 7. 8° 1749. *York.* Conſ. Chapel.
COLMAN. DD.
  * Iſai lx. 8 8° 1741.
COLMAN Ben'am n, M A. late Preacher at Bath.
  * Sermons in 8° 1707. on tne 10 Virgins. *Dr. Wi's L.* Lond.
COLMAN Henry, B. D. Fell. of Trin. Coll. Camb. and R. of Harpley, Norfolk.
  2 Chron. xix. 6. 4° 1711. Elect. Lord Mayor. Government and Obedience.
COLNET William, DD. Fell of All Souls Coll. Oxon.
  Pſ. cxix. 53. 8° 1711. Ref. Manners. *Cb. Cb.* Oxon. *Sion.*
COLVIL John, M. V. D.
  Pſ. cxii. 4. 4° 1753. On a Woman found dead in a Draw-well.
COLVILE William
  * Diſcourſes in 4° 1667.. On effectual Calling.
COMBE Edward, M. A R of St. Martin's, Worceſter.
  Prov x v. 34. 4° 1708 Viſ of a Free-Sch. and Hoſpital.
  Luke vii. 36–50. 4° 1720. *Worceſter.* Aſhwedneſday.
  * Acts ii 32. 8° 1717. Farew. ſ. :
COMBER Thomas, DD. Dean of Durham.
  Heb. vi. 16 4° 1682. Aſſ. Of judicial, vain and falſe Swearing.
    Bod Cb. Cb. Magd Oxon. *Trin.* Camb. *Sion.*
  Pſ. lv. 18. 4° 1687. *Cb. Cb. Queen's.* Oxon. *Sion.*
  Pſ. xxiii. 4. 4° 1691. *Bod..*
  Pſ. cxxii. 6. 4° 1694. Faſt. b. Queen. The Reaſons for the praying for the Peace of our Jeruſalem. *Cb. Cb. Ox.. Pub. L. Trin. Queen's.* Camb.
  Pſ. cxliv 15. 4° 1697. Th. for Peace. *Trin. St. John's.* Cam. *Sion.*
COMER William, M. A. of Baliol Coll. Oxon. and V. of Kingſton, Surry
  2 Cor. iv. 5. 8° 1747. Induction. ſ. at *Richmond.*
CONANT John, DD. R. of Exeter Coll. Oxon. Arch-D. of Norwich and Prebendary of Worceſter.
  Sermons in 4 Vol. 8° 1699. Preached on ſeveral Occaſions. *Bod. Bal. C.C.C. New C.* Oxon. *Trin. Queen's.* Camb. *Sion. Dr. W's. L.* London.
  Sermons Vol. 5. 8° 1708. Vol. 6. 8° 1722.
CONDER John, DD.
  * Acts xx. 32. 8" 1755. Farew. ſ. *Queen's.* Camb.
  * 1 Theſſ. v 12, 13. 8° 1758. Ord.
  * Jer. xxiii. 28. 8° 1759. Ord.
  * Pſ. xxxvii. 37. 8° 1762. Fun. of *Dr. Guyſe.*
  * 1 John iii. 8. 8° 1768. Ref. Manners.
CONEN Geo. B. D. Lecturer of St. George Southwark and Chapl. to Lord Onſlow.
  1 Sam xii. 24. 4° 1745. Rebellion.
CONEY Thomas, DD. Preb. of Wells and Rector of Bath.
  25 Serm. in 8° 1730. Preached on ſev. Subjects and Occaſions.
                                                * Num.

*Num. xiv. 11. 8° 17   Act. f.
Prov. xxix. 2. 8° 1731. Affize.
Micah vi. 8. 8° 1731. Affize.
Sermons and Difcourfes in 8° 1750. Vol. 2. and 3. p. 111.

CONGREVE Charles Walter, M. A. Arch-D of Armagh, and Chapl. to his Grace the Lord Primate of Armagh.
   1 Chron. v. 1, 2 8° 1746. Reb An abfolute, indefeafible, hereditary Right, contrary to Reafon and cripture.

CONINGESBY George, DD. V. of Bodenham, Herefordfhire.
   Rom. i. xxii. 8° 1723. Oxon. The folly of oppofing natural Reafon to the Doctrine of the Trinity. Worc. Bal. Oxon
   Pf xlvii. 7. 8° 1733 Oxon. Church Mufic vindicated, and the Caufes of its Diflike enquired into. Linc. Bal. Cxon.
   Prov. xxix. 2. 8° 1742. Oxon. Admiffion of a Mayor at Hereford. Worc. Oxon.

CONANT Malachi, B. D. Minifter of Beding, Suffex.
   Matt. v. 16. 4° 1669. Vif Unim and Thummim—or the Clergy's Dignity and Duty. Lod. Sion.

CONOLD Robert, M. A. R. of Eerghapton, Norfolk.
   2 Theff. iii. 2 4° 1675 Jan. 30 Bal. Oxon.

CONSERT Thomas, Chapl. to the Brit. Factory at Peterfburgh.
   Pf. lxxxii. 6, 7. 4° 1725. Revel. Fun. of the Czar.

CONSTANTINE Henry, M. A. Preb. of Wells, and Chapl. to Earl Paulet at Hinton St. George, Somerfetf.
   Judges v. 1, 2. 4° 1708. Affize.

CONWAY George, M. A. Mafter of Blandford free-fch. and Chapl. to the Earl of Sandwich.
   *2 Chron. xx 27. 8° 1709. Th. f.
   Acts xx. 35. 8° 1732. The Bleffednefs of giving, above that of receiving. Sion.

CONYBEARE John, Bp. of Briftol and Dean of Ch. Ch. Oxon.
   Heb. ii. 4. 8° 1722. Oxon. Of Miracles. Lod. Ch. Ch. New C. Worc. Linc. Oxon. Queen's. Camb. Sion.
   1 Cor. xiii 12. 8° 1723. Oxon. Myfteries credible. Ch. Ch. New C. Worc. Linc. Oxon. Queen's. Camb.
   1 Tim. vi. 3, 4. 8° 1726. Oxon. Vif. The Cafe of Subfcription to Articles of Religion confidered. Ch. Ch. All S. New C. Worc. Oxon. Queen's. Camb. Sion.
   Ezra vii. 26. 8° 1727. Oxon. Affize. The penal Sanctions of Laws confidered. Ch. Ch. Worc. Oxon. Queen's Cam Brit. M.
   John vi. 45. 8° 1729. Expediency of a divine Revelation reprefented. Ch. Ch. Worc. Oxon. Queen's. Camb. Brit. M.
   2 Pet. iii. 16. 8° 1733. Ox. n. Sch. Feaft. Scripture Difficulties confidered. Cb. Ch. Worc. Linc. Oxon. Queen's. Camb.
   Gal. vi. 9. 4° 1738. An. meet. Char. Sch. Ch. Ch. All S. Worc. Oxon. Queen's. Camb.
   Pf. cxxii. 6–9. 8° 1749. Th. for Peace. b. Commons. True Patriotifm. Ch. Ch. Worc. Oxon. Queen's. Camb.

Prov.

Prov. xi. 17. 8° 1751. Spittal M. The Virtue of being merciful stated and enforced. *Bod. Ch. Ch. Worc.* Oxon.
Pf. lxxviii. 72. 4° 1751. Accell. b. Lords. Of Civil Government. *Bod. Ch. Ch. Worc.* Oxon.
Matt. xviii. 10, 11. 4° 1752. Irish Prot. Sch. *Ch. Ch.* Oxen. *St. John's.* Camb.
James i. 27. 4° 1752. *Oxon.* b. Sons of Clergy, at *Briſtol.* Of Charity. *Bod. Ch. Ch. Braz. N. Worc.* Oxon. *Queen's.* Camb.
‡* Joshua xxiv. 15. 8° 1756. Jan. 30.
* Serm. (Poſth) in 2 V. 8° 1757. *Ch. Ch. All S. New C. Braz. N. C. C. C. Univ. Worc. Wadh. Magd. Bal. Jef. Oriel.* Oxon. *Trin. Queen's.* Camb.

CONYERS Richard, M. A. R. of Kirby-Miſperton, Yorkſhire.
* John xvi. 8–11. 8° 1764. Viſ. The Operation of the H. Ghoſt conſidered.

CONYERS Tobias, Miniſter at St. Ethelbeit's, London.
Luke vi. 36. 4° 1660. b. Lord Mayor and General Monk. Pattern of Mercy, *Worc.* Oxon.

COOK John, M. A. R. of Cuckſtone, Kent.
John viii. 34. 4° 1676. b. Lord Mayor. *Bod Trin.* Camb.

COOK John, R of Merſham, Kent.
Rom. xii. 18. 4° 1683. b. Lord Mayor.

COOKE
* Deut. vi 7, 8. 8° 1752. Anniv. meet. at *Newcaſtle.* The Children having been publickly examined.

COOKE Edward, M. A. V. of Eaſton Neſton, Northamptonſ.
1 Theſſ iv. 14. 8° 1719. Fun. of Will. Ives, Eſq;
Luke i. 46–48. 8° 1722. On the Augment. of a Vicarage.

COOKE Henry M. Fell. of Chriſt's Coll. Camb.
Rev. xiv. 13. 4° 1704. *Camb.* Fun. of Lady Lumley.

COOKE John, M. A. R. of the united Pariſhes of St. George the Martyr, and St. Mary Magdalene, Cant. and R. of Merſham, Kent.
39 Serm in 2 Vol. 8° 1739. On ſeveral Occaſions.

COOKE John, DD. Fell. of C. C C. Oxon.
* Rom xii. 19. 8° 1773. Aſſize. *Oxon.* Unlawfulneſs of private Revenge.

COOKE Shadrach, M. A. Chapl. to the Earl of Ayleſbury, Lecturer of Iſlington, and V. of Feverſham, Kent.
Matt xxi. 32. 4° 1685. Th. *Bod. Sion.*
Mark viii. 38. 4° 1689. An Exhortation to Conſtancy in true Religion.
Pf. xxiii. 4. 4° 1691. Chriſtian Support under the Terrors of Death. *Bod. Sion.*
Job xxiii. 4. 4° 1706.
Rom. xiii 5. 8° 1711. Viſ. *St. John's.* Camb. *Eton.*
Pf. cxix. 120. 8° 1722. Faſt.
Pf. xxxiv. 3. 8° 1723. Th. *Eton.*

COOKE T.
* Exod. xxxi. 13. 8° 1754.

COOKE Thomas, M. A. R. of St. Bennet's and St. Peter's, Paul's
warf, London.
 Rev. xiv. 13. 4° 1709. Fun. of Lady Mary Cooke. Bleſſedneſs
of dying in the Lord. *Brit. M.*
COOKE Thomas, Cur. of Kingſton upon Thame and Ord. of Surry.
2 Theſſ. iii. 10. 8° 1702.
 Pſ. cxxii. 6. } 8° 1712. 2 ſ. { Jan. 6. Faſt.
 Iſai. lvii. 1.   { Jan. 30.
COOKE Thomas, M. A. Chaplain to the Duke of Ormond.
 Heb. xiii. 16. 4° 1704. School Feaſt. The Chriſtian Sacrifices.
Queen's. Camb. *Sion.*
COOKE Thomas, M. A. R. of St Nicholas, Worceſter.
 Luke xiii. 5. 4° 1704. *Oxon* Faſt. Jan. 19.
COOKE Will. DD. Provoſt of King's Coll. Camb. and Dean of Ely.
 2 Pet. i. 19. 8° 1750. Vit. The more ſure Word of Prophecy
conſidered and explained. *Queen's.* Camb. *Eton.*
 * John xviii. 37. 4° 1780. Conc. ad Cl. London.
COOKE William, M. A. Fell. of King's Coll. Camb. and one of
his Majeſty's Preachers at Whitchall.
 * 1 Pet. ii. 16. 4° 1780. 2 ſ. *Camb.* Liberty mor. relig. and civil.
 * Deut. xxviii. 49. 4° 1781. *Camb.* Jan. 30.
COOKSEY John, M. A. R. of St. Antholines, and St. John Baptiſt,
London, and F. R. S.
 1 Pet. iii. 15. 8° 1743. Xnity founded on Argument. *Brit. M.*
 * 1 John ii. 15, 16. 4° 1757. Faſt.
 * 1 Kings iii. 9. 8° 1760. Death of King George 2d.
COOLING Dennis, M. A. V. of Wotton, Bedfordſ.
 Rom. xii. 17. 4° 1708. Aſſize.
COOMBE Thomas, M. A. Chapl. to the Marquiſs of Rockingham.
 * Matt. xxv. 40. 4° 1772. Char. Sch. meeting.
COOPER *David*
 * Heb. iv. 2. 1735.
COOPER Joſeph
 1 Pet. v. 14. 8° 1663. 8 Sermons.
COOPER Miles, LLD. Preſident of King's Coll. New York and
Fell. of Queen's Coll. Oxon.
 * Pſ. vii. 9. 4° 1777. *Oxon.* Faſt. b. Univ. *Worc.* Oxon.
COOPER Samuel, DD. (formerly Fell. of Magd. Coll. Camb.) R.
of Morley and Yelveſton, Norfolk.
 * Matt. v. 42. 4° 1777. The Power of Chriſtianity over malig-
nant Paſſions &c.
 * 1 Theſſ. v. 21. 4° 1777. *Camb.* Commencement. The Neceſſity
and Truth of the three principal Revelations, demonſtrated
from the Gradations of Science and the Progreſs of the mental
Faculties.
COOPER Samuel, DD. Miniſter of Great Yarmouth, Norfolk.
 * Job xii. 23. 4° 1782. Faſt.
COOPER *William*
 * Phil. iv. 9. 4° 1663. V. Coll. Farew. ſ. p. 549.

Gen. ii. 16, 17. 4° 1676. m e. G. p. 84. The Cov. of Works. *Bod.*
1 Theff. v. 18. 4° 1677. m. e. C. p. 405. How we muſt in all Things give thanks.
COOPER *William*, one of the Paſtors at Boſton, New England.
‡ * 4 Serm. in 12° 1765. The Doctrine of Predeſtination explained and vindicated.
COOPER William, DD. Arch. D. of York, and F. R. S.
* Tit. ii. 11, 12. 4° 1763.
* Diſcourſes in 8° 1766. on ſeveral Subjects.
* Rom. x. 2. 8° 1767. Errors in the Church of Rome.
* 1 Tim. vi. 17–19. 4° 1767. Ch. Sch. meeting.
* Luke xxiii. 28. 4° 1773. on the Death of J. Dealtry, M. D.
COPLESTONE John, M. A. V. of Broad Clyſt. Devon, and Preb. of St. Peter's, Exon.
Pſ. lxxvii. 20. 4° 1661. May 29. *Oriel.* Oxon. *Sion.*
COPPING
1 Sam. xv. 3. 8°
COPPING John, Dean of Clogher, Ireland.
Tit. iii. 1. 4° 1739. Dublin. Viſ. *Queen's.* Camb. *Sion. Brit. M.*
COPPING Thomas, R. of St. Olave's Hart-ſtreet, London.
Ezek. xviii. 30. 4° 1702. Faſt.
CORBIN W. Preacher at the Chap. of Bromley St. Leonard, Middleſ.
Ezra iii. 11. 4° 1695. Th. *Trin.* Camb. *Sion.*
CORBYN *Benjamin*
* 2 Sam. iii. 38. 8° 1765. on the Death of the D. of Cumberland.
CORNELL William
* 1 Sam. xii. 24. 8° 1758. Nov. 5.
CORNEWALL Fred. M. A. V. of Bromfield, and Lect. of Ludlow, Salop.
Gal. iv. 18. 8° 1710. Aſſize. Zeal for Relig. recommended. *Bod. Bal. Linc.* Oxon. *Pub. L. Queen's.* Camb. *Sion.*
CORNWALL John, DD. R. of Speldhurſt, and Preacher at Tunbridge-Wells Chapel, Kent.
Prov. viii. 9. 4° 1701. *Camb. All S.* Oxon. *Pub. L. Trin.* Cam.
CORNWALL M. P. ᵃ B. A. late Fell. of Trin Coll. Camb.
* 10 Serm. in 12° 1773 *Saliſbury.*
CORNWALL ᵃ   Chapl. to the Hon. Houſe of Commons.
* Pſ. cx. 15. 1782. Jan. 30. b. Commons.
CORNWALLIS Frederick, Arch-Biſhop of Canterbury.
2 Kings xix. 3. 4° 1751. Jan. 30. b. Lords. *Queen's* Camb.
2 Theſſ. iii. 13. 4° 1752. b. Gov. Lond. Infirmary. *Wadh.* Oxon.
* Acts xxvi. 18. 8° 1756. Prop. Goſpel. *All S. Braz. N.* Oxon.
* Heb. x. 24. 4° 1762. An. meet. Ch. Sch. *Braz. N. Worc.* Oxon.
CORNWALLIS Henry
2 Kings iv. 38. 12° 1694. Viſ. at *Tunbridge*, on Hoſpitality. *Univ. Linc.* Oxon. *Pub. L. Trin. St. John's.* Camb.
* Pſ. cxvi. 9. 12° 1705. The devout Votaries—at Chur. of a Man and his Wife.
* Either i. 8. 12° 1705. Feaſt. The law of drinking.
* Epheſ. v. 19. 12° 1705. Laws reſpecting the ſame.

* Phil. ii. 4. 12° 1705.
* Deut. iv. 23. 12° 1705. Xtning f.
* Gen. xxvi. 12. 12° 1706. Wedding Serm. The Excellency of the Husbandman's Employ. The bridal Bufh.
* Ephef. v. 33. 12° 1732. V. Serm. on Conj. Duty. V. 1. p. 23.

CORNWALLIS James, Bp. of Litchfield and Coventry.
* 1 Tim. vi. 18. 4° 1778. b. Sons of the Clergy.
* Job xii. 23. 4° 1780. Cant. Faft.
* Ifai. xl. 17. 4° 1782. Jan. 30. b. Lords.

COSTARD George, M. A. late Fell. of Wadh: Coll. Oxon.
* Job. xix 25. 8° 1747. Differtation. All S. Oxon.
* Ezek. xiii. 18.
* 2 Kings x. 22. } 8° 1752. 2 Latin Differt. Bod. Queen's. Cam.

COTES Digby, M. A. Principal of Magd-hall, and Pub. Orator of the Univerfity of Oxon.
15 Serm. in 8° 1721. Oxon. On feveral Occafions. Bod. Magd. Worc. Oxon.

COTES Digby, M. A. R. of Door, Herefordfhire, V. of Abergavenny, Monmouthf. and Chapl. to the Bp. of Bangor.
* Pf. lxviii. 4; 5. 4° 1756. Mufick f. ann. meet. of the 3 Choirs.
* 2 Cor. iii. 17. 4° 1771. Affize.

COTT John, B. D. R. of Great Braxted, and V. of Coggefhall, Effex.
* Prov. xiv. 26. 4° 1769. Affize.

COTTON Thomas
1 Sam. xii. 23-35. 12° 1702. Ref. Manners.

COULDWELL William
Pf. xxxix. 9. 8° 1660.

COULTON Richard, M. A. V. of Wootton, Lincolnfhire.
1 Pet. ii. 13, 14. 4° 1685.

COURTAIL John, M. A. R. and V. of Burwafh, Suffex &c.
* Matt. x. 16. 4° 1760. Vif. The Expedience and Neceffity of Wifdom and Innocence towards a due Difcharge of the Minift. Office. Queen's. Camb.

COWPER Allen, M. A. R. of Warbois, Huntingdonfhire.
Rom. xiii. 10. 8° 1722. Affize.

COWPER Charles, M. A. Succentor and Refid. of York.
2 Tim. iii. 2. 8° 1751. Self-love.

COWPER John, M. A. (Fell. of Braz. N. Coll. Oxon.) and V. of Middlewich, Chefhire.
Rom. viii. 33, 34. 8° 1711. Chefter. Affize.
Job xxix. 12, 13. 8° 1713. Ch. f. Excellency of Charity. Queen's, St. John's. Camb.

COWPER Spencer, Hon. DD. Dean of Durham.
8 Difcourfes in 8° 1773. preached on or near the great Feftivals. Exon. Oxon.
* Rom. i. 20.
* 1 Tim. iii. 16 } 8° 1774. Differt. on the diftinct Powers of Reafon and Revelation.

COX Chamberlain Tho. M. A. R. of Brimfield, Glocefter.
Prov. xxix. 2. 8° 1730. Affize. Bal. Oxon.

COX James
  1 Theſſ iv. 1. 4° 1.728. Farew.
COX James, DD. late Maſter of Harrow-School, Middleſex.
  1 Kings x. 3. 4° 1750. on the Earthquake. God's Mercies ſlighted and neglected, a Challenge to his Juſtice.
COX Michael, Arch-Biſhop of Caſhell.
  Pſ. cxii. 9, 10. 4° 1748. *Dublin.* Iriſh. Prot. Schools. *Brit. M.*
COX *Samuel*
  Iſai lvii. 1, 2. 8° 1701. Fun. of Rev. *Sam. Clarke. Dr. Ws's L.* Lond.
COX Thomas, M.A. Lect. of St. Michael's Cornhill, and R. of great Bradfield, Eſſex.
  Acts vii. 22. 4° 1709. Sch. Feaſt. *All S.* Oxon. *Eton.*
  Prov. iv. 7. 4° 1712. Sch. Feaſt.
  2 Sam. xxiii. 3. 4° 1726. Aſſize. Influence of Religion in the Adminiſtration of Juſtice.
  Iſai. xlix. 23. 4° 1727. Aſſize.
COYTE Tobias, B. D. R. of Stratford, Suffolk.
  * 15 (Poſth.) Sermons in 2 Vol. 12° 1761.
CRADOCK John, Abp. of Dublin, Ireland.
  1 Cor. i. 23, 24. 4° 1739. *Camb.* Againſt the Moral Philoſopher. *Worc.* Oxon. *Brit. M.*
  1 Pet. ii 16. 4° 1752. Jan. 30. b. Commons. *Brit. M.*
  * Jer. vi. 8. 4° 1758. Faſt. Earthquake.
CRADOCK William, DD. of Magd. Coll. Oxon.
  1 Theſſ. v. 1.ª 8° 1713. St. Barnabas' day. *St. John's.* Camb.
  2 Cor. iii. 10, 11. 8° 1718. Viſ. Of Catechiſing and confirming Youth. *St. John's.* Camb. *Eton.*
CRADOCK Zechary, DD. Provoſt of Eton and Chapl. in Ord.
  Eccleſ. ix. 2. 4° 1677. b. King. On Providence. *Bod. Ch. Ch. All S. Univ. Linc. Worc. Magd. Jeſ.* Ox. *Trin. Queen's.* C. *Sion.*
  1 Tim. i. 5. 4° 1706. The Great Deſign of Chriſtianity. *Magd. Worc. Jeſ.* Oxon. *Trin. Queen's.* Camb.
CRAFTON
  Acts v. 31. 4° 1676. m. e. G. p. 359. Repentance not to be repented of.
CRAGGE John, M. A.
  Rom. xiii. 1. 8° 1661. Of the King's Supremacy. *Bod. Sion.*
  * Mark xvi. 15, 16. 8° 1741. (2d Edit.) Infant-Baptiſm.
CRAIG *William*, DD, Miniſter of St. Andrew's Church, Glaſgow.
  * 20 Diſc. in 3 Vol. 12° 1775.
CRAIL
  1 Tim. iv. 16. 4° 1673. C. m. e. p. 195. How Miniſters may beſt win Souls.
CRANE Thomas, M. A. Curate of Winwick, Lancaſhire.
  Job xix. 25–27. 4° 1690. Fun. of *Dr. Rich. Sherlock.* Job's Aſſurance of the Reſurrection.
CRANER Henry, M. A. Miniſter of the King's Chapel, Boſton.
  * Nehem. ii. 20. 8° 1749. Rebuild. a Chapel.
  * Iſai. xxxiii. 6. 4° 1763.

CRANER Thomas
    * Pf. xxix. 11. 8° 1763. Th. f.
    * - - - - 1766. Fun. f.
CRAVEN William, B. D. Fell. of St. John's Coll. and Profeſſor of Arabic. Camb.
    * 5 Serm. in 8° 1777. On the Evidence of a future State of Rewards and Puniſhments ariſing from a view of our Nature and Condition. *Queen's.* Camb.
CREED John, M. A. V. of Buckland Monachorum, Devon.
    Pf. lxxii. 1. 8° 1714. Firſt Sund. after the King's Coronation.
    * Rom. xv. 5, 6. 8° 1715. Love and Unity.
CREED William, DD. Can. of Ch. Ch. and Reg. Profeſſor of Divinity, Oxon.
    2 Sam. xix. 14, 15. 4° 1660. Th. for his Majeſty's Return. *Worc.* O.
    Iſai. i. 25, 26. 4° 1660. Aſſize. *Bod.*
CREFFIELD Edw. M A. Chapl. to the Earl of Denbigh.
    * Deut. vi. 7. 12° 17   Duty of catechiſing.
    1 Sam. xxvi. 2. 4° 1711. Jan. 30.
    Prov. xviii. 22. 8° 1717. 2 Wedding f. A good Wife, a great Bleſſing; or the Honour and Happineſs of the nuptial State.
CREMER William, V. of Tillingham near Malden, Eſſex.
    Gal. vi. 14. 8° 1721. 2 f. Palm Sunday.
CRESSET Edward, Bp. of Landaff.
    Pf. lxvi. 7. 4° 1749. Th. May 29. b. Lords.
    * 2 Tim. ii. 9. 8° 1753. Prop. Goſpel. *Braz. N.* Ox. *Queen's.* C.
CREWE Joſeph, DD. R. of Muxton, Stafforſhire.
    * Pf. ci. 4° 1756. *Stafford.* Aſſize.
CREYGHTON Robert, DD. Chantor and Can. of Wells, and Greek Profeſſor, Camb and Chaplain in Ord.
    1 Cor. i. 10. 4° 1682. b. King. *Brit. M.*
    22 Serm. in 8° 1720. *Camb.* On ſeveral Occaſions.
CRISP John
    * Sermons in 2 Vol. 8°
CRISPE Samuel, M. A. V. of Bungay St. Trinity, Suffolk.
    1 Kings xviii. 21. 4° 1686. Viſ. *Bod.*
[CRODACOTT John] Preacher of God's Word at St. Saviour's, Southwark, and St. Sepulchre's.
    Phil. iv. 9. 8° 1663.
CROFT Herbert, Bp. of Hereford.
    * Iſai. xxvii. 13. 4° 16   Faſt.
    Iſai lvii. 21. 4° 1674. Faſt. b. Ls. *Bod. Magd. Queen's.* Ox. Sion.
    Phil. i. 21. 4° 1676. Lent. b. King.
    1 Pet. v. 6. 4° 1678. Faſt. *Bod. Ch. Ch. Magd.* Oxon. *Sion.*
    John v. 39. 4° 1679. 3 f. The Legacy to his Dioceſe. *Bod. Magd.* Oxon. *St John's.* Camb.
CROFT Thomas, M. A. Chapl. to the Earl of Renelagh, and Lect. at Fulham, Middleſex.
    Acts viii. 2. 8° 1711. Fun. of the Rev. Mr. John Hughes. *Magd.* Oxon. *Sion.*

94   AN HISTORICAL REGISTER

CROFTON Zechariah, Minister at Botolph, Aldgate, Lond.
 Pf. xxxiv. 14. 4° 1660.
 Matt. vii. 14. 4° 1662. The hard way to Heaven explained and applied. *Bod.*
 Phil. i. 24. 8° 16
CROMPE J.
 Pf. li. 2.   1660.
CROMPTON William
 * Sermons in 12° 1679.
 * Prov. xxxi. 19. 12° 1732. V. Difc. on conj. Duty. v. 1. p. 225.
CROMWELL *Oliver*
 * Rom. xiii. 1. 4° 1680. Preached in 1649. At Sir P. T's Houfe in Lincoln's-Inn fields, and faithfully taken in Characters by Aaron Guerden in 1680. *Ch. Ch. Queen's.* Oxon. *Trin. St. John's.* Camb.
CROOKSHANK *William*,[a] M. A.
 * - - - - 1743. 2 f.
 Rev. xvii. 6. 8° 1745. Popifh Cruelty reprefented.
CROOKSHANK *William*,[a] DD. at Mile End Academy, near Lond.
 * - - - - 1766.
CROOKE B. M. A. R. of St. Michael Woodftreet, London.
 Acts iii. 19. }
 Mic. iii. 4. } 4° 1695. 2 f. b. Criminals, Newgate, London.
 Pf. cxix. 137. 4° 1698. Fun. of Mrs. Bullivant murdered.
CROOKE-*Henry*, of Leeds, Yorkfhire.
 * Ifai. xxix. 11, 12. 8° 1755. The Spirit no Refpector of Perfons in his Gifts and Graces.
 * Jer. vi 16. 8° 1755.
CROOKE Samuel, of Kinolton and Stanton, Nottinghamf.
 Luke xxi. 34. 8°
CROSLEY David
 Judges xiv. 5. 4° 1691. *Bod.*
CROSS Walter,[b] M. A.
 2 Sam. xxiii. 5. 4° 1693. A Compendium of the Covenant of Grace. *Sion.*
CROSSE Richard, LLB.
 Pf. liii. 5. 8° 1716. Reb. f. *Magd.* Oxon.
 James iv. 1. 8° 1716. Affize. *Magd.* Oxon.
CROSSE Richard, DD.
 Matt. vi. 24.   16
CROSSE Walter,[b]
 Rom. iv. 5, 6. 4° 1695. 2 f. *Eton.*
CROSSE Will. M. A. Chapl. to the Eng. Factory at Conftantinople.
 Heb. i. 14. 8° 1713. Levant Co.
CROSSINGE Richard, B. D. Prefident of Pemb. Hall, Camb.
 Ifai. xxxii. 17. 8° 1718. Peace and Joy, Rewards of Righteoufnefs. *Queen's.* Camb.
 1 Theff. v. 17. 8° 1720. Practical Difc. on Prayer. *Worc.* Oxon.

[a] Q. The fame.   [b] Q. The fame.
                                                          * Sermons

* Sermons in 8° 1722.
1 Pet. iv. 8. 8° 1722. Char. f.
Pf. iv. 6. 8° 1732. The Love and Favour of God, the true and only Happinefs. *Brit. M.*
CROSSMAN Henry, M. A. R. of little Cornard, Suffolk.
* Deut xxiii. 9. 8° 1758. Faft. The fufficiency from Faft-days to avert the divine Judgment without a continued Reformation and Obedience to the divine Laws.
* John ii. 16. 4° 1769. Vif.
CROSSMAN Samuel, DD. Dean of Briftol.
2 Kings xi. 8. 4° 1680. b. Artill. Company.
Lam. iv. 20. 4° 1681. Jan. 30. 2 f.
Pf. cxxxii. 8. 4° 1682.
Matt. xxiv. 12. 4° 1686. Affize.
CROWE William, DD. R. of St. Botolph's Bifhopgate-Street and Chaplain in Ord.
Pf. cxxii. 6. 8° 1724. Jan. 30. b. Lord Mayor. The Duty of promoting the public Peace. *Sion.*
‡ * Ezra ix 13, 14. 4° 1734. b. Lord Mayor. *Brit. M.*
‡ * Prov. xvii. 14. 8° 1735. Jan. 30. b. Commons. *Brit. M.*
Pf. cxlvi. 3–5. 4° 1737. On the Death of Queen Caroline. *Queen's.* Camb.
Phil. ii. 4. 4° 1740. Col. Georgia. The Duty of public Spirit recommended. *Queen's.* Camb.
11 Sermons in 8° 1744. On feveral Occafions. *Queen's.* Camb.
CROWE William, LLB. Fell. of New Coll. Oxon.
* Exod. xii. 2;. 4° 1781. *Oxon.* Nov. 5. b. Univ.
CROWTHER John
* 1 John i. 8, 9. 8° 1745. 3 Wedn. in Lent, at Leed's Chapel.
CROWTHER Jofeph, DD. Preb. of Worcefter.
Matt. xxiii. 23. 4° 1685. Of Tythes.
CROXALL Sam. DD. Chapl. in Ord. and Can. Refid. of Hereford.
John xiii. 35. 8° 1715. Incendiaries, no Chriftians.
Ifai. xxxviii. 18, 19. 8° 1723. Th. f.
1 Tim. iv. 6. 4" 1724. Conf. of Bp. Egerton. *Queen's.* Camb.
Prov. xxv. 5. 8° 1730. Jan. 30. b. Commons. *Bod. Worc.* Oxon. *Queen's.* Camb. *Sion.*
* 2 Sam. xii. 7. 8° 1738. The royal Sin, or Adultery in a King rebuked. *Bal. Linc.* Oxon.
Pf. lxxxvii. 7. 8° 1741. *Hereford.* The Antiquity, Dignity, and Advantages of Mufick. *All S.* Oxon. *Queen's.* Camb.
CRUSO Timothy
* Ecclef. iii. 2. 4° 1688. Fun. of *Henry Brownfword.* *Brit. M.*
* Ecclef. vii. 11. 8° 1688. Fun.
‡ * Num. xxiii. 23. 4° 1689. Th. f. *Pub L.* Camb. *Brit. M.*
* Difcourfes in 2 Vol. 12° 1698 and 1699.
CRUSO Timothy
* Acts xxiv. 14. 8° 1734. Chriftian Worfhipper of God.

CUDWORTH

CUDWORTH John, B. D. R. of Kiddington, Oxon.
  Matt vi. 23. 4° 1688. *Oxon.* Conc. ad Cl. Fides Ecclefiæ Anglicanæ vindicata ab Incertudine. *Bod. Ch. Ch. Magd.* Oxon. *Pub L.* Camb.
CUDWORTH Ralph, DD. Mafter of Chrift's Coll. and Hebrew-Profeffor, Camb.
  1 John ii. 3, 4. 8° 1670. p. 105. *Bod. Univ. All S. C.C.C. Wadh.* Oxon. *Trin.* Camb.
CROWNFIELD Henry, B. D. formerly Vice Prefident of Queen's Coll. Camb. and now R. of South-Walfham, Norfolk.
  2 Tim. xvi. 17 8° 1752. *Norwich.* Effay on the H. Scriptures.
  * Sermons in 8° 1752. Againft Enthufiafm.
CUDWORTH William
  * Luke ii. 29, 31. 8° 1751.
CULL Francis, R. of Snave in Romney Marfh, Kent.
  1 Cor. ix 16. 8° 1731. Vif.
[CULVERWELL Nathaniel]
  * Difcourfes in 4° 1661.
CUMBERLAND Denifon, Bp. of Clonfert, Ireland.
  * Luke xv. 10. 4° 1764. b. Gov. Magd. Hofp
  * John xvi. 2, 3. 4° 1765. *Dublin.* Nov. 5.
CUMING Patrick,[a] Regius Profeffor of Divinity, Edinburgh.
  Pf. xxxv. 12. 8° 1745. Faft. Reb. *Brit. M.*
CUMING Patrick,[a] DD.
  * Matt. ii. 5. 8° 1760. Prop. Chriftian Knowledge. V. Scotch Preacher. V. 1. p. 252. *Queen's.* Camb.
CUMMING John, M. A.
  ‡ * Mark xiii. 37. 8° 1724. Fun. of *Benjamin Robinfon. Brit. M.*
  * 2 Chron. xiv 11. 8° 1739. King Afa's Prayer.
CUMMING *John*, M. A. Minifter of the Scotch Church in Lothbury, London.
  Jofhua xxiii. 14. 8° 1694. Fun.
  * Pf. xii. 1. 8° 1714. b. Diffent. Clergy.
  Pf. xxi. 11. 8° 1717. Nov. 5. *Eton.*
  Jude iii. 8° 1719. b. a Soc. of young Men. Advice to contend for the Faith once delivered to the Saints. *Bod.*
CUMMING Patrick
  James iii. 17. 8° 1726. Open. a Synod in Scotland. *Eton.*
CUMMINGS George
  Rom. xiii. 4. 8° 1713. Th. f. *Sion.*
  Matt. iii. 16, 17. 4° 1713. Trin. S. Human Reafon fatisfied. *St. John's.* Camb.
CUNYNGHAM *Alexander*, Minifter at Synnington.
  * Pf. xxiii. 4. 8° 1770. Fun. of Earl of Eglington.
CURTEIS Thomas, R. of Wrotham, Kent.
  Deut. xxxiii. 29. 8° 1715. Th. for Acceffion. Thankfulnefs and Unanimity the proper Return of National Bleffing.

a *Q.* The fame.

* Ifai-

OF AUTHORS, &c.   97

* Isai. liii. 4. 8° 1715. 2 s. Passion and Easterday.
Isai. xlix. 23. 8° 1716. Th. *Queen's.* Camb.
Isai xxvi. 9 8° 1721. Fast.
Phil. ii 21. 4° 1723. Fun.
Ps. ciii. 15. 4° 1724. Fun. of Hon. John Vane.
Rom. i. 20. 4° 1731. Apoth. Feast. Harmony between natural and revealed Religion. *Queen's.* Camb. *Brit. M.*
* Luke xiv. 23. 8° 1735 At *Tunbridge-Wells* Chapel. Christianity offers no Violence to the Reason or Consciences of Men.

CURTIS William, M. A. V. of Dover Court Essex, and R. of Kettlebaston, Suffolk.
1 Sam. ii. 18, 19. 8° 1713. Ch. s.
* Ps. xcvii 7, 8. 8° 1727. *Ipswich.* Coronation.
1 Pet. ii. 15. 8° 1727. Vis.
Ps. cvii 21–24. 8° 1727. 6 Discourses.

CURTOIS John, M A. R. of Branston, near Lincoln.
Job xxxiv. 29. 4° 1684. On Loyalty. *Bod. Bal.* Oxon.
Rom. xiii. 1. 4° 1685. Death of King Charles 2d.

CURTOIS Thomas, DD.
Phil. i. 21. 4° 1702. Fun.

CUTHBERT Andrew, M. A R. of Wolves Newton and Master of the Free-school at Monmouth.

CUTLORE Joseph, R. of St. Mary Tower, Ipswich.
Exod. xx. 7. 4° 1682. Ass. s. About Swearing. p. 1. *All S.* Ox. *Trin. Pub. L.* Camb. *Eton.*
Rom. xii. 16. 4° 1682. Ass. s. About conceited Wisdom. p. 19.

D.   P. V. of St. Georges's Church, Doncaster, Yorkshire.
Ps. cvii. 43. 4° 1707. Th.

D.   R. formerly of Trin. Coll. Dublin.
Ps. cxii. 6. 8° 1729. Fun. of Abp King.

DAGGE Jonathan, M. A. R. of Endelion, and V. of Fowey at Trum, Cornwall.
Ps. xlv. 6. 4° 17
Matt. xxiv. 46. 4° 1703. *Oxon.* Fun. of Rob. Barton.
Ps. cxxvii. 1. 4° 1709. Assize.

DAGGE Robert, M. A. Fell. of Bal. Coll. Oxon. and R. of Stoke Abbot, Dorsets.
Ps. lvii. 7, 8. 8° 1746. *Sherborne.* Assize. Proteus, or the Jesuit detected in every Shape.

DAHME
* Sermons in 8° 1758. - - - - -
* Sermons in 8° 1775. - - - - -

DAILLE John, Minister of the reformed Church in Paris.
* 49 Sermons in fo. 1672. on St. Paul's Epistle to the Colossians, in 3 parts. Translated by F. S. *Ch. Ch.* Oxon. *Pub. L.* Camb.

DALTON John, DD. Preb. of Worcester, and R. of St. Mary at Hill, London.
Prov. ix. 1. 4° 1745. *Oxon.* 2 s. Rebellion. *All S. Worc. Brit. M.*

Vol. II.   N   Gal.

Gal. ii. 18. 4° 1747. Nov. 5. *Worc.* Oxon.
* Difcourfes in 8° 1757. on feveral Subjects and Occafions.

DALTON J. Minifter of the Gofpel at Coventry.
* 15 Sermons in 8° 1771.
* John xiv. 28. 8° 1773. Fun. Rev. *P. Simpfon.*

DAMPIER Thomas, DD. Dean of Rochefter.
* Ezek. xviii. 3. 4° 1782. Faft. b. Commons.

DANE John, DD. R. of All Saints, Colchefter.
Luke ii. 1, 2. 4° 1705. Vif. Set Forms and Times of Prayer.
2 Cor. i. 10. 4° 1710. Irifh Maffacre. *Bod. Sion.*
Prov. xxix. 8. 4° 1711.
Gal. vi. 9, 10. 4° 1712. Char. f.

DANNYE Robert, DD. R. of Spofforth, Yorkfhire.
Prov. xxix. 2. 4° 1718. *York.* Affize.

DANVERS Arthur, [a] LL. B. R. of Ardagh, Cloyne.
* Heb. ix. 22. 4° 1736. Recantation of a Perfon from Popery.

D'ANVERS Arthur [a]
* Matt. v. 14. 8° 1712. Vif.

DARCH John, V. of Long Benton, Northumberland.
* James i. 27. 4° 1766. b. Sons of Clergy at *Newcaftle. Ex.* Oxon.

DARE William
* John xiii. 34. 8° 1747. b. Free-Mafons.

DARRACOTT *Rifdon William*
* Sermons in 12° 1756. Scripture Marks of Salvation.

DAVENPORT John, B D.
Zach. i. 3. 4° 1669. *Camb.* at 2 public Fafts. *Sion.*

[DAVID R.]
* - - - - - 1781. Faft. Hypocritical Faft.

DAVIDSON Robert, R. of Hayes, Kent.
Ezek. xxxvii. 22. 4° 1707. Th. for Union.

DAVIDSON *Thomas,* [a] M. A.
* 2 Tim. iv. 6-8. 8° 1749. Fun. of Rev. *J. Harrifon. Pub. L.* C.

DAVIDSON *Thomas,* [a] M. A.
* Ecclef. xii. 1. 8° 1772. To young Perfons.

DAVIES E. V. of Dunchurch, Warwick.
Pf. xci. 3. 8° 1720. Faft. from Plague.

DAVIES Edward, M. A. Preb. of Landaff.
* Luke xix. 5. 8° 1769.

DAVIES James, R. of Barton Mills, Suff. and Preb. of Rippon.
Pf. cxix. 57. 4° 1679. Good Man's Portion *Bod. Trin.* Oxon.

DAVIES James, M. A. Cur. of Llandillo, Radnorfhire.
Pf. lxxxv. 8. 4° 1716. Th.

DAVIES Rowland, Dean of Cork, Ireland.
* - - - - 4° 1716. 30 Jan. Xtian Loyalty.
Luke xvi. 9. 8° 1717. *Dublin.* Char. f.

DAVIES Samuel, M. A. V. of Glynd.
* Mark x. 14. 8° 1758. Children invited to Chrift.

[a] *Q.* The fame. [b] *Q.* The fame.

DAVIES

OF AUTHORS, &c. 99

* Pſ. ci. 2. 8° 1777. Viſ. Rational Religion recommended.
DAVIES Samuel, M. A. late Preſident of the College at Princeton, New Jerſey.
* 2 Sam. x. 12. 8° 1755. Religion and Patriotiſm.
* Gen. xviii. 19. 12° 1758. The good Soldier.
* Jerem. xlvii. 10. 8" 1758. b. the Militia in Virginia. The Cure of Cowardice.
* Sermons in 3 vol. 8° 1766 and 1771, on the moſt important and uſeful Subjects, adapted to the Family and Cloſet.
In the firſt Vol. are prefixed 2 Sermons by *Sam. Finley*, DD and *T. Gibbons*, DD.
* Rom. xiv. 7, 8. } on the Death of The Rev. S. *Davies.*
* Epheſ. i. 11. }
DAVIES Thomas
* Amos ix. 2. 8° 16
DAVIES Thomas, M. A. R. of little Hollingbury, Eſſex.
16 Diſc. in 8° 1720. The Faith and Practice of a Xtian.
DAVILLE John, B. A. Maſter of a Grammar Sch. in York.
Epheſ. v. 6. 8° 1745. *York.* Rebellion.
DAVIS George, M. A. Aſſiſtant Preacher at St. Paul's Covent-Garden, London.
* Jon. iii. 10. 4° 1758. Faſt. National Repentance, the only Means of averting national Judgments.
* 2 Chron. xv. 2. 4° 1763. Th. ſ.
DAVIS Richard
Heb. xiii. 17. 8°
DAVISON Thomas, M. A. of St. John's Coll. Camb.
2 Pet. ii. 4. 4° 1683. The Fall of Angels.
Heb. x. 23. 4° 1688.
[DAVY J. Miniſter at Croydon, Surry.
‡ * Eccleſ. xi. 4. } 8° 1715. 2 Acc. ſ. *Brit. M.*
‡ * Pſ. cxxvi. 5. }
DAVYES Hatton, V. of Amwell, Herts.
Epheſ. iv. 14. 4° 1708.
DAWES (lately of St. Pancras) of Hawkſhead, Lancaſt.
* 4 Sermons in 8° 1773.
DAWES Thomas, B. D. Miniſter of St. Mary's in Shrewsbury.
2 Chron. xxv. 24. 4° 1695. Roy. Fun.
DAWES Sir William, Arch-Biſhop of York.
* Exod. xxiii. 9. 8° 16
- Prov. iv. 24. 4° 1687.
His whole Works in 3 Vol. 8° 1733. *Pub. L. Trin.* Camb. *Sien. Occaſ. ſ. St. John's.* Camb.
DAWSON Benj. LL. D. R. of Burgh, Suffolk.
* Prov. xxii. 6. 4° 1759. Religious Education. *Queen's.* Camb.
* 8 Sermons in 8° 1765. At Lady Moyer's Lect. An Illuſtration of ſeveral Texts of Scripture, particularly wherein the *Logos* occurs. *Queen's.* Camb.

N 2 * Luke

*Luke xiii. 3. 4°. 1779. Faſt. National Depravity, the Cauſe and Mark of divine Judgment upon a Land.

DAWSON Eli, Chapl. of his Majeſty's Ship, Sterling Caſtle.
*Pſ. xviii. 49. 4° 1760. on taking of *Quebec*.

DAWSON *Henry*, Miniſter of the Goſpel.
*Rev. i. 10. 12° 1777.

DAWSON William
Phil. iv. 13. 8°

DAY Henry, M.A.
Pſ. cxxii. 6. 4° 1696. Th. *Trin*.

DAY *Robert*
*2 Tim. ii. 6. 8° 1779. b. Educ. Society. *Briſtol*.

DAYE *James*
*John xvii. 4, 5. 4° 1752. Fun. of *Cal. Rotheram*, DD. *Queen's*. C.
*- - - - - 1752. Ord.

DAYRELL Richard, DD. R. of Lillingſton-Dayrell, Bucks.
*Pſ. xcv. 1, 2. 4° 1759 Th. b. Commons.

DEALTRY R. B. M.A. of Trin. Coll. Camb.
*Job xxix. 2. 4° 1782. *York*. Lunatic Aſylum.

D'Aſſigny Marius, B.D.
Rev. ii 10 4° 1670.

D'ASTOR de Lauſſac A. formerly a Prior and Arch-Deacon of the Church of Rome.
*Num. xxiv. 5. 4° 1700. The Xrter of the true Ch. *Ch. Ch*. Ox.

D'AUVERGNE E M A.
Prov. vii. 10, 11. 4° 1705. Sch. Feaſt.

D'COETLOGAN Char. M A Chapl to the Lock-Hoſpital, Lond.
*Judges iii. 20. 12 1773. The Divine Meſſage.
*Sermons on Pſ. v. in 2 vol. 8° 1775. The Portraiture of the Xtian Penitent.
*Iſai. lviii. 13, 14 8° 1776 Obſervation of the Lord's-day.
*Joel ii. 15–18. 8° 1776. National Proſperity and N. Religion inſeparable.
*Eccleſ. xii. 1. 8° 1777. Youth's Monitor.
*Job i. 20–22. 8° 1778. Submiſſion under Afflictions.
*Iſai. lvii. 1, 2. 8° 1778. Fun. of Rt. Hon. Sir. Sidney Stafford Smythe. Death of the Righteous, a public Loſs.
*1 Cor. xv. 10. 8° 1780. Anniv. ſ. On the Converſion of St. Paul. The Scripture Doctrine of Grace.

D'COURCY V. of St. Alkmonds. Shrewſbury.
*2 Sam. xii 7. 8° 1773. Nathan's Meſſage to David.
*Chron. xx 3, 4. 8° 1777. Faſt. 2 ſ.
*Jer. v. 29. 8° 1778. Faſt. 2 ſ.

DEBORDS Lewis, R. of St. Lawrence, and Chaplain to the Duke of Dorſet.
1 Tim. ii. 1, 2. 8° 1723. Aſſize.

DE GOLS Gerard, R. of St. Peter's, Sandwich, Kent.
Pſ. xxiii. 4. 8° 1711. To a condemned Perſon.
Nath. i. 3. 8° 1714. On a Storm.

*John

* John v. 28, 29. 8° 1720.
* 2 Chron. vii. 13, 14. 8° 1721. Faſt.
DELAFAYE Theod. M.A. R. of Mildred and all Saints, Canterbury.
  1 Pet. ii. 13, 14. 8° 1745. Elect. Mayor. Obedience to Governors ſtated and enforced
  Gal. v. 1. 8° 1745. Reb. ſ. The proper Conduct of the Subject under the preſent Troubles explained
  Hoſea vi. 1. 8° 1746. Faſt. Reb. The proper Improvement of national Judgments.
  Pſ. lxv 5. 8° 1751. God, the Mariner's only Hope.
  * Rom. iii. 8. 8° 1753. Inoculation an indefenſible Practice.
  * Amos v. 6. 4° 1757. Faſt.
  * Rev. iii 19, 20. 4° 1758. Faſt.
DELANY Patrick, DD. Dean of Down, Ireland.
  * Prov. xxv. 4, 5. 8° 1738. Jan. 30. b. Ld. Lieutenant. *Queen's*. Camb. *Brit M*.
  John xiii. 34. 4° 1744. Iriſh Prot. School. *All S. Worc.* Oxon. *Queen's* Camb.
  20 Sermons Vol. 1. in 8° 1747. (2d Edit.) On ſocial Duties, and their oppoſite Vices. *Braz. N New. C.* Oxon. *Queen's.* Camb.
  Exod. xx. 17. 8° 1748. Of Tythes.
  * 16 Diſcourſes Vol. 2. in 8° 1754. Againſt the reigning Vanities of the Age. *Braz. N.* Oxon.
  * Pſ cxxii. 6–9. 4° 1763. Th. ſ. *Braz. N.* Oxon. *Queen's. St. John's.* Camb.
  * Mat. v. 27, 28. 4° 1763. b. Gov. Magd Hoſp.
  * 1 Tim. vi. 18, 19. 4° 1763. Ann. meeting Char. School. *All S. Worc.* Oxon. *St. John's* Camb.
  * Matt. xxvi. 26–28. 4° 1766. Ag. Tranſubſtantiation.
  * 18 Diſcourſes Vol. 3. in 8° 1766. Upon various very important and intereſting Subjects. *All S. Univ. Trin Magd. Bal. Or. St. John's. Pemb.* Oxon. *King's. Trin. Cl. H.* Camb.
DE LA ROSE John
  * Rev. xiv. 13. 8° 1715. Fun of Tim. Jollie. *Queen's.* Camb.
DELAP John, DD.
  * Heb. xiii. 8. 4° 1762. *Cantab.* Concio Acad. Mundi perpetuus Adminiſtrator Chriſtus.
DELAUNE William, DD. Preſident of St. John's and Marg. Profeſſor of Divinity, Oxon.
  Matt. xxvii. 25. 4° 1702. Jan. 30. b. Commons. *Ch. Ch. All S.* Oxon. *St. John's.* Camb.
  12 Sermons in 8° 1728. Upon ſev. Subjects. *Bod Ch. Ch. Bal. St. John's. Worc.* Camb. *Pub. L.* Camb. *Sion.*
DELL George LL.B. R. of Foulneſs, Eſſex.
  Prov. iii. 13–15. 4° 1711. b. Comp. Goldſmiths.
[DELL William]
  * Sermons in 8° 1709.
[DELME   ]
  * Jer. x. 22–25. 4° 1701.

DENHAM

DENHAM *Jof.* Minifter in Ayliff-ftreet, Goodman's Fields, Lond.
* Gal. vi. 9, 10. 8° 1741. Char. f.
DENHAM William, M. A. V. of Stoneleigh.
* - - - - 1736.
* 1 John iv. 9. 8° 1742. Chriftmas.
* Ephef. iv. 8. 8° 1743 Afcenfion.
* Rom. xiii. 1. 8° 1745. Jan. 30.
* Heb. viii. 12. 8° 1745. On the Execution of a Malefactor.
DENNE John, DD. Arch-D. of Rochefter, and R. of Lambeth.
 2 Cor. vi. 3. 4° 1720. Conf. Bp. Bradford. The Duty of giving no Offence.
 Ifai. xlix. 1–4. 4° 1723. Vif. The Labours of a Chriftian Minifter, together with his Reward. *Queen's.* Camb. *Brit. M.*
 Mark iv. 30–32. 4° 1725. Ordin. Trin. f. The Miraculous Succefs of the Gofpel in its firft preaching, a good Proof of its divine Origin and Authority. *Queen's.* Camb.
 Acts xix. 5, 6. 4° 1726. and 1737. Conf. The Nature, Defign, and Benefits of Confirmation. *Queen's.* Camb.
 1 Cor. x. 31. 4° 1729. Ref. Manners. The Duty of doing all things to the Glory of God. *Queen's.* Camb.
 Matt vi. 28–30. 4° 1730. Fairchild's Lect. The Wifdom of God in the vegetable Creation. *Queen's.* Camb.
 Mark xvi. 15. 4° 1730. Prop. Gofpel. Want of Univerfality, no juft Objection to the Truth of the Chriftian Religion. *Queen's.* Camb. *Brit. M.*
 Gen. i. 11–13. 4° 1733. Fairchild's Lect. Th. Wifdom and Goodnefs of God in the vegetable Creation. *Queen's.* C. *Brit. M.*
 Deut. vi. 6, 7. 4° 1736. An. meet. Char. Schools.
 2 Chron. ix. 4. 8° 1737. Accefl. b. Commons. The Blefling of a Proteftant King and royal Family to the Nation. *Brit. M.*
 Heb. xiii. 7. 4° 1738. Conf. of Bp. Herring. *Queen's.* Cabm.
 Pf. lx. 10–12. 4° 1740. Spittal T.
 1 Kings xx. 14. 4° 1744. The religious, moral and civil State of the Nation confidered. *Queen's.* Camb. *Brit. M.*
 2 Pet. i. 16. 4° 1745. Conc. ad Cler. Lond. *Queen's.* Cam. *Sion.*
 Pf. viii. 4–6. 8° 1745. Fairchild's Lect. God's regard to Man in his Works of Creation and Providence. *Queen's.* Cam. *Brit. M.*
DENNE John, M. A. Minifter of Maidftone, Kent, and Fellow of C. C. C. Camb.
 * 1 Tim. ii. 2. 4° 1753. Elect. of a Mayor.
DENNIS Samuel, M. A. R. of St. Swithun's, Worceft.
 Ecclef. v 1. 4° 1736. On open. that Church. *Worc.* Oxon.
DENT *Edward*
 Rev. xiv. 13. 4° 1692. Fun. of *Will. Baker.* Everlafting Blefledness. *Bod. Brit. M.*
DENT *Giles*
 2 Sam. v. 3. 4° 1707. Th. for Union. *Pub. L.* Cam. *Eton. Sion.*
 * Pf. lxxxix. 47, 48. 4° 1708. Roy. Fun. *Pub. L.* Camb.
 Pf. cxxiv. 1–3. 4° 1711. Nov. 5. *Eton.*
 * Ifai 32 1, 2. 8° 1712. *Pub. L.* Camb.   Pf.

Pf. xxxvi. 7. 8° 1713. Nov. 5. *Eton.*
DENTON Thomas, late of Queen's Coll. Oxon.
  * Matt. xxv. 36. 8° 1775. Prisoner relieved.
DERBY Richard, V. of Turnworth, Dorfet.
  Pf. cxxii. 6. 8° 1717. Affize. Love to our Church and Nation recommended.
DERHAM Will. DD. R. of Upminfter and Canon of Windfor.
  Pf. iii. 2. 8° 1727. Phyfico—Theology. *Bod. Ch. Ch. Univ New C. Trin. St. John's. Bal. Worc. Wadh. Hert.* Oxon. *Trin. St John's. Queen's. Cl. H.* Camb.
  Acts xxvi. 28. 8° 1730. Xto—Theology. *Ch. Ch. Univ. New C. Trin. St. John's. Bal. Worc. Wadh. Hert.* Oxon. *Queen's.* Cam.
DESAGULIERS John, M. A. Chapl. to the Earl of Caernarvon.
  * Luke xiii. 5. 8° 1717. b. King.
DEVEREL Mary, of Briftol.
  * Sermons in 8° 1777. On various Subjects.
DEVIS *James*
  * - - - - 1756. Nov. 5.
DIBBEN Thomas, DD. Precentor of St. Paul's, London, and R. of great Fontmel, Dorfetfhire.
  2 Cor. iv. 3. 8° 1711. Vif. *Ch. Ch.* Oxon. *St. John's.* Camb.
DICK *Robert*, DD. one of the Minifters of Edinburgh.
  * Deut. xxix. 29. 8° 1758. b. Synod. Simplicity, Popularity and Suitablenefs of divine Revelations. *Queen's.* Camb.
  ‡ * Acts xxxv. 34–39. 8° 1762. *Edinb.* The Counfel of Gamaliel. Prop. Xn. Knowledge. *Brit. M.* V. Scotch Preac. v. 2. p. 281.
DICKENS Charles, LLD.
  * Joel ii. 12, 13. 4° 1757. Faft. for War.
DICKSON *James*
  Practical Difcourfes in 8° 1731. *Edinburgh.*
DICKINSON John,ᵃ
  * Pf. lxxxi. 6, 7. 8° 1737. Roy. Fun.
DICKINSON John,ᵃ
  * Prov. xx. 10. 8° 1779. Ag. falfe Weights and Meafures.
DILLINGHAM William, DD. R. of Woodhil, Bedfordf.
  1 Theff. v. 21. 4° 1661.
  2 Tim. iv. 7, 8. 4° 1678. Fun. of Lady Eliz. Alfton. *Bod. Pub. L.* Camb. *Sion.*
DINGLEY William, B. D. Fell. of C. C. C. Oxon.
  Pf. civ. 33, 34. 8° 1713. *Oxon.* On St. Cecilia's day. Cathedral Service decent and ufeful. *Bod. Worc. Ch. Ch. Linc.* Oxon. *St. John's.* Camb.
DINSDALE Jofhua
  * 2 Cor. vi. 6. 8° 1740. Char. f.
DISNEY John, R. of Kirby fuper Baine, Lincolnf. and V. of St. Mary's, Nottingham.
  John xv. 18, 19. 8° 1720. Nov. 21. *Eton.*
  Acts xxiii. 12. 8° 1720. Nov. 5. *Bod.*

a Q The fame?

1 Pet.

1 Pet ii. 11. 8° 1722.
Prov. xxiv. 21. 8° 1722. *Nottingham.* Jan. 30.
2 Sam. xxiii. 3. 8. 1724.
Ezek. xvii. 18, 19. 8° 1724. *Nottingham.* Aſſize.
Gal. v. 13. 8° 1727. Aſſize. Liberty and the Abuſe of Liberty.
DISNEY John, DD. R. of Panton, and V. of Swinderby, Lincoln, and Chapl. to the Lord Bp. of Carliſle.
 * 4 Serm. in 8° 1771. on Xtmas, Good-Frid. Eaſter, Whitſunday.
 * Pſ. xcvi 9. 8° 1773. Open. a Church after new ſeating it.
 * Rom. xiv. 5. 4° 1777. Viſit.
 * 2 Theſſ. iii. 10. 12° 1781. A Spirit of Induſtry recommended.
DISTERNELL Joſiah, M. A. of Pembroke-Hall, Camb.
 * Heb. xiii. 1. 4° 1777. b. Antigallicans.
DIXON Robert, DD. Preb. of Rocheſter.
 2 Chron. xx. 12. 8° 16
DOBSON John, B. D. Fell. of Magd. Coll. Oxon.
 1 Theſſ. iv. 13. 4° 1670. Fun. of Lady Mary Farmor. *Bod. Magd. Linc* Oxon. *Pub. L. Trin.* Camb. *Sion.*
DOBSON Joſhua
 Coloſſ. iii. 15. ⎫ Relig. Gratitude expl. & relig. & civ. Lib. reform.
 8° 1747. 2 ſ. ⎭ Xty and Loyalty to the preſ. Gov. recommended.
DOBBS Richard, DD.   of Liſburn, Ireland.
 * Rev. vi. 2. 8° 1762. Th. ſ. A remarkable Accompliſhment of a noted Scripture Prophecy.
DOCKWRAY Thomas, M. A. Fell. of St. John's Coll. Camb. and Lecturer of St. Nicholas's Church, Newcaſtle.
 * John iii. 8. 8° 1743. Whitſunday.
 * Pſ. ii. 11. 4° 1754. Conſ. of a Church.
 * Matt. xxii. 37–40. 4° 1754. Infirmary at *Newcaſtle.*
DOD Samuel, M. A. Fell. of Clare-Hall, Camb. and Lecturer of St. Catherine, Colemanſtreet, London.
 1 Pet. vi. 10. 4° 1714. Sch. Feaſt. *Cl. H.* Camb. *Brit. M.*
DOD Thomas, M. A. Fell. of Braz. N. Coll. Oxon.
 Matt. vii. 12. 8° 1717. *Oxon.* Aſſize. Rule of Equity. *Bod. Magd. Linc. Worc* Oxon. *St. John's.* Camb.
DODD W. LL D. V. of Weſtham, and Preach. at the Magd. Hoſp. &c.
 * Gen iii. 16. 8° 1754. b. Gov. Lying-Hoſp.
 * Matt. vi. 6–18. 8° 1757. 2 ſ. Nature and Neceſſity of Faſting.
 * Luke xix. 22. 8° 1755. Sinner condemned by his own Prayers.
 * Sermons in 2 vol 8° 1757. on the Parables of our Saviour.
 * Sermons in 2 vol. 8° 1757. on the Miracles of our Saviour.
 * Deut xxiii. 9. 8° 1758 Faſt. People's Duty when the Hoſt is gone forth againſt the Enemy.
 * Matt. ix. 12, 13. 4° 1759. At the Magdalen Hoſp.
 * Epheſ. iv. 3. 4° 1759. Cautions ag. Methodiſm.
 * Job xxix. 11–13. 4° 1759. b. Gov. of Magd. Hoſp.
 * Pſ. civ. 24. 4° 1759. Apothecary's Feaſt. Wiſdom and Goodneſs of God in the vegetable Creation.
 * Luke xix 10. 4° 1760. At the Magd. Hoſp.
 * 1 Cor. xv 36–38. 4° 1760. Apothecary's Feaſt.

* 2 Sam. xxiii. 4. 4° 1761. Apothecary's Feaſt.
* Luke xv. 13. 8° 1763. Youth diſſuaded from Vice.
* Prov. xiv. 28. 4° 1767. b. Gov. Small pox Hoſp. Innoculation recommended.
* 2 Sam. xii. 23. 8° 1767. Mutual Knowledge in a future State. *Queen's*. Camb.
* James iii. 15. 8° 1768. Popery inconſiſtent with the Rights of Engliſhmen.
* Mark ii. 27, 28. 12° 1768. Sabbath-day well-ſpent, Ground of Comfort throuhout the Week.
* Sermons in 8° 1769. On the Duties of the Great, tranſlated from Monſ. Maſillon.
* - - - - - 1771 For Benefit of Debtors.
* Exod. xx. 13. 8° 1772 Frequent Puniſhments, inconſiſtent with Juſtice Policy and Religion.
* Sermons in 12° 3 Vol. 1772. To Young Men. *Bod. Pub. L.* Camb. *Sion.*
* Exod. ii. 6. 4° 1773. b. Gov. of Diſpenſary for Infant-poor.
* Zech. iv. 6. 4° 1774. b. Gov. of Magd. Hoſp.
* Matt. xxv. 36. 8° 1774. The Priſoner releaſed.
* Luke vii. 22. 8° 1777. Addreſs to Priſoners.

DODDRIDGE *Philip*, DD, late Miniſter at Northampton.
  Rev. ii. 10. 8° 17   Fun.
* 10 Sermons in 12° 1736. On the Power and Grace of Chriſt, or the Evidences of his glorious Goſpel. *Dr. W's. L.*
* Luke ix. 55, 56. 8° 1736. Abſurdity and Iniquity of Perſecution for Conſcience ſake.
* 2 Cor. iv. 5. 8° 1737. Ord.   The Temper and Conduct of a primitive Miniſter of the Goſpel.
* Amos iv. 11 8° 1732. After a Fire.
* Prov. xxiv. 11, 12. 8° 1742. b. Diſſent. Clergy. The Evil and Danger of neglecting the Souls of Men. *Queen's.* Camb.
* Epheſ. ii. 8. 8° 1742. 2 ſ.
* Luke i. 74, 75. 8° 1745. 2 ſ. On the Flight of the Rebels.
* Pſ. vii. 1, 3. 8° 1743. Infirm. at *Northampton.* Compaſſion to the ſick recommended and urged *Queen's.* Camb.
* 4 Sermons in 8° 1743. On the religious Education of Children. *Dr. W's. L. Queen's.* Camb
* 2 Kings iv. 26. 8° 1737. Fun. of a Child. Submiſſion to Divine Providence in the Death of Children.
* 18 Practical ſerm. in 8° 1742. On Regeneration, to which are added 2 ſerm. on Salvation by Grace through Faith.
* Matt xi. 23, 24. 8° 1750. On occaſion of a 2d ſhock of an Earthquake.
* John xi. 35. 8° 1750. Fun.
* Tracts in 3 Vol. 12° 1761.

DODGSON Charles, Bp. of Oſſory, Ireland.
* Prov. iii. 27. 4° 1761. b. Gov. Middleſex Hoſp.
* Iſai. lviii. 6–8. 4° 1768. Ir. Prot. School.

VOL. II.   O   *DODSON*

DODSON *Joseph*, M. A.
* 2 Tim. ii. 24. 8° 1720. b. Diff. Clergy.
* 12 Difc. in 8° 1728.

DODSLEY R.
* Prov. vii. 17. 8° 1745. Pleafure, the beft Religion. V. End of Dodfley's Trifles.

DODWELL William, DD. Arch-D. of Berks, R. of Shottefbrook and Canon Refid. of Sarum.
2 Theff. 1, 7, 9. 8° 1743. *Oxon*. 2 f. Eternity of Hell-torments. *Worc*. Oxon. *Brit. M.*
1 Pet. 1, 8. 8° 1744. *Oxon*. Vif. The Defireablenefs of the Chriftian Faith. *Worc*. Oxon.
1 Pet. iii. 15. 8° 1745. *Oxon*. 2 f. Of a rational Faith, againft Chriftianity not founded on Argument. *Worc*. Oxon.
2 Cor. xiii. 14. 8° 1745. *Oxon*. Practical Influence of the Trinity. *Worc*. Oxon.
Practical Difcourfes on moral Subjects. Vol. 1. 8° 1748. Vol. 2. 8° 1749. *Bod. Braz. N.* Oxon.
Rom xiii. 3. 8° 1750. *Oxon*. Affize. The Nature, Extent and Support of human Laws. *Worc*. Oxon.
Rom. ix. 3. 8° 1752. *Oxon*. St. Paul's Wifh explained. *Worc*. Oxon. *Queen's*. Camb.
* Difcourfes in 8° 1754. Preached before the Univerfity.
* Pf. xxxi. 7. 8° 1754. 2 f. The Nature, Mifchiefs and Remedy of Superftition *Worc*. Oxon.
* Prov xvii. 15. 8° 1755. Affize. Equal and impartial Difcharge of Juftice. *Worc*. Oxon.
* Ifai. xxix 6. 8° 1756. 2 f. Faft. Doctrine of divine Vifitations by Earthquakes.
* Pf. xxxiv. 11. 4° 1758. An. meet. Ch. Schools. *All S. Braz. N.* Oxon. *Queen's*. Camb.
* Exod. xxxiii. 1. 8° 1758. Affize. The falfe Witnefs reproved. *Worc*. Oxon.
* Pf. xxxiii. 13–15. 8° 1760. 2 f. Particular Providence ftated. *Worc Braz. N.* Oxon. *Queen's*. Camb.
* Jerem. xlix. 10. 8° 1760. b. Sons of the Clergy.
* Tit. i. 7–9. 4° 1757. Conf. Bp. of Sarum. *All S.* Oxon.
* Prov. xix. 17. 8° 1768. Inf. at *Salisbury*.

DOLBEN John, Abp. of York.
John xix. 19. 4° 1665. Good-friday b. K. *Bod. Ch. Ch. Magd.* Oxon. *Trin.* Camb. *Sion*
Pf. liv. 6, 7. 4° 1665. Th. b. K. *Bod. Ch. Ch.* Ox. *Trin.* C. *Sion*.
Pf. xviii. 1–3. 4° 1666. Th. b. King. For Victory at Sea. *Ch. Ch. Worc.* Oxon.

DOLBEN Sir John, Bart. DD. Preb. of Durham.
Heb. xiii. 1. 4° 1726. Conc. ad Cl. *Worc*. Oxon.

DOMETT Philobeth, M. A. V. of Axminfter and Bovey-tracy, Devonfhire.
* Tit. ii. 15. 8° 1741. Vif.

DOMINICK

DOMINICK Andrew, DD. R. of Stratfieldsay, Hants.
   Pf. xxii. 12, 13. 4° 1662. Jan. 30. Dies Nefastus.
DONALDSON Thomas, M. A. Minister of the Gospel at Liffe.
   Pf cxxxiii. 1 - 8° 1734. *Edinburgh.* b Synod.
DONGWORTH Richard, M. A. V. of Long Owersby, Linc.
   Deut. v. 29. 4° 1708. *Bod.* Assize.
DOOLITTLE Samuel
   Isai. xxix 6. 4° 1693. On the Earthquakes. *Bod.*
DOOLITTLE Thomas, M. A.
   Jer. vi. 6. 4° 1675. m. e. P. p. 165. Popery a Novelty.
   Joshua xxiv. 15. 4° 1676. s. m. e. p. 295. Concerning Fam. Pray,
   1 John v 13. 4° 1677 m. e. C. p. 240. Assurance possible.
   * 1 Cor. xi. 26. 12° 1582. Lord's last Sufferings.
   2 Cor. iv. 18. 4° 1683. c. m. e. p. 979. Of eying Eternity in all we do.
DOPPING Anthony, Bp. of Meath, Ireland.
   2 Cor. v. 1. 4° 1694. Fun. of Abp. of Dublin.
DORMAN William, M. A.
   12 Sermons in 8° 1742. Preached at the Rolls Chapel. *Sion.*
DORRINGTON Theophilus, M. A. R. of Wittersham, Kent.
   * 1 Cor. vii. 31. 1683.
   Family Devotions for Sunday Evenings in 4 Vol. 8° 1703. *Bod. Ch. Ch.* Oxon. *Trin.* Camb. *Dr. W's L.* London.
   Family Instruction &c. in sev. practical Disc. 8° 1705. *Bod. Dr. W's. L.* London.
   Prov. x. 23. 4° 1706. The Regulations of Play. *Ch. Ch.* Oxon. *Trin.* Camb. *Sion.*
   Ephes. vi. 18. 8° 1708.
   Matt. iv. 10. 8° 1712. Oxon. The Worship of God recommended. *Bod. Ch. Ch. Linc.* Ox. *Trin. St. John's* Camb. *Sion.*
DOVE Hen. DD. Minister of St. Bride's, Lond. and Chap. in Ord.
   Pf. lxiv. 9, 10. 4° 1680. Nov. 5. b. Commons. *All S. Ch. Ch. C. C. C. Magd.* Oxon. *Trin.* Camb. *Brit. M.*
   Tit. iii. 1. 4° 1682. Elect. Lord Mayor. *Ch. Ch.* Oxon. *Pub. L. St. John's.* Camb. *Sion.*
   Acts xvi. 4, 5. 4° 1685. b. King. *C. C. C. Magd.* Oxon. *Pub. L. Trin.* Camb. *Brit. M.*
   Jude 3. 4° 1686. Conc. ad Cler. *Magd. Or. Wadh.* Ox. *Pub. L. Trin.* Camb.
   Pf. xviii. 23. 4° 1691. b. Q. *Bod. Magd.* Ox. *Pub. L.* Cam. *Sion.*
DOVE Richard, M. A. R. of St. Martin's, Birmingham.
   * Rom. xii. 15. 8° 1761. *Salop.* Infirmary.
DOUGHTY
   Mark xii. 41-44. 8° 1742. 2 s. A Persuasive to Charity &c.
DOUGHTY Gregory, M. A. Fell. of King's Coll. Camb.
   Luke ii. 14. 4° 1724. *Camb.* Commem. Benevolence. *Worc.* Ox. *Queen's.* Camb.
DOUGHTY John, M. A. Minister of Clerkenwell, and one of the Sund-Evening Lect. at St. Ann and Agnes, Aldersgate, Lond.
                                                              2 Chron.

2 Cor. i 12. 8° 1740. To be good, is to be happy.
1 Thess. v. 23. 8° 1740. Farewel.
Pf. cvii. 34. 4° 1744. Fast. Fire Lond. b. Lord Mayor.
2 Chron. xx. 27-30 4° 1746. Th. for Reduction of Rebels.
Gal. vi. 2. 4° 1752. b. Gov. Lying-in Hosp. Xtian Sympathy.
* 10 Discourses in 8° 1761. *Waab.* Oxon.

DOUGHTY Thomas
13 Sermons on the Coronation of King George 1st. and Queen Caroline on Chron. xxviii. 10. and 2 Vis. f. on 1 Sam. ii. 30. 8° 1738. *Pub L.* Camb.

DOUGLASS *Thomas*
Gal. iv. 4, 5. 4° 1661.

DOWARS *William*
* Ecclef. iii. 4. 8° 1775. The Expediency and Fitness of things considered and exemplified.

[DOWGLASS Robert]
2 Kings xi. 12, 17. 12° 1660. *Aberdeen. Bod. Trin.* Camb.

DOWNES Henry, Bp. of Meath, Ireland.
Pf. cxii. 9, 10. 4° 1697. The Excellency of public Charity. *Bod. Magd.* Oxon. *St. John's.* Camb.
1 Tim. i. 8. 8° 1708. *Oxon.* Assize. The Necessity and Usefulness of Laws. *Bod. Ch Ch. Univ. Or.* Oxon. *Sion. Eton.*
Pf. lxxvi. 10. 4° 1719. Th. *Eton.*
* 2 Tim. iii. 1, 2. 4° 1725. *Dublin.* May 29.

DOWNES Henry, Bp. of Elphin, then of Derry, Ireland.
2 Pet. iii. 15. 4° 1720. Fast. *Ch Ch.. Oxon. Eton.*
Ecclef. xi. 18. 4° 1721. *Dublin.* Ch. f. *Eton*

DOWNES John, M. A. late R. of St. Michael's Woodstreet, Lond.
2 Chron. vii. 15, 16. 4° 1741. Conf. Chapel. An Apology for public Worship, and Conf. of Churches.
Ecclef. iv. 9, 16. 8° 1742. b. Soc. of Cutlers. *Brit. M.*
1 Kings xii. 14. 4° 1745. Rebellion. A Popish Prince, the Pest of a Protestant People, *Queen's.* Camb.
* 1 Cor. vi. 20. 8° 1757. Fast. The true national Evil—or Cowardice the Cry; but Corruption the Greviance.
* Sermons in 2 Vol. 8° 1761. On various Subjects.

DOWNES Robert, Bp. of Raphoe, Ireland.
*Pf. viii. 2. 4° 1750. Irish Prot. Schools. *Queen's.* Camb.

DOWNING George,[a]
Pf. cxliv. 15. 4° 1734. Assize

DOWNING George,[a] M. A.
* Mark viii. 34. 8° 1760. Ref. Manners.

D'OYLY Robert, M. A.
Pf. lxxiii. 15. 4° 1710. Providence vindicated, as permitting Wickedness and Mischief. *Worc. Jef.* Oxon.

D'OYLY Thomas, LLD. Arch-D. of Lewes, Kent.
* Ecclef. xi. 1. 4° 1766. b. Gov. Small-pox Hosp. London.

a ℞. The same.

DRAKE Francis
* Ephef. iv. 25. 4° 1760. 2 f. Ag. Lying.
DRAKE Nath. M. A. V. of Weighton, then of Sheffield, Yorkfhire.
Matt. xxviii. 15. 4° 1695. Affize. Ag. Bribery.
Prov. xvi. 11. 4° 1697. Ag. falfe Weights and Balances.
DRAKE *Roger*, DD.
* John. i. 12, 13. 4° 1676. m. e. G. p. 320. The Believer's Dignity and Duty opened.
Rom. vii. 23. 4° 1677. m. e. C. p. 271. The Difference between the Conflict in natural and fpiritual Perfons.
DRAKE Samuel,[a] DD. Fell. of St. John's Coll. Camb. and V. of Pontefract, Yorkfhire.
Micah vi. 8. 4° 1670. Affize.
Rom. xiii. 6. 4° 1670. Affize. The civil Deacon's facred Power.
DRAKE Samuel,[a] DD. Fell. of St. John's Coll. Camb.
Matt. xxvi. 29. 8° 1719. Conc. ad Cl. *Cant.* Vino Euchariftico aqua non neceffario admifcenda. *Sion.*
Acts xvii. 22, 23. 4° 1724. *Cant.* Conc. ad Cl. Ara ignoto Deo facra. *Or. Oxon. Queen's.* Camb.
DRAKE W. M. A. Chapl. to Ld Blaney, R. of Full-Sutton, York.
Pf. cxxii. 6-9. 8° 1735. *York.* Rebellion.
DRAYTON Thomas, DD.
2 Cor. vii. 1.
DREW Robert, M. A. R. of St. Margaret Pattens.
Deut. vi. 12. 8° 1725. Admonition to infolvent Debtors. *Sion.*
1 Theff. v. 14. 8° 1735. Ref. Manners. *Queen's.* Camb. *Brit. M.*
DRUMMOND Robert, Arch–Bp. of York.
Ifai. xix. 2-4. 4° 1748. Jan. 30. b. Commons. *Brit. M.*
Pf. cxliv. 15. 4° 1749. b. Lords. Th. for Peace. *Brit. M.*
* Job xxix. 16. 4° 1753. An. meet. Ch. fch. *Braz. N.* Oxon. *Queen's.* Camb.
* Deut. xxix. 29. 4° 1754. Prop. Gofpel. *Braz. N.* Oxon.
* Lament. i. 20. 4° 1759. Faft. b. Lords.
* 1 Kings x. 9. 4° 1761. Coronat. of King Geo. III. and Queen Charlotte. *Queen's.* Camb.
DUBOIS Peter, M A. Mafter of the Free-fchool, Woodftock, Oxon.
Pf. xxxix. 4. 8° 1732. Benefit of dying. b. Corporation.
1 Cor. xii. 13. 8° 1737. *Oxon.* A fpiritual but real Union and Communion of the worthy Receiver with God. *All S.* Oxon.
DUBORDIEU John, M. A. Chancellor of St. Afaph, and V. of Layton, Durham.
2 Sam. xv. 21. 4° 1745. Reb. f. *Sion.*
DOBOURDIEU Jean Armand, R. of Sawtrey-Moines, Huntingdon, and Minifter of the French Church in the Savoy.
Pf. xlvi. 7. 4° 1704. Th. Sep. 7. *Pub. L.* Camb.
Exod. ix. 16. 4° 1707. On the Battle of Ramilies.
Pf. xxxix. 9. 8° 1712. *Bod. Sion.* Eton.
1 Sam. iv. 13. 8° 1714. Affize. *Brit. M.*
1 Sam. x. 24. 8° 1714. Firft Sunday after the King's Entry.

2 Chron.

2 Chron. ix. 8. 8° 1715. Acceſſion.
2 Cor. xi. 26. 8° 1716. Th. June 7.
2 Sam. xix. 30. 8° 1724. *Eton.*
DUBOURDIEU Iſaac, DD. One of the Miniſter's of the French-Church in the Savoy.
    Rom. xiii. 1. 4° 1684. May 29.
DUCHAL *James*
    * Pſ. lxxxiv. 10.
    * Prov. xii. 28. } 8° 1728. The Pract. of Relig. recomm. *Br. M.*
    * —— viii. 6.
    * 10 Serm. in 8° 1753. On preſumptive Arguments for the Truth and divine Authority of the Xtian Religion, to which is added a Sermon on God's moral Government. *Worc. Braz. N.* Oxon. *Publ. Trin.* Camb. *Brit. M.*
    * 18 Sermons (Poſth.) vol. 1. in 8° 1762.
    * 16 Sermons (Poſth.) vol. 2. in 8° 1764. } *Queen's.* Camb.
    * 18 Sermons (Poſth.) vol. 3. in 8° 1764.
DUCHE Jacob, M. A. formerly of Clare-Hall, Camb. and R. of Ch. Ch. and St. Peter's, Philadelphia.
    * Gal. v. 1. 8° 1775. Duty of ſtanding faſt in ſpiritual and temporal Liberties.
    * Diſcourſes in 2 vol. 8° 1779. On various Subjects.
    * Jonah ii. 5, 6. 8° 1781. b. Gov. Humane Society.
DUCKENFIELD *Joſeph*
    2 Cor. 2. 16. 8° 1707. The great Work of the Goſpel Miniſtry.
DUDLEY John, M. A. Arch-Deacon of Bedford.
    Phil. iii. 16. 8° 1729. Viſit.
    1 Tim. v. 17.
    2 Pet. iii. 16. } 8° 1731. 2 ſ. The Privileges of the Clergy.
    - - - - - 8° 1736. Viſ. April 30.
DUKE Rich. M. A. Preb. of Glouceſter, and R. of Witney, **Oxon.**
    1 John ii. 6. 4° 1703. b. Queen. Of the Imitation of Chriſt. *Ch. Ch. Worc. Jeſ.* Oxon. *Trin.* Camb.
    Pſ. xxv. 14. 4° 1704. b. Queen. *Ch Ch.* Oxon.
    John xviii. 36. 4° 1704. Aſſize. Of Chriſt's Kingdom. *Univ. Ch. Ch.* Oxon. *Trin.* Camb. *Brit. M.*
    15 Serm in 8° 1714. *Oxon.* On ſeveral Occaſions. *Bod. Ch. Ch. Or. Worc.* Oxon. *Queen's.* Camb.
DU-GARD William, M. A.
    Pſ. cxxii. 6. 4° 1712. Aſſize.
DUNCH John, of Trin. Coll Oxon.
    1 Sam x. 24. 4° 1660. Th. *Sion.*
DUNCAN John, DD. R. of Southwarmborough, Hants.
    * Matt. v. 20 8° 1769. Viſ. The Condemnation pronounced ag. mere external Pretences to Religion.
    * Matt. xviii. 7. 8° 1775. Viſ. The Intereſts of Truth and Virtue invariably purſued by Providence in the Permiſſion of Error and Vice.

DUNCOMB George
 * James ii. 23. 4° 1697. Abraham's Faith stated & applied. *Ch.Ch.*
DUNCOMB George, M. A. R. of Shere, Surry.
 Exod. xxiii. 2. 4° 1738. Ag. Cursing and Swearing.
DUNCOMB Thomas, M. A. R. of Shere, Surry.
 1 Tim. iv. 12. 4° 1671. Vis. Good Example in the Clergy. *Ch. Ch.* Oxon. *St. John's.* Camb.
DUNCOMBE John, M. A. R. of St. Andrew's, Canterbury.
 * Johua i. 4–7. 4° 1759. Th.
 * 2 Chron. vi. 40. 4° 1774. Cons. of Church.
 * Judges xxi. 6. 4° 1778. Fast.
DUNLOP *William*, Reg. Professor of Divinity in Edinburgh.
 Sermons in 2 vol. 8° 1722. *Edinburgh.* On several Subjects and Occasions, with some Lectures. *Pub. L.* Camb.
DUNSTAN Joseph, Master of St. Olave's School, Southwark, and Lect. of St. And. Wardrobe, and St. Ann, Blackfryars, Lond.
 1 John iii. 10. 4° 1705. Feast. Natives of *London.* Brotherly Love recommended.
DUNSTER Sam. DD. Chapl. to Ld Maynard, and Preb. of Sarum.
 Prov. xix. 8. 8° 1708. Sch. Feast. *Univ.* Oxon. *Trin. Queen's.* C.
DUPONT John, B. A. V. of Aysgarth, Yorkshire.
 Isai. xxxvii. 34, 35. 8° 1745. *York.* Reb. The insolent Invasion of Senacherib against Jerusalem, repelled and defeated by God.
 Psal. cxxxii. 18. 8° 1746. *York.* On the Duke's Victory at Culloden. Rebellion and Treachery defeated by Bravery and Conduct.
 Deut. xxxiii. 29. 8° 1746. Th. Oct. 9. The peculiar Happiness and Excellency of the British Nation.
 * Ps. cxlvii. 12–14. 8° 1751. Th.
 * - - - - - 8° 1757. Fast. National Corruption and Depravity, the principal Case of National Disappointments.
 * 2 Chron. xv. ii. 8° 1759. Fast.
 * Sermons in 8° 1761
DUPORT James, DD. Greek Professor in Camb. and Dean of Peterborough.
 Phil. i. 27. 4° 1661. *Camb.* Evangelical Politie. *Bod. C.C.C. Ox.*
 Acts vii. 6. ⎱   ⎧ Jan. 30.
 1 Pet. ii. 17. ⎬ 4° 1676. ⎨ May 29. ⎬ *Bod. All S.* Oxon.
 Ps. cxxiv. 7. ⎰   ⎩ Nov. 5.
DUPREE Edward, M. A. Fell. of Pemb. Coll. Oxon.
 * 1 Thess. v. 21. 4° 1782. *Oxon.* May 29. b. Univ.
DUPREE John, M. A. Fell. of Ex. Coll. and Min. at Tring, Herts.
 * 13 Sermons in 8° 1782. On various Subjects.
DUREL John, DD. French Minister at the Savoy.
 1 Cor. xi. 16. 4° 1688. The Liturgy of the Church of England asserted. *Bod. All S.* Oxon. *Sion.*
DURHAM *James*
 * 7 Sermons in 12° 1681. The Blessedness of those who die in the Lord.

           * 72 Sermons

*72 Sermons in fo. 1723. On Ifai. liii.
DURHAM William, DD. R: of St. Mildred's, Breadftreet, Lond.
  1 Cor. xvi. 13. 4° 1671. b. Artill. Co. *Bod. Trin.* Camb. *Sion.*
  Prov. xxix. 1. 4° 1675. b. Lord Mayor. *Sion.*
DURHAM William, DD. Chaplain to the Duke of Monmouth and
  R. of Letcombe Baffet, Berks.
  Heb. xiii. 16. 4° 1679. Commem. Encouragement to Charity. *Bod. Ch: Ch.* Oxon.
  James v. 9. 4° 16   Affize.
DURNFORD Thomas, M. A. Cur. of Rogborn, Wilts, and Chapl. to the Earl of Manchefter.
  Ecclef. vii. 10. 8° 1715. Affize. The Folly of thinking the former times better than the prefent.
DYCHE Thomas, M. A. Cur. of Bow, Middlefex, and Mafter of the Free School.
  Acts iii. 19. 8° 1723. b. condemned Criminals.
DYER Richard
  1 Cor. v. 7. 8° 1676. A bleeding Saviour. *Bod.*
DYER Tho. M. A. of Ch. Ch. Ox. and R. of Bedhampton, Hants.
  Prov. x. 7. 4° 1743. Fun.
  * 2 Cor. v. 10. 8° 1758. Religion, a ferious affair.
DYER William
  * Cant. v. 16. 8° 1663.
  * Ifai. v. 16. 8° 1666. Chrift's famous Titles.
  * Rev. iii. 20. 8° 1666. A Call to Sinners.
  Rev. vi. 17. 8° 1666.
  Rev. xiv. 6. 8° 1666.
[DYKE Jeremy]
  * 1 Cor. xv. 13. 8° 1667. The Worthy Communicant.
[DYKES Ofwald,] formerly of Queen's Coll. Oxon.
  * Difcourfes in 8° 1722. Lemuel's Leffons.
E.   E.
  1 John v. 12. 8° 1679. On juftifying Faith. *Bod.*
E.   R. Author of the Duty of Man laid down in exprefs words of Scripture.
  Job xiv. 5, 6. 12° 1679. A Difc. concerning the Period of human Life, whether mutable or immutable.
EARL *Jabez*, DD. Minifter in Hanover-ftreet, London.
  * James i. 22. 4° 1706. Farw. f.
  * Col iii. 16.   } 12° 1708. V. Pract. Difc. on Prayer and
  * 1 Theff. v. 17–20. }   hearing the word.
  2 Cor. v 14. 8° 1719. Char. f. *Eton.*
  ‡ * Matt. iii. 8. 8° 1710. *Brit. M.*
  Matt. xxiii. 9. 8° 1723. Ord.
  * 1 Cor. xiii. 5. 8° 1721.
  * Heb. xii. 9. 8° 1728. Fun.
  * Pf. cxii. 9. 8° 1729.
  * Jude 21. 8° 1729. Fun. *Queen's.* Camb.

Daniel

Daniel ix. 18. 8° 1727. Faſt.
Job v 26. 8° 1733. Fun.
1 John i. 7 8° 1755. Of Purgatory. V. Diſ. ag. Popery. 2 vol. *Braz. N.* Oxon.
Zach. vii. 13. 8° 1737. A ſerious Exhortation to Repentance.
EASTON Thomas, M. A. V. of Nymet Epiſcopi, Devon.
    Pſ. ciii. 15, 16. 4° 1692. Fun. of John Milford. *Bod. Brit. M.*
EATON Samuel, DD.
    * Sermons in 2 Vol 8° 1764. On human Life.
ECCLES Samuel, M. A. late of Braz. N. Coll. Oxon. and Preacher at Bridewell.
    Hoſea iv 3. 4° 1750. On the Return of the Infection among the Cattle.
    1 Cor. xi. 34. 8° 1751. The unworthy Communicant's Plea anſwered and home Baptiſt refuted.
    * Pſ. cvii. 39—41. 4° 1753. Religion, the trueſt Loyalty, Proteſtaniſm, no Fanaticiſm or Judaiſm.
    * Matt. xxvii. 21-23. 8° 1753. b. Univ. of Oxon.
    * Acts xxii. 11. 4° 1754. Jan. 30. The royal Martyr.
    * 16 Sermons in 8° 1755. On different Subjects.
ECHARD Lawr. M. A. Arch-D. of Stowe, and Preb. of Lincoln.
    Prov. ii. 1. 4° 1698. Aſſize. The Heiniouſneſs of Injuſtice. *Eton.*
    Rom. xii. 18. 8° 1726. Acceſſion. Peace and Unity recommended.
ECHLIN John, M. A.
    Matt. v. 10. 8° 1712. *Dublin.* Jan. 30. The royal Martyr.
EDEN Robert, B. D. Arch-D. of Winton, and Preb. of Worceſter.
    Iſai. v. 20. 4° 1743. Aſſize. The neceſſary and unchangeable Difference of moral Good and Evil. *Worc.* Oxon.
    Jerem. xxix. 7. 4° 1743. Aſſize. Connection of private and public Happineſs: *Worc.* Oxon. *Queen's.* Camb.
    * Epheſ. iv. 14, 15. 4° 1754. Viſ. Neceſſary Connection of Faith and Love in matters of Religion. *Worc.* Oxon.
    * Pſ. cxxxvii. 5, 6. 4° 1755. Ann. meet. of 3 Choirs. Harmony of Benevolence. *Braz. N. Worc.* Oxon.
EDGCUMBE James, DD. R. of Exeter Coll. Oxon.
    2 Cor. iii. 5. 8° 1736. 2 ſ. Human Reaſon, an inſufficient Guide in matters of Religion and Morality.
EDGLEY Samuel, M. A. V. of Wandſworth, Surry.
    Pſ. cxxii. 6. 4° 1724. Conc. ad Cl. *Wadh.* Ox. *Queen's.* C. *Eton.*
[EDMONDSON Chriſtopher]
    * Pſ. xxxix. 12. 12° 1664.
EDWARDS David
    * Heb. xi. 4. 8° 1770. 2 ſ. On the Death of Rev. Geo. Whitfield.
EDWARDS Edward, M. A.
    * Pſ. cxxii. 8, 9. 8° 1759. Chriſtian Patriotiſm.
EDWARDS *Jon.* M. A. late Preſid. of New Jerſey, New England.
    * Rev. v. 5, 6. 8° 1738. Excellency of Chriſt.
    * Rom. iii. 19. 8° 1774. God's juſtice in damning Sin.

EDWARDS John, DD. sometime Fell. of St. John's Coll. Camb.
    1 Kings viii. 38. 4° 1665. *Camb.* Of the Plague of the Heart. *Sion.*
    An Enquiry in 2 Vol. 8° 1692. Into several remarkable Texts of the old and new Testament. *Bod. Univ.* Oxon. *Queen's.* Camb.
    12 Sermons in 8° 1698. On special Occasions and Subjects. *Cb. Ch. Queen's. St. John's.* Oxon. *Dr. W's. L.* Lond.
    Ps. cxix. 142. 4° 1699. Commem. Of the Reasons of Good and Evil. *All S.* Oxon. *Trin. St. John's.* Camb. *Sion.*
    Mark v. 12. 8° 1700. *Cant.* Conc. ad Cl. *Bod. All S.* Oxon.
    Exercitations in 2 parts. 8° 1702. On several places of the old and new Testament. *Univ.* Oxon. *Dr. W's. L.* London.
    Lament. i. 8. 8° 1707. Fast. The Heiniousness of England's Sin. *Brit. M.*
    Ezek. xxxvii. 22. 8° 1707. On the Union. One Nation, and one King. *Magd.* Oxon. *Brit. M.*
    * John xiii. 15. 8° 17
    Ps. lx. 12. 8° 1708.
    Ps. cxxvi. 3. 8° 1709. Nov. 5. *Linc.* Oxon. *St. John's.* Camb. *Sion. Eton.*
    Rev. ii. 4, 5. 8° 1711. Fast. March 28.
    Body of Divinity in 3 Vol. fo. 1 and 2. 1713. V. 3. 1726.
    Remains in 8° 1713. { 1 Kings xviii. 21. p. 519. } *Queen's.* Ca.
                        { Phil. i. 21. p. 519. }
    Eccles. vii. 10. 8° 1714. Accession.
EDWARDS Joseph, M. A. Vice-Principal of Magd. Hall. Oxon.
    Acts ii. 46. 8° 1731. Of public Prayer.
    1 Cor. xi. 16. 8° 1736. The Testimony of the antient Church proper &c. *Worc.* Oxon.
    Matt. v. 44. 8° 1743. *Oxon.* Of Forgiveness of Enemies. *Worc.* Oxon. *Queen's.* Camb. *Brit. M.*
    John i. 14. 8° 1749. Christ God man. b. Univ. of Oxon.
EDWARDS Thomas, V. of Keinton, Herts.
    Ps. xv. 2. 8° 1660.
EDWARDS Thomas, DD. late Fell. of Clare Hall, Camb.
    * Jude 3. 8° 1773. Commenc. *Camb.* The indispensable Duty of contending for the Faith &c. *Queen's.* Camb.
EDZARD J. E. Minister to the German Lutherans.
    Ps. cxxxii. 17, 11. 4° 1696. Th. April 16. *Trin.* Camb.
EEDES Richard, V. of Beckford near Cleve, Gloucesters.
    2 Sam. iii. 36. 8° 1660.
EGAN Anthony, B. D. late Confessor gener. of the Kingdom of Ireland.
    Luke xxii. 32. 4° 1673. The Franciscan Convert, or a Recantation sermon &c. *Bod. Queen's.* Oxon. *Pub L.* Camb. *Sion.*
EGERTON Henry, Bp. of Hereford.
    Prov. xxiv. 21. 4° 1727. Jan. 30. b. Lords, *Queen's.* Camb.
    Dan. xii. 3. 4° 1729. Prop. Gospel. *Ch. Ch.* Ox. *Queen's.* Cam.
EGERTON John, Bishop of Durham.
    * 2 Chron. xxxii. 7, 8. 4° 1757. Fast. b. Lords.

                                                                * Hosea

* Hosea iii. 4. 4° 1761. Jan. 30. b. Lords.
*Matt. xxii. 9. 4° 1763. Prop. Gospel. *Braz. N.* Ox. *Queen's.* C.
ELBOROUGH Robert. M. A. Minister of the Parish that was lately
  St. Lawrence-Pountney, London.
  Ezek. xx. 47. 4° 1666. Faſt for the Fire.
ELBOROUGH Thomas, Minister of Chiswick, Middlesex.
  * Discourses in 8° 1663. and 12° 1673. An Exposition of the
    Common Prayer.
[ELIOT Andrew,] M. A. Paſtor of a Church in Boſton.
  * 1 Chron. xii. 32. 8° 1765. Elect. of his Majeſty's Council.
ELLESBY James, M. A. Minister of Chiswick Middlesex.
  Prov. xxx. 31. 4° 1684. Jan. 30. The Doctrine of paſſive Obe-
    dience. *Ch. Ch.* Oxon.
  Heb iii. 7, 8. 4° 1693. Fun. of   The great Danger
    and Uncertainty of a Death-bed Repentance. *Bod.*
ELLINGTON Edward, V. D. M.
  * Heb. xi. 26. 8° 1770. Fun. of Rev. George Whitfield.
ELLIOTT John, B. A. formerly of Bennet Coll. Camb.
  * Gal. ii. 21. 8° 1759. Encouragements for Sinners.
  * Pſ. xxiii. 4. 8° 1762. Fun. of *Joshua Reyner.*
  * 1 Cor. i. 30. 8° 1763. Fun. of *Sarah Elliot.*
  * Sermons in 8° 1764.
  * Rom. vi. 23. 8° 1767. Fun. of *John Hoev.*
  * Matt. xvii. 20. 8° 1769.
  * Acts v. 42. 8° 1769.
  * Isai. lvii. 1. 8° 1770. Fun. of Rev. George Whitfield.
  * Ephes. v. 31–33. 8° 1775. Wedd. f.
ELLIS Clement, M. A. R. of Kirkby, Nottingham, and Preb. of
    Southwell.
  Pſ. cxviii. 22–24. 4° 1661. *Oxon.* May 29. *Bod.*
  Prov. xix. 21. 8° 1684. The Folly of Man's Decrees, and the
    Stability of God's Counsel.
  Phil. ii. 3. 8° 1684. The Practice of true Humility.
  Matt. xi. 28. 12° 1685. Reſt to the heavy-laden. *Queen's.* Camb.
  Prov. xxiv. 21. 4° 1691. Aſſize. Relig. and Loyalty inseparable.
    Magd. Oxon. *Trin.* Camb.
  1 Cor. iii. 7. 4° 1694. The Christian Hearers firſt Leſſon.
  3 Diſc. ⎧ Luke xvi. 19–31. p 1. Par. of Dives and Laz. ⎫ Que.
  8° 1704 ⎨ ———— 1–9. p. 231. ———— unj. Steward.   ⎬ Cam.
          ⎩ Matt xxv. 1–12. p. 385. Par. of the ten Virg. ⎭
  * 2 Chron. xv. 15. 8° 16
  * Pſ. cxii. 7. 8° 16
  * Prov. xvi. 32. 8° 16
  * Luke vi. 25. 8° 16
  * John vi. 33. 8° 16
ELLIS John, R. of Gonalſton, Nottinghamſ.
  Joſh. xxii. 20. 8° 1701. Ref. M. *Bod.*
ELLIS Ph. Monk of the Holy Order of St. Benedict, and of the
    Engliſh Congregation.

* Matt. v. 12. 4° 1685. All Saint's-day. b. King and Queen. *Ch. Ch. Bal. C.C.C. Worc.* Oxon.
* Matt. xxii. 37. 4° 1685. b. King and Queen at Windsor. *Ch. Ch. Bal.* Oxon. *Trin.* Camb.
* Matt. xii. 41. 4° 1686. Lent. b. King and Queen. *Ch. Ch.* Ox.

ELLISON Cuthbert, M.A. V. of Stannington, and Lect. of St. Nicholas, Newcastle.
    Acts xvii. 18. 8° 1748. 2 f. What will this Babbler say.

ELLISON Nath. DD. Arch-D. of Stafford and V. of New-castle upon Tyne.
    Ecclef. viii. 11. 4° 1699. Elect. of a Mayor.
    Acts viii. 14, 15, 17. 8° 1700. Conf. *All S. Bal.* Oxon. *Pub. L. St. John's.* Camb. *Sion.*
    Mark. xiv. 7. 4° 1710. Opening a Char. School. *C.C.C.* Oxon.

ELLYS Anthony, Bp. of St. David's.
    Matt xxii. 21. 4° 1749. Jan. 30. b. Commons. *All S.* Oxon. *Queen's.* Camb.
* 1 Pet. ii. 16. 4° 1754. Jan. 30. b. Lords. *Queen's.* Camb.
* Isai. i. 26. 4° 1758. May 29. b. Lords.
* John. xv. 8. 4° 1759. Prop. Gospel. *Braz. N.* Oxon.

ELSLY William, M.A. Preb. of York.
* 1 Tim. vi. 17–19. 1732.

ELSMERE Sloane, DD. R. of Chelsea, Middlesex.
* Sermons in 2 Vol. 1° 1767. *Bod. Pub. L.* Camb. *Sion.*

ELSTOB Will. M.A. R. of St. Swithun, and St. Mary Bothaw, London.
    Pf. ciii. 10. 4° 1704. Th. for Victory at Hockstet, *Bod. Sion.*
    1 Tim. ii. 1, 2. 4° 1704. Accession. *Bod. Pub. L.* Camb. *Sion.*

ELSTON John, M.A. R. of Langtree, Devon.
    1 Tim. iv. 15. 4° 1681. Vif.

ELWORTHY John, M.A. Minister of South-moulton, Devon.
* 1 Cor. xii. 11. 8° 1753. Vif. Influences of the Spirit, and their Uses considered. *Queen's.* Camb.

EMLYN *Thomas*, Minister at Dublin.
    18 Sermons &c. 8° 1742. *Queen's.* Camb. *Dr. W's L.* London.

ENFIELD William, LL.D. of Warrington, Lancashire.
* Heb. xiii. 22. 8° 1770. Ord. *Queen's.* Camb.
* Sermons in 2 V. 12° 1772. For the Use of Families. *Bod. Sion.*
* 12 Biographical Serm. in 12° 1777. *Bod. Pub. L.* Camb. *Sion.*
* Rom. xi. 13. 4° 1777. Ord.
* 1 Sam. xx. 3. 8° 1777. At the Interment of Mr. John Galway, Student at Warrington Academy.
* 1 Pet. ii. 17. 8° 1778. Ord. of *John Prior Estlin.*
* 1 Cor. xi. 1. 4° 1780. Fun of *John Aikin*, DD
* - - - - - 1780. Progress of Religion and Xn Knowledge.

ENGLAND John, Minister at Sherborne, Dorsetshire.
* Discourses in 8° 1700.
    Esther iii. 15. 8° 1712. Fast.
    1 Tim. ii. 1, 2. 8° 1715. Accession.

ENGLISH

ENGLISH T. of Gosport, Hants.
   * Rev. ii. 5. 8° 1776. Fallen Church delineated.
ENGLISH Thomas, B. D. R. of Friton, York.
   2 Maccab. iv. 50. 4° 1734. Assize. The British Monitor—or the Freeholder's Advocate.
ENOCK Richard, M. A. R. of Stratton, Suffolk.
   Pf cxxxiii. 1. 4° 1707. Th. for Union.
ENTWISLE Edmund, DD. Arch-D. and Preb. of Chester, and R. of Barrow, Cheshire.
   Mark x. 21. 4° 1697. Conc. ad Cl. *Ch. Ch. Magd.* Oxon.
ENTY John, Minister at Exeter.
   Tit. ii. 15. 4° 1707. b. Dissenting Clergy.
   Acts xv. 7, 8. 4° 1716. Jan. 30. The Innocence of Protest. Dissenters cleared and vindicated in reference to the Transactions of 41, and the Death of King Char. 1st. *St. John's.* Cam. *Sion.*
   * Phil. i 8. 8° 1725. Ord.
   * Acts xxvii. 12, 13. 8° 1737. Nov. 5.
ERSKINE Ebenezer
   * Discourses in 3 Vol. 8° 1757.
ERSKINE George, Presbyter of the Church of England.
   Isai. li. 1. 4° 1710.
   Ephef. iv. 3. 4° 1710. June 11.
ERSKINE John,ª DD. Minister of the Gospel at Culross.
   * James iii. 1. 8° 1750. b. Synod. *All S.* Oxon.
   * Isai. lv. 13 8° 1756. b. Soc. for prop. Christian Knowledge. *Queen's.* Camb.
   * 2 Cor. vi. 3. 8° 1765. b. Synod. Ministers of the Gospel cautioned ag. giving offence. V. Scotch Pr. V. 1.
ERSKINE John,ª DD. one of the Ministers at Edinburgh.
   * Judges xx. 21. 8° 1769. War with America.
   * Josh. i. 17. 8° 1779. Elect. of Magistrates at *Edinburgh.*
ERSKINE Ralph, Minister of the Gospel in Dumfermline.
   * Sermons in 2 Vol. fo. 1764. *Bod. Pub. L.* Camb. *Sion.*
EVANKE George
   Matt. xxvi. 39. 4° 1663. V. Coll. Farw. f.
EVANS Caleb, M. A. at Bristol.
   * Pf. xxvii. 13. 8° 1771. Fun. of Mrs. *Ann Robarts.*
   * 3 John xi. 8° 1773. Ord.
   * 2 Tim. iv. 5. 8° 1773. Ord.
   * Ephef. v. 16. 8° 1774. Redeem. of the Time.
   * Gal. v. 13. 8° 1775. Nov. 5. Brit. Constitution and Liberty.
   * Matt. vi. 10. 8° 1775. Educ. f. The Kingdom of God.
   * 1 John v. 20 } 2Difc. 12° 1766. Deity of Son and H. Spirit.
   * Acts v. 4.
   * Pf. lxxiii. 26. 8° 1776. Fun.
   * 2 Sam. iii. 38. 8° 1776. Fun. of Rev. Mr. *Rouquet.*
   * Heb. x. 32. 8° 1778. Nov. 5.

a *Q.* The same.

* Acts

* Acts xx. 37, 38. 8° 1779. Fun. of *J. Ash*, LL.D. Tears of Xn. Friendship.
* Rom. iii. 31. 8° 1779. b. Dissent. Cl.
* 2 Kings ii. 12. 8° 1781. Fun. of Rev. *Hugh Evans*.
‡ * Prov. xiv. 32. 8° 1780. Fun. of Rev. *J. Mason*, DD.

EVANS Hugh, M. A. at Bristol.
    * Phil. ii. 29. 8° 1773. Ord.
    * Col. iv. 17. 8° 1773. Ord.
    * 2 Cor. iii. 6. 8° 1773. Educ. f. The able Minister.
    * Zach. i. 5. 8° 1773. b. Diss. Cl. Ministers described under the Characters of Fathers and Prophets.
    * 1 Thess. ii. 19. 8° 1781. The Hope, Joy, Crown of a faithful Minister.

EVANS John, M. A. R. of St. Ethelborough, Lond.
    Phil. iv. 5. 4° 1682. b. Lord Mayor. Of Moderation. *Ch. Ch. C. C. C. Magd.* Oxon. *Pub. L.* Camb. *Sion.*

EVANS John, M. A.
    * Prov. xxxi. 31. 8° 1695. On the Death of Queen Mary.

EVANS John, V. of Ewell, Surry.
    * Ps. cxii. 6. 8° 1718. Fun.

EVANS John, M. A. One of his Majesty's Chapl. at Whitehall.
    Judges viii. 21. 8° 1751. Welch F. b. Antient Britons. The Christian Soldier. *Queen's.* Camb.

EVANS John, DD. Minister in London.
    - - - - 4° 1704. Th. for Victory at Blenheim.
    Ps. xxi. 3. 8° 1706. Th. for Vict. at Ramallies. *Univ.* Ox. *Trin.* C.
    Ecclef. viii. 11. 8° 1707. Ref. Manners.
    Micah vi. 9. 8° 1715. On the Fire in Thames-Street.
    ‡ * 2 Cor. v. 9. 8° 1716. Fun. of Rev. *Dan. Williams*, DD.
    Acts xx. 32. 8° 1716. On leaving the Lect. at Salter's-Hall. *Qu.* C.
    2 Chron. xv. 2. 8° 1720. God with us, while we are with him.
    Judges x. 11–16. 8° 1720. Nov. 5. Past Deliverances and present Calamities improved.
    2 Sam. xxiv. 14. 8° 1721. David's Choice to fall into the hand of God, rather than into the hand of Man.
    - - - - 1723. Ministers recommended to the Prayers of Xns.
    * Rom. xii. 18. 8° 1725. 2 f.
    Practical Disc. in 2 vol. 8° 1723. Concerning the Xtian Temper.
    7 Sermons in 12° 1725. On various Subjects to young People.
    2 Tim. iv. 7, 8. 8° 1726. Fun. of Mrs *King*. St. Paul's comfortable Reflection and Prospect in view of Death. *Brit. M.*
    Ps. lxiii. 11. 8° 1727. Coron. *Brit. M.*
    Jer. ix. 23, 24. 8° 1727. Fast. Mar. 22.
    2 Tim. i. 5. 8° 1727. To young People.
    2 Kings iv. 26. 8° 1727. Fun.
    * 2 Cor. iv. 7. 8° 1728. Fun. of Mr. *Ratcliffe. Queen's.* Camb.
    ‡ * 1 Pet. ii. 5. 8° 1730. 3 f. Open. Meeting-House. *Brit. M.*

EVANS Robert, M. A. St. Lawrence, London.
    * Prov. iv. 25–27. 4° 1771. El. Lord Mayor.

EVANSON

EVANSON Edward, M.A. late V. of Tewkesbury, Gloucest.
* 3 Difcourfes in 8° 1773. viz.
*Acts xiii. 22. Man after God's own Heart.
*Rom. iv. 22. Abraham's Faith.
*2 Tim ii. 19. Seal of the Foundation of God.
EVERARD John, DD.
   Rev. xi. 17.
EVERSHED William
   * John vi. 30. ⎱ 8° 1780. 2 Difc. A fummary View of the ge-
   * 2 Pet. i. 16. ⎰ nuine Evidences of the Truth of the Xtian Relig.
EVES George, R. of Hartley, Kent.
   Micah vii. 9. 4° 1661. Fun. of Lady Cæcilia Peyton.
EUSTANCE Evans, M.A. V. of Abergavenny, Monmouthf.
   * Prov. xxiv. 22. 4° 1747. Monmouth. Affize.
EWBANCK George
   Job iii. 17. 4° 1661. Fun.
EWER John, Bp. of Landaff.
   * Prov. xxi, 31. 4° 1762. Faft. b. Lords.
   * Heb. xiii. 16. 4° 1766. b. Gov. Lond. Hofp. Wadh. Oxon.
   * Rom. x. 14. 4° 1767. Prop. Gofpel. Braz. N. Ox. Queen's. C.
EYRE John, DD. Curate of Wylye, Wilts.
   * Gen. xix. 27, 28. 4° 1758. Faft. 2 f.
   * Luke xiii. 1-6. 4° 1761. Th. f.
   *Rev. ii. 10. 8° 1777. Vif. An earneft Attempt to reform the times.
EYRE Rich. M.A. Canon of Sarum, and R. of Burghcleer, Hants.
   Pf. xxix. 11. 8° 1713. Oxon. Th. Sion.
   1 Cor. xv. 55. 8° 1713. Oxon. Fun. of Charles Fox, Efq;
   John xvi. 12, 13. 8° 1715. Oxon. Whitfunday. The Neceffity of
      Grace with our Reafon in Xtian Faith. Magd. Oxon. Queen's.
      St. John's. Camb. Eton.
   Prov. iii. 16. 4° 1716. Fun. of Sir Steph. Fox, Knt. Worc. Magd.
      Oxon. Sion. Eton.
   Col. i. 28. 4° 1717. Vif. The Ufefulnefs of Preaching, and the
      Reafons why Men are not more edified by it.
   Jer. ix. 23, 24. 4° 1726. Oxon. Fun.
EYRE Richard, R. of Bright-Walton, Bucks, F.R. & A.S.
   * Pf. cvi. 30, 31. 4° 1765. b. Gov. Small-pox Hofp. London.
   * Jofhua xiii. 33. 4° 1767. b. Sons of Clergy.
   * Matt. x. 8. 4° 1770. An. meet. Ch. Sch. Worc. Oxon.
EYRE Robert, a DD. Fell. of the Coll. near Winchefter.
   Acts xxiv. 16. 4° 1693. Affize. The Nature and Satisfaction of a
      good and inoffenfive Confcience. Bod. Pub. L. Camb.
   1 Sam. xii. 25. 4° 1700. Affize. The Sinner, a Traitor to his
      King and Country. Bod. Worc. Oxon. St. John's. Camb.
   Joel iii. 19. 4° 1708. Jan. 30. b. Commons. Univ. Magd. Worc.
      Or. Oxon. Trin. St. John's. Queen's. Camb. Sion.
EYRE Robert, a DD. R. of Buckland, Surry.

        ª Q. The fame.

Mark

Mark xvi. 16. 8° 1735. Vif. Infidelity without Excufe — or no natural Impoffibility in believing. *Worc.* Oxon. *Sion.*
Matt. iv. 1–10. 8° 1738. 4 f. On Xt's Temptation. *All S.* Oxon.
FAIRCHILD Thomas, of Chigwell, Effex.
* Prov. iii. 77. 4° 1757. Sch. Feaft. St. Paul's.
FAIRCLOUGH Samuel
2 Pet. i. 10. 4° 1675. m. e. P. p. 617. Affurance, Perfeverance.
FAIRWHEATHER Thomas, V. of Great-Grimsby, Lincolnfhire.
Luke ii. 11. 4° 1697. 2 f. Chriftmas.
Heb. xi. 17. 4° 1697.
FALKNER Will. DD. One of the Town Preac. at Lyn. Regis, Norf.
2 Cor. v. 18. Vif. ⎱ ⎰ Bod. Ch. Ch. Magd.
Joel ii. 12. Lent. ⎱ V. End of his Works. ⎰ C. C. C. *Queen's.*
Matt. v. 20. ⎱ ⎰ Oxon.
FALCON Thomas, M. A. of Queen's Coll. Oxon. and of Codrington Coll. Barbadoes.
* Pf. xxvii. 6. 8° 1760. Th. f. Gratitude for divine Mercies, the fpecial Duty of Britons.
FALL James, of Watford, Herts.
* Zach. xi. 4. 8° 1754. Ord.
FALLE Philip, M. A. Chaplain in Ord. R. of St. Saviour's Jerfey, and then of Shenley, Herts.
Luke ii. 14. 4° 1687. At Jerfey. in French.
——— iii. 14. 4° 1692. b. the Garrifon. *Bod.*
Ecclef. viii. 11. 4° 1695. The Impunity of bad men in the world. *Pub. L. Trin.* Camb.
John xvi. 7–11. 4° 1695. b. Lord Mayor. Of the Defcent of the Paraclet.
Acts xvii. 3. 4° 1700. Vif. *St. John's.* Camb.
2 Kings ii. 23, 24. 8° 1715. Opening Char. School.
FANCH James
* 10 Sermons in 8° 1768, On practical Subjects.
FANCOURT Samuel
* Rev. xxii. 14. 8° 1720. Fun.
* 1 Cor. i. 21, 8° 1734. *Sarum.* Ord. *Queen's.* Camb.
* - - - - 1746. Ch. f.
FARBROTHER Roger, V. of Holy Rhoodes in Southampton.
Pf. ii. 12. 4° 1697. Affize. The Magiftrates Concern in Chrift's Kingdom.
FARINDON Anth. B. D. Divinity-Reader of his Majefty's Chapel-Royal at Windfor.
Sermons in 3 Vol. fo. V. 1. 2. 1672. V. 3. 1679. *Bod. Ch. Ch. All S. Mert. Trin. Worc. Queen's.* Ox. *Pub. L. Trin.* Cam. *Sion.*
FARMER Hugh
* Pf. l. 14. 8° 1746. Th. for fuppreffing the Rebellion.
FARMER John,[a] M. A.
20 Sermons in 8° 1744. On various divine Subjects.
FARMER John,[a]   London.
* Sermons in 8° 1756.

a *Q* The fame?

FARMERIE William, M. A.
  Deut. x. 1. 8° 1710. Fast. God the only Judge, and our only Hope in War. *Linc.* Oxon.
  Deut. xxxii. 6. 8° 1716. Th.
  * 1 Tim. ii. 1–3. 8° 1714. The Subjects Duty in praying for Kings &c. *Wadh.* Oxon.
[FARRELL George]
  * 2 Sam. xviii. 28. 8° 1716. Th.
FARRER Isaac, Curate of Eggleston.
  * Pf. xc. 4. 8° 1768. On violent Floods.
FARRINGTON Richard, M. A. R. of Llanarmon, Caernarvonf.
  20 Sermons in 8° 1741. *King's.* Camb.
FARRINGTON William, B D. R. of Warrington, Lancashire.
  * Sermons in 8° 1769. *Warrington.*
FARTHING Ralph, LL. B.
  * Prov. xxiv. 21. 8° 1722. Sessions at *Exon.*
FAWCETT Benjamin, Minister at Kidderminster, Worcesterf.
  * 1 Cor. xvi. 2. } 12° 1758. 2 Disc. The sacred Almoner.
  * Isai. xxxii. 8. }
  * Phil. iv. 1. 12° 1759. Fun. of Rev. *Mr. Darracott.*
  * 1 Chron. xxix. 28. 8° 1760. On the Death of King George 2d and the Accession of King George 3d.
  * Matt. xxv 31–34. 8° 1761. Coron. of King George 3d. Future Coronation of the Saints.
  * 2 Cor. v. 17. 8° 17   2 f. The grand Enquiry.
  * Matt. xxi. 15,16. 12° 1770. On the Death of a Child.
  * 2 Sam. iii. 34. 8° 1771. On the Murder of Francis Belt. Murder lamented and improved.
  * Esther iv. 14. 8° 1773. Rel. Lib. On Dissent. Bill to Parliament.
  * 2 Cor. iv. v. 8° 1774. Ord.   Preach. Xt and not self.
FAWCETT J.
  * Sermons in 8° 1749. On various Subjects.
FAWCETT Richard, DD. V. of Newcastle, Preb. of Durham, and Chaplain in Ord.
  * Ephes. ii. 21, 22. 4° 1768. Conf. St. Anne's Chap. at *Newcastle.*
FAWCETT Samuel, Minister at Kidderminster, Worcesterf.
  Pf. xxv. 22. 8° 1668.
FAWCONER Samuel, M. A. Assistant Preacher at Grosvenor Church, and Lect. of St. Michael, Bassinglaw.
  * Pf. cl. 4. 8° 1763. May 29. Open. an Organ. Church Music an Help to Devotion.
FEARON Joseph, M. A. Fell. of Sidney Coll. Camb.
  * Wisdom vii. 14. 4° 1755. School Feast.
FEATHERSTONHAUGH H. V. of Bethersden, Kent.
  Isai. xxxvii. 3. 8° 1724. Jan. 30.
FEATLY Daniel, DD.
  Deut. xxxii. 29. 8° 1708. Fun. *Univ. Linc. Magd. Ox. King's.* C.
FEATLY Daniel, DD.
  1 Pet. v. 2–4. 4° 1660. *Brit. M.*

FEKE Thomas
    Pf. lxviii. 28. - - - - -
FELL John, DD. Dean of Ch. Ch. and Bp. of Oxford.
    2 Pet. iii. 3. 4° 1675. The Xrter of the laſt days. *Bod. Ch. Ch. Univ. Queen's. Magd. Worc.* Oxon. *Pub. L. Trin. St. John's.* Camb. *Sion.*
    Matt. xii. 25. 4° 1680. Faſt. b. Lords. *Bod. Ch. Ch. Magd. Worc. Jef. Trin. St. John's.* Camb. *Sion.*
FELTHAM Owen
    * Diſc. in fo. 1661.
FELTON George, M. A.
    * John vi. 26. 8° 1715. *Shrewſbury.* Aſſize. Secular Intereſt, Inſincerity, and double Dealing in Religion detected and expoſed.
FELTON Henry, LL. B. R. of Malford, Suff. and Chapl. in Ord.
    Pſ. xvi. 11. 1689. The eternal Joys of God's Preſſence.
FELTON Henry, DD. Principal of Edmund-Hall, Oxon. and R. of Whitwell, Norfolk.
    1 Theſſ. iv. 13. 4° 1711. Fun. of Duke of Rutland. *Linc.* Oxon.
    1 Cor. xv. 23. 8° 1725. The Reſurrection of the ſame numerical Body and its Reunion to the ſame Soul. *Worc.* Oxon. *Queen's.* Camb. *Brit. M.*
    1 Cor. xv 23. 8° 1733. The Univerſality and Order of the Reſurrection. *Worc.* Oxon. *Sion. Brit. M.*
    Matt. xxii. 29. 8° 1735. *Oxon.* The Scripture Doctrine of the Reſurrection as it ſtood before the Law. *Worc.* Oxon.
    Matt. xxii. 29. 2 ſ. 8° 1736. *Oxon.* The Scripture Doctrine in the Books of Moſes and Job. *Worc.* Oxon.
    Prov. xxix 2. 8° 1730. Acceſſion. The Xrter of a good Prince.
    Matt. xxii. 21. 8° 1733. Jan. 30. b. Commons. The Herodian and the Gaulonite. *Worc.* Oxon. *Brit. M.*
    8 Serm. at Lady Moyer's Lect. 1728, 1729. 8° 1732. *Oxon. Bod. Ch. Ch. New C. Worc.* Oxon. *Sion.*
    Job xix. 25. 8° 1736. *Oxon.*
    Serm. in 8° 1748. On the Creation, Fall and Redemption &c.
FELTON William, M. A.
    * Rev. ii. 10. 8° 1773. Fun. of Rev. Mr. Knatchbull.
FELTWELL Richard
    Pſ. xviii. 50. 4° 1660.
FEN James, M. A. V. of Goudhurſt, Kent.
    1 John v. 4. 4° 1686. b. Lord Mayor. *Sion.*
FENNER Ludd John
    * 1 Theſſ. iv. 16. 8° 1777. Fun. of Mrs. *Elizabeth Grundy.* The Scripture Doctrine of the Reſurrection. a Conſolation under the Loſs of Friends.
FENWICK William, R. of South Mediety of Hallerton, Leiceſter.
    2 Cor. vi. 19, 20. 8° 1701.
FENWICKE George, B. D. R. of Hallerton, Leiceſter.
    2Cor. ii. xvi. 8° 1736. Viſ. Plain things delivered to Xt's Miniſters and People.

                                                                        * Matt.

* Matt. xvi. 26. 8° 1737. On the breaking out of the Small-pox.
* Exod. xx. 5. 8° 1738.
* Lam. iii. 40, 41. 8° 1738. } 2 f. Jan. 29. and 30.
FERGUSON Adam, Chapl. to Lord John Murray's Regiment.
   2 Sam. x. 12. 8° 1745. Faſt.
[FERGUSON H.]
   * Pſ. lvi. 6. 8° 1743.
FERNE Robert
   * Heb. xii. 23. 3° 1708. Fun. of Rev. *Edw. Prince. Queen's.* Ca.
   * Sermons in 8° 1721.
FERREBEE Michael, M. A. Student of Ch. Ch. Oxon.
   1 Pet. iii 8. 4° 1732. Ch. f. b. Ld May. *All S.* Oxon. *Brit. M.*
FESTING Michael, M. A. R. of Wyke Regis, Dorſetſ.
   * - - - - 8° 1756. Papiſts, no Chriſtians.
   * Joel ii. 12-14. 8° 1759. Faſt.
FEUILLERADE Peter, R. of Bygrave, Herts.
   Gal. v. 6. 4° 1777. The true Nature and Neceſſity of Faith.
FIDDES Rich. DD. Chapl. to Earl of Oxon. R. of Halſham, Yorkſ.
   52 Practical Diſc. in fo. 1728. *Bod. Ch. Ch. All S. Univ. Mert. Queen's. Magd. St. John's. Bal. Or. Worc. Ox. Pub. L. Trin. C.*
   Exod. xx 1 &c. On the Decalogue, Body of Divinity. fo. 1720. p. 232. &c. Vol. 2. *Ch. Ch. All S. Univ. Queen's. Mert. Worc. Bal.* Oxon. *King's.* Camb. *Sion.*
   Matt. v. 6, 7. On the Serm. on the Mount, Body of Div. fo. 1720. Vol. 2. p. 290. &c. *Bod. Ch. Ch. All S. Univ. Mert. Queen's. Magd. St. John's. Bal. Or. Worc.* Oxon. *Pub. L. Trin.* Camb.
FINA Ferdinand
   Pſ. cxxxix. 7-10. 4° 1704. b. Spaniſh Merchants. On the late Storm. *Pub. L.* Camb. *Sion.*
FINCH Henry, Hon. M. A. Dean of York.
   Epheſ. ii. 18. 4° 1712. b. Queen. Eaſter-day. *Linc. Worc.* Oxon. *Pub. L. Trin.* Camb.
FINCH Robert Pool, DD. R. of St. Michael Cornhill, London.
   Pſ. cxxiv. 1-3. 8° 1746. Th. for Victory at Culloden.
   Jon. iii. 10. 4° 1747. Faſt. The Nat. and Uſe of national Repent.
   Iſai. xxv. 9. 4° 1749. Th. for Peace. April 25.
   * Acts iv. 35. 4° 1768. b. Sons of Clergy. *Broz. N.* Oxon.
   * Mark x. 14. 4° 1774. Ann. meet. Char. Schools. *Worc.* Oxon.
   * Matt. xxiii. 37, 38. 4° 1777. Faſt.
   * Hoſea xiii. 9. 10. 4° 1779. Faſt.
FINCH Will. Lepold, Hon. DD. Warden of All Souls Coll. Oxon. and Preb. of Canterbury.
   Iſai. i. 26. 4° 1704. May 29. b. Commons. *Bod. Ch. Ch. C. C. C. Worc. Jeſ.* Oxon. *St. John's.* Camb.
FINGLASS John, DD. Preb. of St. Audoens, Dublin.
   Iſai. xl. 6-8. 4° 1695. Roy. Fun.
   Iſai. xliii. 2. 4° 1695. b. Trin. Bethren at Deptford.
FINLEY Sam. DD. Preſid. of the Coll. at Princeton, New Jerſey.
   *Rom. xiv. 7. 8° 1761. Fun. of Rev. *Sam. Davies*, late Preſident.

FINNEY John, DD.
　Ifai. v. 30　4° 1746. On the Invafion.
FIREBRACE John, B. A. of Peter-Houfe Camb. and Cur. of Thornham, Lancafterf.
　Matt. x. 16. 8° 1767. Vif. The clerical Character confidered with refpect to times of Improvement.
·FISH Henry, M. A. V. of Middleton, Norfolk.
　*Prov. x. 27. 8° 1737. ·Period of Hum. Life not unalterably fixed.
FISHER John, B. A.
　Pf. xxx. 5. 8° 1723.
　Pf. cxxvii. 1. 8° 1725.
FISHER John, M. A. V. of St. Lawrence, Exon.
　15 Serm. in 8° 1741. On fev. Subjects. *Sherborne.*
FISHER John, M. A. V. of St. John's, Peterborough.
　*　-　-　-　-　4° 1753. Affize.
FISHER Jofeph, M. A. Fell. of Queen's Coll. Oxon.
　Heb. xiii. 14. 4° 1695. Wedd. f. The Honour of Marriage. *Ch. Ch. All S. Trin. Queen's. St. John's.* Camb. *Sion.*
FISHER John, Bp. of Rochefter.
　*John xi. 21. 8° 1708. Fun. of Margaret Countefs of Richmond. *Bod. Ch. Ch.* Oxon.
　*Sermons in 8° 1711.
FISHER *William*
　* Pf. xxi. 11. 8° 1716. Th. f.
FITZWILLIAM John, DD. Chaplain to his Royal Highnefs, and Canon of Windfor.
　Prov. xxiv. 21, 22. 4° 1683. Th. for delivering the King from the late treafonable Confpiracy. *Pub. L. St. John's.* Camb.
　* Ifai. xxxviii. 1. 12° 1696. 6. Sermons. *Magd.* Oxon.
FLAVEL *John,* Minifter of Dartmouth, Devon.
　* His Works in 2 Vol. fo. 1673.
FLEETWOOD William, Bp. of Ely.
　Prov. vi. 10, 11.　17　-　-　-　-
　* Phil i. 27. 8° 17
　* 2 Cor. ix. 20. 4° 17　Prop. Gofpel.
　*Acts xxii. 20. 8° 17
　Tit iii. 10. 8° 1710. Jan. 30.
　Serm. &c. fo. 1737. *Ch. Co. Mert. New C. St. John's. Wadh.* Ox. *Pub L. Cl. H. King's. Trin. Queen's.* Camb. *Dr. W's. L.* Lond.
　N. B. Serm on relative Duties. *Univ.* Oxon. *Pub. L.* Camb.
　Occafional Sermons. *Brit. M.*
FLEMING *Caleb,* DD. Minifter at Pinner's Hall, London.
　* Acts xi. 23, 24. 1° 1753. Fun. of *J. Fofter,* DD. *Brit. M.*
　* Tit. ii. 15　8° 1759. St. Paul's Orthodoxy. *Queen's.* Camb.
　* Matt. xxiii. 8–10. 8° 1760. The Equality of Chriftians in the Province of Religion &c. *Queen's.* Camb.
　* Mark ii. 27, 28. 8° 1771. On the Reaf. and End of Chriftian Sabbath. *Queen's.* Camb.
　* 1 Pet. iii. 15. 8° 1771. Reaf. and End of Xn. Bapt. *Queen's.* C.
　　　　　　　　　　　　　　　　　　　　　* 1 Cor.

 * 1 Cor. xi. 26. 8° 1771. Reaſ. and End of Lord's Supper. Queen's. Camb.
 * Diſcourſes in 8° 1772. On 3 eſſential Properties of the Goſpel Revelation. Queen's. Camb. Dr. W's. L. London.
 * A Supplimental Liſc. on Iſai. 7, 13, 14. On the ſupernatural Conception of Jeſus Chriſt. Queen's. Camb.
 *   - - - - 8° 1775. Ingratitude of Infidelity.
 *   - - - - 1778. 2 Diſcourſes.

FLEMING Robert,[a]
 Eccleſ. vii 1. 8° 169-. Fun. of Mrs. Suſ. Soame. Bod

FLEMING Robert, a V. D. M.
 * Jer. xviii. 7-11. 12° 1692. Ref. Manners. Θεοκρατικ.
 * Diſc. in 8° 1701.
 Job xiv. 14. 8° 1704. Fun.   Eton.

FLETCHER E.
 *   - - - 1742. Fun.

FLETCHER Philip, Dean of Kildare, Ireland.
 * Pſ. lxxii. 3. 4° 1759. Iriſh Prot. Schools. All S. Worc. Oxon. Queen's Camb.
 * Joſhua xxiv. 13, 14. 4° 1763. Iriſh Prot. work School.

FLETCHER Thomas, Bp. of Kildare.
 Prov xiii 23. 4° 1745. Dublin. Iriſh Prot. Schools. All S. Worc. Oxon. Queen's. Camb.

FLETCHER William, Ll D. Dean of Killaloe, Ireland.
 * 20 Sermons in 8° 1772. Dublin.

FLEXMAN R. DD, Miniſter at the old Jewry, London.
 * Rev ii. 10 8° 1774. Fun. of T. Amory, DD. Queen's. Camb.

FLOWER Chriſtopher, M. A. R. of St. Margaret Lothbury, Lond.
 John xviii. 40. 4° 1666. Jan. 30.
 Mal. iv. 5. 4° 1669. Faſt. Fire of London.
 * John xix 42. 4° 1666.

FLOWER John, M. A.
 Matt iv. 9. 4° 1669.

FLOWER Thomas
 * 13 Serm. 8° 17 Union betwixt Chriſt and Believers.
 * Prov. xvi 31. 8° 1754. Fun.

FLUDGER John, M. A. Miniſter at Putney, Surrey, Chapl. to his Grace the Duke of St. Albans, and late Fell. of Pemb. Coll. Oxon.
 * Iſai. xxvi. 9. 4° 1755. Faſt. Earthquake.

FOLEY Samuel, Bp of Down and Connor.
 1 Tim. iii. 1. 4° 1683. Conſ. of 3 Bps. Magd. Oxon.
 1 Tim iv 16. 4° 1683. Viſ. Magd. Oxon.

FOORD Joſeph, Preacher of the Goſpel at Edinburgh.
 19 Sermons in 8° 1719. Edinburgh.

FORD John
 * Gen. ii. 18. 8° 1735. 2 ſ. Wed. ſ. V. Diſc. on Conj. D. v. 1.

[a] Q. The ſame.

FORD

FORD Randolph, B. A. P. Cur. and Lecturer of St. Mary-le-bow, Middlesex.
  Luke xix. 8. 4° 1711.
  Matt. xxi. 38, 39. 8° 1713. Jan. 30.
  Pf. cxxxiii. 1. 8° 1715. Th. Sund. after King George 1st. came.
  1 Cor. xiii. 6. 4° 1716. Th. f.
  Matt. hi. 9, 10. 4° 1721. Faft. ag. Plague.
FORD Thomas, LLD. V. of Melton Mowbray, Leicester, and late Stud. of Ch. Ch. Oxon.
  * 1 Cor. ix 16. 8° 1775. Vif.
FORD Simon, DD. R. of Old Swinford, Worc. and Chap. in Ord.
  2 Sam. xix. 30. 4° 1661. Th for the Exiles Reftoration. Ch. Ch. Worc. Oxon. Pub. L. Camb.
  2 Sam. i. 14. 4° 1661. Jan. 30. The loyal Subject's Indignation for his royal Sovereign's Decollation. Magd. Oxon.
  * Prov. xxii. 6. 4° 16
  Pf. lxxv. 4–7. 16 Aflize. Ch. Ch. Oxon.
  Pf. cvii. 24. 4° 1665. Oxon. The Lord's Wonders in the Deep. Bod. Magd. Ch. Ch. Or. Oxon.
  Acts xxi. 14. 8° 1665. Fun. of Right Hon. Elizabeth Langham. C. C. C. Oxon.
  Acts xx. 35. 8° 1674. Char. f. C. C. C. Oxon.
  Pf. ix. 16. 8° 1678. Of God's Judgments. Bod. Ch. Ch. Ox. Sion.
  1 Cor. xv. 29. 4° 1692. b. Ld May. Baptifm for the dead. Bod.
  Gal. vi. i, 2. 4° 1696. 2 f. On a public Penance. Ch. Ch. Oxon. Trin. Camb.
FORD Stephen
  John iii. 3. 8° 1675. Of Regeneration. Bod.
FORD William, fen.
  * 1 Cor. xv. 55–57. 8° 1733. Fun. of Tim. Shepherd. Pub. L. C.
  * Tim. iv. 14. 8° 1735. Ord. of John Notcutt.
  * —— ii. 12. 8° 1757. Ord.
  * —— i. 11, 12. 8° 1758. Ord.
FORD William, jun.
  * - - - - - 1769. The religious Care of Families.
  * Gen. xviii. 19. 8° 1770.
  ‡ * Pf. lxxiii. 24. 8° 1781. Fun. of Elizabeth Ford. Brit. M.
FORDYCE James, DD.
  * Acts xviii. 24. 1752. Eloquence of the Pulpit.
  * Rev. xviii. 23, 24. 8° 1754. V. Prot. Syftem. V. 1.
  * 1 Cor. xiv. 26. 12° 1755. Ord. The methods of promoting Edification by public Inftitutions.
  * Ecclef. xi. 1. 4° 1757. Fun.
  * Rev. xiv. 6. 8° 1760. Fun. of Rev. Dr. S. Lawrence.
  * Prov. vii. 6, 7. 12° 1775. V. Scotch Pr. V. 1. p 313. The Folly, Infamy and Mifery of unlawful Pleafures. Braz. N. Ox.
  * Sermons in 2 Vol. 12° 1767. To Young Women. Braz. N. Oxon. Queen's. Camb. Sion.

* John

* John xi. 5. 8° 1776. 3 pts. Character of the Fem. Sex, and the Advantages to be derived from the Company of virtuous Women. *Sion.*
* - - - - 1779. Faſt.

FORENESS E. Preſbyter of the Church of England.
Rom. xiii. 2. 4° 1683. Th. Sep. 9.
Acts xiii. 36. 4° 1604. Fun. of Sir Robert Leiceſter. *Sion.*

FORESTER Thomas, M. A. R. of Timpton, Somerſetſhire.
Ezra vii. 25, 26. 4° 1741. Acceſſ. b. Lord Mayor.

FORSTER John, M. A. R. of Beer-Crocombe, Somerſetſhire.
Luke xiv. 23. 4° 1746. A free Proteſtant People, and a Popiſh Prince incompatible.

FORSTER John, M. A. R. of Elton, Huntingdon.
* 1 Tim. ii 2. 8° 1755. 2 f. Aſſize.
* Rom. xiii. 8. 8° 1757. Aſſize.
* Rom. xiii. 5. 8° 1764. Religion and Loyalty inſeparable.

FORSTER Nathaniel, DD. Fell. of C. C. C. Oxon.
Mark vii. 13. 8° 1746. *Oxon.* Nov. 5. Popery deſtructive of the Evidence of Mirlc. All S. C. C. C. *Were.* Ox. *Queen's.* Camb.

FORSTER Nathaniel, DD. R of All Saints Colcheſter, and Chapl. to the Counteſs Dowager of Northington.
* John x. 25. 8° 1767. Evidence from Miracles ſtated and vindicated. *Queen's.* Camb.
* 1 Cor. xiv. 33. 4° 1770. Viſ. The Eſtabliſhment of the Ch. of England defended upon the Principles of relig. Liberty.
* 2 Cor. xiii. 14. 4° 1780. Trin. S. Grace without Enthuſiaſm.
* Heb. xii. 6. 4° 1781. Faſt. Evil providentially good.

FORSTER Nicholas, Ep. of Killaloe.
1 Cor. i. 10. 4° 1716. *Dublin.* Unanimity in the preſent time of Danger recommended. St. *John's.* Camb.
* 1 Tim. ii. 1, 2. 8° 1715. Acceſſion. *Queen's.* Camb.

FORSTER Richard, M. A. R. of Beckley, Suſſex.
Prov. xvii. 26. 4° 1684. Aſſize. Prerogative and Privilege.

FORSTER Thomas
* Judges xii. 23, 34. 8° 1715. Acceſſion.
* 1 Sam. xii. 23, 24. 8° 1715. Acceſſion.
* Rev. xiv. 13. 8° 1718. Fun. of Rev. *Mr. Miller.*

FORSTER Thomas, R. of Haleſworth, Suffolk.
* 1 John iii. 7. 8° 1759. The Neceſſity of actual Holineſs, as well from the Light of Nature as from Scripture.

FORSTER William, R. of St. Clement's Dane, London.
Luke xiv. 21-23. 8° 1714. Prop. Goſp. *Ch. Ch.* Ox. *Queen's.* C.
Heb xii 11. 8° 1714. Royal Fun. *Queen's.* Camb.

FORSTER William, M. A. V. of Heighington.
* - - - - 1755. Aſſize.

FOSS John, M. A. R. of Caſtleford, Yorkſhire.
Matt. vii. 12. 8° 1735. Aſſize.

FOSTER Henry, M. A.
* Acts ix. 11. 8° 1777. Grace Diſplayed and Saul converted. At Newgate Chapel. FOSTER

FOSTER *James*, DD. Minister at Pinner's hall, London.
 Sermons on sev. Subjects. 8° V. 1. 1732. V. 2. 1737. V. 3. V. 4. 1744. Bod. Worc. Wadh. Oxon. Queen's. Trin. Camb. Sion. Dr. W's. L. London.
 Eccles. vii. 2. 8° 1732. On the Death of Mrs. *Mary Wilks*. Bod. Queen's. Camb.
 Heb. vi. 12. 8° 1741. Fun. of *Mr. Emlyn*. Bod. Trin. Queen's. C.
 * Isai. xl. 6. 8° 1742. Fun.
FORT Francis, M. A. Fell. of Sidney Coll. Camb.
 * Acts xxii. 3. 8° 1753. Sch. Feast. *Tiverton*, Devon.
FORTESCUE John
 * Ps. xviii. 47–49. 8° 1760. Th. s.
FOTHERGILL Geo. DD. late Principal of Edmund-Hall. Oxon.
 * Sermons in 2 Vol. 8° 1765. *Oxon*. On sev. Subjects and Occasions. Bod. Queen's. New. C. Worc. Oxon.
FOTHERGILL Thomas, DD. Provost of Queen's Coll. Oxon. and Preb. of Durham.
 Nahum. i. 15. 8° 1749. *Oxon*. Th. for Peace. The Desireableness of Peace and the Duty of a Nation upon the Recovery of it. Worc. Oxon.
 * 2 Chron. xxxv. 25. 8° 1753. *Oxon*. Jan. 30.
 * ———— xiii. 18. Fast. *Oxon*. Qualifications and Advantages of religious Trust in times of Danger. Worc. Oxon.
 * Daniel xii. 10. 8° 1762. Act. *Oxon*. Religion and Learning capable of being rendered mutually serviceable, or prejudicial to one another.
FOULKES Peter, DD. Canon of Ch. Ch. Oxon.
 Tim iii. 1. 4° 1723. *Exon*. Jan. 30.
FOUNTAYNE John, DD. Dean of York.
 * Isai. xxvi. 4, 5. 8° 1756. Fast.
FOURESTIER Paul, of Canterbury.
 * Matt. xxiv. 6. 8° 1758. Lawfulness of just Wars.
FOWLER *Christopher*
 1 Thess. v. 27. 4° 1675. m. e. P. p. 105. The Scriptures to be read by the common People.
FOWLER Edward, Bp. of Gloucester.
 1 Pet. i. 8. 4° 1674. s. m. e. p. 497. *Bod*.
 1 Tim. i. 19. 4° 1681. Ass. All S. C. C. C. Oxon. Pub. L. Trin. St. John's. Camb. Brit. M.
 Matt. xviii. 7. 4° 1683. 2 s. Of Offences. Bod. Ch. Ch. All S. C. C. C. Oxon. Pub. L. Camb. Sion.
 1 Pet. ii. 17. 4° 1685. County Feast. Bod. Ch. Ch. CCC. Oxon. Pub. L. Camb.
 Ps. ci. 5. 4° 1685. Of Slandering. All S. C. C. C. Oxon. Pub. L. Camb. Sion.
 Luke xvi 9. 4° 1688. Spittal W. Bod. Ch. Ch. C. C. C. Oxon. Pub. L. Camb.
 Hosea xi. 8. 4° 1690. Fast. b. Lord Mayor. Bod. All S. Univ. Ch. Ch. Jes. Oxon. Pub. L. Camb.

James

James ii. 10. 4° 1691. b. Queen. *Bod. Ch. Ch.* Oxon. *Pub. L.* Camb. *Sion.*
John xiii 34. 4° 1692. b. Sons of the Clergy. *Bod. Wadh.* Oxon.
1 Cor. vi 14. 4° 1692. Spitt. M. *Magd.* Oxon. *Sion.*
* - - - - 1695. *Camb.* On the Death of Queen Mary.
Pſ. lxxxvi. 12, 13. 4° 1696. Th. b. Lords. For the Diſcovery of a Deſign to aſſaſſinate the King.
Epheſ. vi. 7, 8. 4° 1699. Ref. Manners. *Ch. Ch.* Oxon.
Pſ. xcviii. 1. 4° 1704. Th. after Victory. At Guildhall. *Ch. Ch.* Oxon. *Trin. Queen's.* Camb.
John xvi. 28. 8° 1706. Of the Deſcent of the Man Jeſus Chriſt &c. *St. Paul's.*
Job xxii 25. 8° 1707. On God's Providence.
Job ii. 10. 8° 1707. The great Diſingenuity and Unreaſonableneſs of repining at afflicting Providences &c. *Trin.* Camb.
Pſ cvii. 8. or 10. 8° 1707. Th. The great Duty of Praiſe and Thankſgiving.

FOWLER Matthew, DD. R. of Whitchurch, Salop and Preb. of Litchfield.
Prov. xxiv. 21. 4° 1662.
James iii. 17. 4° 1682. Aſſize. *Trin.* Camb.

FOWLER DD.
* Luke xxii. 19. 4° 1699. Ag. Tranſubſtantiation. Soon after his admiſſion into the Communion of the Church of England.

FOWLER Thomas
* - - - - - 1754. Fun.

FOWNS Richard
2 Theſſ. ii. 3, 4. 1660. Ch. Conc. Lat.

FOWNES Joſeph
* 1 Chron. xxix 26–28. 8° 1760. Faſt. The Connection between the Honour of Princes, and the Happineſs of their People.

FOX Francis, M. A. Surmaſter of St. Paul's School, London.
Exod. xx. 12. 4° 1683. Co. Feaſt. *Bod. Pub. L.* Camb.

FOX Francis, M. A. V. of Potterne, Wilts.
Pſ. xcvii. 1. 4° 1705. May 29 b. Lord Mayor. The Superintendency of divine Providence over human Affairs.
Matt. v. 33–37. 8° 1710. Aſſize. *Bod. Pub.* Camb.
Num xxiii. 23. 8° 1715. 2 ſ. Nov. 5.
Matt. xxiii. 23. 8° 1727. Aſſize.

FOX Joſeph, M. A. V. of St. Michael's, Coventry.
Job. xix. 25–27. 4° 1702. Fun. of Lady Mary Bridgman.

FOXCROFT John, M. A. R. of Widforby, Leiceſterſ.
Acts xxvi. 28, 29. 8° 1695. Sev. ſerm. The altogether Chriſtian's Duty &c.
Prov. xix. 14. 12° 1697. Character and Bleſſing of a prudent and virtuous Wife.
Rom. xiii. 4. 4° 1697. Aſſize.

FOXCROFT Thomas
* Pſ. xcv. 4, 7, 8. 8° 1727 *Boſton.* New Eng. af. an Earthquake.

FOXLEY Thomas, M. A. R. of St. Mary's, Manchester.
* Gen. iv. 26. 8° 1755. Conf. of a Church at Manchester.
FRAMPTON Matt. LLD. ·R. of Bremhill, V. of Westport, Wilts, and Chapl. to the Earl of Berks, and Suffolk.
* 2 Pet. iii. 18. 4° 1769. Act. *Oxon.* Grow in Grace. *Worc.* Ox.
* Pf. lv. 15. 4° 1776. An. Co. meeting.
FRAMPTON Th.
Pf. cxvi. 11–13. 8° 1712. On the Removal of the Small-pox.
FRANCIS John,[a] LLD. Min. of St. Peter's and St. John's, Norw.
Luke xix. 27. 4° 1746. His Majesty's Justice and Clemency vindicated.
FRANCIS John,[a] LLD. R. of Morley, Norfolk.
* Sermons in 2 Vol. 12° 1773.
FRANCIS John, M. A. V. of Lekeham near Norwich.
* Rev. xiv. 13. 8° 1764. Fun. of Rev. B. Froit.
* Prov. xiv. 34. 8° 1766. Religion the truest and best Bulwark of a Nation.
* 1 Theff. iv. 11. 8° 1767. Christians should be quiet &c.
* Rom. xiii. 3. 8° 1770. 3 Assize f. A proper and due Subjection to authority enforced.
FRANCIS   late V. of little Brickhill, Bucks.
* 10 Sermons in 12° 1771. *Queen's.* Camb.
FRANCKEL Hirschel David, at Berlin.
* Pf. xxii. 23, 24. 8° 1757. Th. Translation.
FRANK Augustus Hermannus
Matt. vi. 25–33. 8° 1708. Faith in Christ inconsistent with a solicitous Concern about the things of this World.
* Sermons in 12° 1716.
* John xi. 25. 8° 1731. Easter f.
FRANK John, of Bath.
* Rev. xiv. 13. 8° 1756. Fun. f.
FRANK Le, B. D. Minister of the French Church.
* Discourses in 2 Vol. 12° 1662. The Church of England vindicated from the Errors and Superstitions of Rome.
FRANK Mark, DD. Master of Pemb. Hall. Camb. and Arch-D. of St. Albans.
A Course of 51 Serm. fo. 1672. and one at St. Paul's-Cross in 1641. *Bod. Pemb.* Oxon. *Sion.*
FRANKLIN Thomas, R. of Langton Herring, Dorsetshire.
* Acts xxix. 1, 2, 10. 8° 1756. On Shipwrecks.
FRANKLIN Thomas, DD. late Fell. of Trin. Coll. and Greek-Professor Camb. R. of Brasted, Kent, and Chaplain in Ord.
Eccles[us]. vii. 34. 4° 1748. On the Fire in Cornhill, Lond.
Gal. vi. 9. 4° 1750. Col. Georgia. *Brit. M.*
* 2 Sam xii. 23. 8° 1756. Fun. of Rev. Mr. Sturges.
* Jonah iii. 7, 8. 4° 1758. Faft.

a *Q.* The same.

* Luke

OF AUTHORS, &c. 131

  * Luke x. 37. 4° 1758. b. Gov. of Middlef. Hofp.
  * 2 Chron. xxxii. 33. 4° 1760. Death of K. George 2d.
  * Jer. xlix. 11. 4° 1763. b. Sons of the Clergy.
  * Serm. in 8° 1765. On the Relative Duties. *All S*. Oxon.
  * Hofea xiv. 3. 4° 1768. b. Gov. of the Afylum.
  * Mark x 14. 4° 1774. b. Gov. of Difpenf. for Infant poor.
  * Matt. xviii. 32, 33. 4° 1774. Benefit of fmall Debtors.
FRANKLYN Francis, M. A. Prieft Vicar of St. Andrew, Wells, Somerfet.
  Rom. xiii. 8. 8° 1724. At a Quarter feffions. The perpetual Debt, and mutual obligation of mutual Love.
FREE John, DD. formerly Chaplain of Ch. Ch. Oxon. and V. of Runcorn, Chefhire.
  12 Serm. in 8° 1750. Preached before the Univerfity.
  * Pf. liii. ii. 8° 1739. Act. f.
  * Exod. xxxiv. 14. 8° 1753. Jan. 30.
  * Jerem. ii. 18. } 8° 1753.
  * 1 Pet. iii. 8. } 8° 1756. } b. Antigallicans.
  * 1 John iv. 1. 8° 1758. Whitfunday. b. Univerfity.
  * Gen. i. 2. 8° 1764. b. Soc of Florifts. *Braz. N.* Oxon.
  * ——— 26. 8° 1764. The Analyfis of Man *Braz. N.* Oxon.
  * 1 Cor. ix 13, 14. 4° 1765. Poetical f. The voluntary Exile.
  * Levit. xxiv. 21. 8° 1768. On the Murder of Mr. Allen, jun.
  * Gen. xiv. 14. 8° 1769. Anniv. f. On the fame Occafion. *Dr. W's. L.* London.
FREEMAN *Francis*
  Luke xii. 15. { 8° 1722. }
  ——— xiv. 14. {   2 f. } Ag. Covetoufnefs. Fun.
FREEMAN Samuel, DD. R. of St. Paul's Cov. Garden Lond, and Dean of Peterborough.
  John i. 47. 4° 1681. Fun.   The Ifraelite indeed. *Sion. Trin.* Camb.
  1 Theff. iv. 14. 4° 1682. Fun. of Sir Tho. Bludworth. *Bod. All S. C. C. C.* Oxon. *Pub. L.* Camb. *Brit. M.*
  Pf. xxxiv. 12–14. 4° 1682. b. Lord Mayor.
  Pf. lxxxii. 6. 4° 1690. Affize. *Bod. All S. Or. Jef.* Oxon. *Pub. L. Trin. Cl. H.* Camb. *Sion.*
  Pf. lxxxix. 21, 22. 4° 1690. Nov. 5. b. Commons. *Bod. All S. Ch Ch.* Oxon. *Pub. L. Cl. H.* Camb. *Sion.*
  1 John v. 4. 3° 1643. b. Queen. *Ch. Ch. Oriel.* Oxon. *Pub. L. Trin.* Camb. *Sion.*
  Matt. xxv. 46. 4° 1694. Spittal T. *Ch. Ch. Magd.* Oxon. *Trin.* Camb. *Sion.*
  1 Cor. xv. 58. 4° 1698. Spittal   *Ch. Ch.* Oxon.
  ——— ix. 25. 4° 1700. Fun. of Duke of Bedford. *Ch. Ch.* Oxon. *Cl. H.* Camb. *Sion.*
FREEMAN William. B. A. Lect. of St. Botolph's, Aldergate.
  1 Tim. ii. 1, 2. 4° 1730. Acceff. b. Lord Mayor.

FREKE Thomas
  ‡ * Jonah i. 16. 4° 1704. Faſt. *Brit. M.*
  ‡ * John v. 40. 8° 1715. Liberty of Will.
  * Rom. xiv. 17. 12° 1704. Ref. Manners.
  * Pſ. cxxii. 9. 8° 1713.
  * Job xxiv. 13. 8° 1716. 15 Diſc. Ignorance of God.
  * Matt. i. 21. 8° 1716.
FRIEND Robert, DD. R. of Whitney, and Can. of Ch. Ch. Oxon.
  Jer. iii. 25. 4° 1711. Jan. 30. b. Commons. *Ch. Ch. Univ. Magd. Linc.* Oxon. *Queen's. St. John's.* Camb. *Sion.*
FRIEND William, DD. Preb. of Weſtminſter.
  * 1 Pet. ii. 16. 4° 1755. Jan. 30. b. Commons. *Braz. N.* Oxon.
  * Gal. v. 1. 4° 1761. Conc. ad Cler. *Queen's.* Camb.
FROST B. M. A. Cur. of Glamsforth, Suffolk.
  Eccleſ. v. 5. 8° 1741. 2 ſ. Office of Godfathers and Godmothers.
FROST *Richard*, of great Yarmouth, Norfolk.
  Ruth. ii. 4° 1729. *Norwich.* Harveſt ſ.
  * Prov. xxiii. 29—25. 8° 1729. Danger and Folly of Drunkenneſs. *Queen's.* Camb.
  Levit. xix. 16. 8° 17   Againſt Talebearing.
  * 2 Cor. ii. 16. 8° 1745. Ord.
  * Rev. ii. 1. 8° 1752. Fun. of *P. Dodderidge*, DD.
FROYSELL *Thomas*, Miniſter at Clunne, Salop.
  * Serm. in 8° 1678. Concerning Grace and Temptations. *Bod. Sion.*
FRY *Samuel*
  * - - - - 1755.
  * 1 Pet. iv. 18. 8° 1759. Fun.
FULHAM John, M. A. Chaplain to the Houſe of Commons, and Canon or Windſor.
  Deut. ix. 6. 8° 1749. May 29. b. Commons.
FULLER Francis
  1 Cor. vii. 29. 12° 1700. Shortneſs of Time.
FULLER Ignatius, of Sherrington, Bucks.
  Mark ix. 50. Viſ. ſ. 8° 1672. p. 1. *Bod. Queen's. Pemb.* Oxon.
  1 Tim. vi. 3—5. 8° 1672. To a great preſence. p. 47. *Bod. Queen's. Pemb.* Oxon.
  Rom. viii. 2. Fun. of Mrs. Anne Norton. *Bod. Queen's. Pem.* Ox.
FULLER John, M. A.
  Acts v. 38. 4° 1681. Faſt. Seaſonable Advice in trying Times.
FULLER Samuel, DD. Dean. of Linc. and Chaplain in Ord.
  Matt. vi. 23. 4° 1682. At Court. *Ch. Ch. Magd.* Oxon.
  —— xxii. 21, 22. 4° 1682. b. King. June 25. *Magd. Ch. Ch.* Oxon. *Trin. St. John's.* Camb. *Sion.*
FULLER Thomas, DD. R. of Biſhop's Hatfield, Herts.
  Phil i. 27, 28. 4° 1703. Viſ. *Ch. Ch. All S.* Ox. *St. John's.* Cam.
FULLWOOD Francis, DD. Arch-Deacon of Totnes, and Canon of Exon, Devon.
  Heb. xii. 23. 4° 1667. Neceſſity of receiving the Communion &c. *Bod. Ch. Ch.* Oxon.   1 Cor.

1 Cor. xi. 22. 4° 1672. Aſſize. The Neceſſity of keeping our Churches. *Univ. Queen's. Magd. Worc.* Oxon.

FULLWOOD Peter, M. A. R. of South Normanton, Derbyſhire.
Prov. xiv. 34. 8° 1673. Conc. ad Magiſt. A Nation's Honour, and Diſhonour. p. 1.
1 Tim. v. 17. 8° 1673. Conc. ad Cler. Viſ. The Miniſter's Duty and Due. p. 19.
Col. i. 10. 8° 1673. Conc. ad Plebem. The Xn's Guide. p. 35.

FURLY Samuel, B. A. of Queen's Coll. Camb.
* John vii. 17. 4° 1779. Viſ. at *Truro*, Cornwal.

FURNEaUX *Philip*, DD. of Clapham, Surry.
* Prov. xxii 26 8° 1755. An. meet. Char. Sch. *Queen's.* Camb.
* Iſai xlix. 4, 5. 8° 1758. Faſt.
* 2 Tim. iv. 7, 8. 8° 1763. Fun. of *Henry Miles*, DD. *Queen's.* C.
* 1 Cor iv. 1. 8° 1766. Ord.
* John vii 46. 8° 1769. Ord. Character of Jeſ. Chriſt as a public Speaker conſidered. *Queen's.* Camb.
* Rom 14. 7. 8° 1755. Char. Sch. meeting.

FURSMAN John, M. A. R. of Trevalga, Cornwal.
* Matt. v. 33. 34. 8° 1715. Aſſize. *Eton.*

FYLER Samuel, M. A. R. of Stockton, Wilts.
Matt. vi 9. 4° 1680. Viſ. *Pub. L.* Camb.

FYSH Henry, M. A. V. of Middleton, Norfolk.
Prov. x. 27. 8° 1738. Period of human Life. *Queen's.* Camb.

FYSH Thomas, M. A.
Zech. xii. 8. 4° 1685. May 29. *St. John's.* Camb. *Sion.*

FYSON Tho. M. A. Chaplain to the Earl of Uxbridge and Lect. of St. Bartholomew, near the Royal Exchange, London.
1 Cor xv. 58. 8° 1715. Farew. ſ.

GAIRDEN George, DD.
Phil. i. 21. 8° 1726. Fun. of Dr. Scougal. V. his works. p. 395.

G. S.
1 Tim. iii. 16. 8° 1730. On the Trinity. Chriſtmas.

GALE *John*, D.P.
Serm. in 4 Vol. 8° 1726. Preached upon ſev. Occaſions.

GALE *Theophilus*, M. A. Fell. of Magd. Coll. Oxon.
* Luke xix. 41. 8° 1672. Anatomy of Infidelity.
1 John ii. 15. 4° 1676. ſ. m. e. C. p. 64. Wherein the Love of God is inconſiſtent with the Love of the World.

GALE Thomas, DD. Dean of York.
Serm. in 8° 1704. Preached on ſev. Holy-days. *Pub. L. C. Sion.*

GALLAWAY Cole, John, V. of Hinkley, Leiceſter.
* 1 Tim. i. 9. 8° 1779. Aſſize. Chriſtianity, the true Foundation of civil Liberty.

GALLAWAY Will. M. A. Chaplain to the Train of Artillery, and Preb. of Worc.
Deut. xx. 3, 4. 4° 1692.
Iſai. xiv. 16–18. 4° 1697. Th.

GALLIMORE Francis, M. A. Chapl. to the Earl of Scarſdale.
  Eccleſ. xii. 1. 4° 1694. The Happineſs of ſuch as mind their Creator betimes.
GALLY Henry, DD. R. of St. Giles's in the Fields, and Chaplain in Ord.
  Job v. 7. 8° 1723. 2 ſ. On the Miſery of Man.
  1 Tim. ii 1, 2. 4° 1739. Acceſſ. b. Commons.
GALPINE Calvin, B. A. R. of Port-royal in Jamaica.
  * Matt. vii. 1 8° 1721.
  Pſ. lxxxii. 6, 7. 4° 1722. *Jamaica.*
[GALPINE John]
  * Zech. iv. 6. 12° 1703. Ref. Manners.
  * 1 Pet. i. 3, 4. 8° 1703. Fun.
GAMBOLD John, M. A. V. of Stanton-Harcourt, Oxon.
  Luke ii. 10. 8° :741. *Oxon.* Xnity, Tidings of Joy. *Worc. Ox.*
  * Pſ. cxiv. 7. 8° 1756. Faſt. Earthquake. The Reaſonableneſs and Extent of religious Reverence.
GANE John, M. A. V. of Winterbourn, White Church, and Turnworth, Dorſet.
  Gal. v. 15. 8° 1728. Aſſize.
GARBUTT Richard, B. D. Fell. of Sidney-Coll. Camb.
  1 Cor. xv. 20. 12° 1699. A Demonſtration of the Reſurrection. p. 1. *St. Paul's,* London.
  Num. xxvi. 10. 12° 1669. A Perſervative ag. Judgments. p. 169. *St. Paul's,* London.
  1 Sam. i. 16. 8° 1675. A ſober Teſtimony ag. Drunkards and Whoremongers. *Bod.*
GARDINER James, Bp. of Lincoln.
  Pſ. lxxiv. 9. 4° 1695. Faſt. b. Lords. *Magd. Ox. Queen's. Trin. Camb. Sion.*
  Acts x. 31. 4° 1701. Spittal. *C. C. C. Oxon.*
GARDINER James, M. A. R. of St. Michael Crooked Lane, Lond.
  2 Tim. iii. 1. and 4. 4° 1696. Th. April 16. *Sion.*
  Zech. xi. 2. 4° 1700. Fun. of Duke of Gloucefter.
  Pſ. lxxvi. 10. 4° 1706. Th. June 27. *Sion.*
  2 Cor. ii. 16. 4° 1713. *Oxon.* Conc. ad Cl. Lond. *Bod. Sion.*
GARDINER James, M. A. Sub-Dean of Lincoln.
  Rom. xiv. 19. 8° 1713. The Duty of Peace &c. *Linc.* Oxon. *St. John's.* Camb.
  A Pract. Expoſition of our Saviour's ſerm. on the Mount. 8° 1720. *Ch. Ch. Hert.* Oxon.
GARDINER John, M. A. V. of Henbury, Gloucefter.
  * Pſ. cxix. 9. 4" 1752. Elect. of Mayor. Religious Zeal.
[GARDINER R.   ]
  * Rom. viii. 11. 8°
  * 1 Tim. ii. 1, 2. 8°
GARDINER Samuel, M. A. Chaplain in Ord.
  2 Cor. v. 20. 4° 1672; Viſ. *C. C. C.* Oxon. *Pub L.* Camb. *Sion.*

GARDINER

GARDINER William, LL.B. V. of Hambleton, Rutlandſ.
  Iſai. vii. 14. ⎫ 8° 17   A literal Expoſition of 2 remarkable
  Deut. xviii. 15. ⎭ Prophecies.
GARDNER William, DD. R. of St. Olave's, Southwark.
  1 Pet. ii. 17. 4° 1726. Aſſize.
  1 Sam. ii. 35. 8° 1745. Act. Oxon. The faithful Paſtor. *All S.*
    Worc. Oxon.
GARMSTON John, M. A. Maſter of the Free-ſchool, Linc. and
    late Fell. of Magd. Coll. Camb.
  * Lam. v. 16. 4° 1712. *Lincoln* Jan. 30. *Queen's.* Camb.
  Luke xiii. 3. 8° 1715. To Priſoners for Debt.
  Phil. i. 21. 8° 17   Fun.
  Pſ. xc. 12. 8° 1717.
  Exod. xx. 5. 8° 1727. On the Juſtice of God in viſiting &c.
    Queen's. Camb.
GARMSTON Shadrach, M.A. V. of Hanſtape, Bucks.
  Pſ. iv. 4. 8° 1716. Th. *Bod.*
  Amos iv. 11. 8° 1716. Nov. 5. *Bod.*
  2 Chron. xxxv. 25. 8° 1724. Jan. 30.
  Eccleſ. viii. 2. 8° 1724.
GARNER *John,* M. D.
  * Iſai. i. 19, 20. 8° 1760. Faſt.
GARNET John, Bp. of Clogher.
  Gal vi. 15. 4° 1740. The new Creation, a State of Proſelytiſm.
    Queen's. Trin. Camb.
  2 Sam. xx. 19. 4° 1741. *Camb.* Aſſize.
  Rom. xii. 11. 4° 1745. *Camb.* Reb. and Commemoration. *Queen's.*
    Camb. *Brit. M.*
  Job i. 5. 4° 1745. Faſt. Jan. 8. p. 313.
  Job xlii. 10. 4° 1748. Whitſunday. May 29. p. 331.
  2 Chron. xxix. 20, 21. 4° 1747-8. Faſt. Feb. 17. p. 347.
  James v. 11. 4° 1744. At Whitehall. Feb. 26. p. 363.
  N. B. Theſe 4 laſt Sermons are added to his Diſſertation on Job.
    4° 1749. *Camb.*
  * Luke xv. 7. 4° 1756. Iriſh Prot. Schools.
[GARTSHERE George]
  * - - - - - 1736.
GASKARTH John, DD. Fell. of Pemb. Hall Camb. and V. of All
    Saints, Barking.
  Pſ. lxxxii. 6, 7. 4° 1683. Fun. of Duke of Lauderdale. *All S.*
    Queen's. Oxon. *Pub. L.* Camb.
  Acts xi. 34. 4° 1685. Viſ. *Ch. Ch. Magd.* Ox. *Pub. L. C. Sion.*
  Rom. viii. 14. 4° 1700. Conc. ad Cl. *Cant.* Enthuſiaſmi Refu-
    tatio. *All S.* Oxon. *Pub. L. Trin. Queen's. St. John's.* Camb.
  Epheſ. ii. 1. 4° 1700. *Camb.* Commenc. A Deſcription of the
    unregenerate and the truly Chriſtian Temper or State. *All S.*
    Oxon. *Trin. Queen's. St. John's.* Camb.
  Iſai. vi. 13. 4° 1705. Open. a Ch. The beautiful Sanctuary. *Sion.*
  Gal. iv. 18. 4° 1713. Ref. Manners. *Pub. L.* Camb.

GASPINE

GASPINE John
* Luke xii. 32. 4° 1663. V. Coll. Farew. f.
GASTRELL Francis, Bp. of Chester.
Heb. xi. 6. 8 Serm. at Boyle's Lect. 8° 1703. or fo. 1739. V. 1.
p. 275 Ch. Ch. C.C.C. Magd. Oxon.
Pf. xlvi. 1–3. 4° 1704. Faft. b. Commons. Ch. Ch. Jef. Oxon. Trin. Camb. Brit. M.
Pf. cxlvii. 12, 13. 4° 1704, Ann. meeting Char. Sch. Bod. Univ. Ch. Ch. All S. C.C.C. Magd. Oriel. Jef. Oxon. Queen's. St. John's. Camb. Sion. Eton.
Rom. xiv. 18. 4° 1712. b. Queen. Univ. C.C.C. Linc. Oxon.
Prov. xxi. 31. 4° 1714. May 29. b. Lords. Ch. Ch. Linc. Oxon. Queen's. Camb.
GATAKER Thomas, B. D.
* Sermons in fo. 1737.
* Prov. xix. 14. } V. Difc. on Conj. Duty. V. 2. p. 499.
* Prov. xviii. 22. }
[GATCHELL Thomas]
Pf. xxi. 1. 4° 1706. Th. f.
GATTON Benjamin, V. of Dinton, Bucks.
John xvi. 2, 3. 4° 1704. Nov. 5. A view of the Cruelty and Ignorance of the Romifh Church.
Rom. xiii. 2. 4° 1710. Nov. 5. Non-refiftance. Bed. Sion.
18 Serm. in 8° 1732. Oxon. On feveral Occafions.
GAUDEN John, Bp. of Worcefter.
Ecclef. vii. 2. 4° 1660. Funerals made Cordials. 8° Bod.
2 Kings ii. 12. 12° 1660. Fun. of Bp. Brownrig. Bod. Univ. St. John's. Oxon. Pub L. Camb.
Jer. viii. 11. 4° 1660. Th. b. Ld Mayor. [Feb. 28. 1659.] Bod. Univ. Worc. Oxon. Sion.
Micah vi. 8. 4° 1660. Faft. b. Commons. Bod. Pub. L. Camb.
Pf. lxxiv. 22. 4° 1661. 2 f. Caufa Dei. Bod. Univ. Oxon.
GAUNT John, M. A. Lect. of St. Martin's, Birmingham, and late of C.C.C. Camb.
* James ii. 24. 8° 1769. Birmingham. 3 f. The Impoffibility of obtaining Salvation by Faith without Obedience.
GEARING William, R. of Chrift Church. Surry.
Job xix. 12. 12° 1667. Faft. for Fire of London.
Matt xi 19. 12° 1668. A Vol.
Ifai. xxiv. 15. 4° 1668. Faft. for Fire of London. Sion.
* Heb. xiii. 14. 16 2 f.
GEE Edward, R. of St. Benedict, Paul's Warf, and Chapl. in Ord.
Ephef. v. 16. 4° 1692. b. Queen. Of the Improvement of time Bod. Univ. Ch. Ch. Jef. Oxon. Sion.
GEORGE William, DD. Provoft of King's Coll. Camb. and Dean of Lincoln.
Pf. xcvii 1. 4° 1732. May 29. b. Commons.
John x. 16. 4° 1749. Prop. Gofpel. All S. Ox. Trin. Queen's. C.
* Deut. xv. 11. 4° 1752. Char. School-meeting. Lincoln.

[GELL

[GELL Robert, DD.]
 * His Remains in 2 Vol. fo. 1676. *King's.* Camb.
GERARD *Alex.* DD. Profeffor of Divinity in King's Coll. Aberdeen.
 * Ezek. xxxvi. 32. 8° 1759. Th. f. *Queen's.* Camb.
 * Tit. i. 7. 8° 1760. b. Synod.
 * Deut. vi. 24. 12° 1776. Influence of Piety on the public Good. V. Scotch Preacher. v. 2. p. 307.
 * 1 Pet. ii. 16. 8° 1778. Faft.
 * 19 Serm. in 8°. 1780. *Bod, Pub, L.* Camb.
GEREE John, M.A. Fell. of C.C.C. Coll. Oxon.
 1 Cor. x. 24. 4° 1706. *Oxon.* Affize. The Excellency of a public Spirit. *Bod. Ch. Ch. C C.C. Jef.* Oxon.
GERY Robert, V. of Iflington, R. of Allhallows the Great, Lond. and Preb. of Lincoln.
 Pf. xcvi. 9. 4° 1706. Open. a Church. *Sion. Trin.* Camb.
GIBB John, M.A. V. of Bedminfter, and St. Mary Redcliffe in Briftol and Abbots Leigh, Somerfet. and Preb. of Sarum.
 Rom. xiii. 6, 7. 4° 1721. *Briftol.* May 29.
GIBBES Charles, DD. R. of Stanford Rivers, Effex, and Preb. of Weftminfter.
 31 Serm. in 4° 1677. *Bod. Pemb.* Oxon. *Sion.*
GIBBON   , fometime Preacher at Black-fryers, London.
 Rom. v. 1 4° 1676. m. e. G. p. 297. The true Nature of Juftification.
 Gal. v. 16. 4° 1676. m. e. C. p. 79. How we may be fo fpiritual, as to check Sin in the firft rifings of it.
GIBBON Will. M.A. V. of St. Dunftan in the Weft, and Preacher of Bridewell, London.
 2 Sam. xxiii. 3. 4° 1743. Elect. Lord Mayor.
 Pf. cxv. 1. 4° 1747. May 29. b. Lord Mayor. *All S.* Oxon.
GIBBONS *Thomas,* DD.
 * 1 Kings. viii. 66. 8° 1746. Th. f. The Deliverance and Triumph of Great Britain.
 * Dan. ii. 44. 8° 1747. b. Diffent. Clergy.
 * Micah vi. 9. 8° 1748. On a Fire in Cornhill, London.
 * Matt. xiii. 45, 46. 8° 1752. Ch. Society.
 * Hab. iii. 2. 8° 1755. Faft. Earthquake.
 * Amos vi. 6. 8° 1755. 2 f. On the cruel oppreffions of the Proteftants in France.
 * Jer. iv. 19. 8° 1756. On Declaring War ag. the French.
 * 1 Pet. i. 24, 25. 8° 1760. Death of King George 2d.
 * Ephef. i. 11. 8° 1761. Fun. of Rev. *S. Davies. Queen's.* Cam.
 * Sermons in 8° 1762. On various Subjects.
 *   - - - 1764. Ch. Sch. meet.
 * Gal. v. 13. 8° 1764. Ord.
 * Ifai. xxi. 6. 8° 1770. State of the World in general, and Britain in particular as to Religion.
 * Ifai. iii. 10. 8° 1772. Fun. of *Will. Cromwell,* Efq; Character and Bleffedness of the righteous. *Queen's.* Camb.
Vol. II.   S   * Rev.

* Rev. xiv. 13. 8° 1775. Fun. of Rev. *Will. Langford*, DD.
* Ecclef. xii. 1. 8° 1776. Fun. of Mr. *Thomas Wilton*. The Remembrance of our Creator &c.

GIBBS John, of All Soul's Coll. Oxon.
 Job. xxx. 23. 1698.
 ‡ * Prov. xiv. 32.
 ‡ * Pf. lxxxix. 4.

GIBBS William, M. A. R. of Gayton, Northampton.
 1 Theff. iv. 13. 4° 1699. Fun. of Edward Reynolds, DD. *Oriel.* Oxon. *Trin.* Camb.

GIBSON Edmund, Bp. of London.
 1 Theff. v. 12, 13. 4° 1702. Conf. of Bp. Nicholfon. *Ch. Ch. C. C. C.* Oxon. *Pub. L. St. John's.* Camb.
 1 Cor. v. 12,13. 4° 1715. Conc. ad Synod. De Excommunicatione. *Ch. Ch.* Oxon. *Cl. H.* Camb.
 Dan. xii. 13. 4° 1716. An. meet. Ch. Sch. *Ch. Ch. Magd.* Ox. *Queen's.* Camb. *Brit. M.*
 2 Theff. iii. 3, 4. 8° 1717. Farewel f.
 Pf. cxix. 136. 4° 1723. Ref. Manners. *All S. Ch. Ch. Worc.* Ox. *Queen's.* Camb.
 4 Sermons in 8° 1729. On fev. Subjects, *Ch. Ch. Univ. Or. Worc. Hert.* Oxon. *Trin. Queen's. Cl. H. St. John's.* Camb. *Brit. M.*
 Acts xxiii. 5. 4° 1706. Affize. p. 1.
 Hofea vii. 9. 4° 1706. Affize. p. 33.
 Jer. vii. 3, 4. 4° 1715. Affize. p. 63.
 Pf. cvi. 43, 44. 4° 1716. b. L's. On fuppreffing the Reb. p. 93.
 1 Cor. ix. 25. 8° 1743. Ag. Intemperance. *Queen's.* Camb.
 Pf. cxii. 7. 12° 1749. Truft in God.
 * Acts xvii. 30. 17

GIBSON John, DD. Provoft of Queen's Coll. Oxon. and Preb. of Linc. and Peterborough.
 Pf. lxxxiv. 10, 11. 8° 1719. *Oxon.* Conf. of Queen's Chapel. *Magd. Worc.* Oxon.

GIBSON John, V. of Kirby in Le Soken, Effex.
 Judges viii. 34, 35. 8° 1727. *Ipfwich.* On the Death of K. Geo. I.

GIBSON John, Minifter of St. Ninians.
 * 2 Pet. i. 16. 8° 1761. On the Credibility and Importance of Scripture-Hiftory. *Queen's.* Camb.

GIBSON Sam. Minifter of Burleigh, Rutland.
 2 Chron. xxx. 27. 8° 1709. V. the Sacerdotal Benediction. *C.C.C.* Oxon. *Sion.*

GIFFARD Francis, M. A.
 1 Sam. xii. 17. 4° 1681. Affize. *Magd.* Ox. *Pub. L. Trin.* Camb.

GIFFARD John, M. A. R. of Maynftone, Salop.
 * Jer. x. 25. 12° 1713. Family-Religion, the principal fupport of the Church of England.

GIFFORD A.
 * John iii. 8. 8° 1733. On a Storm. *All S.* Oxon.

GIFFORD Bonaventura, DD. of Sorbone.
 Luke ii. 14. 4° 1687. *Eton.*

GIFFORD George, late Minister of St. Dunstan's in the East, Lond.
Gen. xlv. 8. 4° 1695. Subst. of sev. Sermons. The great Mystery of Providence.
GILBANK Jos. jun. Minis. of the Gosp. at Cockermouth, Cumb.
* Ephes. iv. 25. 4° 1779. b. Friendly Society.
GILBERT John, M. A. Canon of St. Peter's, Exon. and V. of St. Andrew's, Plymouth, Devon.
2 Sam. xxi. 1. 4° 1698. *Exon.* Jan. 30. *Magd.* Ox. *St. John's.* C.
Rom. xiii. 7. 4" 1699. *Exon.* Assize.
Practical Disc. in 8° 1724. Upon several Subjects. *Ch. Ch.* Oxon.
GILBERT John, Arch-Bp. of York.
2 Tim. i. 7. 4° 1724. Cons. of Bp. Weston. *Or.* Oxon.
Ephes. iv. 26. 4° 1742. Jan. 30. b. Lords. *Worc.* Oxon.
Gal. vi. 10. 4° 1743. Spitt. M. *Worc.* Oxon. *Brit. M.*
Rom. i. 16. 4° 1744. Prop. Gosp. *All S. Worc.* Oxon. *Sion.*
Matt. vii. 12. 4° 1745. London-Infirmary. *Worc. Wadh.* Oxon. *Queen's.* Camb.
Prov. xxiv. 21. 4° 1746. May 29. b. Lords.
GILBERT John, R. of Whippingham in the Isle of Wight.
Rom. xiii. 1. 8° 1744. Jan. 30. The Duty of Prince and People.
Prov. xxiv. 21, 22. 8° 1746. *Sarum.* Th. after Rebellion.
GILL *John*, DD.
*Acts xxvi. 8. 8° 1732. 2 s. V. Lime-s. s. v. 2. p. 372. Resurrection.
*1 Tim. iv. 16. 8° 1734. Ord.
*1 Cor. xii. 25. 8° 1758. Fun. of Rev. *Jos. Stennett*, DD.
*1 John v. 3. 8° 1765. At the Baptism of Mr. *Carmichael.* Baptism a divine Command to be observed.
* - - - - 8° 1765. Ord.
*1 Cor. xii. 25. 8° 1766. St. Paul's Character.
* - - - - 8° 1767. Fun. of Mr. *Anderson*.
* His Sermons and Tracts in 3 vol. 4° 1773.
* 115 Disc. 4° 1776. An Exposition of Solomon's Song.
GILLING *Isaac*, of Exeter, Devon.
* Phil. i. 21. 8° 1704. Fun.
* Col. iv. 17. 8° 1708. b. Dissent. Clergy.
* Matt. vii. 1. 8° 1719. b. Dissent. Cl. The Mischief of rash and uncharitable judging.
GILLMAN John, DD. R. of Creek, Northampton.
1 Pet. iii. 15. 8° 1721. *Northampton.* Vis. *Sion.*
GILPIN Bernard, R. of Warmington, Warwickshire.
Judges xvii. 6. 8° 1717. Accession.
GILPIN Rich. Min. of the Gospel at Newcastle upon Tyne, Staff.
Ps. ii. 12. 4° 1700. Assize. Sept. 10. 1660.
GIPPS Tho. Fell. of Trin Coll. Camb. and R. of Bury, Lancast.
Rom. xiii. 1. } 4° 1683. Assize. p. 1. } *Ch. Ch.* Ox. *St. John's.* C.
Tit. iii. 1. } 2 s. p. 27, 54. }
Prov. xxx. 6. 4° 1697. Ag. corrupt. the word of God. *Ch. Ch.* O.
GITTINS Dan. LL.B. R. of Southstoke, and V. of Leominster, Suff.
* Jer. v. 9. 8° 1744. Fast.

Pf. l. 16–20. 8° 1745. Faſt. Dec. 18.
GLANVIL. Joſeph, F. R. S. R. of Bath, Preb. of Worceſter, and Chapl. in Ord.
Rom. xii. 1. 4° 1670. Conc. ad Cl. Λογε θρησκεία. Bod. Ch. Ch. O.
Some Diſc. Serm. and Remains in 4° 1681. Magd. Worc. Oxon.
GLAS Adam, late a diſſenting Teacher, now a Presbyter of the Ch. of England.
Heb. i. 5. 8° 1712. Chriſtmas f.
GLASCOCKE T.
* Rev. v. 8–14. 4° 1702.
GLASCOTT Cradock, M. A. Chapl. to the Earl of Buchan, and one of Lady Huntingdon's Preachers.
* Joel ii. 13. 8° 1777. Faſt.
GLASSE Sam. DD. R. of Hanwell, Middleſex, and Chapl. in Ord.
* Hoſea iv. 3. 4° 1773. b. Sons of the Clergy.
* Job xxx. 25. 4° 1774. b. Preſid. and Gov. of Marine Society.
* Exod. xx. 24. 8° 1776. Opening a Church.
* John viii. 11. 4° 1777. b. Govern. of Magd. Hoſpital.
* Rom. xii. 8. 4° 1778. b. Pref. and Govern. of Mar. Society.
* Pf. xliv. 6, 7. 4° 1779. b. King. Chriſtian Fortitude particularly recommended in times of Danger.
* Luke ii. 13. 4° 1778. Meet. of the 3 Choirs.
* Lev. xix. 30. 8° 1781. A devout Obſervance of the Xn. Sabbath.
* Rom. vi. 21. 8° 1781. The Sinner's Account fairly ſtated.
* Matt. xxv. 35, 36. 8° 1781. b. Govern. of the Aſylum.
GLEN A. M. A. Fell. of Jeſ. Coll. Camb. and R. of Hathern, Leic.
Rom. vi. 21. 4° 1707. Aſſize. Brit. M.
GLOVER Henry, R. of Shrotton, Dorſet.
Pf. cxxii. 6. 4° 1663. Aſſize. An Exhortation to pray for Jeruſalem's Peace.
Gen. iv. 10, 11. 4° 1664. Jan. 30. Bod.
Rom. xii. 19. 4° 1664. Of Vengeance.
GLOVER William, M. A. formerly Chapl. of Ch. Ch. Oxon.
James iv. 1. 17
GOAD John, B. D. Head-Maſter of Merch. Taylor's School, Lond.
Luke xxi. 34. 4° 1663. Advent. ἡ ἡμέρα ἐκείνη.
1 Theſſ. v. 21. 4° 1664. Of the Trial of all Things by the Scriptures. C. C. C. Oxon.
GODDARD Peter Stephen, DD. Maſter of Clare-Hall, Camb. and Preb. of Peterborough.
* Luke xxxiii. 43. 8° 1756. The intermediate State. Queen's. C.
* Deut. xxxiii. 29. 8° 1759. Th. f. Queen's. Camb.
* Matt. xxi. 13. 4° 1769. Conf. of Clare Hall-Chapel. Queen's. C.
* Sermons in 8° 1781. preached before the Univerſity.
GODDARD Philip, V. of Beneham, Berks.
James v. 19, 20. 8° 1714. Oxon. Ref. Manners.
GODDARD Thomas, M. A. Canon of Windſor, and R. of St. Bennet Fink, London.
Prov. xxiv. 21. 8° 1703. Jan. 30.

James iii. 1. 4° 1710. Of Cenſure. *Bod. Ch. Ch. Worc.* Oxon.
Pub. L. Camb. *Sion.*
Pſ. cxxvi. 2, 3. 8° 1710. Th. The Mercy of God to this Church
and Kingdom. *Bod. Linc.* Oxon. *Pub. L.* Camb. *Sion.*
6 Sermons in 8° 1715. On ſeveral Occaſions.
GODDARD Thomas, M. A. R. of Swell, Somerſetſ.
* John xvii. 3. 8° 1772. Reform. the Liturgy. *Queen's.* Camb.
GODDEN Thomas, DD. Preb. in Ord. to her Majeſty.
Luke ii. 15, 16. 16 Xtmas.
* Matt. xvi. 18. 4° 1686. On St. Peter and Paul. *Jeſ.* Oxon.
Magd. Camb.
Matt. xvii. 1, 2. 4° 1687. Tranſfiguration.
GODFREY Robert
* Acts ii. 47.
GODMAN William, B. D. Fell. of King's Coll. Camb.
Eccleſ. x. 17. 4° 1660. Th. May 24. The Son of Nobles. *Trin.* C.
GODWIN *Edward*
* Pſ. cxix. 60. 8° 1721.
* Pſ. cvii. 8. 8° 1727.
* Mark xiii. 35-37. 8° 1728. Fun. of *Will. Voyce.*
* John i. 14. 8° 1729. At Coward's Lecture.
GODWIN R.
* - - - - 1780. On relig. Zeal with a comparative View
of the Proteſtant Diſſenters of the laſt and preſent Age.
GODWIN Timothy, Bp. of Kilmore and Ardagh, then Abp. of
Caſhel, Ireland.
Pſ. xcviii. 1. 4° 1716. Th. b. Lords Juſtices &c. *Ch. Ch.* Ox.
Ezek. xvii. 19. 4° 1716. b. Lords Juſtices &c. *Ch. Ch.* Oxon.
Heb. xiii. 16. 4° 1724. *Dublin.* Ch. ſ.
GODWYN Morgan, Student of Ch. Ch. Oxon.
* Jer. ii. 34. 4° 1685. Relating to the Plantations. Trade before
Religion. *Bal. Univ.* Oxon.
GOLDWIN William, M. A. Fell. of Eton, and V. of St. Nicholas,
Briſtol.
Pſ. cxliv. 15. 4° 1707. Th. ſ.
Rev. xviii. 23. 4° 1715. *Briſtol.* b. Merchants. The Honoura-
bleneſs, Uſefulneſs, and Duty of Merchants.
* Iſai. xxvi. 9. 8° 1722. Th. for Plague.
2 Cor. i. 10. 4° 1726. Nov. 5.
Matt. v. 16. 8° 1734. Sch. Feaſt.
Pſ. lxxii. 17. 4° 1781. Elect. *Eton.*
GOLTY Richard, M. A. Miniſter of Hutton, Eſſex.
Matt. xiii. 29, 30. 4° 1688. Aſſize. *Bod.*
GOOCH Thomas Sir, Bp. of Ely.
Pſ. xi. 3. 4° 1711. Jan. 30. b. Commons. *Univ. Bal. Linc. Worc.*
Hert. Oxon. *Trin. Queen's.* Camb. *Sion.*
1 Tim. iii. 1. 8° and 4° 1713. Fun. of Bp. Compton. *Magd. Linc.*
Hert. Oxon. *Sion.*
2 Chron. xx. 15. 4° 1740. Faſt. b. Lords. *Queen's.* Camb.

GOOD

GOOD Thomas, M. A. R. of Afhley, Worcefterfhire.
    Matt. v. 9. 4° 1715. *Worcefter.* Th. July 7. Bleffednefs of Peacemakers.

GOODALL Henry, DD. Arch-Deacon of Suffolk.
    * 2 Cor. vi. 3. 4° 1741. Duties of Miniftry. *Queen's.* C. *Brit. M.*
    1 Tim. vi. 17–19. 4° 1751. Spittal W. *Queen's.* Camb.
    * Jude 3. 4° 1760. Vif. f. Nature of true Zeal, confidered with a view to the prefent defign of collating the Heb. MSS.

GOODMAN James
    Pf. lxxvi. 10.   Th.

GOODMAN John, DD. R. of Hadham, Herts, Arch-Deacon of Middlefex, and Chaplain in Ord.
    Serm. in 8° 1697. Preached upon feveral Occafions—to which is added the golden Rule. *Ch. Ch.* C. C. C. *All S. Bal. Pemb. Pub. L. Trin.* Camb. *Brit. M.*
    * Prov. xvii. 1. 4° 1683. The Interefts of divine Providence in the Government of the World.
    Luke xv. 11–31. (4° 1697.) 8° 1707. The Penitent pardoned—or a Difcourfe of the Nature of Sin, and the Efficacy of Repentance. *Bod. Ch. Ch. Bal. Or. St. John's.* Ox. *Trin.* Camb.

GOODRICK John, M. A. Chapl. to Lincoln's Inn, and the Bp. of Norwich.
    Pf. xlvi. 10, 11. 4° 1685. Th. July 26. For Victory over the Rebels.

GOODWIN John, M. A. R. of Clapham, Surrey.
    Prov. xxix. 2. 4° 1738. Elect. Lord Mayor. The righteous in Authority.

GOODWIN Nathaniel
    Ifai. v. 1–4. 4° 17   Th.
    Pf. xxxvii. 37. 4° 1705. Fun.

GOODWIN Peter, M. A. late Minifter in Rope Maker's Alley, Lond.
    * Rom. v. 19. 8° 1732. Adam's Sin. V. Lime f. S. V. 1. p. 251.
    * Pf. li 5. 8° 1732. Original Corrup. V. Lime f. S. V. 1, p. 287.
    * - - - - 1732. Ord.
    * Heb. xiii. 7. 8° 1737. Fun.
    1 Pet. v. 2–4. 8° 1740. Ord.

GOODWIN Thomas, DD
    * James i. 1–6. 8° 1666. Patience.
    * John xiii. 1. 8° 16   Chrift's Heart toward Sinners.
    * Rom. viii. 38, 39. 8° 16
    * Expofitions on the firft, and part of the fecond Epiftle to the Ephefians in 50 Sermons in fo. 1681. to which are fubjoined 13 Sermons upon feveral Occafions confifting of 3 parts, All publifhed by T. G. *Trin.* Camb.
    Pf. lxxiii. 24. 4° 1695. Roy. Fun. *Pub. L. St. John's. Trin.* Cam.
    Heb. ii. 14. 4° 1699. Fun. of *Stephen Lob. Sion.*
    * Phil. i. 23, 24. 4° 1702. Royal Fun.
    * Pf. lxxxv. 8. 4° 1716. Th.

GORDON

GORDON   A Layman.
   * Job xxxiv. 30. 8° 1732. b. Soc. at Lincoln's Inn. *Queen's.* Ca.
GORDON John, DD. Arch-D. of Linc. and Chaplain to the Lord
   Bp. of that Diocese.
   * Matt. xviii. 33. 4° 1767. *Camb.* Addenbrook-Hosp. *Queen's.* C.
   * Acts xxiii. 5. 4° 1771. Access. Causes and Consequences of
      Evil-speaking.
GORDON Will. M.A. R. of St. James's and St. Michael's, Barbadoes.
   1 John iii. 2. 4° 1710. Fun. of Col. Codrington. *Brit. M.*
   Ps. cxxxii. 18. 8° 1717. Th. for suppressing the Rebellion.
GORDON Will. M. A. Lect. of St. Matthew's, Bethnal Green.
   Exod. iii. 5. 8° 1746. Sund. after Cons. of the Church.
GORDON *James*, M. A.
   * - - - - 1735. Ord.
GORDON *William*, Pastor of the 3d Church at Roxbury.
   * Lam. iii. 22. 8° 1776. Th. s. Relig. and civil Liberty.
GOSTWYKE William, M. A. Fell. of Trin. Coll. Camb. and R.
   of Purley, Berks.
   John xi. 21. 4° 1685.
   Prov. xi. 21. 4° 1685. *Camb.* Th. July 26. *Pub. L. Trin.* Camb.
   Ps. cxxii. 6. 4° 1692. Vis. Pray for the Peace of Jerusalem.
   Matt. xiii. 45, 46. 4° 1696.
[GOSWELL John]
   * Discourses in 8° 1715.
GOUGE *Thomas*
   Joshua xxiv. 16. 4° 1663. The Christian Householder Joshua's
      Resolution.
   1 Tim. i. 17–19. 4° 1677. m. e. C. p. 202. How Alms may be
      acceptable to God.
   * Discourses in 8° 1706.
   * 1 Sam. xxiv 17–20. 1717. Accession.
GOUGH Strickland a
   * Sermons in 8° 1709.
   * Tit. i. 9. 8° 1713. Ord.
   * Isai. xlix. 23. 8° 1714. Accession.
GOUGH Strickland. a M. A. R. of Swafield. V. of Swinstead, Linc.
   Matt. vii. 10. 4° 1733. Nov. 5. b. Lord Mayor. *Queen's.* Camb.
   Ps. cxx. 5, 6. 8° 1745. Reb. The Wickedness of a factious Dis-
      position. *Sion.*
   16 Serm. in 8° 1751. To which is added a Dissertation on
   1 Cor. xi. 10. *Queen's.* Camb. *Sion.*
[GOUGH William]
   * Disc. in 12° 1695.
GOULD Will. R. of Stapleford-Abbots, Essex and R. S. S.
   * Isai. xliv. 28. 4° 1774. Conc. Acad. pro Grad. Doct. *Wadh.* Ox.
GOULDE William, a Son of the Church of England, R. of Ken
   near Exeter, Devon.

a *Q.* The same.

Matt.

Matt. xxi. 13. 4° 1672. Palm. S.
1 Cor. xiv. 40. 4° 1674. Vif. Conformity according to Canon
  juftified. *Bal. Oxon. Pub. L. St. John's. Camb.*
1 Cor. xiii. 5. 4° 1676. The Generofity of Chriftian Love. *Bod.
  St. John's. Camb.*
Job xxxvi. 21. 4° 1682. The primitive Xtian juftified. *Pub. L.
  St. John's. Camb.*

GOWER Humphrey, DD. Mafter of St. John's Coll. Camb. Margaret-Profeffor in Divinity, and Preb. of Ely.
  Gal. iii. 21, 22. 4° 1685. b. King. Xtmas. *Bod. Magd. C.C.C.
  Oxon. St. John's. Camb.*
  2 Kings ii. 11, 12. 4° 1685. *Camb.* 2 f. Fun. of Bp. Gunning.
  Bod. C.C.C. Oxon. Trin. St. John's. Camb.

GOWER John
  *Ephef. v. 8. 4° 1772. b. Free-mafons.
GOWER Nath. M. A. V. of Batterfea, Surry.
  Pf. cxix. 59, 60. 4° 1769. b. Lord Mayor. The Neceffity of Self-reflection in order to an holy Life.

GRACE Job, Treafurer of the Cathedral Church of Litchfield, and Minifter of Watford, Northamptonfhire.
  2 Chron. xix. 5, 6. 4° 1710. Affize. Judicium Auguftale.

GRAILLE John, R. of Blickling, Norfolk.
  4 f. 8° 1685. Of Reformation and Loyalty.
  Prov. xxiv. 21, 22.⎫ Pious Reverence tow: God and the King. p. 1.
  ———— 23–25. ⎬ Juft Abhor. of ufurp. Republicans. p. 41 & 77.
  ———— xxviii. 2. ⎭ Due Affection to the Monarchy. p. 127. *All
  S. Oxon.*
  Jerem. xiii. 15. 8° 1685.
  ———— xxxv. 14. 8° 1685. The Reform. of ourfelves. *All S. Ox.*
  Pf. cxviii. 8, 9. 4° 1702. *Norwich.* Royal Fun. Trufting in God better than trufting in Man or Princes: *St. John's. Camb.*
  Ecclef. xii. 1. 8° 1708. Fun.
  Pf. xcii. 14. 8° 1720. Fun. of Rev. Mr. W. Haylett. *St. John's. C.*

GRANGER James, M. A. V. of Shiplake, Oxon.
  * Prov xii. 10. 8° 1772. Apology for Brute-Creation.
  * Rom. xii. 11. 8° 1772. Nature and Extent of Induftry.

GRAHAM W. M. A. of Leeds, Yorkfhire.
  (* Matt. x. 34. 8° 1759. Ord.
  * Matt. iv. 7. 8° 1771. b. Diffent. Clergy. *Queen's. Camb.*

GRANT James, LL.D. Lect. of St. Leonard's, Shoreditch, London.
  * 16 Sermons in 8° 1775. On various Subjects.
  * Pf. lvi. 7. 8° 1777. Faft.

GRANT John, M. A. Preb. of Rochefter, and V. of St. Dunftan's in the Weft, London.
  Judges v. 12. 4° 1704. Th. *Bod. St. John's. Camb.*
  * Ezek. xxxvii. 22. 4° 1707. Th. for Union. *Magd. O. Pub. L. C.*

GRANTHAM Tho. M. A. Curate of High Barnet near London.
  1 Pet. ii. 17. 4° 1674.

Gen.

Gen. xxix. 25. 4° 1681 and 8° 1709. Wedd. f. V. Difc. on conj.
Duty, vol. 1. p. 94.
GRAY *Andrew*, Minifter of the Gofpel at Glafcow.
Sermons in 8° 1679. *Bod. Pub. L.* Camb.
GRAY *Andrew*, DD. of Abernethy, Scotland.
* Pf. lxxxv. 6. 12° 1779. Caufe, Symptoms, and Cure of Indiffe-
rence to Religion. V. Scotch Pr. v. 3. p. 234.
[GREAVES Thomas]
* - - - - 1763. Fun. f.
* f. - - - 1764. Th. f.
GREEN John, late Curate of Thurfcoe, Yorkfhire.
* 2 Tim. iii. 16, 17. 8° 1711. *Camb.* 9 Difc. Demonftration of the
Truth and Divinity of the Chriftian Religion.
* Heb. xi. 1. 8° 1711. *Camb.* Matters of Faith are equally, if not
more demonftrable than thofe of Reafon.
* 2 Pet. i. 10. 8° 1763.
GREEN John, Bp. of Lincoln.
1 John iv. 21. 4° 1749. *Camb.* Commencement. *Queen's.* C. Brit. M.
1 Cor. iii. 9. 4° 1752. *Camb.* Conf. of Bp Keene. *Queen's.* C. Br. M.
* Ifai. xxvi. 9. 4° 1756. Faft. b. Lords.
* Ecclef. vii. 3. 4° 1759. Faft. b. Commons. *Queen's.* Camb.
* Rom. xiii. 7. 4° 1763. Jan. 30. bef. Lords. *Braz. N.* Oxon.
Queen's. Camb.
* Luke xvi. 19, 20. 4° 1763. b. Govern. of the Small-pox. Hofp.
Queen's. Camb.
* Rom. i. 16. 4° 1768. Prop. of Gofpel. *Queen's.* Camb.
* Tit. iii. 8. 4° 1767. Ir. Prot. Schools.
* Mark i. 34. 4° 1771. Infirm. at *Lincoln*.
* James iii. 17. 4° 1773. An. meet. Char. Sch.
GREEN John, Curate of St. Saviour's, Southwark, and Lect. of St.
John's, Wapping, London.
* Pf. xc. 12. 4° 1757. Fun. of Rev. J. Creyk.
* 9 Sermons in 8° 1758. *All S.* Oxon.
GREEN John, M. A. Minifter of St. George's, Norwich.
* 1 Tim. ii. 2. 4° 1764. *Norwich.* Elect. of Mayor.
GREEN Richard,[a] DD. Fell. of St. John's Coll. Oxon.
Exod. xx. 7. 4° 1745. Affize. The Benefit of Oaths to Society.
GREEN Richard,[a] DD. R. of Belbroughton, Worcefterf.
* Rom. xiii. 5. 4° 1756. Accefs. Confcientious Obedience to
Governors recommended. *Braz. N. Worc.* Oxon.
GREEN Robert, DD. Fell. of Clare-Hall. Camb.
2 Tim. iii. 16. 8° 1711. 9 Difcourfes. *All S.* Oxon.
Heb. xi. 1. 8° 1711. 9 Difcourfes. p. 187.
GREEN T. M. A. V. of Wymefwould, Leicefter.
Pf. lxviii. 10. 12° 1750. Inftructions for the Poor.
* Phil. ii. 2. 12° 1754. On the New-Style.
GREEN Thomas, DD. Dean of Sarum.
* 1 Chron. xxix. 14. 8° 1767. Infirm. at *Sarum*.

a *Q.* The fame?

GREENE John
Prov. xxiii. 26. 8° 1713. A new Yr's Gift to young perfons. *Sion.*
GREENE John
* Ephef. iv. 28. 8° 1737. On occafion of the Church being robbed at Chelmsford.
GREENE Thomas, Bp. of Ely.
Matt. v. 33. 8° 1715. The great Wickednefs of Perjury, and of the prefent Rebellion. *St. John's.* Camb. *Eton.*
Pf. lxv. 7. 4° 1716. Th. June 7. *Ch. Ch.* Oxon. *Eton.*
Ifai. xxvi. 9. 4° 1721. Faft. b. Lords. Dec. 8. The End and Defign of God's Judgments. *Worc.* Oxon. *Cl. H.* Camb.
Phil. i. 27. 4° 1723. Farewel.
Luke ii. 32. 4° 1724. Prop. Gofpel. *Ch. Ch.* Oxon.
Ephef. v. 11. 8° 1726. Ref. Manners. *Queen's.* Camb.
Heb. xiii. 16. 4° 1727. Spitt. b. Lord Mayor. *Or.* Oxon.
GREENFIELD Nathaniel
Rev. vi. 15–17. 8° 1660.
GREEFFIELD Thomas, M. A. of Pemb. Coll. Oxon. and Preacher at Lincoln's Inn, London.
Ifai. lviii. 5–7. 4° 1661. Faft. b. Commons. *Univ. Magd.* Oxon. *Trin.* Camb.
GREENHILL Jofeph, M. A. R. of Eaft-Horfley and Eaft Clandon, Surry.
* Luke xviii. 18. 4° 1756. Decreafe of Chriftian Faith.
* Rom. x. 1. 8° 1757. Preparatory to a Faft.
* John xviii. 36. 4° 1768. Chrift's Kingdom, not of this World.
* Matt. ix. 12. 4° 1771. On the Millenium.
* 1 Pet. iv. 7. 4° 1773. Duty of patiently and chearfully waiting at all times for Salvation.
* Rev. xx. 4. 8° 1774. On the Millenium.
GREENHILL William
Sev. Serm. in 8° 1671. *Bod. Sion.*
Ezek. xviii 32. 4° 1677. m. e. C. p. 29. What muft and can perfons do towards their own Converfion.
GREENWOOD Daniel, M. A. R. of Steeple Afton, Oxon.
2 Cor. vi. 7. 8. 1672.
Ifai. lvii 1, 2. 4° 1680. *Oxon.* Fun.
GREENWOOD William, DD.
* 1 Cor. xv 8° 1761. A Paraphraftical Expofition. *Queen's.* Cam.
* Gen. i. 1 to end 8° 1763. Effay with a paraphraftical Expofition.
GREGORY Fran. DD. Chap. in Ord. and R. of Hambleton, Bucks.
2 Sam. xix. 30. 4° 1660. Th. May 27 Reftoration.
Acts xxi. 13. 4° 1660. 2 f. *Oxon. Magd.* Oxon.
1 Tim. iv. 16. 4° 1675. Vif. *Bod. Bal.* Oxon. *St. John's.* Camb.
Matt. xiii. 37. 4° 1673. b. the Gregorians. Spiritual Watchfulnefs *Bod. Worc.* Oxon.
Deut. xxiii 9. 4° 1673. Faft. b. Lord Mayor. *St. John's.* Camb.
1 Theff. v. 21. 4° 1674. The Trial of Religions. *Bod.*
Jude 12. 4° 1675. Co. Feaft. The Feaft of Love. *Bod. Queen's.* Oxon. *Sion.*

John

John xvi 2. 4° 1679. Nov. h. Lord Mayor. The relig. Villain.
Matt. ii. 2. 4° 1680. Epiphany.
2 Sam. xix. 3. 4° 1680. Nov. 5.
Pf. xviii. 50. 4° 1696. Th. *Trin.* Camb.
Pf. cxxxii. 7. 4° 1697. Th. *St. John's.* Camb.
— cxxii. 7. 4° 1697. Th.
GREGORY John, M. A. of Ch. Ch. Oxon.
    1 Cor. xv. 20. His Works Pofth. 4° 1664. p. 57. Of the Refurrection. *Bod. Brit. M.*
GREGORY John, Arch-Deacon of Gloucefter.
    Exod. 20. 8-11. 12° 1681. The Morality of the Sabbath. *Bod.*
GREGORY Thomas, M. A. late Fell. of Wadh. Coll. Oxon. and Lect. of Fulham, Middlefex.
    James i. 27. 4° 1696.
    Difc. in 8° 1696. Upon feveral divine Subjects. *Ch. Ch.* Oxon. *Queen's.* Camb.
    Several practical Sermons &c. in 8° 1708. *Brit. M.*
GREGSON *Moses*
    *Tit. i. 1. 8° 1770 Fun.
GRENVILLE Denis, DD. Dean of Durham.
    John i. 29. 4° 1684. Epiphany. The compleat Conformift. *Bod. Magd.* Oxon. *Trin.* Camb.
    Rom. xii. 11. 4° 1685. Advent. *Bod. Magd.* Oxon.
    Gen. xiii. 14. 4° 1689. *Roven.* 2 f.
GRETTON Phillips, D D. Rector of Springfield, Effex.
    Exod. xxxiii. 23. 8° 1732. *Cant.* Conc. ad Cler. Ag. the Argument à Priori. *Sion.*
    John i. 17. 8° 1732. *Camb.* Commencement. The Infufficiency of Reafon, and Affurance of Revelation, in Matters of Religion.
[GREW Obadiah, DD.] Minifter at Coventry.
    * Acts xx. 32. 4° 1663. V. Coll. Farw. f.
GREY Richard, DD. Preb. of St. Paul's, Lond. and R. of Hinton, Northamptonfhire.
    Matt. xvi. 16. 8° 1730. *Oxford.* Vif. The Perpetuity of Chrift's Church. *Braz. N. Linc.* Oxon.
    2 Cor. v. 10. 4° 1732. Affize. The great Tribunal.
    Matt. x. 16. 8° 1736. Vif. The Duty and proper Conduct of the Clergy &c. *Queen's.* Camb.
    Matt. xxv. 37-40. 8° 1744. *Northampton.* Infirm f.
    *Pf. xciii. 5. 4° 1752. Open a Chapel. *Worc. Ox. Queen's.* C.
GREY Thomas,[a] M. A. Minifter of Dedham, Effex
    Tit. iii. 1. 4° 1685. Rebell. in the Weft. Submiffion, Obedience and Loyalty.
GREY Thomas,[a]   of Cambridge.
    Luke xvi. 24, 25. 12° 1706. *Brit. M.*
GRIFFITH Evan, M. A. Minifter of Alderly, Gloucefterfhire.
    Ifai. lvii. 1. 4° 1677. Fun. of Sir Matthew Hale. *Bod.*
GRIFFITH John, M. A. Curate of Edenfor, Derbyfhire, and Chapl. to the Duke of Devonfhire.

[a] Q. The fame.

John vi. 60. 4° 1701. Ag. Transubstantiation.
  1 Tim. vi. 19. 4° 1703. Sch. Feast. The Sacrifice of Gratitude.
  Pſ. lxxxix 32. 4° 1704. Faſt for the great Storm.
  Lament. iv. 20. 4° 1707. Jan. 30.
  2 Cor. vi. 10. 8° 1707. Fun. of Duke of Devon.
GRIFFITH John
  * Diſc. in 1707.
GRIFFITH Matthew, DD. R. of St. Mary Magdalen near Old Fiſh-ſtreet, and Preacher at the Temple, London.
  Prov. xxiv. 21. 12° 1660. Lady-day. The Fear of God and the King. *Bal.* Oxon.
  Rom. xii. 4, 5. 4° 1661.
  1 John i. 7. 4° 1662. Communion ſ. The ſpiritual Antidote to cure our Souls.
  1 Cor. v. 7. 4° 1662.
  1 Sam. xxvi. 9. 4° 1665. Jan. 30. At the Temple.
GRIFFITH Owen
  Heb. xi. 10. 4° 1681. Fun.
GRIFFITH Robert, R. of Woolaſton, Glouceſterſhire.
  1 Cor. iii. 5-7 4° 1711. b. Lord Mayor. Of the Neceſſity of parochial Communion. *Sion.*
  Gal. vi. 6. 8° 1716. Viſ.
  ‡ Eccleſ. vii. 10. 4° 17 Faſt.
GRIFFITH Thomas, DD. late Fell. of Pemb. Coll. Oxon. and R. of Biſhops-Stoke, Hants.
  * Matt. x. 16. 8° 1757. *Oxon.* b. the Univerſity. The Difficulties of the Miniſterial Office. *Pemb. Jeſ. Worc.* Ox. *Queen's.* C.
  * Acts xvii. 21. 8° 1760. *Oxon.* Evils ariſing from miſapplied Curioſity. *Pemb. Jeſ. Worc.* Oxon. *Queen's.* Camb.
  * Phil. ii. 13. 8° 1763. *Oxon.* b. the Univerſity. The Uſe and Extent of Reaſon in Matters of Religion. *Pemb. Worc.* Oxon. *Queen's.* Camb.
  * Prov. iv. 14. 8° 1773. *Oxon.* Act ſ. *Pemb.* Oxon. *Queen's.* C.
GRIFFITHS Lemuel
  * 1 Sam. xvii. 44, 45. 8° 1760. Faſt.
GRIFFYTH John, M. A. V. of White Waltham, Berks.
  1 Theſſ. iv. 11. 4° 1695. On the Day the Mayor was ſworn. *Bod.*
GRIGMAN Stephen, M. A. Cur. of St. Botolph's, Biſhopſgate, and Lect. of St. Michael's Cornhill, London.
  Lev xix. 30. 4° 1728. Open. a Church. Reverence due to God's Sanctuary.
GROSVENOR *Benjamin*, DD. Miniſter at Croſby-Square, London.
  * Hoſea viii. 7. 8° 1704. Faſt. for Storm.
  * Prov. xi. 11. 8° 1705. Ref. Manners.
  Pſ ii. 11. 8° 1710. Th. ſ.
  * Pſ xlviii. 3. 8° 1710. Nov. 5.
  * Heb. xi. 13. 8° 1712. Fun. ſ.
  Pſ. xviii. 23. 8° 1714. To Young perſons.
  * Pſ. cxvi. 15. 8° 1716. Fun.

* Pſ.

* Pf. cxxxii. 18. 8° 1716. Coron. *Brit. M.*
* Luke xii. 47. 8° 1721. 2 f.
* Heb. vi. 12. 8° 1723. Fun.
* Luke xxiv. 47. 8° 1724. Jefus's Temper.
* Matt. i. 21. 8° 1724. Name, Jefus
* Acts xi. 26. 8° 1728. Chriſtian Name.
John xvi. 2. 8. 1735. Perfecution and Cruelty of the Church of Rome. V. 2 Vol. Ag Popery. *Braz. N.* Oxon. *Brit. M.*
* Pf. cii. 27. 8° 1740. Fun. of *Will. Harris*, DD.
* 2 Cor. v. 11. 8° 1713. Fun.

GROVE Edward, M. A. R. of Chevington, Suffolk.
Ecclef. ii. 1,2. 4° 1702. *Norwich.* The Vanity of Man's Laughter.

GROVE Henry, of Taunton, Somerfetf.
Serm. and Tracts in 4 Vol. 8° 1741. *Wadh.* Oxon. *Queen's.* Cam.
Sermons, being 2 additional Vol. in 8° 1742. *Queen's.* Camb.
* 3 Serm. in 1° 1746. On Rom. xiv. 16. Pointing out fome of the Errors and Imperfections in the Conduct of Chriſtians &c. *Queen's.* Camb.
Serm. and Tracts (publiſhed in his Life-time.) in 4 Vol. 8° 1747.

GROVE Robert, Bp. of Chichefter.
1 John ii. 15. 4° 1690. b. K. and Queen. *Ch. Ch. Magd. Jef* Ox.
1 Cor. xiii 3. 4° 1695. Spittal M. Profitable Charity. *Queen's.* Camb. *Sion.*

GRUCHY Martin, M. A. Curate of Scale, Surrey.
1 Cor. xii. 5. 8° 1723. A clear and diftinct Account from Scripture of the firſt Inſtitution of the 3 Orders of Deacons, Prieſts, and Biſhops by our Lord and Saviour Jefus Chriſt.

[GUISE Samuel,] M. A.
* Pf. cxxxii. 18. 8° 1724.

GUNHILL DD.
Matt. ix. 15. 4° 1661.

GUNNING Peter, Bp. of Ely.
Luke v. 35–38. 4° 1662. On Lent-faſt. *Bod.*

GURDON Brampton, M. A. R. of St. Edmond the King, and Arch-Deacon of Sudbury, Gloucefterf.
Boyle's Lect. 1721, 1722. 8° or fo. 1739. V. 3. p. 277 &c. *Ch. Ch. St. John's. New C. Jef.* Oxon. *Queen's.* Camb.
Ephef. iv. 11, 12. 4° 1723. Conf. of Bp. Leng. The Diſtinction of Chriſtianity into Clergy and Laity juſtified. *Queen's.* C. *Eton.*

GURNALL William, M. A. late Fell. of Eman. Coll. Camb. R. of Lavenham, Suffolk.
Sermons in 4° 1660.
Ephef. vi. 17. 4° 1662. The Chriſtian in compleat Armour. *Bod.*
1 Cor. xv. 58. 8° 1672. Fun. of Lady Mary Vere. *Bod. Trin.* Camb. *Brit. M.*

GUTHRIE James, M. A. Ordinary of Newgate.
* Pf cxix. 85–87. 8° 1732. b. Robert Hallam. For the Murder of his Wife.
* Matt. xiv. 22–24. 12° 1738.

GUYSE

GUYSE John, DD. Minister in New Broad-street Buildings, Lond.
* Rom ix. 5. 8° 17. 9. Jesus Christ, God-Man.
* Disc. in 2 Vol. 8° 1721.
* 5 Serm. in 8° 1724.
* Matt. xix. 22. 8° 1728.
Prov. viii. 17. 8° 1729. 2 s. Christ, Son of God. *Queen's*. Cam.
* Matt. xxv. 8, 9. 8° 17
* Phil. i. 9–11. 8° 17   Ord.
* John xi. 25, 26. 8° 1730. Fun. of Rev. *J. Asty*. *Queen's*. Cam.
* Prov. xi. 24. 8° 1741.
* 6 Sermons in 8° 1742. To Youth. *Sion. Brit. M.*
* Phil. i. 21. 8° 1743. Fun. of Rev. *J. Hubbard*. *Queen's*. Camb.
* Discourses in 12° 1747. Youth's Monitor.
* Isai. liv. 10. 8° 1750. Fun. of Rev. *Mord. Andrews*.
* 17 Pract. Discourses in 8° 1756.

GWYNE Will. B. A. Master of the Grammar-Sch. at Lewes, Sussex.
* Rom. iii xviii. } 8° 1780. Ass. s.
* Mark ix. 50.

H.   A. M. A. Chapl. to the Duke of Richmond.
James i. 19. 8° 1702. Against Detraction.

H.   E.
- - - - - - 1700. Jan. 30.

H.   G.
1 John iii. 4. 8° 1669. The Excellency and Equitableness of God's Law, the Unreasonableness of Sin. *Bod.*

H.   H.
Ezek. ix. 5, 6. 4° 1686. 2 Sund. East. *St. John's*. Oxon.

H.   J.
* Luke vii. 35. 8° 1699. Wisdom justified.

H.   J.
Ps. cxix. 136. 4° 1732. Relig. Society.

H.   J. B. A.
1 Sam. xii. 24. 25. 8° 1746. Th. after the Rebellion.

H.   O.
* Gen. xxiv. 22. 12° 1693. Worship in private Houses.

H.   S. R. de S.   Comit. Suff.
Eccles. xi. 9. 4° 1673. Fun.   The Young Man's Monitor.

H.   T.
Ps. cxxxix. 5. 4° 1676.

H.   W.
Prov. xxiv. 21, 22. 4° 1660. A Changling, no Company for Lovers of Loyalty.

HACKET John, DD. Chaplain in Ord.
Acts xv. 39. 4° 1660. Lent. b. King. *Ch. Ch. Linc. Worc.* Oxon. *St. John's*. Camb.

HACKET John, Bp. of Litchfield and Coventry.
A Century of Serm. in fo. 1675. *Ch. Ch. Bod. Queen's. Worc.* Oxon. *Trin. King's. Queen's.* Camb.

HACKET

HACKET Lawrence, Chapl. to the Factory at Conſtantinople.
 Micah. vi. 8. 4° 1707. Levant-Co. *Magd.* Oxon. *Sion.*
[HACKET Roger]
 * Gen. ii. 22. 12° 17.   V. Diſc. on conj. D. v. 2. p. 430.
HACKET Thomas, Bp. of Downe and Connor.
 1 Cor. xiv. 16. 8° 1660. b. Convoc. at *Dublin.*
 Matt. vi. 19–21. 4° 1672. Spittal T. *Bod.*
HADFIELD Thomas, M. D.
 * - - - - 1733. Fun. ſ.
 * Acts xiv. 23. 8° 1737. Ord.
HAILES William, M. A.
 Matt. v. 44. 8° 1722.
HALES James, M. A. V. of Chart-Sutton, Kent.
 * 24 Serm. in 2 Vol. 8° 1766. On ſolemn Occaſions.
HALES John,   Fell. of Eton Coll. and Canon of Windſor.
 Golden Remains and 4 Serm. in 4° 1673. *Bod Mert. Bal. Univ.*
 St. John's. Oxon. *Pub. L. Queen's.* Camb. *Sion.*
HALES Stephen, DD. and F. R. S. R. of Farrington, Hants, and
  Miniſter of Teddington, Middleſex, and Clerk of the Cloſet
  to her royal Highneſs the Princeſs of Wales.
 Gal. vi. 2. 4° 1735. Col. Georgia. *Queen's.* Camb. *Brit. M.*
 Job x. 11, 12. 4° 1751. b. Phyſicians. The Wiſdom and Good-
  neſs of God in the Formation of Man. *Worc.* Oxon. *Queen's.*
  Camb. *Brit. M.*
 * Iſai. lvi. 12. 8° 1754. Ag. drink. ſpirituous Liquors. V. Bel-
  lamy's Fam. Preacher. V. 2. p. 21. (1ſt. Edit.)
HALEY William, M. A. Fell. of All Soul's Coll. Oxon.
 * Prov. viii. 18. 4° 1686. b. Levant-Co.
HALL Archibald.
 * 2 Diſc. in 8° 1777. Entitled grace and Holineſs, *viz.*
 * Rom. viii. 3. Redemption by Chriſt without Law.
 * Gal. ii. 19. Believer's Death to the Law.
HALL Charles, DD. late Fell. of C. C. C. Oxon. R. of Bocking,
  and Chapl. in Ord.
 * Matt. xxviii. 20. 4° 1756. The Goſpel-Credibility defended.
  All S. Braz. N. Oxon. *Queen's.* Camb.
 * Job. i. 5. 8° 1760. Faſt. b. Commons. National Humiliation
  ſeaſonable in times of national Succeſs. *Braz. N.* Oxon.
HALL Edmund, M. A. of Pemb. Coll. Oxon. and R. of Great Ri-
  ſington, Glouceſter.
 Ezek. xxiv. 16. 8° 1664. *Oxon. Bod.*
HALL George, Bp. of Cheſter.
 Pſ. vii. 9. 4° 1666. Faſt. b. Lords for Plague. *Sion. St. John's.* C.
HALL Joſeph, Bp. of Exeter.
 * Serm. in 2 Vol. fo. 1661. *Queen's. Cl. H.* Camb.
HALL Robert
 Prov. xvi. 7. 8° 1713. Th. for Peace.
 4 Sermons or Catechetical Lectures.
 12 Sermons on the Apoſtles Creed.

HALL Thomas, B. D.
  * Pſ. lxxxii. 1 &c, 4° 1660. The Beauty of Magiſtrates.
  Hoſea xiii. 12. 4° 1660. Samaria's Downfall.
  * Matt. v. 13. 4 1660.
HALL Thomas, Miniſter of the Goſpel.
  * Phil. i. 6. 8° 1732. 2 ſ. V. Lime-ſtreet. S. v. 2. p. 271. Perſeverance in Grace.
  * - - - - 1742. Faſt.
  * Phil. iii. 8,9. 8° 1747. Fun.
  * Luke x. 23. 8° 1759. Introduct. to Ord.
  * - - - - 1754. Fun. of *Dr. Marryatt.*
  * Zech. i. 5. 8° 1759. Fun.
HALL Timothy, Bp. of Oxford.
  Heb. ii. 15. 4° 1684. Fun. *Sion.*
  Levit. xix. 17. 4° 1689. *Sion.*
HALLET *Joſeph*, Miniſter at Exeter.
  * 1 Tim. i. 15. 8° 1714. Fun.   V. G. *Troſſe*'s Life.
  John xiii. 17. 8° 1726. Fun. of Rev. *J. Peirce. Brit. M.*
HALLEY George, M. A. Succentor of the Vicars Choral, and R. of St. Cuthbert, and Preb. of Ripon, York.
  Pſ. cvii. 2. 4° 1689. Th.
  Deut. xxxii. 29. 4° 1691. To condemned Priſoners at *York. Bod.*
  Pſ. cxxii. 6. 4° 1695.
  2 Cor. i. 10. 4° 1698. Nov. 5.
HALLEY *William*, DD.
  * Rev. x. 5, 6. 8°   Fun.
HALLIFAX James, DD. R. of Cheddington, Bucks, V. of Ewell, Surrey, and F. R. S.
  * Jerem. xviii. 7. 4° 1756. Faſt. for Earthquake.
  * 2 Sam xxiii. 3. 4° 1757. Elect. Lord Mayor.
  * Gen. xlvii. 22. 4° 1765. b. the Sons of the Clergy.
  * Prov. xxix. 15. 4° 1766. b. Gov. of Aſylum.
  * Job. ii. 7. 4° 1768. b. Gov. of Small-pox Hoſpital.
  * Deut. vi. 6, 7. 4° 1771. An. meet. Char. Sch. *All S. Worc.* Ox.
HALLIFAX Samuel, Bp. of Gloucester.
  * Rom iii. 28. 8° 1760. 3 ſ. St. Paul's Doctrine of Juſtification by Faith. *Braz. N.* Oxon.
  * Gal. v. 13. 4° 1769. Jan. 30. *Camb.* b. Commons. *Queen's.* C.
  * Eccl. i. 18. 4° 1769. 2 ſ. *Camb.* Com. of Benefactors. *Queen's.* C.
  * Matt. xxv. 40. 4° 1770. *Camb.* Addenbrook-Hoſp.
  * 2 Cor. ii. 17. 8° 1772. 3 ſ. *Camb.* On Subſcription. *Queen's.* C.
  * Sermons in 8° 1776. On the Prophecies, preached at Lincoln's Inn Chapel, at the Lecture of (Warburton) Bp. of Gloucester. *Bod. Sion. Pub. L. Queen's. Trin.* Camb.
HALLIFAX Will. DD. R. of Old Swinford. Worceſterſ.
  2 Kings ix. 31. 4° 1701. Jan. 30. *C. C. C.* Oxon.
HALLYWELL Henry, M. A. V. of Cowfield, Suſſex.
  Phil. iv. 8. 8° 1692. The Excellency of moral Virtue in ſeveral Diſcourſes. *Bod. Magd.* Oxon.

John

John i. 47. 8° 1692. p. 144. On Sincerity. *Bod.*
Rom. i. 16. 8° 1694. 6 f. A Defence of revealed Religion. *Bod.*
All S. C.C.C. Pemb. Oxon.
HALSEY James
Pf. cvii. 8. 8° 1676. An Essay. *Bod.*
* Luke xiii. 5. 8° 1676. Duty of Amendment of Life.
HAM Robert, M. A.
Pf. cxxxiii. 1. 8° 1713. Vis.
HALWARD John, M. A. late Cur. of St. Giles's, Reading, Berks, and Fell. of Worc. Coll. Oxon.
* Tit. iii. 8. 8° 1774. Anniv. of Mr. West's Charity.
HAMILTON William, Arch-D. of Armagh.
* - - - - - 4° 1700. *Dublin.* 2 f. Concerning Zeal. Ag. Immorality and Profaneness.
* - - - - - 4° 1722. Nov. 5. } b. House of Commons.
* - - - - - 4° 1725. Nov. 5. }
HAMILTON Anthony, DD. Arch-D. of Colchester, and Chaplain in Ord.
* 1 Thess. iv. 9. 4° 1775. An. meet. Ch. Sch.
HAMILTON Hugh, DD. F. R. S. Dean of Armagh.
* Tit. iii. 1. 4° 1772. Assize. On the late Disturbances in the North of Ireland. *Queen's.* Camb.
HAMILTON William
* Phil. iii. 7, 8. 8° 1732.
HAMMATT John. M. A. V. of Stanton-Berry, Bucks.
John v. 35. 4° 1684. Fun.
HAMMOND George
Col. iv. 5. 4° 1690. C. m. e. p. 300. *Bod. Pub L.*
2 Tim. 2. 15. 8° 1693. Fun. of Rev. *Rich. Steel. Bod. Pub. L.* Camb. *Brit. M.*
HAMMOND Henry, DD. Can. of Ch. Ch. Ox. and Chapl. in Ord.
31 Sermons in fo. 1684. *Bod. Ch. Ch. Univ. Trin. Magd. New C. Jes. Oriel. Bal. Mert. Queen's.* Oxon. *Pub. L. Trin. Queen's. Cl. H.* Camb.
HAMMOND Humfrey, M. A. of Bennet-Coll. Camb. and R. of East Guilford, Sussex.
1 Sam. x. 24. 8° 1715. Th.
Acts xvi. 17. 8° 1715. Vis.
HAMMOND John, DD. R. of Catsfield, Sussex.
Acts xiii. 36. 4° 1702. Royal Fun.
HAMMOND William, B. A. of St. John's Coll. Camb.
* Serm. in 12° 1745. On Christian Liberty and Holiness.
HAMMOND William, M. A.
* James v. 4, 5. 12° 1776. Vis. On Non-residence.
HAMPTON William, R. of Blechingley, Surrey.
2 Chron. xxxv. 24, 25. 4° 1660. 2 f. Jan. 30.
Gen. xviii. 25. 4° 1667. Assize. The Man of Judgment—or a Pattern for Judges.

HANCOCK John, DD. R. of St. Margaret's Lothbury, Lond. and Preb. of Cant. and Chapl. to the Duke of Bedford.
 Rom. i. 20, 21. 4° 1697. Th. for Peace. The great Duty of Thankfulnefs. *Ch. Ch.* Oxon.
 Jer. v 29. 8° 1699 Ref. Manners. *Bod. Ch. Ch.* Oxon.
 Acts xvii. 23. Boyle's Lect. 1706. fo. 1739. Vol. 2. p. 201–258. *Ch. Ch. Magd. St. John's.* Oxon. *Queen's. St. John's.* Camb.
 Rev. xiv. 13. 4° 1713. Fun. of J Poftlewait, the Xn Schoolmafter. *Brit M.*

HANCOCK Thomas Saul, R. of Wormfhill, and V. of Hollingbourn, Kent.
 Rom. xiii. 4, 8° 1735. Affize at *Maidftone.*

HANCOCKE Robert, Fell. of Clare-Hall Camb. and R. of Northill, Bedfordf.
 Luke xix. 42. 4° 1680. b. Lord Mayor. *Bod. Pub. L.* Camb.

HANCORNE Thomas, R. of St. Donats, Glamorganf.
 1 Sam. ii 30. 1710. Affize.

HANDLEY William
 * Luke xii. 17, 18. 8° 1720. Char. f.

HANNES William, M. A. R. of Newton Purcel, Oxon. and Mafter of the Free-School, Stamford.
 Rom xiii. 7. 8° 1717. Affize. *Magd* Oxon.
 1 John iv. 9. 8° 1717. *Oxon.* The Love of God to Mankind. *Sion.*
 Pf. lxxi. 5, 6. 4° 1725. *Stamf. rd.* Char. f. for Children.

HARCOURT James, DD. V. of All-S and Preb. of Briftol.
 Pf. cxii. 9. 4° 1721. On the Death of Mr. Colfton. *Linc. Worc.* Oxon. *Trin.* Camb.
 2 Cor. vi. 3. 4° 1735. Vif.

HARDCASTLE Thomas
 Sev. Serm. in 8° 1674. Chriftian Geography and Arithmetick, being a Survey of the World. *Bod.*

HARDING Nathaniel
 * 1 Kings viii. 66. 8° 1704. Acceffion.

HARDING Robert, V. of Potterfbury, Northampton.
 * Pf. xviii. 7. 8° 1756. Faft. for Earthquake.

HARDINGE Gideon, M. A. V. of Kingfton upon Thames, Surrey.
 2 Tim. ii. 8. 8° 1700. Ref. Manners.

HARDINGE George, M. A. V. of Kingfton, Surrey.
 Pf. xx 7. 4° 1709. Th. Victory and Succefs from God alone.

HARDY John, R. of Elfing, Norfolk.
 Pf. cxxxiii 1. 8° 1707. Th. for Union.

HARDY Nathaniel, DD. V. of St. Martin's in the Fields, Dean of Rochefter, and Chaplain in Ord.
 Ifai lvii. 19. 4° 1660. Faft. b. Lords. *Ch. Ch.* Oxon.
 Rev. iii. 9. 4° 1661. Conf. of 7 Bps. The Hierarcy exalted, and its Enemies humbled.
 1 Tim. ii. 1, 2. 4° 1661.
 Zech. xii. 11. 4° 1662. Jan. 30. b. Commons. A loud Call to great Mourning. *Univ. Ch. Ch.* Oxon.

               Luke

Luke xix. 41. 4° 1666. Sund. after Fire at London. Lamentation, Mourning, and Woe. *Univ. Ch. Ch.* Oxon. *Brit. M.*
Phil. i. 23. 4° 1666. Fun. The Pilgrim's Wish— or the Saints longing. *Ch. Ch.* Oxon.
Acts xiii. 36. 4° 1663. Fun of Sir Thomas Adams. The royal Common-wealth's Man. *Ch. Ch. Pub L.* Camb.
* Ephef. v. 3. V. Difc. on Conj. D. V. 2. p. 510.
Serm. from 1646. to 1666. *Sion.*

HARDY Samuel,[a] Curate of Layham, Suffolk.
Heb. x. 14. 8° 1748. Palm S. The Euchariſt, a material Sacrifice.

HARDY Samuel,[a] V. of Little Blakenham, Suffolk.
* Difcourfes in 8° 1770. On principal Prophecies of the old and new Teſtament.

HARE Francis, Bp. of Chicheſter.
Luke ii. 32. 4° 1700. *Camb.* Epiph. *Univ. Magd.* Oxon. *Trin. Queen's. Cl. H.* Camb. *Sion.*
Pf. lxxi. 17-19. 4° 1709. Th. b. Commons. For Succefs under the Command of the Duke of Malborough. *Ch. Ch. Or. Worc.* Oxon. *Trin. Queen's.* Camb. *Brit M.*
Joſhua i. 9. 8° 1711. b. Duke of Malborough. Th. for paſſing the Lines, and taking Bouchain. The Charge of God to joſhua. *Bod. Queen's. Worc.* Oxon. *Queen's.* Camb. *Sion.*
Rom. xiii. 4. 8° 1716. Acc. *Ch. Ch.* Oxon. *Cl. H. Queen's.* Cam. *Brit. M.*
Heb. xiii. 17. 4° 1719. Vif. Of Church-Authority. *Bod. Magd. Ch. Ch. Linc. Worc.* Oxon. *Queen's. Trin.* Camb.
Tit. ii. 8. 4° 1722. Conc. ad Synod.
Rom. xiii. 1, 2. 4° 1723. 2 f. Concerning the Duty of the Subject—Setting forth the Sin and Folly of entring into Confpiracies ag. the prefent Government. *Ch. Ch. Ox. Queen's.* Cam.
Prov. xiv. 34. 4° 1730. Ref. Manners. *Queen's.* Camb.
Prov. xxiv. 21. 4° 1731. Jan. 30. b. Lords. *Worc.* Oxon. *Trin. Queen's.* Camb.
Rom. x. 13-15. 4° 1735. Prop. Gofpel. *Ch Ch. Worc. Jef.* Ox. *Queen's.* Camb.
All thefe Serm. are printed together in his Works. V. 1. 8° 1746. *All S.* Oxon. *Pub. L.* Camb.

HARE Tho M. A. Maſter of the Free Sch. of Crewkerne, Somerf.
Prov. xix. 2. 4° 1747. *Sherborne.* School Feaſt. The Advantage and Abufes of Learning confidered.
* Serm. in 2 V. 8° 1748. On fev. important, practical Subjects.

HARGRAVES James, M. A. of Cl-Hall. Camb. R. of Eaſt Hoadly, Suffex, and Chaplain in Ord.
Deut. vi. 13. 4° 1723. Affize. The evil Confequences of Perjury. *Cl. H.* Camb.
1 Tim. v. 22. 4° 1724. Conf. of 2 Bps. *Cl. H.* Camb.

HARGREAVES Robert, M.A. Fell. of Trin. Coll. Camb.
2 Cor. xiii. 11. 8° 1745. *York.* Rebel. Unanimity recommended.

[a] The fame.

Luke xiii. 34. 8° 1745. *York*. A patriotic Spirit recommended.
HARMER John, V. of Butlers Marston, Warwick.
    * Judges xvi. 20. 8° 1777. At the Magd. Hosp.
HARPER John, M. A. V. of Beckford, Gloucesters.
    Rom. xi. 21. 8° 1721.
    2 Kings iii. 15. 8° 1730. The Nature and Efficacy of Musick to prepare the Mind for good Impressions.
HARPER William,   Chapl. to Lord Viscount Malpas.
    Gen. ii. 15. 4° 1732. Gardener's Feast. The Antiquity, Innocence, and Pleasure of gardening.
HARRINGTON J.
    * Ps. lxxii. 1. 8° 1714. David and Solomon. *Queen's*. Camb.
HARRIS Daniel, B. A.
    Ezek. xvii. 19. 8° 1722. Assize. *Queen's*. Camb.
HARRIS Higgins, B. A. R. of Brobury, Herefords.
    Luke x. 16. 4° 1710. Gospel-Ministers great Duty and Dignity. *Linc*. Oxon.
HARRIS John, DD. and F. R. S. R. of St. Mildred, Bread-street, London
    Luke vi. 24.   1718.
    Ps. x. 4.   ⎫ (Boyle's Lect. 1698.) fo. 1739. Vol. 1. p. 356–
    John. iv. 24.   ⎬ 425. *All S. Ch. Ch. C. C. C. Magd. Oriel*. Oxon.
    Jerem. ix. 24.   ⎭ *Queen's. St. John's*. Camb.
    Isai. i. 16, 17. 4° 1701. Fast. The Practice of religious and moral Duties, the best way to make a Nation happy. *Brit. M.*
    Jerem. xviii. 11. 4° 1703. Fast.
    Rom. xiv. 22, 23. 4° 1705. The modest Christian's Duty as to indifferent things in the Worship of God. *Ch. Ch.* Ox. *Pub. L. Queen's.* Camb.
    Eccles. ix. 7. 4° 1706. Co. Feast. The Lawfulness and Use of public Fasting.
    Luke ix. 55. 8° 1710. Evil and Mischief of a fiery Spirit. *Brit. M.*
    John xvi. 2. 8° 1715. Rebellion. Nov. 5.
    Prov. xxv. 5. 4° 1715. Accession.
HARRIS John, Bp. of Landaff.
    Isai. v. 10. 8° 1716. Nov. 5.
    1 Cor. ii. 15. 4° 1725. b. Soc. of Antient Britons. *Queen's*. Cam.
    Hosea x. 6. 4° 1734. Jan. 30. b. Lord..
HARRIS John, LL. B.
    * Deut. xxxiii. 29. 4° 1759. Th. s.
HARRIS R. DD.
    * Rev. xxii. 3, 4. 8° 1767. Fun.
[HARRIS Samuel,[a]]
    1 Pet. iii. 8. 8° 1711.
HARRIS Samuel,[a]
    Prov. xxii. 6. 8° 1715. Child's Educat. in Xtian Knowledge.

a *Q*. The same.

HARRIS Tho. M. A. R. of Gravesend and V. of Northfleet, Kent.
   Pf. cxviii. 18-20. 8° 1733. Open. a Church rebuilt after a Fire. The Duty of Gratitude to God and Man.
   Acts vii. 26. 4° 1749. Th. for Peace. The Bleſſings and Obligations ariſing from Peace.
   * Luke xxiv. 44. 8° 1755. David's prophetic Character vindicated.
HARRIS William, DD. Miniſter at London.
   * Iſai. xxix. 6. 12° 1704. Faſt. for Storm.
   Prov. i. 10. 8° 1707.
   Eccleſ. xii. 5. 8° 1708. Death of Prince George. *Queen's*. Cam.
   * 1 Tim. ii. 1. 12° 1711. V. Pract. Diſ. on Prayer. 12° 1711.
   * Matt. xxii. 29. 12° 1717. V. Pract. Diſ. on hearing the Word &c. 12° 1713. p. 121.
   * Matt. xvi. 18. 8° 1713. Nov. 5. Pope's Supremacy.
   * Luke viii. 18. 12° 1713. V. Pract. Diſ. on Hearing the Word &c. 12° 1713.
   * 2 Tim. ii. 6. 8° 1716. On Confideration.
   * Pſ. lxxviii. 20. 8° 1716. Th.
   * Matt. xii. 31, 32. 8° 1718. Sin ag. Holy Ghoſt.
   Pſ. xcvii. 1. 8° 1721. Coron. *Brit. M.*
   * Pract Diſcourſes in 8° 1724. On the principal Repreſentations of the Meſſiah. *Braz. N.* Oxon. *Dr. Ws's. L.* London.
   * 1. Pet. v. 1-4. 8° 1725. Ord.
   John xi. 45, 46. 8° 1728. 2 ſ. Ag. Woolſton. *Cl. H.* Camb.
   * 1 Cor. iv. 1, 2. 8° 1729. Ord.
   * Pſ. cii. 23, 24. 8° 1729. Fun. of Rev. *Mr. Harvey. Queen's.* C.
   * Acts xx. 24. 8° 1730. Fun.
   * 1 Tim. iv. 12. 8° 1730. Ord.
   * 2 Pet. iii. 14. 8° 1733. Fun. of Rev. *Dan. Mayo.*
   Luke xxii. 19, 20. 8° 1735. Of Tranſubſtantiation. V. Diſc. ag. Popery. Vol. 1. *Braz. N.* Oxon.
   John vi. 53. 8° 1735. V. Diſc. ag. Pop. V. 2. *Braz. N.* Oxon.
   1 Cor. xi. 24, 25. 8° 1735. On the Sacrament.
   * Funeral Diſc. in 8° 1736.
   * - - - - 1737. On Aug. 1.
   1 Cor. iv. 2. 17 Ord.
HARRISON John, DD. R. of Pulborow, Suſſex.
   2 Sam. xviii. 28. 4° 1683. Th. Sept. 9. *St. John's.* Camb.
HARRISON John, V. of Burnham, Eſſex.
   2 Cor. vii. 1. 8° 1710. A Perſuaſive to Holineſs. *Univ. Or. Linc.* Oxon. *Trin.* Camb.
HARRISON John, B. A. Curate of Hadleigh, Suffolk.
   Pſ. cxxii. 6. 4° 1717. *Ipſwich.* Nov. 5.
HARRISON Joſeph
   John v. 14. 8° 1713. Th. *Linc.* Oxon.
HARRISON Michael, Miniſter of Caſfield, Bucks.
   Rom. iii. 22. 8° 1691. Sev. Sermons of Juſtification. *Bod.*
   * Iſai. xlv. 24, 25. 8° 1691. Subſt. of ſev. Sermons. *Bod.*
   Matt. xxii. 1, 2 &c. 8° 1691. The Believ. Marriage with Xt. *Bod.*

HARRISON R.[a]
  * Job xiii. 15. 8° 1765. On a Fire at *Honiton*, Devon.
HARRISON R.[a] M. A.
  * Luke ix. 56. ⎫
  * Matt. v. 22. ⎬ 8° 1781. *York*. The Catholic Proteſtant.
  * Epheſ. iv. 26. ⎭
HARRISON Richard, Lect. of St. Peter's Cornhill, and joint Lect. of St. Martin's in the Fields, London, and Miniſter of Brompton-Chapel.
  * Jerem. iii. 1. 4° 1768. b. Gov. of Magd. Hoſp.
  * Deut. xv. 11. 4° 1769. b. Gov. of Small-pox Hoſp.
  * Gal vi. 10. 4° 1775. b. the Humane Society.
  * - - - - 1779. Faſt.
  * Exod. viii. 20. 8° 1781. Faſt.
HARRISON Robert M. A. Student of Ch. Ch. Oxon. R. of Wyfordley, Staffordſ.
  Amos v. 23, 24. 4° 1672. Aſſize. *Bod*.
  Prov. xiv. 34. 4° 1672. Aſſize. *Bod*.
HARRISON *Thomas*
  * Matt xxv. 21. 8° 1700. Fun. of *Mord. Abbott*, Eſq;
  * Pſ. lxxii. 18. 8° 1715. Th. for Acceſſion.
  John xvii. 23, 24. 8° 1720. Fun.
  * 2 Tim. iv. 7, 8. 8° 1728. Fun. of *Mary Page*. *Queen's*. Camb.
  ‡ * Phil. i. 20. 8° 17   *Brit. M.*
  ‡ * Rom. xv. 29. 8° 17   Mutual Duties of Cler. & Laity. *Br. M.*
HARRISON William,   R. of Stanton, Glouceſterſ.
  Exod. xxxii. 26. 12° 1702. ⎫
  Prov. xiv. 34. 8° 1704.   ⎬ Ref. Manners.
HART John, DD.
  * Diſc. in 12° 1702.
HART John, M. A. V. of Stockland, Somerſetſ.
  Rom. xiv. 10. 4° 1726. Liberty of Conſcience aſſerted.
HART Richard, M. A. V. of St. George, Glouceſter.
  * Jerem. ii. 4. 8° 1767. 2 ſ. Importance of the Word of God.
HARTCLIFFE John, B. D, Fell. of King's Coll. Camb. and Canon of Windſor.
  Jonah i. 8, 9. 4° 1684. Oxfordſhire Feaſt.
  Job xxxi. 19. 4° 1694. Spitt. W. *Brit. M.*
  Pſ. xc. 15. 4° 1695. Jan. 30. b. Commons. *Ch. Ch. Magd.* Ox. *Trin. Cl. H.* Camb. *Eton.*
HARTE Walter, M. A. Canon of Windſor.
  John xiv. 1. 8° 1737. *Oxon*. Union and Harmony of Reaſon, Morality and revealed Religion. *Bod. Worc. Linc.* Oxon. *Queen's.* Camb. *Brit. M.*
  ‡ * Num. x. 9. 8° 17
[HARTLEY F.]
  * - - - 1756.

[a] *Q.* The ſame.

[HARTLEY James,] of Hull, Yorkſ.
* - - - - 8° 1774. Fun.
HARTLEY Thomas, M. A. R. of Winwick, Northampton.
  1 Chron. iv. 10. 8° 1737. On Prayer and Charity.
  1 Tim. vi. 17–19. 8° 1737. The Duty and Reward of Charity.
  John iv. 23. 8° 1747. Viſ. A ſpirit. Worſhip, the Religion of the Law and the Goſpel.
  Acts ii. 37. 8° 1748. Converſion founded on Conviction of Sin.
  1 Cor. xii. 31. 8° 1750. *Northampton.* Infirmary.
  * 7 Additional Serm. publiſhed in 8°. (viz.)
  * Rom. i. 6.
  * Pſ. xliv. 14.
  * Matt. xiv. 24.
  * Heb. vi. 12.   } 1755.
  * John viii. 36.
  * Col. i. 26.
  * Jer. xxxi. 33.
HARTWELL William. DD. Sub-Dean of Durham.
  Pſ. lxxxv. 8. 8° 1713. Th.
HARVEST George, M. A. Fell. of Magd. Coll. Camb.
  Luke xiii. 5. 4° 1746. Rebellion. The Grounds and Reaſons of temporal Judgments conſidered. *Queen's.* Camb.
  * 8 Sermons in 8° 1754. On various Subjects.
HARVEY Francis, M. A. R. of Lawſhall, Suffolk.
  James i, 8. 4° 1721. Viſ. *Ch. H.* Camb.
HARVEY William, V. of Hambledon, Hants, and Chap. on board her Majeſty's Ship Edgar.
  Prov. xvi. 28. 4° 1705.
[HARWARD   ]
  ‡ * Pſ. xvi. 18. 8° 1732. *Boſton.* Fulneſs of Joy in the Preſence of God. *Brit. M.*
HARWARD Thomas, M. A. Cur. of Madington, Wilts.
  1 Tim. iii. 9. 4° 1709 Viſ.
HARWOOD *Edward,* DD.
  * Iſai. lvii. 1. 8° 1761. Fun. of *J. Taylor*, DD. *Queen's.* Camb.
  * 2 Cor iv. 18. 12° 1767. Thoughts on Time and Eternity.
  * 5 Diſſertations in 8° 1772.
  * 7 Sermons in 12° 1776. On the Parable of the Sower — to which are added
  * 3 Sermons on the Nature and Deſign of the Chriſtian Religion. *Queen's.* Camb.
HARWOOD James
  Pſ. lxxvii. 20. 4° 1661. p. 21.
  Phil. iv. 5. 4° 1662. p. 67.
  1 Pet. iii. 2. 4° 1662. p. 76.
  * Diſcourſes in 4° 1662.
HASCARD Gregory, DD. Dean of Windſor and Chapl. in Ord.
  Rom. xiii. 4. 4° 1668. Aſſize.

Pf. cxxiv. 7. 4° 1672. Nov. 5. *Bod. All S. Ch. Ch.* Ox. *Queen's.* C.
Jude 8. 4° 1680. Elect. Lord Mayor. *All S. Ch. Ch.* Oxon. *St. John's.* Camb. *Brit. M.*
Ephef. iv. 32. 4° 1685. Spitt. T. *Brit. M.*
Acts xvi. 30, 31. 4° 1696. b. King. *Magd.* Oxon. *Trin.* Camb.
Micah vii. 2. 4° 1696. Jan. 30. b. Commons. *Bod. Magd.* Ox.

HASLEWOOD Francis, M. A. R. of Chinkford, Effex, and Preb. of Warwell, Hants.
Ifai. i. 26. 4° 1720. Nov. 5. b. Lord Mayor. *Sion.*
Zech. vii. 5. 8° 1720. Jan. 30. b. Lord Mayor.

HASLEWOOD John, DD. R. of St. Olave's, Southwark.
Ifai. lv. iii. 4° 1701. Recantation of a Quaker. *Sion.*
2 Sam. xv. 4. 4° 1707. Or. Oxon. *St. John's. Trin.* Camb. *Sion.*
Deut. i. 16, 17. 4° 1707. Affize.

HASSEL S.
1 Kings iii. 9. 8° 1719. Affize.

HAVETT John, M. A. Chapl. to Lady Ann Franklyn.
13 Serm. in 8° 1703. *Trin.* Camb.

HAWEIS Tho. LL.B. R. of Allwinkle Northampton, and Chaplain to the Countefs of Huntingdon.
* 14 Sermons in 8° 1762. Entitled Evangelical Principles and Practices. Preached at St. Mary Magdalen, Oxford.
* Ifai. v. 25. 8° 1778. *Bath.* Faft.

HAWKER Robert
* Acts x. 7. 4° 1781. A devout Soldier. b. the North-battallion of Glouc. Militia at Roborough-Down near Plymouth, Devon.

HAWKINS William, M. A. late Poetry-Profeffor, and Fell. of Pemb. Coll. Oxon. Preb. of Wells and R. of Cofterton, Rutland.
Jerem. xii. 1. 8° 1752. *Oxon.* Jan. 30. *Bod. Braz. N. Bal.* Oxon.
* 1 Cor. xiii. 13. 4° 1755. On Mr. Colfton's birth-day. The Nature, Extent and Excellence of Chriftian Charity.
* Luke xii. 57. 8° 1756. Reafonablenefs of Belief in the Doctrines of Chriftianity.
* 2 Tim. ii. 15. 8° 1768. Pretences of Enthufiafts confidered and confuted.
* Job xxxvi. 26. 8° 1769. *Oxon.* Enthufiat. Pretences, as grounded in the Articles of the Church, confidered and confuted.
* 1 Cor. i. 10. 8° 1773. 2 f. Principles of the Confeffional confidered.

HAWKYNS George, M. A. R. of St. Mary at Hill, London.
Ecclef. xii. 13. 3° 1731. Elect. of Lord Mayor.
1 Tim. ii. 2. 4° 1744. Nov. 5. b. Lord Mayor. Godlinefs and Honefty, the Foundation and Support of Government.

HAWKSHAW Benj.   of St. John's Coll. Camb.
* - - - - 17   On St. Cæcilia's Day.

HAWORTH R.   R. of Eaft Hothley, Suffex.
* Pf. cxi. 4. 8° 17

HAW.

HAWTAYNE Will. M. A R. of Datchworth, Herts, and Chapl.
to the Princefs of Wales.
   Pf. xcii. 4. 8° 1714. Th. *Ch. Ch.* Oxon.
   Rom. ii. 3. 8° 1716.
HAWYS Charles,   V. of Chebfey near Stafford.
   Acts xv. 41. 4° 1705. Vif.
HAYDON John, late Preacher at the Baptift-meeting at Tewkefbury,
   Gloucefterf.
   *Rom. vii. 24. 8° 1770. 2 f. Saints Complaint under Remains of
   indwelling Sin.
   * Phil. iii. 8° 1772.
HAYLEY Tho. DD. Can. Refid. of Chichefter and Chapl. in Ord.
   Gal. v. 1. 4° 1711. Prop. Gofpel. The Liberty of the Gofpel
   explained. *Ch. Ch.*. Oxon. *Queen's*. Camb.
   Pf. lxxxi. 13, 14. 8° 1712. Faft. *Bod. Linc.* Oxon. *Pub. L. Cl. H.*
   Camb. *Sion*.
   Matt. xv. 9. 8° 1716. b. King. The Vanity and Sinfulnefs of
   human Impofitions in Doctrines of Religion. *Worc. Ox. Eton.*
   Col. iii. 14. 8° 1718. b. King. Of mutual Charity. *Bod. Ch. Ch.*
   Oxon. *Sion.*
   Pf. cxix. 158. 4° 1718. Ref. Manners. *Ch. Ch* Oxon.
   Ifai. xli. 17-20. 4° 1721. May 29. b. Commons. *Eton.*
HAYLEY William, DD. Dean of Chichefter, and R. of St. Giles's
   in the Fields, and Chapl. in Ord.
   Prov. viii. 18. 4° 1687. Jan. 30. Levant Co. *C. C. C. Ox. Sion.*
   Ezra viii. 21. 4° 1695. Faft. b. Commons. *Ch. Ch. Magd.* Oxon.
   Trin. Cl. H. Camb. *Sion.*
   Prov. xiv. 34. 12° 1699. Ref. Manners. *Ch. Ch.* Ox. *St. John's.*
   Camb. *Brit. M.*
   Pf. xc. 12. 4° 1699. Fun. of Dr. Connor. *Ch. Ch.* Ox. *Queen's.*
   Cl. H. St. John's. Camb. *Brit. M.*
   Matt. xxv. 34-36. 4° 1700. Spitt T *Pub. L.* Camb.
   Rom. xiv. 19. 4° 1701. Conc. ad Synod. *Ch. Ch. Magd. Linc.*
   Oxon. *Trin. St. John's.* Camb. *Brit. M.*
   Ephef. iv. 11, 12. 4° 1702. Conf. of Ep. Evans. *Ch. Ch.* Oxon.
   Trin. St. John's. Camb.
HAYTER Thomas, Bp. of London.
   Pf. lxxxix. 20-24. 4° 1746. Acc. b. Com. *Queen's. C. Brit. M.*
   1 Pet. ii. 17. 4° 1750. Jan. 30. b. Lords. *Queen's.* Camb.
   1 Cor. vii. 31. 4° 1752. b. King. *Bal.* Ox. *Queen's. C. Brit. M.*
   *Pf. cxxii. 8, 9. 4° 1753. Ir. Prot. fch. *All S. Braz. N. Ex.* Ox.
   * Rev. xiv. 6, 7. 4° 1755. Prop. of Gofpel. *Ex.* Ox. *Queen's. C.*
   * Matt. xviii. 10, 11. 4° 1755. An. meet. Ch. Sch. *Ex.* Oxon.
   Queen's. Camb.
   * Luke ix. 11. 4° 1759. b. Gov. of Lond. Hofp. *Ex. Wadh.* Ox.
   Queen's. Camb.
HAYTER John, B. A. Fell. of King's Coll. Camb.
   * 2 Tim. iv. 2-4. 4° 1780. Vif.

HAYWARD Roger, DD. Chapl. in Ord.
  2 Theff. 2. 10, 11. 4° 1673. b. King. The Alliance of Wickedness to Error. *Bod. Ch. Ch. Magd.* Oxon. *Sion.*
  Mal. iii. 14. 4° 1676. b. King. *Bod. Magd.* Oxon. *St. John's.* C.
HAYWARD Samuel
  * Pf. cvii. 31. 8° 1746. Advice to Sailors.
  * Serm. in 8° 1758.
HAYWOOD William, DD. V. of St. Giles's. Preb. of Weſtm. and Chapl. in Ord.
  Rom. v. 5. 4° 1660. Fun. of Walter Norbane, Efq;
  Acts xxiii. 5. 4° 1663. Ag. ſpeaking ill of Governors. *Pub. L. C.*
HAZELAND William, M. A. V. of Bruges, Herts, and Lect. of St. Mary White Chapel, London.
  * Job xxxvii. 14. 4° 1756. Faſt.
  * Prov. xv. 8. 4° 1760.
  * Ephef. v. 16. 4° 1761. b. Gov. of the Afylum.
HEAD Erafmus, M. A. Preb. of Carliſle.
  1 Tim. iv. 16. 8° 1746. Ord. Trin. Sunday.
  * 1 Pet. xiii. 14. 8° 1747. Affize. Loyalty recommended on proper Principles.
HEAD Henry, Maſter of the Free-ſchool at Ambroſbury, Wilts.
  2 Cor. v. 18–20. 8° 1714. Nature of the Xtian Relig. *Linc.* Ox.
HEALD Peter, M. A. Preb. of Chicheſter.
  Tit. iii. 1. 4° 1697. Affize.
HEATH J.   late of New Coll. Oxon.
  * Matt. viii. 25. 4° 1760. Th.
HEATHCOTE Ralph, DD. Preacher-Affiſtant at Linc. Inn, Lond.
  * Micah vi. 8. 8° 1756. *Leiceſter.* Affize. *Queen's.* Camb.
  * Coloff. ii. 8. 4° 1759. Conc. Acad. pro Grad. Doctor.
  * Rom. i. 20. 4° 1763. 2 f. at Boyle's Lect. *Queen's.* Camb.
HEBDEN Samuel, of Wrentham, Suffolk.
  * Acts xxiv. 25. 8° 1738. Sev. Sermons.
  * Job i. 20, 21. 8° 1739. On the Death of a Child.
  * Acts xvi. 14, 15. 8° 1745.
  * ——— xxiii. 24. 8° 1746.
HEBER John,   R. of Marton in the Dioceſe of York.
  - - - - 1732. *York.* Vif. The Labours and Difficulties of the miniſterial Function.
HECKFORD Thomas, M. A.
  * Ecclef. xii. 13, 14. 8° 1721. Farw. f.
HECKSTALL Abraham, M. A.
  Pf. cxxii. 6. 4° 1728. May 26. b. Lord Mayor. Peace the Fruits of Piety.
HELLENBROECK Abraham
  * Cant. xi. 15. 8° 1742. V. *Tennent's* Sermons.
HELLIER Henry, DD. Fell. of C. C. C. Oxon.
  Pf. xv. 4. 4° 1688. *Oxon.* The Obligation of Oaths. *Bod. Ch. Ch. Queen's. Werc.* Oxon. *St. John's.* Camb. *Sion.*

HELME

HELME J.
 * Heb. ii 3. 8° 1762. Specimen of preaching among Methodists.
HELMES Thomas, M. A. fometime of Jef. Coll. Camb.
 Pf. cxxi. 1. 4° 1668.
HELVETIUS Sangallo, V. D. M.
 * 1 Cor. vii. 36. 8° 1775. Latin Differtation.
HENCHMAN John
 * Exod. xxii. 28. 4° 1683.
HENCHMAN Richard, DD. Treafurer of St. Paul's, and V. of Chigwell, Effex.
 Pf. xxxix. 5. 4° 1661. Fun. of Mrs Ellen Harcourt.
 Rom. xv. 5, 6. 4° 1661. *Queen's.* Oxon.
HENDLEY William, Lecturer of St. James's, Clerkenwell, Lond.
 Acts xxiv. 14. 8° 1715.
 2 Tim iv. 2, 3. } 8° 1716. The Paftor's Duty.
 1 Tim. vi. 20. }
 Jerem. xlviii. 10. 8° 1716. 2 f.
 Rev. 19. 9. 8° 1718. Ch. [The Author was tried and convicted for this Sermon.] *Bod.*
HENLEY John, (Orator) M. A. R. of Chelmondifton, Suffolk.
 1 Sam. iii. 1. 8° 1727. Speaking and Action. *Queen's.* Camb.
 * 2 Cor. vi. 8, 9. 8° 1728. An academical Difquifition. Defence of Oratory. *Bod.*
 * Pf. viii. 6. 8° 1729. The Butcher's Lecture. *Bod.*
 Job. xviii. 14. 8° 1729. *Bod.*
 Luke xix. 22. 8° 1729. Theolog. Lecture. *Queen's.* Camb.
 * Heb. xii. 7. 8° 1729. Pangs of expiring Penitents.
 * Rev. xxi. 10, 11. 8° 1729. Heaven of Heavens.
 * Col. iv. 14. 8° 1729. Advantages of divine Revelation.
 1 Kings xviii. 24. 8° 1730. *Bod.*
 * Acts ii. 42. 8° 1731. Homily.
 * 2 Tim. i. 13. 8° 1731. Homily.
 * Gen. xviii. 19. 8° 1732. Ref. Manners.
 * Acts xxiv. 25. 8° 1753. Second St. Paul &c.
 * 1 Pet. ii. 12. }
 * Ifai. vii. 4 &c. } 17 2 Dif. a Vindicat. of the Univ. of Oxon.
HENLEY S. Profeff. of Mor. Philofophy in Will. and Mary Coll.
 * Heb. xiii. 16. 4° 1771. Ch. f. For Support of the Coll.
 * Mark xii. 17. 4° 1772. Diftinct Claims of Religion and Government confidered.
 * Jer. xiv. 3. 4° 1776. Anniv. of Founder of the Coll. *Queen's.* C.
 * Jude 5–7. 8° 1778. Differtation.
HENRY *Matthew,* Minifter of the Gofpel.
 * Acts xv. 36. 8° 1704. Right Management of friendly Vifits.
 * 1 Cor. xvi. 19. 8° 1704. Family-Religion.
 * Pf. lxv. 11. 8° 1706. Th.
 * Acts xx. 37, 38. 8° 1706. Fun. of - - - *Owen.*
 * Ifai. lxiii. 4. 8° 1707. New Year's-day.
 * Matt. vi. 12. 8° 1711.

* Pf.

* Pſ. vii. 9. 12° 1712. Ref. Manners.
* Prov. xxxi. 28. 8° 1712. Fun. of *Mrs. Henry*.
* Phil. ii. 27. 8° 1712. Fun. of *Mr. Lawrence*. *Pub. L.* Camb.
* Diſcourſes in fo. 1726.
* 3 Diſc. in 12° 1731. For daily Communion with God.
* 20 Diſc. in 12° 1770. (3d Edition.)

HENRY Robert, DD.
* - - - - 1773. For propag. Xtian Knowledge.

HENRY William, DD. R. of Urney in the Dioceſe of Derry and Chaplain to his Grace (Joſeph) Abp. of Tuam.
  Pſ. cxlvii. 12–14. 8° 1749. Th. for Peace. The Advantages of Peace, and the Means to perpetuate the preſent Peace.
* Matt. v. 48. 4° 1751. Viſ. Chriſtian Perfection.
* Pſ. cxii. 6. 1753.
* 2 Sam. xxiii. 1–3 1754.
* Luke xxiv. 5. 8° 1756. *Dublin*. The Anniv. of *St. Patrick*.
* Deut. xxxiii. 28–31. 8° 1758. Faſt.

HENWOOD James
  John vi. 53. } 4° 1701. On the Sacrament.
  1 Cor. xi. 28.

HERNE Samuel, Fell. of Clare-Hall Camb. and Chaplain to the Duke of Monmouth.
  Heb. iv. 13. 4° 1679. Of Divine Providence. *Magd*. Ox. *Trin*. Camb. *Sion*.

HERRIES John, M. A.
* Job xiv. 14. 4° 1774. Againſt Suicide.

HERRING Thomas, Abp. of Canterbury.
* Acts xxvi. 18. 4° 1756. Prop. Goſpel. *Braz. N.* Oxon.
* 7 Serm. (republiſhed) in 8° 1763. On public Occaſions. *Queen's*. Camb. *Dr. Ws's L.* London.

HERRING Tho. M. A. Preb. of York and R. of Culleſden, Surrey.
* 1 Tim. iv. 16. 4° 1765. Viſ.

HERVEY James, M. A R. of Weſton Flavel, Northamptonſ.
* Gal. vi. 14. 8° 1753. Viſ. Croſs of Chriſt the Xtian's Glory.
* 2 Cor. v. 18. 8° 1759. Reconciliation.
* Heb. xi. 28. 8° 1759. 2 ſ. Time of Danger, Means of Safety.
* 8 Sermons in 12° 1759.
* Rom. v. 19. 8° 1769. 2 ſ. Many made righteous by the Obedience of one.
* Phil. iv. 4. 12° 1770. The Grounds and Duty of Christian rejoicing.
* Mark vi. 2. 12° 1770. 2 ſ. On Repentance.
* Phil. i. 21. 12° 1775. Fun. of Mr. Abraham Donn, Teacher of the Mathematics at Biddeford, Devon.

HESKETH Henry, DD. R. of Charlewood, Surrey, V. of St. Helen's, London, and Chapl. in Ord.
  2 Sam. i. 17, 18. 4° 1678. Jan 30. b. Lord Mayor. *Pub. L.* Cam.
  Ezek. xxxvii. 3. 4° 1679. The dangerous and almoſt deſperate State of Religion.

Lam,

Lam. iii. 22. 4° 1679. Faft. for Fire of London. b. Lord Mayor. *Ch. Ch. Univ.* Oxon.

Lam. iii. 20, 21. 4° 1682. Faft. for Fire at London. *Brit. M.*

Ecclef. xi. 10. 4° 1683. Fun. of Sir Tho. Vinor. The Importance of Religion to young perfons. *Ch. Ch. Ox. St. John's. C.*

2 Sam. xxii. 51. 4° 1684. A private Peace-offering for the Difcovery of the late horrid Confpiracy. *Pub. L. Trin. Cam. Sion.*

1 Pet. ii. 15. 4° 1684. Th. Sept. 9. b. Lord Mayor. *Univ. Ch. Ch.* Oxon. *Brit. M.*

Matt. v. 17. 4° 1684. b. King. *Bod.*

1 Cor. xi. 26. 12° 1684. Subft. of 2 Serm. Exhortation to frequent Communion.

1 Pet. ii. 13. 8° 1685. Th. for the late Victory over the Rebels. *Magd.* Oxon.

1 Cor. xi. 29. 12° 1689. The Cafe of eating and drinking unworthily.

Jer. v. 5. 4° 1699. Great men's Advantages and Obligations to Religion. *Trin. Camb. Sion.*

1 Tim. i. 9. 4° 1699. Affize. *Linc.*

HESKITH Thomas, M. A. R. of St. John's at Nevis in America.
- - - - - 4° 1699. Fun. of Col. Francis Collingwood and of his Lady.

* Jofhua xxiv. 14. 4° 1700. Ref. Manners. The Excellency and Advantages of Religion. *St. John's.* Camb.

Acts xx. 26, 27. 4° 1702. Farewel at *Nevis.* Piety and Learning, the great Ornament and Character of the Priefthood. *Eton.*

HESLEDEN Thomas, M. A.

Pf. cvii. 43. 4° 1696. *York.* On the late horrid Confpiracy.

HEWERDINE Thomas, M. A. R. of Abington, and V. of Bafingbourn, Camb.

Ifai. lvii. 1. 8° 1711. Fun. of Mrs. Nightingale.

Acts xxiv. 14. 8° 1718. The Common-prayer-book, no Mafs-book.

HEWERTSON
* Prov. xiii. 11. 8° 1775. b. a Society of Artificers at *Blackbourn,* Lancafter.

HEWGOE Walter, R. of Holy Trinity, Exon.
* Rev. xiv. 13. 4° 1728. Fun.

[HEWYTT]
* 9 Select Sermons. - - - - - -

HEY John, DD. Fell. of Sidney Coll. and Norrifian Profeffor of Divinity Camb. and Preacher at Whitehall.

* Heb. viii. 13. 8° 1773. *Camb.* Affize. Nature of obfolete Ordinances. *Queen's.* Camb.

* 1 Pet. ii. 16. 8° 1774. *Camb.* Nov. 5. *Queen's.* Camb.

* Ephef. iv. 31. 8° 1774. 2 f. *Camb.* Nature of malevolent Sentiments. *Queen's.* Camb.

* Jerem. xlvii. 6. 8° 1771. *Camb.* Faft.

* Ephef. iv. 28. 4° 1777. *Camb.* Addenbrook-Hofpital.

HEYLIN John, DD.
* Difcourfes in 2 Vol. 4° 1761.

HEYLYN John, DD. Preb. of Weſtminſter, R. of St. Mary-le-
    ſtrand and Chaplain in Ord.
    Iſai. li. 7. 8° 1720. Ref. Manners. *Brit. M.*
    Rom. xiii. 4. 8° 1728. Ref. Manners. *Queen's.* Camb. *Eton.*
    Theolog. Lectures &c. in 4° 1749. *Bod. Magd. New C. Wadh.
    Hert.* Oxon. *Pub. L. Queen's.* Camb. *Sion.*
HEYLYN Pet. DD. Sub-Dean of Weſtminſter, and Chapl. in Ord.
    Pſ. xxxi. 21. 4° 1661. May 29. *Univ. Worc.* Oxon. *Brit. M.*
HEYNES John, M. A. Preacher. of the New Church, Weſtminſter.
    Phil. iii. 21. 4° 1669.
HEYNES Matthew, M. A. Miniſter of Wroxall, Warwickſhire.
    Rom. xiii. 3, 4. 4° 1701. Aſſize.
    Prov. xx. 1. 4° 1701. Ref. M. Ag. Drunkenneſs.
HEYRICK Richard, M. A. Warden of Mancheſter College.
    2 Kings xi. 12° 1661. Coron.
    1 Kings ii. 12. 4° 1661. *Sion.*
HEYRICK Thomas,   Miniſter of Market-Harborough, Leiceſter.
    Prov. xxi. 1. 4° 1685. On proclaiming K. James II.
    2 Sam. xv. 11. 4° 1697. Th. The Character of a Rebel. *Oriel.*
    Oxon. *Pub. L.* Camb.
HEYWOOD Oliver
    *Iſai. lv. 3. 8° 1672. The ſure Mercies of David. *Bod.*
    Pſ. xxx. 5. 8° 1679. Subſt. of ſev. ſ. Life in God's Favour. *Bad.*
    1 Cor. xv. 19. 8° 1701. Fun.   The two worlds
        preſent and future. *Sion.*
HEYWOOD James
    *Dan. vi. 21. 8° 1756. On the Kings Indiſpoſition.
HIBBERT Hen, DD. Miniſ. of St. Olave's in the Old Jewry, Lond.
    Pſ. cxviii. 24. 4° 1661. May 29. b. Lord Mayor. *Univ.* Oxon.
    A Body of Divinity with 12 ſ. on ſev. Occaſions. fo. 1662. *Sion.*
HICKERINGILL Edmond.   R. of All Saints, Colcheſter.
    Judges v. 23. 4° 1680. b. Lord Mayor. *Bod. Ch. Ch. Bal. Magd.
    Queen's.* Oxon. *Trin. St. John's. Magd.* Camb.
    Jerem. v. 25, 26. 4° 1681. The horrid Sin of Man-catching. *Bod.*
    2 Sam. x. 12. 4° 1692. The good old Cauſe. *Pub. L.* Cam. *Sion.*
    1 Kings xxi. 12, 13. 4° 1700. Jan. 30.
    N. B. Theſe Serm. are reprinted in his works. 2 Vol. 8° 1716.
    Magd. Oxon.
HICKES George, DD. Dean of Worceſter.
    Rom. xiii. 4. 4° 1683. *Ch. Ch. Magd.* Oxon.
    Prov. xxx. 31. 4° 1684. 3 ſ. Jan. 30. Ag. Non-reſiſtance. *Bod.*
    Serm. in 2 V. 8° 1713. *Ch. Ch. C. C. C. Balſ Magd. New C.* Ox.
    13 Serm. (Poſth.) 8° 1726. On practical Subjects. *Bal.* Oxon.
    Dr. W's. L. London.
HICHMAN Charles, Bp. of Derry.
    1 Kings xviii. 21. 4° 1680. b. L. May. *All S. Ch. Ch. Magd.* Ox.
    John iv. 21–23. 4° 1681. b. Levant Co. *Ch. Ch. Magd.* Oxon.
    Pub. L. Camb. *Sion.*

Prov.

Prov. iii. 8,9, 4° 1686. b. Lord Mayor. *Bod. Magd.* Oxon. *Sion.*
Ifai. lx. 10. 4° 1690. b. Commons. *Bod. All S. Jef.* Oxon. *Sion.*
Pf. iv. 4. 4° 1690. b. Queen. *Ch. Ch. Univ. Magd. Jef.* Oxon. *Pub. L. Trin.* Camb. *Sion.*
Deut. xxx. 15. 4° 1692. b. Queen. Lent. On Contentment. *Univ. Magd. Jef. Ch. Ch.* Oxon.
Phil. iv. 11. 4° 1693. b. Queen. Lent. *Bod. Magd. Jef.* Oxon. *Sion. Pub. L.* Camb.
Pf. c. 1. 4° 1695. On St. Cæcilias's day. *Ch. Ch.* Oxon. *Trin.* Camb. *Sion.*
14 Serm. in 8° 1706. *Bod. All S. C. C. C. Magd. St. John's. Pemb.* Oxon. *Pub. L.* Camb.
12 Serm. in 8° 1713. On the principal Feftivals. *Bod. C. C. C. New C. Magd. St. John's. Worc.* Oxon. *St. John's.* Camb.

HICKS Edward, DD. R. of Margaret Pattens, Lond. and of Buckland, Herts.
Gen. xviii. 25. 4° 1682. Affize.

HICKS H.
Phil. iii. 20,21. 4° 1681. Fun.

HICKS Samuel, R. of Wreftlingworth, Bedfordfhire.
* 6 Difc. in 12° 1767.

HICKSON James, M. A.
Prov. xx. 8. 8° 1682. Affize.

HIERON John, M. A. fometime R. of Breadfall, Derbyfhire.
Pf. xxxii. 11. 8° 1680. Subftance of fev. Sermons.

HIGDEN Will. DD. R. of St. Paul's, Shadwell, and Preb. of Cant.
Luke xxiii. 28. 4° 1710. Jan. 30. b. Queen. *Bod. Univ. Linc.* Oxon. *Queen's. St. John's.* Camb. *Sion.*

HIGDON William, M. A.
Ifai. lvii. 1, 2. 4° 1688. Fun. of Mrs Parr.

HIGGINS Francis, M. A. Preb. of Ch. Ch. Dublin.
1 Chron. xvi. 34-39. 8° 1705. Th. *Trin.* Camb. *Sion.*
Rev. iii. 2, 3. 4° 1706. Afh-wednefday. *Univ. Worc. Jef.* Oxon. *Queen's.* Camb.

HIGGINS John, or D. F.
Ifai. liii. 8. 4° 1688. [Found in an Oxford-Scholar's Pocket.]

HIGHAM John, M. A. R. of Wotton in Surrey.
Prov. xxiv. 21. 8° 1675. Sev. Serm. Looking-glafs for Loyalty. *Bod.*

HILDEYARD John, LL. D. Commiffary of the Arch-Deaconry of Norfolk, and R. of Cowfton in the Diocefe of Norwich.
Rev. iv. 4. 4° 1683. Fun. of E. of Yarmouth, *Trin. St. John's.* C.

HILDROP John, DD. R. of Wath near Rippon, Yorkfhire.
A Treatife in 8° 1711. Of the three Evils of the laft Times, the Sword, the Peftilence, and the Famine &c.
A Commentary on the 2d Pf. 8° 1742.
John iii. 19. 8° 1746. Immorality, Root of Infidelity. *Queen's.* C.

HILDYARD Chriftopher, M. A. R. of Claxby, Lincolnfhire.
Mic. vi: 8. 4° 1707.

HIL.-

HILDYARD Chrift.   R. of Rowley near Beverley, Yorkfhire.
  Job xxvii. 5, 6. 8° 1732. Uprightnefs and Integrity, requifite to attain and preferve a good Confcience.
HILDYARD Francis
  Jude 14, 15. 8° 1703. Preached at Weft-Acre, Norfolk.
HILL
  * Phil. iv. 5. 4° 1677. m. e. C. p. 320. In what things we muft ufe Moderation and in what not.
HILL Anthony, M. A. Lect. of Stratford-le-Bow, Middlefex, and Chaplain to the Duke of Richmond.
  Rom. vi. 18. 8° 1702. Afer baptizatus. *Ch. Ch.* Oxon. *Sion.*
  1 Cor. xiii. 13. 4° 1702. County-Feaft.
HILL Bryam, B. A. Chapl. to the Earl of Leven.
  * Gal. iv. 18. 8° 1780. b. Gov. of the *Salop* Infirmary.
HILL Daniel, M. A. Preb. of Rochefter.
  Rev. xix. 3. 4° 1707. Th. for Victory.
HILL H.
  * Ecclef. xii. 7. 8° 1667.
HILL J. S. DD. Chapl. to the Abp. of Canterbury.
  John ii. 17. 8° 1745. *York.* Falt Zeal and Chriftian Zeal diftinguifhed or the Effentials of Popery defcribed. *Brit. M.*
HILL John. M. A. R. of St. Mabyn, Cornwal.
  Rev. xviii. 4. 4° 1680. The grand Apoftacy of the Church of Rome from her primitive Purity and Integrity.
  2 Sam. xxi. 16, 17. 4° 1693. Faft and Affize. Ifhbibenob defeated and David fuccoured. *Brit. M.*
HILL *John*, Minifter of the Gofpel in London.
  * 2 Tim. ii. 2. 8° 1726.
  * Serm. in 8° 1755. (Republifhed with Additions.)
HILL Jofeph, B. D. Chancellor of St. David's.
  Gen. xxxv. 19. 4° 1685. *Rotterdam.* Fun. of Mary Reeve. *Brit. M.*
HILL Jofeph
  * 2 Tim. iii. 15. 12° 1735. Char. f.
HILL N.
  * - - - - 8° 1773. Nov. 5.
  * Acts xxi. 26. 8° 1779. Fun.
  * - - - 8° 17   Ch. f. The Knowledge of national Benefits and Deliverances to the rifing Generation.
HILL Robert,   R. of Stanhow, Norfolk.
  Exod. xx. 8-11. 6 f. in 2 Vol. 8° Vol. 1. 1728. V. 2. 1730.
HILL Samuel,   R. of Kilmington, Somerfet.
  1 Cor. xi. 19. 4° 1688. The Neceffity of Herefies.
HILLIARD Samuel, M. A. Preb. of Lincoln, R. of Stafford, Effex.
  Luke xvi 29. 8° 1709. b. Lord Mayor. *Univ. Linc. Worc.* Ox. *Tr. n.* Camb.
  Pf. cxxii. 1. 4° 1712. Conf. of Chapel.
  Col. iii. 15. 8° 1713.
  Pf. cxliv. 10. 8° 1713. Th. for Peace. *St. John's.* Camb.
  Matt. vi. 13. 8° 1714. b. Co. of Parifh Clerks. On Amen. *Ch. Ch.* Oxon. *Eton.*   Pf.

Matt. vi. 10. 8° 1714. The Nature of the Kingdom or Church of Xt.
Col ii. 4. 8° 1717. A seasonable Caution to Saducers.
HILTON Thomas, M. A. V. of Brackley, Northamptonſ.
Eccleſ. xii. 5. 4° 1700. Fun.
HINCHLIFFE John, Bp. of Peterborough, and Maſter of Trin. Coll. Camb.
*Phil. iv. 4. 4° 1773. Jan. 30. b. Lords.
*Acts x. 34. 35. 4° 1776. Prop. of Goſpel.
HINCKLEY John, DD. R. of Northfield, Worceſter. and Preb. of Litchfield.
Gen. xxv. 8. 4° 1661.
HIND Richard, DD. V. of Rochdale, and of Skipton upon Craven, Yorkſhire.
* 1 Cor. xiv. 23. 4° 1755. Abuſes of miraculous Powers in the Church of Corinth. *Worc.* Oxon.
* Rom. xiv. 16. 4° 1764. b. Sons of Clergy.
* 2 Cor. ii. 17. 4° 1765. Jan. 30. b. Commons.
HIND Thomas, M. A. Fell. of Linc. Coll. and R. of Lillinſton Lovel, Oxon.
John i. 14. 8° 1717. *Oxon.* Act. The Divinity of our Saviour proved from the Scriptures of the old and new Teſtament. *Magd. Linc.* Oxon. *Queen's.* Camb.
HINDE Samuel, one of his Majeſty's Chaplains and Incumbent of St. Mary's Church in Dover.
Hoſea ix. 7. 4° 1663. Viſ. England's perſpective Glaſs. *Bod.*
HINDES Thomas, R. of Avon-daſſet, Warwickſ.
* Acts v. 42. 8° 1765. Viſ. Duty of Inſtruction recommended.
HINDMARSH Thomas, M. A. V. of Long Ouriſby, Linc.
Acts xxiv. 25. 4° 1680. *Lincoln.* Aſſize. *Pub. L.* Camb.
HINGESTON James, M. A. V. of Raydon, Norfolk.
* Exod. xxxiv. 6, 7. 8° 1772. Diſſertation.
HINTON Edward, M. A. R. of Shering, Eſſex.
2 Tim. ii. 24. 4° 1720. Viſ. *St. John's.* Camb.
HINTON John, M. A. R. of Newbury, Berks, and Preb. of Sarum.
2 Sam. xviii. 28. 4° 1685. Th. for Victory over the Rebels.
HITCHCOCK John, M. A.
Heb. xi. 6. 4° 1697. b. Lord Mayor. The Reaſonableneſs and Neceſſity of the Chriſtian Faith manifeſted. *Trin.* Camb.
HITCHCOCK Thomas, DD. Fell. of St. John's Coll. Oxon. and one of his Majeſty's Preachers at Whitehall.
* 2 Pet. ii. 5. 8° 1761. *Oxon.* Act. Mutual Connection between Faith, Virtue and Knowledge. *Worc.* Oxon.
HITCHIN Edward
* Epheſ. v. 20. 8° 1759. Th. ſ.
* 1 Theſſ. iv. 13. 8° 1751. Fun. of *Martha Tate.*
HITCHMOUGH Richard, M. A. V. of Whenby, Yorkſ.
Matt. v. 12. 8° 1722. *York.*
Acts ii. 1. 8° 1722. *York.* Whitſunday.

HOADLY Benjamin, Bp. of Winchester.
  Matt. x. 34. 8° 1703. 2 f. Concerning the Evils of which Christianity has been the Occasion, or in Tracts. 8° 1715. p. 67–82.
  Pf. xcv. 2. 4° 1705. Accession. *Pub. L.* Camb.
  Rom. xiii. 1. 4° 1705. Elect. Lord Mayor. The Measures of Submission to the civil Magistrate. *Bod. Sion.*
  1 Sam. viii. 9. 4° 1708. Assize. *Brit. M.*
  Acts xxii. 25. 4° 1708. Assize. St. Paul's Behaviour towards the civil Magistrate. *Pub. L.* Camb. *Brit. M.*
  Sev. Serm. or Disc. in 8° 1711. Concerning the Terms of Acceptance with God. *Bod. Ch. Ch. Univ.* Oxon. *Pub. L. Trin. Cl. H.* Camb.
  1 Theff. v. 21. 4 f. in Tracts. 8° 1715. Concerning an impartial Enquiry into Religion. p. 455 &c.
  2 Theff ii. 11. 8° 1715. Nov. 5. The present Delusion of many Protestants considered. *Trin.* Camb. *Sion.*
  Pf. cxxvi. 3. 8" 1716. May 29. b. King. The Restoration made a Blessing to us by the protestant Succession. *Bod. Trin. C. Sion.*
  Phil. ii. 4. 4° 1716. b. Welch Soc. The Nature and Duty of a public Spirit. *Magd.* Oxon. *Brit. M.*
  Ecclef. viii. 2. 8° 17
  John xviii. 36. 4° 1717. b. King. The Nature of the Kingdom or Church of Christ. *Bod. Sion.*
  Rev. xiv. 13. 8° 1719. Fun. of Mrs. Mary Howland.
  1 Cor. x. 11. 4° 1721. Jan. 30. b. Lords. *Bod. Trin.* Cam. *Sion.*
  N. B. All these (except that on Ecclef. viii. 2. 8° 17) are reprinted in 1 Vol. *Trin.* Camb.
  * Serm. in 2 Vol. 8° 1754. *Ch. Ch. All S. Wore. Wadh.* Oxon. *Queen's. Pub. L.* Camb. *Dr. Ws's. L.* Lond.
  1 Vol. At the End are added 6 preached upon public Occasions.
  2 Vol. 9 of these were preached before the King.

HOADLY John, Abp. of Armagh.
  Joel ii. 12, 13. 4° 1704. *Norwich.* Faft. for the Storm. *Pub. L. C.*
  Phil. iv. 5. 4° 1707. The Nature and Excellency of Moderation. *Trin. Queen's.* Camb. *Sion.*
  Dan. iv. 37. 4° 1708. Th. and Affize. The Abasement of Pride. *Pub. L. Trin. St. John's.* Camb.
  2 Cor. i. 12. 8° 1716. Conf. of Bp. Benj. Hoadly.
  1 Cor. x. 11. 8° 1717. Jan 30. b. Commons. *St. John's. Queen's.* C.

HOARD Samuel, B. D. Parson of Morton, Effex.
  1 Cor. xiv. 40. 8° 1709. The Church's Authority afferted. *Bod. Sion.*

HOCKIN John, M. A. V. of Launceston, Cornwal.
  * Rom. x 3. 4° 1764. Vif.

HODGE John.
  * 52 practical Difc. in 8° 1758. On the principal Evidences in Favour of the Christian Religion. *Dr Ws's L.* London.
  * Phil. i. 21. 8° 1763. Fun. of Rev. *John Mason. Queen's.* Cam.
  * Acts xxvi. 22. 8° 17 Char. Sch. meet.

HODGES John, B. A.
  1 John iv. 11. 8° 1731. Co. Feast.

HODGES Moses, DD. V. of St. Mary's in Warwick.
   Prov. xxix. 15. 8° 1711. Char. f.
   Isai. xxvi 12. 8° 1712. Fast.
HODGES Thomas, B. D. R. of Kensington, Middlesex.
   Pf cxxvi. 3. 4° 1660. Th *Bod. St. John's.* Camb.
HODGES Thomas, DD. R. of Souldern, Oxon.
   Gen. i. 31. 4° 1675. 2 f.
   Prov. xx. 10. 4° 1675. 2 f.
   Pf. xxxix. 5. 4° 1676. Sch. Feast. The Vanity of Man in his Estate. p. 1.
   Luke xvi. 30, 31. b. Univ. The Vanity of Dives's Desire, p. 27. *St. John's.* Camb.
   Matt. v. 13. 4° 1685. The Duty of Ministers. *All S.* Oxon. *St. John's.* Camb. *Eton.*
   * Job xi. 12, 13. 8° 16   b. Sons of Clergy.
HODGES Thomas, M. A. Fell. of Bal. Coll. Oxon.
   1 Cor. xv. 20. 8° 1730. Easter.
HODGES Thomas, M. A. Curate of Church-Hulme.
   * Rom. xiii. 4. 8° 1766. Assize.
HOFFMAN Benjamin, M. A. Lect. of St. George's Botolph Lane, and R. of   Sussex.
   Rom. xv. 5–7. 4° 1683. Farew. f. Mutual Forbearance. *Pub. L.* Camb. *Brit. M.*
HOGG John
   * Isai. xxv. 9. } 8° 1759. Th.
   * Isai. xliv. 23. }
   * Rev. ii. 5. 8° 1775. Declensions in Religion.
HOGGART Will.   Cur. of Tandridge, and Crowhurt, Surrey.
   Prov. xi. 11. 8° 1740. *York.* Fast.
   1 Sam. xvii. 26. 8° 1748. Fast.
HOLBERRY Mark,   late of Eman. Coll. Camb.
   * John xiv. 27. 8° 1770. Farew. f.
HOLBROOK Anthony, M. A. R. of Waltham Parva, Essex.
   Tit. iii. 1. 8° 1715. Th. after Rebellion.
   1 Sam. xv. 28. 4° 1715. Accession. No Security for Protestants under a Popish Prince.
   Matt. xvi. 19. 8° 1722. On Church-Authority.
   1 Sam. xvii. 48. 8° 1727. Against Duelling. *Queen's.* Camb.
   1 Thess. iv. 7. 8° 1727. 2 f. Universal Chastity the Xtian Calling. *Queen's.* Camb.
   Judges xi. 30, 31. 8° 1731. A Letter to Tindal. The Case of Jepthah's Vow. p. 18.
   Exod. xii. 35, 36. 8° 1731. A Letter to Tindal. The Case of Israel's borrowing Jewels of Egypt. p. 28.
HOLCOMBE   M. A. Canon-Resid. of St. David's.
   * - - - - 4° 1755. Vis.
HOLDEN *Anthony*
   2 Tim. iv. 7, 8. 8° 1710. Fun.

HOLDEN *Lawrence*, of Malden.
  * 22 Serm. in 8° 1755. On interesting Subjects.
  * Exod. xiv. 15. 8° 1757. Faſt. The Vanity of crying to God, unleſs a people proceed in the Path he hath preſcribed them.

HOLDEN Richard, M. A. R. of St. Dunſtan's in the Eaſt, and V. of Deptford, Kent.
  Dan. xii. 4. 4° 1680. b. Corp. Trin-Houſe. *Sion.*

HOLDEN Samuel, M.A. of Linc. Coll. Oxon. and Chapl. to Lord Lexington.
  Eccleſ. vii. 1. ⎱ 4° 1676. At Lord Lexington's Fun. ⎱ *Trin. Queen.*
  Job xiv. 12. ⎰ 4° 1676. At Lady Lexington's Fun. ⎰ Camb.

[HOLDER James]
  * Rom. xiv. 33.

HOLDSWORTH John, M. A.
  Pſ. cvii. 43. 8° 1725. May 29.
  1 Cor. x. 12. 8° 1725.

HOLDSWORTH Winch. DD. Fell. of St. John's Coll. Oxon. R. of Chafont St. Peter's, and of Gatton, Surrey.
  John v. 28, 29. 8° 1719. *Oxon.* Eaſter. *Worc. Linc.* Oxon. *St. John's.* Camb *Sion.*

HOLE Matthew, DD. R. of Exeter Coll. Oxon. and Preb. of Wells.
  Acts ii. 23. 4° 1670. Good-friday. On our Saviour's Paſſion. *St. John's.* Camb.
  Luke ii. 14. 4° 1689. b. Militia.
  Matt. xiii. 27, 28. *Briſtol.* Aug. 1.
  Lam. v. 16. 4° 1710. *Briſtol.* Jan. 30.
  Prov. xxiii. 23. 8° 1710. *Briſtol.* At the Fair-time.
  Job v. 12, 13. 8° 1711. *Briſtol.* Jan. 30.
  - - - 12° 17 Of Deiſm.
  Pſ. xxix. 2. 8° 1713. *Briſtol.* Beautifying a Church.
  2 Kings xx. 19. 8° 1713. Th. for the Peace. *St. John's.* Camb.
  Jerem. xxvi. 14, 15. 4° 1713. On the Expiration of the Sentence againſt Dr. Sachiverell. *St. John's.* Camb.
  Pſ. cxxxii. 18. 4° 1714. Coron.
  Rev. ii. 10. 1714.
  Matt. vi. 34. 8° 1715. *St. John's.* Camb.
  1 Theſſ. iv. 11. 8° 1715. *St. John's.* Camb. *Sion.*
  A practical Expoſition of the Church-Catechiſm in 2 vol. 8° 1715. *Magd.* Oxon. *Queen's.* Camb.
  Pſ. cii. 13, 14. 8° 1716. *Oxen.* Act. *Magd. Worc.* Oxon.
  Practical Diſcourſes on all the Parts and Offices of the Liturgy. Vol. IV. 8° 1716.
  N.B. The IV Vol. On the Epiſt. and Goſpels contains 3 parts. *Magd.* Oxon.
  Practical Diſcourſes on the Communion Service. Vol. V. 8° 1717. *Bod. Magd.* Oxon.
  Practical Diſcourſes on the Offices of Baptiſm, Confirmation and Matrimony in 3 parts. Vol. VI. 8° 1719. *Magd.* Oxon.
  Matt. x. 32. 8° 1720. 2 ſ.

Acts

Acts xiv. 17. 8° 1720.
Matt. xi. 6. 8° 1721. *Oxon.*
Acts v. 38, 39. 8° 1721.
1 Tim. vi. 9, 10. 8° 1721. *Sion.*
Pract. Discourses on the Nature, Properties and Excellencies of Charity &c. 8° 1725. *Oxon. Bod.*

HOLE William, B. D. Arch-Deacon of Barnstaple, Devon, and V. of Maynhinneot, Cornwal.
Haggai i. 8. 4° 1743. Conf. of a Church. *Eton.*

HOLLAND *John*
* Luke xxxi. 24. 8° 1750. b. Diss. Clergy. On the Folly and Guilt of Intemperance. *Queen's.* Camb.
* 37 Serm. in 2 Vol. 8° 1753. On various Subjects.

HOLLAND *Philip*, at Manchester.
* Acts vii. 32. 8° 1760. The Importance of Learning.
* - - - - 8° 1780. b. Diff. Clergy. Character, Offices and Qualifications of a Christian Preacher.

HOLLAND Richard, M. A. R. of St. George's, Stamford.
Exod. xiv. 13. 4° 1685 Assize. *Ch. Ch.*

HOLLAND Rich. M.A. Chapl. to the Duke of Richmond, and Cur. of St. Magnus, and Lect. of All-Hallows the Great. Lond.
Esther vi. 13. 4° 1698. Fast.
Acts ii. 38. 4° 1700. At the baptizing of some Persons of riper Years. *Sion.*
Luke x. 37. 4° 1700. Ch. f. The good Samaritan. *Ch. Ch. Ox.*
Pf. cxlvi. 1. 4° 1702. Th. on Praise. *Sion.*
John xiii. 34. 4° 1702. Co. Feast. *Brit. M.*

HOLLINGWORTH Richard, DD. V. of Westham near London, and R. of St. Botolph's, Aldgate.
Tit. iii. 1. 4° 1673. Assize. *Pub. L.* Camb. *Sion.*
John vi. 68. 12° 1676. A modest Plea for the Ch. of Eng. *Bod.*
Acts ii 17, 18. 4° 1680. Vis. An Account of Spirits working upon the Minds of Men in the several Ages of the Christian Church. *C. C. C.* Oxon.
Pf. lxxiv. 20. 4° 1680. b. Lord Mayor. Christian Principles, no Abettors of Popish Practices.
John i. 47. 4° 1682. Nov. 5. b. Ld Mayor. *Pub. L. St. John's.* C.
Matt. xix. 18. 4° 1693. Jan. 30. The Death of the King, down-right Murder. *Bod. Ch. Ch. Pub. L.* Camb. *Sion.*

HOLLOWAY Benjamin, LL.B. R. of Blayden, and Middleton-Stoney, Oxon.
1 Cor. ii. 23–26. 8° 1736. *Oxon.* Vis. The commemorative Sacrifice. *Worc.* Oxon.
Acts ii. 38. 8° 1739. *Oxon.* 3 s. The Nullity of Repentance without Faith by Jesus Christ, proved from Scripture.
Originals physical and theological &c. in 8° 1750. Vol. II.
Rev. ii. 17. On the hidden Manna, p. 379.
Rev. ii. 7. On the Tree of Life, p. 400.

HOLME Thomas, R. of Wilden, and Chapl. to Lord Hume.
- - - - 1739. Assize. Luke

Luke xvi. 9. 8° 1745. *Northamp.* Infirmary. *All S.* Ox. *Queen's.* C.
HOLMES David
 * Heb. xiii. 17. - - - -
HOLMES Robert. M A. Fell. of New Coll. Oxon.
 * Phil. iii. 21. 4° 1777. *Oxon.* Refurrection of the Body deduced from that of Xt's, and illustrated from his Transfiguration.
 * 8 Serm. in 8° 1782. Preached before the University of Oxon, at Bampton's Lecture.
HOLMES William, Master of the Grammar-school at Pontefract and Cur. of Ferry-fryston, York.
 Matt. vii. 7. 8° 1746. *York.* Rebellion. The Frauds of Popery and the Abettors of the present Rebellion set in a true light.
HOLT Ludlow, LLD. V. of Dedham, Effex.
 * Isai. xxxiii. 6. ⎫
 * Prov. xiv. 34. ⎬ 4° 1780. Affize.
HOLWELL John, M. A. R. of Torbryan, Devon.
 Phil. iii. 8. 4° 1721.
HOLYDAY Barton, DD. Arch-Deacon of Oxon.
 4 Serm. in 8° 1661. *Oxon.* Against Disloyalty.
HOMES *Nathaniel*, DD.
 * Exercitations in fo. 1664.
HOOD *Rob.* M. A. Minister of the Chapel in Hanover Square, New Castle upon Tyne, Stafford.
 * Luke xvii. 20, 21. 8° 1781. b. Diff. Clergy. The Nature of Christ's Kingdom.
HOOK
 Matt. xxv. 10. 4° 1676. f. m. e. p. 760. Preparation for Death and Judgment. *Bod.*
HOOK Christopher
 1 John iii. 1. 8°   *Bod.*
HOOKE Richard, M. A. R. of Thornton in Craven, Yorkf.
 Acts xxiv. 16. 8° 1660. Affize.
 Pf. cxliv. 10. 8° 1662. The royal Guard, or the King's Salvation.
 * Acts vii 56 8° 1663. Fun. of Lady Rogers.
HOOKER Richard, M. A. Fell. of C. C. C. Oxon. and Master of the Temple.
 Matt. vii. 17. 8° 1678. V. Walton's Life of Bp. Sanderson. p. 254. *Bod. Queen's. C.C.C.* Oxon.
 * Hab. i. 4. ⎫ 8° 1705. Justif. by Works. ⎫
 * Hab. ii. 4. ⎬ 8° 1705. On Pride.   ⎬ V. His Works abridged 8° 1705.
 * Jude 17–21. ⎭ 8° 1705. 2 f.   ⎭
HOOLE Joseph, M. A. R. of St. Ann's in Manchester.
 Serm. in 2 Vol. 8° 1741. On sev. important Subjects.
HOOPER George, Bp. of Bath and Wells.
 Gal. v. 22, 23. 4° 1681. b. Ld Mayor. *Bod. Magd.* Ox. *Brit. M.*
 Matt. xxii. 21. 4° 1681. Nov. 5. b. Kirg. *Bod. C.C.C. Magd. Worc.* Oxon. *Sion.*
 Luke xvi. 31. 4° 1691. b. Queen. *Bod. All S. Magd. Or.* Oxon.
 John vii. 17. 4° 1694. b. K. and Q. *Bod. Magd. Trin.* Cam. *Sion.*
                1 John

1 John iii. 20. 4° 1695. b. King. *Bod. All S. Magd. Worc.* Oxon. *Trin.* Camb.
Phil. iii. 20. 4° 1701. Faſt. b. Commons. April 4. *Bod. Magd. C.C.C. Worc.* Oxon. *Sion.*
2 Cor. x. 3, 4. 4° 1704. Jan. 30. b. Lords. *Bod. Ch. Ch. C. C. C. Worc.* Oxon. *Sion.*
Pſ. cxxii. 7. 4° 1713. Th. b. Lord Mayor. July 7. *Bod. C.C.C. Magd. Worc.* Oxon. *Sion.*
N. B. All theſe are to be found at the End of his Works publiſhed in fo. 1757. *Ch. Ch. C. C. C. All S. Bal. Wadh. Pemb.* Oxon. *Pub. L. King's. Cl. H.* Camb.

HOOPER William, Min. of Trinity Church, Boſton, New England.
 * Eccleſ. vii. 1. 4° 1763. Fun. of Thomas Green, Eſq;

HOOTON Henry
 * Sermons in 8° 1709.

HOPKINS Ezekiel, Bp. of London-derry.
 * Diſc. in 4° 1692. An Expoſition on the 10 Commandments. *Bod. Trin.* Camb.
His Works or Serm. &c. fo. 1710. *Ch. Ch. New C. Magd. Queen's. Worc.* Oxon. *Queen's.* Camb.
Death Diſarmed. 8° 1712.
Doctrine of the Covenants. 8° 1712.
Doctrine of the Sacraments. 8° 1712. *Bod.*

HOPKINS John, B. D. V. of Cropedy, and late Fell. of Pemb. Coll. Oxon.
 * Nehem. iv. 23. 8° 1771. The true Reading of the Verſe.

HOPKINS Mar. M. A. R. of St. Vedaſt Foſter Lane, London.
1 Cor. x. 10. 4° 1689. Murmurers reproved. *Brit. M.*

HOPKINS William, DD. Lect. of St. Lawrence-Jewry, Lond. and Preb. of Worc.
John v. 14. 4° 1683. Faſt. b. Lord Mayor. *Pub. L. Trin. Queen's.* Camb. *Sion.*
17 Serm. 8° 1708. *Bod.*

HORBERY Matt. DD. Fell. of Magd. Coll. Oxon. and Preb. of Litchfield.
2 Tim. iii. 16, 17. 8° 1745. *Oxon.* Viſ. The Inſpiration of the moral parts of the Scripture aſſerted. *Worc.* Oxon. *Queen's.* C.
1 Cor. xii. 31. 8° 1747. *Salop.* Infirmary. The Pre-eminence of Charity. *Queen's.* Camb.
1 Tim. iii. 9. 8° 1749. *Oxon.* Trinity. The Athanaſian Creed defended and explained. *Worc.* Oxon. *Queen's.* Camb.
 * 18 Serm. in 8° 1774. On important Subjects.

HORDEN John, R. of St. Michael's, Queen-Hithe, Lond: and V. of Iſleworth.
2 Sam. 19. 14, 15. 4° 1676. May 29. *Bod. Univ.* Oxon. *Sion.*

HORLER Joſeph, B. A. Maſter of the Free-ſchool at Wilton.
Matt. xxv. 40. 4° 1729. County-ſeaſt.
Acts xxiv. 16. 8° 1742. Aſſize.
 * Acts

. * Acts xx. 35. 8° 1750. *Briſtol.* Bleſſedneſs of giving ſuperior to that of receiving.

HORN J.
Pſ. cxxxiii. 1. 4° 1713. Viſ.

HORNE Geo. DD. Preſid. of Magd. Coll. Oxon. and Dean of Cant.
* Prov. xx. 27. 8° 1756. *Oxon.* Chriſt and H. Ghoſt, the Supporters of ſpiritual Life. *All S.* Oxon.
* Iſai. xl. 3–5. 8° 1756. *Oxon.* 2 ſ. Repentance, the Forerunner of Faith. *All S.* Oxon.
* Rev. xi. 13, 14. 8° 1756. *Oxon.* Faſt. The Almighty glorified in Judgment.
* 1 Pet. ii. 21. 8°1761. *Oxon.* Jan. 30. The Xtian King. *All S.* Ox.
* James ii. 24. 8° 1761. *Oxon.* Works without Faith, a Condition of our Juſtification. *Worc.* Oxon.
* Lament. v. 3. 8" 1762. *Oxon.* b. Sons of the Clergy.
* Tit. ii. 11, 12. 8° 1773. Aſſize. The Influence of Chriſtianity on civil Society. *All S. Linc. Worc.* Oxon.
* Acts xx. 35. 4° 1774. *Oxon.* b. Gov. of the Aſylum.
* 1 Sam. ii. 30. 8° 1775. *Oxon.* Aſſize. The Providence of God manifeſted in the Riſe and Fall of Empires. *Worc.* Oxon.
* Rom. x. 13. 8°1775. *Oxon.* Chriſt the Object of relig. Adoration and therefore very God.
* Diſc. in 2 Vol. 8° 1778. On ſeveral Subjects and Occaſions. *Bod. Trin.* Camb.
* Deut. xxiii. 9. 4°1780. Faſt. b. Commons.
* Iſai. xxvi. 9. 4° 1781. Faſt. b. Univerſity.

HORNE John
Jude 20, 21. 8° 1671. Exerciſe for Chriſtians in the worſt of times. *Bod.*

HORNE John, late Miniſter of New Brentford, Middlſex.
* Pſ. lv. 12–14. 4° 1769. Nature of Friendſhip.

HORNE Thomas, M A. Fell. of Eton Coll. and Chapl. in Ord.
Prov. xxii. 6. 4° 1679. Eton-ſchool Feaſt. *All S.* Oxon. *Pub. L.* Camb. *Sion.*
1 Theſſ. v. 19. 4° 1685. Sund. after the Death of King Charles. II. *C. C. C,* Oxon.

HORNE Thomas, M. A. Chapl. of St. Saviours, Southwark.
Prov. xiv. 34. 8° 1713. Aſſize. *Linc.* Oxon.

HORNE Thomas, M. A. late Fell. of Trin Coll. Oxon. and Cur. of St. Peter's, Hereford.
* Matt. v. 14. 4° 1778. *Hereford.* Viſ.
* Prov. xiv. 34. 4° 1778. Faſt.

HORNECK Anthony, DD. Preacher at the Savoy, Preb. of Weſtminſter, and Chapl. in Ord.
Rom. viii. 20. 4° 1677. Fun. of a young Lady. *Bod. Worc.* Ox.
Pſ. xcix. 1. 4° 1681. Jan. 30. God's Providence in the midſt of Confuſions.
* Eccleſ. xi. 9. 12°1684. A Vol. entitled Delight and Judgment.
‡ * Matt. v. 20. 1689. b. King and Queen. *Brit. M.*

Eccleſ.

Eccles. 12. 1. 12° 1686. *Trin.* Camb.
Rom. viii. 18. 8° 1687. Easter. The Glories of the other World. *Univ.* Oxon. *Queen's. Trin.* Camb.
2 Tim. i. 6. 4° 1689. Cons. of Bp. Burnet. *Bod. Ch. Ch. Magd.* Oxon. *Pub. L. St. John's. Cl. H.* Camb.
* Ephes. v. 16. - - - -
Rev. xx. vi. 4° 1695. Fun.   The Happiness of being saved from the second Death. *Trin.* Camb.
Matt. v. 21, 22. 8° 1697. Ag. Revenge. 4 Tracts, p. 1. *Ch. Ch.* Ox.
39 Serm. in 2 Vol. 8° 1706. on Matt. v. being Part of Christ's Sermon on the Mount. *Ch Ch. Pemb.* Oxon. *Trin.* Camb.
1 Tim. iv. 7. 8° 1724. Bett Exercise.

HORNECK Philip, LL. B. Chapl. to Lord Guilford.
    Prov. xxxi. 31. 4° 1699. Fun. of Lady Guilford.

HORSEY John
    * Judges v. 2. 8° 1746. Th. after Rebellion.

HORSENAILE Thomas
    * - - - - 1742.

HORSLEY Sam. LL.D. Secretary to the Royal Society, and Chapl. to the Bp. of London.
    * Matt. xvi. 21. 4° 1778. Good-friday. Provid. and Free-agency.

HORSMANDEN Samuel, LL. B. R. of Purleigh, Essex.
    1 Cor. xiii. 12. 8° 1744. Sch. Feast. Hum. Knowledge difficult, short, and imperfect.

HORSNELL John, B. D. V. of Fordingbridge, Hants.
    Num. xvi. 24. 4° 1705. Assize and Accession.

HORROBIN Robert,   Curate of Warrington, Lancast.
    * 1 Tim. xvii. 19. 8° 1719. *Liverpool.* Ch. Sch. meet. *Queen's.* C.

HORT Josiah, Abp. of Tuam.
    Ps. cxlix. 6-8. 4° 1707. Th. for Successes. *Ch. Ch.* Ox. *Brit. M.*
    2 Pet. i. 12. 8° 1709. Vis. Great Knowledge, no Excuse for neglecting to hear Sermons.
    16 Serm. in 8° 1738. On practical Subjects. *Dublin.*

HORT Rob. M.A. R. of Temple Michael, and Chapl. to Abp. Hort.
    Matt. vi. 10. 8° 1748. *Dublin.* On the Millenium. *Queen's.* Cam.

HORTON Joseph,   Curate of Tewin, Herts.
    1 Pet. ii. 13. 8° 1727. Assize.

HORTON Thomas, DD. Master of Queen's Coll. Camb. and V. of Great St. Helen's, London.
    Luke xvi. 9. 4° 1661. Fun.   The unrighteous Mammon exchanged for the true Riches.
    2 Cor. iv. 7. 4° 1663. Fun.
    2 Chron. xix. 6. 4° 1672. Assize. *Bod. Sion.*
    * 8 Serm. in fo. 1675. on Ps. iv. 1–8.
    * 7 Serm. in fo. 1675. on Ps. lxiii. 1–11.
    * 10 Serm. in fo. 1675. on Ps. xlii. 1–11.
    * 20 Serm. in fo. 1675. on Ps. li. 1–19.
    100 Select Sermons in fo. 1679. *Bod. Ch. Ch. All S. Bal.* Oxon. *Pub. L. Trin. Queen's.* Camb.

HOTCHKIS Thomas, M.A. R. of Stanton, Wilts.
   1 ev. xxvi. 23, 24. 8° 1675. Sev. Sermons. *Bod.*

HOUGH John, Bp. of Worcester.
   Pf. cxxvii. 1. 4° 1701. Faft. b. Lords. April 4. *Ch.Ch. C.C.C. Magd. Worc.* Oxon. *St. John's.* Camb. *Brit. M.*
   Col. iii. 1. 4° 1702. Spittal. M. *Ch.Ch. C.C.C. Magd. Jef.* Ox. *St. John's.* Camb.
   Rom. ii. 28, 29. 4° 1704. Ref. of Manners. *Ch.Ch. C.C.C.* Ox. *Brit. M.*
   Acts xvii. 30, 31. 4° 1705. Prop. of Gospel. *Ch.Ch. C.C.C. Magd.* Oxon. *Pub. L. Queen's.* Camb.
   Prov. xxix. 2. 4° 1705. b. Queen. Accession. *Ch.Ch. C.C.C.* Ox. *Pub. L. St. John's.* Camb.
   Pf. xxxi. 23. 4° 1709. Th. b. Lords. Nov. 22. *Magd. Or.* Ox. *Pub L. Trin. St. John's.* Camb. *Brit. M.*
   Luke xvi. 25. 4° 1712. Spittal M. *Ch.Ch.* Oxon. *Brit. M.*
   Mal. iv. 2. 4° 1715. Fun. of Lady Marrow.

HOUGH Nathaniel, DD Fell. of Jef. Coll. Camb. and R. of St. George's, Southwark.
   Pf. cxliv. 15. 4° 1704. Th. Sept. 7. *Pub. L.* Camb. *Brit.M.*
   Pf cxxiv. 2, 3. 4° 1706. Nov. 5. *Trin.* Camb. *Sion.*
   Isai. xlix. 23. 4° 1712. Accession. *St. John's.* Camb.
   Pf. lxxxvi. 10. 8° 1715. Nov. 5 *Trin.* Camb. *Eton.*
   Jude 3. 8° 1716. Vif. Ag. Nonjurors.
   Isai. lviii 6. 4° 1724. Jan. 30. b. Com. *AllS. Magd. Worc.* Ox.

HOUGH Thomas, M.A. Fell. of Trin. Coll. Camb. and Lect. of Huntingdon.
   Acts xxii. 3. 4° 1728. *Camb.* School Feaſt. The Happineſs and Advantages of a liberal and virtuous Education. *Brit. M.*

HOUGHTON William
   Acts v. 3. 4° 1661.

HOULTON Robert, M.A. V. of Milton Clavedon, Somerſet, and Chapl. on board the Superbe.
   * 1 Sam. 37. 8° 1740. March. At Spithead.

HOULTON Robert, M.A. late Demy of Magd. Coll. Oxon. and Chapl. to the Earl of Ilcheſter.
   * Prov. xv. 2, 3. 4° 1765. Detraction expoſed.
   * John xi. 4. 8° 1767. The Practice of Inoculation juſtified.

HOUSER Henry
   Exod. xviii 21. 4° 1672.

HOW James, M.A. R. of Milton, Kent, and of St. Margarets Lothbury, London.
   * Luke xiii. 2, 3. 8° 1728 On a Fire at Gravefend.
   Luke vii. 5. 8° 1731. On rebuilding a Church. Gratitude to Benefactors.
   Pf. cxxii. 6–8. 8° 1732. Peace and Unity recommended.
   * Luke xiii. 2, 3. 8° 1756. Faſt. on the Earthquake.
   * 13 Diſc. in 8° 1761. On the prodigal Son.

                                                                          * Diſc.

* Disc. in 8° 1764.
* 2 Thess. iii. 11. 8° 1769. Busy Bodies anatomized.

HOW John, M. A. of Magd Coll Oxon.
* 1 Thess. iv. 18. 4° 1060. Fun. of Mr. Thomas Ball.
* Ps. xvii. 15. 8° 1668.
* Ps. xxxvii. 4. 8° 1674. Treatise in 2 parts. Delighting in God.
* Eccles. vii 29 4° 1676. m. e. G. p. 73. Man created holy, but in a mutuable State.
* 1 Cor. xi. i. 6. 12° 1681. Charity in reference to other Men's Sins. *Bal.* Oxon.
* 2 Cor. v. 8. 4° 1681. Fun. of Mrs. *Baxter.*
* Jerem. xiv. 21. 8° 1682 Prayer.
  Col. ii. 2. 4° 1683. C. m. e. p. 76. Remedies against Animosities among Christians.
* Luke xix 41,42. 12° 1684. A Treatise. The Redeemer's Tears wept over lost Souls.
* Luke xiii. 16. 4° 1690. Fun. of Mrs. *Esther Sampson.*
* Disc. in 12° 1693.
  Heb. xii. 23. 4° 1695. Royal Fun. *Pub. L.* Camb. *Sion.*
* Ps. xxix. 11. 4° 1697. Th. *St. John's.* Camb.
* Rom. xiii. 14. 12° 1698. Ref Manners.
  John xi. 16. 8° 1699. Fun. of Dr. *Bates*——or in his Works. fo. 1700. p. 951. *New C.* Oxon. *St. John's.* Camb.
* Acts v. 20. 8° 1702. Fun.
* Rom. xii. 1. 8° 1702. Of yield. ourselves to God. *Brit. M.*
* 8 Serm. in 8° 1726. Office of the Spirit.
  Ezek. xxxix. 29. 8° 1726. 15 s. The prosperous State of the Christian Interest before the End of time by a plentiful Effusion of the Holy Spirit.
* Discourses in 2 Vol. 8° 1744 On the Love of God.
* - - - - - Fun. of *Richard Fairclough.*
* - - - - - —— Mrs. *Jud. Hammond.*
* - - - - - —— Rev. *Rich. Adams.*
* - - - - - —— Rev. *Matthew Mead.*
* - - - - - —— Rev. Mr. *Vink.*
* - - - - - —— John Houghton, Esq;
* - - - - Enquiry whether or no we truly love God.
* - - - - 2 s. The Carnality of relig. Contentions.
* - - - - 2 s. Of Enmity and Reconciliation to God.

HOWARD John, M. A. R. of Marston-Trussel, Northampton, and afterwards V. of Kidderminster, Worcesters.
  Prov. xiv. 34. 4° 1692. Assize. Of the true Interest of a Nation. *Bod Magd.* Oxon.
  Ephes. v. 16. 4° 1698. Vis. The Evil of our Days with the Remedy of it. *Pub. L.* Camb.
  1 John v. 7. 4° 1700. b. Lord Mayor. Trin. S. The Trinity asserted.
  1 John v. 7. 4° 1701. b. Lord Mayor. Trin. S. The Doctrine

of the Trinity a reasonable and necessary Condition of Salvation. *Ch. Ch.* Oxon. *Pub. L. Cl. H.* Camb.
James v. 11. 12° 1710. The Happiness of enduring Afflictions.
Matt. xvi. 24. 12° 1710. 3 f. On Self-denial. *Bal.* Oxon.
Micah vi. 8. 8° 1713.
Tit. ii. 15. 8° 1728. 2 Disc. The Duties between Pastors and their People.

HOWARD Leonard, DD. R. of St. George's, Southwark, and Chapl. to the Prince of Wales.
1 Thess. iv. 11. 8° 1736. The christian Study of Peace and Quietness.
Job xxviii. 14. 4° 1742. Assize.
13 Sermons in 8° 1742. On several Occasions.
Acts xxii. 28. 4° 1745. Assize. The Advantages of a free People, and ill Consequences of Licentiousness considered.
2 Kings xix. 32–34. 4° 1745. On the Invasion.
Jude 8. 4° 1751. Jan. 30. The Sin and evil Consequences of speaking evil of Dignities.
* Isai. xxxii. 1, 2. 4° 1753. May 29. b. Commons. The good Government of a Country, its great Object. *Brit. M.*
* Luke xxiii. 19. 8° 17   On the Sacrament. V. newest Manual of private Devotions.
* 2 Sam. xxiii. 4° 1761. Accession.

HOWARD Robert, Bp. of Elphin.
Isai. xlv. 7. 8° 1721. Fast. b. Com. in Ireland. Ag. the Plague.
Ps. c. 5. 4° 1722. *Dublin.* Th. f.
* Prov. xxii. 2. 4° 1730. Ann. meeting Char. School.
Gen. iii. 19. 4° 1738. *Dublin.* Irish Prot. School. *All S. Wore.* Oxon. *Queen's. Cl. H.* Camb.

HOWARD Samuel
* - - - - 1746.

HOWDELL William, M. A. Minister of East-hardwick in the Parish of Pontefract, Yorks.
* Phil. iv. 4. 8° 1744. Religion productive of Joy, and consistent with Politeness.
Ps. xliv. 7, 8. *York.* Rebellion. The Duty and Interest of true Englishmen to oppose a popish Pretender.

HOWE Jasper
* 1 Tim. iv. 12. 8° 1718. b. Diff. Clergy.

HOWE Obadiah, DD. V. of Boston, Lincoln.
Ps. lxxxii. 6. 4° 1663. Elohim.
Isai. lx. 13. 4° 1664. Vis. The royal Present. *Bod.*

HOWE Thomas, of Yarmouth, Norfolk.
* Heb. xi. 4. 8° 1767. Fun. of Rev. S. *Wood,* LLD.
* - - - - 8° 1770. Fun.
* Ps. xcvii. 2. 8° 1778. Fun. of Rev. Mr. *Frost.*
* - - - - 1780. Fast. Virtue and Patriotism founded on Religion.
* 5 Serm. in 8° 1771.

HOWELL George, M. A. R. of Buckland, Surrey.
  Matt. x. 33. 4° 1684.
HOWELL James, M. A. Student of Ch. Ch. Oxon. and V. of Ardington, Berks.
  * Rom. xiii. 11. 4° 1780. Bod.
HOWELL William, V. of Fittleworth, Suffex.
  Col. iv. 17. 4° 1676. Vif. Bod. Ch. Ch. Ox. Pub. L. St. John'. C.
HOWELL Will M. A. of Wadh. Coll. and Cur. of Twelme, Oxen.
  1 John v. 7. 8° 1711. Oxon. The Doctrine of the Trinity proved. Bed. Bal. Linc. Oxon. Sion.
  Col ii. 15. 8° 1712. Oxon. Peace and Unity recommended. Bod. Linc. Oxon. Sion.
HOWES John, of Eman. Coll. Camb. and R. of Abington near Northampton.
  1 Theff. iv. 18. 4° 1660. Chrift, God-Man.
  2 Chron. xix 5, 6. 4° 1669. Affize. Ch. Ch. Oxon.
HOWSON John, Bp. of Durham.
  Luke xii. 41, 42. 4° 1661.
HOWSON Robert, M. A. Lect. of St. Nicholas, Cole-abby, and R. of Stanford-Deanly, Berks.
  John xiii. 34. 4° 17 Cole-Abby-Society.
  Acts i. 18. 8° 1703. On the unparalleled and untimely Death of John Harrifon of Bradfield, Berks, who pulled out his own Bowels, and cut them in feveral Pieces, cafting them about the Room before his Eyes, and lived 11 Hours in that Condition.
HUBBARD Henry, B. D. Fell. of Eman. Coll. Cambridge.
  2 Kings iv. 1. 4° 1750. Camb. bef. Governors for the Relief of Clergymen's Widows at Ipfwich. Queen's. Trin. Camb.
HUBBARD John
  * Ephef. i. 11. p. 81.
  * Rom. v. 12.   p. 293.   V. Berry-ft. Serm. Vol. I.
  * ——viii. 34. p. 399.
  * Ecclef. vii. 5. p. 135.
  * Exod. xx. 7.   p. 32.
  * 1 John ii. 6. p. 128.
  * Ephef. vi. 13. p. 226. V. Berry-ft. Serm. Vol. II.
  * Prov. xviii. 34. p. 329.
  * 2 Tim. ii. 10. p. 429
HUDDESFORD Will. M. A. R. of Bourton upon Dunfmore, and V. of Lemmington Haftings, Warwickfhire
  Pf. cxxii. 8, 9. 8° 1745. Rebellion. The Chriftian Patriot.
HUDDLESTON Curwen, M. A. Minifter of the Old Chapel at Whitehaven.
  * 2 Chron. xix. 6, 7. 4° 1753. Affize. The Advantage of an impartial Adminiftration of Juftice.
HUDDLESTON Will. (late a Benedictine) R. of Navenden, Kent.
  1 Kings 22. 21, 22. 8° 1729. Recantation. Queen's. Camb Sien.
HUDDY Matthew, of Exeter, Devon.
  Jude 3. 8° 1718. b. Diff. Clergy.

HUDSON

HUDSON Samuel, R. of Earles Stonham, Suffolk.
 Acts xiii. 36. 4° 1689. Fun. David's Labour and Rest.
HUGHES John, M.A. Fell. of Bal. Coll. Oxford.
 Pf. cvii. 23, 24. 4° 1683. Levant-Co.
HUGHES John
 * 2 Tim. iv. 7. 8° 1768. Fun. of Rev. Mr. *Hart*.
 * Jerem. v. 3. 8° 1779. Fast.
HUGHES *Obadiah*, DD. Minister of the Gospel at Westminster.
 Isai. xxvi. 20, 21. 8° 1722. On the Plague.
 * Pf. cxix. 158. 8° 1728. Ref. of Manners.
 * Isai. lvii. 2. 8° 1730. Fun. *Queen's*. Camb.
 Isai. xlii. 8. 8° 1735. The Veneration of Saints and Images taught and practised in the Church of Rome examined. V. Vol. I. Ag. Popery. *Braz. N.* Oxon.
 * Pf. cxxiv. 1 &c. 8° 1739. National Deliverances thankfully acknowledged and improved.
 * Luke xxix. 30. 8° 17 Fast.
 * Luke ii. 10, 11. 8° 17 Christmas.
 * Eccles. xii. 1. 8° 1742. New Year's-day.
 * Prov. xiv. 32. 8° 17
 * 2 Sam. xii. 22, 23. 8° 1744. Fun.
 * Daniel xii. 13. 8° 1744. Fun.
 * Zech. xiv. 7. 8° 1745. Fast.
 ‡ * Matt. xxviii. 18. 8° 1746. Christ present with his faithful Ministers. *Brit. M.*
 * Luke ii. 29. 8° 1746. Fun.
HUGHES William, M.A. Hospitaller of St. Thomas, Southwark, and Minister of Kimbolton, Huntingdonshire.
 Pf. cxix. 59, 60. 8° 1682. Several Sermons. Summons to Sinners to think and turn. *Sion.*
 Pf. xxi. 1. 4° 1684. 2 Th. f. Sep. 9. *Bod.*
 Pf. xxxix. 9. 8° 1694. Of Silence and Submission under the severest Providences. *Bod. Pub. L.* Camb.
HUGHES William, M.A. Minor Canon of Worcester.
 1 Sam. xviii. 6. 8° 1749. Music-meet. The Efficacy and Importance of Musick.
HULSE John, M.A.
 Rom. xiii. 3, 4. 4° 1745. Assize. The Necessity and Usefulness of Laws in the natural and moral World.
HULSIUS Anthony, DD. Pastor of the Walloon-Church of Breda.
 Pf. xxi. 1–5. 4° 1660. Accession. On proclaiming K. Char. II.
HUME John, M.A. R. of Yelling, Huntingdonshire.
 Phil. iii. 20. 4° 1670 *Camb. Trin.* Camb.
HUME John, Bp. of Salisbury.
 Jerem. xxxi. 13. 4° 1747. May 29. b. Commons. *Eton.*
 * Joshua xxiv. 15. 4° 1757. Jan. 30. b. Lords.
 * Luke viii. 24. 4° 1758. Fast. b. Lords. *All S.* Oxon.
 * Matt. ix. 36–48. 4° 1762. Prop. of Gospel. *Braz. N.* Oxon.
 * Prov. iii. 27. 4° 1762. b. Gov. of Lond. Hosp.

HUME Robert,   V. of Lafenby, Cumberland.
  James iv. 14. 4° 1695. Fun.
HUMFREY John
  * Difc. in 8° 1704.
  Luke xi. 28. 8° 1709.
HUMPHREYS A. R. of Barton, Bedfordfhire.
  Rev. xiv. 13. 4° 1706. Fun. of T. Pomfret. *Brit. M.*
HUMPHREYS David, B. A.
  1 Cor. vi. 18. 4° 1707. Soc. of Batchelors.
HUMPHREYS Francis, M. A. Lect. of Hampstead, Middlefex.
  * Rom. xvii. 6. 4° 1776. Fast.
HUMPHREYS Humphrey, Bp. of Hereford.
  Hof. x iii 4° 1695. Jan. 30. b. Lords. *Jef.* Ox. *St. John's.* C.
HUMPHREYS John, M.A. V. of Mywood, Montgomeryfhire.
  Pf. lv. 3. 8° 1727. *Salop.* Acceffion.
HUMPHREYS Thomas, M. A. of Pemb. Coll. Oxon. Curate of
    Morton-in-Marfh, Gloucefterfhire.
  1 Theff. iv. 8. 8° 1712. *Oxon.* The divine Authority of the New
    Teft. proved and vindicated. *Bod. Or. Linc. Worc.* Ox. *Queen's.* C.
  Phil. iv. 13. 8° 17
HUMPHREYS Thomas, M.A. V. of Dreffield, Gloucefterfhire.
  Heb. xiii. 4. 8° 1742. Wedd. f. Marriage an hon[ble]. State. *Br. M.*
HUMPHRIES Thomas,   R. of St. Chads, Shrewsbury.
  * Luke xxi. 3. 8° 1771. *Salop*-Infirmary.
HUNT
  2 Sam. i. 25, 26.
HUNT *Jerem.* DD. Minifter of the Gofpel at Pinner's Hall, Lond.
  * Deut. xxxii. 29. 8° 1716. Ref. of Manners.
  * Prov. xiv. 32. 8° 1717. Fun. of Rev. *J. Maifters. Queen's.* C.
  * James i. 27. 8° 1723. Fun. of Grey Neville. *Queen's.* Camb.
  * 1 Kings x. 9. 8° 1725. Acceffion.
  Mark vi. 12. 8° 1735. The Sources of corrupting both natural
    and revealed Religion exemplified in the Romifh Doctrine of
    Penance and Pilgrimages. V. vol. 1. Ag. Popery. *Braz. N.* Ox.
  * 1 Pet. i. 24, 25. 8° 1736. Fun.
  * Serm. in 4 Vol. 8° 1748. On the Being and Attributes of God,
    on moral Obligations, and on various Subjects. *Ch. Ch.* Ox.
HUNT Ifaac, M.A. Preac. at Bentwick-Chapel St. Marylebone, Lond.
  ‡ * Matt. vi. 11. 8° 1781. Occafioned by the general Diftrefs of
    the Parifh of Mary le bone, on the improvident Accommoda-
    tion of the poor Inhabitants for the Purpofe of public Worfhip.
  * Sermons in 8° 1781. On public Occafions.
  * Nehem. ii. 3. 4° 1782. For the Benefit of the Weft-India-Suf-
    ferers of the Ifland of Jamaica and Barbadoes.
HUNT Thomas, DD. Heb. Profeffor, and Laudian Profeffor of
    Arabic, and Canon of Ch. Ch. Oxon.
  Prov. vii. 22, 23. 4° 1743. *Oxon.* Differtation. *Bal.* Oxon.
  * Differtations in 4° 1775. At the end of which are 2 Serm. on
  * Prov. xix. 21. ⎱ *Ch. Ch. Univ.* Oxon.
  * Matt. ii. 23. ⎰

HUNTER

HUNTER *Andrew*, DD. of Dumfries.
* Deut. xv. 17. 8° 1778. Anniv. of St. Andrew.
* Joſh. 24, 14. 12° 1779. 2 ſ. Fam-Worſhip recommended. V. Scotch Pr. Vol. 3.
HUNTER *Henry*, DD.
* - - - - 1775. Ord.
HUNTER *John*, Miniſter of the Goſpel at Gateſchaw.
* Exod. iii. 1, 2. 12° 1743. *Edinburgh*. The burning Buſh, yet not conſumed. *Brit. M.*
‡ * Mark xvi. 21 to end. 8° 1743. *Edinburgh*. A Lecture. *Brit M.*
HUNTER Joſiah, M. A. Miniſter in York.
Acts ix. 36, 37. 4° 1660.
Numb. xvi. 46. 4° 1666. Faſt. The Dreadfulneſs of the Plague. *Univ.* Oxon.
HUNTER Richard, M. A.
Pſ. i. 3. 4° 1703. Fun. of the Counteſs of Derby. *Ch. Ch.* Oxon. *Brit. M.*
HUNTER Thomas, V. of Garſtang, Lancaſter.
* Luke xxiii. 50. 4° 1754. Fun. of Will. Stratford, Eſq; LLD.
HUNTER Thomas, M. A. V. of Weaverham, Cheſhire.
* Moral Diſc. in 4 Vol. 8° 1754. *Warrington*. On Providence and other important Subjects.
HUNTER William, M. A. Fell. of Braz. Noſe. Oxon. and Miniſter of St. Paul's, Liverpool.
* - - - - 8° 1771. On Friendſhip.
* Joel ii. 15. 4° 1778. Faſt.
* Matt. iii. 8. 4° 1780. Faſt. National Calamities founded on national Diſſention and Diſſipation.
HURD Richard, Bp. of Worceſter.
* James iii. 18. 4° 1752. *Camb*. Aſſize. Enthuſiaſm and Bigotry. *Queen's.* Camb.
* Prov. xxii. 6. 8° 1753. *Camb.* Ann. meeting Ch. Sch. *Bod.*
* Pſ. cxix. 35. 4° 1776. Faſt. b. Lords.
* Serm. in 2 Vol. 8° 1776. Preached at Lincoln's Inn-Chapel at (Warburton's) the late Bp. of Glouceſter's Lecture. *Bod. Worc.* Oxon. *Sion.*
* 6 Sermons in 8° 1777. Preached at Lincoln's Inn-Chapel to which is ſubjoined a Diſc. on our Saviour's driving the Buyers and Sellers out of the Temple. *Pub. L. Queen's.* Camb.
* Serm. in 2 Vol. 8° 1780. Preached at Lincoln's Inn Chapel. *Trin.* Camb.
HURLY James,[a] B. A. Cur. of Wilton, Somerſetſ.
John i. 1. 8° 1746. *Oxon*. Viſ. The Divinity of Chriſt aſſerted, and the Cenſures of the Athanaſian Creed conſidered.
HURLY James,[a] B. A. Preſbyter of the Church England.
* Matt. xi. 29. } 12° 1763. V. vol. 2. Of the divine Orator.
* 1 Theſſ. v. 17.
HURRION *John*, Miniſter of the Goſpel in London.
* 1 Theſſ. iv. 13, 14. 8° 1712. Fun.

a ℞. The ſame. Heb.

Heb. xiii. 17. 8° 1721. Rights and Duties of Ministers & People.
* Disc. in 3 Vol. 8° 1727.
Col. iii. 3. 8° 1728. Fun.   The Xtian's hidden Life.
* 1 Thess. v. 12, 13. 8° 1731. Ord.
* Tit. ii. 14. 8° 1731. 4 f. V. Lime-street Serm. Vol. I. p. 325. Script. Doctrine of particular Redemption.

HURST Henry, M. A. Fell. of Mert. Coll. Oxon.
* Rom. vii. 7. 8° 1660.
Acts xxvi. 2. 4° 1675. m. e. P. p. 44. Kings and Emperors, not rightful Subjects to the Pope.
* 3 Serm. in 12° 1660. On the Inability of the highest improved natural Man to attain a sufficient Knowledge of indwelling Sin.
* Ps. cxvi. 12–14. 4° 1677. m. e. C. p. 465. Whether well-composed Vows do not exceedingly promote Religion.
Gal. iii. 13. 8° 1678. *Bod.*
Prov. xxvi. 28. 4° 1683. C. m. e. p. 182. Against Flattery.
Acts xvii. 21. 4° 1690. C. m. e. p. 400. *Bod.*

HUSBANDS Thomas, M. A. One of the Vicars of the Coll. of Hereford, and V. of Canon Pion, Herefordshire.
Eccles. x. 20. 8° 1713. Jan. 30. The great Sin and certain Punishment of traiterous Thoughts and rebel. Practices. *Bal. Ox.*

HUSSEY Christopher, DD. R of Westwickham, Kent, and Chapl. to his Grace the Duke of Dorset.
* Serm. in 3 Vol. 8° 1755.
* 20 Serm. in 8° 1758. *Queen's.* Camb.

HUSSEY Joseph, Pastor at Cambridge.
* John iii. 8. 4° 1704. Public Humiliation. On Account of a Storm. *St. John's.* Camb.
* Ephes. ii. 2. 4° 1704. Exposition. *All S.* Oxon.

HUTCHIN John, B. D. Fell. of St. John's Coll. Cambridge.
Matt. xvi. 18. 4° 1689.

HUTCHINS R.
* 2 Cor. xiii. 8. 8° 1773. *Lond.* b. Diff. Clergy.

HUTCHINS Richard, DD. R. of Linc. Coll. Oxon.
* 10 Serm. in 8° 1782. N. B. 3 first Serm. published in 8° 1771.

HUTCHINSON Francis, Bp. of Down and Connor.
2 Cor. v. 19. 4° 1692. Vis. *Brit. M.*
Ps. ix. 10. 4° 1698. *Camb.* Commencement. *Queen's.* Oxon.
Pub. L. Trin. *St. John's.* Camb. *Brit. M.*
Judges xviii. 7. 8° 1707. Assize. *Pub. L.* Camb.
Ps. lxviii. 8. 8° 1707. On the Union. *Pub. L. Trin. Cl. H.* Cam.
— cxlviii. 2. 8° 1720. Concerning Angels. Historical Essay concerning Witchcraft. p. 312.
— cxxxi. 1. 4° 1723. *Dublin.* Jan. 30. *Eton.*
* — — — 1731. Nov. 5.

HUTCHINSON Michael, DD. Minister of All-Saints, Derby, and afterwards of Hammersmith, Middlesex.
2 Sam. x. 10–12. 8° 1717. *Nottingham.* Birth-day.
Mark xiv. 6, 7. 4° 1727. b. Sons of the Clergy. *Wadh.* Oxon.

HUTCHINSON Samuel, Bp. of Killala and Achonry, Ireland.
　*Gal. vi. 9. 4° 1760. Irish Prot. Sch.
HUTCHINSON Thomas, DD. Preb. of Chichester, and V. of Horsham, Sussex.
　Luke xiii. 32. 8° 1738. Oxon. The usual Interpretation of δαί-μονες and δαιμόνια in the New Testament asserted. Bod. All S. Linc. Wroc. Oxon. Queen's Camb. Brit. M.
　Gal. iii. 19. 8° 1740. Oxon. The Use and Scope of the ceremonial Law briefly represented. Bod. Linc. Worc. Ox. Queen's. C.
　*Ps cvii 2. 8° 1745. Nov. 5.
　Ps. l 21. 8° 1746. Fast.
　—— 15. 8° 1746. Th. Oct. 9.
HUTTON Charles, M. A. R. of Uplime, Dorsetshire.
　Joshua xvii. 22 4° 1685. Th. July 26. The Rebels Text opened, and their solemn Appeal answered. Bod. Ch. Ch. Oxon. Sion.
HUTTON Matthew, Abp. of York.
　1 Pet. ii. 17. 4° 1741. Jan. 30. b. Commons. Queen's. Camb.
　Matt. xii. 25. 4° 1744. Jan. 30. b. Lords.
　—— vii. 12. 4° 1744. Spittal M.
　2 Cor. viii. 21. 4° 1744. An. meet. Ch. Sch. All S. Worc. Ox.
　1 Tim. iv. 8. 4° 1745. Irish Prot. Sch. All S. Jes. Worc. Oxon. Queen's. St. John's. Camb.
　John viii. 32. 4° 1746. Prop. of Gospel. All S. Oxon. Queen's. Camb. Sion.
　Luke xvi. 20, 21. 4° 1746. b. Govern. of Lond. Inf. Wadh. Ox.
　Joshua i. 7. 4° 1746. Accession. b. Lords. Brit. M.
HYDE Edward, DD. R. resident of Brightwell, Berks.
　* Eccles. viii. 2–4. 8° 1662. Sev. Sermons. Allegiance and Conscience not fled out of England. V. a Book entitled " the true " Catholick's Tenure."

J.　　G.　　DD.
　Num. xi. 5, 6. 1689.
JACKSON
　* 1 Cor. xi. 26. - - - -
JACKSON John
　Rom. xiii. 3. 4° 1685. Magistrate.
JACKSON John, M. A. late Minister of Dursly, R. of West-Birth, Gloucesters.
　Ps. ciii. 3. 4° 1707. On Bath-waters.
　Deut. xxxi. 16, 17. 8° 1710. Fast.
　Heb. xii 16. 8° 1710. Erect. a Char. School. Univ. Oxon. Trin. Queen's. Camb.
　Matt. xiii. 57. 8° 1711. Vis.
　Rom. xiii. 1. 8° 1723.
JACKSON John, DD. R. of Rossington, York.
　8 Practical Disc. on 12° 1728. On the Lord's Prayer, and Sacrament of the Lord's Supper.
JACKSON Matthew
　*Phil. i. 21. 8° 1756. Christ the Christians Life.

JACKSON Thomas, DD. President of C. C. C. Oxon.
　His Works in 3 Vol. fo. 1673. *Bod. Ch. Ch Univ. New C. Mert. Bal. Or. Wash. Pemb.* Oxon. *Trin. Queen's.* Camb. *Sion.*
JACKSON William, DD.
　Jude 3. 4° 1675. *Camb.* Vif. The Rule of Faith. *Bod. Univ.* Oxon. *St. John's.* Camb.

JACOB Joseph
　Numb. xxiii. 23. 4° 1702. 2 f. Th for Succeſſes.
　* Ezek xxi. 27. 4° 1705. Th.

JACOMB Samuel
　* 1 John v. 7. 4° 1676. m.c.G. p. 44. Trin. proved by Scripture.
　* 2 Tim iii. 16. 4° 1676. m.c.G. p. 85. Trin. proved by Scripture.

JACOMB Thomas, DD.
　Phil. iv 11. 4° 1675. f.m.c.C. p. 663. Contentment in every State.
　Rom. viii. 14. 4° 1683. C. m. e. p. 939. The Leading of the Spirit of God.
　* Rom viii. 1–4. 8° 1672. A Volume.
　* Iſai. liii. 10. 4° 1676. m. e. G. p. 155. The Covenant of Redemption opened.

JACOMB William,　　V. of Marden, Kent.
　* Gen. xviii. 19. 8° 1719. 2 f. Family-Inſtruction, *Queen's.* Cam.
　Jerem. xxxv. 8. 8° 1736. Upon the Act ag. ſpirituous Liquor.

JAGO Richard, M. A. R. of Harbury, Warwickſ.
　* Luke xvi. 31. 8° 1755. Cauſes of Impenitence conſidered &c. *Braz. N.* Oxon.
　* Rev. xiv. 13. 8° 1763. Fun.

JAMES David
　* Rev. xiv. 13. 8° 1780. *Malborough.* Fun. of Dr. *Collett.* The good Chriſtian happy in Death.

JAMES Henry, DD. Maſter of Queen's Coll. Camb. and Chaplain in Ord.
　Luke i. 74, 75. 4° 1674. b. King. *Univ. All S. Ch. Ch. Magd.* Oxon. *Trin. Queen's. St. John's.* Camb. *Sion.*

JAMES Hugh, M. A. R. of Upwell, Norfolk.
　Pſ. xcvii. 2.　17.　Aſſize.
　Prov. viii. 15, 16. 4° 1707. Aſſize.

JAMES John, M. A. R. of Latimer's, Bucks.
　1 Cor. iv. 1, 2. 4° 1678. Viſ. *Pub. L. Trin. St. John's. Queen's.* Camb. *Sion.*
　1 John iii. 8. 4° 1682. b Lord Mayor. *Magd.* Oxon. *Sion.*

JAMES John, Miniſter of Llanderfiſon, Carmarthen.
　Tit. i. 16. 8° 1720. *Gloucefter.*

JAMES Ptolemy, M. A. Miniſter of St. Helen's, and Preb. of St. Paul's, London.
　Pſ. xxvii. 15. 4° 1717. Fun. of Mrs. Durley.

JAMES William, M. A. V. of Clyrow, Radnorſhire.
　Acts viii. 30. 8° 1729. *Oxon.* The proper Interpretation of the Scriptures vindicated. *Queen's.* Camb. *Eton.*

JANE Will. DD. Dean of Gloucester and Canon of Ch. Ch. Oxon.
  Acts xx. 28. 4° 1675. Conf. of Bp. Compton. *Bod. Ch. Ch Univ. Magd. Queen's. Or. Oxon. Pub. L. St. John's. Camb. Sion.*
  Hosea vii. 9. 4° 1679. Fast. b. Commons. *Bod. Ch. Ch. C. C. C. Magd. Worc. Oxon. Pub. L. St. John's. Camb. Sion.*
  Pf. xcvi. 10. 4° 1691. *Oxon.* Th. b. Commons. *Bod. All S. Ch. Ch. Magd. Worc. Oxon. Cl. H. Queen's. Camb. Sion.*
  Pf. cxix. 106. 4° 1692. *Oxon.* b. King and Queen. Of religious Resolution. *Bod. Ch. Ch. C. C. C. Magd. Oxon. Sion.*

JANEWAY James
  * Pf. lxxxix. 44. 12° 16   *Trin.* Camb.
  * Rev. xiv. 13. 12° 1669. Fun. of Tho. Mowsley, Apothecary. *Pub. L.* Camb.
  Ephes. vi. 5–9. 4° 1676. s. m. e. C. p. 442. Duties of Masters and Servants.
  * Job xxii. 21. 8° 1677. Sev. serm. Heaven upon Earth, or the best Friend in the worst of times.

JAY Stephen,   R. of Chinner, Oxfordshire.
  Heb. xi. 33. 4° 1682. On the Lord President's Imprisonment. Daniel in the Den.
  Gen. xi. 4. 4° 1689. Tragedies of Sin &c. *Bod. Sion.*

IBBETSON James, DD. Arch-Deacon of St. Albans.
  Gen. xlix. 4. 8° 1746. *York.* Assize. Public Virtue and Happiness of any People.
  a Num. xxv. 5. 4° 1746. Assize.
  Luke xvii. 20. 8° 1748. *Oxon.* Pro. Grad. Bac. in S. Th. De Miraculis in Ecclesia Christiana.
  * Gal. vi 10. 4° 1758. b. Sons of the Clergy.
  * John v. 6. 4° 1759. Spitt. W. *Queen's.* Camb.
  * Acts viii. 17. 8° 1774. Confirmation.
  * Luke xxii. 19. 8° 1775. 6 Disc. on the Lord's Supper.
  * Acts xx. 35. 4° 1777. Ch. s.
  * Ezek. xxxv. 6. 8° 1778. Fast.

IBBETSON Richard, DD. late Fell. of Oriel Coll. Oxon. and R. of Lambeth, and Chapl. to the Abp.
  1 Tim. iii. 16. 8° 1712. *Oxon.* Epiphany. The Divinity of our Saviour proved from Scripture and Antiquity. *Bod. Bal. Worc. Oxon. Pub. L. Camb. Sion..*
  Rom. xiii. 4. 4° 1722 Assize. Obedience to Governors. *Ch. Ch. Oxon. St. John's. Camb. Sion. Eton.*

IBBOT Benj. DD. R. of St. Paul's Shadwell, and Chapl. in Ord.
  36 Disc. in 2 Vol. 8° 1726. (Republished 1776.) On practical Subjects. *Ch Ch. Magd. New C. Oxon. Cl. H. Camb. Brit. M.*
  N. B. His Sermons at Boyles Lect. V. p. 731.

JEACOCKE Abraham,   of Birmingham.
  Ephes. iv. 4. 8° 1702. Of Church Communion.
  Matt. xv. 4. 8° 1702. Of Rites and Ceremonies.

a Q. Levit. xxv. 3.

OF AUTHORS, &c. 189

JEBB John, M.D. late Fell. of St. Peter's Coll. Camb.
 * Acts xx. 35. 8° 1773. The Excellency of Benevolence. *Queen's.* C.
JEFFERSON Jacob, DD. late Fell. of Queen's Oxon. and V. of
 Carisbrook in the Isle of Wight.
 * Prov. xvi. 7. 8° 1763. Th for Peace. *Worc.* Oxon.
JEFFERY John, DD. Asch-Deacon of Norwich.
 16 Select Disc. in 8° 1710. On divers important Subjects. *Pub. L.*
 Camb *Brit. M. Dr. W's. L.* London.
 * John i. 1. 8° 1726. Logology.
 A Compleat Collection of his Serm. and Tracts in 2 V. 8° 1751.
 Pub L. Queen's. Camb. *Sion. Dr W's. L.* London.
JEGON William, M.A. late Fell. of King's Coll. Camb. and R. of
 Swanton Morley, Norfolk.
 Rom. xiii. 2. 4° 1685. May 29. The damning Nat. of Rebellion.
 Tit. ii. 15. 4° 1707. *Norwich.* Vis.
JEKYLL Thomas, DD. Preacher of the New Church, Westminster,
 and V. of Rowd, Wilts.
 Heb. xii. 14.   } 4° 1675. Peace and Love recommended and
 1 John iv. 20, 21. } Jan. 30.   persuaded. *Ch. Ch. Queen'..* O. *Sion.*
 2 Thess. ii. 7. 4° 1680. Fast. Dec. 22. Popery, Mystery of Ini-
  quity. *Magd.* Oxon.
 Jerem v. 29. 4° 1681. Fast. b. Lord Mayor. Righteousness and
  Peace, the best means to prevent Ruin *Ch Ch.* Oxon. *Pub. L.*
  Camb. *Brit. M.*
 Prov. xxiv. 21. 4° 1682. May 29. True Religion, the best Loy-
  alty. *Ch. Ch. Magd.* Oxon.
 Matt. v. 16. 4° 1697. Spitt. W. Public Charity. *Ch. Ch.* Oxon.
 Prov. xvi. 17. 8° 1698. Ref. of Manners. *Bod.*
[JELLINGER Christopher, M.A.]
 1 Pet. i. 9 4° 1664.
 * Serm. in 12° 1676. The spiritual Merchant.
JEMMAT Samuel, M.A. V. of St Nicholas, Warwick.
 2 Chron. xix. 6. 4° 1683. *Oxon.* Assize. *Trin.* Camb.
JENINGS
 Heb. x. 26, 27.   Farewel.
JENKINS Joseph, M.A. of Wrexham, Danbyshire.
 * 2 Cor. xii. 10. 8° 1775. Christian's Strength.
 * Disc. in 12° 1779. On select Passages of Scripture-History.
 * Matt. xxii. 21. 8° 1781. Fast. The National Debt.
JENKINS William
 * Collection of Farew. Serm. in 4° 1663. *Magd.* Camb.
JENKINS William
 Rom. vi. 2, 3. 4° 1675. m e. P. p. 261. No Sin venial.
 * 2 Pet. i. 15. 4° 1675. Fun.
 1 Cor. vi. 1, 2. 4° 1676. f. m. e. C. p. 86. How we may improve
  the present Season of Grace. *Bod.*
 2 Pet. ii. 7, 8. 4° 1683. C. m. e. p. 106. *Pub L.* Camb.
JENKINSON Richard
 Ps. xi. 3. 8° 1715. *Exon.* At Sessions. The Methods of subvert-
  ing Government. *St. John's.* Camb.   JENKS

JENKS Benjamin, M. A. R. of Harley, Salop, and Chapl. to the
    Earl of Bradford.
  Pſ. lxxxv. 1. 4° 1689. Th.
  — xxxiv. 3. 4° 1689. Nov. 5.
  Iſai. lii. 7. 4° 1697. Th.
  Rom. x 3. 8° 1700. Subſtance of ſeveral Sermons. Submiſſion
    to the Righteouſneſs of God
  *Gen. xxxix. 9. 12° 17   On Chaſtity.
JENKS Richard, M. A. Lect. of St. Mary at Hill, and St. Andrew,
    Hobart, and Preacher of St. Dunſtan's in the Weſt, Lond.
  Rom. vi. 23. 4° 1707. b. Lord Mayor. The Eternity of Hell-
    torments aſſerted and vindicated. *St. John's* Camb. *Sion.*
[JENKYN William]
  ‡*2 Pet. i. 15. 4° 1675. Fun. of Laz. Seaman.
JENNER Char. DD. R. of Buckworth, Huntingd. and Chapl. in Ord.
  *1 Pet. iii. 15. 4° 1753. Conf. of Bp. Ellys. *Queen's.* Camb.
JENNER Dav. B.D. Fell. of Sidney-Suſſex-Coll. Camb. and Preb.
    of Sarum.
  2 Tim. iv. 11. 4° 1676. On St. Luke's day. Of the Life and
    Death of St. Luke. *Bod. Ch. Ch.* Ox. *Trin. St. John's.* C. *Sion.*
  Gen. iv 15. 4° 1681. Jan. 30. Cain's Mark and Murder.
JENNER Thomas, DD. Preſident of Magd. Coll. and Margaret Pro-
    feſſor of Divinity in Oxford
  2 Cor. ix. 12. 8° 1752. *Oxon. Worceſter* Infirmary. Charity and
    Compaſſion towards Men, the Occaſion of Thankſgiving to
    God. *Worc.* Oxon.
JENNINGS David, DD.
  *2 Cor. iv. 5. 8° 1742. Ord. *Queen's.* Camb.
  *1 Cor. xv. 22. 8° 1743. Fun. of *David Neale.* *Queen's.* Camb.
    Brit. M.
  *Sermons in 12° 1743. to young Perſons. *Dr. W's L.* Lond.
  Heb. xi. 4. 8° 1749. Fun.
  *Serm. in 12° 1752.
  *Phil. i. 23. 8° 1757. Fun. of *Tim. Jollie.*
  ‡*Prov. xxii. 6. 8° 17
JENNINGS John, M. A. V. of Great Granſden, and Gamlingham,
    Cambridgeſhire.
  1 Cor. ii. 12. 4° 1701. Whitſunday. Of the Chriſtian Revela-
    tion. *Bod. Queen's* Camb. *Brit. M.*
  Acts iv. 16.   1710. Jan. 30.
  Pſ. cxxxii. 17, 18. 8° 1711. Acceſſion. *Linc.* Ox. *Pub. L.* Camb.
    Sion. Brit. M.
  Acts xxiv. 16. 8° 1711. Jan. 30. *Queen's.* Camb.
  2 Sam. xviii. 28. 8° 17   Th.
  2 Chron. xx. 9. 8° 1711. Faſt. *Linc.* Oxon. *Pub. L.* Camb.
  2 Tim. i. 5. 4° 1712. Viſ. *Ch. Ch.* Oxon.
  *Pſ. cxlvii. 6, 7. 8° 1713. Th.
  Tit. ii. 1. 8° 1715. Acceſſion.
  *2 Tim. i. 13. 8° 1719. Commem. of Dedication of a Church.
    Ch. Ch. Oxon.   *Dan.

* Dan. ix. 9, 10. 8° 1721. Faſt.
JENNINGS Nathaniel, of Iſlington.
   * Rev. xv. 3. 8° 1774. Fun. of Sarah Johnſon.
JENNY Jehu, M. A. V. of Hammondſworth, Middleſex.
   Matt. xxiv. 46. 4° 1673. Fun. of Lady Paget. *Pub. L.* Camb.
JEPHCOT John, DD. Preb. of Worceſter, and R. of All Saints in Eveſham, Worceſterſhire.
   Tit. iii. 8. 4° 1698. Ch. Sch. Of good Works.
JEPHSON Alexander, M. A. Maſter of Camberwell Free-ſchool, and R. of Bell-Haye, Eſſex.
   Prov. xxix. 15. 4° 1669.
   Judges v. 12. 4° 1705. Th. for Victory at Blenheim. *Sion.*
   Iſai. xliii. 3, 4. 8° 1715. Th.
JEPHSON Alexander, B. A. R. of Craike, Yorkſhire, and Dioceſe of Durham.
   * Matt. xvi. 24. 8° 1742. On Self-denial. *Queen's.* Camb.
   * Matt. xxv. 46. 2 f.
   * Acts xvii. 21. } 8° 1742. On a future Judgment.
   Mark xvi. 17, 18. 8° 1750. Ag. Dr. Middleton. Miracles continued beyond the Times of the Apoſtles.
   * Heb. xiii. 4. 8° 1754. Heinous Sins of Fornication and Adultery.
   * Matt. xix. 24. 8° 1765. The great Difficuty of rich Men entering into the Kingdom of Heaven conſidered.
JERVIS William, M. A. R. of Standon, Staffordſhire.
   1 Tim. ii. 1, 2. 4° 1722. Viſ.
ILES Henry
   Judges ii. 16. 4° 1709. Aſſize.
IMBER John, L.L.B. V. of Micheldever and R. of Kingſworthy, Hants.
   Pſ. cxxii. 6, 7. 8° 1721. Nov. 5. The Chriſtian Patriot.
IMRIE David, M. A. Miniſter of the Goſpel at Dalton.
   Pſ li. 10–13. 8° 1748. *Edinb.* b. Synod of Dumfries. The Neceſſity of Almighty Power, and the Grace of God to cure the Infection of Sin.
INETT John, DD. V. of Nun-Eaton, Warwickſ.
   Prov. xiv. 34. 4° 1682. Aſſ. *All S.* Ox. *Pub. L.* Camb. *Brit. M.*
INGELO Nathaniel, DD. Fell. of Eton College.
   Luke xxiv. 47. 8° 1677. *Queen's.* Oxon.
INGLIS Charles. DD.
   * Phil. iii. 20, 21. 8° 17   Fun.
INNES Alexander, DD. Aſſiſtant-Preacher at St. Margaret's, Weſtminſter, and R. of Wrabneſs, Eſſex.
   Matt. xviii. 17. 8° 1717. Ag. Bp. Hoadly. The abſolute Authority of the Church.
   Matt. xxvi. 41. 8° 1719. Char. ſ. The Danger of Corruptions from an unhappy Education.
   Pſ. cxxii. 1. 4° 1726. Conſ. of Ch. *Queen's.* Camb.
   12 Sermons in 8° 1726.
JOHNSON Andrew
   James iv. 17.

JOHNSON Chrift. M. A. Schoolmafter at Richmond, Surrey.
Num. xxiii. 23. ⎫   ⎧ Acceffion. p. 3.
1 Sam iv. 22   ⎬ 4° 1696.   ⎨ Roy. Fun. p. 21.
2 Sam. xxii. 47. ⎭   ⎩ Th after Affafination. p. 41.
Num. xxiii. 23. 4° 1698. Th. Dec. 2.
JOHNSON George
    John xi. 26. 8° 1733. Reafon, Judge of Doctrines.
JOHNSON James, B. D. Fell. of Sidney-Suffex-Coll. Camb.
    Deut. xvi. 13, 19. 8° 1670. Camb. Affize. The Judges Authority or Conftitution. Bod.
    Amos vi. 12. 4° 1670. Camb. Affize. Nature inverted. Bod.
JOHNSON James, M. A. R. of Melford, Suffolk.
    Matt. vii. 12. 8° 1723.
JOHNSON James, Bp. of Worcefter.
    * Pf. iii. 4. 4° 1753. May 29. b. Lords. *Queen's.* Camb.
    * Pf. cxliv, 15. 8° 1758. Prop. Gofpel.
    * Daniel ii. 20. 4° 1759. Th. b. Lords.
JOHNSON John, M. A.
    Matt. xiii. 43. 4° 1680. Fun. of Stephen Charnock. *Sion.*
JOHNSON John, M. A. V. of Cranbrook and of Appledore, Kent.
    Pf. xciv. 16. 8° 1701. Affize. Cl. H. Camb.
JOHNSON John, Minifter of the Gofpel at Liverpool.
    * Pf. lxv. 9. 8° 1756. The River of God enriching his Church.
    * 2 Theff. iii. 5. 8° 1758. Fun.   The Love of God.
    * Prov. viii. 15, 16. 8° 1762. Coron. Jefus, the King of Kings.
    * 12 Difcourfes in 2 Vol. 8° 1776. The Riches of Gofpel Grace opened.
JOHNSON Ifaac, B. A.
    Ecclef. xi. 1, 2. 8° 1739. At Swalecliffe and St. Paul's, Cant.
    * Matt. xi. 30. 8° 1740. Feb. iv. At St. Paul's, Cant.
JOHNSON Samuel,   Chaplain to Lord Ruffel, and R. of Corrington, Effex.
    Works fo. (1710) 1713. *Bod. Sion.*
JOHNSON Sam. M. A. V. of Great, and R. of Little Torrington, Devonfhire.
    * Ecclef. i. 2. 8° 1711.
    Rev. v. 13, 14. 8° 1729. Vif. The Divinity of Chrift from his Right to worfhip.
    John iii. 16. 8° 1729. Chriftmas. The Neceffity of believing the Divinity of the Son of God. *Sion.*
    Phil. ii. 6–12. 8° 1729. Vif. The Humiliation and Exaltation of the Son. of God.
    Matt. ii. 1, 2. 8° 1729. Chriftmas. Chrift King of the Jews both before and after his Incarnation.
    Matt. ii. 1, 2. 8° 1729. Chriftmas. The Beginning, Extent, and Duration of Chrift's mediatorial Kingdom.
    Matt. ii. 1, 2. 8° 1729. Epiph. The natural Supremacy of God the Son.
    *John vii. 24. 4° 1730. Vindication of himfelf.

                                                                                    1 Cor.

1 Cor. xv. 36–38. 8° 1733. The Resurrection of the same Body, as asserted and illustrated by St. Paul.
Select Disc. &c. in 2 Vol. 8° 1740.
John vi. 51. 8° 1741. The Doctrine of the Eucharist explained and vindicated.
Jonah i. 14. 8° 1745. Jan. 30. National Sins to be deplored by the innocent as well as the guilty.

JOHNSON Thomas, M. A. Fell. of Magd. Coll. Camb.
2 Cor. iii 5. 8° 1731. *Camb.* The Insufficiency of the Law of Nature. *Worc.* Oxon.

JOHNSON Will. DD. Chapl. in Ord. and Sub-Almoner and Preb. of St. Paul's, London.
Ps. xci. 15. 12° 1664. Th. On a great Deliverance at Sea. *Bod. C. C. C.* Oxon. *Pub. L.* Camb.

[JOHNSON William,] M A.
* - - - - 8° 1770. Fun.

JOHNSON William, P. G. C. Cur. of St. Mary's Castlegate, and St. Olive's in Mary Gate, York.
* - - - - 4° 1779. b. the provincial Grand Lodge of the most antient Society of Masons.

JOHNSTON George
‡* John ix. 26. 8° 1733. Religion plain, not mysterious. *Brit. M.*

JOHNSTON Henry
Amos iv. 12. 8° 1720. Fast. *Eton.*

JOHNSTON Samuel, B. D. V. of St. Mary's, and R. of St. Nicholas in Beverley, York.
Prov. xiii. 23. 8° 1726. *York.* The Advantage of employing the poor in useful Labour, and the Mischief of Idleness or ill-judged Business.

JOHNSTON William, M. A. R. of St. Andrew, Liguania.
Deut. i. 16. 4° 1718. *Kingston,* Jamaica.

JOHNSTON William. M. A.
* 2 Tim. i. 10. 12° 1764.

JOLLIE Timothy
* - - - - 1739. Ref. of Manners.

JONES Charles, L.L. B. R. of Nettlecomb and Higham, Somerset.
Josh. xxiv. 14. 4° 1705. Assize. Ag. Hypocrisy.
——— 15. 4° 1705. Assize. Ag. Indifference in Religion *Ch. Ch.* Oxon.

JONES David, M. A. V. of Marcham, Berks.
1 Tim. vi. 17. 4° 1690. *Bod. Trin.* Camb.
Josh. xxiv. 15. 4° 1692. The absolute Necessity of Family-Duties. *All S. Pub. L.* Camb.
Gal. iv. 16. 4° 1692. Farwel. *Bod. All S. Magd.* Oxon. *Trin.* Camb. *Sion.*
Ephes. iv. 16. 4° 169
Gal. ii. 20. 4° 1698. *Oxon.* Act.
Matt. ix. 36–38. 4° 1699. Ord. Ember-Week. *All S. Worc.* Ox. *Trin.* Camb.

Jerem. xxiii. 10. 4° 1699. Ag. curfing and fwearing.
Matt. iv. 17. 4° 1703. Faft. for Fire of London.
JONES David, M. A. R. of Upper Hardres, Kent.
    Prov. xxii. 6. 4° 1729. Sch. Fcaft. Some Remarks upon modern Education. *Brit. M.*
JONES Edward, B. A.
    Prov. xxix. 2. 8° 1719. Affize.
JONES Evan, V. D. M.
    * 2 Cor. xiii. 11. 8° 1764. St. Paul's Farewel to the Church of Corinth.
JONES Gibbon, B. A. R. of Sudburn and Oreford Suffolk, and Chaplain to Earl of Radnor.
    * 2 Cor. xiii. 11. 8° 1741. Farewel.
    1 Pet. ii. 17. 8° 1746. Reb. Fear God, and honour the King.
JONES HENRY, Bp. of Meath.
    Pf. cxviii. 24–26. 4° 1660.
    * - - - - 4° 1667. Conf. of Bp.
    2 Theff. ii. 3–13. 4° 1676 *Dublin.* Of Antichrift. *Bod. Ch. Ch. Magd.* Oxon. *St. John's.* Camb.
    1 Cor. xv. 24–28. 4° 1679. Fun. of J. Margetfon Abp. of Armagh. *Bod.*
JONES Herbert, Joint-Lect. of St. James's Duke's Place, London.
    * Luke x. 36, 37. 12° 1774. At Mifericordia-Hofp.
    * Lev xvii. 8, 9. 12° 1775. Precepts of Lev. Law ftill in force.
    * Gen. xxviii. 19. 8° 1777. Opening of Northampton-Chapel.
JONES John, B. D. Proctor for the Clergy of St. Afaph.
    Luke xi. 2. 4° 1704. Acceffion. Kingdom of God.
JONES John, M. A. Fell. of Bal. Coll. Oxon.
    Col. ii. 8. 8° 1728. *Oxon.* Sch. Feaft. *Bal. Worc.* Oxon.
JONES John, M. A. Preb. of Lincoln.
    * Luke iii. 21, 22. 4° 1668. At baptizing Theoph. Ld. Haftings.
JONES J.   Cur. of St. Clement's Dane.
    * Lament. iii. 39, 40. 4° 1759. Faft.
JONES Lewis, M. A. of Jef. Coll. Oxon. and   of Ely.
    1 Tim. ii. 1. 4° 1750. On the Common-prayer and Communion.
JONES R.   at Peckham, Surrey.
    * Haggai i. 5. 8° 1778. Faft.
JONES Samuel, M. A. R. of St. John's of Maddermarket, Norwich.
    Col. ii. 8. 4° 1701. *Norwich.* Vif.
    Acts xx. 32. 1720. Fun. of Dr. Jeffery.
JONES Samuel, E. C. C.
    1 Theff. iv. 13, 14. 8° 1726. *Salop.* Fun.
JONES Thomas,   of Ofweftry, Chapl. to the Duke of York.
    * Col. iii. 23. 8° 1678. The Heart, and its right fovereign.
JONES Thomas,   R. of Llandurnog, Denbyfhire.
    2 Tim. iv. 7, 3. 4° 1681. Fun. of Rev. *Ez. Tongue*, DD. *Or.* Ox. *Brit. M.*
JONES Tho. M. A. late Chapl. of St. Saviour's Southwark, Lond.
    * Acts xx. 26. 8° 1755. Vif.

* James

OF AUTHORS, &c.   195

* James iv. 9, 10. 8° 1756. Repentance and Reconciliation with God recommended.
* Disc. in 8° 1756. (Republished in 1763.)
* 2 Cor. v. 14. 8° 1761. For promoting Christian Knowledge among the poor.

JONES Walter, DD. Chapl. in Ord.
  1 John iv. 7. 8° 1720. Assize. *Brit. M.*
  17 Serm. in 8° 1741. Upon several Subjects.

JONES William
  * Isai. xl. 16. 8° 1712. Fun. of Mrs. *Joanna Brooks.*
JONES William,   R. of Plukley, Kent.
  * 3 Dissertations in 8° 1772. On Life and Death.
JONES William, B. A. R. of Paston, Northampton, Minister of Nayland, Suffolk, and F. R. S.
  * 1 Pet. ii. 17. 8° 1778. 2 s. Fear of God and the Benefits of civil Obedience.

JORDEN Humphrey, M. A. R. of Newland, Gloucester.
  Levit. xix. 17. 12° 1702. Ref. of Manners.

JORTIN John, DD. Arch-Deacon of London.
  4 Serm. in 12° 1730. On the Truth of the Christian Religion. *New C. Hert.* Oxon. *Pub. L. Queen's.* Camb. *Sion.*
  Heb. x. 25. 8° 1748. Conf. of Bp. Pearce. *Brit. M.*
  * 6 Dissertations in 8° 1755. *Bal. Wadh.* Oxon. *Pub. L.* Camb.
  * Serm. in 7 Vol. 8° 1774. *All S. Trin.* Ox. *Trin. Queen's.* C. *Sion.*

JOSS Torial
  * Isai. lvii. 2. 8° 1770. Fun.

IRONSIDE Gilbert, Bp. of Hereford.
  1 Pet. iv. 15. 4° 1685. *Oxon. Bod. Ch. Ch. C. C. C. Queen's.* Ox. *Trin.* Camb.
  Ps. lxxxv. 8. 4° 1690. *Bod.*
  Ps. cxliv. 10, 11. 4° 1690. *Bod.*
  Ps. xii. 1. 4° 1691. *Bod. Eton.*
  Prov. xx. 28. 4° 1691. *Bod.*

ISAAC John, M. A. R. of Ashwell, Rutland, and Chapl. to the Countess of Gainsborough.
  1 Cor. xv. 55. 8° 1715. Fun.   , *Magd.*

ISHAM Zach. DD. R. of Solyhull, Warwick, Preb. of St. Paul's, and Can. of Canterbury.
  Phil. iii. 20, 21. 4° 1695. Fun. of Dr. Scott. *Bod. All S. Ch. Ch. C. C. C. Magd.* Oxon. *Pub. L. Trin. St. John's. Queen's.* Camb.
  Luke x. 37. 4° 1696. b. Sons of Clergy. *Ch. Ch. C. C. C. Jes. Wadh.* Oxon. *Sion.*
  Acts xx. 35. 4° 1700. Spittl. W. *C. C. C. Jes.* Ox. *St. John's.* C.
  1 Sam. iv. 13. 4° 1701. Fast. b. Convocation. April 4. *All S. Ch. Ch. Queen's. Jes. Worc.* Oxon. *Queen's. St. John's. Trin.* Camb. *Sion.*
  1 Tim. iv. 14. 4° 1704. Conf. of Bp. Hooper. *Ch. Ch. C. C. C. Magd. Queen's. Oriel. Jes.* Oxon. *St. John's.* Camb. *Sion.*

Acts viii. 17. 4° 1705. Vif. Of Confirmation. *Cb. Cb. C. C. C. Queen's. Magd. Jef.* Oxon. *St. John's.* Camb.

JUXON John (or Joseph) V. of Twyford and Hungarton, Leicesterf. Exod. xxii. 18. 4° 1736. On Witchcraft.

JUXON William, Abp. of Canterbury.
Luke xviii. 31.

K.   R. M. A. R. of Royden, Suffolk.
Ezek. xxiv. 16. 4° 1688.

KAY Matthew, LL. D. V. of Holme Cultram cum Newton Arloifh, Cumberland.
* Ecclef. vii. 28. 8° 1765. Fun. of Mr. Rose. Man's Defection from his original Urightnefs chargeable on himfelf.

KAY Richard, LL. D. Sub-Almoner, and Chapl. in Ord. to his Majefty, R. of Kirkby, Nottingham &c.
* John xxi. 15, 16. 4° 1776. Ann. meet. ch. Sch.

KEACH Benjamin, Minifter of the Gofpel in London.
* Exod. xxviii. 12. 8° 16
Matt. iii. 10. 4° 1692. 3 f. The Axe laid ro the Root &c. *Bod.*

KEACK Elias
Rom. iii. 24. 4° 1694. 4 f. On Juftification. *Bod. Pub. L.* Camb.

KEARNY John, DD.
* Heb. xiii. 3. 4° 1747. *Dublin.* For Benefit of the poor Remains and Defcendants of the Proteftants who defended Enifkilling and Derry.
* Prov. xiv. 6. 8° 17   A Scorner defcribed.

KEATE Will. M. A. Preb. of Wells, and R. of Launton, Somerfetf.
* Micah. vi. 8. 8° 1775. Affize.

KEENE Edmund, Bp. of Ely.
Rom. xiv. 16. 8° 1748. b. Sons of Clergy, at Newcaftle upon Tyne. *Brit. M.*
* 1 Cor. x. 11. 4° 1753. Jan. 30. b. Lords. *Queen's.* Camb.
* Jerem. xxix. 7. 4° 1755. Ir. Prot. Sch. *Braz. N.* Ox. *Queen's.* C.
* Matt xxiv. 12. 4° 1757. Prop. of Gofp. *Braz. N.* Ox. *Queen's.* C.
* Matt. xi. 5. 4° 1767. Ann. meet. ch. Sch.

KEITH George, M. A. (formerly a Quaker) R. of Edburton, Effex.
Ifai. xxxviii. 19. 4° 1696. Th. for the Deliverance of the King and Kingdom. *Trin.* Camb. *Sion.*
1 Pet iii. 16. 4° 1700. Good Confcience. *Bod. Cb. Cb.* Oxon. *Cl. H.* Camb.
* Ephef. ii. 20-22. 4° 1700. Apoftles and Prophets Doctrine, the Foundation of the Church of Chrift.
Luke i. 6. 4° 1700. 2 f. *Bod. All S. Cb. Cb.* Oxon. *Sion.*
2 Cor. v. 14, 15. 4° 1703. *Bod. Magd.* Oxon.
* 1 Theff. i. 5. 4° 1703. Power of the Gofpel in the Converfion of Sinners.
Acts ii. 41, 42. 4° 1704. The Notes of the true Church.
1 Cor. xii. 13. 4° 1704. The Ufe of the Holy Sacraments.
Rom. i. 16. 4° 1705. 2 f. *Cb. Cb.* Oxon.
Heb. xi. 6. 4° 1707. Ag. the Quakers.

KEDDING.

OF AUTHORS, &c.   197

KEDDINGTON R. DD. R. of Keddington, Suffolk.
  * Serm. in 8° 1754. On public Occasions.
  * Gen xlix. 21. 8° 1758. Jacob's Prophecy on Napthali explained.
    Worc. Oxon. *Queen's.* Camb.
KEELING Barthol. M. A. R of Tiffield and Bradden, Northampt.
  * Ephes. iv. 11, 12. 8° 1754. Vis.
  * Rom. ix. 3. 8° 1766. 3 Disc. On St. Paul's Wish. *Queen's.* C.
  * Exod. xxxii. 31–33. 8° 1767. 3 Dis On Moses's Petition.
  * Luke xxiii. 39, 40. 8° 1767. 4 Dis. Crucified Malefactor.
   1 Cor. iii 8. 8° 1767. 4 Dis. Alliance of Heresy with Deism &c.
KELLO John
  * Hosea ix. 12. 8° 1777. Fast.
  * 4 Serm. in 12° 17   On secret Prayer.
KELLY George, jun. B. A. of Bal. Coll. Oxon.
  * Joel ii. 15. 4° 1777. Fast.
KELSAL
   John v 24.   Fun.
KELSAL Edward, M. A. V. of Boston, Lincolnshire.
   Phil iv 5. 8° 1710. The true Nature of Moderation. *Ch. Ch.*
   Oxon. *Queen's.* Camb.
   Deut. xvi. 19. 8° 1712. Ag. Bribery.
KELSEY Joseph, B. D. Arch-Deacon and Canon of Sarum, R. of
    Newton Tony, Wilts.
   1 Kings ix. 3. 4° 1674. Cons. of a Chapel. *Bod. C.C.C.* Ox. *Sion.*
   1 Cor. i 23, 24. 4° 1691. Christ crucified. *Bod. St. John's.* Cam.
   Heb. vi. 10. 4° 1691. Vis. De æterno Christi Sacerdotio. *Bod.*
    Ch. Ch Univ. St. John's. Linc. Oxon. *Cl. H.* Camb. *Sion.*
   Serm. (2d Edit.) in 8° 1721. On sev. Occasions. *Trin.* C. *Brit. M.*
KEMP Edward, B. D. Fell. of Queen's Coll Camb.
   2 Cor. v. 17. 4° 1668. *Camb.* The Sunday before Sturbridge Fair.
    Trin. Camb
KEN Thomas, Bp of Bath and Wells.
   Prov. xi. 16. 4° 1682. Fun. of Lady Maynard. *Magd. C.C.C.* Ox.
    Trin. St. John's. Cl. H. Camb.
   - - - - 1687. Ascension.
   Dan. x. 11. 8° 1713. ⎱ p 57. V. his Life by Hawkins. *Bod.*
   Mic. vii 8, 9. 8° 1713. ⎰ Palm Sund. p. 99.
KENDAL Nicholas, M. A. R. of Sheviock, Cornwal.
   1 Sam ii. 25. 4° 1685. Assize.
[KENNEDY George, M. A.]
   - - - - 1749. Th.
KENNET Basil, DD. President of C. C. C. Oxford.
   20 Serm in 8° 1715. preached on several Occasions to a Society
    of Merchants in foreign Parts. *Ch. Ch. C.C.C. New C. St. John's.*
    Oxon. *Queen's. St. John's.* Camb.
KENNET White, Bp. of Peterborough.
   Isai. lvii. 1. 4° 1695. Roy. Fun. The righteous taken away from
    the Evil to come. *Ch. Ch.* Oxon. *St. John's.* Camb.
   Gal. iv. 18. 12° 1702. Ref. of Manners. *Pub. L.* Camb.
                                                        Prov.

Prov. xvii. 6. 4° 1703. b. Sons of Clergy. The Glory of Children in their Fathers. *Wadh.* Ox. *Trin. Queen's.* Cam. *Brit. M.*
Jerem. xliv. 23. 4° 1704. Jan. 30. Enquiry into the Causes of the civil War. *Univ. Ch. Ch. Worc. Jes.* Ox. *Pub. L. St. John's.* C.
1 Theff. iv. 6. 4° 1704. Affize. Christian Honefty recommended. *Ch. Ch.* Oxon. *Pub. L.* Camb. *Brit. M.*
Jerem. l. 22, 23. 4° 1764. Th. Sep. 7. *Magd.* Oxon. *Trin.* C.
Pf. cxliv. 15. 4° 1705. Acceffion. b. Lord Mayor. *Ch. Ch.* Ox. *Pub. L. St. John's. Queen's.* Camb.
Gen. xlii. 21. 4° 1706. Jan. 30. b. Commons. *Ch. Ch. Univ. Magd.* Oxon. *Trin. Queen's.* Camb. *Sion.*
1 Tim. iii. 1. 4° 1706. Conf. of Bp. Wake. The Office and good Work of a Bifhop. *Ch. Ch. C. C. C. Magd.* Ox. *Queen's. Cl. H.* Camb. *Sion.*
Pf. cxliv. 12. 8° 1706. Ann. meet. ch. Sch. *Pub. L. Queen's.* Cam.
Ecclef. vii. 14. 4° 1706. b. Queen. The Duty of rejoicing in a Day of Profperity. *Ch. Ch. C. C. C.* Oxon. *Trin.* Camb. *Sion.*
Pf. xxxix. 4. 8° 1708. Fun. of Duke of Devonfhire. *Bod. Bal. Ch. Ch. Worc.* Oxon. *Pub. L. Trin. St. John's.* Camb. *Sion.*
Prov. xxxi. 29. 8° 1708. Char. for Girls. The excellent Daughter. *Bod.*
Luke xvii. 17, 18. 8° 1709. Th. b. Queen. Nov. 22. Glory to God, and Gratitude to Benefactors. *Univ.* Ox. *Pub. L. Queen's.* Camb. *Sion.*
John vi. 10. 8° 1710. Spitt. T. The Works of Charity. *Linc.* Oxon. *Pub. L. St. John's.* Camb.
Luke xiv. 27. 8° 1710. b. Convocation.
John xiv. 27. 4° 1710. Conc. ad Synod. *C. C. C.* Oxon. *Pub. L. Trin. St. John's. Queen's.* Camb. *Sion. Brit. M.*
Luke x. 29. 4° 1711. El. of Lord Mayor. The Chriftian Neighbour. *Ch. Ch.* Oxon. *Pub. L. Queen's.* Camb. *Brit. M.*
1 Cor. ix. 12. 4° 1712. Prop. of Gofpel. The Letts and Impediments in planting and propagating Chrift's Gofpel. *Ch. Ch. C. C. C.* Oxon. *Pub. L. Queen's.* Camb. *Sion.*
Matt. xix. 16. 4° 1712. Spit. T. Doing good, the way to eternal Life. *Ch. Ch.* Oxon. *Pub. L.* Camb.
1 Cor. xiii. 4. 8° 1714. Spit. T. *Bod. Ch. Ch.* Oxon. *Queen's.* C.
1 Sam. xv. 13. 4° 1715. Rebellion. The Wichcraft of the prefent Rebellion. *Queen's.* Camb.
2 Sam. xv. 23. 8° 1715.
Pf. lxxv. 1. 4° 1715. Nov. 5. Providence protecting the Proteftant Religion. *Queen's.* Camb. *Brit. M.*
Prov. i. 12. 4° 1715. Nov. 5. b. Lord Mayor. *Brit. M.*
Luke xvi. 1, 2. 4° 1716. Spittal T. The faithful Steward. *Ch. Ch.* Oxon.
Pf. xxxiii. 1. 8° 1716. Th. for fuppreffing the Reb. *Ch. Ch.* Ox.
Luke xix. 8. 8° 1719. Spitt. M. Charity and Reftitution.
Mark xiv. 19. 4° 1720. Jan. 30. b. L. *Magd.* Ox. *St. John's.* C.

KENNI-

KENNICOTT Benjamin, DD. Canon of Ch. Ch. and Keeper of the Radcliffe Library and V. of Culham, Oxon. &c. &c.
* Gen. ii. 8–24. 8° 1747. Critical Differtation. On the Tree of Life in Paradife. *Bod. Queen's.* Camb. *Eton.*
* Gen. iv. 1–5. 8° 1747. Critical Differtation. On the Oblation of Cain and Abel. *Bod. Queen's.* Camb. *Eton.*
Jerem. xxxiii. 10, 11. 8° 1749. Th. for Peace. The Duty of Thankfgiving for Peace in general, and the Reafonablenefs of Thankfgiving for our prefent Peace. *Bod. Queen's.* Camb.
* 1 Chron. xi. 1 &c. 8° 1753. V. State of the printed Heb. Text of the Old Teftament. *Bod. Queen's.* Camb. *Eton.*
* Rom. viii. 35–37. 8° 1757. On St. Paul's-day. Chriftian Fortitude. *Bod. Queen's.* Camb.
* Ifai. vii. 13–16. 8° 1765. Text explained. *Bad. Worc.* Oxon. *Queen's.* Camb.
* Gen. ii. 3. 8° 1781. The Sabbath.

KENRICK Daniel, M. A. V. of Kemfey, Worcefter.
Rom. xiii. 4. 4° 1688. Affize. *Magd.* Oxon.

KENRICK Van Ivjik
* Numb. xiv. 9. 8° 1691.

KENWRICK George, M. A. Minifter of Horming, Norfolk.
Pf. cxviii. 8, 9. 8° 1721. Nov. 5.
Acts xvi. 30, 31. 8° 1729. *Norwich.* 2 f.

KEPPEL Frederick, Bp. of Exeter.
* James iii. 17. 4° 1766. Jan. 30. b. Lords.
* Matt. xxviii. 19. 4° 1770. Prop. of Gofpel. *Queen's.* Camb.

KERRICK Samuel, DD. Fell. of C.C.C. Camb.
1 Pet iv. 10. 8° 1735. Commencement. *Queen's.* Cam. *Brit. M.*
* Pf. cxxiv. 7. 8° 1749. Th. Oct. 9.

KERRICK Walter, M. A. Canon Refid. of Sarum, and late Fell. of Catherine Hall, Camb.
* Joel ii. 12, 13. 4° 1781. Faft.

KERRICK Charles, Curate of Redenhall, Norfolk.
1 Kings xii. 10, 11. 8° 1746. *Norwich.* Faft.

KERSWEL John. B. D. R. of Goddington, Oxon.
* Pf. cxvi. 12. 4° 1665. May 29. David's Thankfulnefs to God. *Bal.* Oxon.

KETTLEWELL John, B. D. V. of Colefhill, Warwickfhire.
5 Difc. in 8° 1696. On fo many important Points of practical Religion. *Bod. Ch.Ch. Univ. Or. Pemb. Ox. Trin. St. John's.* C.
To which are added 4 Sermons publifhed by the Author in his life-time, *viz.*

1 Cor. xiv. 12. 4° 1684. Vif. Of Edification. *Bod. Ch.Ch. Magd.* Oxon. *Pub. L.* Camb.
Prov. xiv. 32. 4° 1684. Fun. of Lady Digby. *Bod. Ch.Ch. C.C.C. Magd.* Oxon. *Sion.*
Heb. vi. 12. 4° 1685. Fun. of Lord Digby. *Ch. Ch. C.C.C. Ox.*
Matt. xxii. 21. 4° 1685. Vif. The religious Loyalift. *Ch.Ch.* Ox.
N.B. All thefe are printed in the firft Vol. of his Works, fo. 1719. *Ch. Ch. Bal. Mert. New C. Jef.* Oxon. *Sion.*

KIDDEL John, of Tiverton, Devon.
    * 2 Cor. vi. 3, 4. 8° 1747. b. Diff. Clergy.
    * Jerem. ix. 23, 24. 8° 1759. Th.
    * 2 Tim. iii. 16. 8° 1779. 3 Differt. On the Infpiration of the H. Scriptures
KIDDER Richard, Bp. of Bath and Wells.
    Pf. xxxix. 5. 4° 1673. Fun.
    Ephef vi. 4. 4° 1673 Of the Education of Youth.
    1 Pet. iii. 11. 4° 1682. b. Lord Mayor. *All S*. Ox. *Trin*. C. *Sion*.
    Heb. xiii. 14. 4° 1686. Fun. of Mr. Allen. *Bod Ch. Ch. St. John's*. Oxon. *Pub. L. Camb. Sion*.
    1 Tim. vi 17–19. 4° 1690 Spitt. T. The Duty of the rich. *Bod. Ch Ch. Oxon. Pub. L. St John's. Camb. Sion*.
    Matt. xxiii. 35. 4° 1692. Jan. 30. b. Lords. *Bod. Magd.* Oxon. *Ch. H. Camb. Sion*.
    1 Pet. i. 3. 4° 1694. Spitt. M. On the Refurrection. *Bod. Sion*.
    ‡ * Matt. v. 43, 44. 4° 1693 b. King and Queen. *Brit. M*.
    Zechar. vii. 5. 4° 1694. b. Queen. Of Failing. *Bod. Ch. Ch.* Oxon. *Sion*.
    12 Serm. in 8° 1797. *New C. Magd. Pemb.* Oxon. *Dr. W's. L.*
KIDGELL John, M. A. R. of Wolverfton, Suffolk.
    * Ifai. xxvi. 20. 8° 1756. Faft. Earthquake. *Queen's*. Camb.
    * Pf. xx. 9. 8° 1761. Faft.
KILBOURN Robert, LL. D. Preb. of St. Paul's, R. of St. Mary Aldermary and St. Thomas, and of Barnes in Surrey.
    Mal. ii. 7. 8° 1727. Conf. of Bp. Hare. *Brit. M.*
    1 Cor. ix. 5. 4° 1729. b. Sons of Clergy. *Worc. Wadh.* Oxon. *Brit. M.*
    Pf. cxxii. 6. 8f 1729. Acceffion.
KILBY George, M. A. late of King's Coll. Camb. and R. of the Heath, Colchefter.
    Rom. xii. 18. 8° 1733.
KILLIGREW Henry. DD. Preb. of Weftminfter, and Mafter of the Savoy.
    Matt. xxi. 9. 4° 1666. b. King. Advent. *Ch. Ch. Magd.* Oxon. *Trin*. Camb.
    22 Serm. in 4° 1685. *Queen's. Pemb.* Oxon.
    Pf. cx. 7. 4° 1689. Sund. b. Eafter. *Bod.*
KILLINBECK John, B. D. Fell. of Jef. Coll. Camb. V. of Leeds and Preb. of York.
    Luke xiv. 14. 8° 1710. Ch. f.
    18 Serm. in 8° 1717. *Nottingham.*
KILNER James, M. A. R. of Lexden, Effex, and Chapl. in Ord.
    1 Sam. viii. 18. 4° 1745. Rebellion. Nov. 5.
    * Matt. x. 29. 4° 1756. Earthquake. Faft.
KIMBER Ifaac
    * 20 Serm in 8° 1756. On the moft interefting, religious, moral and practical Subjects. *Queen's.* Camb.

KIMBERLEY Jonathan, M. A. of Pemb. Coll. Oxon. Chaplain in Ord. Dean of Litchfield and Preb. of Westminster.
 Rom. xiii. 5. 4° 1683. Assize. *Sion*.
 Exod. xv. 2. 4° 1702. Nov. 5. b. Convocation. *Ch. Ch. Magd. Jes.* Oxon. *St. John's.* Camb.

KINCH *John*
 ‡ * 1 Thess. iv. 13. 8° 1722. Fun. of Rev. *J. Gale. Brit. M.*

KING Arnold, L L. B. R. of St. Michael's Cornhill, London.
 Luke ix. 54–56. 4° 1748. Nov. 5. b. Lord Mayor.
 Ps. cxxii. 7. 4° 1749. Th. for Peace. b. Lord Mayor.
 Exod. xviii. 21. 4° 1749. Elect. Lord Mayor.
 2 Kings iv. 1. 4° 1751. b. Sons of the Clergy.
 * Heb. ix. 27. 4° 1753. Fun. of Dr. Hay. *Brit. M.*
 * Ps. cxxvii. 2. 4° 1756. Fast. Earthquake.

KING Henry, Bp. of Chichester.
 Ezek. xxi. 27. 4° 1661. May 29. *Worc.* Oxon. *St. John's.* Camb.
 Ps. cxvi. 15. 4° 1662. Fun. of Bp. Duppa, *C. C. C.* Oxon.
 Tit ii. 1. 4° 1663. Vis.
 * Matt. vi. 9–13. 4° 1664. *Or.* Oxon.
 2 Chron. xxxv. 24, 25. 4° 1665. Jan. 30. *Pub. L. Trin.* Camb.

KING James, M. A. Lect. of St. Martin's, Ludgate, London.
 Luke x. 37. 4° 1707. Co. Feast. The good Samaritan exemplified in the charitable Christian. *Univ.* Ox. *Queen's. Trin.* Cam.

KING James, DD, R. of St Michael's Crooked Lane, Lond. afterwards of Cheam, Surrey.
 Luke xiii. 7–9. 4° 1743. Fast. b. Lord Mayor.
 Ps. cvii. 39–41. 4° 1743. Col. Georgia.

KING James,   Dean of Raphoe.
 * Rom. xiii. 5. 4° 1771. Jan. 30. b. Commons.

KING John, Bp. of London.
 * Ps. cxxviii. 3. 12° 1740. V. Disc. on conj. Duty. V. 1. p. 235.

KING John, DD. R. of Chelsea near Lond. and Preb. of York.
 Eccles[us]. xvi. 22. 4° 1698. Fun. of Willoughby Chamberlain.
 Joel ii. 18. 4° 1701. Fast. The divine Favour, the best alliance.

KING John, M. A. late Fell. of Queen's Coll. Oxon. Minister of Rumsey, Hants.
 Ephes. vi. 4. 8° 1725. *Oxon.* The Necessity and Benefit of Confirmation. *Worc.* Oxon.

KING Richard, M. A. Cur. of St. Mary's at Hill, Lecturer of St. George's Middlesex, and Chaplain in Ord.
 2 Cor. xiii. 11. 4° 1748. Farewel.
 Ps. cxxii. 6. 4° 1751. b. Antigallicans.
 Ps. cxliv. 15. 4° 1751. Nov. 5. b. Lord Mayor.

KING *Samuel*
 * Exod. ix. 3. 8° 1750. Distemper among Cattle.
 * ———— 1767. Ord. of   *Symonds.*

KING William, Abp. of Dublin.
 * Isai. lix. 6, 7. 4° 1685. *Dublin.* b. Lord Justices.
 Acts xxiv. 14–16. 4° 1686. *Ch. Ch.* Oxon. *Sion.*

Pſ. cvii. 2, 3. 4° 1691. Th. Nov. 16. Europe's Deliverance from France and Slavery. *Bod. All S. Ch. Ch.* Oxon. *Sion.*
Pſ. cxxvi. 3. 4° 1704. Th. Sept. 7. *Ch. Ch.* Oxon. *St. John's.* Camb. *Sion.*
Phil. ii. 3–5. 4° 1705. b. Queen. Palm. S. Of Humility. *Ch. Ch.* Oxon. *Pub. L.*
Prov. xxii. 6. 4° 1705. Char-School. The Advantages of Education. *Ch. Ch.* Oxon. *Sion.*
Eccleſ. viii. 11. 4° 1706. b. Lord Mayor of Dublin. *Sion.*
Rom. viii. 29, 30. 8° 1709. Divine Predeſtination and Foreknowledge conſiſtent with the Freedom of Man's Will. *Ch. Ch. Bal. Magd. St. John's. Worc.* Ox. *Pub. L. Trin. Queen's. Cl. H. St. John's.* Camb.
* Pſ. cxii 6. 4° 1714. Fun. of Narciſſus Abp. of Armagh.
Gen. ii. 16, 17. 4° 1731. On the Fall of Man. Appendix to an Eſſay on the Origin of Evil. p. 113. *St. John's.* Oxon.

KINGS William
 Mal. iv. 2. 4° 1667.

KINGSTON Richard, M. A. Chapl. in Ord.
 2 Chron. vii. 13, 14. 4° 1665. Spiritual Receipt for Cure of the Plague. *Sion.*
 Matt. xviii. 7. 4° 1682. Subſtance of ſev. Serm. The Cauſe and Cure of Offences. *Bod. Sion.*
 1 Sam. x. 24. 4° 1683. The Aſſaſſination-plot. *Pub. L.* Camb.

KINNERSLEY Thomas, M. A. R. of Lavenham, Suffolk, and Miniſter of Trinity Minories, London.
 Micah. vi. 6–8. 8° 1718. In the King's Bench-Priſon. *Sion.*

KIPPIS *Andrew*, DD.
 * 1 Cor. xi. 29. 8° 17 On the Lord's Supper.
 * - - - - 1756. Religious Knowledge.
 * Pſ. cxxvi. 3 8° 1759. Th. ſ.
 * Pſ. xxi. 3. 8° 1761. Coronation.
 * John vii. 46. 8° 1769. Ord.
 * Prov. x. 7. 8° 1769. Fun. of Rev. *Tim. Laugher. Queen's.* Cam.
 * Matt. xi. 5. 8° 1777. b. Society for Prop. Xtian Knowledge.
 * Luke ii. 52. 8° 1780. Char. School. The Example of Jeſus in his Youth recommended to Imitation.

KIRKUP J.
 * - - - - 1761. Roy. Fun.

KIRKWOOD James, R. of Aſtwick, Bedfordſhire.
 * Epheſ. v. 16. 12° 1693. Redeeming the Time.

KITCHIN *John*, M. A. Miniſter of St. Mary Abchurch, London.
 Heb. ix. 27. 4° 1660. Fun.
 1 Tim. v. 22. 4° 1677. m. e. C. p. 111. How we muſt reprove and not partake of other Men's Sins.

KNAGGS Thomas, M. A. Lect. of St. Giles in the Fields, Lond.
 Pſ. lxviii. 28. 4° 1691. Nov. 5.
 — lxiv. 9. 4° 1693. Nov. 5. b. Lord Mayor. *Pub. L.* Cam. *Sion.*
 1 Theſſ. v. 13. 4° 1696. Th. April 16.
              * Eccleſ.

* Eccles. x. 20. 8" 1697. Nov. 5.
Acts xxiv. 16. 4° 1697. Assize.
Heb. xii. 5, 6. 4° 1700. Of Contentment. *Univ. Worc.* Oxon. *Queen's.* Camb. *Sion.*
Heb. iv. 13. 4° 1701. Assize. Of the Omnipresence.
Prov. xiv. 9. 4° 1701. Ag. Atheism.
1 Cor. iv. 7. 4° 1702. Roy. Fun. The Vanity of the World.
Prov. xxiii 17, 18. 4° 1702. Nov. 5. b. Ld Mayor. Divine Providence.
Ps. cxxvi. 4. 8° 1704. Th. Sep. 7.
2 Cor. xiii. 11. 4° 1705. Ag the French King.
1 Pet. iii. 13. 4° 1706. Th. for Victory at Ramellies. God with us. *Magd.* Oxon. *Pub. L.* Camb. *Sion.*
Mark vi. 12. 8° 1707. Exhortation to national Repentance. *Univ. Worc.* Oxon. *Trin Queen's.* Camb
Ps cvi. 21. 8° 1708. Th. Aug. 19. *Univ.* Ox. *Queen's.* C. *Eton.*
1 Kings xix. 4. 8° 1708. Ag. Self-murder. *Sion.*
Prov. xxii. 1. 8° 1708. Pr. George's Fun. *Univ.* Ox. *Trin.* Cam.
Luke xvii. 15, 16. 8° 1709. For the Victory of Mons.
Prov. iii. 5, 6. 8° 1710 Fast. *Magd. Linc. Wadh.* Oxon.
Ps. xvi. 12. 8° 1710. Fun.
Matt. vi. 34. 8° 1712. God governs the World.
* Luke viii. 52. 8° 1714.
Phil. i. 23, 24. 8° 1714. Fun. of Arch-Bp. Sharp.
Ephes. v. 7. 8° 1714. Ag. Riots.
Prov xiii. 10. 8° 1715. June 12.
John v. 14. 8° 1716. June 10.
Esther v. 13. 8° 1716. Nov. 5. b. Ld Mayor. Haman and Mordecai. *Queen's.* Camb.
2 Sam. xviii. 3. 8° 1717. Jan. 30.
Ps. cxxv. 5. 8° 1720. Nov. 5.
Isai. lvii. 1. 4° 1721. *Brit. M.*
* Gen. xviii. 32. 4° 1721. Fast. Plague in France.
‡ * Matt. xiv. 6-8. 8° 1722. Death of John Baptist.

KNAPP William,   R. of Ingoldworth, Norfolk.
Job xxii. 21. 12° 1685.

KNELL Paul, M.A. of Clare-hall, Camb. and Chapl. to a Regiment of Cuirasiers.
5 Serm. in 8° 1660. Israel and England parallelled. *Brit. M.*

KNIGHT *Henry*, M. A.
* Serm. in 8° 1747. On the Being and Attributes of God. *Queen's.* Camb. *Dr. W's L.* Lond.

KNIGHT James, DD. V. of St. Sepulchre's, London.
Deut. xvii. 12. 4° 1719. Vis. *Linc.* Ox. *St. John's.* Camb. *Sion.*
Ps. lxxii 4. 4° 1720. An. meet. Ch. Sch. *Sion.*
8 Sermons in 8° 1721. At Lady Moyer's Lect. *Bod. Ch. Ch. Univ. Bal. Worc. Hert.* Oxon. *Dr. W's L.* Lond.
Deut. xvi. 18. 4° 1730. El. of Lord Mayor.
Isai. lix. 19. 8° 1733. Ref of Manners.

2 Pet. iii. 10–13. 8° 1736. On the Conflagration and Renovation of the World. *Worc.* Oxon. *Queen's.* Camb. *Sion.*

KNIGHT John, of New-Inn-Hall, Oxon. V. of Banbury, and R. of Broughton, Oxon.
    Hosea x. 4. 4° 1682. Assize. The Samaritan Rebels perjured. *Ch. Ch. Oriel. Bal.* Oxon. *Trin. St. John's.* Camb.
    Num. xxiii. 10. 4° 1700. Fun. of Lady Guilford. *St. John's.* C.

KNIGHT John, Minister of Poplar.
    * - - - - 1764.

KNIGHT Robert, M. A. V. of Harewood, Yorkshire.
    * Heb. xii. 28. 8° 1728. The Nature and Obligation of relative Holiness.

KNIGHT Samuel, DD. Preb. of Ely, and Chapl. in Ord.
    Rev. xiv. 13. 8° 1721. Fun.
    Tit. iii. 1. 8° 1724. Cor. *Eton.*
    2 Kings xi 19, 20. 8° 1725. May 29. b. Commons. *Trin. Queen's.* Camb.
    Heb. vi. 10. 8° 1729. Spitt. T. *Queen's.* Camb.
    Luke xvi. 10. 8° 1731. Cons. of 2 Bishops. *Queen's.* Camb.
    * Luke ii. 52. 8° 17
    Rom. xiii. 5. 4° 1738. Accession. *Brit. M.*

KNIPE Rest
    * - - - - 8° 1769. The new Birth.

KNOWLES J. C. B. A. Minister of Pointon and Norbury, Cheshire.
    * 12 Serm. in 8° 1769.

KNOWLES Thomas, M. A. R. of Ickworth, and Fell. of Pemb. Hall, Cambridge.
    12 Serm. in 8° 1750. The Scripture-Doctrine of the Existence and Attributes of God. *Queen's.* Camb.

KNOWLES Thomas, DD. Preacher of St. Mary's in Bury, Suffex.
    * Rom. xiv. 16. 4° 1772. Objections to Charity Schools answered.

[KNOX Hugh] Min. of the Gosp. in the Island of Saba, West Indies.
    * Disc. in 2 Vol. 8° 1768. On the Truth of revealed Religion, and other important Subjects.

KYTE Joshua, DD. R. of Windlebury, Oxon.
    * Prov. xxviii. 1. 8° 1758. Fast. True Religion, the only Foundation of true Courage.

LABONNEILLE Samuel,   R. of Braylsford near Derby.
    1 Cor. xiii. 13. 4° 1709. Vis. The Pre eminence of Charity.

LACY *Benjamin*
    Ps. lxviii. 1–3. 8° 1706. Th.
    * Disc. in 12° 1720. Of the Vanity of the World.

LACY James,   V. of Sherborne, Dorsetshire.
    Ps. lxxxiv. 1. 8° 1715. Cons. of Church. *St. John's.* Camb. *Sion.*

LAFITE Dan. M. A. R. of Woolavington, Suffex.
    Rom. x. 15. 4° 1712. Vis.

LAKE Edward, DD. R. of the united Parishes of St. Mary at Hill, and St. Andrew, Hobart, Middlesex.
    2 Sam. i. 18. 4° 1684. Jan. 30. b. Lord Mayor. *Ch. Ch. Magd.* Oxon. *Sion.*   Heb.

Heb. xiii. 7. 4° 1693. b. Sons of Clergy. *Ch.Ch. Wadh.* Oxon. *Pub. L. St. John's.* Camb. *Brit. M.*
Rev. xxi. 8. 4° 1703. b. Lord Mayor. Of Hell torments. *Univ.* Oxon. *Queen's. St. John's.* Camb.
16 Serm. in 8° 1705. On several Occasions. *Bod. Univ. Ch. Ch. Magd. Bal.* Oxon. *Dr. W's L.* Lond.

LAKE John, Bp. of Chichester.
Pf. ii. 6. 4° 1670. May 29.
* John v. 12. 8° 16
Rev. ii. 10. 4° 1671. Fun. of Will. Cade. Character of a true Christian. *Ch Ch. Magd.* Oxon.

LAKE Neal *John*, Minister at Abingdon, Berks.
 * Acts ii. 39. 8° 1781. On Account of the Baptism of his own Child   Infant-Baptism a reasonable and script. Service.

LAMB Charles, Curate of Enfield, Middlesex.
1 Chron. xvi. 8. 4° 1706. Th. s.

LAMB P. Minister of the Gospel.
* John xiv. 33. V. Coll. of Farew. s. 4° 1663. *Magd.* Camb.
* Pf. xxxvii. 37. 8° 1679. Fun.

LAMB Robert, Bp. of Peterborough.
* James iii. 16. 4° 1768. Jan. 30. b. Lords.

LAMBE Charles, M. A. Minister of St. Catherine's Cree Church, and Lect. of All-Hallows, Barkin.
10 Serm. in 8° 1717. On several Occasions. *Ch. Ch.* Oxon.

LAMBE Henry, LL.D. Minister of Stratford le Bow, and Lect. of St. Mary Magdalen, Bermondsea, and R. of Nursling, Hants.
James iii. 17. 8° 1707. Assize. Christianity from above.
Pf. xlix. 17. 4° 1709. Accession.
Col. ii. 6. 8° 1710. Spitt. W. *Cl. H.* Camb. *Sion.*
Rom. xii. 18. 8° 1717. Assize.
——— x. 2. 8° 1723. Nov. 5 b. Ld Mayor. Xtian Zeal displayed.

LAMBE John, DD. Dean of Ely, and Chapl. in Ord.
2 Thess. iii. 2. 4° 1673. b. Lord Mayor. *Bod. Queen's.* Oxon. *Pub. L. Trin. St. John's.* Camb. *Sion.*
Matt. xvi. 26. 4° 1680. b. King. *Pub. L.* Camb. *Sion.*
Pf. cxix. 165. 4° 1682. b. Lord Mayor. *All S.* Oxon. *Pub. L.* Camb. *Eton.*
1 Cor. vi. 12. 4° 1684. The Liberty of human Nature. *All S.* Oxon. *Pub. L.* Camb. *Sion.*
Prov. xxii. 4. 4° 1686. b. King. On Humility. *Magd.* Oxon.
Tit. ii. 10. 4° 1691. b. Queen. *Bod. Pub. L.* Camb.
Isai. lvii. 21. 4° 1693. b. King. *Bod. Pub. L. Trin.* Camb.
2 Pet. i. 4. 4° 1693. b. Queen. *Bod. Univ. Ox. Pub. L. Trin.* C.
Job v. 2. 4° 1695. b. King. Ag. Envy. *Ch. Ch. Magd.* Ox. *Sion.*
Prov. iii. 6. 4° 1696. b. King. *Sion.*
Col. iii. 1, 2. 4° 1701. Spitt. T. *Magd.* Oxon.
Isai. lx. 1. 4° 17   Fun.

LAMBE William, M. A. R. of Gateshead, Durham.
* Acts iii. 6. 4° 1755. *Newcastle*-Infirmary.

LAMBERT

LAMBERT George
 *Serm. in 8° 1779. On various useful and important Subjects.
LAMBERT Ralph, DD. Bp. of Meath.
 Ezek. xxiv. 15, 16. 4° 1693. Fun. of Mrs. Ann Margetson.
 Isai. lii. 10. 4° 1702. Th Nov. 12.
 Isai. lix. 7, 8. 4° 1708. Commem. Irish Prot. *Univ*. Ox. *Pub. L. Trin. Queen's.* Camb. *Brit. M.*
LAMOTHE Charles G.
 Phil. ii. 6, 7. 4° 1693. 2 s. On the Divinity of our Saviour.
LAMOTTE Charles, DD. Chapl. to the Prince of Wales.
 *Ps. cxi. 2. 8° 1740 b. Florists. The Greatness of God's Works in the vegetable world.
LAMPLUGH Thomas, Abp. of York.
 Luke ix. 55, 56. 4° 1678 Nov. 5. b. Lords. *Bod. Ch. Ch. Magd. Queen's. Or. Oxon. Pub L. Trin. Magd. Cam.). Brit. M.*
 Luke xiii. 5. 4° 1678. Fast.
LANCASTER Nathaniel, L.L.D. R. of Stanford Rivers, Essex.
 Ps. cxxxvii. 5, 6. 4° 1746. Rebellion. Public Virtue, or the Love of our Country.
LANCASTER William, DD. Provost of Queen's Coll. Oxon. and V. of St. Martin's in the Fields, London.
 Lam. v. 16. 4° 1696. Jan. 30. b. Commons. *Bod. Ch. Ch. Jes.* Oxon. *Trin. St. John's.* Camb. *Sion*.
LAND H. M. A. late Fell. of Oriel Coll. Oxon. and R. of Clare-Portion in the Church of Tiverton, Devon.
 *Gal. v. 5, 6. 8° 1771. Against Methodism.
LANDON (or Langdon) John, L.L.D.
 Matt. xix. 23, 24. 4° 1726. Spitt. W. The Case of Riches under the Gospel-Dispensation considered.
LANE Edward, M. A. V. of Sperfholt, Hants.
 Heb. xiii. 8. 4° 1663.
LANE William, M. A. Lecturer at Hereford Cathedral.
 Ezek. xxxvi. 32. 8° 1746. Th. Oct. 9.
LANEY Benjamin, Bp. of Ely.
 1 Pet. ii. 25. 4° 1662. b. King. The Shepherd. *Bod. Bal. Magd. Ch. Ch.* Oxon. *Pub. L. St. John's.* Camb. *Sion.*
 Heb. xiii. 15. 4° 1663. 2 s. b. King. *Bod. Ch. Ch. Magd.* Oxon. *St. John's.* Camb. *Sion.*
 Matt. xix. 8. 4° 1663. *St. John's.* Camb.
 Mark iv. 24. 4° 1665. b. King. Of hearing God's word. *Bod. Ch. Ch. Magd.* Oxon. *Sion.*
 1 Thess. iv. 11. 4° 1665. b. King. 2 s. Study of Quietness. *Bod. Ch. Ch. Magd. Bal.* Oxon. *Pub. L. Trin.* Camb. *Sion.*
 Gal. vi. 7, 8. 4° 1675. b. King. *Ch. Ch. C. C. C. Univ. Magd. Worc.* Oxon. *Pub. L. Trin. St. John's.* Camb. *Sion.*
LANGFORD Emanuel, DD. Chaplain of Chelsea-College.
 Isai. liii. 7. 4° 1697. Jan. 30. b. Commons. *All S.* Oxon. *Trin. St. John's.* Camb.

LANG-

LANGFORD John, Minif. of the Gofpel at Horfley-down, Southwark.
* Dan. xii. 3. 8° 1770. Death of Rev. George Whitfield.

LANGFORD *William*, DD.
‡ * Pf. xxiii. 4. 8° 1737. Fun. *Brit. M.*
* Deut. viii. 2. 8° 1748. Char. School.
* 2 Cor. v 18 8° 1749. Ord.
* Numb. xxiii. 23. 8° 1759. Aug. 1.
* John xii. 26. 8° 1764. Fun. of Rev. *Edw. Godwin, Queen's.* C.
* Acts xxiii. 11. 8° 1770. Ord.

LANGHORNE *John*, DD. R. of Blagdon, Somerfetf.
* Serm. in 2 Vol. 12° 1773. *Queen's.* Camb.
* Deut. xxviii. 2, 3. 4° 1776. Vif Happinefs of ecclefiaft. Life.
* Acts vii. 26. 4° 1777. Ann. Co meeting. The Love of mankind, the fundamental Principle of the Chriftian Religion.

LANGHORNE *William*, M. A.
* Sermons in 2 Vol. 12° 1773.

LARDNER Nathaniel, DD. Minifter of the Gofpel in London.
Rom. xii 2. 8° 1739. 2 f. A caution ag. a Conformity to the World.
* 2 Theff. i. 10. 8° 1740. Fun. of Rev. *William Harris*, DD.
Rom. xi. 11. 8° 1743. 3 Difc. *Brit. M.*
Matt. x. 16. 8° 1743. Counfels of Prudence for the Ufe of young People.
* John xiv. 2. 8° 1748. Fun. of *J. Hunt*, DD. *Queen's.* Camb. *Brit. M.* V. Dr. *Hunt's* Serm.
* Rom xi. 11. 8° 1743. 3 Difc. The Circumftances of the Jewifh people, an argument for the truth of the Chriftian Religion.
* John xiv. 2–4. 8° 1744. Fun.
18 Serm. in 8° 1751. Upon various Subjects. *Queen's.* Camb.
* Serm. in 8° 1760. Dr *W's* L. London.
* Mark v. 19. 4 Difc. On Demoniacs. *Queen's.* Camb.

LATHAM Ebenezer, M. D. Minifter at Derby.
* Zech. i. 5. 8° 1743. Fun. of *Matt. Erafshaw. Queen's.* Camb.
* Col. i. 12. 8° 1745. Fun. of *Dan. Madock. Queen's.* C. *Brit. M.*
* Judges v 9. 8° 1746 Th. f. *Queen's.* Camb.
* Serm. in 8° 1774. *Queen's.* Camb.

LATHAM *Paul*, M. A. of Pemb. Coll. Oxon. and Preb. of Sarum.
1 Cor. xv. 57. 4° 1676. Fun. of Mr. Peter Adams, *Bod.*
Rom. i 20. 4° 1678. God manifeft in his Works. *Magd.* Oxon St. *John's.* Camb. *Sion.*
Prov viii. 15. 4° 1683. June 29. On the Detection of the Plot.
Acts xxvi. 9. ⎫   ⎧ p. 151. Vif.
Ephef. iv 14. ⎬ 8° 1666. Xt crucified. ⎨ p. 20..
James iii. 17. ⎭   ⎩ p. 235.

LATHROP John, M. A. Paftor of the 2d Church in Bofton, America.
* Gen. iii. 10. 4° 1770. Innocent Blood crying to God from the ftreets of Bofton.

LAVINGTON *George*, Bp. of Exeter.
1 Cor. v. 7. 8° 1724. 2 f. The Nature and Ufe of a Type. *Ware.* Oxon. *Queen's.* Camb.

Ephef.

Ephef. v. 18–20. 8° 1725. The Influence of Ch. Mufick. *Worc.* Ox.
1 Pet. ii. 17.   1726. Affize. *Queen's.* Camb.
1 Theff. v. 13. 4° 1735. b. Sons of Clergy. *Queen's.* Camb.
Deut. xxix. 9. 8° 1745. Rebellion. *Sion.*
Jerem. v. 4, 5. 4° 1746. Ann. meeting Char. Sch. *All S. Worc.* Oxon. *Queen's.* Camb. *Sion.*
Pf. xlvii 7. 4° 1747. May 29. b Lords. *Queen's.* Camb.
* Pf. xlvi. 8. 8° 1756. *Exon.* Faft. Earthquake. *Queen's.* Camb.

LAVINGTON *John*
  * Deut. v. 12. 8° 1743.
  * 1 Chron. xv. 13. 8° 1757. Fun.

LAUGHTON George, DD.
  * Prov. xiv. 34 4° 1775. Inauguration. Righteoufnefs the fure Foundation of national Security, Reputation and Happinefs.

LAUGHTON John
  2 Cor. i. 12.   Affize.

LAUGHTON Richard, DD. Fell. of Clare-hall, Camb. and Preb. of Worcefter.
  Rom. vi. 23. 4° 1717. *Camb.* b. King, at King's Coll. Chapel. *Cl. H. Queen's.* Camb.

LAW Edmund, Bp. of Carlifle. -
  Matt. v. 40. 8° 1743. *Camb.* Affize. Litigioufnefs repugnant to the Laws of Chriftianity. *Queen's.* Camb.
  Confiderat. in 8° 1745. *Camb.* On the State of the World &c. *viz.*
  Acts vii. 30. p. 1. Want of Univerfality in natural and revealed Religion.
  Gal. iv. 4. p. 49. Of the fev. Difpenfations of revealed Religion.
  Ecclef. vii. 10. p. 203. The Progrefs of natural Rel. and Science.
  * Jerem. xxix. 7. 4° 1755. Ir. Prot. Sch.
  * Micah vi. 8. 8° 1768. Fun. of Dr. Bland. The true Nature and Intent of Religion. *Queen's.* Camb.
  * Dan. ii. 21, 22. 4° 1771. Jan. 30. b. Lords.
  * Mal. i. 11. 4° 1774. Prop. of Gofpel.

LAW John, DD. Arch-Deacon of Rochefter, and R. of Much-Eafton, Effex.
  * Acts v. 38, 39. 4° 1768. Vif.
  * Pf. lxviii. 5. 4° 1780. b. Sons of the Clergy.

LAW Robert
  2 Sam. xv. 6. 8° 1683. Jan. 30.

LAW William, M. A. Fell. of Emanuel Coll. Camb.
  Tit. iii. 1. 8° 1713. Th. *Queen's. St. John's.* Camb.
  1 Cor. xii. 3. 8° 1718.

LAWRENCE *Edmund*
  * Matt. viii. 5–14. 8° 1662.
  * 1 Cor. vi. 12. 12° 1690. 2 f. Fun. Ufe and Happinefs of hum. Bodies.

LAWRENCE *George*, M. A. Minifter of the Hofpital of St. Crofs near Winchefter.
  1 Cor. xi. 23–25. 4° 1675. m. e. P. p. 729. No Tranfubftan-tiation in the Lord's Supper.   LAW-

LAWRENCE John, M. A. R. of Yelvertorft, Northamptonſ.
Rom xiii. 4. 8° 1717. Aſſize. Chriſtian Religion, beſt Friend to Government.
2 Cor. iv 5. 8° 1720. V. end of his Treatiſe on Xtian Prudence.
Prov. xvii. 25. 8° 17
LAWRENCE Thomas, M. A. Preb. of Sarum.
Acts ii. 37, 38. 4° 1669. Jan. 30.
LAWSON George, R. of More, Salop.
Matt. xxviii. 18-20. 8° 1680. Magna Charta Eccleſiæ univerſæ.
LAWSON John, DD. ſen. Fell. of Trin. Coll. Dublin.
* Occaſional Serm. in 8° 1764. reſpecting the Office, and Duty of Biſhops &c. Pub. L. Camb. Sion.
LAXTON Thomas, M. A
1 Theſſ. iv. 13. 4° 1682. Fun. of Chriſt. Sherard, Eſq; Grief allayed, Death ſwetened, Hope raiſed.
LAYARD Peter Charles, M. A. Fell. of St. John's Coll. Camb.
* Rev. xiv. 13. 4° 17-6. Fun. of Matthew Matty, M. D.
LAYNG Henry, M. A. R. of Pauler'pury Northampton and Preb. of Lincoln.
1 Pet iv. 8. 8° 1746. Northampton-Infirmary.
LAYTON Joſeph, V. of Ringwood, Hants.
Rom. xii. 1. 4° 1684. School Feaſt. Trin. Camb.
LEAKE Martin William, L.L. B.
* 1 Cor. xv. 33. 8° 1773. On account of 2 Soldiers under ſentence of Death.
* 1 King's v. 12. 8° 1778. Colcheſter. St. John's-day. b. Freemaſons.
LEATHES William, V. of Iſell, Cumberland.
Eccleſ. xii 13. 8° 1724.
LEAVESLY Thomas, Miniſter of the Goſpel in London.
* Luke xvi. 9. 8° 1727. Charity.
* —— xii. 14. 8° 1730. Ref. of Manners.
Heb. xi. 8. 8° 1735. The Reaſons and Neceſſity of the Reformation. V. Diſc. 2 Vol. ag. Popery. Braz. N. Oxon.
LE Broq Philip
* Jerem. xlvii. 6. 4° 1777. Faſt.
LECHE Thomas
Luke xvi. 8. 8° 1712, Aſſize. Linc. Oxon.
LE FRANK James, B. D. Miniſter of the French Church, Norwich.
* Diſc. in 2 Vol. 8° 1662. Trin. Camb.
LEE Henry, DD. R. of Tichmarch, Northamptonſhire.
James i. 27. 4° 1728. Fun. of Mrs. Creed.
Philip. iii. 15. 8° 1730. Viſ.
LEE Henry, LL. B. Lect. of St. Olave's, Southwark.
Pſ lxxvii. 12. 8° 1751. b. relig. Societies. Divine Meditation, or a Key to the Scriptures.
* Amos iv. 12. 4° 1756. Faſt. God's Summons of deſpiſed Forbearance.

LEE James
   Rom. xvi. 27.
LEE Richard, DD. R. of King's Hatfield, Herts.
   Pſ. li. 17. 4° 1663. Cor. humiliatum et contritum. *Queen's*. Ox.
   St. John's. Camb. *Sion*.
LEE Richard,   R. of Eſſenden and Beryford, Herts.
   Col. iii. 15. 4° 1720. Aſſize.
LEE *Samuel*, M. A. Miniſter of Great St. Helen's, London.
   Matt. xvi. 18. 4° 1675. m.e.P. p. 839. Viſibility of the true Ch.
   Matt. vi. 6. 4° 1676. S.m.e.C. p. 268. Secret Prayer ſucceſs-
   fully managed.
   Rom. x. 1. 4° 1677. m.e.C. p.132. Converſ. of our carnal Relations.
LEE Thomas
   * 1 Theſſ iv. 1. 4° 1704.
LEECHMAN *William*, DD. Principal of the Univerſity in Glaſcow.
   1 Tim. iv. 16. 8° 1741. *Glaſcow*. b. Synod. The Temper, Cha-
   racter and Duty of a Miniſter of the Goſpel. *Queen's*. Camb.
   Brit. M.
   Matt. xxvi. 41. 8° 1743. *Glaſcow*. The Nature, Reaſonableneſs,
   and Advantage of Prayer. V. Prot. Syſt. vol.2. Scotch Pr. v.1.
   p. 138. *Dr. Enfield's* Eng. Pr. vol.6 p.25. *Queen's*. C. *Brit. M.*
   * 1 Cor. i. 2. 12° 1758. Opening the general Aſſembly of the
   Church of Scotland. V. Sch. Pr. v. 2. p. 215. *Queen's*. Camb.
   * 2 Tim. i. 7. 12° 1768. 2 ſ. The Excellency of the Spirit of
   Chriſtianity. V. Scotch Pr. v. 3. p. 287. *Queen's*. Camb.
LEEKE Robert, B. D. Fell. of St. John's, Camb. and R. of Great
   Snoring, Norfolk.
   Acts vii. 37. 8° 1728. *Camb.* The Interpretation of the Law and
   the Prophets made by Jeſus and his Apoſtles vindicated. *Worc.*
   Oxon. *Queen's*. Camb.
   John xiv. 1. 8° 1729. On St. Thomas's day. No Act of Religion
   acceptable to God without Faith in Jeſus Chriſt. *Queen's*. C.
   1 Sam. ii. 30. 8° 1730. Aſſize. Some ſpecial methods of ho-
   nouring God.
   Gal. ii. 21. 8° 1735. The Neceſſity of Chriſt's Satisfaction.
   * Rom. xiii. 1,2. 4° 1739. *Norwich*. Jan. 30.
   * Joel ii. 12,13. 4° 1740. Faſt. Feb. 4.
   * Pſ. cxxxii. 18. 4° 1746. Th.
   * Acts x. 4–6. 4° 1748. Viſ. A new Cauſe of Infidelity peculiar
   to the preſent Age
LEIGH Thomas, B.D. V. of Biſhop's Stortford, Herts.
   Pſ. cxviii. 24. 4° 1684. Viſ. The keeping Holy-days recom-
   mended. *All S. Ch. Ch.* Oxon, *Sion.*
LEIGHTON Robert, Abp. of Glaſcow.
   His ſelect Works in 8° 1746. *Edinb. Bod. New C. Were* Oxon.
   Queen's. Cl. H. Camb. *Dr W's. L.*
   * Mediations and Expoſ. Lectures in 2 Vol. 8° 1748.
LEIGHTONHOUSE Walter, M. A. R. of Waſhingburgh near Linc.
   ‡ * 2 Cron. xix. 6,7. 4° 1692. Aſſize. *Brit. M.*
   12 Serm. in 8° 1697. *Pemb.* Oxon.   LE-

LEMOINE Abraham, R. of Everly Wilts, and Chaplain to the Duke of Portland.
   Gen. iii. 6. 4° 1751. Vif. A Vindication of the literal account of the Fall. *Brit. M.*
   * Deut. xxxi. 24–26. 4° 1753. Vif. Ag. Bolingbroke. A Defence of the facred Hiftory of the old Teftament. *Brit. M.*

LELAND *Thomas,* DD.
   * Sermons in 4 Vol. 8° 1769. *Magd.* Oxon. *Queen's.* Camb.

LELAND Tho. DD. fen. Fell. of Trin. Coll. & V. of St. Ann's, Dubl.
   * Judges xxi. 2, 3. 4° 1777. Faft.
   * Ezek. xxviii. 17. 4° 1779. Faft.

LENG John, Bp. of Norwich.
   Ecclef viii. 11. 4° 1699. *Camb.* b. King. *Pub. L. Trin. Queen's. St. John's.* Camb. *Brit. M.*
   Levit. xxvi. 2. 4° 1704. *Camb.* Conf. of Cath-Hall-Chapel. *Ch. Ch. All S. Queen's.* Oxon. *Trin. Queen's. St. John's.* Camb. *Sion.*
   * Matt. xxii. 21. 8° 1706. Acceffion. *Worc.* Oxon.
   1 Cor. xii. 31. 4° 1713. St. Paul's Sch. Feaft. *Queen's.* Camb.
   Pf. ix. 10. 4° 1715. Knowledge of the Nature and Providence of God, an Inducement to believe and truft in him. *All S. Ch. Ch.* Oxon. *Queen's.* Camb.
   1 Tim. ii. 1, 2. 8° 1715. Nov. 6. *Ch. Ch.* Oxon.
   * Phil. iv. 5. 4° 1715. Duty of Moderation.
   Rom. xiii. 3, 4. 8° 1716. Affize. (Sep. 4. 1715.) Advantages of Government and Duty of preferving it. *Ch. Ch.* Ox. *Brit. M.*
   Pf. xcii. 1. 8° 1716. Aug. 1.
   Pf. xcvii. 1. 4° 1716. Affize. (March 22. 1715.) *Queen's.* Camb.
   Boyle's Lect. 8° 1717. 1718. or fo. 1739. Vol. 3. *Bod. Ch. Ch. Magd. New C. St. John's. Worc.* Oxon. *Cl. H. Queen's.* Camb.
   Matt. v. 16. 8° 1719. Ref. of Manners. *Eton.*
   * James iv. 1. 4° 1726. Jan. 30. b. Lords. *Brit. M.*
   Ephef. iii. 5, 6. 4° 1727. Prop. of Gofpel. *Ch. Ch. Oriel.* Oxon. *Pub. L. Queen's.* Camb.
   1 Cor. xii. 7. 4° 1727. School Feaft. *All S.* Oxon.

LESTLEY DD.
   Acts ix. 36, 37.

LESTLEY Charles, Chancellor of the Cathedral of Connor.
   Rev. xii. 7. fo. 1721. p. 799. or 4° 1698. Of Angels. *Bod.*
   Ezra x. 4. fo. 1721. p. 745. or 8° 1702. Ag. Marriages in different Communions. *Ch. Ch.* Oxon.
   * Sermons in 8° 1720.
   His Works in 2 V. fo. 1721. *Bod. Ch. Ch. Bal. St. John's. Queen's. Trin.* Oxon.

LESTLEY George, Minifter of Olney, and R. of Witttering, Northampton.
   4 Serm. in 8° 1684.

LESTLEY Henry, Bp. of Down and Connor.
   1 Cor. xiv. 15. 4° 1660. 2 f. Of praying with the Spirit, and the Underftanding.

1 Cor. ii. 8. 4° 1660. and 8°: 709. Of the Authority of the Ch. In Bibliotheca Scriptorum ecclesiæ Anglicanæ. p. 34. Bod.

LEWIS Edward, M. A. R. of Waterstock and Emington, Oxon.
Isai. vii. 5–7. 8° 1741. Fast. On the French Invasion.
Isai. ix. 13. 8° 1747. Fast. Mercy and judgment—or intestine War, but soon over; Cattle die, but men are not obliged to eat their Carcases.
* 1 Tim. i. 15. 8° 1756. Vis. Sinners saved by Jesus Christ as preached in Scripture; but Church-Fathers and Clergy are no sure Guides to Heaven
* Rom xiii. 1–11. 4° 1776. Fast. Translated from St. Chrysostom.

LEWIS Ellis, V. of Ruddlan Flintshire.
*Gen. ii. 20–24. 8° 1716. Wedding s.

LEWIS George, M. A. V. of Westram, Kent,
Acts viii. 17. 8° 1717. On Confirmation.
Eccles. vii. 14. 4° 1725. Fun. of Lord Whitworth.
Eccles xi. 3. 4° 1727 Fun. of Mr. Missenden.
Acts xxvi. 26–22. 8° 1729. The Conference between King Agrippa and St. Paul. *Queen's*. Camb.
John iv. 9. 8° 1729. The Conference between Christ and the Woman of Samaria.
Heb. xiii. 14. 8° 1731. Fun.
John ii. 11. 8° 1735. After the high-Wind.

LEWIS George, M. A. Student of Ch. Ch. Oxon. and Cur. of Hever, Kent.
Deut. iv. 8. 4° 1740. Assize.

LEWIS Henry, DD. of New Inn-Hall Oxon. Preb. of Hereford, and Chaplain to the Duke of Ormond.
Isai. lx. 1. 8° 17
Prov. i. 10. 8° 1710. *Oxon.*. Act. *Bod. Magd. Or. Bal.* Oxon. *St. John's.* Camb. *Sion.*
Ps. cxxxiii. 1. 8° 1714. Accession.

LEWIS John, M. A. Minister of Margate, Kent.
1 Cor. iv. 13. 8° 1710. The Clergy of the Church of England vindicated. *St. John's.* Camb.
2 Sam. i. 14. 8° 1718. Jan. 30. *St. John's.* Camb.

LEWIS Lewis, little Ayliffe street Goodman's Fields, London.
* - - - - 1771. Fun. s.
* - - - - 1775. Farew. s.

LEWIS Samuel. B. A. Cur. of Great Oakley, Essex.
Prov. xxiv. 21. 8° 1746. Fast. for Rebellion.

LEY Ross, R. of St. Matthews Friday-street, London.
*Prov. xi. 30. 8° 1712. Char. School. Subst. of sev. Serm.
Nehem. vi. 16. 4° 1727. May 29. b. Lord Mayor.

LEY Thomas, M. A. V. of Crediton, Devon.
Luke xiii. 5. 8° 17 Fun. of Son and Daughter who perished by Fire.
Ps. xviii. 7–10. 4° 1704. Fast. for the late Storm.
Ps. cxix. 120. 8° 1721. Fast. for the Plague.

LEYBORNE

LEYBORNE Robert, DD. of Braz. N. Coll. Oxon.
  ‡ * Prov. iii. 2. 8° 1753. Infirmary.
LIDGOULD Charles, M. A. Fell. of Clare-hall Camb. Reader at
  the Charter-houfe, and R of Dunfby. Lincoln.
  Jerem. vii. 17. 4° 1699. On Proclamation againft Atheifm &c.
  1 Pet iv. 10. 4° 1699. Faft. April 5. Charity to our poor per-
  fec ted Brethren abroad
LIGHTFOOT J. DD. Mafter of Cath. Hall, Camb. & Preb. of Ely.
  His Works 2 Vol. fo. 1684. *Bod. Univ. Ch. Ch. Bal. Mert. St.*
  John's. Queen's. New C. Oxon.
LIGHTFOOT Robert, B. D R. of Odel, Bedfordf.
  Acts xx. 28. 8° 1707. Vif. The Duty of a good Minifter with
  refpect to himfelf and his Flock. *Univ. Ox. Trin. Cam Sion.*
LILIENTHAL William, M. A. Fell. of the Roy. Soc. in Pruffia.
  * 1 Cor. xv. 26. 8° 1750. Fun. of Godfrey Gowart, public Execu-
  tioner. Origin, Inftitution and neceffity of that Office confidered.
LIMBORCH Hugh
  * Prov. xxxi. 3. 8° 1740. Royal Laft Tranflation.
LINDSAY John, DD. R. of the Metropolis at Jamaica.
  * 2 Kings xx. 1. 8° 1777. Fun. of Sir Bafil Keith, Governor.
LINDSEY Theophilus,   late V. of Catterick, Yorkf.
  * Ephef. iv. 3. 8° 1774. Open of a Chapel, Effex-ftreet, Strand.
  * John iv. 23, 24. 8° 1778.
LINDESAY Thomas, Abp. of Armagh.
  Gal. vi. 10. 4° 1692. County-Feaft. *Sion.*
LINGARD Ric. DD. Dean of Lifmore, and Divin-Profeffor, Dublin.
  2 Chron. xxix. 30. 4° 1668. b. King. In defence of our Liturgy.
  Bod. Magd. Queen's. Oxon. *Queen's. Cl. H.* Camb. *Sion.*
LINGUE John,   V. of Yalding, Kent.
  Pf. xviii. 50. 4° 1661. Coron.
LIPTROTT B.
  Matt. v. 20. 8° 1745. Reb. Pharifaifm revived in Popery. *Brit. M.*
LIPTROTT John, M. A. Chaplain to the Earl of Stamford.
  Rom. xiii. 1. 8° 1724. Jan. 30.
  * Acts iv. 12. 8° 1741. Calviniftical Truths (but not calviniftical
  Errors) the Doctrine of the Church of England.
LISLE Samuel, Bp. of Norwich.
  Heb. xiii. 17. 4° 1723. Conf. of Bp. Baker. *Or.* Oxon. *Queen's.*
  Camb. *Brit. M.*
  1 Cor. i. 21. 4° 1735. Conc. ad Synod. *Queen's.* Camb.
  Ifai. v. 4. 4° 1744. Faft. b. Lords. *Brit. M.*
  Rev. ii. 5. 4° 1745. Faft. b. Lords. *Queen's.* Camb.
  Ifai. xlix. 6. 4° 1748. Prop. of Gofpel.
LITTELL Tho. DD. Preb. of Norwich, R. of Tydd St. Mary's, Linc.
  1 Tim iv. 16. 4° 1708. Vif. *All S.* Ox. *Queen's. St. John's* Cam.
[LITTLETON Adam]   Prieft.
  ‡ * Prov. xxxi 30. 4° 1669. Fun of Lady Jane Newcaflle. *Br. M.*
LITTLETON Adam, DD. of Ch. Ch Oxon. Chaplain in Ord. and
  Preb. of Weftminfter.
  Pf. xxxvii. 5. 4° 1680. County Feaft. *Sion.*

61 Serm. in fo.1680. *Magd. Mert. Pemb.* Ox. *Trin. Queen's.* C. *Sion.*
LITTLETON Edward, L.L.D. Fell. of Eton Coll. and V. of Ma-
plederham, Oxon. and Chaplain in Ord.
1 Pet. ii. 16. 4° 1730. Jan. 30. b. Commons. *All S. Wroc.* Oxon.
Queen's. Camb. *Brit. M.*
24 Serm. in 2 Vol. 8° 1735. Upon fev. practical Subjects. *Bod.*
St. John's. Wadh. Oxon.
LIVESEY James, M. A. V. of Great Budworth, Cheshire.
Micah ii. 7. 8° 1674. 3 f. An Apology for the Power and Li-
berty of the Spirit. *Bod. Sion.*
2 Chron. xix. 6. 8° 1660. Jehosaphat's Charge to his Judges.
Bod. Sion.
2 Sam. iii. 38,39. 8° 1660. Fun. of John Atherton, Esq; *Bod. Sion.*
LIVESEY John
Matt. xvi. 26. 8° 1660. The greatest Lofs. *Bod. Sion.*
LLEWELIN David
Rom. iii. 31. 4° 1678. Affize. *Bal. All S.* Oxon. *Pub. L.* Cam.
LLOYD John, of Braz. Nofe Coll- Oxon.
Prov. xix. 29. 4° 1713 Aug. 30.
LLOYD Robert Lumley, Hon. R. of St. Paul's Covent Gar-
den, London.
Pf. lx. 11. 4° 1704. Inauguration. *Pub. L.* Camb.
Heb. xii. 14. 4° 1705 Christian Charity.
Jerem. xxx. 10. 4° 1705. Affize. *Pub. L.* Camb.
Luke xiii. 2, 3. 8° 1709. Jan. 30.
Pf. cxxiv. 7. 8° 1711. Nov. 5. *Wadh.* Oxon. *St. John's.* Camb.
Luke xiii. 3. 8° 1712. Jan. 30.
Isai. viii. 10. 8° 1712. Nov. 5.
Matt. xxii. 21 8° 1716. Acceffion.
LLOYD P. M. A Cur. of Roxwell, Effex.
*Gen. i. 14. 8° 1753. New Style, the true Style. *Brit. M.*
LLOYD Peirfon, DD. late Arch-Deacon of the Church of York.
*16 Serm, in 8° 1765. On fev. Occasions. *Wadh.* Ox. *Trin.* C.
LLOYD William, Bp of Worcester.
John vi. 14. 4° 1668. b. King. Advent. *Ch. Ch. C. C. C. Univ.*
Queen's. Jef. Oxon. *Pub. L. St. John's.* Camb.
Pf. xxxvii. 37. 4° 1671. Fun. of Mr. Mitchel.
Heb. xiii. 7. 4° 1673. Fun. of Bp. Wilkins. *Bod. Ch. Ch. C.C.C.*
Queen's. Magd. New C. Univ. Trin. Oxon. *St. John's.* C. *Sion.*
Rom. viii. 13. 4° 1674. Lent. b. King. Of Mortification. *Bod.*
Univ. Ch. Ch. Magd. Queen's. Pub L. Trin. St. John's. Camb.
2 Sam. iii. 33. 4° 1678. Fun. of Sir Edmunbury Godfrey. *Ch. Ch.*
C.C.C. Magd. Or. Worc. Ox. *Pub. L. Trin. Magd. St. John's.* C.
John xvi. 2. 4° 1679. Nov. 5. *Bod. Ch. Ch. C. C. C. Magd.* Ox.
Trin. Camb.
Acts ii. 42. 4° 1679. b. King. Ag. Popery. *Bod. Ch. Ch. Queen's.*
Univ. Magd. Wadh. Oxon. *Pub. L. Trin. St. John's.* C. *Sion.*
Pf. cxxiv. 1-3. 4° 1681. 5 Nov. b. Lords. *Ch. Ch. C.C.C. Magd.*
Oxon. *Pub. L. St. John's.* Camb.
Luke xvi. 9. 4° 1688. Pf.

Pf. lvii. 6, 7. 4° 1689. b. King and Queen. *Bod. Ch. Ch.* Oxon.
Pub. L. Camb. *Sion. Brit. M.*
2 Pet. iii. 9. 4° 1690. Faſt. b. King and Queen. *Bod. Pub. L.*
St. *John's.* Camb. *Sion.*
2 Chron. xxv. 24, 25. 4° 1691. Jan. 30. b. Lords. *Bod. Pub. L.* C.
* Acts xv. 28. 4° 1661. Conc. ad Synod. *Magd.* Oxon.
Pf. lxxv. 6, 7   4° 1691. Of God's Ways of diſpoſing of Kingdoms. *Bod. Bod. Ch. Ch. Sion.*
Pf. cxviii. 23, 24. 4° 1692. May 29. b. Queen. *Pub. L.* Camb.
Zechar. vii. 5. 4° 1697. Jan. 30. b. Lords. *Magd.* Oxon. *Trin.*
St. *John's.* Camb. *Sion.*

LLOYD William, Bp. of Killala.
John viii 13. 8° 1695.
1 Tim ii. 1, 2. 8° 1715. Th. *Eton.*

LOBB Samuel, M. A. R. of Hungerford Farley. (A Convert from Popery, then from Presbyterianiſm)
Matt. v 44. 8° 1746. Aſſize. The Benevolence incumbent on us as Men and Chriſtians conſidered.

LOBB Stephen, Miniſter of the Goſpel in London.
Rom. xi. 13. 4° 1683. C. m. c. p. 491.

LOBB Stephen,   Chapl. of Penzance-Chapel, Cornwal.
4 Diſcourſes in 8° 1717. On public Occaſions.

LOBB Theophilus, M D
* Diſcourſes in 8° 1708.

LOCKIER Francis, DD. Dean of Peterborough, and Chapl. in Ord.
Lam. v. 7. 4° 1725. Jan. 30. b. Commons. *Or. Worc.* Ox. *Brit. M.*

LOCKIER *Nicholas*, M. A.
* Sermons in 12° 1671. *Pub. L.* Camb.

LODINGTON Thomas, M. A. R. of Welby, Lincolnſhire.
Ff. lxxxii. 6, 7. 4° 1674. Aſſize. *Bod. Univ. Ch. Ch. Queen's.* Ox.
Trin. Camb.
2 Cor. v. 20. 4° 1674. Viſ. *Bod. Ch. Ch.* Oxon. *Trin.* Camb.

LOEFFS Iſaac
Phil. i. 23 8° 1670. The Soul's Aſcenſion in a ſtate of Seperation. *Bod.*

LOMBARD Daniel, DD. Fell. of St. John's Coll. Oxon.
Rom xii. 18 8° 1714. *Oxon.* At Hanover. *Bod. Worc.* Oxon.
Queen's. Camb. *Sion.*

LONG Roger, DD. Maſter of Pemb. Hall. Camb. and R. of Cherry-Horton, Huntingdonſ.
John xx 29. 8° 1728. *Camb-* Commenc. The bleſſedneſs of believing. *All S.* Oxon. *St. John's.* Camb.

LONG Thomas, B. D. Preb. of St. Peter's, Exon, and V. of St. Lawrence Clyſt, Devon.
1 John i. 3. 8° 1672.   *Brit. M.*
* Matt. ix. 13. 8° 1677. Phariſee's Leſſon.
* Jude xix. 8° 1677. Tract. Senſuality, Ground of Separation.
Eccleſ. vii. 10. 4° 1680. May 29. Ag. murmuring. *Bod.* Oxon.

Deut.

Deut. iii. 7. 4° 1681. May 29.
Pf. iv. 9. 4° 1683. Th. Sept. 9. For Difcovery of the Plot. King David's Danger and Deliverance.
Joſh iii. 7. 4° 1684. May 29.
James iv. 1. 4° 1684. The original of War, or the Caufes of Rebellion.
Deut. xxxiv. 5. 4° 1684. Jan. 30 Mofes and King Charles Ift. parallelled.
Pf. ii. 1. 4° 1685. Th. July 26. For Victory over the Rebels. The Unreafonablenefs of Rebellion.

LONGWORTH John, L.L.B. R. of Port Royal.
Prov xxiv. 21. 4° 1687. Loyal Society Feaſt.

LORRAIN Paul, ordinary of Newgate,
Gen. v. 24. 8° 1703. Fun. of *Tho. Cook.* Walking with God. *Bod.*
Jerem. v 3. 8° 1707. Faſt. Sept. 2. Fire of London.
James i. 27 8° 1712. Ag. Popery, *Bod. Pub. L. Camb. Sion.*

LORT Michael, DD late Fell. of Trin. Coll. and Greek Profeffor, Camb. Preb. of St. Paul's, London.
* Pf. cxxxiii 1. 4° 1763. Acceffion. *Queen's.* Camb.
* Luke xi. 13. 4° 1769. Conf. of Bp. Hinchliffe. *Queen's.* Cam.

LORTIE Andrew, late R. of Barton, Nottinghamfhire.
* Matt xxviii. 19. 12° 1717. 2 f. On the H. Trin. *Ch. Ch.* Ox.
Practical Diſc. in 8° 1720. On fev. Subjects.

LOTHIAN William, V. D. M. of the Canongate.
* 1 Sam. xvi. 7. 12° 1776. V. Scot. Pr. vol. 2. p. 188.
* John xi. 35. 12° 1776. V. Scot. Pr. vol. 2. p. 201. On Jefus's weeping.

LOVE Barry, M. A. Minifter of Great Yarmouth, Norfolk.
Exod. iii. 5. 4° 1715. *Norwich.* Conf. of Yarmouth-Chapel. *Ch. Ch.* Oxon.

[LOVE Chriſtopher] a
* Sermons in 8° 1676.

[LOVE Chriſtopher] a
* Sermons in 8° 1754.

LOVE Samuel, M A. Fell. of Bal. Coll. Oxon. and Minor Canon of the Cathedral of Briſtol.
* Job xxix. 11–13. 8° 1772. b. Grateful Society. *Exon.* Oxon.

LOVEDAY Joſeph
* 1 Tim. i. 9. 4° 1736.

LOVEDAY Ralph, R. of Taplow, Bucks.
Matt. v. 33–37. 8° 1741. Ag. raſh ſwearing.

LOVEDER Thomas, V. of little Stambridge, Effex.
* 8 Pract. Diſc. in 8° 1756. *All S.* Oxon.

LOVELING Benjamin, M A. V. of Banbury, Oxon.
Judges v. 2. 4° 1702. Th ſ.
Pf. xlvii. 7. 8° 1704. Th. Sept. 7.
Prov. iii. 9. 4° 1706. Char. School. The beſt Uſe of Riches.

a Q. A Republication.

Pſ.

OF AUTHORS, &c. 217

Pſ. cxxii. 6. 8° 1712. Faſt. *Linc. Magd.* Oxon.
Deut. xii. 10, 11. 8° 1713. Th.
John xviii. 36. 8° 1717. *Ch. Ch.* Oxon.
LOVELL Edw. DD. Chapl. in Ord. R. of St. Mary Rotherhith, Lond.
 * 1 Kings v. 4, 5. 4° 1713.
 Prov. xxiv. 21. 8° 1715. Acceſſion.
 Gal. v. 1. 4° 1715. 2 ſ. Nov. v. and 13. Popery deſtructive of Church and State. *Queen's.* Camb.
 Rom. xiii. 3–5. 8° 1716. Acceſſion. The Duty of the Magiſtrate to employ his Sword againſt the rebellious and obſtinate.
 1 Tim. ii. 1, 2. 8° 1718. Aſſize.
 John i. 47. 8° 1727. Aſſize.
LOVELL Edmund, LL.D. late of Mert. Coll. Oxon. and Canon of the Cathedral of Wells.
 * Iſai. ii. 2, 3. 4° 1774. Frequent Worſhip at the Lord's Houſe recommended.
LOWDE James, M. A. Fell. of Clare-Hall, Camb. and R. of Eſington, Yorkſhire.
 1 Cor. i 23, 24. 4° 1684. Viſ. Reaſonableneſs of the Chriſtian Religion. *Magd.* Oxon. *Pub. L.* Camb.
LOWMAN *Moſes*, Miniſter of the Goſpel at Clapham, Surrey.
 ‡ * Luke xx. 25. 8° 1720. Ref. of Manners. *Erit. M.*
 Rom. xi. 22. 8° 1735. The Principles of Popery ſchiſmatical. V. Diſ. againſt Popery. *Braz. N.* Oxon.
LOWTH Robert, Bp. of London.
 * 1 Theſſ. iv. 9. 4° 1757. *Newcaſtle*-Infirmary. *Queen's.* Camb.
 * Matt. vi. 10. 4° 1758. Viſ. *Queen's.* Camb.
 * Deut. iv. 7–9. 4° 1764. Aſſize. *Ex.* Oxon. *Queen's.* Camb.
 * Prov. xxiv. 21. 4° 1767. Jan. 30. b. Lords. *Braz. N. Ex.* Ox.
 * Acts ii. 39. 4° 1771. Prop. Goſpel. *Magd Worc.* Oxon.
 * Gal. vi. 10. 4° 1771. *Oxon. Radcliffe*-Infirmary.
 * Rom. ii. 11. 4° 1773. Ir. Prot. Sch. *Worc.* Oxon.
 * Luke xiii. 1–3. 4° 1779. b. King. Aſh-wedneſday.
LOWTH Will. DD. Fell. of St. John's, Oxon. Preb. of Wincheſter.
 Job xxviii 28. 8° 1714. Aſſize. Religion, the diſtinguiſhing Character of human Nature.
 Matt. xi. 19. 8° 1714. Aſſize. The Wiſdom of acknowledging divine Revelation.
 Acts ii. 42. 8° 1722. The Character of an Apoſtolical Church fulfilled in the Church of England. *Sien.*
LOWTHIAN S.
 * 2 Tim. iv. 7, 8. 8° 1760. Fun. of Rev. Mr. *Rogerſon.*
 ‡ * Matt. ix 37, 38. 8° 1763. *Brit. M.*
LUCAS Richard, DD. V. of St. Stephen, Coleman-ſtreet, and Preb. of Weſtminſter.
 Heb. vi. 1. 8° 1697. Religious Perfection.
 Tit. iii. 14. 4° 1699. Company of Goldſmiths.
 Rom. xii. 10. 4° 1704. b. Queen. Of Humility.
 24 Serm. in 2 Vol. 8° 1710. On ſev. Occaſions. *Pemb.* Ox. *Sien.*

Vol. II.   E e   15 Serm.

15 Serm. Vol. I. (Pofth.) in 8° 1722. On Death and Judgment. *Pub. L.* Camb.
16 Serm. &c. Vol. II. (Pofth.) 8° 1716. *Pub. L. Trin. Queen's.* Camb. *Brit. M.*
Difc. Vol. III. (Pofth.) in 8° 1717. On Repentance, the Severity and Goodnefs of God. *Pub. L.* Camb.

LUCAS *Thomas*
* Luke xiv. 23. 8° 1718.
* Pf. cxix. 165. 8° 1720. Fun.
* Pf. xxxiv. 19. 8° 1728. Fun. of Mr. *Robert Webb.*

LUCE Richard, a Prefbyter of the Church of England.
* 1 Pet. ii. 16. 4° 1672. Chriftian Liberty not to be abufed. Or. Oxon. *Trin.* Camb.

LUCK R.
* Pf. cxii. 2. 1734.

LUKE John, B. D. Fell. of Sidney-Suffex-Coll. Camb. Preacher to the Englifh Factory at Smyrna.
1 Cor. xv. 29. 4° 1664. b. Levant-Co. *Trin.* Camb.

LUMLEY George, of Merton Coll. Oxon.
- - - - 1737. Jan. 30.

LUNN William, DD. of Bennet Coll. Camb. Arch-Deacon of Huntingdon, and Preb. of Linc.
Col. ii. 8. 4° 1710 Sch. Feaft. The Ufe and Abufe of Philofophy in Matters of Religion. *Queen's.* Camb. *Sion.*

LUPTON William, DD. Preacher at Lincoln's-Inn, and Preb. of Durham.
12 Serm. in 8° 1729. *Bod. Bal. St. John's. Worc. Wadh.* Oxon. *Pub. L.* Camb. *Sion. Brit. M.*

LUSHINGTON Thomas, B. D. Preb. of Sarum, and Chapl. in Ord.
Matt. xxviii. 13. (12 1624.) 8° 1741. Eafter S. *Bal. Worc.* Ox. *St. John's.* Camb.

ᵃ LUZANCY Hippolytus Du Chaftelet de, B. D. V. of Dover. Court and Harwich, Effex.
John viii. 32. 4° 1676. On the Day of his Abjuration. *Bod. Ch. Ch. Magd. Queen's.* Oxon *St. John's.* Camb.
2 Tim. i. 13. 4° 1697. At the Bifhop of London's Conference with his Clergy. *Ch. Ch.* Oxon. *Sion.*

ᵃ LURANCY Hippol de, B. D. V. of South-Weald, Effex.
Acts xxiii 3. 8° 1710. Affize. *Eton.*

LYDIAT Simon, M. A. Mafter of the Free School in Felftead, Effex.
Acts xvii. 28. 4° 1707. Sch. Feaft. The Advantage of human Learning.

LYE *Thomas*, M. A. Minifter of All-Hallows Lombart-ftreet, Lond. (before the Ejection. 1662.)
Phil. iv. 1. 4° 1662. Farewel. Aug. 17. The fixt Saint. *Bod. Magd.* Camb.
Luke xvii. 10. 4° 1675. m.c.P. 548. No works of Supererogation.

a 𝒬 The fame.

Prov.

Prov. xxii. 6. 4° 1676. f. m. e. C. p. 203. By what Rules may catechizing be best managed.

* 1 Cor. vi. 17. 4° 1676. m. e. G. p. 279. The true Believer's Union with Christ Jesus.

Pf. lxii. 8. 4° 1677. m. e. C. p. 340. How we are to live by Faith on the divine Providence.

John xi. 11. 4° 1681. Fun. Death the sweetest Sleep.

{ Mal. iv. 6. 4° 1683. C. m. e. p. 151. What may gracious Parents best do, for the Conversion of their Children, where Wickedness is occasioned by their sinful Severity or Indulgence.

Ephes. vi. 4. 4° 1683. C. m. e. p. 151. What may gracious Parents best do, for the Conversion of their Children, where Wickedness is occasioned by their sinful Severity or Indulgence. }

LYNCH John, DD. Dean of Canterbury.

Acts v. 38, 39. 4° 1735. Prop. of Gospel. *All S*. Ox. *Queen's*. C.

LYNCH John, LL. D. R. of Adisham, Kent.

* Acts xx. 24. 8° 1771. Conf. of Bp. St. Paul's Xrter considered and his Example recommended.

LYNFORD Thomas, DD. R. of St. Edmond the King, and St. Nicholas Acons, Lond. Preb. of Westm. and Chapl. in Ord.

Pf. xii. 7. 8° 16 On Divine Assistance.

2 Chron. xx. 17. 4° 1679. b. Lord Mayor. *All S*. Oxon. *Trin*. *Queen's*. Camb. *Sion*.

Pf. cxxvii. 1. 4° 1689. b. Lord Mayor. God's Providence, the City's Safety. *Ch. Ch*. Oxon. *Trin*. Camb.

Matt. vi. 6. 4° 1691. b. Queen. Worship of God in private. *Bod*. *Ch. Ch*. Oxon. *St. John's*. Camb.

1 Tim vi. 17-19. 4° 1698. Spitt. W. *Ch. Ch*. Ox. *Trin*. C. *Sion*.

Acts ii. 42. 8° 1709. Primitive Christianity revived. *Bod*. *All S*. *Magd*. Oxon. *Trin*. Camb. *Sion*.

Jerem. v. 29. 8° 1709. Fast. *Trin*. Camb.

John xv. 18. 4° 1712. Spitt. W. The charitable Man bears much Fruit. *Ch. Ch*. Oxon. *Queen's*. Camb. *Eton*.

Dan. xii 3. 4° 1715. b. King. The Advantage of being good, and making others so. *Ch. Ch. Linc*. Oxon.

2 Sam. xxii. 51. 4° 1715. Accession. b. Commons. God a Tower of Salvation to the King. *Ch. Ch*. Oxon. *Queen's*. Camb.

- - - - 17 Charity-Schools recommended.

LYNG William, a Priest of the Church of England, Minister of Yarmouth, Norfolk.

Mark iii. 24. 4° 1703. b. Mayor of Norwich. Concerning the Causes, Mischiefs and Cures of national Divisions. *Pub. L*. *St. John's*. Camb.

LYTTLETON Charles, Bp. of Carlisle.

* Luke ii. 14. 4° 1765. Jan. 30. b. Lords.

LYTTON William, M. A. R. of Knebworth, Herts.

2 Cor. vi. 1. 8° 1716. Vis.

M. R. a Friend of Anthony Farindon.

Phil. iv. 17. V. Farindon's Serm. fo. 1674. Vol. III. p. 13.

MACE Charles, V. of Chrift Church, York.
  Ephef. v. 1, 2. 8° 1714.
MACE Daniel
  * 19 Serm. in 8° 1751.
MACGILL William, V. D. of Ayr.
  * John xvii. 20. 12° 1779. 2 f. Our Saviour's Prayer for the Union of his Followers confidered. V. Scotch Pr. Vol. III. p. 119.
MACHAM N.
  * Col. i. 7. 1667.
MACHIN Richard
  * Heb. iv. 15. 8° 1735.
  * 2 Sam. xxiv. 14. 8° 1740. David's Choice.
MACLAINE Archibald, Min. of the Eng. Church at the Hague.
  Lament. iii. 28, 29. 8° 1752. Hague. On the Death of the Prince of Orange. The Difficulties of Refignation allieviated by Hope.
MACLAURIN John
  * Serm. in 12° 1772.
MACKENZIE John,   V. D. M. of Port-patrick.
  * Job iii. 17-19. 12° 1779. The Peace of the Grave. V. Scotch Preacher. Vol. 3. p. 257.
MACKEIVEN Robert, M. A.
  2 Tim. iv. 7, 8. 8° 1734. Fun. of Vifcount Barrington. V. Dr. Enfield's Eng. Preacher. Vol. 5. p. 287. Queen's. Camb.
MACKGOWEN John,   Grafton-ftreet, London.
  * - - - - Fun.   The fure Foundation.
  * - - - - Fun.   Cleanfing Fountain opened.
MACKQUEEN John,   one of the Minif. of the City of Edinb.
  Pf. ii. 6. 4° 1687. King's birth-day.
  Acts xiii. 36. 4° 1693. Elect. of Magiftrates.
  Luke vii. 4, 5. 4° 1694. Edinb. The good Patriot.
MACKQUEEN John, M. A. Minifter of St. Mary's in the Town and Port of Dover.
  Efther vi. 6. 4° 1711. Effay on Honour.
  Difc. in 8° 1715. Britifh Valour triumphing over French Courage.
MACRO Thomas, DD. Minifter of Yarmouth, Norfolk.
  1 Cor. xiii. 3. 8° 1731. Nov. 5. Charity of Temper. p. 11.
  Gal. v. 14. 8° 1731. Charity of Affiftance. p. 29.
  Ephef. v. 19. 8° 1734. Opening an Organ. The Melody of the Heart. Queen's. Camb.
MADAN Martin, B. A. Chapl. of the Lock-Hofpital, Weftminfter.
  * James ii. 24. 8° 1761. Juftification by Works.
  * Luke x. 28. 8° 1762. Hofpital f.
  * John viii. 7. 4° 1764. Opening of the Chapel.
  * 2 Cor. viii. 9. 8° 1777. At the Lock-Hofpital.
MADDOCK Thomas, M. A. Lecturer of St George's, Liverpool.
  2 Sam. xxii. 38-41. 4° 1746. Th. Oct. 9.
  * Deut. v. 29. 4° 1771. Affize. Religion neceffary to the Being and Happinefs of Society.

MAD.

MADDOX Isaac, Bp. of Worcester.
 Tit. ii. 11–13. 4° 1734. Prop. of Gospel. *Queen's.* Camb.
 Pf. cxxvi. 6. 4° 1736. Ref. Manners. The Love of our Country recommended. *Queen's.* Camb.
 Matt. xxv. 36. 4° 1739. *Westminster*-Infirmary.
 Pf. cxi. 4. 4° 1739. Accession. b. Lords.
 Job xxix. 16. 4° 1741. Ann. meet. Char. School. *Queen's.* Cam.
 Ruth ii. 20. 4° 1742. b. Sons of the Clergy. *Queen's.* Camb.
 Ezra ix. 9. 4° 1742. May 29. b. Lords.
 Pf. xli. 1. 4° 1743. *London*-Infirmary The Duty and Advantages of encouraging public Infirmaries. *Wadh* Ox *Qyre's* Camb.
 Luke xi. 2. 4° 1744. *London* Infirmary. *Wadh* Ox. *Queen's.* Cam.
 Pf. lii. 1, 2. 4° 1746. Th. after Rebellion. *Worc.* Oxon. *Queen's.* Camb *Brit. M.*
 Gal. vi. 9, 10. 4° 1748. *Worcester*-Infirmary.
 Isai. xi. 13. 4° 1749. Irish Prot. School. *Queen's.* Cl. H. Camb. *Worc.* Oxon.
 Job v. 16. 4° 1750. Spitt. M. *All S.* Oxon. *Queen's.* Camb.
 Isai. lviii. 7. 4° 1752 Small pox-Hosp *Queen's* Camb. *Eton.*
 *Pf. xxvii. 12. 4° 1753.   Hosp. *Queen's* Camb.
MAGILL Moses, M. A. Curate of St. Mary's, Dublin.
 Judg. v. 2, 3. 4° 1746. Th. after Rebellion.
MAJENDIE J. J.   one of the Preachers of the Savoy, and Chapl. to the Earl of Grantham.
 *2 Cor. v. 9–11. 8° 1741. : e But. des Afflictions.
 Acts xv. 10. 4° 1745. Rebellion. The Yoke of the Church of Rome proved to be insufferable.
 *Pf. cxxiv. 6, 7. 4° 1755. Nov. 5. The double Deliverance.
MAINWARING Edward, M. A. Preb. of Chester.
 *   -   -   - 1762. Accession.
MAINWARING John. B. D. Fell. of St. John's Coll. Camb. and R. of Church-Stretton, Salop.
 * Serm. in 8° 1780. *Camb.* On several Occasions.
MALBON Samuel
 *Matt. xvi. 27. 8° 1673. 2 f. Xt's Appearance in Judgment. *Bod.*
 *Disc. in 12° 1715.
[MALEVERER   ]
 2 Sam. xv. 12. 4° 1683. Th. Sep. 9. Achitophel's Policy defeated.
MALLERY Thomas
 Gen xviii. 37. 4° 1677. m. e. C. p. 350. How must we have suitable Conceptions of God in Duty.
MALTON William, M. A. R. of South Collingham, Nottinghamsh.
 Rev. xiii. 14. 4° 1715. Fun, of Lady Cath. Neville.
MALTUS Farmerie,   Cur. of St. Mary Magdalen Bermondsey, Surrey and of Wymeswould, Leicestersh.
 *Rom. xii. 10. 4° 1752. b. Gregorians.
 *Matt. vii. 21. 8° 1762. The Gospel-Terms of Salvation by Xt.
MANBY Peter,   Dean of Derry.
 *Matt. iv. 2. 4° 1682. *Dublin.* Ashwednesday.
                                    MANGEY

MANGEY Thomas, DD. Preb. of Durham.
- Lvke xvi. 9. 8° 1716. Ch. f. The wife Steward. *Sion*.
- Pract. Difc. in 8° 1717. On the Lord's Prayer. *Univ. C.C.C. Magd.* Oxon. *Queen's. St. John's.* Camb.
- Pf. xciii 5. 4° 1719. Conf. of Church. The Holinefs of Xtian Churches *Worc.* Oxon. *Queen's.* Camb. *Sion.*
- Heb. xiii. 8. 4° 1719. Vif. The eternal Exiftence of our Lord. Jefus Chrift. *Queen's.* Camb. *Sion.*
- Matt. i. 23. 8° 1719. Chriftmas. Plain Nations of our Lord's Divinity. *Worc.* Oxon. *Queen's.* Camb.
- Ifai. lvii. 1. 4° 1720. Jan. 30. b. Commons. The providential Sufferings of good Men. *All S. Magd. Linc. Worc.* Oxon. *Queen's.* Camb.
- Matt xi. 5. 8° 1726. Ann. meeting Char. School. The Gofpel preached to the poor. *Queen's.* Camb.
- Pf. xxix. 2. 8° 1729. Hutchin's Lect. The Duty and Method of honouring God as contained in the Common Prayer of the Church of England. *Queen's* Camb.
- Ecclef. xi. 1, 2. 8° 1731. Spitt. W. The Rules of public Charity.
- Mal. ii. 7. 4° 1733. b. Sons of the Clergy. The Ufefulnefs and Authority of the Chriftian Clergy's Inftructions. *Queen's.* Cam.

MANN Ifaac, DD. Arch-Deacon of Dublin.
- *Pf. cxxii. 1, 2. 12° 1769. Open. St. Catherine's Church, Dublin.

MANNINGHAM Thomas, Bp. of Chichefter.
- Pf. cxix. 67. 8° 1679. b. Lord Mayor. Of Afflictions. *Magd. C.C.C.* Oxon. *Sion. Eton.*
- Pf. cxix. 67. 8° 1679. b. Lord Mayor. Of Afflictions. *Magd. C.C.C.* Oxon. *Pub. L. Queen's.* Camb. *Sion Eton.*
- Pf. ciii. 1. 4° 1681 Trin. f. Of Praife and Adoration. *C.C.C.* Oxon. *Pub. L. Queen's.* Camb. *Sion.*
- Pf. ii. 1. 4° 1685. May 29. At the Rolls. *Worc. C.C.C.* Oxon. *Pub. L. Trin. Queen's.* Camb. *Sion.*
- Pf. lxxix. 8. 4° 1084. Jan 30. *C.C.C.* Oxon. *Pub. L. Queen's.* Camb. *Sion.*
- Phil. iv. 8. 4° 1686. County-Feaft. *C.C.C.* Ox. *Queen's.* C. *Sion.*
- Pf. xv. 1, 2. 4° 1687. Fun. of Sir John Norton. *Bod. Magd. C.C.C.* Oxon. *Pub. L. Queen's. St. John's.* Camb. *Sion.*
- Ifai. lvi. 7. 4° 1692. b. Queen. Of public Worfhip. *Ch. Ch. Univ* Oxon. *Trin.* Camb. *Sion.*
- Acts xvii 22 4° 1692. Nov. 5. b. Commons. The Nature and Effects of Superftition. *Ch. Ch. Magd.* Oxon. *Pub. L. St. John's.* Camb. *Sion.*
- Luke xv. 7. 4° 1693. b. Queen. A Comparifon between a juft Perfon and a ferious Penitent. *Bod. Ch.Ch. Magd.* Ox. *Pub. L. Trin.* Camb. *Sion.*
- Prov. viii. 12. 4° 1694. b. Queen. Of religious Providence. *Bod. Ch. Ch. Pub. L.* Camb. *Sion.*
- Pf. cxxxix. 23, 24. 4° 1694. Of Integrity of Heart. *Ch. Ch.* Oxon. *Sion.*

Amos

OF AUTHORS, &c.

Amos viii. 9, 10. 4° 1695. Roy. Fun. *Ch. Ch. Magd.* Ox. *Pub. L. Trin. St. John's. Cl. H.* Camb. *Sion.*
Pf. lxxxii. 6, 7. 4° 1695. Roy. Fun. *Sion.*
1 Cor. ii. 6. 4° 1701. *Lond.* Conc. ad Cl. *Magd.* Oxon. *Pub. L. Trin. Queen's. St. John's.* Camb.
1 Cor. ii. 9. 4° 1703. Fun. of Lady Dorothy Norton. *Ch. Ch.* Ox.
Ifai. xxvi. 9. 4° 1704. On the late Storm. *Ch. Ch. Magd.* Oxon. *St. John's.* Camb. *Brit. M.*
Rom. viii. 6. 4° 1706. b. Queen. *Ch. Ch. Maga. Hert.* Oxon. *Trin.* Camb. *Sion.*
Ecclef. vii. 1. 4° 1706. Fun. of Dr. Umphreville. *Trin.* Camb.
Rom. xiv. 7. 8° 1707. Th. for Union. *Hert.* Oxon. *Sion.*
Pf. xlvi. 10, 11. 1° 1708. b. Queen. Th. for Victory. July 11. *Worc.* Oxon. *Trin.* Camb. *Sion.*
1 Cor. xv. 28. 6° 1708. b. Queen. *Univ.* Oxon. *Trin. Queen's.* Camb. *Brit. M.*
Ecclef. vii. 14. 4° 1709. Th. b. Queen. *Ch. Ch. Magd. Hert.* Oxon. *Pub. L. Queen's.* Camb. *Brit. M.*
Col. i. 11. 8° 1713. Farewel. *Pub. L. Queen's.* Camb.
Prov. xxiv. 21. 4° 1722. Jan. 30.

MANNINGHAM Thomas, DD. Preb. of Weftminfter.
Matt. xiii. 58. 4° 1724. Con. Acad. pro Grad. Doct. *Queen's.* C.

MANSELL John, L.L.B. R. of Furthoe, Northamptonf.
Pf. lxxxii. 1. 4° 1694. Affize. *Or.* Oxon. *Pub. L. Queen's.* Cam.
1 Tim. i. 16. 4° 1694. Vif. *Or.* Oxon. *Pub. L. Queen's.* Camb.

MANSTON Joseph, of Exeter, Devon.
* 2 Cor xi. 26. 8° 1718. *Exon.* The Perils from falfe Brethren. *St. John's* Camb.

MANTON *Thomas*, DD. Minifter of the Gofpel in London.
2 Theff. ii. 15. 4° 1675. m e. P. p. 149. The Scripture fufficient without unwritten Tradition.
Acts ii. 38. 4° 1676. f. m. e. C. p. 191. How ought we to improve our Baptifm.
* Rom. v. 6. 4° 1676. m. e. G. p. 144. Man's Impotency to help himfelf out of Mifery.
Matt. xv. 7, 8. 4° 1677. m. e. C. p. 390. How we may cure Diftractions in holy Duties.
* Difc. in 4° 1678.
* Difc. in 8° 1685.
* Difc. in 4 Vol. 1693. and 1708.
‡ * Phil. i. 27. 8° 1726. Farewel. *Brit. M.*

MAPLETOFT John, DD. V. of St. Lawrence Jewry, London.
1 Theff. v. 17, 18. 4° 1687. A Perfuafive to the confcientious frequenting of the daily public Prayers of the Church of England *Bod. Pub. L.* Camb. *Sion.*
Luke xii. 21. 4° 1695. Spitt. W. The rich man's Bounty, the true meafure of his Wifdom. *Ch. Ch.* Oxon. *Pub. L. Queen's.* Camb. *Brit. M.*

1 Sam.

1 Sam. ii. 30. 4° 1700. Ref. of Manners.
Matt. vii. 12. 4° 1714. Affize. *Cl. H.* Camb.
MARCH John, B. D. V. of St. Nicholas, New Caftle.
Matt. xxi. 9. 4° 1666. Advent.
Judges xix. 30. 4° 1677. Jan. 30. *Jef.* Oxon. *Sion.*
Pf. xxxiv. 11. 4° 1682. Ch. f. Erect. a Char-Sch. *Ch. Ch.* Ox.
Matt. vii. 15,16. 4° 1683. Jan. 30.
Hofea iii. 5. 4° 1684. May 29.
12 Serm. in 4° 1693. To which is added an Affize Serm. 8° 1699.
Trin. Queen's. Camb.
MARIOTT Thomas, M. A. R. of Canfield, Effex.
1 Sam. xv. 23. 4° 1661.
John xx. 9, 4° 1689. Eafter. b. Lord Mayor. *Bod. Pub. L. St. John's.* Camb. *Sion.*
Luke xi. 17. 4° 1689. Elect. Lord Mayor. The Danger of Divifion, and Neceffity of Union. *St. John's.* Camb
MARKHAM William, Abp. of York.
* 2 Tim. i. 7. 4° 1752. Conf. of Bp. Johnfon. *Bod. Ex.* Oxon. *Queen's.* Camb. *Brit. M.*
* Col. ii. 8. 4° 1769. *Lond.* Conc. ad Cl. *Braz. N. Worc.* Oxon.
* 1 Cor. iii. 9. 4° 1773. *Radcliffe-*Infirmary, Oxon.
* Ifai. iii. 5. 4° 1774. Jan. 30. b. Lord's. *Worc.* Oxon.
* Dan. vii 14. 4° 1777. Prop. of Gofpel.
MARKHAM Robert, DD. R. of St. Mary's Whitechapel, London. and Chaplain in Ord.
* James v. 20. 4° 1776. At the Magdalen-Hofp.
* Pf. ciii. 4 8° 1778 b. Gov. of Humane Society, for the Recovery of drowned Perfons.
* Matt. xviii. 14. 8° 1778. b. Gov. of the Afylum.
* Prov. xix. 17. 4° 1779. b. Gov of Marine Society.
* Luke x. 24. 4° 1779. Ann. meeting Char. School.
‡ * Ezra. vii. 5. 4° 1780. The Wifdom of appointing and fupporting the civil Magiftrate.
* Jerem. xlix. 11. 4° 1781. b. Sons of the Clergy. Sympathy in Diftrefs.
* Gal. vi. 2. 4° 1781. On a Brief for Sufferers in the Weft Indies.
MARKLAND Abraham, DD. Preb. of Weftminfter, and Mafter of St. Crofs Hofp. near Winchefter, Hants.
Luke xix. 41, 42. 4° 1682. b. Court of Aldermen. *Pub. L.* Cam.
* Jer. li. 15. 8° 17
Serm. in 2 Vol. 8° 1729. Preached at the Cathedral Church at Winchefter.
MARKWICH Nathaniel, B. D. V. of Eaft-Brent, Somerfetf.
Dan. ix. 24–27. 8° 1728. Stricturæ Lucis—or a Calculation of Daniel's 70 Weeks.
MARRIOTT George. R. of Alphamftone, Effex, Lect. of St. Luke's, Middlefex and late Chapl. of the Britifh Factory at Guttenburgh.
* - - - - 1768. Mofes's Prefervation in the Ark of Bulrufhes fymbolically explained. * Heb.

* Heb, xiii. 14. 4° 1773. Farw. Hum. Life, State of Pilgrimage.
* 3 Serm. in 8°. 1775. On the intermediate State. *Queen's*. Cam.
* Rom. viii. 10. 8° 1775. 2 f. On Mortality. *Queen's*. Camb.
* 1 Pet. iv. 17. 4° 1776. Faſt. Judgment begun in the Houſe of God, to be finiſhed on its Enemies.
* 10 Diſc. in 8° 1774. An Eſtimate of hum. Life.

MARRYATT Zephaniah, DD
 * John xx. 28. 8" 1719. The exalted Saviour.

MARSDEN Robert, B. D. late Fell. of Jeſ Coll. Camb. Arch-D. of Nottingham and Preb. of Southwell.
 Rom. v. 1. 4° 1701. *Cant.* Conc. ad Cl. *All S. Or. Pub. L. Trin. St. John's. Queen's.* Camb.
 Gal. iv. 18. 8° 1713. Aſſize.
 Prov. xii. 26. 8° 1729. Fun.

MARSH George, B. A. R of Ford, Northumberland.
 Zech. viii. 16. 8° 1722. *York.* Aſſize.

MARSH George, M. A. V. of Milton-Abbas, Dorſetſhire.
 12 Serm. in 8° 1737.

MARSH Richard, M. A. Fell. of St. John's Coll. Camb.
 Job xxxviii. 4. 4° 1701. *Camb.* The Vanity and Danger of modern Theories. *Trin. Queen's. St. John's.* Camb. *Sion.*

MARSH Richard, V. of St. Margaret's at Cliff, Canterbury.
 1 Cor. ii. 4, 5. 8° 1715. Sch. F. The Advantage of Learning in Religion. *All S.* Oxon.

MARSHALL John, L.L. D. one of his Majeſty's Chaplains at Whitehall.
 Matt. iv. 2. 12° 1706. A ſhort and pract. Diſc. upon the holy Faſt of Lent being the Subſtance of 2 Sermons.
 Levit. vi. 22. 1706.
 Iſai. lvii. 1 8° 1714. Fun. of Mr. Nelſon. *Magd. Linc. Worc. Oxon. Sion.*

MARSHALL John, M. A. V. of Widecombe, and Maſter of the Grammar-School at Exon.
 * Luke x. 37. 8° 1780. b. Gov. of *Deven.* and *Ex.* Hoſp.

MARSHALL Nathaniel, L.L. D. R. of Finchley, Middleſex, and Chaplain in Ord.
 Deut. iv. 7. 4° 1707. Th. for the Union.
 Gal. vi. 10. 4° 1701. b. Sons of the Clergy. *Wadh.* Ox. *Brit. M.*
 Pſ. lxxxii. 6, 7. 8° 1714. Royal Fun. The royal Pattern. *Worc. Oxon. Queen's.* Camb. *Sion.*
 Epheſ. iv. 11–13. 8° 1719. Viſ. A regular Succeſſion of the Chriſtian Miniſtry. *Queen's.* Camb. *Sion.*

MARSHALL Nathaniel, DD. R. of St. Vedaſt's Foſter lane, Canon of Windſor and Chaplain in Ord.
 Pſ. xxxvii. 37. 8° 1718. Fun. of Mr. Blundell. The juſt man's Character, or the Recompence of Virtue. *Worc.* Ox. *Eton. Sign.*
 Exod. xx. 5. 4° 1721. Jan. 30. b. Commons. *Worc.* Ox. *Cl. H.* Camb. *Sion.*

Isai. liv. 13. 4° 1721. An. meet. Char. School. *Sion.*
2 Cor. v. 10, 11. 4° 1722. *Sion.*
Acts xx. 35. 8° 1722. Spitt. W. *Ch. Ch.* Oxon.
*Luke vii. 5. 8° 1727. Conf. of St. John's Chapel. *Brit. M.*
Rom. x. 15. 8° 1717. Open. a Lecture. *Eton.*
Phil. i. 23, 24. 8° 1729. Fun. of Dr. John Rogers. *Queen's.* Camb. *Sion.*
Sermons in 3 Vol. 8° 1731. *Bod. All S. St. John's. Pemb. Worc. New C.* Oxon. *Brit. M.*
An additional 4 Vol. 8° 1750. *Worc. New C.* Oxon.

MARSHALL *Walter*
  Rom. iii. 23–26. 8° 1692. On Justification. *Bod.*

MARSTON Edward
  Prov. xx. 25. 4° 1699. Of Simony and Sacrilege. *Pub. L. Queen's. St. John's.* Camb.

MARSTON William, M. A. V. of Redbourn, Herts.
  Pf. cxi. 4. 4° 1709. Th.

MARSTON William, M. A. Chaplain to the Duke of Bridgwater, and V. of Redbourn, Herts.
  Pf. ci. 1. 8° 1772. Affize. *All S.* Oxon.

MARTEN Edmond, L. L. D. Dean of Worcester.
  Heb. x. 24, 25. 8° 1738. b. Sons of the Clergy. *Queen's.* Camb. *Brit. M.*

MARTIN David
  1 John v. 7. 8° 1719. Differtation. *Bod. Bal.* Oxon.

MARTIN John, B. A. R. of Horfey's Melcombe, Dorfetfhire, and Preb. of Sarum.
  Pf. cxviii. 22–25. 4° 1660. *Oxon.* Hofannah, or Thankfgiving Serm. June 28.
  Deut. xvii. 12. 4° 1664. Affize. Lex. pacifica, or God's own Law of determining Controverfies. *Sion.*

MARTIN *John*
  * – – – – 8° 1766. Fun.
  * Rom. x. 3. 8° 1771. The Rock of Offence, the Sinners laft and only Refuge.
  * Exod. xii. 26. 8° 1772. Faft.
  * Matt. v. 29, 30. 12° 1779. Chrift's Counfel to Chriftians.

MARTIN S   M. A. R. of Gotham, Nottinghamf.
  *Prov. xxv. 26. 8° 1760. 2 f. Self-confidence.
  *Rom. v. 1. 8° 1760. Juftification.
  * – – 8° 1767. Blafphemy ag. Holy Ghoft.

MARTYN Thomas, B. D. R. of Ludgerfhall, Bucks and Profeffor of Botany, Camb.
  *Ifai. liii. 4. 4° 1768. *Camb. Addenbrook*-Hofp. *Queen's.* Camb.

MASON Charles, DD. R. of St. Peter's-le-poor and Preb. of St. Paul's, London.
  2 Cor. ii. 16. 4° 1663. Conc. ad Cl. Officium Miniftri. *Queen's.* Camb. *Sion.*
  2 Tim. ii. 2, 3. 4° 1673. b. Artillery-Co. Miles Chriftianus. *St. John's.* Camb.   Col.

Col. i. 18. 4° 1676. *Lond.* Conc. ad Cl. Solus Christus totius mundi Episcopus.
2 Thess. iii. 10. 4° 16
2 Pet. iii. 10, 11. 4° 1676. b. Lord Mayor. The Day of the Lord, or a Caution to the City of London after the many dreadful Fires.

MASON Francis, DD. Fell. of Mert. Coll. Oxon.
1 Cor. xiv. 40. (1605.) 4° 1705. reprinted. The Authority of the Ch. in making Canons &c. *Bod. Magd. Queen's. Jes.* Oxon.

MASON John, M. A. R. of Water-Stratford, Bucks.
Matt. xxv. 1, 2. 4° 1691. The Midnight-Cry. *Bod.*

MASON John, of Clare-Hall. Camb. R. of Arwarby Linc. and Preb. of Litchfield.
Heb. ix. 27, 28. 4° 1671. Fun.
Phil. i. 21. 4° 1726. Fun. of Lady Whitchcote. The good Xtian's Gain by Death.

MASON John, M. A. Minister of the Gospel at Cheshunt, Herts.
Rom. xiii. 1, 2. 8° 1741. Nov. 5.
2 Cor. xiii. 11. 8° 1746. The Christian Farewel.
Amos iv. 12. 8° 1750. On the Earthquakes. *Queen's.* Camb.
52 Pract. Discourses in 8° 1752. The Lord's day Evening Entertainment.
* Ps. xlvi. 10. 8° 1756. Fast. *Queen's.* Camb.
* 15 Disc. in 8° 1758. Devotional and practical, suited to the Use of Families.
* Christian Morals or Disc. in 2 Vol. 8° 1761. On the several human, divine, christian, and social Virtues, being a Sequel to the Lord's day Evening-Entertainment.

MASON Richard, Gent. Commoner of Magd. Coll. Oxon.
Luke xv. 11, 12. 8° 1742. The indulgent Father.
Ps. viii. 4. 8° 1742. The Vanity of Man.
Acts xxvi. 8. 1° 1742. On the Resurrection.
Prov. xx. 2. 8° 1742. The mutual Advantages of Subordination.
Phil. iv. 11. 8° 1742. The Benefits of Contentment.
Matt. vii. 1, 2. 8° 1742. Dissuasive from rash Censures.
Hosea x. 12. 8° 1742. Exhortation to Repentance.
‡ * Dan. ii. 20, 21. 8° 1745. On the Invasion.
‡ * Ps. vii. 14. 17 Th. s.

MASSEY Edmund, M. A. Lect. of St. Alban, Woodstreet, and R. of Colne Engaygne, Essex.
Jer. v. 29. 8° 1721. Fast. for the Plague. b. Lord Mayor. The Signs of the Times. *Brit. M.*
Job ii. 7. 8° 1722. Against the dangerous and sinful Practice of Inoculation. *Bod. Queen's.* Camb. *Sion.*
Deut. i. 16, 17. 4° 1723. Assize.
Luke ix. 54–56. 8° 1724. Nov. 5.
Ps. lxxxii. 6, 7. 8° 1725. Accession. *Queen's.* Camb.
Luke xiii. 24. 8° 1725. Elect. of Lord Mayor. The strait Gate made unpassable by the Abuse of Riches, Titles and Places of public Trust. *Queen's.* Camb. *Sion.*

Iſai. i. 25, 26. 8° 1736. b. Lord Mayor. May 29.
MASTER Thomas, B. D. Fell. of New Coll. Oxon.
 Luke i. 26, 27 (1641.) 1710. reprinted. The Virgin Mary. V. Diſc. on conj Duty. 12° 1740. Vol. 1. p. 123. *Univ. Magd.* Oxon. *Queen's.* Camb.
MASTERS Robert, M. A. Fell. of C. C. C. Camb.
 Pſ. xvii. 14. 8° 1745. *Camb.* The Miſchiefs of Faction and Rebellion conſidered.
MASTERS Samuel, B. D. Preacher to Bridewell Hoſp. Preb. of St. Paul's, Cur. of Litchfield.
 Prov. xvii. 17. 4° 1685. Co. Feaſt. Of Friendſhip. *C.C.C. Ox.*
 * Job. ii. 10. 12° 1689.
 Phil. iv. 5. 4° 1690. b. Lord Mayor. The Chriſtian Temper of Moderation deſcribed and recommended. *All S. Ch. Ch.* Oxon. *Brit. M.*

MASTERSON George
 1 Pet. ii. 4, 5. 12° 1661. Sev. ſerm. The ſpiritual Houſe deſcribed. *Lod. Sion.*

MATHER *Cotton*, DD. Paſtor of a Church in Boſton, New England.
 Eſther iv. 14. 12° 1690.
 ‡ * Zach. x. 1. 8° 1712. *Boſton.* Rainbow. *Brit. M.*
 * Rev. x. 1. 8° 1714.

MATHER *increaſe*, Teacher of the Church at Boſton, New England.
 * Sev. Serm. in 12° 1674. About Converſion. *Bod.*
 * Num. xiii. 6. 8° 1690. *Bod.*

MATHER John, DD. Preſident of C. C. C. Oxon.
 John v 14. 4° 1705. *Oxon.* May 29. *Bod. C.C.C.* Oxon. *Sion.*

MATHER *Nathaniel*
 * Rom. iii. 22. 4° 1694 *Oxon. Brit. M.*
 * 23 Select ſerm. in 8° 1701. Preached at the Merchant's Lect. at Pinner's Hall, London.

MATHER *Samuel*
 * Serm. in 4° 1683. On the Figures and Types of the old Teſtament. *Brit. M.*

MATTHEWS J.[a]
 Iſai. xxxii. 8. 1712. Ch. ſ.

MATTHEWS John,[a] M. A. Paſtor of the Church of Tewkeſbury, Glouceſterſhire.
 Luke xxiii. 34. 4° 1706. *Oxon.* Forgiveneſs of Enemies, and praying for Enemies. *Bod.*

MATTHEWS M.
 Pſ. lxxviii. 8, 9. 4° 1673.

MAUDUIT *Iſaac*, V. D. M.
 2 Cor. xiii. 14. 8° 1694. Tri-Unity, or the Doctrine of the Holy Trinity aſſerted. *Bod.*
 Epheſ. v. 2. 8° 1704. Sermons on Chriſt's Satisfaction. *St. Paul's L.* London.
 * Matt. v. 19. 8° 1710. Little Sins.

   a Q. The ſame.

MAULDEN

MAULDEN J   of Burwell, Camb.
 * Prov. iii. 9. 8° 1738. Collection for the Support of poor Ministers &c.
 * Prov. iii. 6. 8° 1762. Ag. Inoculation. *Queen's.* Camb.
MAULE Henry, Bp. of Meath.
 Pf. cxxiv. 5. 4° 1733. *Dublin.* (*Lond.* 12°) Anniv. of Deliverance from Pop. *All S. Worc. Ox. Pub. L. Queen's. Ca. Brit. M.*
MAUNDRELL Henry, M. A. Fell. of Ex. Coll. Oxon. and Chapl. to the Factory at Aleppo.
 Eccles. vii. 16, 17. 4° 1690. Levant Co. *Queen's.* Camb. *Eton.*
[MAURICE Antoine]
 * Disc. in 8° 1722.
MAURICE David, B. D. formerly Chapl. of New Coll. Oxon.
 Matt. xii. 20. 4° 1700. The bruised Reed. *Jes.* Oxon. *Sion.*
MAURICE Henry, DD. Margaret-Professor of Divinity Oxon. and Preb. of Worcester.
 Isai. xxxvii 3. 4° 1681. (8° 1764.) Jan. 30. b. King. *Bod. All S. Ch. Ch. Ex. Worc. St. John's.* Camb.
MAURICE *Matthias*
 * - - - 1736. Open. Meeting-House,
MAURICE Peter, M. A. Fell. of Jes. Coll. Oxon. Dean of Bangor.
 Tit. ii 15. 8° 1728. The true Causes of the Contempt of christian Ministers. *Bod. Wadh.* Oxon. *Queen's.* Camb. *Brit. M.*
MAURICE T   B. A. of Univ. Coll. Oxon.
 * Jer xviii. 8. 8° 1779. Fast.
MAWER John, DD.
 * Rev. i. 8. 8° 1735. Vis. May 6.
 1 Cor. v. 7, 8. 8° 1736. *York.* Palm S. The Nature and design of the Lords Supper.
 * Rom. xi. 22. 8° 1737. Roma Meretrix.
 Deut. xx. 1, 2 8° 1741. The Priest of War among the Hebrews.
MAWSON Matthias, Bp. of Chichester.
 Matt. vii. 12. 4° 1723. Sch. Feast. *Eton.*
 Rom. xiii. 1. 4° 1733. Jan. 30. b. Commons. *Worc.* Oxon.
 1 Sam. vii. 6. 4° 1740. Fast. b. Lords Feb. 4. *Queen's.* Camb.
 1 Cor. vii. 17. 4° 1741. Spitt. M. *Queen's.* Camb.
 Rom. x 14, 15. 4° 1743. Prop. Gospel. *All S.* Ox. *Queen's.* Cam.
 James iii. 16. 4° 1746. Jan. 30. b. Lords. Mischiefs of Divisions. *Queen's.* Camb.
 Prov. xix 6. 4° 1750. *London-*Infirmary. *Wadh.* Oxon.
MAXWELL Henry, Bp. of Dromore.
 * Gal. vi. 9. 4° 1770. Irish Prot. School.
MAXWELL J   A Layman.
 * Isai. lxi. 1–3. 8° 1757. Christmas.
MAXWELL James,   Chapl. to the Asylum.
 * 1 Tim. v. 8. 4° 1759. b. Gov. of Christ-Hosp.
 * Rom. xii. 15. 4° 1763. b. Gov. of the Asylum.
MAY *William*
 * 6 Serm. in 8° 1744. To young People.
 * 20 Pract. Serm. in 8° 1757.

MAYHEW *Jonathan*, DD. Paſtor of Weſt Ch. Boſton, New England.
* Serm. in 4 Vol. 8° 1750. *Dr Wʃ's L.* London.
* Matt. xxv. 21. 8° 1754. Election.
* Serm. in 8° 1756.
* Pſ. cxxvi. 3. 8° 1759. 2 ſ. The Reduc. of Quebeck. *Queen's.* C.
* Amos iii. 8. 8° 1760, Fire at Boſton.
* Pſ. cxxiv. 7, 8. 8° 1767. Repeal of the Stampt-Act. *Queen's.* C.
* 15 Serm. in 2 Vol. 8° 1767. To young Men. *Bod. Pub L. C. Sion.*
* - - - - 1770 2 ſ. A Name in Heaven, ſureſt Ground of Joy. Publiſhed by The Rev Mr. Toplady.
MAYNARD Edward, DD. of Magd. Coll. formerly Preacher at Lincoln's Inn, now R. of Boddington, Northamptonſ.
   10 Serm. &c. 1 Vol. 8° 1722. With 2 Diſcourſes on natural and revealed Religion- *Ch. Ch. Magd.* Oxon.
   14 Serm. and 2 Vol. 8° 1724. *Ch. Ch. Magd.* Oxon.
MAYNE Jaſper, DD. Canon of Ch. Ch. Oxon. and Chapl. in Ord.
   1 Tim. iv. 14. 4° 1662. Conſ. of Bp. Croft. *Univ. Bal. Or. Magd. Wore.* Oxon. *Trin.* Camb *Brit. M.*
   Gal. v. 1. 4° 1664. *Oxon.* Conc. ad Acad. *Bod. Univ.* Oxon.
MAYNE *Zachariah*
‡ * Rom. vi. 22. 4° 1693. *Brit. M.*
MAYNWARING Roger, DD.
   Eccleſ. viii. 2. [4° 1627.] 2 ſ. reprinted 8° 1709. Religion and Allegiance. *Magd. Wore.* Oxon. *Sion.*
MAYO *Daniel*, M. A.
* Matt. xxviii. 19, 20. 8° 1713. On Baptiſm.
* 1 Pet. i. 24, 25. 8° 1723.
* 2 Cor. iv. 7. 8° 1732. Fun. of Rev. *Edm. Calamy. Queen's.* Cam.
MAYO *Richard*, M. A. Miniſter of the Goſpel in London.
   Rom. x. 14. 4° 1675. m. e. P. p. 519. Invocations of Saints and Angels unlawful.
   2 Cor. xii. 7. 4° 1683. C. m. e. p. 452. To prevent and cure ſpiritual Pride. *Bod. Pub. L.* Camb.
   Heb. ii. 15. 4° 1690. C. m. e. p. 64. From what Fear of Death are the Children of God delivered by Chriſt, and by what means doth he deliver them from it? *Bod. Pub. L.* Camb.
MAYO Richard,   V. of Great Kimbel, Bucks, afterwards Miniſter of St. Thomas's Hoſpital, Southwark.
   Acts xx. 32. 12° 1707. Farewel.
   2 Cor. v. 1. 4° 1708. Fun. of Lady Diana Aſhurſh. *Bod. Pub. L.* C.
MAYO Richard, DD. R. of St. Michael's, Crooked Lane and Chap. to Lady Torrington.
   Micah vi. 4. 8° 1723. b. Lord Mayor. Anniv. of Queen Elizabeth's Acceſſion.
   Heb iv. 14. 4° 1724. Conſ. of Bp. Clavering. *Or.* Oxon. *Br. M.*
[MAYO William]
* Prov. xxix. 1. 12° 1700. Ref. of Manners.
MAYS Chriſtopher, M. A. of King's Coll. Camb.
   2 Sam. xxii. 48. 8° 1746. *Camb.* Th. after Rebellion.

MEAD

OF AUTHORS, &c.   231

MEAD Henry,   Afternoon Preacher at Trin. Church in the Minories, London.
   * Phil. ii. 6-8. 8° 1780. Christ both God and Man.
MEAD Matthew,   Pastor of a Church of Christ at Stepney—of Sepulchre's, London, before the Ejection. 1662.
   Ephes. v. 15, 16. 4° 1660. Trin. Camb.
   1 Cor. i. 3. 4° 1662. Farew. s. The Pastor's Valediction.
   * Acts xxvi. 28. 8° 1666. 7 s. The almost Christian. Brit. M.
   * Lam. iii. 27. 8° 1683. Good of early Obedience.
   * Ezek. x. 13. 4° 1689. Vision of the Wheels. Ch. Ch. Oxon.
   Job xxxiii. 23, 24. 4° 1691. Fun. of Tho. Rosewell. Sion.
   Rom. viii. 11. 4° 1698. Fun. of Rev. Timothy Cruso.
   * Luke i. 26, 27. 8° 1740. V. Disc. on conj. Duty. V. 1. p. 123.
MEAD Norman, M. A. Lect. of St. Vedast Foster Lane, Preb. of Linc. and Chaplain to the Lord Mayor.
   Isai. vii. 5-7. 4° 1745. Nov. 5. b. Lord Mayor.
   Exod. xviii. 21. 4° 1746. Sept. 29. Elect. Lord Mayor.
   2 Chron. xx. 27, 28. 4° 1746. Th. b. Ld Mayor, after Rebell.
MEADES William,   R. of Rampton, Cambridgeshire.
   1 Cor. x. 11. 4° 1750. b. Lord Mayor. Fast. for Fire of Lond.
MEADOWCOURT Richard, M. A. Fell. of Mert. Coll. Oxon. and Preb. of Worcester.
   1 Tim. i. 5. 8° 1721. The Duty of Preachers explained &c. Wadh. Oxon. Queen's. Camb. Eton.
   Acts vi. 9-11. 8° 1722. The sinful Causes, and fatal Effects of the practice of Calumny and Defamation in religious Controversies. Wadh. Worc. Oxon. Queen's. Camb.
   * Heb. xiii. 3. 8° 1753. Worcester-Infirmary.
   Ps. lxxvi. 19. 4° 1723. The Ground and Rule of interpreting &c. extraordinary Events. Queen's. Camb.
   John xvii. 17. 8° 1724. Nature of Truth defined &c. Or. Oxon. Queen's. Camb. Brit. M.
   Prov. xxiv. 21. 8° 1726. Nov. 5. At Westminster-Abby. Queen's. Camb. Eton.
   Ps. iv. 4. 8° 1729. b. Ld May. Self-communion recommended.
   Ps. cvi. 34, 35. 8° 1740. Nov. 5. Popery disarmed Queen's. Cam.
   Haggai i. 5. 8° 1744. Fast. The Duty of considering our Ways.
   Ps. x. 1. 8° 1745. Fast. The Causes of our national Dangers and Distresses assigned. Brit. M.
   Ps. cxxix. 1, 2. 8° 1746. Nov. 3. The Rise and Progress and Effects of papal Power.
MEADOWS Samuel
   * Prov. xviii. 10. 8° 1765. Fun.
   * Prov. xxiv. 30-32. 8° 1768. Warning to Sluggards.
MEDCALF Augustine, M. A. Minister of Berwick, Sussex, and Preb. of Chichester.
   Phil. iv. 4 24° 1679
MEDE Joseph, B. D. Fell. of Ch. Coll. Camb.
   His Works fo. 1672. Bod. Oriel. Oxon. King's. Queen's. Cl. H. Camb. Sion.   M'FAR-

M'FARLAN *John*, DD. of Canongate.
  * Rom. xii. 10. 12° 1779. 2 f. On kind Affections. V. Scotch Pr. V. 3. p. 95.
[M'GEORGE William]
  * Serm. in 8° 1729.
MEDLEY *Samuel*
  * Prov. iii. 14. 8° 1778. The fpiritual Merchant defcribed, and the Gain of true Godlinefs proved.
MEGGOT Richard, DD. Dean of Winchefter and Chapl. in Ord.
  John v. 14. 4° 1662. May 29. The new cured Cripple's Caveat.
  Job xiv. 14. 4° 1663. Fun. of Dean Hardy. *Brit. M.*
  Tit i. 16. 4° 1675. b. King. *Bod. Univ.* Oxon. *Sion.*
  Ecclef. iii. (1. or) 21. 4° 1683. Lent. *C.C.C.* Oxon. *Eton. Sion.*
  * Pf. xi. 3. 4° 1674. *Queen's.* Oxon.
  * Gen ii. 28. 12° 1740. V. Difc. on conj. Duty. V. 2. p. 541.
  10 Serm. in 8° 1696. On feveral Occafions. *Ch. Ch. Queen's. Or. Bal.* Oxon. *Pub. L.* Camb. *Dr. W's L.* London.
MELDRUM George
  * Pf. cxxxvii. 5,6. 4° 1690.
MELVIL Thomas, M. A.
  Zach. viii. 17. 8° 1719. Affize.
MENZIES John.   Profeffor of Divinity in Aberdeen.
  Pf. xc. 12. 4° 1681. *Edinburgh.* Fun.
MERITON Henry,   R. of Oxborough, Norfolk.
  1 Sam. x. 24. 4° 1696. Coron. April 11. *Ch. Ch.* Oxon. *Sion.*
MERITON John, DD. R. of St. Michael's, Cornhill, London.
  Ecclef. x. 20. 4° 1660. Jan. 30. Curfe not the King. *Trin.* Cam.
  Jofh. i. vii. 4° 1673. b. Artillery Co. Religio Militis.
  * Phil. ii. 8   4° 1676. in. e. G. p. 211. Chrift's Humiliation.
MERITON John, M. A. V. of St. Ives, Huntingdon, and R. of St. Mary Bothaw, Lond.
  Rom. xiii. 5. 4° 1670. Affize. The Obligation of a good Confcience to civil Obedience. *Bad.*
  Matt. iii. 8,9. 4° 1677. b. King.
MERITON Thomas,   R. of St. Nicholas, Coleabby. London.
  Job xiv. 12. 4° 1690. Fun. of Sir Chrift. Lethieullier. *Brit. M.*
MERREL Zachary
  * Mal. iii. 16. 12° 1709. Ref. of Manners.
MERRICK James, M. A. of Trin Coll. Oxon.
  Prov. ix. 1–6. 4° 1744. *Oxon* Differtation.
MERRICK M. Marfhal, L.L.B. Lect. of St. Ann's, Weftminfter, and Chapl. to the Earl of Verney.
  * John xv. 5. 4° 1753. The Parable of the Vineyard—and Chrift the true Vine.
  * Matt. xix. 9. 4° 1754. 2 f. Marriage, a divine Inftitution.
  * Jerem. xiv. 12. 4° 1761. Faft. A national Faft, a national Mockery of God, without Amendment in Principle and Pract.
MICHEL Humph. M. A. R. of St. Giles's at Blafton, Leicefter.
  Ifai. xlix. 23. 4° 1702. Coron. *Bod.*

Rom.

Rom. xiii. 5. 4° 1702. 2 f. St. Paul's triumphant Confutation of all the late Jacobitical Schifm and Sedition. *Bod.*
2 Sam. i. 14. 4° 1702. 2 f. Jan. 30. *Bod.*

MICHELL, Ch.
   Heb. xiii. 17.   Vif.

MICHELL Gilbert, M. A. R. of Breadfall near Derby.
   Tit. ii. 11, 12. 8° 1731. The Defign of publifhing the Gofpel.
   20 Difc. in 8° 1737. The Laws and Liberties of the Gofp. &c.

MICKLEBOURGH John, B.D. Minifter of St. Andrew the Great, Camb.
   * 1 Theff. iii. 10. 8° 1751. For a general Work-houfe. *Queen's.* Camb. *Brit. M.*

MIDDLETON Erafmus,   Lect. at St. Bennet's Grace Church-ftreet, London.
   * Ephef. ii. 8. 8° 1775. Fun. of Tho. Jackfon. Grace triumphant.

MIDDLETON John, DD. of Mert. Coll. Oxon. Lect. of St. Bride's, and R. of St. Peter's Cornhill, London.
   Pf. cvi. 48. 4° 1730. May 29. b. Lord Mayor. The Duty and Excellence of Thankfgiving. *Worc. Oxon. Queen's.* Camb.
   Prov. xxix. 2. 4° 1732. Elect. of Lord Mayor. A good Magiftrate, a public Blefling. *Worc. Oxon. Brit. M.*

MIDDLETON P
   * Gen. xxii. 12. 8° 1740. Cafe of Abraham's being commanded by God to offer up his Son Ifaac. *Worc. Oxon.*

MILBOURNE Luke, M. A. R. of St. Ethelberg and Lect. of St. Leonard Shoreditch, London.
   Acts xxv. 8. 4° 1682. Jan. 30. The Originals of Rebellion—or the Ends of Separation. *Sion.*
   Ezra iv. 1–5. 4° 1683. Th. Sept. 9. Samaratanifm revived. *Trin. St. John's.* Camb.
   1 Cor. xiii. 3. 4° 1698. b. Lord Mayor. A falfe Faith not juftified by Care of the poor. *St. John's.* Camb. *Sion.*
   Phil. iv. 9. 4° 1699. Farewel.
   Judges v. 12. 4° 1704. Th. Sept. 7. Great Britain's Acclamation to her Deborah.
   Zech. i. 5. 4° 1704. Fun. of Rev. Mr. Copping. The Mortality of God's Prophets; and what good Chriftians ought to learn from it.
   1 Cor. xv. 19. 4° 1704. Fun. of Dr. Symfon. The Hope of a future Life, the fole Foundation of a Chriftian's Happinefs. *St. John's.* Camb. *Sion.*
   1 Pet. ii. 17. 4° 1704. County Feaft. Chriftian good Fellowfhip.
   Rom. xiii. 1. 8° 1707. Jan. 30. The People, not the Original of civil Power. *Hert. Oxon. Trin.* Camb. *Sion. Eton.*
   Ifai. xiv. 20, 21. 8° 1708. Jan. 30. *Trin. St. John's.* Cam. *Brit. M.*
   Acts xxv. 10, 11. 8° 1709. Debtor and Creditor made eafy. *St. John's.* Camb.
   Rom. xiii. 2. 8° 1710. Jan. 30. *Linc. Oxon.*
   1 Sam. xxiv. 13. 8° 1711. Jan. 30. *Linc. Oxon.*

Gen. xlix. 5–7. 8° 1712. Jan. 30.
Rom. xiii. 3. 8° 1713. Jan. 30. b. Lord Mayor. Of Charity.
Matt xxii. 21. 8° 1712. May 29.
2 Chron. xxix. 30. 8° 1713. b. Co. of Parish Clerks. Psalmody recommended. *Eton.*
Isai. lvii. 19–21. 4° 1713. Th. for Peace. Peace the Gift of God. *Sion.*
2 Sam. i. 16. 8° 1714. Jan. 30. *St. John's.* Camb.
Heb. xi. 38. 8° 1714. Royal Fun.
Prov. xxiv. 21, 22. 8° 1715. Jan 30. *St. John's.* Camb. *Sion.*
Matt. xxv. 46. 8° 1715. *Lond.* Conc duæ ad Cl. *Lond.* De Æternitate Pænarum gehennalium.
2 Cor. i. 12. 8° 1715. Conc. ad Cler.
John xviii. 36. 8° 1716. Jan. 30.
Isai. i. 26. 4° 1716. May 29.
Rom. iii. 8. 8° 1717. Jan. 30.
1 Pet. ii. 15. 8° 1719. Jan. 30.
Nehem. ix. 33. 8° 1720. Jan. 30.

MILES Henry
 * Heb. xiii. 16. 8° 1738. b. Society for the Relief of Widows of dissenting Ministers. *Pub. L.* Camb.

MILL John, DD. Principal of Edmond-Hall, Oxon. and Chaplain in Ord.
 Luke i. 28. 4° 1676. On the Feast of the blessed Virgin. *Univ. Queen's.* Oxon. *Sion.*

MILLECHAMP Richard, M. A. R. of Rudford, Glouceſt. and V. of great Marlow, Bucks.
 * 1 Cor. xvi. 13. 8° 1703.
 1 Tim. i. 19. 4° 1705. Aſſize. *Eton.*
 James v. 9. 4° 1708. Aſſize. The Unreaſonableneſs and Danger of grudging.
 Eſther ix. 21. 4° 1711. Fun. of Mr. James Harman.

MILLER James, of Wadh. Oxon.
 22 Serm. in 8° 1749. On various Subjects. *Wadh.* Oxon.

MILLES Jeremiah, DD. Dean of Exon.
 Luke v. 31. 8°.1748. b. Gov. of *Devon* and *Exon* Hoſp. *Eton. Brit. M.*

MILLES Thomas, Bp. of Waterford.
 1 Pet. iiit 14. 8° 1701. Oxon. Jan. 30. *Bod. Ch. Ch. Magd. Jeſ. Oxon. Pub. L. St. John's.* Camb.
 Jude 3. 4° 1707. Oxon. Coram Acad. Ox. *Ch. Ch. C.C.C. Jeſ.* Oxon. *Pub. L.* Camb.

MILLS Benjamin
 2 Pet. i. 13, 14. 8° 1733.
 – – – – – 1741. Nov. 5.

MILLS Thomas, B. A. late of Pemb. Coll. Oxon.
 * Matt. xxv. 40. 8° 1781. In behalf of the Sufferers by the late Fire in the Strand.

MILLS William, M. A.
 * Rev. ii. 5. 8° 1741. Fun. of Rev. Mr. *John Gaſpine.*

MILNE Colin, L.L.D. R. of North Chapel, Suſſex, Lecturer of St.
Paul's Deptford, and Preacher at the Lying Inn Hoſp. Lond.
* Rom. xiv. 7. 8° 1778. b. Humane Society.
* 9 Serm. in 8° 1780.
MILNER John, DD. Miniſter of the Goſpel at Peckham, Surrey.
2 Cor. i. 24. 8° 1739. Ord.   The Principles of
religious Liberty aſſerted, and the Abuſe of them diſclaimed.
* Eccleſ. iii. 2. 8° 1743. Ch. New Year's-day. *Brit. M.*
Pſ. cv. 42. 8° 1745. Rebellion.
* Luke xvii. 17, 18. 8° 1746. Th.
* Phil. ii. 20. 8° 1756. Ord.   The paſtoral Care.
Queen's. Camb.
* Acts xx. 25. 8° 1746. Fun.
* Pſ. xxvi. 8–10. 8° 1748. Faſt. 2 ſ.
* Matt. xviii. 20. 8° 1748. Chriſt's Promiſe to his Church.
Job xiv. 2. 8° 1749. Fun.   The fading Flowers of life.
* Rev. xiv. 13. 8° 1749. Fun. of Dr. *Iſaac Watts. Queen's.* Cam.
Luke vii. 22, 23. 8° 1750. 3 ſ. On the Honour and Happineſs of
the poor.
2 Tim. iv. 7, 8. 8° 1750. Fun. of Rev. Mr. *Thomas Coad.*
Iſai. xxvi. 20, 21. 8° 1750. On the Earthquake.
* Serm. in 12° 1751.
* 1 Tim. iv. 16. 8° 1755. Ord.   *Queen's.* Camb.
* Matt. xvi. 3. 8° 1757. Faſt.
MILNER William, M. A. V. of Shephall, Herts, and Preb. of York.
Rev. xiv. 13. 4° 1698. Fun. of Mrs. Eliz. Fiſher. *St. John's.*
Camb. *Brit. M.*
MILNER William, M. A. Chapl. to the Bp. of Cheſter.
2 Cor. vi. 3. 8° 1708. Conſ of Bp. Dawes. *Univ. Magd. Hert.*
Oxon. *Queen's. St. John's. Cl. H.* Camb. *Sion.*
MILWARD John, M. A. Fell. of C. C. C. Oxon.
Matt. xxii. 39. 4° 1676. ſ. m. e. C. p. 41. How ought we to
love our Neighbour as ourſelves. *Bod.*
* Rom. xii. 21. 4° 1683. C. m. e. p. 553. To do our Duty.
MILWAY Thomas
Zach. i. 5, 6. 4° 1692. Fun. of Francis Holcroft. *Bod. Brit. M.*
MILWAY Thomas
* Phil. iii. 9. 8° 1751. The Righteouſneſs of Faith explained.
* - - - - 1761.
MITCHELL Andrew, M. A. Miniſter of the Goſpel at Muirkirk
* - - - - 1765.
MITCHELL Jonathan
Some Serm. in 4° 1677. *Bod. Pub. L.* Camb.
MITCHELL John, M. A.
* - - - - 1745. Th.
MITCALFE Phil. P. of the Society of Jeſus.
* Matt. viii. 26. 4° 1688. Th. New Caſtle upon Tyne. *Pub. L. C.*
MOGRIDGE Anthony, B. A. V. of Himbleton, Worceſter.
* Matt. xxiii. 1–3. 8° 1766. The Rules of Behaviour which Xt
has

has commanded his Disciples to observe, when the Practice of the chief Pastors and Guides in the Church of God is manifestly contrary to what they preach.

MOIR Henry
 * Disc. in 12° 1759.
MOIR John
 * 7 Disc. in 12° 1776. On practical Subjects. *Bod. Sion.*
MOISES Edward, R. of Kegworth, Nottinghamsh.
 Isai. xxxii. 17. 8° 1736. Assize.
MOLE Thomas, Minister at Uxbridge Middlesex.
 * Pf. xi. 7. 1732. Foundation of Virtue. *Brit. M.*
 * Jonah iii. 8, 9. 8° 1745. Rebellion.
 * - - - - 1776. Repentance.
 * - - - - 1778.
MONCRIEF Alexander
 * Disc. in 1757.
MONOUX Lewis, M. A. R. of Sanby, Bedfordsh.
 John iv. 48. 8° 1733. Vis. Christianity proved and supported by a sufficient Evidence &c. *Queen's.* Camb.
 Pf ci. 2. 8° 1745. Vis. Understanding in the way of Godliness.
 Luke ii. 52. 4° 1751. School Feast. *All S.* Oxon.
MONRO Alexander, DD. Principal of the Coll. of Edinburgh.
 13 Serm in 4° 1693. On several Occasions. *Bod. C.C.C. New C. Bal. Pub. L.* Camb. *Sion. Dr. W's. L.* London.
MONTGOMERY J Chapl. to the 10th. Infantry.
 * Ezek. xxxiii. 11. 8° 1780. Anniv. of Queen Elizabeth's Release from the Tower.
MOODY Samuel, DD. R. of Dudinghurst. Essex.
 Jonah iii. 10. 8° 1723. Th. f.
 Pf. xxxv. 11, 12. 4° 1733. Jan 30. b. Lord Mayor. *Queen's.* C.
 Gen. xviii 25. 4° 1736. Assize. The impartial Justice of the divine Administration.
 Matt. v. 13. 8° 1749. *Cant.* Conc. Acad.
MOOR John, Curate of Brislington, Somersetsh.
 * Sev. serm. in 12° 1696. Sin of Corah, Dathan and Abiram.
MOOR John, Bp. of Bangor.
 * 1 Pet. ii. 17. 4° 1777. Jan. 30. b. Lords.
 * 2 Chron. xv. 2. 4° 1781. Fast. b. Lords.
MOORE Benjamin, M. A.
 * 2 Kings ii. 12. 8° 17 Fun.
MOORE George, M. A. Canon Residentiary of Exon.
 * Matt. v. 48. 4° 1770. b. Gov. of *Devon* and *Exon* Hosp.
MOORE Henry
 * Pf. xviii. 50. 8° 1746. Th.
MOORE Jean
 * Rev. xiv. 13. 12° 1782.
MOORE John, Bp. of Ely.
 * Serm. in 2 Vol. 8° 1715.

MOORE Philip, R. of Kirk-Brides.
* Pf. cxii. 6. 17 Fun. of Bp. Wilſon. V. the Bp's works. 4° 1781. Vol. 2.
(MOORE Richard]
‡ * 2 Cor. iv. 7.
‡ * Heb. ii. 4. } 8° 1675. Fun. of T. Hall. *Brit. M.*
MOORE Thomas
Heb. xiii. 4. 4° 1677. Fornication condemned.
MORE Henry, DD. Fell. of Chriſt's Coll. Camb. and Preb. of Glouceſter.
Diſc. in 8° 1692. On ſeveral Texts of Scripture. *Bod. Ch. Ch. Or. Worc.* Oxon. *Pub. L.* Camb.
MORELL Thomas, DD. Fell. of King's Coll. Camb. R. of Buckland, Herts.
Pſ. cxix. 96. 8° 1737. Royal Fun. *All S.* Oxon.
1 Kings viii. 44, 45. 8° 1739. Faſt. Jan. 9. *All S.* Oxon.
Matt. ii. 1, 2. 8° 1742. Epiphany, and Dr. Snape's Character. *Queen's.* Camb.
Pſ. cvii. 31, 32. 8° 1747. Muſick at *Worceſter.* The Uſe and Importance of Muſick in the Sacrifice of Thankſgiving *Eton.*
* Iſai. xxxv. 5, 6. 4° 1753. Spitt. W. The charitable Diſpoſition of the preſent Age.
* Ruth ii. 20. 4° 1772. b. the Sons of the Clergy.
* Matt. xviii. 7. 4° 1774. On Trin. At Lady Moyer's Lect. *Bod.*
MORER Thomas, B. D. R. of St. Ann's Alderſgate, and Lect. of St. Lawrence-Jewry, London.
Iſai. i. 26. 4° 1699. May 29. b. Lord Mayor. *Ch. Ch.* Oxon.
Luke i. 74, 75. 4° 1699. Nov. 5. b. Lord Mayor.
9 Serm. in 8° 1708. On ſev. Occaſions. *Pub. L.* Camb.
15 Serm. in 8° 1717. On ſev. Occaſions. *Magd.* Oxon.
MORES Edward, M. A. R- of Tunſtall, Kent.
* Funeral Entertainments in 12° 1702.
Heb. xi. 4. 8° 1725. Fun.
MORGAN Cæſar, M. A. Minor Canon of Ely, and late Fell. of Chriſt's Coll. Camb.
* Judges v. 23. 4° 1708. The Duty of Patriotiſm vindicated and enforced.
* Iſai. lviii. 3. 4° 1781. Faſt.
MORGAN John, Lect. of the united Pariſhes of St. Edmond the King, and St. Nicholas Acons, London.
Pſ. cxxxiii. 1. 8° 1723.
1 Pet. ii. 21. 8° 1728. Welch-Feaſt.
MORGAN Sutton, of St. Margaret's Weſtminſter.
Gal vi. 10. 8° 1719. Welch-Feaſt. The Duty of doing good.
[MORICE William, Eſq;]
* Diſc. in fo. 1660. On the Lord's Supper.
MORLEY George, Bp. of Wincheſter.
Prov. xxviii. 2. 4° 1661. Coron. April 23. *Magd. C. C. C. Bal. Queen's. Worc.* Oxon. *Pub. L. Trin. St. John's.* Camb.
1 Cor. xiv. 33. 4° 1683. Nov. 5. *Sien.*

MORRICE John, of Lincoln Coll. Oxon. and Cur. of Lam-
bourn, Wilts.
2 Cor. xiii. 11. 8° 1712. Farewel.
MORRICE John. DD. Lect. of St. Bartholomew Exchange, Lond.
Rom. xiii. 1, 2. 4° 1740. Accession. b. Lord Mayor.
MORRICE Thomas
Pf. cix. 59. 8° 1740.
MORRIS Joseph, Minister of the Gospel in London.
Heb. xiii. 7. 8° 1728. Fun. of Rev. *Thomas Kirby*.
16 Sermons in 8° 1743. On several Subjects. *Queen's*. Camb.
Dr. *W's. L.* Lond. *Brit. M.*
* 20 (Posth.) Serm. in 8° 1757. On various Subjects
MORRIS Thomas, M. A. Chapl. to Earl of Orrery.
Rev. xiv. 13. 4° 1681. Fun. of Earl of Orrery.
MORSE Robert, M. A. R. of Willersy, Master of the Free-School.
at Campden, Gloucesterf.
1 Theff. v. 17–20. 4° 1692. Vis. *Magd*. Oxon.
MORTON Thomas, DD. R. of Baffingham, Lincolnf.
‡ * Matt. xxvii. 25. 4° 1754. *Linc.* The inexcusable Behaviour
of the Jews exemplified, and the divine Authority of Moses
and Christ asserted.
MORUS Monsieur
Isai. xl. 6–8. 4° 1694. Royal Fun. Translated by Dan la Fite.
Trin. Camb.
MOSELEY John, M. A.
John xv. 14. 8° 1750. *Gloucester*. b. Free-masons.
MOSELEY Richard, M. A. R. of St. Saviour's, and of Wiggin-
ton, Yorkshire.
Rom. xii. 18. 8° 1735. *York*. Assize.
MOSS Charles, Bp. of Bath and Wells.
Matt. xxv. 40. 4° 1750. Spitt. T. *All S.* Oxon *Brit. M.*
* Isai. xxvi. 9. 4° 1756. Fast. Earthquake. *All S. Brit. M.* Ox.
* 1 Theff iv. 9. 8° 1769. *Salisbury*-Infirmary.
* James iv. 1. 4° 1769. Jan. 30. b. Lords.
* Rom. xi. 25, 26. 4° 1776. Prop. of Gospel.
MOSS Robert, DD. Dean of Ely, and Preacher at Grays Inn, Lond.
Serm. and Disc. in 4 Vol. 8° 1732. On practical Subjects. *Bod.*
Worc. Oxon. *Pub. L.* Camb. *Brit. M.*
Serm. and Disc. in 8° Vol. 5. 1733. Vol. 6. and 7. 1737. Vol.
8. 1738. *Bod. Bal New C. Worc.* Oxon. *Trin.* Camb. *Sion*.
* Eccles. ix. 11. 17 Th. f.
MOSS Thomas, B. A. Minister of Brierley-Hill, Staffordf.
* Pf. cxvi. 12. 4° 1778. Ch. f.
* Phil. iv. 5. 4° 1779. Assixe. *Worcester*. The Importance and
Necessity of Christian Moderation.
MOSSOM Robert, Bp. of London-derry.
Pf. lxxv. 1. 4° 1660. Th.
Ezek. xvii. 22. 4° 1660. Fun.
Preacher's Trippartite pt. 3. fo. 1685. *Sion.*

MOTTE

MOTTE de la Francis, A Convert from the Carmelites.
 Rom. v. 20. 4° 1675. Recantation f. The Abominations of the Church of Rome. *Bod. St. John's.* Camb. *Sion.*
MOTTERSHEAD *Joseph*, of Manchester.
 * John iii. 2. 8° 1745. Ord.
 * Discourses in 12° 1759.
MOULD Bernard, M. A. Fell. of Wadh. Coll. Oxon. and Minister to the English Factory at Smyrna.
 Isai. xxxiv. xvi. 8° 1717. 3 f. b. Levant Co, The Christian's Altar of Prayer and Praise. *Brit. M.*
 Phil. i. 9–11. 4° 17:7. Farewel.
 2 Sam. xxiv. 25. 4° 1725. 3 f. After the Plague.
MOULIN du Peter, DD. Canon of Cant. and Chaplain in Ord.
 Dan. xii. 2, 3. 4° 1669. Fun. of Lady Fordwich. *Univ. Linc.* Oxon. *Queen's.* Camb.
 Phil. i. 21. 4° 1672. Fun. of Dr. Tho. Turner, Dean of Canterbury. *Ch. Ch. C.C.C.* Oxon *St. John's.* Camb. *Sion.*
 Rev. xviii. 4, 5. 4° 1674. 2 f. Papal Tyranny. *Bod. Univ.* Oxon.
 Rom. i. 16. - 16 - -
 10 Occasional Serm. in 8° 1684. *Queen's. Magd.* Oxon.
MOXON Mordecai
 Matt. v. 28. 12° 1708. Ag. Adultery. *Linc.* Oxon. V. Disc. on conj. Duty. Vol. 1. p. 57.
MUDGE Zechary; Preb. of Exon, and V. of St. Andrew's, Plymouth, Devon.
 11 Sermons in 8° 1739 On different Subjects. *Worc.* Oxon.
 2 Cor. x. 8. 4° 1748. Vis. The Nature and Extent of Church Authority. *Queen's.* Camb.
MUIR *George*, M. A. of Paisley, Scotland.
 * Matt. viii. 11. 8° 1766. Prop. of Christian Knowledge.
 ‡ * Luke viii 5. 12° 1769. Parable of the Sower.
MULES Walter, V. of Nymet-Episcopi, Devon.
 Jude 3. 8° 1710. Assize. *Exon. Linc.* Oxon.
MULSO John, M A. late R. of Witney, Oxon.
 2 Cor. ix. 5. 8° 1751. Subscription for rebuilding a Church.
MUNTON Anthony, M. A. Minister of New Castle upon Tyne.
 * 22 Serm. in 8° 1756. *Univ.* Oxon.
MURDIN Cornelius, M. A. Curate of All-Hallows, Barking, and Lect. of St. Mary at Hill, London.
 Prov. xiv. 34. 4° 1752. Jan. 30. b. Lord Mayor.
 * - - - - 4° 1779. 3 f. Fast.
MURDOCK John, V. of South Halsted, Essex.
 Col. iii. 18, 19. 4° 1738. Wedding f.
MURRAY *James*, of Newcastle.
 * Sermons to Asses in 12° 1771.
 * Sermons to Doctors in Divinity. 12° 1771.
 * New Serm. to Asses in 8° 1772.
 * Lectures in 2 Vol. 8° 1777. On the most remarkable Characters and Transactions recorded in the book of Genesis.

* Sermons to Minifters of State in 8° 1781.
MUSCUTT James, M. A. late R. of little Straughton, Bedfordfi and Fell. of C. C. C. Oxon.
   * 12 Serm. in 8° 1760. On feveral Subjects. *C.C.C. AllS.* Ox.
MUSGRAVE William
   * Tit. iii. 1. 4° 1766. Vif.
MUTTER Thomas,   V. D. M. of Dumfries.
   * John i. 14. 12° 1776. The Character of Chrift. V. Scotch Pr. V. 2. p. 21.
MYNORS Willoughby, M. A.
   Pf. lxxiii. 12, 13. 8° 1716. Comfort under Affliction.
   Ifai xxx. 10. 8° 1716. True Loyalty. *Queen's.* Camb. *Sion.*
   Ezra ix. 13, 14. 8° 1717. May 29.
MYONNETT John, DD. R. of Swafield, Lincoln, and Weft-Tilbury, Effex.
   Rev. xiv. 13. 8° 1725. Fun. of his Mother. *Eton.*
   Gal. v. 13. 8° 1734. Affize. The Nature and Grounds of civil Liberty.
   1 Theff. v. 21. 8° 1736. Nov. 5. b. Lord Mayor. *Brit. M.*
   * - - - - 1766.

N.   G.
   * Rom. viii. 38, 39. 4° 1663. V. Coll. of Farew. f.
N.   J.   M. A.
   - - - - 1706. Th. at Sea for Succefs. June 27.
N.   T.
   John v. 24. 4° 1686. Fun. of Mr. Bond.
NADEN Thomas, M. A.
   1 Cor. xii. 25. 8° 1712. To reduce Diffenters. *Ch. Ch.* Oxon.
[NAILOR J   ]
   * Matt. vii. 5. 8° 1662. Ref. of Manners.
NAILOUR William
   2 Sam. iii. 38. 4° 1675. Commem. for the Hon. Charles Cavendifh flain 1643. *Bod. Magd. Queen's.* Oxon. *Pub. L. Trin. St. John's.* Camb. *Sion.*
NAISH James, M. A. late of Jef. Coll. Oxon. R. of Kelham, Nottinghamf.
   Rev. xiv. 13. 4° 1723. *Nottingham.* Fun. of Lord Lexington.
NAISH Thomas, Sub-Dean of Sarum.
   Rev. xix. 1. 4° 1700. Mufick. *Trin. St. John's.* Camb.
   Rev. xix. 3. 4° 1726. Mufick.
   Matt. vi. 10. 4° 1727. Mufick.
   Acts vii. 26. 4° 1729.
NALSON Valentine, M. A. Preb. of Ripon, Yorkf.
   20 Serm. in 8° 1724. and 1737. On feveral Subjects.
NALTON *James,*   Minifter of St. Leonard's Fofter Lane, Lond.
   2 Cor. iv. 17. 8° 1661. Fun.
   * John vi 35. 8° 1664.
   20 Sermi. in 8° 1677. Upon fev. Texts. *Trin.* Camb.

NANFAN

OF AUTHORS, '&c. 241

NANFAN Bridges, Esq;
   Ecclef. xii. 1. 8° 1680. Essays. *Sion.*
   2 Cor. iv. 17. 8° 16.
NASMITH R.
   Gen. vi. 3. 8° 1725.
NATION William
   * Tit. ii. 11, 12. 8° 1731. *Exon.* b. Diffent. Minif. *Queen's.* C.
NAYLOR Quintus,   R. of Lyminge, Kent, Cur. of St. Mary
   Aldermary, and Chapl. to Lady Abergavenny.
   Luke ix. 55, 56. 8° 1724. Nov. 5. The Spirit and Practices of
   the Papifts &c. *Brit. M.*
NEALE *Daniel,* M. A. Minifter of the Gofpel in Jewin-ftreet, Lond.
   * Ezek. ix. 4. 8° 1721. Solemn Prayer ag. Plague. *Queen's.* Cum.
   * Pf. xciv. 16. 8° 1722. Ref. of Manners. *Queen's.* Camb.
   Job xxix. 12, 13. 8° 1723. Ch. Sch. On New Year's day.
   * Matt. xxv. 21. 8° 1726. Fun. of Rev. *Matt. Clarke. Queen's.* C.
   * 1 Theff. iv. 13, 14. 8° 1727. Fun. of Mrs. Phillibrowne.
   Queen's. Camb.
   Matt. xvi. 18, 19. 8° 1735. The Supremacy of St. Peter and his
   Succeffors. V. Difc. V. 1. Ag. Popery. *Braz. N. Ox. Brit. M.*
   * Dan. iv. 9. V. 1. p. 117.
   * Rom. vii. 22. V. 1. 418. Vital Religion.
   * Acts iii. 19. V. 1. 438. Confeffion of Sin.
   *John xiii. 34, 35. V. 2. 258. Lov. our Neighbour.   8° 1757. v. Berry-
   *Gal. iv. 4, 5. V. 1. 230. Incarnation of Xt.   ftreet Sermons.
   * 1 Cor. xi. 23-26. V. 2. 162. Sacrament.
   *2 Tim. iii. 16. V. 1. 21. Antiq. & Proof of Script.
   *———— i. 9. V. 1. 332. Effectual Calling &c.
NEAST Thomas, M. A. R. of St. Stephen's Coleman-ftreet, Lond.
   Ephef. v. 24. 4° 1677. m. e. C. p. 158. The Characters of the
   Love of Chrift &c.
   Ezek. ix. 4. 8° 1721. Faft. Ag. the Plague.
NEEDHAM John,[a] M. A. R. of Bedhampton, Hants.
   1 Cor. iii. 4. 8° 1710. 2 f. Vif. *Bod. Linc. Wroc.* Oxon. *Sion.*
[NEEDHAM John[a]]
   * Pf. cxxii. 8, 9. 8° 1726. Fun.
   * Pf. cvi. 10-13. 8° 1753. Nov. 5.
NEEDHAM Peter, B. D. Fell. of St. John's Coll. Camb. R.
   Conington. Camb.
   Luke xiv. 23. 8° 1716. *Camb.* On St. Paul's-day. *Queen'*
Cl. H. Camb. *Brit. M.*
NEEDHAM Robert, M. A. late Fell. of Queen's Coll. Camb.
   6 Serm. in 8° 1679. *Camb. Bod. All S. Magd. Pemb. Ox. Pub. L.*
   Queen's. Camb. *Dr. Ws's. L.* London.
NEEDHAM William, DD. R. of Alresford Hants, and one of the
   Proctors for the Diocefe of Winton,
   Pf. cv. 4-6. 4° 1702. Th. b. Convocation. *Ch. Ch. Magd. Jef.*
   Oxon. *Queen's. St. John's.* Camb. *Sion.*

                   a *Q.* The fame.

Vol. II.   H h   *NEEDLER*

NEEDLER Benjamin, L.L.B. Fell. of St. John's Coll. Oxon. and Minister of Margaret Moses, Friday-street before the Ejection. 1662.
    Matt. iv. 10. 4° 1675. m.e.P. p.458. God not to be worshipped as represented by an Image.
    1 John v. 7. 4° 1676. m.e.G. Vol. II. p.63. The Trinity proved by Scripture. *Bod.*
    Matt. v. 29,30. 4° 1677. m.e.C. p.41. How may beloved Lusts be discovered and mortified.
NEGUS Thomas, DD. R. of St. Mary Rotherhithe, London.
    * 1 Tim. i. 5. 4° 1761. Ann. meeting Charity School. *Braz. N.* Oxon. *Cl. H.* Camb.
    * 1 Tim. iv. 16. 8° 1764. Vis. St. Paul's Charge to Timothy.
NELME John, M.A. of Magd. Hall, Oxon.
    Ps. cxviii. 21–26. 4° 1660.
NELSON G.   R. of Oakley, Suffolk.
    Prov. xxiii. 23. 8° 17   Happiness of Man in this life.
NELSON Hen.   R. of Hunsdon, and V. of Stansted Abbots, Herts.
    Lev. xix. 12. b° 1704. Assize.
    Ephes. iv. 2, 3. 8° 1707. School-Feast. Charity and Unity. *Univ.* Oxon. *Trin. Queen's. St. John's.* Camb. *Sion.*
NESBITT John, Minister of the Gospel, London.
    Ps. cxix. 9. 8° 1713. To young Persons.
    Job ix. 12. 8° 1714. Fun. of Mr. *Russel.*
    Heb. xiii. 7. 8° 1719. Fun.
NEST
    * Ephes. vi. 24. 4° 1677. m.e.C. p.158. What are the Characters of a Soul's sincere Love to Christ? and how that Love to him may be kindled and enflamed.
NETTO Isaac, Arch-Synagogus of the Portuguez-Jews Synagogue.
    * Deut. x. 16. 4° 1756. Fast. for the Earthquake. *Worc.* Oxon.
NEVE Timothy, DD. Arch-Deacon of Huntingdon, R. of Middleton Stoney, and Chapl. of Merton Coll. Oxon.
    Matt. vii. 28, 29. 8° 1747. *Oxon.* Vis. Teaching with Authority. *Queen's.* Camb.
    * Ephes. v. 8. 8° 1759. *Oxon.* Act s. Comparative Blessings of Christianity. *Worc.* Oxon. *Queen's.* Camb.
    * 8 Serm. in 8° 1781. *Oxon.* Preached before the University at Bampton's Lecture.
NEVILLE Robert, B.D. late Fell. of King's Coll. Camb. R. of Ansty, Herts.
    Tit. iii. 10. 4° 1673. Vis. *Bod. Queen's.* Oxon. *St. John's.* Cam.
    Luke xxii. 19. 4° 1678. The Necessity of receiving the Holy Sacrament.
    Heb. ix. 27. 4° 1679. b. Lord Mayor. Future Judgment. *Bod. Queen's.* Camb.
    Prov. xix. 2. 4° 1681. The Excellency, Usefulness, and Necessity of human Learning. *Pub. L.* Camb. *Brit. M.*
    Ephes. i. 4. 4° 1682. The absolute Decree of Election reprobated. *Pub. L.* Camb.   Col.

Col. iii. 2. 4° 1683. The things above proved to be the moſt proper objects of the Mind and Affections. *Pub. L.* Camb.

Heb. iii. 15. 4° 1683. The Nature and Cauſes of Hardneſs of Heart.

1 Pet. iii. 13. 4° 1687. Innocent's day. Goodneſs the beſt protection from the Arreſts of Harms.

NEWCOMB
   Pſ. cv. 8.

NEWCOME
   2 Sam. xix. 14.

NEWCOME Daniel, M. A. R. of Whimple, Devon.
   Acts vii. 39. 8° 1717. *Exon.* Aſſize.
   *Exod. xx. 5, 6. 12° 1728. Aſſize. Againſt Perjury and common Swearing.

NEWCOME Daniel, DD. Dean of Glouceſter.
   Gal. vi. 10. 4. 1735. Spitt. T.

NEWCOME Henry, M. A. R. of Tatten-Hall, Cheſhire.
   1 Pet. iii. 13. 4° 1689. Aſſize. *Bod.*

NEWCOME Henry, M. A. R. of Middleton, Lancaſhire.
   Matt. xxv. 35. 8° 1711. *Warrington.* Anniv. Meet. of the Clergy for the Relief of Widows and Orphans. Some Motives purely Chriſtian to Alms-deeds.
   Tit. ii. 15. 8° 1712 Viſ. *Eton.*

NEWCOME John, DD. Maſter of St. John's Coll. Camb. and R. of Morton, Eſſex.
   1 Theſſ. v. 21. 8° 1720. Ord. The Conduct required in matters of Faith. *New C. Ox. St. John's. C. Sion.*
   2 Pet. i. 19. 8° 1724. *Camb.* The ſure Word of Prophecy. *New C. Oxon. Queen's. St. John's. Cl. H.* Camb.
   Prov. xvii. 14. 4° 1744. *Camb.* Jan. 30. b. Commons. *Queen's.* C.

NEWCOME Peter, M. A. V. of Aldenham, Herts.
   Pſ. xviii. 23. 4° 1686. Of boſom-Sins. *Bal. Ch. Ch.* Oxon.
   Nehem. ix. 17. 4° 1696. Th. April 16.

NEWCOME Peter, M. A. V. of Hackney, Middleſex.
   A catechetical Courſe of Serm. in 2 Vol. 8° 1702. For the whole Year. *Magd. Mert. Pemb.* Oxon. *Queen's.* Camb.
   Eccleſ. vii. 1. 4° 1705. Fun. The Bleſſing of a good Name at Death. *Eton.*
   Matt. xxiv. 12. 8° 1710. Ref. of Manners. *Linc.* Oxon.
   Matt. v. 33. 8° 1715. The Religion of an Oath. *Eton.*
   Heb. ii. 3. 8° 1719. 4 ſ. On Goſpel-Salvation.
   Luke xii. 40. 8° 1737.

NEWCOME Richard, M. A. V. of Hurſley, Hants.
   1 Theſſ. iv. 9. 8° 1728. Aſſize. *Queen's.* Camb.

NEWCOME Richard, Bp. of St. Aſaph.
   *Heb. xii. 5. 4° 1756. Jan. 30. b. Lords.
   *Rom. ix. 26. 4° 1761. Prop. of Goſpel.
   *Gal. vi. 10. 4° 1764. b. Gov. of *Lond.* Hoſp. *Wadh.* Oxon.

NEWCOME William, Bp. of Waterford.
  * Tit. iii. 1. 4° 1767. Anniv Irish Rebellion.
  * John viii. 47. 4° 1769. Nov. 5. b. Lords. Oppofition between Scripture and Popery ftated.
  * Ephef. vi. 4. 4° 1772. Irifh Prot. Schools.
NEWCOMEN Matthew
  * Rev. iii. 3. 4° 1663. V. Coll. of Farew. f. Magd. Camb.
NEWLIN Thomas, B. D. Fell. of Magd. Coll. Oxon. and V. of Beeding, Suffex.
  Dan. xv. 11. 8° 1718. Oxon. Magd. Oxon.
  2 Pet. ii. 19. 8° 1718. Oxon. The Sinner enflaved by falfe Pretences. Bod. Magd Worc. Linc. Oxon.
  18 Serm. in 8° 1720. Oxon. On feveral Occafions. Bod. All S. Magd. Oxon.
  Pf. lxxviii. 50. 8° 1721. Faft. Ag. the Plague. God's gracious Defign in inflicting national Judgments.
  21 Serm. in 8° 1726. and 1728. Oxon. On feveral Occafions. Bod. All S. Magd. Or. Oxon.
  1 Sam. iii. 12, 13. 8° 1729. Oxon. Affize.
  2 Tim. iv. 8. 8° 1736. Fun.   Crown of Righteoufnefs.
NEWMAN Henry
  * 2 Sam. xix. 14. 4° 1661.
NEWMAN Henry, B. A. of Trin. Coll. Camb.
  * Pf. cxxiv. 4. 4° 1780. b. Humane Society.
NEWMAN John,   Minifter of the Gofpel at Salter's Hall, Lond.
  * Ephef. v. 19. 12° 1708. V. pract. Difc. on Prayer &c. p. 146.
  * Mark viii. 38. 12° 1710. Ref. of Manners.
  * Ifai. xxxii. 1, 2.   1716. Nov. 5.
  * Serm. in 12° 1717.
  * Ecclef. i. 4.   1720. New Year's-day.
  * Acts xiii. 36. 8° 1722. Fun. of Richard Mount. Queen's. Cam.
  1 Cor. ii. 2. 8° 1728. 2 f. The Importance of knowing Jefus Chrift &c.
  * Acts ii. 47. 8° 17.
  Rom. iv. 4. 8° 1735. The popifh Doctrine of Merit and Juftification. V. Difc. Vol. II. Ag. Popery. Braz. N. Oxon.
NEWMAN Richard,   V. of Keynton, Warwickf. and Evening-Preacher at St. Ann's within Alderfgate, Lond.
  2 Sam. i. 14. 4° 1694. Jan. 30. Bod.
NEWMAN Thomas,   Minif. of the Gofpel in Carter Lane, Lond.
  Pf. lxxiii. 24. 8° 1727. Fun.
  * Rom. xii. i. 8° 1727. Ch. f.
  * Luke xi. 2. 8° 1729.
  2 Cor. vii. 1. 8° 1735. Nov. 5. The Spirit of Popery repugnant to the Spirit of Chriftianity.
  ‡ * Pf. i. 1. 8° 1738.
  * Pf. lxvi. 13, 14. 8° 1746. Th. f.
  ‡ * Micah vi. 9. 8° 1746. Faft. Brit. M.
  * Ifai. v. 12. 8° 1750. On difregarding alarming Providences.
                                                  * 1 Tim.

* 1 Tim. vi. 19. 8° 1750. Char. School meeting.
　　　* - - - - 1751. Penitent Thief on the Crofs.
　　　* Serm. in 2 Vol. 8° 1760. On Happinefs and various Subjects.
　　　　Wadh. Oxon.
NEWSON John, M. A. K. of Conington, Camb. and V. of Elm cum Enneth in the Ifle of Ely.
　　　* 8 Serm. in 8° 1781. On plain and practical Subjects.
NEWTE John, M. A. Fell. of Bal. Coll. Oxon, and R. of Tiverton, Devon.
　　　Pf. cl. 4. 4° 1696. The Lawfulnefs and Ufe of Organs in Chriftian Churches. *St. John's.* Camb. *Eton. Sion.*
　　　Prov. iii. 9 4° 1711. The Impiety of Tythe-ftealing.
NEWTE Samuel, M. A. R. of Tidcomb-Portion in Tiverton Church, Devon.
　　　Ecclef. xii. 11. 8° 1725. *Exon.* Char. School meeting.
NEWTON Benjamin, M. A. V. of Lantwit, Glamorganfhire.
　　　Acts xxiii. 5.　1715. Jan. 30.
　　　Serm. in 2 Vol. 8° 1736. on fev. Occafions. *Queen's.* Camb.
NEWTON Benjamin, M. A. Fell. of Jef. Coll. Camb. and V. of Sandhurft, Gloucefterf.
　　　* 2 Tim. iii. 1, 2. 4° 1758. *Camb.* Jan. 30.
　　　* Pf. xcvi. 9. 4° 1760. Mufick-meeting of 3 Choirs.
　　　*Tit. ii. 15. 4° 1779. Con. of Bp. Warren.
NEWTON George, M. A. V. of Taunton St. Magdalen, Somerfetf.
　　　Pf. xci. 16. 12° 1661.
　　　Luke xxiii. 28. 8° 1673. Fun. of Jofeph Alleyne. *Bod.*
NEWTON James
　　　* Luke xvi. 2. 8° 1776. The good Steward.
NEWTON John, M. A. of Clare-Hall Camb. V. of St. Martin's, Leicefter.
　　　Gen. xlii. 21. 4° 1684. On burning a Woman for poifoning her Hufband. *Sion.*
NEWTON John, M. A. V. of Taynton, and Minor Canon of Glouc.
　　　1 Sam. x. 5, 6. 8° 1748. Mufick. The Nature, Morality, and divine Influences of Mufick.
NEWTON John,　　R. of St. Mary Woolnoth, London.
　　　* 6 Serm. in 8° 1760.
　　　* 3 Serm. in 8° 1767.
　　　* 20 Serm. in 8° 1767. *Sion.*
　　　* Ephef. iv. 15. 8° 1780. Vif. The Subject and Temper of the Gofpel-Miniftry.
　　　* Jerem. v. 29. 8° 1781. Faft. The Guilt and Danger of fuch a Nation as this.
NEWTON Jofeph,　　V. of Colefhill, Berks.
　　　* Ezra vii. 26. 8° 1755. Affize.
NEWTON Richard, DD. Principal of Hertford Coll. Oxon.
　　　1 Pet. ii. 17. 4° 1712. Acceffion. b. Commons. *Ch. Ch. C. C. C. Bal. Magd Worc. Linc.* Oxon. *Queen's. St. John's.* Camb.
　　　Rom. x. 2, 3. 4° 1713. Nov. 5. b. Queen. *Bod. Ch. Ch. Bal. Or. Worc.* Oxon. *Sion.*　　　　　　　　　　　　　Pf.

Pf. xxvi. 8. 4° 1716. *Oxon.* Conf. of Hart Hall Chapel. *Magd. Or. Worc.* Oxon. *Sion. Eton.*
2 Tim. ii. 24. 8° 1740. Anniv. f. The miniſterial Duty ſet forth. *Worc. Linc.* Oxon. *Queen's.* Camb. *Brit. M.*

NEWTON Robert, M. A. late Fell. of Jeſ. Coll. Camb. R. of St. James Garlick-Hyth, London.
Prov. xxii. 6. 4° 1702. School-Feaſt. Religion and Learning, the happy Effects of an early Education. *St. John's.* Camb.
2 Sam. xix. 30. 4° 1703. May 29. b. Ld May. *St. John's.* Cam.

NEWTON Robert, M. A. R. of St. Auſtin's, and St. Faith, Lond.
Pf. xcvi. 9. 4° 1713. Open. the Church. *Linc.* Oxon. *Sion.*
Pf. xvi. 9. 8° 1713.

NEWTON Thomas, Bp. of Briſtol.
Luke xi. 1. 8° 1745. Hutchin's Lect. Of Forms of Prayer, and and particularly thoſe of the Church of England.
Matt. xxiii. 13. 8° 1745. Reb. Phariſaiſm and Popery parallelled.
Rev. ii. 5. 8° 1745. Faſt. b. Commons. Dec. 18.
* Differtations in 8° 1759. V. the Biſhop's Works publiſhed in 4° 1782.
* Mark iii. 14. 8° 1760. Conf. of Bp. Warburton, *Braz. N.* Ox.
* 2 Pet. ii. 17. 4° 1761. Acceſſion.
* Luke x. 37. 4° 1716 . *Briſtol*-Infirmary.
* Phil. iv. 5. 4° 1764. Jan. 30. b. Lords. Chriſtian Moderation. *Queen's.* Camb.
* Matt. xi. 5. 4° 1765. Ann. meeting Charity School. *Braz. N. Worc.* Oxon.
* John x. 16. 4° 1769. Prop. of Goſpel. Imperfect Reception of the Goſpel. *Braz. N.* Oxon. *Queen's.* Camb.

NEWTON William, R. of Wingham and Stodmarſh, Kent.
Iſai. xxvi. 9. 8° 1720. Faſt. Dec. 16.
2 Cor. i. 10. 8° 1722. Th. Nov. 4.
Deut. xxix. 29. 8° 1723. Trin. Sunday.
- - - - - 1727. On the Death of King George I.

NICHOLETS Charles, Miniſter of the Loyal Eagle Ship.
Eccleſ. xii. 5. 4° 1682. Fun. of a Sea-Surgeon.

NICHOLETS Charles, . Preacher of the Goſpel and Paſtor.
Pf. cxxvi. 3. 4° 1687. The Diſſenters Jubilee. *Brit. M.*

NICHOLL John, M. A. of Jeſ. Coll. Oxon. V. of Weſtham, Suſſex.
Rom. xii. 13. 8° 1741. Welch Feaſt. Antient Britiſh Hoſpitality. *Queen's.* Camb.
* Nehem. v. 12. 8° 1763. Viſ. Againſt Simony.

NICHOLS Benjamin, M. A. Chaplain to the Earl of Uxbridge, Aſſiſtant Cur. of St. Ann's, Mancheſter.
Prov. xvii. 11. 8° 1745. Rebellion. Rebellion greatly aggravated in a Proteſtant Subject.
Matt. v. 10. 8° 1746. Falſe Claims to Martyrdom conſidered.

NICHOLS Will. DD. Fell. of Mert. Coll. Ox. R. of Selſey, Suſſex.
Acts xxii. 3. 4° 1698. Sch. Feaſt. The Advantages of a learned Education. *Trin.* Camb. *Brit. M.*

* 2 Sam.

* 2 Sam. xii. 14, 15. 4° 16   Affize.
5 Practical Difc. in 8° 1701. The Duty of Inferiors to Superiors.
John v. 4. 4° 1702.   On mineral Waters at *Tunbridge*. *Ch. Ch.* Oxon. *St. John's.* Camb. *Sion.*
Heb. xii. 7, 8. 8° 1709. On the Death of Prince George. Afflictions, the Lot of God's Children. *Trin.* Camb. *Eton.*

NICHOLS Nathaniel, B. D. R. of All Saints, Evefham, Worcefterf.
1 Pet. ii. 13. 8° 1728. *Camb.* Admiffion of a Mayor.

NICHOLS Nicholas, M.A. formerly Fell. of Clare-Hall, Camb. and R. of Patrinton, Holdernefs.
Ifai. vii. 5–7. 8° 1746. *Hull.* Th. After Rebellion.

NICHOLSON Edward, M. A. of Caftlecuna in the County of Rofcommon, Ireland.
1 John ii. 15. 12° 1715. *Dublin.*

NICKOLLS Boucher Rob. LL. B. R. of Stoney Stanton, Leicefter.
* 1 Tim. iv. 15. 8° 1782. Vif. The general Objects of clerical Attention confidered with particular reference to the pref. times.

NICOLL Richard, DD. R. of Drayton, and late Fell. of Linc. Coll. Oxon.
* Prov. xix. 27. 8° 1775. *Oxon.* Act f. Pretences to Sciences pointed out, and true Knowledge recommended. *Worc.* Oxon.

NICOLLS Chrift. Lect. of St. Michaels, Woodftreet, London.
* Ecclef. xii. 1. 4° 1767. Char. School meeting.
* Pf. iv. 4. 4° 1768. Fun. of Rev. Mr. Doughty.

NICOLLS John, DD. Preb. of Ely.
* 1 Theff. iv. 9, 10. 4° 1767. b. Gov. of *Lond.* Lying-in Hofp.

NICOLLS John, DD. V. of St. Lawrence. Reading, Berks.
* Job xxxi. 15. 4° 1781. On Weft's Charity.

NICOLLS Samuel, LL. D. Mafter of the Temple, R. of St. James's Weftminfter, and Chapl. in Ord.
Pf. cxxii. 8, 9. 8° 1745. Rebellion. *Trin.* Camb.
John xix. 26, 27. 8° 1746. b. Sons of the Clergy. *All S.* Oxon. *Trin.* Camb.
Pf. lvii. i. 4° 1748. Faft. b. Commons. *Brit. M.*
Ifai. lx. 22. 4° 1749. Irifh Prot. School. *All S.* Ox. *Trin.* Camb.
* Jude 20, 21. 8° 1750. Farewel.
* Pf. lxxviii. 5–7. 4° 1756. Ann. meet. Char. School. *Braz. N.* Oxon. *Queen's.* Camb.
* Heb. xiii 7. 4° 1762. On the Death of Bp. Sherlock. *Queen's.* C.

NICOLS Daniel, M. A. Fell. of St. John's Coll. Oxon. R. of Scotton, Lincolnfhire.
1 Sam. xii. 14, 15. 4° 1681. Affize. *Pub. L.* Camb. *Brit. M.*

NICOLS John, M. A. Reader at the Charter Houfe, and Fell. of Mert. Coll. Oxon.
Matt. xxiii. 11. 8° 1730. Commem. of Founders. *Queen's.* Camb.

NICOLSON John, M. A. Minifter of Lingfield, Surrey, and Chapl. to Lord Effingham.
Rev. ii. 17. 4° 1707. b. the Armourers. The conftant Pay of the Church militant.

NICOLSON William, Bp. of Gloucester.
 Exposition on the Apostles Creed in several Sermons. fo. 1661.
 Univ. Oxon.
NICOLSON William, Abp. of Cashel.
 Prov. xxiv. 21. 4° 1685. Accession.
 2 Tim. ii. 11, 12. 4° 1703. Jan. 30. b. Lords. *Ch. Ch.* Oxon.
 Pub. L. Cl. H. St. John's. Camb.
 Judges v. 8. 4° 1706. Ref. of Manners. *Univ. Or.* Oxon. *Trin.*
 Camb. *Sion*
 Lev. xxv. 20, 21. 4° 1707. Accession. b. Queen. The Blessings
  of the 6th Year. *Or. Worc.* Oxon. *St. John's.* Camb. *Sion.*
 2 Kings ii. 11. 4° 1712.
 Ephes. ii. 8, 9. 4° 1716. Ch. s. *Ch. Ch.* Oxon.
 Esther ii. 8, 9. 4° 1716. Spitt. M.
NIXON John, M. A. R. of Cold Higham, Northampt. and F. R. S.
 Ps. xc. 16, 17. 8° 1749. *Northampton*-Infirmary.
NOBLE Daniel
 * Heb. vi. 11, 12. 8° 1755. Fun.
 * Dan. vi. 21. 8° 1760. Royal Fun.
 * 1 Pet. i. 22–25. 8° 1761. Fun. of Rev. *Jos. Burroughs. Queen's.* C.
 * John viii. 32. 8° 1767. Fun.
NOONE George, M. A. R. of Widford, Essex.
 2 Kings xxiii. 25. 8° 1714. On the Death of Queen Ann. *St.*
 John's. Camb.
NORMAN John, Minister of the Gospel at Portsmouth.
 * John iv. 22. 8° 1718.
 * Isai. i. 4. 8° 1720. Fast.
 Joel ii 12, 13. 8° 1721. Fast. Ag. the Plague.
 * Ephes. i. 22, 23. 8° 1722. Open. meeting-house.
NORRIS John, M. A. Fell. of All Soul's Coll. Oxon. R. of Bemer-
 ton near Sarum.
 Rom. xii. 3. 4° 1685. *Oxon.* (or Miscell. 12° 1723. p. 264.)
 Midlent s. *Worc. Jes.* Oxon. *Brit. M.*
 John xxi. 15. 8° 1691. Treatises. Vol. II. p. 264. *Bod. New C.*
 All S. Oxon. *Trin.* Camb.
 Pract. Disc. in 8° (1694.) 1728. *Bod. Univ. All S. Ch. Ch. New C.*
 Oxon. *Queen's. Trin.* Camb. *Dr. W's's L.* London.
 Pract. Disc. in several Divine Subjects. Vol. II. (8° 1691. *Bod.*
 Vol. III. 8° 1693. *Bod.*) III. IV. 9° 1728. *Univ. All S. New C.*
 Mert. Pemb. Oxon.
NORRIS Richard
 Lam. v. 16. 4° 1702. Fun.
 Ps. cxviii. 24. 4° 1704. Th. After a Victory. *Ch. Ch.* Oxon.
 Pub. L. Camb.
NORTH Brownlow, Hon. Bp. of Winchester.
 * Prov. xxix. 7. 4° 1771. b. Gov. of *Lond.* Lying in Hosp.
 * Jer. xxxi. 13. 4° 1774. b. Gov. of *Magd.* Hosp.
 * 1 Tim. vi. 18. 4° 1774. b. Gov. of *Lond.*-Hosp.

＊ Phil. iv. 3. 4° 1775. Jan. 30. b. Lords.
　＊ Gal. iii. 14. 4° 1778. Prop. of Gospel.
NORTH John, Hon. DD. Master of Trin. Coll. Camb. Clerk of the Closet, and Preb. of Westminster.
　Ps. i. 1 4° 1671. *Camb.* b King. *Univ. Ch. Ch. C. C. C. Jes.* Oxon. *Trin. Pub. L. St. John's.* Camb. *Sion.*
NORTON Edward, DD. V. of Saffron Walden, Essex, and Preb. of St. Paul's, Lond.
　Prov. xxvii. 1. 4° 1701. b. Lord Mayor.
[NORTON Joseph]
　‡ ＊ Matt. v. 16. 4° 1693. Public Charity. *Brit. M.*
NORTON Robert, M. A. R. of Southwick, Sussex, and Chaplain to the Duke of Richmond.
　＊ Ps. cxii. 9. 4° 1755. *Charter-House*-School Feast.
NOTCUTT *William,*　　Minister at Ipswich.
　＊ 2 Thess. ii. viii. 8° 1729. Nov. 5.
　＊ Isai. ix. 6.　1733. 6 Sermons.
　＊ Serm. in 2 Vol.　1733.
　＊ Phil. iii. 8. 9. 8° 1734. 7 Sermons.
NOURSE Peter, DD. Fell. of St. John's Coll. Camb. and Chaplain in Ord.
　2 Cor. iv 3. 4° 1698. *Camb.* Commencement. *All S.* Ox. *Trin. St. John's.* Camb.
　1 Cor. iv. 1, 2. 4° 1708. Vis. A Vindication of the Christian Priesthood.
NOWELL Thomas, DD. Principal of St. Mary Hall, and Professor of Modern History, Oxon.
　＊ Num. xvi. 3. 8° 1772. Jan. 30. b. Commons.
NOWELL William. M. A. R of Wolsingham, Northumb.
　＊ Ps. xviii. 7. 4° 1756. Fast. *Newcastle* upon Tyne.
　＊ Ephes. vi. 4. 4° 1757. Char. School meeting.
　＊ Ps. cxii. 9.　4° 1763. b. Gov. of *Lying-in* Hosp. *Braz. N.* Ox.
NOYES *Nicholas*
　＊ Jer. xxxi. 23. 12° 1698. New England's Duty and Interest.
NOYES *Robert*
　＊　 -　-　-　- 1756.
　＊　-　-　- 8° 1771. Fun.
NYE Stephen,　　R. of little Hormead, Herts.
　1 Cor xv. 10. 8° 1700. Vis. The System of Grace and Free-will. *Eton.*
[OAKES A.　　　LL. D.]
　‡ ＊ 1 Cor. ii. 27. 8° 1739. Sacramental Worthiness.
OAKES *John*
　＊ Luke x. 20. 8° 1689.
　＊ Serm. in 32° 1747. To young people.
OAKEY
　Prov. xxx. 8, 9. C. m. e. p. 468. A middling Condit in most eligible.

OAKELY Simon, B. D. Professor of Arabic, Camb.
   Mal. ii. 7. 8° 1710. The Dignity of the Christian Priesthood. *Pub. L.* Camb.
   Deut. vi. 6, 7. 8° 1713. Ch. f. *St. John's.* Camb.

OATES Titus, DD.
   Matt. xviii. 11. 4° 1679. *Bod. Ch Ch. Queen's. Worc.* Oxon. *Trin. St. John's.* Camb. *Sion.*

O'BEIRNE   Chapl. to Lord Howe at St. Paul's, New York.
   * Jerem. xii. 15. 4° 1776. On taking New York.

OBOURN Thomas, M.A. R. of Laverstoke, Hants.
   * Pf. cxxxi. 4. 8° 1759. Th.

OFFLEY Walter, M. A. Dean of Chester, and Preb. of Litchfield.
   Prov. xvii 13. 4° 1717. Assize. *Ch. Ch.* Oxon.

OFFLEY William. M. A. late Fell. of King's Coll. Camb. and Preb. of Lincoln, and R. of Middleton Stoney, Oxon.
   * Job i 21. 4° 1696. Fun. of Rev. Jeffery Shaw. Warning given to the Flock by the sudden Death of a good Shepherd. *Br. M.*
   Pf. cxlviii, 8. 4° 1704. Fast. Jan. 19. For the great Winds. The Power and Providence of God considered and asserted. *Pub. L.* Camb.

OGDEN Samuel, DD. Woodwardian Professor, Camb.
   * 1 Thess. v. 13. 4° 1758. May 29. *All S.* Ox. *Queen's.* Camb.
   * Deut. iv. 6. 4° 1758. Accession *All S.* Oxon. *Queen's.* Camb.
   * 10 Serm. in 8° 1770. On the Efficacy of Prayer and Intercession. *Pub. L. Queen's.* Camb.
   * 23 Serm. in 8° 1770. On the Commandments. *Trin.* Camb.
   * 14 Serm. in 8° 1777. On the Articles of the Christian Faith. *Trin.* Camb.
   . N. B. republished in 2 Vol. 12° 1780. With 5 additional Serm. on the Lord's Supper.

OGILVIE *John*, DD. Minister at Midmar, Scotland.
   * 6 Serm. in 8° 1767. On several Subjects.
   * Lam. i. 12. 12° 1779. Christ's Sufferings compared &c. V. Scotch Pr. Vol. III. p. 208.

OGLE N.   DD. Dean of Winchester and Can. Resid. of Sarum.
   * John viii. 10, 11. 4° 1766 At the *Magd.* Hosp.
   * Luke x. 35. 8° 1770. *Solisbury*-Infirmary.
   * Matt. xi. 5. 4° 1775. Ann. meeting Ch. School. *Worc.* Oxon.

OKES John, M. A. R. of Shinfield, Berks.
   Mark xii. 17. 4° 1681. Assize. *Pub. L.* Camb.

OLDFIELD Joshua, DD.
   * Prov. viii. 15. 12° 1699. Ref. of Manners.
   * Ezek. xxxvii. 32. 8° 1707. On the Union. *Ch Ch.* Oxon.

OLDHAM George, B. D. V. of St. Paul's Walden, Herts, and Fell. of St. John's Coll. Camb.
   Acts iv. 29. 8° 1710. Vis. *St. John's.* Camb.
   1 Cor. i. 10. 4° 1713. *Camb.* School-Feast. *St. John's.* Camb.

OLDING

OLDING John,   Minister at Deptford, Kent.
  * 1 Tim. iii. 15. 8° 1759. Ord.
  * Nehem. ii. 4. 8° 1767. Ejaculatory Prayer.
  * Isai. lv. 6. 8° 1775. Fun.
OLDISWORTH Giles, M. A. R. of Bourton on the Hill, Glouc.
  2 Cor. vii. 1. 4° 1662. Vis.
  John xiv. 1, 2. 4° 1663.
  Hosea vi. 2. 4° 1663. Fun. of Mrs. Dor. Rutter.
  1 Cor. ix. 24. 4° 1666. *Oxon.* A necessity laid upon Gospel-Believers to run with Diligence through all Gospel-Duties. *Bod.*
  Heb. xi. 17. 4° 1677. *Oxon.* Fun.   The Father of the faithful tempted.
OLIVE R.   M. A. R. of Burnham, Kent.
  * Ps. cxxii. 6. 4° 1759. Fast.
  * Isai. lv. 1. 4° 1759. *Bath*-Infirmary.
OLIVER Edward, M. A. Fell. of C. C. C. Camb. and Chaplain to the Earl of Northampton.
  John iv. 24. 4° 1698. b. Lord Mayor. *St. John's.* Cam. *Brit. M.*
OLIVER Edward, B. D. R. of St. Mary Ab Church, and Preb. of St. Paul's, London.
  Rom. xiii. 3. 4° 1726. Elect. of Lord Mayor. The relative Duties of a Magistrate and People. *All S.* Oxon. *Queen's.* Camb.
OLIVER John. M. A. Minister of St. Peter's, and V. of Audlam, Chester.
  2 Cor. v. 10. 4° 1682. Assize.
  Prov. x. 9. 4° 1699. Assize.
  Eccles. xii. 7. 4° 1709. Fun.
  Tit. ii 15. 4° 1709 Vis.
  Ps. xiv. 1. 4° 1710. Assize. Ag. Atheism.
  Ps. xxxvii. 37. 4° 1710. *Chester.* Assize.
  Ps li. 3 8° 1711. *Chester.* Jan. 30.
OLIVER Richard,   Curate of Midhurst.
  1 Cor. vii. 30. 4° 1700. Fun. of George Payne.
OLIVER R.   Cur. of St. George's Chapel Preston, Lancas.
  * Rom. xiii. 1. 8° 1746. Subjection to the present Government a Duty. *Worc.* Oxon.
  * Matt. xxii. 21. 8° 1749.
OLLYFFE George, M. A. R. of Hedgerly, Bucks.
  Jerem. xxxii. 17. 8° 1707. *Eton.*
  Gal. v. 7. 8° 1709. The Hindrance of a Reformation.
  Col. iii. 12. 8° 1710.
OLLYFFE John, LL. B. R of Almer, Dorsetshire.
  Ps. cxxvi. 3. 4° 1689. Th. Feb. 14. England's Call to Thankfulness. *Bal. Sion. Eton.*
  * 2 Pet. i. 2. 12° 1694. Farewel.
OLLYFFE John,   R. of Durton and Hedgerly, Bucks.
  Ps. cxix. 136. 12° 1701. Ref of Manners
  Ezek. xxxvii. 22. 8° 1707. Th. May 4. For the Union. *Trin. C.*
  Prov. viii. 15, 16. 8° 1709. Assize.

Pf. lxxii. 1. 8° 1715. Affize.
Pf. lxxxv 8. 8° 1721. Acceffion.
OLLYFFE John
   Rev. xiv. 13. 4° 1699. Fun. of Hen. Cornifh. B. D.
OLLYFFE William
   Job xiv. 14. 4° 1707. Fun. of Tho. Ligoe, Efq;
ORAM Richard
   Prov xxviii. 2. 8° 1725. Jan. 30.
ORME William,   V. of St. Bartholomew the lefs, London.
   Phil. i. 27. 4° 1682. Pub. L. Camb.
ORR John, DD. Arch Deacon of Ferns, Ireland.
   14 Serm. Vol. I. in 8" 1739
   13 Serm Vol. II. in 8° 1749. Queen's. Trin. Camb. Brit. M.
   * Serm. in 3 Vol in 8° 1772. Trin. Camb.
ORTON Job,   of Shrewefbury.
   * 1 Cor. xv. 24. 8° 1752. Fun. of Dr. Dodderidge. Queen's. Cam.
   * Heb. xi. 7. 8° 1756. Faft. Earthquake.
   * 2 Cor. iv. 18. 24° 1764. 3 Difc. on Eternity.
   * Religious Exercifes recommended, or Difcourfes in 8° 1769. On fecret and family Worfhip, and religious Obfervation of the Lord's day—with 2 Difc. on the heavenly State.
   * Difc. in 12° 1771. To the Aged. Queen's. Camb.
   * Phil ii. 21. 24° 1773. 3 Difc. on Chriftian Zeal.
   * 2 Tim ii. 7. 24° 1775. Hearing the Word.
   * 1 Cor. xiv. 16. 24° 1775. Public Prayer.
   * Pf. c. 4. 24° 1775. Pfalmody.
   * 36 Difc. in 2 Vol. 12° 1776. On practical Subjects.
OSBALDESTON Richard, Bp of London.
   * James ii. S. 8° 1723. Affize.
   Lum. xxi. 5, 6. 4° 1748. Jan. 30. b. Lords.
   Matt viii. 11. 4° 1752. Prop. of Gofpel. St. John's. Camb. Eton.
OSBORNE George,   of C. C. C. Oxon V. of Batterfea, Surrey.
   Rom. xiii. 3. 8° 1730. Affize. Doing good the beft perfervative againft the Fear of the civil Power.
   Prov. xiv. 34. 8° 1732. Affize. Righteoufnefs the Exaltation of a Nation.
   Ezra vii. 26. 8° 1733. Affize. The civil Magiftrate's Right of inflicting Punifhment. The End of penal Laws, and the Neceffity of a due Execution of them.
   Tit. iii. 1. 8° 1735. Affize. Subjection to Principalities, Powers and Magiftrates.
OSWALD James, DD. Minifter of the Gofpel at Methven,
   * Pf xvi. 6. 8° 1766. Open general Affembly. Queen's. Camb.
OSWALD Thomas,   Minifter of the Scotch Church, Ruffel-ftreet, Covent Garden, London
   * - - - - 8° 1771. Fun.
OVERING John, M. A.
   2 Chron xxxv. 24, 25. 4° 1670. Jan. 30. Hadadrimmon—or Jofiah's Lamentation.

OVING-

OF AUTHORS, &c. 253

OVINGTON John, DD. Chaplain to the Queen.
 Matt. vii. 22, 23. 4° 1705. Vif. The plaufible Plea filenced. *Ch. Ch.* Oxon. *St. John's.* Camb.
 1 Cor. vii. 2. 8° 1712. Chriftian Chaftity, or a Caveat ag. vagrant Luft.
 Matt. xvii. 21. 8° 1712. Lent.
 Matt. xviii. 21. 8° 1716.

OWEN Charles ᵃ
 * Jude 11. 8° 1717. Th.
 * Pf. xxxix. 5. 8° 1737. Death of a young Woman.

OWEN *Charles*, ᵃ DD.
 ‡ * Pf. xxix 5. 8° 1758. Fun. of Mr Lythgoe.
 ‡ * Heb. xiii. 4. 8° 1758. On Marriage.

OWEN E.   M. A. Mafter of the Free Sch. Warrington, Lanc.
 * 1 Sam. xxvi. 10, 11. 8° 1765. *Liverpool* Infirmary. V. Dr. *Enfield's* Eng. Pr. V. 8. p. 93. *Queen's.* Camb.
 * Matt. xi. 5. 8° 1779. Ch. f.
 * 2 Theff. iii. 13. 8° 1782. Ch. f.

OWEN Edward, DD. Fell. of St. John's Coll. Oxon. V. of great Houghton, Huntingdonf.
 Exod. xx. 16. 4° 1746. Affize.
 Pf. cl. 5. 6. 4° 1749. Opening an Organ.

OWEN Hen. DD. R. of St. Olave's, Hart-ftreet, Lond. and F. R S.
 * Serm. in 2 Vol. 8° 1773. On the Intent and Propriety of Scripture Miracles (preached at Boyle's Lect.) confidered and explained *Queen's.* Camb.

OWEN *Jeremiah*
 * 1 Sam. xii. 24. 8° 1717. On St. David's-day.

OWEN John, DD. Dean of Ch. Ch. Ox. before the Ejection. 1662.
 Luke xvi. 29. 4° 1675. m. e. P. p. 312. Concerning the Authority of the Scripture.
 Pf. cxli. 5. 4° 1676. f. m. e. p. 683. How we may bring ourfelves to bear Reproofs.
 * John v. 14. 4° 1681.
 1 Pet. ii. 3. 4° 1683. c. m. e. p. 217. Antidote againft Popery.

OWEN John,   Chapl. to Lord Grey of Ruthin.
 2 Sam. xii. 21-23. 1° 1680. Fun.
 Tit. iii. 1 4° 1684. The true way to Loyalty.

OWEN *John*
 * 17 Serm. in 2 Vol. 1720.
 * Pf. cxvi. 12. 1742.
 ‡ * 2 Sam. xviii. 20. 8° 1746.

[OWEN John, DD.]
 * Serm. in 12° 1760.

OWEN Jonathan
 Ezek. v. 8. 4° 1694. England's warning. *Bod.*

OWEN R.   V. of Ilford near Lewes, Suffex.
 Matt. xix. 27. 8° 1713.
 2 Sam. xix. 27. 8° 1713. b. Freeholders.

   ᵃ Q. The fame.

OWEN Rich. DD. Fell. of Oriel Coll. Oxon. R. of St. Swithin's, London-ftone.
    1 Cor. ix. 22. 4° 1666. Conc. ad Cler. Paulus multiformis.
OWEN Thomas, M. A. Fell. of St. Peter's Coll. Camb. and Chapl. to the Factory at Aleppo.
    Pf. cxix. 59. 4° 1706. Levant Co. *Sion.*
OWTRAM William, DD. Preb. of Weftminfter and Chapl. in Ord.
    5 Serm. in 8° 1680. On Faith, Providence, and other Subjects. *Or. Oxon. Sion.*
    20 Serm. in 8° 1697. On feveral Occafions. *All S. Bal. C. C. C. Oxon. Pub. L. Camb. Brit. M.*

P.   C.   M. A.

‡ * 1 Cor. xi. 29. 12° 1693. The Danger of a total and wilful Neglect, equal to the Danger of an unworthy receiving of the Lord's Supper &c.

[PACK Samuel]
    * Rom. ix. 5. 4° 1691. Myftery of the Gofpel unveiled.
PACKWOOD Samuel, E. A. P.
    Pf. cxix. 138. 8° 1712. Affize.
PAGE Thomas, M. A. R. of Wheatacre, Norfolk.
    1 Chron. xxix. 22, 23. 4° 1715. Th.
PAGET Simon,   R. of Truro, Cornwall.
    Luke ii. 14. 4° 1698. Th for Peace. *Trin.* Camb.
PAGET Thomas, M. A. Lecturer of Staines, Middlefex.
    * Rom. x. 2. 4° 1730. Nov. 5.
    * 2 Cor, v. 17. 4° 1739. New Year's day. Tranflated from Monfieur Superville.
PALEY William, M. A. late Fell. of Chrift's Coll. Camb. V. of Dalitone, and St. Lawrence in Appleby, Carllile, and Chapl. to the Bp. of Carlifle.
    * 2 Pet. iii. 15, 16. 4° 1777. Vif. Caution recommended in the Ufe and application of Scripture-Langüage.
    * 1 Tim. iv. 12. 4° 1781. Ord. f.
PALKE William
    John xx. 28. 8° 1719. The Divinity of Jefus Chrift proved. *Sion. Eton.*
PALMER Anthony, M. A. R. of Bourton on the Water, Gloucefterf.
    Matt. viii. 23-27. 8° 1673. Extract of feveral Sermons. *Bod.*
    Pf. xxv. 11. 8° 1674. The Gofpel a new Creature. *Bod.*
PALMER Charles, M. A. V. of Towcefter, Northamptonf.
    Ifai. lix. 8. 4° 1702. *Oxon.* Faft. June 10.
    * 2 Cor. xi. 29. 12° 1710. Sacrament.
PALMER John
    * 1 Chron. xxix. 27, 28. 8° 1760. Death of King George II.
    * - - - - 8° 1766. Infanity of the Senfualift.
    * Prov. xiii. 20. 8° 1769. Char. School-meeting.
    * 2 Cor. i. 12. 8° 1779. Fun. of Dr. *Caleb Fleming.*
PALMER Robert, DD. Fell. of St. John's Coll. Camb. and Lecturer of Ealing, Middlefex.

Prov.

Prov. xiv. 34. 4° 1726. Pro Gradu Doctoratûs.
Ezek. xviii. 24. 4° 1730. Par. The Danger of falling from Grace.
PALMER Samuel, Prefbyter of the Church of England.
* 1 Sam. xvii. 29. 12° 1706. Ref. of Manners.
Pf. xxxvii. 12. 8° 1709. Anniv. of Ir. Prot. *Linc.* Oxon. *Sion.*
* Ecclef. ix 2. 8° 1726. Jan. 30. b. Lords.
PALMER Samuel, of Hackney, Middlefex.
* 1 Pet. v. 4. 8° 1766. Fun. of Rev. Mr. *S. Sanderfon.*
* Haggai ii. 9. 8° 1771. 2 f. Opening Meeting Houfe.
* Exod. ii. o. 8° 1774. Char. School-meeting. Compaffion to poor Children recommended from the Example of Pharaoh's Daughter.
* Luke x. 2. 8° 1775. Fun. of *Caleb Afhworth,* LL.D. *Queen's* C.
* John xxi. 15. 12° 1777. The good Shepherd's Care for the Lamb's of his Flock.
* 2 Tim. i. 12. 8° 1778. Fun. of Rev. *Sam. Wilton,* DD.
PANTING Matthew, DD. Mafter of Pemb. Coll. Oxon.
    Gen. xxviii. 20-22. 4° 1732. *Oxon.* Conf. of *Pemb.* Coll. Chapel. Religious Vows. *Were.* Oxon.
PARADISE John, B. A. of Mert. Coll. Oxon. Minifter of Weftbury, Wilts.
    2 Sam. xxiv. 5, 6. 4° 1660. } Jan. 30.
    1 Sam. xxiv. 5, 6. 4° 1661. }
PARGITER Thomas, DD. R. of Gritworth Northamptonf.
    1 Theff. iv. 6. 4° 1682. b. Lord Mayor.
PARIS John, DD. Fell. of Trin. Coll. Camb.
    Pf. cxliv. 15. 8° 17   Th.
    John xiv. 1. 8° 1726. *Camb.* On Faith. p. 83. Mifcellanea practico-theoretica; or a Mifcellany concerning Faith and Manners. *Bod.*
PARKER Henry, M. A. R. of St. Michael's, Crooked Lane, Lond.
    - - - - - 1726. Jan. 30. b. Lord Mayor. The Wifdom of Providence vindicated.
    Amos iii. 6. 4° 1727. Sept. 2. b. Lord Mayor. The Original of public Calamities. *Brit. M.*
    1 Cor. iv. 5. 4° 1727. Sept. 29. b. Lord Mayor. Of Slander and Defamation.
    1 Pet. iii. 8. 4° 1727. School-Feaft.
PARKER J.
    1 Cor. xiii. 12. 8° 1729.
PARKER James, E. A. P.
    Deut. xxxii. 29. 8° 1728. The great Wifdom of confidering our latter End.
PARKER James, M. A. V. of Ewell, Surrey, and Chapl. to the Bp. of Litchfield and Coventry.
    Luke xvi. 31. 4° 1750. At Serjeant's Inn.
PARKER John, Abp. of Dublin.
    2 Sam. xix. 14. 4₀ 1663. b. both Houfes of Parliament in Ireland. *Univ.* Oxon.

PARKER John G. Chapl. V. of St. Helen's, York.
* - - - - 4° 1779. b. moſt ancient grand Lodges of all England.
PARKER Robert, DD. R. of Wolſingham, Durham.
Rom. xiii. 3. 4° 1740. Aſſize. *Queen's.* Camb. *Brit. M.*
PARKER Stavely, M. A. Fell of Jeſ. Coll. Camb and Chaplain to the Britiſh Factory at Liſbon.
Prov. xiv. 34. 8° 1746. At Liſbon.
PARKER Timothy, R. of Eaſt Hothley, Suſſex.
Matt. v. 16. 4° 1675. Viſ. *Bod. Eton. Pub. L.* Camb.
PARKER William, DD. R. of St. James's Weſtminſter, Chapl. in Ord. and F. R. S.
Matt ix. 38. 8° 1746. *Oxon.* Ordination. The Nature and Reaſonableneſs of the inward Call and outward Miſſion to the holy Miniſtry conſidered. *Worc. Queen's.* Camb.
Iſai. xxvi. 9. 8° 1748. *Oxon.* Sept. 2. b. Lord Mayor. The natural Effect, and religious Improvement of extraordinary divine Judgments, and of ſolemn Faſts inſtituted in remembrance of them. *Queen's.* Camb.
Mark xvi. 17, 18. 8° 1749. *Oxon.* 2 ſ. p. 9. The Expediency of the miraculous Powers of the Chriſtian Fathers, and p. 39. The Inexpediency of thoſe that are claimed by the Church of Rome conſidered. *Bod.*
2 Cor xi. 3. 8° 1750. 2 ſ. *Oxon.* The Moſaic Hiſtory of the Fall conſidered. *Bod.*
* Iſai. xliv. 28. 8° 1752. Acceſſion. The Grounds of Submiſſion to Government, the Origin of the different Modes of civil Polity, and the Happineſs of our own Form of Legiſlation in particular. *Braz. N.* Oxon. *Brit. M.*
* Pſ. cxlvii. 1. 8° 1753. Ann. meeting of the 3 Choirs. The Pleaſure of Gratitude and Benevolence improved by Church Muſick *Braz. N.* Oxon. *Brit. M.*
* John xviii. 38. 8° 1754. 2 ſ. The Nature, Evidence, and Importance of Truth.
* Phil. iv. 8. 8° 1755. Act. ſ. Of academical Education. *Bod. Brit. M.*
* Prov. xvii. 4. 4° 1757. Jan. 30. b. Commons. *Braz. N.* Oxon.
* Rom. viii. 30. 8° 1758. 2 ſ. The Scripture Doctrine of Predeſtination. *Braz. N. Worc. Jeſ.* Oxon.
* Iſai. iv. 11. 4° 1762. Conſ. of Bp. Lyttleton. *Braz. N.* Oxon.
* 2 Cor. viii. 3. 4° 1771. b. the Sons of the Clergy. *Bod.*
* Prov. xi, 25. 4° 1781. Ann meeting Char. Sch.
PARKHURST Nathaniel, M. A. V. of Yoxford, Suffolk.
1 Cor. xv. 58. 12° 1684. Fun. of Lady Eliz. Brookes. *Trin.* C.
John xi. 11. 4° 1692. Fun. of S. Fairclough. *Bod.*
* Phil. i. 23. 8° 1704. Treatiſe. On being willing to live and deſirous to die. *Queen's.* Camb.
* Rev. xx. 11, 12. 8° 1704. Treatiſe. On the laſt Judgment. *Queen's.* Camb.

* Zach.

* Zach. i. 5. 8° 1704. Fun. of Rev. Mr. Burkitt.
Pſ. xc. 12. 8° 1705. Fun. of Thomas Neale, Eſq;
Matt. xxv. 21. 8° 1705. Fun. of Rev. Mr. G. Jones.
10 Select. Diſc. Vol. I. 8° 1706.
Select Diſc. Vol. II. 8° 1707.
PARNE Thomas, DD. Fell. of Trin. Coll. Camb. R. of Walking-
 ton, Yorkſ. and Chapl. in Ord.
 Gen. vi. 4. 8° 1722. Commem. *Bod. Queen's*. Camb.
 Iſai. ii. 22. 4° 1724. *Camb.* Fun. of Anthony Earl of Harold.
 Queen's. Camb.
 Judges ix. 8. 8° 1744. *Camb.* Acceſſion. *Queen's* Camb.
PARR Richard, DD. V. of Camerwall, R. of St. Mary Magdalen,
 Southwark, and Canon of Armagh.
 Luke xix. 41, 42. 8° 1661. Chriſt's gracious Intention to Sinners.
 Matt. xxiv. 46. 4° 1672. Fun. of Dr. Rob. Bretton. *Brit. M.*
PARR Samuel, M. A.
 * Gal. iv. 4. 4° 1780. 2 ſ. *Norwich* Xtmas-day and Char. Sch.
PARRY George, M. A. Fell. of Oriel Coll. Oxon.
 Exod. xx. 7. 8° 1723. Lawfulneſs, Nature and Oblig. of Oaths.
PARRY John, Bp. of Oſſory.
 * Pſ. lxxiii. 1 &c. 8° 1660.
 Luke xxiii. 27, 28. 8° 1666. Tears well directed, or pious Re-
 flections upon our Saviour's Sufferings, and our Sins.
 * Pſ. lxii. 18. 8° 1666. Pious Reflections on the Pentecoſt.
 * Phil. iii. 10. 8° 1666. Pious Reflections on the Reſurrection.
 * Matt. ii. 9–12. 8° 1666. Pious Reflections on the Adoration
of wiſe Men &c.
 * Nehem. xiii. 14. 4° 1670. *Bod. Queen's.* Oxon. *Trin.* Camb.
PARRY Joshua
 * 1 John iv. 20. 8° 17   2 ſ. Againſt Popery.
PARRY Richard, B. D. Miniſter of Market Harborough, Leiceſterſ.
 and Chapl. to Lord Vere.
 * 1 Cor. xi 26. 8° 1755. 2 ſ. The Scripture Account of the
 Lord's Supper.
 * Mark ii. 27. 4° 1752. The Xtian Sabbath as old as the Creation.
PARSLEY Henry, M. A. R. of Hedgerley, Bucks.
 Rev. xiv. 13. 4° 1692. Fun. of Mr. Whitchurch. *Bod.*
PARSLEY Henry, M. A. R. of Smarden, Kent.
 Heb. xiii. 16. 8° 1702. Several Diſcourſes.
PARSON Thomas
 Acts xvi. 31. 4° 1676. m. e. G. p. 336. Of ſaving Faith. *Bod.*
PARSONS Bartholomew, B. D. V. of Collingbourne Kingſton, and
 R. of Luggerſhall, Wilts.
 Matt. ii. 1, 2. (4" 1618.) 8° (reprinted) 17   3 ſ. The firſt Fruits
 of the Gentiles. *Linc.* Oxon.
 * Ruth iv. 1. 12° 1740. V. Diſc. on conj. Duty. V. 1. p. 253.
PARSONS Jonathan, M. A. Miniſter of the Preſbyterian Church at
 Newbry Port.
 * Phil. i. 21. 8° 1770. On the Death of Rev. George Whitfield.

PARSONS John, M. A. R. of St. Martin's, Birmingham.
* Acts iv. 12. 8° 1770. 2 f. *Birmingham.* Doctrine of Salvation.
PARSONS Joseph, M. A. V. of Hemnall, and Bedingham, Norfolk.
Pf. cvi. 30. 8° 1746. On the Diftemper of the Cattle. The Nature and Means of prevalent Prayer to avert divine Judgments.
PARSONS Joseph, M. A. V. of Hemenhall, Suffolk.
* Deut. xxi. 1–9. 8° 1763. On the Murder of Mrs. Spoile.
PARSONS Joseph, M. A. late Minifter of Stanton Harcourt, and South Leigh, Oxon.
* 2 Kings xix. 19. 4° 1760. Faft. *Bed. Braz. N.* Oxon.
* 30 Lect. in 8° 1761. On the Principles of the Chriftian Religion, according to Dr. Bufby's Plan. *Worc.* Oxon.
* 1 Theff v. 21. 4° 1767. Apology for the Church of England. *Bod. Braz. N.* Oxon.
PARSONS Robert, M. A. of Univ. Coll. Oxon. and R. of Addington, Gloucefterf.
Luke xv. 7. 4° 1680. Fun. of Earl of Rochefter. *Bod. Univ. Ch. Ch. All S. C. C. C. Linc. Worc. Or.* Oxon. *Trin Queen's.* Cam.
PARSONS Robert
* 2 Cor. iii 6. 8° 1774. Abilities for the Miniftry from God alone.
PARSONS Thomas, M. A. R. of Suckley, Worcefterf.
Modern Sadducifm confuted, or a Treatife concerning the Refurrection from the dead
Matt. vii. 13, 14. 8° 1711. *Worcefter.*
Gen. ii. 5. 8° 1721. *Oxon.* The Being of God. *Brit. M.*
2 Tim. i. 10. 8° 1721. *Oxon.* The Immortality of the Soul.
PARTINGTON John, M. A.
* Matt. x. 32. 8° 1733. Ref. of Manners. Duty and Intereft infeparable. *Queen's.* Camb. *Brit. M.*
* Jerem. xxxvi. 7. 8° 1740. Faft.
PARTRIDGE Nathaniel, M. A. R. of Ardingworth, Northampton.
* Matt. viii. 36, 37. 8° 1720. On the great worth of Men's Souls.
* Exod. xx. 8. 8° 1720. Neceffity of religious Obfervance of the Sabbath.
PASTON James, M. A. R. of Tinningham, and of little Livermere, Suffolk.
Rom. xiii. 5. 4° 1673. The Magiftrate's Authority afferted. *Bod. Sion.*
Luke ix. 55. 4° 1688. Of penal Laws in matters of Relig. *Bed.*
PATE Robert, M. A. Mafter of the Free School, Norwich.
* Rom. i. 16. 4° 1708. 1 Sund. in Lent.
PATERSON James, M. A.
Gen. vi. 3. 8° 1721. Ag. the Plague. *Queen's.* Camb.
Col. iii. 15. 8° 1737. Th. At the Chapels of the Fleet-prifon and Poultry-Compter, London.
[PATERSON James, M. D.
* Luke xiii. 1–6. 8° 1779. Faft. The Light in which public Calamities ought to be viewed, and the Ufe we fhould make of them.

OF AUTHORS, &c.   259

P*A*TERSON *John*. M. A. Minifter of the Gofpel at Aberdeen.
* Pf. cxxvi. 1, 2. 4° 1660. Th. *Worc.* Oxon.
Ezek. vii. 23. 4° 1661. *Edinburgh.*

PATRICK Simon, M. A.
  Rom. xiv. 10. 4° 1707. b. Queen. Ag. Cenfuring and judging.
    Univ. Oxon. *Sion.*

PATRICK Simon, Bp. of Ely.
  Pf. xc. 12. 4° 1660. Fun. of Mr. Jacomb. Divine Arithmetick.
    Ch. Ch. C. C. C. Oxon. *Sion.*
  2 Cor. v. 1. 4° 1670. Fun. of Dr. Hardy. *Bod. Ch. Ch.* Oxon.
  ——— 9. 4° 1670. Fun. of Rev. Mr. Grigg *Univ.* Ox. *Sion.*
  Acts xvi. 33. 8° 1670. Aqua genitalis. Difc. concerning Baptifm. *Bod.*
  Micah vi. 8. 8° 1670. At the end of Jewifh Hypocrify. *Queen's.*
    Oxon. *Pub. L.* Camb. *Sion.*
  2 Kings ii. 12. 4° 1673. Fun. of Rev. John Smith. *Bod. All S.*
    Univ Oxon. *Sion.*
  1 John v. 7, 8. 8° 1675. The Witneffes of Chriftianity. *Bod. St.*
    John's. Oxon.
  Act vii. 59. 4° 1676 b. King. On St. Stephen's day. *Bod. All S.*
    Queen's. Oxon. *Pub. L. St. John's.* Camb.
  1 John v. 11. 8° 1677. part 2. The Witneffes of Xnity. *Bod.*
  Ifai v. 25. 4° 1678. Faft. April 24. Angliæ Speculum. *Bod.*
  Jerem. xiv. 9 4° 1678. Faft. Nov. 13. *Ch. Ch. Magd. Worc.* Ox.
    Pub. L. Trin. Camb. *Sion.*
  Rom. xv. 4. 4° 1678. b. King. The Ufe of the Holy Scriptures.
    Queen's. Magd. Oxon. *Pub L.* Camb *Sion.*
  Ephef. vi. 10. 4° 1680. b. Lord Mayor. *Ch. Ch. Queen's.* Oxon.
    Pub. L. Camb. *Sion.*
  Rev. ii. 16. 4° 1681. Faft. April 11. Chrift's Counfel to his
    Church. *Ch. Ch. Magd.* Oxon. *Pub. L. Trin.* Camb. *Sion.*
  Rev. iii. 3. 4° 1681. Faft. Dec. 22. Chrift's Counfel to his Ch.
    Ch Ch. Magd. Oxon. *Pub. L. Trin.* Camb. *Sion.*
  1 Cor. xi. 26. 4° 1684. 3 Sacra. f.
  * 2 Pet. iii. 16. 12° 1685. Search the Scriptures.
  Pf. lxxii. 15. 4° 1686. Acceffion. Ad Teftimonium.
  Ephef. iv. 14. 4° 1686. On St. Mark's day. *Bod. Univ. Ch. Ch.*
    Jef. Oxon. *Pub. L.* Camb. *Sion.*
  Matt. xvi. 18. 4° 1687. On St. Peter's day. *Bod. Ch. Ch. Magd.*
    Bal. Univ. Oxon. *Sion.*
  1 Tim. iii. 15. 4" 1687. The Pillar and Ground of Truth. *Bod.*
  Pf. lxxv. 1. 4° 1689. Th. Jan. 30. For the Deliverance of this
    Kingdom by the Prince of Orange. *Ch. Ch. Or. Magd. Worc.*
    Jef. Oxon. *Trin. St. John's.* Camb. *Sion.*
  1 Cor. iv. 5. 4° 1689. ⎱ Ag. Cenfuring. ⎧ *Bod. Ch. Ch. Magd.*
  ——— x. 10. 4° 1689. ⎰ Ag. Murmuring. ⎩ Oxon. *Pub. L.* Camb.
  Ifai. xi. 6. 4° 1689. 2 f. b. Prince of Orange. *Bod. All S. Ch. Ch.*
    Magd. Oxon. *Pub. L. Cl. H.* Camb. *Sion.*

K k 2   Col.

Col. iii. 15. 4° 1689. b. Queen. *Bod. C.C.C. Ch. Ch. Magd.* Oxon. *Trin. Cl. H.* Camb. *Sion.*
Prov. xxiv. 34. 4° 1690. Faſt. April 16. b. King and Queen. *Bod Univ. Ch. Ch. Magd.* Oxon. *Trin* Camb. *Sion.*
Deut iv. 9. 4° 1691. Th. Nov. 26. b. Lords. *Bod. Ch. Ch. Magd.* Oxon. *Pub. L. Cl. H.* Camb *Sion.*
Num. x. 9 4° 1692. Faſt. April 8. b. Queen. *Bod. Sion.*
John v 39. 12° 1697. Search the Scriptures.
2 Tim. ii. 8. 4° 1696. Spitt. M. *Pub. L.* Camb. *Sion.*
Dan iv. 35. 4° 1696. Nov. 5. b. Lords. *Oriel.* Oxon. *Trin. St. John's.* Camb.
Rev xvi. 9. 12° 1704. Diſcourſe on the late Storm.
John xiv. 1. 12° 1707. The Hearts Eaſe. *Ch. Ch.* Ox. *Pub. L.* C.
15 Serm. 8° 1719. On Contentment and Reſignation to the Will of God &c.
2 Serm. on the Miniſtration of Angels.

PATTEN Robert, Chapl. to General Forſter.
Gal. v. 1. 8° 1716.

PATTEN Thomas, DD. late Fell. of C. C. C. Oxon. and R. of Childrey, Berks.
 * 1 Pet. iii. 15, 16. 8° 1735. *Oxon.* Act. The Chriſtian Apology in matters of Religion. *Queen's.* Camb.
 * Col. ii. 8. 8° 1759. Oppoſition between Chriſt's Religion and that of Nature. *Queen's.* Camb.

PAUL William, R of Gittiſham, Devon.
 * Pſ. cxxxiii. 1–3. 8° 1707. Th. ſ. *Worc.* Oxon.
 * 2 Tim. iii. 16. 4° 1724. Exon. Aſſize. *Queen's.* Camb.

PAYNE Denis
 * Matt. xi. 5. 8° 1731.

[PAYNE John]
 * 9 Evangelical Diſc. in 8° 1763.

PAYNE Thomas, M. A. R. of High Halden, Kent, and Chaplain to the Engliſh Factory at Conſtantinople.
Eccleſ. viii. 2 4° 1718. b. Levant Co. *Eton.*

PAYNE Thomas, M. A. Cuſtos of the Coll. of Hereford, and V. of Hom-Lacy, Herefordſ.
Prov. iv. 25. 8° 1728.
Pſ lxvi. 1, 2 8° 1738. *Oxon.* Muſick at *Hereford.* A Defence of Church Muſick. *Bal.* Oxon

PAYNE William, L'D. R. of White Chapel, and Chapl. in Ord.
Prov i. 7. 4° 1682. School-Feaſt. Learning and Knowledge recommended. *All S.* Oxon. *Sion.*
1 Sam. xxvi 9. 4° 1683. Jan 30. The unlawfulneſs of ſtretching forth the hand to reſiſt Murder. *All S. Ch. Ch. C.C.C.* Oxon. *Pub. L. St. John's.* Camb.
1 Sam xxvi 9. 4° 1683. Sept. 9. Th. for the Deliverance of the King and Kingdom from the treaſonable Conſpiracy. *All ſ. Ch. Ch. C.C.C.* Oxon. *Pub. L. St. John's.* Camb.
Joſh xxiv. 15. 4° 1691. Family-Religion. *Univ. Ch. Ch.* Oxon.
Pſ.

Pſ. lxxxii. 6, 7. 4° 1695. Royal Fun. *Ch. Ch. Magd.* Ox. *Pub. L.*
Trin. St. John's. Camb.
Pſ lxxii. 6, 7. 4° 1695. Fun.
1 Tim. iii. 9. 12° 1697. 3 ſ. The Myſtery of the Xtian Faith, and of the Trinity vindicated, and the Divinity of Chriſt proved. *Jeſ.* Oxon. *Pub. L.* Camb.
12 Diſc. in 8° 1698. Upon ſeveral practical Subjects. *C. C. C.* Oxon. *Trin.* Camb. *Dr Wſ's. L.* London.

PEACOCK John
* 1 Cor. xv. 55–57. 8° 1768. Fun. of Rev. *Johnſon.*

PEAD Deuel, Chapl. to the Duke of Newcaſtle, and Miniſter of St. James's Clerkenwell, London.
Matt. xiii. 58. 8° 1694. Jeſus is God—or the Deity of Jeſus vindicated in an Abſtract of certain Sermons. *Bid.*
Luke xxiii. 28. 4° 1695. Royal Fun.
Iſai. xxx. 1. 4° 1695. Faſt. Dec. 11.
2 Sam. xx. 1. 4° 1696. On the national Aſſociation. *Trin.* Cam.
Pſ. ii. 1–6. 4° 1696. Th. April 16. *Trin.* Camb.
Epheſ. ii. 1. 4° 1701. The Sinner converted. *Sion.*
Acts xiii. 36. 4° 1702. Fun. of King William. Greatneſs and Goodneſs reprieve not from Death.
Iſai. xxvi. 16. 4° 1704. Faſt.
Iſai. xxvi. 16. 4° 1704. Faſt.
Pſ. ii. 4. 8° 1706. Th. Dec. 31. *Worc.* Oxon. *Trin.* Camb.
Ezek. xxxvii. 22. 4° 1707. May 1. On the Union.
Pſ. x. 2. 8° 1709. Th. Feb. 17. *Pub. L* Camb.
Pſ. lxviii. 11. 8° 1709. On Mr. Preſton's being tore in pieces by his own Bear.
2 Sam. v. 1. 4° 1715. Th. for King's Acceſſion.

PEAKE William, M. A. R. of Seaton, Rutlandſ.
Exod. xviii. 2. 4° 1709. Election of a Mayor. *Pub. L.* Camb.

PEARCE Zachary, Bp. of Rocheſter.
Pſ. cxxx. 5. 4° 1723. b. Lord Mayor. Th. April 25. After the Plague.
Acts xx. 32. 4° 1724. Farewel.
Gen. xxviii. 18. 4° 1727. Conſ. of St. *Martin's* Church in the Fields, London. *Worc.* Oxon. *Queen's.* Camb. *Brit. M.*
Iſai. xlix. 6. 4° 1730. Prop. of Goſpel. *Queen's.* Camb.
1 Cor. x. 21. 4° 1735. Ann. meet. Ch. School. *Queen's.* Camb.
Job ii. 10. 12° 1736. Ag. Self Murder. *Eton.*
Acts xx. 28. 4° 1741. Conc. ad Synod. *Worc.* Ox. *Queen's.* Cam.
Matt. xviii. 33. 4° 1743. Spitt. T. *Queen's.* Camb.
Pſ. xx. 6. 4° 1747. Acceſſion. b. Commons.
Acts xxiii. 5. 4° 1749. Jan. 30. b. Lords. *Queen's.* Camb.
* Prov. xxxi 31. 4° 1760. *Weſtminſter*-Jubilee. *Queen's.* Camb.
* Pſ. xx. 7. 4° 1760. Faſt. b. Lords. *Worc.* Ox. *Queen's.* Camb.
* Serm. (Poſth.) in 4 Vol. 8° 1779. On various Subjects.

PEARSE Edmund
* Matt. xxviii. 20. 8° 1728.

PEARSE *Innes*, M. A. Minister of the Gospel at Tadley, Hants.
 * 21 Serm. in 8° 1763.
PEARSE Robert, M. A. Vice Principal of Edmund Hall, Oxon.
 Pf. lxviii. 19, 20. 8° 1716. *Oxon.* Th. June 7. The Duty of praising God for private and public Benefits. *Bal. Magd.* Ox. *Queen's.* Camb.
 Matt. xi. 30. 8° 1717. *Oxon.* Lent.
 Acts xxiv. 16. 8° 1720. At the Temple.
 Lam. iii. 39, 40. 8° 1721. *Oxon.* Nov. 5. An Exhortation to the Successors of the Apostles.
 * Jerem xxxv. 18, 19. 8° 17
PEARSHALL John,   Curate of St. Pancras, London.
 *Sev. Serm. in 8° 1751. The Importance of daily public Prayer.
PEARSHALL *Richard*
 * Job xiv. 2. 8° 1740. Fun.
 * Rom. x. 16. 8° 1747. Ord.
 * 2 Chron. xxxiv. 3. 8° 1758. Fun. for a Youth.
 * Pf. xvii. 15. 8° 1758. Fun. of Mrs *Tristram*.
PEARSON John, Bp. of Chester.
 Luke xi. 2. (4° 1644.) reprinted in 8° 1701. The Excellency of Forms of Prayer, especially the Lord's Prayer. *Bal.* Oxon. *Trin.* Camb.
 Pf. cxi. 4. 4° 1673. Nov. 5. b. Lords. *Queen's. Or.* Oxon. *Trin.* Camb *Sion.*
PEARSON Richard, DD. Chapl. to the Earl of Eglin.
 Heb. xi 5. 4° 1664. Fun. of Earl of Eglin. Enoch's Translation. *Univ. Magd.* Oxon. *Sion.*
PEARSON Richard, DD. R. of St. Michael's Crooked Lane, Lond.
 Pf. lxxvi. 10. 4° 1684. Th. Sept. 9. Providence bringing good out of evil. *Ch. Ch.* Oxon. *Pub. L.* Camb.
 1 Thess. iv. 11. 4° 1684. b. Lord Mayor. The Study of Quietness. *Ch. Ch. C. C. C.* Oxon. *Pub. L.* Camb. *Sion.*
 1 Thess. iv. 13. 4° 1684. Fun. of Dr. Atfield.
 Rom. ii. 21. 4° 1690.
PEARSON Richard,   Priest of the Church of England.
 2 Kings v. 18, 19. 4° 1704. Naaman vindicated.
PEARSON William, LL. D. Chancellor of York, Arch Deacon of Nottingham and Residentiary of York.
 2 Chron. xxxii. 7, 8. 4° 1704. *York.* Th. Sept. 7. For Victory at Blenheim. *Queen's.* Oxon. *St. John's.* Camb.
 Luke xvi. 9. 4° 1708. Charity. The Duty of Char. to the poor.
 13 Serm. in 8° 1718. On sev. Occasions. *Bod. Ch. Ch.* Oxon.
PECK Fran. M. A. R. of Goodeby Maurewood, and Preb. of Linc.
 Prov. xxix. 2. 8° 1720. *Stamford.* Inauguration of a Mayor. Ad Magistratum.
 4 Disc. in 8° 1742. *viz.*
 Ezek. xxxiii. 32. Vis. p. 3. Of Grace and how to excite.
 John vi. 14. Vis. p. 25. Jesus Christ the true Messiah from his Miracles.

John xx. 12. East. p. 53. Jesus Christ the true Messiah from his Resurrection.
Judges xviii. 7. Assize. p. 81. The Necessity and Advantage of good Laws and good Magistrates.

PECK John,   V. of Welford, Warwicks.
  2 Cor. viii. 11. 4° 1703.
  Eccles. xii. 1. 4° 1686. Fun. of Mrs. Eliz. Bell *Brit. M.*
  Joshua vi. 26. 4° 1689. Th. for Deliverance from Popery.

PECK Samuel,   Minister of Poplar, Middlesex.
  2 Cor. v. 1. 4° 1684. Fun. of Sir Henry Johnson.
  Isai. lix. 11. 4° 1693. Assize.

PECKARD Peter, M. A. late Fell of C. C. C. Oxon.
  * 1 Cor. ix. 20. 8° 1753. Popular Clamour against the Jews indefensible.
  * 1 Pet. ii. 16. 8° 1754. The Nature and Extent of civil and religious Liberty.
  * Rev. xi. 13. 8° 1755. Dissertation. Earthquake at Lisbon.
  * 1 Cor. i. 21. 8° 1770. The proper Style of Christian Oratory. *Queen's.* Camb.
  * Rom ix. 28. 4° 1772. Vis.
  * Isai. v. 20. 8° 1775. Ag. Lord Chesterfield. The unalterable Nature of Vice and Virtue. *Queen's.* Camb.

PECKWELL Henry, DD. R. of Bloxham-cum Digby, Lincolns.
  * Heb. ii. x. 8° 1774. Christmas.
  * John xi. 3. 8° 1782. b. Gov. of *Lond.* Dispensary.

PEERS Richard, M. A. V. of Faringdon, Berks, and Preb. of Worcester.
  Matt. v. 17. 8° 1730. Christmas. The great Tendency of the positive Precepts of the Gospel to promote the Observance of nat. Religion. Ag. Tindal's Christianity as old as the Creation.

PEGGE Samuel, M. A. V. of Godmersham, Kent.
  John i. 5. 8° 1742. On St. John's day. *Queen's.* Camb. *Brit. M.*
  Isai. v. 20. 8° 1746. Rebell. Popery an Encourager of Vice and Immorality.

PEIRCE *James*,   of Exeter, Devon.
  ‡* 1 Cor. i. 3. 8° 1719. Evil and Cure of Divisions. *Brit. M.*
  ‡* 1 Cor. iii. 2. 8° 1720. *Brit. M.*
  15 Serm. in 1° 1728. On several Occasions. *Queen's.* Camb. Dr. *Ws's. L.* London.
  * 6 Dissertations in 4° 1737. *Ex.* Oxon. *Queen's. Cl. II.* Camb.

PEIRCE Thomas, DD.
  * Deut. vi. 12. 4° 1661.

PELIER V   DD.
  Wisd. xiv. 3. 8° 1737. Of Grace.
  Matt. v. 44. 8° 1737.
  Luke vii. 47. 8° 1737.
  John v. 14. 8° 1737.

PELLING Edward, DD. R. of Petworth, Sussex, Chapl. in Ord. and Preb. of Westminster.
  Prov. viii. 15. 4° 1679. Jan. 30. *Bod. Trin. St. John's.* Camb.

Luke iii. 14. 4° 1679. b. Artillery Co. *Ch. Ch. Jef.* Oxon. *Trin. St. John's.* Camb. *Brit. M.*
2 Theff. ii. 11. 4° 1679 3 f. Ag. Popery. Antient and modern Delufions compared. *Ch. Ch.* Oxon. *Pub. L.* Camb.
Lament. v. 16 4° 1682. Jan. 30. *Ch. Ch.* Oxon. *Pub. L. Trin.* Camb. *Sion.*
Pf. xxxiv. 19 (or 135.) 4° 1683. Th. Sep. 9. For a Deliverance from a fanatic Confpiracy. *Magd Worc* Oxon.
Prov. xxiv 21. 4° 1683. County-Feaft. *Brit. M.*
2 Sam. i. 14. 4° 1683. Jan. 30. David and the Amalekite upon the Death of Saul. *Ch. Ch. C.C.C. Magd.* Oxon.
Luke xix. 42. 4° 1683. Nov. 5. b. Lord Mayor. *Magd.* Oxon. *Pub. L.* Camb. *Sion.*
Rom. xiii. 2. 4° 1683. Jan. 30. b. the Judges. *Magd.* Oxon. *Pub. L.* Camb.
Pf. cxxxvii. 1. 4° 1685. Jan. 30. *Ch. Ch.* Oxon. *Trin.* Camb.
Rom. i. 8. 4° 1685. Nov. 5. The true mark of the Beaft; or the prefent Degeneracy of the Church of Rome. *Magd.* Ox.
Pf. cxxiv. 6. 4° 1685. Th. for Victory over the Rebels. *Bod. Ch.* Oxon. *Sion.*
1 Pet. iii. 3. 4° 1685. Sept. 27.
Luke i. 71. 4° 1690. b. King and Queen. *Magd. Ch. Ch.* Oxon. *Trin. St. John's.* Camb. *Sion.*
Acts xxiv. 16. 4° 1691. b. King and Queen. *Magd. Pub. L.* Camb. *Sion.*
Col. i. 12. 4° 1692. b. Queen. *Bod. Ch. Ch. Magd.* Ox. *Trin.* C.
1 Tim. iv. 16. 4° 1693. Vif. *Boa.*
John iii 16. 8° 1694. God's Love to mankind. *Pub. L.* Camb.
Pf. cix. 27. 4° 1695. b. King.
Rom. v. 5. 4° 1703. b. Queen.

PELLING John, DD, R. of St. Ann's, Weftminfter and Canon of Windfor.
Exod. xx. 5. 4° 1709. Jan. 30. b. Commons. *Ch. Ch. All S. C.C.C. Univ. Or. Jef. Hert.* Oxon. *Trin. Queen's.* Camb. *Sion.*

PEMBERTON Ebenezer
*Serm. in 8° 1726. On feveral Occafions.

PEMBERTON Ebenezer, DD. Paftor of a Church in Bofton.
*1 Pet. i. 4. 8° 1770. On the Death of Rev. Mr. Whitfield.

PENDLEBURY William, M. A. R. of Burythorp, and V. of Acklam, Yorkfhire.
Joel ii. 12-18. 8° 1744. Faft.
Rom. i. 25. 8° 1746. *York.* p. 5. Errors and Mifchiefs of Pop.
Rom. xiii. 4. 8° 1746. *York.* p. 45. The fatal Confequences of arbitrary and defpotic Power.
Matt. v 16. 8° 1748. Vif.

PENN James.   Undermafter of Chrift's Hofpital, London, and V. of Clavering-cum Langley, Effex.
*2 Sam. xvii. 23. 4° 1756. b. Gov. of *Lond.*-Hofpital.
*Matt. ix. 36. 4° 1758. Faft.

* Tracts

* Tracts in 8° 1756.
* Judges xvi. 25. 4° 1758.
* Gen. xxv. 14. 4° 1761. b. Gov. of Christ-Hospital.
* Isai xlix. 23. 8° 1761. Accession.
* Acts viii. 17. 12° 17
* Matt. xv. 9. 8° 1761. Against Popery.
* Prov. xx. 1 8° 1767. Caution to the Livery men of London. Ag. the general Election.
* Acts xx. 9. 8° 1769. Sleepy Sermon.
* Serm. in 8° 1769.

PENNINGTON John, M. A. R. of All Saints Huntingdon, and Preb. of Lincoln.
 2 Chron. xix 5–7. 8° 1728. Assize. King Jehoshaphat's Charge to his Judges; or Justice without Corruption, or Partiality recommended.
 Rom. xiii. 3–5. 8° 1728. Assize. St. Paul's Charge to civil Magistrates—shewing their Duty in defence of Christianity.
* Rom. xi. 22. 8° 1756. Fast. On the Earthquake. Serious Call to Repentance. *Queen's*. Camb.
* 1 Tim. iv. 16. 8° 1756. Vis. St. Paul's Instruction to the Christian Preacher. *Queen's*. Camb.

PENROSE Thomas, M. A. V. of Newberry, Berks.
* 2 Chron. xx. 3, 4. 8° 1745. Fast for Rebellion. Dec. 9.
* Deut. xxiii. 9. 8° 1759. b. Militia.
* Tit. iii. 1. 8° 1760. Accession. Duty of Subjects to their Princes set forth.

PENROSE Thomas, jun.   R. of Beckinton and Standerwick, Somersetshire.
* Rev. xiv. 13. 4° 1774. Fun. of Rev. J. Gerce, L.L.B.
* Ps. xxiv. 14. 4° 17-6. Fast.

PENTYCROSS Thomas, M. A. R. of St. Mary's the Moor, Wallingford, Berks, and Chaplain to the Right Hon. the Earl of Selkirk.
* 20 Serm. in 8° 1781. speculative, practical, and experimental.
‡* 1 Cor. xv. 56, 57. 4° 1782. Fun. of Mrs. Ann Walcott at Bath.

PEPLOE Samuel, Bp. of Chester.
 1 Kings xviii. 21. 8° 1716. Assize of the Rebels. *Sion*.
 1 Sam. xii. 7. 8° 1716. *Sion*.
 Matt. xxv. 40. 4° 1730. Ann. meeting Char. Sch.
 Matt. x. 34. 4° 1733. Jan. 30. b. Lords.
 1 Cor. x. 14. 4° 1745. Rebellion. Popish Idolatry, a strong Reason why all Protestants should zealously oppose the present Rebellion.

PEPPER John, B. A. Master of the Free School, Lecturer of Odyham, and R. of Windslade, Hants.
 2 Pet. ii. 10. 12° 1716.
 Prov. xiv. 34. 8° 1721. Assize.

PERCIVALE William, M. A. Arch-Deacon of Cashel, Ireland.
 Nehem. xiii. 14. 4° 1713. Cons. of a Church. *St. John's*. Cam.

PERCY Thomas, Bp. of Dromore, Ireland.
 * John xiii. 35. 4° 1769. b. the Sons of the Clergy.
PERIAM George, M. A. late Student of Ch. Ch. Oxon. and V. of Lathbury, Bucks.
 * Matt. v. 39. 8° 1755. Affize. The means of redreffing, and Duty of forgiveneſs.
PERKINS Joſeph, M. A. Cur. of Little Hampſtead, Devon, afterwards of little Oakley, Eſſex.
 Epheſ. i. 7. 4° 1693. Palm Sunday.
 Acts xx. 33. 4° 1699.
 John i. 14. 8° 1707. Chriſtmas.
PERKINS Joſeph, A Priſoner in the Marſhalſea.
 Col. iii. 1. 8° 1707. Eaſter. *Trin. Queen's.* Camb.
 Matt. v. 8. 8° 1707.
PERRINCHIEF Richard, DD. Preb. of Weſtminſter.
 Lev. xxvi. 18. 4° 1666. Faſt. b. Commons for the Plague. *Ch. Ch. Magd.* Oxon. *Pub. L.* Camb. *Sion.*
PERRONET Vincent, M. A. V. of Shoreham, Kent.
 Rom. xii. 13. 8° 1745. Of Divine Hoſpitality.
PERROT Humphrey, M. A. Fell. of Oriel Coll. Oxon.
 1 King. xxii. 43. 8° 1738. *Oxon.* Affize. *Worc.* Oxon.
PERROTT Thomas, M. A. R. of St. Martin's, Yorkſ.
 * Epheſ. iv. 25. 8° 1726. Affize. Truth, Cement of Society.
PERSAL A Jeſuit.
 ‡ * Matt. xxviii. 19. 4° 1687. b. King and Queen. *Brit. M.*
PERSE Will. M. A. Fell. of King's Coll. Camb. Miniſter of Malton, and R. of Heſlerton, Yorkſhire.
 Acts xxii. 3. 4° 1682. *Eton.* Sch. Feaſt. *Trin. St. John's.* Camb. *Eton. Sion.*
 Pſ. cxxix. 1, 2. 4° 1689. Nov. 5. *Trin.* Camb.
 Matt. xxvi. 13. 4° 1695. Royal Fun.
 Eccleſ. x. 20. 4° 1696. Th.
 Exod. xvii. 13-15. 4° 1706. *York.* Th. June 27. For Victory over the French Army.
PERSEHOWSE Thomas, M. A. of Trin. Coll. Camb. Curate of Barnes, Surrey.
 Zech. iv. 6. 4° 1744. May 29. b. Lord Mayor.
 Rom. iii. 16-18. 8° 1745. Jan. 30. b. Lord Mayor.
PETER Charles, M. A. R. of St. Mabyn's, Cornwall.
 * Serm. (Poſth.) in 8° 1776.
PETERS John, M. A. R. of St. Clement Old Romney, Kent, Lect. of St. Clement Danes.
 Rom. xiv. 16. 4° 1724. b. Antient Britons. The univerſal Obligation to Chriſtian Charity.
 Phil. i. 28. 4° 1745. Rebellion. Error in Religion deſtructive of Government.
PETERS Richard
 1 Cor. x. 13. } 2 ſ. 4° 1737. *Philadelphia.*
 Rom. xii. 21. }

PETTER

OF AUTHORS, &c.

PETIT Peter, M. A. V. of Wymondham, and Commiſſary of Norf.
* - - - - 1755. Faſt.
* Iſai. xxxiii. 1. 4° 1779. Faſt. The Spoilers ſpoiled.
PETRIE Robert,   V D. M. Of Canobie.
* Heb. xiii. 15–17. 12° 1779. The Reaſonableneſs and Neceſſity of public Worſhip. V. Scotch Pr. V. III. p. 39.
[PETTER George]
* Lect. in fo. 1661.
PETTER John, M. A. Chaplain to Brigadier Lumley's Regiment of Horſe.
* John xxi. 22. 4° 1685. July 5. On occaſion of the late Rebellion. *Pub. L.* Camb.
1 Sam. iv. 9. 4° 1694. b. the Forces in Flanders. *Pub. L. Trin.* C.
Iſai. xxxii. 8. 4° 1698. County-Feaſt.
PHELPES *Charles*
* Epheſ. v. 18. 12° 1676. Caveat. ag. Drunkenneſs. *Pub. L.* C.
PHILIPPS Henry, M. A. of both Univerſities, and ſometime Fell. of Magd. Coll. Oxon.
* 3 Sermons in 12° 1705.
PHILIPPS Philip, M. A. Chapl. to the Earl of Berkley.
1 Pet. ii 15. 8° 1715. Welch Society. Loyalty and Love. *Ch. Ch.* Oxon.
PHILIPS David, DD. R. of Stackpoole Elidor, Pembrokeſhire.
Pſ. cxxxiii. 1. 8° 1710. 3 ſ. Unity recommended to Pract. *Sion.*
PHILIPS F   E. A. P.
Eccleſ. v. i. 8° 1717. The Church of England man directed how to worſhip in public and private.
PHILIPS John, B. D. Fell. of Magd. Coll. Camb. V. of Ayleſham, Norfolk.
Pſ. xxi. 1. 4° 1661. Th. May 29. God and the King. God's Strength, the King's Salvation. *Univ.* Oxon. *Pub. L.* Camb.
PHILIPS John, M. A. Chap. to Lord Churchill's Regm. of Marines.
Deut. iv. 7, 8. 4° 1725. On occaſion of the Expedition into Sardinia. *Worc.* Oxon.
PHILIPS Michael
* Occaſional ſerm. in 12° 1775. For the royal Navy.
PHILIPS Nicholas,   Chapl. to the Garriſon in Scilly,
Heb. xi. 15. 4° 1679. The Holy Choice.
Dan. vi. 21. 4° 1681. Loyalty and Piety.
Acts ii. 47. 4° 1681. The way to Heaven clearly diſcovered.
PHILIPS William,   V. of St. Peter's, Worceſter.
* Rom. xiv. 19. 4° 1730. May 29. The things which make for Peace.
Pſ. lxxxiv. 4. 8° 1731. Muſick.
PHILLIPS Robert, DD.
Pſ. lxxv. 7. 4° 1712. Th. May 29. b. Commons.
PHILPOT Thomas, DD. R. of Turveſton and Akeley, Bucks.
Eccleſ. iii. 20. 4° 1660. Fun. An adieu to the Duke of Glouc.
John v. 7. 4° 1663. Sept. 29. The Cripple's Complaint. *Bod.*

PICKARD Edward
  * Luke i. 74,75. 8° 1747. Vaſt Import. of Delivery from Popery.
  * 1 Kings iii. 9,10. 8° 1752. b. young perſons. Solomon's Preference of Wiſdom.
  * Phil. i. 23,24. 8° 1758. Fun of *Tim. Wild.*
  * 2 Tim. i. 12. 8° 1758. Fun. of Rev. *T. Newman. Queen's.* Ca.
  * Prov. xxii. 6. 4° 1760. Charity to Orphans.
  * Pſ. cxlvii. 1. 8° 1761. Aug. 1.
  * Matt. xxv. 21. 8° 1762. Fun. of Rev. *George Benſon,* DD. *Queen's.* Camb.
  * Gen. xviii. 19. 8° 1763. 3 Diſc. Relig. Governm. of a Family.
PICKERING Robert, M. A. R. of Cowling, Kent.
  Tit iii. 1. 8° 1712. Lent. The Sovereign's Power, and Subject's Duty. *Bal.* Oxon.
PICKERING *Roger,*   F. R. S. late Miniſter of the Goſpel in Silver ſtreet, and Lect. at Salter's Hall, London.
  Pſ. cxxxix. 7–10. 8° 1751. On the Earthquake.
PICKERING Thomas, DD. V. of St. Sepulchre's, London.
  2 Sam. i. 27. 4° 1750. Jan. 30. b. Lord Mayor. *Worc.* Oxon.
PIDDLE John,   late of St. Mary Hall, Oxon. Curate of Sherborne, Dorſetſhire.
  * Ezek. xxxiii. 30,31. 8° 1777. Abuſe of hear. God's word.
[PIERCE John]
  ‡ * Pſ. lxxxv. 9,10. 8° 1704. Aſſize.
PIERCE John, M. A. R. of Cotteſbrooke, Northamptonſhire.
  15 Serm. in 8° 1731. on ſeveral Occaſions.
PIERCE Tho. DD. Preſid. of Magd. Coll Ox. and Dean of Sarum.
  ‡ * Acts xi. 28. 4° 1661. Ad Synod. Lond.
  A Collection of Serm. in 4° 1671. *Oxon.* upon ſeveral occaſions &c. *Bod. Univ. Magd. Queen's. New C.* Oxon. *Sion.*
  A Decad of Caveats to the people of England. 4° 1679. *Bod. Magd.* Oxon. *Sion.*
  The Sinner impleaded in his own Court. 4° 1679. *Pub. L. C. Sion.*
  The Signal Diagnoſtic. 4° 1679. *Bod. Sion.*
  2 Diſc. of the Law and Equity of the Goſpel on John xiii. 13.— With other Serm. V. III. 4° 1686. *Bod. Queen's.* Ox. *Pub. L.* Camb. *Sion.*
PIERS Henry, M. A. of Trin. Coll. Dublin, V. of Bexley, Kent.
  1 Cor iv. 1,2. 12° 1742. Viſ.
  Iſai. vii. 14. 8° 1743. Chriſtmas. Chriſt born, that we may be born again. *Queen's.* Camb.
  Luke xiii. 3. 12° 1744. Faſt. Goſpel Repentance.
  Pſ. cvii. 2. 8° 1746. *Briſtol* Th., Oct. 9. Religion and Liberty reſcued from Superſtition and Slavery.
  Job xxviii. 28. 12° 1747. Fun.   True Wiſdom from above; or Chriſtianity the beſt Underſtanding.
  Heb. iii. 18,19. 12° 1748. Faſt. Infidelity the Ruin of a People; or Unbelief the damning Sin.
  Epheſ. ii. 12. 12° 1748. The Subſtance of 3 Sermons. Atheiſm a commoner Sin than thought of.

OF AUTHORS, &c. 269

    * Diſc. in 1748.
    * Luke i. 17. 12° 1758.
    * Pſ. lxviii. 19. 8° 1759. Th. for Victory and Harveſt.
    Matt. xvii. 11, 12. 4° 1761. On a Legacy left to Danſon Pariſh, Kent, by Mr. Styleman.
PIERSON J   DD.
    * Pſ. lxxv. 1. 4° 17   Th. ſ.
PIETY Thomas
    * Diſc. in 8° 1737.
    * Epheſ. ii. 4, 5. 8° 1737. Chriſtmas.
    * Pſ. xcvii. 1. 8° 1746. Th. on the Duke's (Cumberland) Return.
PIGG Thomas, M. A. V. of Watton, and R. of Bodney, Norfolk.
    Exod. xx. 16. 4° 1736. *Camb.* Aſſize.
PIGGOTT George
    *   -   -   -   1735. Chriſtmas.
PIGGOTT John
    * 1 Theſſ. iv. 13, 14. 8° 1700. On the Death of *Mord. Abbott*, Eſq;
    * Eccleſ. iv. 11. 8° 1714.
    * 11 Serm. in 8° 1714. *Dr. W's L.* London.
PIGOTT Edward
    * Serm. in 12° 1702.
PIGOTT Henry, B. D. Miniſter of Rochdale, Lancaſhire.
    Acts xvii. 6. 4° 1676. Aſſize. *Bod. Queen's.* Camb.
PIGOTT James, M. A. V. of Wigſton Magna, and late of Pemb. Hall Camb.
    * Gen. v. 27. 4° 1762. The Age of Methuſelah, and the Houſe of Mourning.
PIKE Samuel
    * Rom. iv. 16 8° 1748. Connect. between Faith, and true Grace.
    * Phil. i. 27. 8° 1753. Education for Miniſters.
    * Exod. xxxiii. 19. 8° 1758. Saving Grace, ſovereign Grace.
    * Iſai. xxxiii. 17. 8° 1761. Coronation.
    * Heb. xi. 1.   17
PILKINGTON Matthew, L.L.B. Preb. of Litchfield.
    2 Sam. xxiii. 3. 4° 1733. Elect. of a Lord Mayor. *Queen's.* Cam.
    * John v. 39. 8° 1755. Viſ. The Paſſages in Moſes and the Prophets, in which are Expreſſions of eternal Life, illuſtrated. *Queen's.* Camb.
    * Gen. xvii. 11. 8° 1760. Baptiſm of an Adult.
PILLOK Thomas
    ‡* 1 Cor. x. 15. 8° 1734. *Edinburgh.* Immortality of the Soul. *Brit. M.*
PINDAR Thomas
    ‡* 2 Tim. iii. 16. 8° 1728. *New York.* Divinity of the Scriptures. *Brit. M.*
PINDAR William, M. A. Fell. of Univ. Coll. Oxon. and Chapl. to Ford Lord Grey of Werke.
    Prov. vii. 27. 4° 1677. b. Ld. Mayor. *Bod Cb. Ch. C.C.C. Univ. Worc. Magd.* Oxon. *Pub. L.* Camb. *Sion.*

Pſ.

Pf. cxxvii. 1. 4° 1679. Of Divine Providence. *Ch. Cb. C. C. C. Univ. Magd.* Oxon. *Pub. L. St. John's.* Camb.

[PINE William,] of Briftol.
* - - - - - 1770. A word in reafon—or Submiffion to Government.

PINNELL Peter, M. A. R. of St. Mary Magd. Bermondfey, Surrey.
Pf. lxxxiii. 18. 4° 1748. May 29. b. Lord Mayor.
Prov. xxix. 2. 4° 1750. Affize.

PINSENT John, M. A. V. of Colefhill, Berks.
Job xiv. 14. 8° 1705. Fun. of Mrs. Barker.

PITTIS Thomas, DD. Chapl. in Ord. and R. of St. Botolph without Bifhopfgate, London.
Luke iii. 14. 4° 1677. b. Artillery Co. *All S. Univ. Queen's.* Ox. *Pub. L. St. John's.* Camb. *Sion.*
1 John ii. 24. 4° 1682. An old way of ending new Controverfies. *Pub. L.* Camb. *Brit. M.*
Ecclef xi. 6. 4° 1684. Spitt. W. *Ch. Ch.* Oxon.

PITTMAN William, M. A.
Prov. iii. 9, 10. 8° 1735. Conf. of a Ch.

PITTS Jofeph
* Pf. xxvii. 13. 8° 1742. Farewell.
* Job i. 21. 8° 1742. Fun. of a Child.
‡ * Pf. lvi. 3. 8° 1746. Rebellion.
* - - - - 1756. Faft.
* 1 Chron. xxix. 28. 8° 1760. Royal Fun.

PLACE Conyers, M. A.
Matt. xxiii. 35, 36. 4° 1702. Jan. 30.
Acts vii. 26. 4° 1705. Affize.

PLATTS John
* Serm. in 8° 1701.

PLAXTON John, M. A. R. of Sutton upon Derwent, Yorkf.
1 Cor. i. 10. 8° 1746. *York.* Rebellion. An Exhortation to Unanimity and Concord.

PLEDGER Elias
Gen. xlii. 21, 22. 4° 1677. m. e. C. p. 224. How a Chriftian fhould behave himfelf, when inward and outw. Troubles meet.

PLEYDELL Jofias, B. D. Arch-D. and Minor Preb. of Chichefter.
Rev. xiv. 13. 4° 1681. Fun. of Mr. Glanville. V. Glanville's Remains. *Brit. M.*
Rom. xiii 4. } 4° 1682. 2 f. Loyalty and Conformity afferted.
Ecclef. v. 1. } *Brit. M.*

PLUMPTREE Charles, DD. Mafter of Queen's Coll. Camb.
* 2 Cor. iv. 2. 4° 1754. Conc. ad Cler. *Queen's.* Camb.

[POCOCK T.]
* - - - - 1738. Acceffion.

POCOCKE Richard, M. A.
* Serm. in 8° 1702. in 2 parts.
Matt. vi. 6. } 4° 1707. 2 f.
Matt. vi. 24. }

* Heb.

POCOCKE R.　　　Bp. of Offory.
　　* - - - - 1755.
　　* Heb. xiii. 16. 4° 1761. At the *Magdalen*-Hofp.
　　* 1 Theff. ii. 19, 20. 4° 1762. Irifh Prot. Schools.
POLLARD Thomas,　　Minifter of St. Peter's, Dublin.
　　Lev. xix. 17. 4° 1698. b. relig. Societies in Dublin.
POMFRET Samuel
　　* Ezra x. 4. 12° 1701. Ref. of Manners. *Pub. L.* Camb.
POMFRET Tho. M. A. R. of Umpthill, and V. of Luton, Bedfordf.
　　Rom. xiii. 5. 4° 1682. Affize. *Trin.* Camb.
　　1 Pet. ii. 20, 21. 4° 1683. Th. Sep. 9. Paffive Obedience ftated
　　　and afferted. *Ch. Ch.* Oxon. *Trin. St. John's.* Camb.
POOL *Matthew*, M. A. of Emanuel Coll. Camb. Minifter of St. Mi-
　　chael in le Querne (before the Ejection. 1662.)
　　John iv. 23, 24. 4° 1660. b. Lord Mayor. Evangelical Worfhip,
　　　fpiritual Worfhip. *Bod. St. John's.* Camb. *Sion.*
　　Matt. xi. 19. 4° 1673. 2 f. A feafonable Apology for Relig. *Bod.*
　　Matt. xxiii. 8–10. 4° 1675. m. c. P. p. 1. Pope and Councils
　　　not infallible.
　　Col. i. 20. 4° 1676. m. e. G. p. 254. Xt's Satisfaction difcuffed.
　　Pf. xv. 3. 4° 1676. f. m. c. C. p. 527. The Prevention and Cure
　　　of Detraction.
　　Job xxxiii. 23, 24. 4° 1677. m. e. C. p. 101. How muft we vifit
　　　fick Perfons.
POOLEY Giles, DD. V. of St. Leonard's Shoreditch, London.
　　John xiii. 35. 4° 1705. Nov. 5. b. Lord Mayor. *Ch. Ch.* Oxon.
　　　Queen's. St. John's. Camb.
　　Pf. cvii. 2. 8° 1716. Th. After Rebellion.
POPE James
　　Matt. xx. 1–13. 8° 1675. Kingdom of Heaven explained. *Bod.*
[POPE John]
　　* Matt. xxvii. 51. 4° 1777. Shock of an Earthquake.
POPE Michael
　　* Difc. in 8° 1701. *Pub. L* Camb.
　　* 2 Chron. xx. 12. 4° 1703. Faft
　　* Pf. lxxxix. 22, 33. 8° 1716.
PORTAL Andrew, M. A. V. of St. Helen's, Berks.
　　* Acts xvi. 29, 30. 8° 1750. 2 f. On the Earthquake.
　　* Pf. lxxvi. 10. 4. 1763. Th. for Peace.
PORTEOUS *William*,　　one of the Minifters of Glafcow.
　　* Luke ix. 55, 56. 8° 1779. Faft. The Doctrine of Toleration
　　　applied to the prefent times.
PORTEUS Beilby, Bp. of Chefter.
　　* 1 Sam. xiii. 14. 8° 1761. Character of King David. *Braz. N.*
　　　Oxon. *Queen's.* Camb.
　　† Matt. vi. 33. 4° 1767. Jan. 30. b. Commons. *Braz. N.* Oxon.
　　　Queen's. Camb.
　　* Tit. ii. 6. 4° 1767. *Camb.* Commencement. *Queen's.* Camb.
　　* John iii. 19. 4° 1772. b. King and Queen. *Ex.* Oxon.
　　* 2 Tim. iii. 4. 4° 1772. Love of Pleafure.

  * Luke vi. 30. 4° 1773. b. Gov. of the *Afylum*.
  * 2 Kings iv. 1. 4° 1776. b. Sons of the Clergy.
  * - - - - 4° 1777. Faſt. b. Lords.
  * Pſ. xxii. 28. 4° 1778. Jan. 30. b. Lords.
  * Jer. xviii. 11. 4° 1779. Faſt. b. Commons.
PORTER J.
  * 2 Tim. ii. 22. 8° 1708 Fun.   Caution againſt ſinful Luſts.
PORTER *John*,   of Hinkley, Leiceſterſ.
  * Mark iii. 24. 8° 1768. Evil of national Diviſions.
PORTER Thomas, M. A.
  2 Tim. iii. 15. 8° 1661. Character of a formal Profeſſor in Relig.
[PORTER William,]   Miles Lane, London.
  * Pſ. xxxi. 5. 8° 1763. Fun.
POSTLEWAITE Matthew, M. A. R. of Denton, Norfolk.
  Heb. v. 12. 4° 1715. School-Feaſt.
  Acts xxvi. 9 4° 1719. *Norwich*. Nov. 5.
POSTLEWAITE T.   B. D. Fell. of Trin. Coll. Camb.
  * Iſai. vii. 14–16. 4° 1781. *Camb*. Diſc. in 2 parts.
POTTER Francis, M. A. V. of Burford, Oxon.
  Jerem. xxii. 30. 8° 1745. Rebellion.
POTTER Francis, M. A. Arch Deacon of Wells.
  * Pſ. cxxii. 3. 8° 1757. Faſt.
  * - - - - 1761. Ag. murmuring.
POTTER   Reymarſton, Norfolk.
  * John iii. 5. 8° 1758. On the pretended Inſpiration of the Methodiſts.
POTTER John, M. A. V. of Cloford, Somerſetſhire.
  Rom. xii. 18. 8° 1712. Aſſize. *Linc*. Oxon. *St. John's*. Camb.
  ——— 19 8° 1712. Aſſize. *Queen's*. Camb.
POTTER John, Abp. of Canterbury.
  * Serm. in 8° 1753. V. Vol. I. Of his theological Works. *Ch. Ch. Braz. N*. Oxon. *Pub. L*. Camb.
POTTS *John*,   V. D. M.
  * Serm. in 8° 1758. On Jonah's Commiſſion.
POVEY Joſiah,   of St. Catherine's.
  * Pſ cxix. 1 8° 1698.
POWELL Charles, M. A. late Student of Ch. Ch. Oxon. and R. of Cheddington, Bucks.
  Pſ. x. 10. 4° 1683. Th. Sept. 9. Religious Rebellion. *Bod. Sion*.
POWELL Joſ. M. A. R. of St. Mary in the Wall, Colcheſter, Eſſex.
  Luke ii. 29. 4° 1692. Fun. of Rev. Thomas Gregory. *Bod. Sion. Brit. M*.
  2 Chron. xxxv. 24. 4° 1695. Royal Fun. *Pub. L. Trin*. Camb.
POWELL Matthew, B. A.
  * Haggai i. 5. 8° 1748. *Camb*. Diſtemper among horned Cattle. *Queen's*. Camb.
POWELL *Thomas*
  * Eccleſ. xii. 1. 12° 1676. The beauty, vigor and ſtrength of Youth beſpoke for God. *Pub. L*. Camb.

POWELL William, M. A. Dean of St. Afaph.
  Pf. cix. 2. 12° 1716. *Shrewsbury.* Jan. 30. The Ways that lead to Rebellion laid open.
  1 Sam. iii. 13. 8° 1742. Vif. *Queen's.* Camb.
POWELL William, M. A R. of Waldingfield, Suffolk.
  * Acts xi. 16. 12° 1730. What it is to be a Christian indeed.
POWELL William Samuel, DD. late Arch-Deacon of Colchester, and Master of St. John's Coll. Camb.
  * 1 Cor. i. 23, 24. 4° 1767. *Camb.* Commencement.
  * Serm. in 8° 1776. on various Subjects. *Queen's.* Camb.
POWER Lawrence, M. A. of Trin. Coll. Dublin, Preb. and R. of Tandrogee &c.
  Pf. cxii. 6. 4° 1680. Fun. - The righteous Man's Portion.
POYNTING *John*
  * Pf. cxxxii. 16. 8° 1768. b. Diffenting Clergy.
POWYS Thomas, M. A.   Fawley, Bucks.
  * Pf. xc. 12. 8° 1766. *Reading.* On Recovery from a fall from a Horfe.
PRAT Samuel, DD. Chapl. to the Duke of Gloucefter, and Minifter of the Savoy.
  Col. iii. 15. 4° 1697. Co. Feaft. *Pub. L. Trin.* Camb.
  Ifai. i. 5. 4° 1697. Faft. Sep. 2. b. Ld May. *Trin. St. John's.* C.
  1 Cor. x. 24. 4° 1700. School-Feaft. Public Spiritednefs recommended. *C. C. C.* Oxon. *Brit. M.*
  Nahum. i. 3. 4° 1704. Faft. *C. C. C.* Oxon.
  Zech. i. 16. 4° 1704. b. Lord Mayor. Returns of Mercy.
PRATT Benjamin, DD. Provoft of Trin. Coll. Dublin.
  Pf. cxxxiii. 1. 4° 1706. Anniv. Char. School-Feaft. The Excellency of the duty of religious Unity among brethren in Judgment and affections.
  Ifai. i. 26. 4° 1709. May 29.
PRENTICE *Thomas*,   at Nottingham.
  * Tit. iii. 1. 8° 1777. Faft.
PRESSICK George,   of Dublin.
  * Several ferm. in fo. 1662.
  * 8 Serm. in 4° 1664.
  * Others in 4° 1666.
PRIAULX John, DD. Canon Refid. of Sarum.
  Acts viii. 17. 4° 1662. Confirmation confirmed and recommended from Scripture, Antiquity and Reafon. *Bod.*
PRICE James
  James iv. 17.
PRICE John, DD. Fell. of King's Coll. Camb. Fell. of Eton, R. of Petworth and Preb. of Sarum.
  1 Sam. ii. 9. 4° 1660. b. Commons. *Cb. Cb. Worc.* Oxon.
  1 Cor. ix. 10. 4° 1683. Th. Sept. 9. *Cb. Cb.* Oxon.
PRICE John, M. A. of Univ. Coll. Oxon. and Cur. of Holywell.
  Matt. v. 47. 8° 1661. *Oxon.* The Chriftians Excellency.

Vol. II.   M m   Gal.

Gal. iv. 16. 8° 1661. *Oxon.* Truth beg. Enmity.
Ecclef. x. 17. 8° 1661. *Oxon.* A nation's Happ. in a good King.
Heb. xiii. 16. 8° 1661. *Oxon.* Praife of Charity.
Phil. iv. 5. 4° 1663. Moderation and Sedition.
PRICE John, M. A.
* Pf. cxviii. 24. 8° 1748. b. antient Britons. The Advantages of Unity recommended.

PRICE John, B. D. R. of Newton Tony, Wilts.
* 1 John iii. 17. 8° 1730. Brief for relief of German and French Proteftants at Copenhagen.

PRICE *Richard*, DD. and F. R. S.
* Pf. cxlvii. 20. 8° 1759. Th.
* Job xxxii. 8. 8° 1766. Char. School meeting. The Nature and Dignity of human Soul. *Queen's.* Camb.
* John xiii. 17. 8° 1770. Vanity, Mifery, and Infamy of Knowledge without fuitable Practice.
* Gen. xviii. 32. 8° 1779. Faft.
* 1 Pet. i. 11. or } 8° 1781. Faft.
* 2 Pet. iii. 13. }

PRICE Samuel
Ecclef. iii. 1.

PRICE *Samuel*
* Rev. xiii. 3. 8° 1724.
* Deut. viii. 11. 8° 1725. Ref. of Manners.
* Heb. xiii. 16. 8° 1726. 6 f.
* Phil. i. 23. 8° 1749. Fun. of *Mary Abney*.
* Matt. v. 48. V. I. p. 54. Moral Perf. of God. ⎤
* Luke i. 72. V. I. p. 196. Var. Difp. of Gofp. ⎟
* Rom. xiii. 7. V. II. p. 291. Duty to Superiors. ⎟
* Rom. xv. 13. V. II. p. 368. Peace of Confcience Hope and holy Joy. ⎬ V. Berryftreet f.
* Gal. v. 5, 6. V. II. p. 94. Faith and Hope in Jefus Chrift. ⎟ 8° 1757.
* Tit. ii. 11, 12. V. II. p. 196. On Sobriety &c. ⎟
* Heb. vi. 2. V. II. p. 389. The Refurrection of the Body, and the laft Judgment. ⎟
* 1 Pet. iii. 18. V. I. p. 263. Xt's Sufferings &c. ⎦

PRICE William, B. D. late Preacher at Covent Garden, now to the Reformed church in Amfterdam.
Pf. cxviii. 23. 4° 1663. On the King's Reftoration.

PRIDEAUX Humphrey, DD. Dean of Norwich.
* 1 Sam. xii. 24. 4° 1703. Th. for Victory. *Cl. H. St. John's.* Camb. *Brit. M.*

PRIDEAUX John, DD. R. of Exeter Coll. and Reg. Profeffor of Divinity, Oxon.
* Matt. v. 25. 4° 1661.

PRIEST Ifaac, Prefbyter of the Church of England.
1 Tim. vi. 7-19. 8° 1730.
Pf. xcvi. 9. 8° 1750. Defence of the Liturgy.
* Serm. in 8° 1753. on 10 different Subjects.

PRIEST Simon, V. of Bisley, Gloucesterſ.
  Pſ. cxix. 115. 8° 1710. Danger of bad Company. *Sion*
  Eccleſ. v. 14. 8° 1711.
PRIESTLEY *Joseph*, L.L.D. and F. R. S.
  * Rom. xiv. 7. 8° 1764. b. diſſent. Clergy. The duty of not living to ourſelves. *Queen's*. Camb.
  * 1 Pet. i. 13 8° 1773. On reſigning his paſtoral Office at *Leeds*.
  * Matt. xiii. 3–10. 8° 1779. The Doctrine of Divine Influence on the human Mind.
  * - - - - 1782. 2 ſ. On habitual Devotion.
PRIESTLEY T. V. of Snettiſham, Norfolk.
  * Micah vi. 8. 8° 1776. Aſſize.
  * Matt. xvi. 27. 8° 1776. Aſſize.
PRINCE John, M. A. V. of Berry Pomeroy, Devon.
  1 Tim. iv. 16. 4° 1674. Viſ. *Bod. Univ. St. John's.* Camb.
  * Pſ. cxxvii. 1. 8° 1722. Th. for Plague.
PRINCE John, B. A. Lect. of St. Mary Aldermanbury, London.
  * Pſ. cxxii. 6–9. 8° 1781. b. Antigallicans.
PRINCE Tho. M. A. Paſtor of the South Ch. Boſton, New England.
  ‡ * Pſ. lxviii. 71, 72. 8° 1728. *Beſton.* Civil rulers. *Brit. M.*
  Pſ. cxviii. 23. 8° 1745. *Boſton.* Th. on taking Cape Breton. Extraordinary Events the Doings of God, and marvellous in pious eyes. *All S.* Oxon. *Queen's.* Camb.
  Exod. xiv. 13. 8° 1747. *Boſton.* Th. Nov. 27. The Salvations of God in 1746. *Queen's.* Camb.
  * Ezra ix. 13, 14. 8° 1747. Th. for Victory near Culloden. *Queen's.* Camb.
  Pſ. cvii. 33–35. 8° 1749. Th. Aug. 24. For Rain. The natural and moral government and agency of God in causing Droughts and Rains.
PRIOR *William*, DD. London.
  * Rev. xviii. 4. 8° 1750. Aug. 1. Popery not Xnity. *Brit. M.*
  * Matt. xi. 30. 8° 1754. Ch. ſ. Pleaſure of Xtian Life. *Brit. M.*
PRIOR William, Cur. of Sawbridgeworth, Herts.
  * Prov. xiv. 34. 8° 1758. Faſt.
PRITCHARD Thomas, M. A. late R. of Weſt Tilbury, Eſſex.
  Heb. xiii. 14. 4° 1693. Fun. of Mrs. Dawes. *Bod. Univ. Linc.* Oxon. *Queen's.* Camb. *Eton. Sion.*
  Heb. ix. 27. 4° 1693. Fun. of Lady Lumley. *Bod.*
[PROCTER Henry]
  * Matt. xxv. 4. 8° 17
PROSSER Jacob, Chapl. to the Garriſon of Portſmouth.
  Pſ. lxxxv. 8. 8° 1713. Th. July 7. For Peace.
PROUDMAN John, R. of the Mediety of Trowell, Northampt.
  Eccleſ. xii. 14. 8° 1719. *Nottingham.* Aſſize.
PROVOSTE John, M. A.
  Pſ. xxxvii. 37. 4° 1698. Fun. of Lady Cutts. *Ch. Ch. Ox. Cl. H. Trin.* Camb. *Brit. M.*

PROWDE Francis, M. A. N. of Woollavington, Somerſetſ.
  Acts viii. 17. 4° 1694. Conf. *Ch. Ch. Ox. St. John's.* C. *Brit. M.*
PRUDE John, M. A. Chapl. to the Duke of Norfolk, and Cur. of St. Clement's Danes, Middleſex.
  Eccleſ ii. 16. 4° 1697. Fun. of Mrs. Baynard. *Brit. M.*
PUDDICOMB J.   M. A.
  * Pſ. li. 17. 4° 1782. Faſt.
PUGH Hugh,   Miniſter of the Church of England.
  Gal. iv. 18. 8° 1710. Of relig. Zeal. *Linc.* Oxon *Queen's.* Cam.
PUGH William,   Cur. of Tottenhoe, Bucks.
  * Rom. xiii. 4. 4° 1764. Aſſize.
PULLEN Tobias, Bp. of Dromore.
  Pſ cxviii. 24. 4° 1695. Nov. 5.
PULLEYN John, M. A. Preb. of St. Paul's, London.
  Acts xx. 34. 4° 1699. School-Feaſt. *St. John's.* Camb.
  Phil. iv. 11. 4° 1700. The Art of Contentment.
  2 Cor. x. 5. 4° 1702. Aſſize.
PURKIS William, M. A. Fell. of Magd. Coll. Camb.
  * Matt vii. 13. 4° 1771. Aſſize.
PYKE William, M. A. R. of Stokes Climeſland, Cornwall.
  1 Cor xv. 31. 4° 1680. Fun. of Mrs. Warren. The Myſtery of dying daily.
PYLE Benjamin, LL. D.
  * Matt. xiii. or Mark iv. 36. 8° 1781. Viſ. *Durham.*
PYLE Tho. M. A. R. of Lynn Regis Norfolk, and Preb. of Sarum.
  1 Kings iii. 9. 4° 1706. *Norwich.* Anniv. of Coron. The great Charge and Difficulties of ſupreme Government, with the Duties of chriſtian Subjects to make it proſperous and eaſy.
  Ezek. xxxvii. 22. and part of 24. 4° 1707. Th. May 1. National Union, a national Bleſſing.
  Iſai. v. 20. 8° 1716. The heinous ſin and danger of prevaricating with God and the Government.
  Num. xvi. 41. 8° 1716. Aſſize. The Wiſdom of Government in diſtributing Puniſhment or Mercy to State-criminals.
  2 Cor. xiii. 5. 8° 1717. The proteſtant Rule of judging of the Way to Salvation. *Ch. Ch.* Oxon. *Cl. H.* Camb.
  1 Tim. iii. 15. 8° 1718. The Scriptures, only Teſt of Truth.
  * Serm. (Poſth.) in 2 Vol. 1° 1771. On practical Subjects. *Trin. Queen's.* Camb.
QUICKE John,   of Exon Coll. Oxon. Miniſter of the Goſpel.
  Deut. xxxii. 29. 4° 1681. Fun. of Philip Harris, Eſq; The Teſt of true Godlineſs.
  * Zach. i. 5. 4° 1691. Fun.
QUINCY Samuel,   Lect. of St. Philip's Charles Town; South Carolina.
  * 20 Serm. in 8° 1750.
RADCLIFFE E.   at Walthamſtow.
  * Luke xxii. 36. 8° 1758. Faſt.
  * Exod. xv. 1. 8° 1759. Prince Ferdinando's Victory.

* Jer.

* Jer. iv. 21. 8° 1762. Faſt.
* John xviii. 36. 8° 17
* 2 Tim. ii. 19. 8° 17   Chriſtmas. Confiſtency of the Xtian Character recommended. V. Dr. *Enfield's* Eng Pr. V.9. p.267.
* Acts v. 29. 8° 1772. reſpecting Subſcription.
* Pſ. lxxxix. 31, 32. 8° 1776. Faſt.

RAINBOW Edward, Bp. of Carliſle.
 * John vi. 17. 8° 16
 Prov. xiv. 1. 4° 1677. Fun. of the Counteſs of Pembroke. *Bod. Pub. L. St. John's.* Camb. *Sion.*

RAINSFORD Giles, M. A. R. of St. Paul's at Upper Malborough in Prince George County, Maryland.
 1 Kings ii. 10. 8° 1724. Fun. of Mr. Levett, Merchant.

RAINSTORP John, M. A. Maſter of the Free School in Briſtol.
 2 Sam. xv. 21. 4° 1683. b. Co. of Merchants. Loyalty recommended.

RALEIGH Walter, DD. Dean of Wells and Chapl. in Ord.
 Difcourſes (Reliquiæ Raleighanæ) in 4° 1679. on ſev. Subjects. *Bod. Ch Ch. Or.* Oxon. *Sion.*

RAMSAY John,   R. of Langdon, Kent.
 John xvi. 2. 4° 1714. Th. Iriſh Prot. *Bod. Pub. L.* Camb. *Sion.*

RAMSAY William,   E. A. P. late a Franciſcan.
 Gal. i. 8. 4° 1672 The tridentine Goſpel, or Papal Creed.

RAMSAY William, Eſq; B. D. Lect. of Iſleworth, Middleſex.
 Prov. xiv. 25. 4° 1680. Nov. 5. Mirmah, or the deceitful Witneſs. *Ch. Ch.* Oxon. *Trin.* Camb.
 Prov. xiv. 25. 4° 1680. Nov. 5. Maromah. The Lord of Rome, the Antichriſt. &c. *Ch. Ch.* Oxon. *Trin.* Camb.
 Iſai. xxiv. 21. 4° 1680. Maroum. The Deſtruction of the Lord of Rome &c. *Trin.* Camb.
 Acts xxvii. 15. 4° 1681. The Julian Ship, or Paul's Tranſportation to Rome. *Trin.* Camb.

RAMSEY James,   Chap. of his Majeſty's Ship the Prince of Wales.
 * Deut. xxxii. 29, 30. 4° 1778. Republiſhed in the Volume.
 * 12 Serm. in 8° 1782. For the Uſe of the royal Navy.

RAMSEY John
 2 Kings ix. 31. 4° 1661. 2 ſ.

RANDOLPH Herbert, M. A. R. of Deal, and Wood Church, Kent.
 Ezra vii. 26. 4° 1722. Aſſize. Legal Puniſhment confidered. *Bod.*
 *Mark xiii. 23. 8° 1752. Divinity of Chriſt. *Brit. M.*

RANDOLPH John, B. D. Stud. of Ch. Ch. Profeſſor of Greek, and Poetry, Oxon.
 * 1 Cor. xii. 31. 4° 1779. *Oxon.* Ord. ſ.
 * Acts ii. 42. 4° 1782. *Oxon.* Conſ. of Bp. Bagott.

RANDOLPH Thomas, DD. Preſident of C. C. C. Margaret-Profeſſor of Divinity, and Arch-Deacon of Oxon.
 2 Kings iv. 38. 8° 1733. *Oxon.* School-Feaſt. The Advantages of a public Education. *All S. Worc.* Oxon.

2 Cor.

2 Cor. iii. 5. 8° 1739. *Oxon*. An enquiry into the Sufficiency of Reason in matters of Religion. *Worc*. Oxon.

1 Cor. iii. 3. 8° 1752. *Oxon*. b. Univ. Party-Zeal censured. *Worc* Oxon.

* Ecclef. xii. 14. 8° 1755. *Oxon*. Assize. Certainty of a future State asserted and vindicated ag. the exceptions of the late Lord Bolingbroke. *Worc*. Oxon. *Cl. H.* Camb.
* Rom. i. 20. 8° 1762. *Oxon*. Use of Reason in religious matters. *Worc*. *Braz. N.* Oxon.
* Judges xi. 30, 31. 8° 1767. *Oxon*. Jepthah's Vow, with a Dissertation on Lev. xxvi. 28, 29. &c. *Worc*. Oxon.
* Rom. viii. 16. 8° 1768. *Oxon*. Witness of the Spirit. *Worc*. Ox.
* Rom. iii. 28. 8° 1768. *Oxon*. Doctrine of Justification by Faith explained. *Worc*. Oxon. *Queen's*. Camb.
* John xii. 41. 8° 1769. *Oxon*. Xt the Lord of Glory. *Worc*. Ox.
* Deut. iv 5 8° 1777. 2 f. Excellency of the Jewish Law; to which is added an appendix and a short Comment on Pf. cix. 55. *Worc*. Oxon. *Queen's*. Camb.
* Acts v 38, 39. 8° 1777. 2 f. Truth of the christian Religion proved from its speedy Propagation. *All S.* Oxon.

RANKEN David,   one ot the Episcopal Ministers at Edinburgh.
  1 Pet. iii. 13. } 8° 1716. 3 Disc. *Edinburgh*.
  1 Pet. iii. 14. }

  1 Pet. iii. 14–16. }
  1 Pet. iii. 14.   } 8° 1716. 3 Disc. *Edinburgh*.
  1 Pet. iii. 15.   }

  1 Pet. iii. 13–16. 8° 1717. *Edinburgh*.

RASTRICK John, M.A. sometime V. of Kirkton near Boston, Linc. and now Minister of the Gospel at King's Lynn, Norfolk.
  Matt. xxviii. 20. 8° 1714. Ord. s.

RAWLIN Richard
  *7 Disc. in 8° 1741. On Justification. Preached at Pinner's Hall, London.

RAWLINS Gershom,   Chapl. to the Earl of Bradford.
  2 Chron. ix. 7. 8° 1715. Accession. b. the second Regiment of Footguards. *Bal. Sion. Brit. M.*

RAWLINS John, M.A. R. of Leigh, Minister of Badsey, and Wickamford, Worcester, and Chapl. to Lord Archer.
* Rev. xix. 10. 8° 1761. Scripture-Prophecies.
* John xiv. 22. 8° 1763. Christmas f. Plan of divine Revelation justified in answer to the Objections of unbelievers.
* Deut. iv. 8. 8° 1766. Assize.
* Rom. xi. 20. 8° 1768. 2 f. Infidelity and Faith.
* Matt. xiv. 14. 8° 1770. *Worcester*-Infirmary.
* Pf. lvii. 78. 8° 1773. Meeting of 3 Choirs at *Worc*. Compassion.

RAWLINS Thomas
  Ephes. iv. 25. 8° 1713. Ag. lying.

RAWLINS William,   V. of Stockland, Dorsetshire.
  John v. 2–4. 8° 1751. The Discovery and due Use of *Glastonbury* Waters considered.   RAW-

RAWSON Jof. DD. Fell. of King's Coll. Camb. R. of St. Stephen, Walbrook, and Canon of Litchfield and Coventry.
    Ecclef. ii. 13. 4° 1703. Sch. Feaft. Wifdom the beft Poffeffion.
    2 Cor. xiii. 11. 4° 1704. Farewel.
    Prov. vi. 19. 4° 1708. Lond. Conc. ad Cler. Ch. Ch. Oxon. Queen's. Camb.
    Pf. xxxvii. 38. }
    Pf. xxxvii. 37. } 4° 1708. b. Queen. Mag. Ox. Queen's. Trin. C.
    Acts xv. 39. 4° 1709. Conc. pro. Grad. Doctor. Ch. Ch. Oxon. Queen's. Camb. Eton. Sion.
    Prov. xiv. 34. 8° 1714. Affize Eton.
    1 Cor. xvi. 14. 4° 1715. Spittal.
    2 Sam. xxiv. 14. 4° 1715. Affize.
    Pf. lxvi. 12. 8° 1716. Th. May 29. b. Ld Mayor. Ch. Ch. Ox.
RAY Charles, M. A. V. of St. Peter's in St. Alban's, and of King's Langley, Herts.
    Judges vi. 14. 4° 1746. Th. after Rebellion.
RAYMOND George, M. A. Minifter of St. Lawrence, Ipfwich.
    Ephef. iv. 12. 4° 1692. Vif. Brit. M.
    Tit. iii. 3 &c. 4° 1705. Norwich. Loyalty and Peaceablenefs.
    2 Chron. xix. 9. 4° 1708. Norwich. Affize.
    Tit. iii. 1. 8° 1716. Affize. Chriftian Loyalty.
RAYNER William, M. A.
    John xxi. 15. 8° 1717. Ex. Conf. of Bp. Blackburne. Ch. Ch. Ox.
    Tit. ii. 15. 8° 1718. Exon. Vif.
RAYNER William, B. A. of Caius Coll. Camb. Cur. of Walingworth, Suffolk.
    * Serm. in 4° 1767.
READ J.
    ‡ * 1 Pet. ii. 5. 8° 1730. Opening a Church.
READ Henry
    ‡ * James ii. 25. 8° 1728. Hearing infufficient without Practice.
    * - - - - 1737. Fun.
    * - - - - 1739. New Year's-day.
    * Deut. xxxiii. 29. 8° 1746. Th. Britain faved by Chrift.
    * - - - - 1755. David's Charge.
READER Samuel,   of Wareham, Dorfetfhire.
    * 13 Serm. in 8° 1765. On the parable of the 10 Virgins.
    * 3 Serm. in 8° 1765. On perfonal and family-Religion.
    * Jofh. xxiv. 15. 8° 1766. Family-Religion.
READER Thomas
    * Luke xii. 40. 12° 1778. Fun. of a perfon killed by the Fall of a Wall.
READING John, DD. Preb. of Canterbury.
    2 Kings iii. 15, 16. 4° 1663. Of Church-Mufick. C. C. C. Ox.
READING Will. M. A. Keeper of the Library at Sion Coll. Lond.
    1 Sam. xxiv. 5, 6. 8° 1714. Jan. 30. Magd. Oxon. St. John's. Camb. Sion.

23 Serm. in 8° 1724. Of Mortification &c. *Bod. Pub. L. C. Sion.*
52 Sermons in 8° 1728. Vol. I. and II. for every Sunday in the year at Morning Prayer. *Bod. Univ. All S. Ch. Ch. Wadh.* Oxon. *Sion.*
58 Serm. in 8° 1730. Vol. III. and IV. for every Sunday in the year at Evening Prayer with an Appendix of 6 Sermons &c. *Bod. Univ. All S. Ch. Ch. Wadh.* Oxon. *Sion.*
Luke xvi. 24. 8° 1731. Ag. profane curfing and fwearing. *Queen's.* Camb. *Sion.*
* Luke xix. 27. } 8° 1739. Tracts on Government.
* Ecclef. viii. 11. }

RECKS Robert, R. of Maningford-Abbots, Wilts.
Prov. xi. 4. 4° 1713. Fun..

REECE Richard, B. A.
* Efth. viii. 8. 4° 1776. In honour of the royal Favour to infolvent Debtors.

REES Abraham, DD.
* 1 Cor. ix. 24. 8° 1770. Ch. f. Acceptable Religion illuftrated and recommended.
* John v. 39. 8° 1779. Nov. 5. b. Society at Salter's Hall. The Obligation and Importance of fearching the Scriptures as a Prefervative from Popery.

REES David
* 1 Cor. ix. 14. 8° 1728. Modeft Plea for the maintenance of the Chriftian Miniftry.

REEVE Thomas, DD. Preacher of Waltham Abbey, Effex.
Heb. xi. 4 4° 1660. Jan. 30.
* Difcourfes in 4° 1661.
Judges vi. 12. 4° 1661. p. 95.
2 Sam. xix. 12.. 4° 1661. Faft.
Prov. xxviii. 2. 4° 1661. Sev. ferm. England's Reftitution.
Zach. xi. 2. 4° 1661. Fun. of Earl of Carlifle. *Brit. M.*

REEVES J.
Phil. iv 13.

REEVES Jonathan, Chapl. of the Magd. Hofp. London.
* Luke xv. 20. 4° 1758. Open. of the *Magdalen*-Hofp. -The loft Sheep found.

REEVES William, M. A. R. of Craneford, Middlefex.
Ecclef. iii. 21, 22. 4° 1704. Apothecary's Feaft. Of the natural Immortality of the Soul.
Rom. i. 19. 4° 1705. Apothecary's Feaft. Of the Wifdom of God in the works of Nature. *Queen's. St. John's.* C. *Sion. Eton.*

REEVES William, M. A. V. of St. Mary's Reading, Berks, and Chapl. in Ord.
Ephef. iv. 25. 4° 1712. b. Queen. The nature of Truth and Falfehood. *Bod. Ch. Ch.* Oxon. *Queen's.* Camb. *Sion.*
2 Tim. iii. 4. 4° 1713. b. Queen. The Folly and Danger of mifplacing our Affections. *Queen's.* Camb. *Sion.*
Prov. xxiv. 21. 4° 1713. Ox. Aff. At *Abingdon.* Berks. *Linc. Ox. Col.*

Col. iv. 3. 4° 1714. b. Queen. The great Importance of redeeming time. *Ch. Ch. Magd.* Oxon.
Mark vi. 16. 4° 1714. On the Sund. b. the Queen's Death. *Ch. Ch. Magd. Linc. Worc.* Oxon.
14 Serm. in 8° 1729. On several occasions. *Bod. Ch. Ch. Worc. Wadh.* Oxon.
* Matt. xxvii. 3, 4. 8° 1754. Elect. of Memb. of Parliament.

REGIS Balthasar, DD. R. of Adisham, Kent, Canon of Windsor, and Chapl. in Ord.
* Matt. v. 9. 8° 1718. Advantages of Peaceableness.
1 Tim iii. 16. 8° 1721. Vis.
* Ps. cxlv. 18, 19. 8° 1745. Fast.
Matt. xvii. 20. 8° 1750. Of Faith.
2 Pet. ii. 9. 8° 1751. Of the immediate State between Death and the Resurrection.
* Rom. vi. 6, 7. 8° 1751. On the vile mischievous Issue of the Devil, the old Man crucified with Christ, and the body of Sin destroyed.
* Ps. cxlv. 3. 8° 1752. On the Greatness of God.
* Ps. cxliv. 3. 8° 1752. The Knowledge all ought to have of their Body and Soul.
* Matt. vi. 24. 8° 1752. The glorious Service of God certainly rewarded for ever, and vile Service of Mammon doubtfully rewarded even during a short time.
* Gen. iii. 15. 8° 1753. The Antientness of the Xtian Religion.
* Deut. xi. 26. 8° 1753. A Parallel between the people of Israel and England.
* John i. 1. 8° 1753. Jesus Christ over all, God blessed for ever.

RELLY James
* Isai. xlii. 6 &c. 8° 1762. Salvation compleated, and secured in Christ as the Covenant of the people.
* 1 John iv. 1. 8° 1762. Trial of Spirits.
* John xiv. 19. 8° 1762. The Life of Christ, the Perseverance of the Christian.
* Matt. xix. 12. 8° 1762.
* Ephes. iv. 5. 8° 1762. The true christian Baptism delineated according to Reason and Spirit.

RENNELL Thomas, M.A. Fell. of Exon Coll. Oxon.
1 Cor. iii. 3, 4. 4° 1705. *Oxon.* Of Divisions for greater Edification. *Bod. Ch. Ch. Magd.* Oxon.
1 Tim. ii. 1–3. 4° 1709. Accession. *Univ. Or. Ox. Pub. L. Trin. Queen's.* Camb.

RERESBY William, DD.
Amos iv. 12. 12° 1664.

RESBURY Nathaniel, DD. R. of St. Paul's Shadwell, Lond. and Chaplain in Ord.
Isai. lvii. 1. 4° 1681. Fun. of Sir Alan Broderick. *Magd.* Oxon. *Pub. L. Trin Queen's.* Camb. *Sion.*

Matt. xxv. 40. 4° 1681. School-Feaſt. *C. C. C.* Oxon. *Pub. L.* Camb. *Sion.*
Matt. vi. 26. 4° 1689. b. Lord Mayor. Of Providence. *Bod. Ch. Ch. Magd.* Oxon. *Eton. Sion.*
Job xxxvi. 26. 4° 1691. b. Queen. *Bod. Ch. Ch. Magd.* Ox. *Eton.*
Job xxxiii. 22–24. 4° 1692. b. Queen. The Advantages of Sickneſs. *Bod. Univ. Magd.* Oxon.
Matt. vi. 6. 4° 1693. b. Queen. Of Cloſet-Prayer. *Trin.* C. *Sion.*
Rev. ii 1. 4° 1703. b. the Sons of the Clergy. *Worc.* Ox. *Trin. Queen's. St. John's.* Camb. *Sion.*

REYNELL Carew, B. D. Fell. of C. C. C. Oxon.
Ma.t. xi. 2–6. 4° 1724. *Oxon.* De Immanuele. Or. *Worc.* Oxon. *Queen's.* Camb.
Acts x. 40, 41. 8° 1726. Eaſter. Ag. Woolſton.

REYNELL Carew, Bp. of Derry, Ireland.
Pſ. cxviii. 24. 4° 1729. Nov. 5.
1 Tim. ii. 1, 2. 4° 1729. Jan. 30.
Matt. xxv. 40. 4° 1738. On erect. the Infirm at *Briſtol.*

REYNER Allen
Pſ. ci. 1. 12° 1666.
* Prov. xxviii. 14. 12° 1667.

[REYNER Kirby]
2 Tim. iv. 7, 8. 4° 1713. Fun. of Mr. Tho. Kipping.
* Select ſerm. in 8° 1745.

REYNER Samuel, M. A. R. of St. Peter's, Dorcheſter.
Iſai. iii. 1–3. 4° 1680. Fun. of John Holle. *Bod.*

REYNOLDS   M. A. R. of   Salop.
* 1 Cor. xiii. 1. 8° 1759. b. Gov. of *Salop*-Infirmary.

REYNOLDS
* Pract. Diſc. in 12° 1713. On hearing the Word.

REYNOLDS Edward, Bp. of Norwich.
His Works in fo. 1679. (2d Edit.) *Bod. Univ. Ch. Ch. Oriel.* Oxon. *Sion.*

REYNOLDS John, M. A.
Pſ. cxxix. 1, 2. 4° 1678. Nov. 5. *Bod. Ch. Ch.* Oxon. *Sion.*
Pſ. xxvi. 8. 8° 1684.

REYNOLDS John, V. D. M. in London.
Matt. xxv. 8. 8° 1714.   *Eton.*
* Matt. xxv. 21. 8° 1714. Fun. of the Rev. *Matt. Henry.*

REYNOLDS Joſeph
Matt. x. 16.

REYNOLDS Richard, Bp. of Lincoln.
1 Kings xii. 19. 4° 1721. Jan. 30. b. Lords. *Queen's.* Camb.
1 John iii. 8. 4° 1727. Prop. of Goſpel. *Ch. Ch.* Ox. *Pub. L.* C.
2 Cor. ix. 8. 4° 1735. Spittal M. The Retributions of Charity.

REYNOLDS Thomas
Prov. ix. 7, 8. 8° 1699. Ref. of Manners.

REYNOLDS Thomas
* Heb. xi. 13. 8° 1707. Fun.

‡ * Exod.

‡ * Exod. xxiii. 29, 30. 8° 1710. Th. f.
‡ * Pf. cvi. 21–23. 8° 1711. Nov. 5.
* John xiv. 3. 8° 1713. Fun. of *Eleanor Murdin*. *Queen's*. Camb.
* Acts xx. 37, 38. 8° 1722. Fun. of Rev. Mr. *William Hocker*.
* —— 31, 32. 8° 1722. Fun. of Rev. Mr. *Pomfret*. *Queen's*. C.
RICE Theophilus, B. A. R. of Edingthorpe and Edington, Norfolk.
    Matt. x. 34. 12° 1711. *Norwich*. The Weaknefs of the Latitudinariam plea of Peace &c.
    1 Theff. iv. 8. 8° 1722.
RICH Charles
    * Ifai. i. 16, 17. 8° 1753. Ag. profaning Chriftmas-day &c.
RICH Edward Pickering, M. A. of Baliol. Coll. Oxon.
    Ecclef. i. 2. 4° 1750. At *Cheltenham*. *Bod*.
    * Pf. xxvii. 3. 4° 1759. Th. f.
RICH Samuel, M. A. R. of Stalbridge, Dorfetfhire.
    Rom. xiii. 2. 4° 1685. b. his Majefty's Forces. *Pub. L*. Camb.
RICHARDS
    John xii. 26.   Fun.
RICHARDS Thomas,[a] M. A. R. of Llanfyllin, Montgomeryfhire.
    Luke ii. 10, 11. 8° 1727. Chriftmas.
    Rev. xiv. 13. 8° 1732. Fun. of Lady Price. The Happinefs of good Chriftians after Death.
RICHARDS Thomas[a]
    * Ifai. v. 4. 8° 1757. Faft. Earthquake.
RICHARDSON John
    * Gal. v. 13. 8° 1752. Chriftian Liberty and Love reprefented and earneftly recommended. *Pub. L*. Camb. *Brit. M.*
    * - - - - 1763.
RICHARDSON Jofhua, M. A. R. of All-Hallows on the Wall, London.
    Prov. xiv. 34. 4° 1682. b. Lord Mayor. *Ch. Ch*. Oxon. *Brit. M.*
RICHARDSON Robert, DD. R. of Si. Ann's, Weftminfter, F. R. S. and S. A.
    * Pf. cxlvii. 12. 4° 1763. Faft. Preached at the Hague. *All S*. Ox.
    * Pf. cxxii. 8, 9. 4° 1779. b. the Sons of the Clergy.
RICHARDSON Thomas,   Cur. of All Saints, Northampton.
    * 2 Tim. iv. 7, 8. 8° 1729. Fun. of Mrs. Page. *Queen's*. Camb.
RICHARDSON William,   lately a diffenting Teacher.
    Heb. v. 4, 5. 4° 1711. God's call of his Minifters. *Bod*. *Ch. Ch*. *C. C. C*. *Linc*. *Worc*. Oxon. *Sion*.
RICHARDSON William, M. A. Preb. of Linc. and Lect. of St. Olave's, Southwark.

Acts xvii. 4.	p. 5.		
Phil. ii. 11.	p. 27.	8° 1730. 4 f.	On the Ufefulnefs and Neceffity of divine Revelation.
Deut. xviii. 15.	p. 49.		
1 John ii. 8.	p. 77.		

[a] Q. The fame.

RICHARDSON William, DD. Master of Emanuel Coll. Camb.
   Exod. iii. 5. 4° 1733. Conf. of a Chapel. Relative Holiness.
   * Matt. xxii. 21. 4° 1764. Jan. 30. b. Commons. *Queen's*. Cam.
RICHMOND Henry,   R. of Liverpool.
   Prov. i. 22. 8° 1710.
   —— 29. 1. 8° 1710. } Assize. Linc. Oxon. *Queen's*. Camb.
RICHMOND Richard, Bp. of Sodor and Man.
   * 11 Serm. in 4° 1764.
RIDER William, B. A. formerly of Jes. Coll. Oxon. Assistant at St.
   Paul's School, London.
   *Pf. xxi. 3. 8° 1761. Coronation. The Expediency of the Coro-
   nation-Oath, and the peculiar Felicity of the Eng. Nation.
   *John xi. 35. 4° 1764. Fun. of Rev. William Reyner.
RIDLEY Glocester, DD. late Fell. of New Coll. Oxon. Canon of
   Salisbury, and R. of Weston, Norfolk.
   The Xtian Passover (4 serm. in Lent 1736.) 8° 1742. *Queen's*. C.
   8 Serm. on the Divinity and Operations of the Holy Ghost, at
   Lady Moyer's Lecture. 1740, 1741, 8° 1742. *New C.* Oxon.
   Queen's. Camb. *Dr. W's. L.* London.
   Rev. ii. 5.
   John xvi. 2. } 8° 1745. Rebell. Constitution in Ch. and State.

   Gen. ix. 27. 4° 1746. Col. of Georgia. *Queen's*. Camb.
   John xi. 26. 4° 1750. Fun. of Dr. Berriman. *Queen's*. Camb.
   Jerem. xviii. 6–8. 8° 1750. On the Earthquake. God's threat-
   ning ag. sinful Nations exemplified and improved.
   * Pf. cxlvii. 19. 4° 1753. *Norwich.* Assize.
   * Luke xi. 1, 2. 4° 1755. Hutchin. Lect.
   * Jerem. xvii. 6–8. 8° 1756. Fast. Earthquake.
   * Prov. xxii. 6. 4° 1757. Ann. meeting Ch. Sch. *Queen's*. Cam.
   *.Ecclef. ix. 16. 4° 1757. b. Sons of the Clergy. *Braz N.* Oxon.
   * Pf. cxxvii. 3–5. 4° 1764. b. Gov. *Lond.* Lying-in Hosp.
RIDGLEY Thomas, DD.
   * Pf. cxvi. 7. 12° 1711. Fun of *Eliz. Banks.*
   * Exod. xxxiii. 6. 8° 1711. Abuse of fealting.
   * Rom. v. 18. 8° 1725. 2 s. On original Sin. *Queen's*. Camb.
   * - - - - 1733. Fun.
RILAND John, M. A. Arch-D. of Coventry, and R. of Birmingham.
   Acts vii. 26. 4° 1662. Confirmation. *Bal.* Oxon *Trin.* Camb.
   Isai. i. 26. 4° 1662. Assize. *Bal.* Oxon. *Trin.* Camb.
   Pf. 1. 3. 4° 1663. Confirmation. revived. p. 1.
   Rev. xx 12. 4° 1663 Ass. Doom's-day books opened: p. 35. *Bod.*
RILAND John, M. A. Chapl. of St. Mary's Chapel, Birmingham.
   * 2 Cor. ii. 17. 8° 1762. Christian, new Creat. in Christ.
   * Hosea iv, 6. 8° 1764. 2 s. Ignorance, the Destruction of God's
   people, and the ways and means to prevent it..
   * Ezek. xxxiii. 1–6. 12° 1775. 2 s. The sinful state of the Nation.
   * Exod. xx. 13. 8° 1777. Ag Self-murder.
RINGER Thomas, M. A. of Worc. Coll. Oxon.
   12 Disc. &c. in 8° 1734. *Bod. Worc.* Oxon. *Brit. M.*

OF AUTHORS, &c.   285

RIVELY Benedict, M. A. Chapl. to the Bp. of Norwich.
  Job xxx. 23. 4° 1677. Fun. of Bp. Reynolds. *All S. Or. Queen's.* Oxon. *Trin.* Camb.
  Rom. xiii. 4 4° 1679. Admiſſion of a Mayor.
RIVERS Sir Peter, Bart.   R. of Woolwich, Kent.
  * Epheſ. vi. 4. 4° 1764. An. meet. Char. School. *Braz. N. Ox.*
RIVERS Tho. LL. D. Preb. of Wincheſter, Fell. of All S. Coll. Ox.
  Pſ. lxxvii. 14, 15. 4° 1710. Th. *Bod. Univ. C. C. C. Jeſ. Worc. Ox.*
ROBERTS Charles,   Miniſter of the licenſed Chapels of Muſſelburgh, and Dalkirk.
  * Iſai lvii. 1. 8° 1750. *Edinburgh.* Fun. of Earl of Dalkeith.
ROBERTS Edward, M. A. Lect. of St. Magnus the Martyr, Lond.
  3 John 2. 4° 1693. *Sion.*
ROBERTS Edward, M. A. R. of Raleigh, Eſſex, and Miniſter of Queenborough, Kent.
  2 Sam. xxiii. 10. 4° 1704 Th. ſ.
  Mark xi. 24. 4° 1704. Farewel.
  * Jonah iii. 4, 5. 8° 1708. a Vol.
  Luke viii. 23, 24. 8° 1716.
ROBERTS Francis, DD. R. of Wrington, Somerſetſhire.
  1 Cor. iii. 21–23. 4° 1662. Fun.   The Chriſtians advantagē both by Life and Death.
ROBERTS Richard, M. A. Chapl. to the Duke of Beaufort, V. of All Saint's in Briſtol.
  1 Pet. ii. 17. 4° 1685. Young Men's Feaſt. *Ch. Ch.* Oxon.
ROBERTS *Samuel,*   Miniſter of the Goſpel at Sarum.
  Pſ. cxxii. 6–8. 8° 1745. Rebel. Love of our Country. *Brit. M.*
  * Micah vi. 6. 8° 1748. Faſt
ROBERTS William,   R. of Jacobſtow, Devon.
  Heb. v. 4. 4° 1709. *Exon.* Viſ. The divine Inſtitution of the Goſpel-miniſtry, and the Neceſſity of epiſcopal Ordination. *Linc. St. John's. Worc./*Oxon. *Trin. Queen's. St. John's.* Camb.
ROBERTSON J.   B. A. V. of Harriad, Hants.
  * Rom. xi. 22. 8° 1761. Faſt. Subverſion of antient Kingdoms &c.
ROBERTSON *Thomas,*   Miniſter at Dalmeny.
  * - - - - 1778. Faſt.
ROBERTSON Will. DD. Principal of the Univerſity of Edingburgh.
  * Col. i. 26. 8° 1755. Prop. of Chriſtian Knowledge. The Situation of the world at the time of Chriſt's appearance, and its Connection with the Succeſs of his Religion conſidered. V. Prot. Syſt. V. II. and Scotch Pr. V. I. p. 102. *Queen's.* Cam.
ROBETSON J.   Cur. of Whitby, Yorkſhire.
  * - - - - 1779. b. friendly Society.
  * 1 Chron. xix. 13. 4° 1781. b. Battallion of Volunteers.
ROBINSON *Benjamin*
  * Pſ. cvi. 30, 31. 12° 1701. Ref. of Manners.
  * Acts xiii. 36. 4° 1702. On the Death of King William III. *Pub. L.* Camb.
  Rom. xiv. 6. 8° 1707. The practical improvement of Xtmas-day.
  * Pſ. cxviii. 22–24. 8° 1719. King's birth-day. *St. John's.* Cam.

ROBINSON Chriſtopher, M. A. R. of Welby, Lincolnſ.
  8 Diſc. in 8° 1733—1740. The Excellence and Neceſſity of a Revelation. *Cl. H.* Camb.
ROBINSON J.   DD.
  Jer. xvii. 9, 10. 8° 1
ROBINSON John
  Matt. v. 5. 4° 1704. *Norwich.* Aſſize. Meekneſs.
ROBINSON John, Bp. of London.
  Pſ. xxi. 1. 4° 1710. b. Queen. Acceſſion. *Ch. Ch. Magd. Linc.* Oxon. *St. John's.* Camb.
  Matt. xix. 14. 4° 1714. Ann. meet. Ch. School. *Ch. Ch.* Oxon. *Queen's.* Camb. *Sion.*
[ROBINSON Ralph]
  * Serm. in 4° 1660. on Chriſt.
ROBINSON *Robert,*   of Cambridge.
  * Pſ. cxliv. 11, 12. 8° 1772. To young perſons. Early Piety.
  * 2 Tim. iii. 14, 15. 8° 1776. Proper Behaviour at rel. Aſſemblies.
  * Rom. xiii. 1–7. 8° 1780. *Camb.* Jan. 30.
  * 2 Cor. iv. 3, 4. 8° 1781. Xn Doct. of Ceremonies. V. Saurin J.
ROBINSON T.   R. of Ouſeby, Cumberland.
  James v. 12. 8° 1710.
ROBINSON Thomas, DD. Fell. of Mert. Coll. Oxon.
  2 Tim, 22. 8° 1730. *Oxon.* Youthful luſts inconſiſtent with the Miniſtry. *Worc.* Oxon. *Queen's.* Camb.
ROBOTHAM Charles, B. D. R. of Reiſam, Norfolk.
  Iſai. xlix. 23. 12° 1680. May 29. The royal nurſing Father. *Sion.*
  Rom. xvi. 26. 12° 1680. The Obedience of Faith. *Sion.*
  Heb. xiii 16. 12° 1680. Commem. on Charity.
ROBOTHAM Charles
  * Serm. in 8° 1756.
ROBY William
  ‡ * 2 Sam. v. 12. 8° 1715. Acceſſion.
  1 Kings viii. 27. 8° 1721. Opening meeting-Houſe.
RODERICK Richard, DD. Stud. of Ch. Ch. Oxon. V. of Blandford-Forum, Dorſetſhire, and afterwards R. of St. Michael's Baſiſhaw, London.
  Acts ii. 42. 4° 1683. Viſ. *Ch. Ch. Jeſ.* Oxon. *Sion.*
  2 Chron. vii. 16. 4° 1684. Conſ. of a Chapel. *Pub. L.* Cam. *Sion.*
  Jer. vii. 12. 4° 1707. Conc. ad Cler. Lond. *Sion.*
  Mark xiii. 13. 4° 1723. Conc. ad Cler. Lond. *Sion.*
ROE James, M. A. Prime Curate of the parochial Church of Macclesfield, Cheſhire.
  * 20 Serm. in 8° 1766. *AllS.* Oxon.
ROE Stephen, M. A. Morning Preacher at Stepney, Middleſex.
  * Num. xxv. 17, 18. 8° 1756. b. Antigallicans.
ROE William
  * Acts xv. 29. 8° 1662. Chriſtian Liberty rightly ſtated.
ROGERS John, M. A. Chaplain to the Earl of Berkeley.
  Jonah. i. 6. 4° 1681. At Trinity-Houſe. *Sion.*
  Pſ. xxvii. 6. 4° 1702. Th.

ROGERS John, DD. V. of St. Giles's Cripplegate, Sub-Dean and Canon of Wells, and Chapl. in Ord.
    6 Serm. in 8° 1727. Vol. I. The Necessity of a divine Revelation. *Bod. Univ. Ch. Ch. C.C.C. St. John's. New C. All S. Worc. Pemb.* Oxon. *Queen's. Cl. H.* Camb.
    12 Serm. in 8° 1730. Vol. II. (Posth.) *Bod. Uivn. Ch.Ch. C.C.C. St. John's. New C. All S. Worc. Pemb.* Ox. *Queen's. Cl. H.* Cam.
    19 Serm. in 8° 1735. 1738. Vol. III. (Posth.) *Bod. Univ. Ch.Ch. C.C.C. St. John's. New C. All S. Worc. Pemb.* Oxon. *Queen's. Cl. H.* Camb.
    17 Serm. in 8°1736. Vol.IV. (Posth) *Bod. Univ. Ch. Ch. C.C.C. St. John's. New C. All S. Worc. Pemb.* Ox. *Queen's. Cl. H.* Cam.

ROGERS *John*
    * - - - - 1752. Fun.
    * 2 Cor. iv. 5. 8° 1767. Ord.

ROGERS Samuel, M.A.
    Rom. viii. 18. 8° 1714. Fun. of the Earl of Gainsborough.
    1 Thess. iv. 13, 14. 4° 1714. Fun.

ROGERS *Thomas*
    Eccles. xii. 1. 4° 1683. Fun. of *Robert Linager. Brit.M.*
    * Disc. in 8° 1691. on Sickness and Recovery. *Brit. M.*
    * Disc. in 8° 1692. on a friendly correspondence between Conformists and Non-conformists.
    Gen. xlv. 24. 8°1692. 2 s. on the Death of *Anthony Duncell. Pub. L.* Camb. *Sion.*
    * Zech. xii. 15. 8°.16   May 29.
    Heb. xi. 7. 12° 1701. Ref. of Manners.

ROGERS William
    * Phil. iv. 13.

ROLLS Samuel, DD.
    1 Sam. xxiv. 5. } 8° 1678. 2 s. on Conscience. { *Bod. Bal. Pub. L.* Jan. 30. { Camb. *Sion.*

ROLLS William, B.D. R. of Chalfont St. Giles's, Bucks.
    1 Cor. i. 10. 4° 1672. The Necessity of christian Charity.

ROMAINE William, M.A. formerly of Ch. Ch. Oxon. R. of St. Ann's Blackfryars, Lect. of St. Dunstan's in the West, Lond.
    Mark xii. 24-27. 8°1739. The Divine Legation of moses demonstrated from his having made express mention of a future State.
    Mark xii. 24-27. 4° 1742. Future Rewards and Punishments proved to be the Sanctions of the Mosaic Dispensation.
    Rom. ii. 14, 15. 4° 1741. b. Lord Mayor. No Justification by the Law of Nature.
    Judges xi. 30, 31. 8° 1744. Jeptha's Vow. Ag. Sacrifice.
    * John i. 14. 8° 1755. Self-existence of Jesus Christ.
    * Amos iv. 12. 8° 1755. an Alarm to a careless World.
    * Ps. cvii. 1 &c. 12° 1755. Pract. Comment. in several Lectures.
    * Ezek. xxxvi. 25-27. 8° 1755. A Gift serm. by Miss Hill. Benefit of Holy Spirit to Man.
    * Ezek. xxxvii. 4. 8° 1756. Parable of dry Bones.

                                                              * Isai.

  *Ifai. xxviii. 16. 8° 1756. 2 f. The fure Foundation.
  *Matt xxv. 13. 8° 1756. Duty of Watchfulnefs enforced.
  *Ifai. xlv. 8. 8° 1757. 2 f. Lord our Righteoufnefs.
  *Matt. xv. 19, 20. 12° 1757. for preventing frequency of Robberies and Murders.
  * Luke ii. 29, 30. 8° 1759. Death of Rev. Mr. Hervey.
  * John viii. 24. 17
  * 12 Difc. in 8° 1759. upon fome pract. parts of Solomon's Song.
  * 12 Difc. in 8° 1760. upon the Law and the Gofpel.
  * Pf. cxvi. 15. 8° 1762. Fun. of Rev. Mr. Jones.
  * 2 Cor. iv. 5. 8° 1764. on Earthquake.
ROMAN William, LL. B. Chapl. to the Lord Mayor.
  * Matt. v. 16. 4° 1752. Elect. of Lord Mayor.
ROOTES Richard, M. A. R. of Chilmark, Wilts.
  Prov. xix. 8. 8° 17 *Oxon.* p. 38. St. Paul's Epift. to the Romans vindicated from unconditional Predeftination. *Hert. Ox.*
  Acts ii. 42. 8° 1711. *Oxon.* Sacrament. *Bod.*
ROPER Jofeph. DD. Fell. of St. John's Coll. Camb. R. of St. Nicholas Cole-Abbey, and St. Nicholas Olave's, London.
  1 Cor. ix. 11. 4° 1725. b. Sons of the Clergy. *Wadh.* Ox. *Sion.*
  John vii. 17. 4° 1728. Commenc. *St. John's.* Camb. *Brit. M.*
  Prov. xi. 25. 4° 1734. Spitt. W. The Character of a liberal Man.
  1 Cor. ix. 16. 4° 1737. Conc. ad Cler. Lond. *Queen's.* Camb.
[ROSE Jonathan]
  * Rom. xii. 2. 4° 1711. 3 f.
ROSE William, M. A. V. of Eaft-Clandon, Surrey.
  Ifai. liv. 8. 8° 1715. Th. for Acceffion.
ROSEWELL
  Prov. iii. 15. Nov. 5.
ROSEWELL H.
  Pf. lxxxiv. 1. 8° 1711. at a Country-revel.
ROSEWELL *Samuel*
  * Serm. in 1706.
  * Prov. xiii. 6. 4° 1706. Nov. 5.
  * John xxi. 21, 22. 8° 1708. One's own Bufinefs.
  ‡ * Deut. xxxiv. 5. 8° 1708. Fun. of Lady Clinton.
  * Pf. cxxxii. 17, 18. 8° 1714. Coronation.
  * Mark x. 21. 8° 1714. Warning to Youth.
  Matt. xxvi. 41. 8° 1715. of Temptation, and the Means to prevent its Prevalence.
  ‡ * Acts xix. 40. 8° 1715. ag. Riots.
  * Num. xxvi. 10. 8° 1715. on an Execution.
  * Prov. xxiv. 21. 8° 1716.
  ‡ * Pf. xxxvii. 34. 8° 1719. Farewel. At Founders Hall. *Brit. M.*
  * Nehem. xi. 2. 8° 1719. Ref. of Manners.
ROSS John, Bp. of Exeter.
  * Ifai. xxxiii. 6. 4° 1756. *Camb.* Commencement. *All S. Braz. N.* Oxon. *Queen's.* Camb.
  * Ifai. xxvi. 9. 4° 1756. Faft. *All* S. Oxon.
                * Hofea

* Hosea xiii. 9. 4° 1759. Jan. 30. b. Commons. *Braz. N.* Oxon. *Queen's.* Camb.
* Prov. xxiv. 21. 4° 1779. Jan. 30. b. Lords.
* - - - - 4° 1779. Faſt. b. Lords.
ROSSINGTON James,   R. of Lezant, Cornwall.
  1 Cor. xi. 16. 4° 1676. Vis. *Bod. Pub. L.* Camb.
  Col. ii. 12. 8° 1700. Infant-Baptiſm.
ROST John, M. A. R. of Offwell, and Gittiſham, Devon.
  Jam. v. 12. 4° 1695. ag. raſh and vain ſwearing.
ROTHERAM John, M. A. R. of Houghton Le ſpring, and V. of Seaham, and Chapl. to the Bp. of Durham.
  * John x. 37, 38. 8° 1761. *Oxon.* Origin of Faith. *All S. Worc. Braz. N.* Oxon. *Queen's.* Camb.
  * Dan. ii. 20, 21. 8° 1762. *Oxon.* Inauguration. Wiſdom of Providence in the Adminiſtration of the World. *Braz. N. Worc.* Oxon. *Queen's.* Camb.
  * Gen. ix. 6. 8° 1763. Aſſize. Influence of Religion on human Laws. *Braz. N. Worc.* Oxon. *Queen's.* Camb.
  * Rom. xiii. 1. 8° 7766. *Oxon.* May 29. Government a divine Inſtitution. *Queen's.* Camb.
  * Pſ. cxxxix. 14. 4° 1771. *Newcaſtle*-Infirmary.
  * Luke ix. 55, 56. 8° 1780. againſt Perſecution.
ROTHWELL
  Pſ. lxxiii. 1. 4° 1684. Th.
ROW *Benjamin*
  ‡ * 2 Cor. v. 5. 8° 1704. at Pinmaker's Hall.
ROWDEN John,   Preſbyter of the Church of England.
  Pſ. x. 16. 8° 1714. *Oxon.* on the Death of Queen Ann. *Linc.* Ox.
ROWLAND Daniel,   Chapl. to his Grace the Duke of Leinſter.
  * 8 Serm. in 12° 1774. on practical Subjects.
  * 3 Serm. in 12° 1778. Tranſlated from the Britiſh Language by J. Davies, R. of Sharnecotte, Wilts.
ROWLAND Parker.
  * Mal. iii. 3. 4° 1775. againſt Perjury.
ROWLEY John,   R. of Hemmingford Abbots, Huntingdonſ.
  Prov. xi. 11. 4° 1680. b. Lord Mayor. The Cities exaltation by Uprightneſs. *Pub. L.* Camb.
ROYSE Geor. DD. Dean of Briſtol, Provoſt of Oriel Coll. Oxon. and Chapl. in Ord.
  1 Cor vi. 20. 4° 1689. Palm. S. b. Lord Mayor. *Bod. Sion.*
  Heb. xi. 33. 4° 1690. b. King. *Trin.* Camb. *Sion.*
  1 John v. 3. 4° 1690. b. King and Queen. *Bod.*
  John xvi. 32. 4° 1705. *Oxon.* b Queen. Government of the Paſſions. *Bod. Univ. Or.* Oxon. *St. John's.* Camb.
RUDD A.   M. A. Preb. of Hereford, and Maſter of the Free-School.
  * Prov. xiv. 31. 8° 1-81. *Hereford*-Infirmary. The Advantages of general Infirmaries illuſtrated.

Vol. II.   O o   RUDD

RUDD James
    Matt. xxviii. 19. 8° 1740. 2 f. *Kendal.* on Baptifm.
RUDD Sayer, M. D. Minifter of Walmer in Kent.
    2 Theff. ii. 16, 17. 8° 1730. Fun. of Mrs. *Clarke.*
    * - - - - 1737.
    * - - - - 1739. on the Trinity.
    * John xvii. 5. 8° 1740. 6 f. on the Doctrine of Chrift pre-exifting his State of Incarnation &c.
RUE de la
    Dan. iv. 11. 4° 1695. Fun. (from the French.) *Trin.* Cam. *Sion.*
RUFFORD Francis, B. A. Fell. of Wadh. Coll Oxon.
    * Matt. ix. 36-38. 4° 1779. Prop. of Gofpel. Compaffion to men's Souls. the greateft Charity.
RUMLEY John. M. A.
    Exod. xxiii. 2. 1° 1732. againft Sodomy.
RUNDLE Thomas, Bp. of London-derry, Ireland.
    Acts x. 34, 35. 8° 1718. Nov. 5. *Eton.*
    Deut. xv. 11. 4° 1734. Col. of Georgia. *Queen's.* Cam. *Brit. M.*
    Zach. xii. 5. 4° 1735. *Dublin.* Anniv. of Irifh Rebellion. *Queen's.* Camb. *Brit. M.*
    Rev. iii. 15-19. 4° 1736. *Dublin.* Incorp. Soc. for Englifh Prot. School. *Pub. L.* Camb.
RUSSEL J.
    ‡ * 1 John v. 16. 8°   *Brit. M.*
RUSSEL John,   R. of Brundal, Norfolk.
    1 Cor. x. 10. 4° 1693. *Camb.* Affize. *Pub. L. St. John's.* Camb.
RUSSEL John, M. A. R. of Poftwick, Norfolk.
    Luke xix. 41, 42. 8° 1716. Norwich. Jan. 30. *St. John's.* Cam.
RUSSEL Patrick
    * Tit. ii. 13. 8° 1719. The Deity of Chrift.
RUSSEL Richard, M. A. formerly of Univ. Coll. Oxon. V. of Alfrifton and Selmefton, Suffex.
    * Rom. xiv. 43. 8° 1716. Far. f. on Oaths.
RUSSEL Robert
    * Difc. in 12° 1746.
RUSSELL J.
    1 Pet. iv. 8.   1695.
RUSSELL John,   R. of St. John's of Wapping.
    Luke ix. 62. 12° 1697. Ref. of Manners.
RUSSELL John, M. A. Fell. of Mert. Coll. Oxon. Preb. of Peterborough, and Lincoln, and R. of Fifkerton, Lincolnfhire.
    1 Tim. iv. 16. 8° 1719. Ord. The Duty and Reward of the Clergy. *Linc.* Oxon.
    Acts xx. 28. 8° 1721. Conf. of Bps. Reynolds and Wilcocks. *Eton.*
RUSSEN Benjamin,   Affiftant Preacher at Mr. Maxfield's Chapel, little Moor-Fields.
    * Pf. xlvi. 4. 8° 1771. The Chriftian Mariner.
    * Jerem. xxiii. 6. 8° 1774. Probation f. Lord our Righteoufnefs.
                                                         RUST

RUST George, Bp. of Dromore, Ireland.
  2 Tim. i. 10. 4° 1663. *Dublin.* Fun. of the Earl of Mount-Alexander.
  1 John iii. 2. 4° 1668. Fun. of Bp. Taylor. *Univ. St. John's. All S.* Oxon. *Brit. M.*
  1 Pet. iii. 15. 4° 1683. Use of Reason in Relig. *Ch. Co.* Ox. *Sion.*
  Rom. iv. 16. 4° 1686. Remains.
  1 John iv. 16. 4° 1686. p. 1. *Camb.* God is Love.
  Prov. xx. 27. 4° 1686. p. 21.
  John xviii. 38. 4° 1686. p. 43.
  Ps. xi. 3. 4° 1673.
RUTHERFORTH Thomas, DD. Fell. of St. John's Coll. and Regius Professor of Divinity, Camb. and Arch-Deacon of Essex &c.
  Isai. lviii. 4. 4° 1746. *Camb.* Jan. 30. b. Commons. *Worc.* Ox. *Trin. Queen's.* Camb.
  Ps. cvii. 2. 4° 1747. May 29.
  1 Pet. ii. 17. 4° 1747. June 11.
  John xx. 30, 31. 4° 1751. Vis. The Credibility of Ministers defended. *Braz. N. Worc.* Oxon. *Trin. Cl. H. Queen's.* Camb.
  * 1 Tim. iv. 13. 4° 1765. Conc. ad Cler. De Artibus et Doctrinis quibus Theologiæ studiosos erudiri oportet. *Braz. N.* Ox. *Queen's.* Camb.
  * John v. 7. 4° 1771. *Camb.* b. Gov. of *Addenbrook*-Hosp.
RUTHERFORTH *William*, M. A, Master of the Academy at Uxbridge, Middlesex.
  * - - - - 1781. Ord.
RYE George, DD. Arch-Deacon of Oxon. Canon of Ch. Ch. and R. of Islip, Oxon.
  Luke xx. 25. 8° 1714. *Oxon.* The Supremacy of the Crown, and the Power of the Church. *Bod. Bal.* Ox. *Worc. Queen's.* C. *Sion.*
  Heb. xiii. 17. 4° 1715. Cons. of Bp. Potter. *Or.* Oxon. *Queen's.* Camb. *Eton.*
RYLAND *John*, jun.   of Northampton.
  * Prov. xvii. 3. 12° 1780. b. Dissenting Clergy. God's experimental Probation of intelligent Agents.
RYMER Thomas, DD. Fell. of Queen's Coll. Camb. and one of the 6 Preachers of the Diocese of Canterbury.
  Exod xx. 17. 8° 1726. Commencement.
  2 Pet. ii. 19. 4° 1773. May 29. b. Commons. Obedience to Government. *Worc.* Oxon. *Queen's.* Camb.
RYTHER *John*
  * Sev. serm. in 8° 1672. *Pub. L.* Camb.
  Acts xxvii. 18–20. 8° 1674. Sea-Dangers and Deliverances. *Bod. Pub. L.* Camb.
  * Exod. xxxii. 26. 1° 1699. Ref. of Manners.
RYVES Edmund, DD. late Fell. of Magd. Coll. Oxon. R. of Swinnerton, Staffordshire.
  2 Cor. iv. 2. 8° 1715. Vis.

  Luke xvii. 10. } 8° 1724. ag. Popery.
  John vi. 52. }
  Tit. ii. 15. 8° 1726. Vif.
S. A.
  Pf. ix. 16. 4° 1696. Th. God glorified, and the wicked fnared.
8. H.
  * Rom. xii 2. 12° 1695. p. 1. Non conformity to the World.
  * Ezek xxiv. 13, 14. 12° 1695. p. 87. God's Severity for Iniquity.
  * 2 Theff. iii. 16. 12° 1695. p. 141. God's gracious Prefence, the Saints great Privilege. *Dr. W's. L.* London.
S. J. M. A.
  Matt v. 28. 4° 1672. ag. Adultery.
S. J.
  1 Theff. iv. 14. 12° 1708. Fun. of Nath. Parkhurft. *Pub L.* Ca.
S. M.
  1 Sam. iii. 18. 4° 1683. Submiffion to the Will of God.
S. T.
  2 Tim. ii. 12. 1683.
SACHEVERELL Henry, DA. Fell. of Magd. Coll. Oxon. and R. of St. Andrews Holborn, London.
  Prov. viii. 15. 4° 1702. *Oxon.* The political Union. *Bod. Univ. Ch. Ch. Bal. Magd. Or. Jef. Trin. St. John's.* Camb.
  2 Chron. vi. 34, 35. 4° 1702. *Oxon.* Faft. A Defence of her Majefty's Title to the Crown. *Bod. All S. Ch. Ch. Bal. Magd.* Oxon. *Trin. Queen's. St. John's.* Camb. *Sion.*
  1 Tim. v. 21. 4° 1704. *Oxon.* Affize. The Nature and Mifchief of Prejudice and Partiality. *Bod. C. C. C. Univ. Bal. Magd. Or. Jef.* Oxon. *Trin. Queen's.* Camb. *Sion.*
  Acts xxiii. 1. 4° 1706. *Oxon.* Affize. The Nature, Objection, and Meafures of Confcience. *Bod. Or. Magd. Worc.* Oxon. *St. John's.* Camb. *Sion.*
  Num. xv. 30, 31. 4° 1708. *Oxon.* The Nature, Guilt, and Danger of prefumptuous Sins. *Bod. C. C. C. Or. Worc.* Oxon. *Sion.*
  1 Tim. v. 22. 4° 1709. Affize. The Communication of Sin. *Univ. Ch. Ch. Or. Hert. Worc.* Oxon. *Trin.* Camb. *Sion.*
  2 Cor. xi. 26. 4° 1709. Nov. 5. Perils of falfe brethren both in Church and State. *Ch. Ch. Magd. Linc. Or. Worc.* Oxon. *Trin. Queen's. St. John's.* Camb. *Sion.*
  Luke xxiii. 34. 4° 1713. Palm S. The Chriftian Triumph — or the Duty of praying for our Enemies. *Bod. All S. C. C. C. Or. Bal. Linc. Worc. Magd. Hert.* Oxon. *Trin. St. John's. Queen's.* Camb. *Sion.*
  1 Pet. ii. 16. 4° 1713. May 29. Falfe Notions of Liberty in Religion and Government, deftructive of both. *Bal. Linc.* Ox. *Queen's.* Camb.
  1 Tim. v. 1. 4° 1714. b. Sons of the Clergy. *Wadh.* Oxon. *Sion.*
SACK A. W. F.
  * Pf. cxxvi. 3. 4° 1758. Th. f. at *Berlin.*
SADLER Anth. DD. V. of Mitcham, Surrey, and Chapl. in Ord.
  Matt viii. 25. 4° 1661. Th. May 29. Mercy in a Miracle.

SAINT George Arthur, DD.
* 4 Difc. in 12° 1757. on the miniſterial offices of the Church. V. Arch-Deacon's Examination for Holy Orders.

SAINT John Pawlet, DD. R. of Yelden, Bedfordſhire, Preb. of Hereford, and Chapl. in Ord.
3 John 11. 8° 17
Matt. xxviii. 20. 4° 1710. Viſ. *C. C. C.* Oxon. *St. John's.* Camb.
Job xvii. 5, 6. 4° 1711. Fun. of Dr. Sacheverell. *C. C. C. Magd.' Or. Jeſ. Bod. Bal.* Oxon. *Pub. L.* Camb. *Sion. Brit. M.*
14 Serm. in 8° 1737. on practical Subjects

SALISBURY William, B. D. Fell. of St. John's Coll. Camb. and R. of Newton, Bucks.
Deut viii. 10. 8° 1738. Sch. Feaſt. Commemoration.

SALISBURY William, B. D. R. of Moreton, and little Halingbury, Eſſex.
* Prov. xiv. 24. 8° 1773. Viſ. *Queen's.* Camb.

SALKELD John, M. A. Fell. of Queen's Coll. Camb.
John xi. 44. 4° 1673. on the King's Declaration for Liberty of Conſcience.

SALL Andrew, DD. Chapl. to the Earl of Eſſex, Lord Lieutenant of Ireland, and Preb. of Swords &c.
Matt. xxiv. 15–18. 8° 1674. *Dublin.* Recantation. Ag. Popery. *Bod. Univ. Ch. Ch.* Oxon. *Queen's.* Camb.

SALMON Thomas, M. A. R. of Mepſal. Bedfordſ.
Mark x. 14. 4° 1701. Upon Baptiſm &c. *Brit. M.*

SALMON Thomas, LL. D.
John i. 14. 4° 1753. 2 ſ. p. 1. The perſonal Union of the divine and human Nature in Jeſus Chriſt.
Job xxvii. 5, 6. 4° 1753. 2 ſ. p. 13. The Comforts of a good Conſcience and Torments of an evil one.

SALTER John,   V. of Mary Church, Devon.
* Jerem. v. 22. 8° 1756. Faſt. Earthquake at Liſbon.

SALTER Samuel, M. A. V. of St. Stephen's, Norwich.
Pſ. cxxxii. 18. 8° 1714. Coron.

SALTER Samuel, M. A. Preb. of Gloucester
1 Sam. xvi. 23. 8° 17   Muſick at *Gloucester.*
Luke xiii. 1–5. 4° 1740. Faſt. b. Lord Mayor. for Fire of London, *Brit. M.*

SALTER Samuel, DD. Maſter of the Charter-Houſe.
* Ezek. xxxvii. 3. 4° 1755. b. Sons of the Clergy. *Braz. N. Ox. Queen's.* Camb.
* Prov. xvii. 14. 4° 1762. Jan. 30. b. Commons. *Queen's.* Cam.

SALWEY John, M. A. R. of Richard's Caſtle, Herefordſ.
2 Pet. iii. 18. 8° 1722. Viſ. Divine Worſhip due to Xt &c. *Br. M.*

SAMPSON John, M. A. late Fell. of Mert. Coll. Oxon. and R. of Croſcombe, Somerſetſ.
* Pſ. cxliv. 15. 8° 1771. Th.
* Luke xxii. 35, 36. 8° 1771. Viſ.
* Prov. xi. 26. 8° 1771. on withholding the Corn.

SANCROFT

SANCROFT William, Abp. of Canterbury.
  Tit. i. 5. 8° 1694. p. 1. Advent. Conf. of 7 Bps.
  Ifai. xxvi. 9. 8° 1694. p. 59. b King. Faft. for Fire of Lond.
  Pf lxxvii. 1. 8° 1694. p. 121. Faft. b. King. *Bod. Ch. Ch. Magd. C. C. C. Or. Queen's Bal.* Oxon. *Pub. L. Trin. Queen's.* Camb. *Sion. Dr. W's L.* London.
  * Jerem. xxvi. 9. 4° 1666. Lexignea.
SANDERCOCK *Edward*, of Rotherhithe.
  ‡ * Matt. xiii. 10. 8° 1733. on Parables. *Brit. M.*
  * Serm. in 2 Vol. 8° 1776.
SANDERS Thomas. M. A. R. of Avon Daffet, and Chapl. to the right Hon. Harry Earl of Stamford.
  * Jude xiv. 15. 4° 1724. Affize.
SANDERSON Robert, B. of Lincoln.
  * 36 Serm. in fo. 1689. (reprinted) *Bod. Ch. Ch. Magd.* Oxon. *Pub. L. King's. Trin. Cl. H.* Camb.
  *Cafes of Confcience in 2 V. 8° 1722. (Tranflated by Lewis) *Bod.*
SANDFORD *Benjamin*
  *Tit. ii. 6. 8° 1760. Fun. of a young Perfon.
SANDFORD William, DD. Minifter ot Aldermanbury, and Chap. to the Lord Mayor.
  Pf. cxviii. 24. 4° 1750. May 29.   ⎫
  1 Tim. ii. 1, 2. 4° 1750. Acceffion.   ⎬ b. Lord Mayor.
  2 Sam. xxiii. 3. 4° 1750. El. of Ld May.   ⎭
SANDIFORD Rowland, Lect. of St. Bartholomew near the Exchange, and Chapl. to the Lord Mayor.
  Dan. iv. 27. 4° 1746. Nov. 5. b. Lord Mayor.
  Pf. cxxii. 6, 7. 4° 1747. Elect. of Lord Mayor.
SANDWICH Robert, Cur. of Lucker, Northumberland.
  * Luke x. 37. 8° 1774. The good Samaritan.
  * John xviii. 38. 8° 1774. Pilate's Queftion.
SAVAGE John, R. of Morcot, Rutlandf.
  Acts viii. 17. 4° 1683. The facred Rite of Confirmation.
SAVAGE John, DD. of Eman. Coll. Camb. R. of Bygrave, then of Clothall, Herts, and Lecturer of St. George's Hanover Square, London.
  Col i. 18. 4° 1704. *Camb.* Vif. Chrift's Body the Church. *All S.* Oxon. *Queen's.* Camb.
  Deut. iv. 6. 4° 1704. *Camb.* Affize. Security of the eftablifhed Religion, the Wifdom of the Nation. *Ch. Ch.* Ox. *St. John's. Queen's*. Camb *Sion.*
SAVAGE *Morton Samuel*
  * Heb. xii. 9, 10. 8° 1732. Submiffion to divine Chaftifements.
  * Prov. xiv. 34. 8° 1745. Faft.
  * - - - - 1749. Fun.
  * 1 Pet. ii. 17. 8° 1760. Acceffion of King George III.
  * Luke ii. 29, 30. 8° 1762. Fun. of the Rev. Dr. *D. Jennings. Queen's.* Camb.
  * Job xxviii. 28. 8° 1763. Charity-School.
                                                              * 1 Cor.

* 1 Cor. xi. 24. 12° 1763. Lord's Supper.
* Jerem. xviii. 7,8. 8° 1782. On the prefent State of public affairs.
SAVAGE William, DD. Mafter of Eman. Coll. and R. of St. Andrew Wardrobe, and St. Ann's Blackfryars, London.
 Prov. xxix. 2. 4° 1707. Elect. of Lord Mayor. *All S*. Ox. *Trin. Queen's*. Camb. *Eton*.
 1 Cor. ix. 13, 14. 4° 1715. b. Sons of the Clergy. *All S. Wadh*. Oxon. *Sion*.
SAUNDERS Erafmus, DD. V. of Blockley, Worcefterf.
 * Jofh. xxiv. 14. 12° 1701. Houfehold-Government.
 Matt. x. 16. 8° 1708. Vif. *Jef*. Oxon.
 Matt. v. 13. 8° 1713. Act. The divine Authority, and Ufefulnefs of the Paftors of the chriftian Church. *Or*. Oxon.
 Pf. lviii. 11. 8° 1721. Affize. of judicial Providence.
 Ifai. v. 4, 5. 8° 1721. b. Commons. Faft for the Plague. *All S. Ch Ch*. Oxon. *Eton*.
SAUNDERS Will. DD. Chap. to his Grace the Duke of Chandois.
 * Pf. cxxxiii. 1. 8° 1744. The Neceffity and Advantages of Union afferted.
SAURIN James,   Paftor of the French Church at the Hague.
 * 1 Vol. (13 ferm.) 8° 1775. on the Attributes of God.
 * 2 Vol. (14 ferm.) 8° 1775. on the Truth of Revelation.
 * 3 Vol. (14 ferm.) 8° 1777. on the principal Doctrines of Xnity. Tranflated and publifhed by *R. Robinfon*, at Cambridge.
SAWBRIDGE Thomas,   V. of Hungerton, Leicefter.
 Ifai. i. 26. 4° 1689. Affize.
SAWBRIDGE Wanley, M. A. Chapl. to the Lord Mayor.
 * Prov. xi. 3. 4° 1776. Elect. of Lord Mayor. Duty and Advantage of Integrity both in private and public life.
SAWLE William,   V. of Cholfey, Berks.
 Pf. xxxiii. 12. 8° 1716. Affize.
SAY Samuel
 * Ifai. xlix. 4. 8° 1736. Ref. of Manners. *Queen's*. Cam. *Brit. M*.
 * Ifai. v. 4. 8° 1740. Faft. f.
SAYER Fr.   M. A. R. of Chackenden, Oxon.
 Col. iv. 17. 4° 1705. Vif. *Bod*.
SAYER Jofeph, B. D. R. of Newbury Berks, and Arch-Deacon of Lewes, Suffex.
 Rom. xiii. 5. 4° 1673. Affize. *Bod Ch. Ch*. Oxon.
SAYER T.   Lect. of St. Giles's, Cripplegate, London.
 1 Cor. xi. 29. 12° 1708. Cafe of unworthy receiving the Lord's Supper.
SAYWELL Samuel, B. D. Fell. of St. John's Coll. Camb. and R. of Bluntham, Huntingdon.
 Phil. ii. 21. 4° 1696. Conc. ad Cler. Vif. *St. John's*. Camb.
 Acts viii 14–17. 12° 1701. The divine original of Confirmation.
SCAMLER Robert, M. A. R. of Taverham, Norfolk.
 Pf. xxxiv. 19. 4° 1677.
 John iii. 16.
 * Sev. ferm. in 4° 1685. on feveral Occafions.

SCARISBRIKE *Edward*,   (a Jefuit.)
 Prov. viii. 15. 4° 1688. b. King and Queen. Jan. 30. Catholic Loyalty. *Bod Sion.*
 Luke xvii. 12. 4° 1688.   *Sion.*
SCATTERGOOD Anthonie, DD. R. of Winwick and Yelvertoft, Northamp. and Preb. of Linc. and Litchfield.
 Exod. xviii. 21. 4° 1664. Affize. Jethro's Character of worthy Judges. *Bod. Pub. L.* Camb.
SCATTERGOOD Samuel, M. A. Fell. of Trin. Coll. Camb. and V. of Blockley, Worcefterf.
 Job xxviii. 28. 4° 1676. *Camb.* b. King. *Queen's.* Oxon. *Sion.*
 Pf. lxiv. 5–10. 4° 1683. Th. Sept. 9.
 12 Serm. in 8° 1700. upon feveral Occafions. *Bod.*
 52 Serm. in 2 Vol. 8° 1725. upon feveral Occafions.
SCHREVELIUS C.   · Minifter of the Dutch Ch. Colchefter.
 Rom. i. 16. 8° 1708. Introduction f.
SCHWAB Chrift. Erneftus.
 * Ifai. xii. 1–6. 4° 1765. Fun. of Henry Buckman, Efq; Tranflated from the German.
SCLATER Edward, M. A. Minifter of Putney, Surrey:
 Pf. cvi. 16. 4° 1681. April 21. *Worc.* Oxon.
SCLATER William, DD. R. of Clifton, Bedfordf. and Minifter of Clerkenwell, London.
 Rev. ii. 10. 4° 1671. b. Military company. *Bod.*
SCOFFIN William
 * - - - 12° 1692. 2 f. on the Death of Mrs. Cath. Difney.
SCOLEFIELD *Radcliffe*,   of Birmingham.
 * 1 Kings xxii. 14. 8° 1769. b. diffenting Clergy. Numbers, no Criterion of Faith.
SCOTLAND *John*, V. D. M. of Wefterkirk.
 * Hofea iii 5. 12° 1776. The Fear of the divine Goodnefs. V. Scotch Pr. V. II. p. 66.
SCOTT Alexander, M. A.
 Gal. v. 22, 23. } p. 5.
 Luke xi. 13.   } p. 16, 29.   8° 1711. 3 f. *Linc.* Oxon.
SCOTT James, DD. late Fell. of Trin. Coll. Camb. and R. of Simonbourn, Northumberland.
 * 2 Sam, xi. 20, 21. 4° 1764. How far a ftate of Dependence, and a fenfe of Gratitude fhould influence our Conduct.
 * 2 Cor. i. 12. 4° 1769. *Leeds.* Farw. f. *Queen's.* Camb.
 * Luke vii. 44–47. 4° 1769.
 * Matt. xxi. 21. 4° 1769. *Leeds.* Vif.
 * John v. 6. 4° 1777. *Newcaftle*-Infirmary.
 * Mark v. 15. 4° 1780. The Lunatic Afylum at *York.*
 * Luke xiii. 2, 3. 4° 1781. Faft.
SCOTT John,   Minifter of St. Thomas, Southwark.
 † * Luke ix. 56. 4° 1673. Nov. 5. b. Lord Mayor.
SCOTT John, DD. R. of St. Giles's in the Fields, Can. of Windfor.
 * Gal. vi. 11. 8° 1673.
                Matt.

* Gal. vi. 11. 8° 1673.
Matt. xxv. 46. 4° 1685. Fun. of Mrs. Crown. *Jef.* Oxon.
* Ecclef. ii. 8. 4° 1688.
4 Difc. in 8° 1700. V. Chriſtian-Life. Vol. V.
11 Praƈt. Difc. V. I 8° 1700. on feveral Subjeƈts.
11 Praƈt. Difc. V. II. 8° 1701. concerning Obedience and the Love of God.
11 Serm in 8° 1704. upon feveral Occaſions.
All his ferm. are comprized in the 2 Vol. of his Works. fo. 1718. *Bod. Magd. Ch. Ch C. C. C. Bal. Univ. Trin. Mert. Worc. Jef. St. John's.* Oxon. *Pub. L Queen's. King's. Cl. H. Trin.* Camb. *Dr. W's L.* London.

SCOTT John, M. A. Fell. of Queen's Coll. Oxon. V. of Cariſbrook in the Iſle of Wight.
    Heb. xiii. 17. 8° 1708. Viſ. of fpiritual Rule.

[SCOTT John]
    * Serm. in 8° 1764. on feveral Occaſions.

SCOTT *Jof- Nicoll*, Miniſter at Norwich.
    * Serm. in 2 Vol. 8° 1743. in defence of all Religions.

SCOTT Thomas, M. A. V. of Wakefield, Yorkſ.
    Rev. xxi. 8. 8° 1710. *York.*

SCOTT Thomas
    * Prov. xiv. 12.   *Queen's.* Oxon.

SCOTT *Thomas*
    * Jude 3. 8° 1739. Chriſtian Zeal. *Queen's.* Camb.
    * Pf. cviii. 13. 8° 1759. *Ipſwich.* Th. The Reaſonableneſs, Pleaſure and Benefit of the Nation.

SCOTT William
    * Difc. in 8° 1701. on the Wiſdom of God. *Jef.* Oxon. *Brit. M.*

SCOTT William, M. A. Sch. of Eton and Trin. Coll. Camb.
    * 1 Tim. ii. 1, 2. 8° 1772. Acceſſion. *Bod.*
    * - - - - 8° 1773. 2 f. New year's Gift for a Prime Miniſter.
    * 2 Kings iv. 7. 8° 1773. on Bankruptcy.
    * - - - - - 8° 1774. ag. Duelling. ⎫
    * - - - - - - - on Xtms-day. |
    * - - - - - - - Aſcenſion.   ⎬ Tranſlated from St. Chryſoſtom's Difc.
    * - - - - - - - Whitfunday. |
    * - - - - - - - Trinity Sunday. |
    * Luke x. 37. 8° 1778. Fun. ⎭

SCOUGAL Henry, M. A. of the Church of Scotland.
    9 Serm. in 8° 1726. on important Subjeƈts. To which is fubjoined a fermon preached at his Fun. by G. Gairden, DD. *Ch. Ch.* Oxon. *Brit. M.*

SCROPE John, DD. R. of Caſtle Combe in the dioceſe of Sarum.
    * 1 Cor. viii. 1. 8° 1760. Viſ. *Bod.*

SCURLOCK David, M. A. Fell. of Jef. Coll. Oxon. V. of Waltham St. Lawrence, Berks, and of Pottern, Wilts.
    Jerem. viii. 9, 10. 8° 17   Eleƈt. of Burgeſſes.
    Aƈts xxiii. 5. 8° 1725.

Rom. xiii. 7. 8° 1725. 2 f.
1 Pet. ii. 13, 14. 8° 1727. Affize.
Tit. iii. 2. 8° 1733. of speaking evil of Governors. *Queen's.* C.
Pf. cxix. 24. 4° 1736. Welch Feaft.
* 2 Tim. ii. 22. 8° 1748. at the grand Seffions at *Carmarthen.* A warning to all christian Governors and Subjects to follow Righteousnefs and Faith.

SEABURY *Samuel*, DD.
* 2 Tim. iii. P6. 8° 17   Ufe of Scripture.
* 1 Pet. ii. 17. 8° 17   Fear God and honour the King.

SEAGRAVE *Robert*, M. A. late of the Church of England, now Preacher at the Bull and Mouth-meeting, Alderfgate ftreet, London.
Gal. iii. 24. 8° 1737. 6 f. of Juftification.

SEAMAN
* Heb. xiii. 20, 21. 4° 1663. V. Coll. of Farew. f. *Magd.* Camb.

SEATON Thomas, M. A. V. of Raunfton, Bucks.
* Difc. in 12° 1720. Duty of Servants.
Luke xxiv. 27. 8° 1726. Vif.

SECKER William, Abp. of Canterbury.
* 14 Serm. in 8° 1766. on feveral Occafions. *Bod. All S. Pemb. Queen's. Triu.* Oxon. *Pub. L.* Camb.
9 Sermons. (reprinted in 8° 1771.) on the Rebellion 1745. *Bod. All S. Ch Ch Worc. Wadh.* Oxon. *Queen's.* Camb.
* Serm. (Pofth). in 4 Vol. 8° 1770. on feveral Subjects, as alfo
* Lectures in 2 Vol. 8° 1771. on the Catechifm, to which is added a fermon on Confirmation. *Bod. All S. New C.* Ox. *Queen's.* C.

SECKER *Will.* Preacher of the Gofpel at Tewkefbury, Gloucefterf.
Matt. v. 47. 8° 1660. 7 f. entitled the non fuch Profeffor in his meridian Splendor. *Bod.*
* Gen. ii. 18. 12° 16   V. Difc. on conjugal Duty. V. I. p. 34.

SEDGEWICK *Obadiah*
* Difc. in fo. 1660.
* Acts xvi. 30, 31. 4° 1660.

SEED Jeremiah, M. A. Fell. of Queen's Coll. Oxon. and R. of Enham, Hants.
Difc. in 2 Vol. 8° 1743. on feveral important Subjects, to which are added 8 Serm. at Lady Moyer's Lect. *Brit. M.*
His pofthumous Works in 2 Vol. 1750. *Univ. All S. New C. Wadh.* Oxon. *Brit. M.*

SEIGNIOR George,   Fell. of Trin. Coll. Camb.
Exod. iv. 16. 4° 1670. *Camb. St. John's.* Camb. *Brit. M.*
8 Serm. in 8° 1670. God, the King, and the Church. *Bod. Sion.*
James i. 21. 4° 1674. f. in. e. p. 153. Hearing the Word. *Bod.*

SENHOUSE Peter, M. A. V. of Linton, and Preb. of Brecon.
Gen. xxvii. 4. 8° 1727. The right Ufe and Improvement of fenfitive Pleafures, more particularly of Mufick.

SEPPENS Robert,   R. of Higham, Norfolk.
1 Cor. ix. 27. 4° 1679. Shrove-Sunday.

SERMON

SERMON Edmund, M. A. of St. Mary Hall, Oxon.
    James iii. 13. 4° 1679. b. Lord Mayor. Wisdom of pub. Piety.
SEVILL William, M. A. Fell. of C. C. C. Oxon.
    Rev. xiv. 13. 4° 1694. designed for the Fun. of Edm. Wiseman, Esq; *C. C. C.* Oxon.
SEWARD Thomas, M. A. Canon of Litchfield, R. of Eyham, Derbyshire, and of Kingsly, Staffordshire.
    Pf. cxxxiii. 1. 4° 1750 Affize. The folly, danger and wickedness of Disaffection to the Government.
    * Luke xiii. 4, 5. 8° 1756. Falt. Earthquake. *Queen's.* Camb.
SEWELL *Joseph*
    ‡ * Pf. cxix. 115. 8° 1728. *Boston.* ag. Duelling. *Brit. M.*
SEWELL Thomas
    Isai. lx. 1. 4° 1697. Fun.   *Sion.*
SHAKESPEAR Edward, M. A. R. of Northmeals, and V. of Leyland, Lancastershire.
    1 Tim. i. 9, 10. 8° 1740. Affize.
    * 2 Tim. ii. 19. 8° 1742. Vis. Mutual obligation of Clergy and Laity to Holiness of life.
SHANK John, B. A. R. of   Bedfordshire.
    Jonah iii. 8. 4° 1694. Falt. *Brit. M.*
    Pf. xiv. 1. 8° 1725. Vis.
[SHARP Granville]
    * Isai. vii. 8.
    * Isai. vii. 13–16. } 8° 1769. Dissertations.
    * Gen. xlix. 10.
SHARP Gregory, LL. D. Master of the Temple, and Chap. in Ord. F. R. S. and A. S.
    * Acts ii. 22. 8° 1755. Arguments in defence of Christianity. *Queen's.* Camb.
    * Pf. xxix. 9. 8° 1765. Rise and Fall of the City of Jerusalem. *Braz. N. Worc.* Oxon. *Queen's.* Camb.
    * Col. i. 23. 8° 1766. Want of Universality, no Objection to the christian Religion. *Braz. N. Worc.* Oxon. *Queen's.* Camb.
    * Ephef. vi. 4. 4° 1770. b. Gov. of the *Asylum*. Rel. Education.
    * 18 Serm. in 8° 1772. on various Subjects. *Queen's.* Camb.
SHARP John, Abp. of York.
    Prov. iii. 6. 8° 1693.
    15 Serm. Vol. I. 8° 1729. on several Occasions.
    8 Serm. and 2 Disc. Vol. II. 8° 1729.
    16 Casuistical serm. Vol. III. 8° 1729.
    18 Serm. Vol. IV. 8° 1729. on several Occasions.
    8 Disc. Vol. V. 8° 1734. with 4 serm. on the Imitation of Christ.
    19 Serm. Vol. VI. 8° 1734. on several Subjects.
    15 Sermons. Vol. VII. 8° 1735. with an Appendix. *Bod. All S. C. C. C. Bal. Or. New C. St. John's. Worc. Pemb.* Oxon. *Trin. Queen's.* Camb. *Sion. Dr. W's. L.* London.

SHARP J. M. A. Chap. to the Queen's Forces New York, America.
Job xiv. 14. 8° 1706. Fun. of Lady Cornbury. *Univ.* Oxon. *Trin.* Camb. *Sion.*
* Pſ. xciv. 19. 8° 17

SHARP Tho. DD. Arch-D. of Northumberland, Preb. of Durham.
* Serm. in 8° 1763. on ſev. Occaſions. *Sion. Dr. W's. L.* Lond.

SHARP William, DD. Profeſſor of Greek, Oxon. and R. of Eaſthamſtead, Berks.
* Rom. xiv. 16. 8° 1754. *Oxon.* Act. *All S.* Oxon.
* Pſ. lxxii. 1 &c. 4° 1755. *Oxon.* Acceſſion. National Proſperity the joint Product of juſt Government and dutiful Subjection. *All S.* Oxon.
* Mark x. 13–16. 8° 1755. Charity-School. The Amiableneſs and Advantages of making a ſuitable proviſion for the Education and Employment of poor Children. *All S.* Oxon.

SHARPE Lewis,   R. of Moreton Hampſtead, Devon.
Matt. xxv. 29. 12° 1674. The reward of Diligence. *Bod.*
Rom. iii. 2. 8° 1692.

SHARROCK Robert, LL. D. Preb. of Wincheſter.
Sev. Diſc. in 4° 1673. *Oxon.* De Finibus virtutis Chriſtianæ, or the Ends of chriſtian Religion. *Bod. Sion.*

SHAW
Lev. xiv. 4, 8.

SHAW Ferdinando, M. A. at Derby.
* Pſ. lxxv. 7. 8° 1714. Death of Queen Ann, and Acceſſion of King George I.
Pſ. cxxxii. 18. 8° 1714. Coron.
Job xii. 16.   } 8° 1716. 2 ſ. on the Pretender's landing.
2 Kings xix. 28. }
1 Chron. xxviii. 9. 8° 1729. on Prince Frederick's birth-day.

SHAW S.
Prov. xxv. 5.   1660.

[SHAW Samuel]
* Serm. in 8° 1751.
* 2 Cor. v. 6. 8° 1751. A farewel to life.

SHAW Thomas, M. A. late of Queen's Coll. Oxon.
* Prov. viii. 12. 8° 1765. Viſ. The uſe and office with ſome inſtances of the Weakneſs and Imperfections of Reaſon in matters of Religion.

SHAW William, M. A. of Stanford, Berks.
* Prov. xxviii. 7. 8° 1723. at a ſpecial Commiſſion for trying the Waltham Blacks.

SHEELES James,   of Trin. Coll. Camb.
* 2 Jerem. iii. 21, 22. 4° 1762. Faſt.

SHEFFIELD John
Heb. xii. 14. 4° 1676. m. e. G. p. 410. of Holineſs. *Bod.*
Heb. vi. 4–6. 4° 1677. m. e. C. p. 63. What Relapſes are inconſiſtent with Grace.
* 1 John iii. 8. 12° 1705. Ref. of Manners.

SHELDON

SHELDON Gilbert, Abp. of Canterbury.
 Pf. xviii. 49. 4° 1660. b. King. Th. David's Deliverance and Thanksgiving. *Ch. Ch/Magd. Worc.* Ox. *St. John's.* C. *Br. M.*
SHELLEY Peter, M. A. R. of Woodford, Eflex.
 1 Pet. ii. 17. 4° 1700. County-Foaft. *Ch. Ch.* Ox. *Queen's.* Camb.
 Dan. vi. 31. 4° 1702. Acceffion.
SHELTON William, R. of St. James's, Colchefter, Effex.
 Pf. xcvii. 1. 4° 1680. b. Lord Mayor. Divine Providence, the Support of good men under all Events.
 1 Theff. iv. 17. 4° 1690. Fun. of Mr. Glafcock. *All S.* Oxon.
SHEPHEARD Richard, B. D. late Fell. of C. C. C. Oxon.
 *Gal. v. 1. 4° 1771. Requifition of Subfcription to 39 Articles and Liturgy.
 ‡*Rom. ii. 14, 15. 8° 1776. on Confcience. V. Mifcell. v. II. p. 151.
 ‡*Tim. iii. 16. 8° 1776. Whitf. on Infpiration. p. 175.
 ‡*Ecclef. vii. 30. 8° 1776. Conc. Acad. de Statu Paradif. p. 199.
SHEPHEARD Will. M. A. R. of Afhreigney, Devon, and Chapl. to the Bp. of Gloucefter.
 10 Serm. in 8° 1748. *Sherborne.* on feveral religious and important Subjects.
SHEPHERD *James*
 *9 Serm. in 12° 1748.
SHEPHERD *Thomas*
 * Matt. xxv. 1–14. fo. 1660. Parable of the ten Virgins.
 * Sol. Song v. 2. 8° 1680. V. fincere Convert p. 206.
 * 2 Cor. vii. 1. 8° 1680. V. fincere Convert p. 187.
 * Serm. in 12° 1702.
 * Gen. ii. 18. 8° 1713. Wedd. f.
SHEPPARD *William*
 * Ephef. v. 16. 8° 17. Redeeming the time.
SHEPPEY Thomas, formerly of Pemb. Hall Camb. and Chapl. to Lord Biron.
 1 Theff. iv. 10, 11. 4° 1682. Affize. τὰ πρὸς εἰρήνην.
SHERARD Bennet, M. A. Chapl. to the Duke and Dutchefs of Rutland, and R. of Aileftone, Leicefter.
 Prov. xiv. 34. 4° 1720. Affize. The advantages of Righteoufnefs to a Nation.
SHERIDAN William, Bp. of Kilmore and Ardagh, Ireland.
 Ifai. xxxviii. 1. 4° 1665. Fun. of Sir M. Euftace.
 Pract. Difc. in 3 Vol. 8° 1720. upon the moft important fubjects. *Bod. Wadh.* Oxon. *Dr. W's. L.* London.
SHERLEY William, B. D. R. of Huifh Comb-flower.
 1 Cor. xi. 34. 4° 1662. *Oxon.* Vif. The Excellency of the order of the Church of England under Epifcopal Government.
SHERLOCK Richard, DD. R. of Winwick, Lancafterf.
 Acts xx. 28. 4° 1669. *Oxon.* Vif. *Bod.*
SHERLOCK Thomas, Bp. of London.
 * Sermons in 4 Vol. 8° 1772. *Bod. All S. Bal. Ch. Ch. Or. New C. St. John's. Wadh. Worc.* Oxon. *Trin. Queen's. Cl. H.* Camb.
               Occafional

Occasional serm. 5 Vol. 8°1774. (republished) except Matt. xxiii. 23. and
2 Pet. i. 19. 8° 1740. 6 s. to which are added
* 6 Dissertations. *Bod. All S. Worc. Wadh.* Oxon.

SHERLOCK William, DD. Dean of St. Paul's, and Master of the Temple.
    Ps. xviii. 50. 4° 1683. Th. on the Discovery of the Plot. *Magd. Or. Bal.* Oxon. *Pub. L.* Camb.
    Eccles. x. 17. 4° 1685. May 29. b. Commons. *Bod. All S. Ch. Ch. Magd. Or. Worc.* Oxon. *Pub. L. Trin.* Camb. *Sion.*
    ‡ * Matt. xxiv. 25, 26. 4° 1686. Fun. of Rev. Benjamin Calamy, DD. *Brit. M.*
    Heb. ix. 27. 8° 1689. (and 1705. *Bod.*) A practical Disc. concerning Death. *Univ. Magd. New C. Worc. Hert.* Oxon. *Pub. L. Queen's.* Camb.
    Acts xvii. 31. 8° 1691. (and 8° 1699. *Bod.*) A practical Discourse concerning a future Judgement. *Univ. Magd. Wadh.* Oxon. *Pub. L. Queen's.* Camb.
    Ps. xc. 15. 4° 1692. Jan. 30. b. Commons. *Bod. Ch. Ch. Univ. Magd. Or. Jes.* Oxon. *Pub. L.* Camb.
    1 Tim. ii. 1, 2. 4° 1692. May 29. at the Temple. *Bod. Ch. Ch. Magd.* Oxon. *Pub. L.* Camb. *Sion.*
    ‡*Phil. i. 23, 24. 4°1693. Fun. of Rev. Rich. Meggott. *Brit. M.*
    Jude 3. 4° 1701. Conc. ad Synod. *Bod. All S. Or. Queen's.* Cam. *Sion. Eton.*
    Ps. lviii. 11. 4° 1704. Th. b. Queen. *Magd.* Oxon. *Queen's.* Camb. *Sion.*
    17 Serm. Vol. I. 8° 1719. (3d Edit.) upon sev. Occasions.
    19 Serm. Vol. II. 8° 1719. upon useful Subjects. *Univ. All S. Ch. Ch. C. C. C. St. John's. Or. Pemb.* Oxon. *Pub. L.* Camb. *Dr. W's. L.* London.

SHERMAN T.
    * Prov. xiv. 32. 8° 1729. Fun.   *Queen's.* Camb.

SHERWILL Thomas, M. A. Fell. of Christ's Coll. Camb.
    Matt. xxiii. 23. 4° 1704. *Camb.* Church-conformity asserted and vindicated. *Trin. Queen's.* Camb. *Sion.*
    2 Tim. iv. 3. 4° 1704. *Camb.* The Degeneracy of the present age as to Principles. *Ch. Ch. Pub. L. Trin. Queen's. Cl. H.* Camb. *Sion.*
    Eccles. ix. 17. 8° 1709. *Camb.* Accession. b. Univ. *All S.* Oxon. *Trin. Queen's.* Camb.
    Prov. xxii. 6. 4° 1710. School-Feast.

SHERWIN W
    * 2 Cor. iii. 18. 1° 1661.

SHILL
    Matt. xxvii 29.

SHIPLEY Jonathan, Bp. of St. Asaph.
    * Isai. xxxiii. 6, 4° 1770. Jan. 30. b. Lords. *Queen's.* Camb.

                                                              * Luke

* Luke ii. 14. 4° 1773. Prop. of Gospel
* Prov. xxii. 6. 4° 1777. Ann. meeting Char. School.
SHIPPEN William, DD. Fell. of Univ. Coll. Oxon.
   1 Cor. xv. 55. 4° 1688. Fun.
SHIRLEY Walter, Hon. B. A. R. of Loughrea in tne County of Galway.
   * 12 Serm. in 12° 1762. on several Occasions.
SHORE John,   R. of Hamsey, Sussex.
   2 Sam. i. 19. 4° 1695. Royal Fun. The Threnody of the Bow, or the Countryman's Lamentation. *St. John's.* Camb.
SHOREY William, M. A. R. of St. Lawrence Jewry, London.
   2 Kings viii. 12, 13. 8° 1715. b. Lord Mayor. Jan. 30. *Ch. Ch.* Oxon. *Sion.*
   14 Disc. in 8° 1725. on several Occasions. *Sion.*
SHORTHOSE Hugh, L. C. S. Chapl. to the Duke of Chandos, and Lect. of Chelsea, Middlesex.
   14 Serm. in 8° 1738. on several Occasions. *Brit. M.*
SHOWER *John*,   Minister of the Gospel in London.
   ‡ * Phil. i. 23. 3° 1682. Fun. of Ann Barnardiston. *Brit. M.*
   2 Sam. xv. 26. 4° 1684. on Resignation. *Wadh.* Oxon.
   * Isai. xxi. 11, 12. 4° 1688. Repentance and Union.
   ‡ * Ps. cxix. 9. 4° 1692. Fun. of Rich. Walter.
   * 2 Kings ix. 22. 4° 1694. Fast. no peace to the wicked.
   1 Cor. x. 9. 8° 1694. of tempting Christ. *Bod.*
   Ps. lxxxi. 11, 12. 8° 1694. 4 l. The Day of Grace. *Bod.*
   Isai. lxvi. 10. 4° 1696. Th. April 16.
   Isai. lix. 4. 12° 1698. Ref. of Manners.
   * Fun. Disc. in 2 Vol. 12° 1699. *Pub. L.* Camb. *Brit. M.*
   * Luke xvi. 26. 12° 1700.
   * Sacram. Disc. in 2 parts. 8° 1702. *Pemb.* Oxon.
   2 Cor. v. 9. 4° 1702. Fun.   *Eton.*
   Ps. cxlvii. 15–18. 8° 1709. Winter-Meditations on Frost and Snow. *Pub. L. St. John's.* Camb.
   * Gen. v. 24. 8° 1712. Fun. of *N. Grew.*
SHUCKBURGH George, M. A. R. of Caston, Norfolk.
   Zach. viii. 17. 4° 1715. Assize. *Ch. Ch.* Oxon.
   Eccles. i. 15. 4° 1722. Insufficiency of human Reason in the discovery of divine Truth.
SHUCKFORD Samuel, DD. Preb. of Cant. and Chapl. in Ord.
   Ps. cxxxiii. 1. 4° 1723. *Camb.* Vis. *Queen's.* Camb.
   Deut. xxix. 24. 4° 1724. Jan. 30. *Queen's.* Camb.
   Prov. xxiv. 21. 8° 1734. Norwich. Jan. 30. *Brit. M.*
   Ps. lxxxiv. 10. 4° 1737. Cons. of Bp. Gooch. *Queen's.* C. *Brit. M.*
   Eccles. v. 1. 8° 1752. Hutchins Lect. The use of a Liturgy, and the Excellency of the Liturgy of the church of England considered. *Queen's.* Camb.
SHUTE Christopher, DD. R. of St. Vedast's Foster Lane, Arch-D. of St. Alban's, and Chapl. in Ord.

Luke xxi. 34. 4° 1661. A feasonable Watchword to all sober Christians. *Pub. L.* Camb.

Ecclef. ix. 14, 15. 4° 1662.

SHUTE Henry, M. A. Chapl. to the Earl of Orford, Lect. of St. Mary's White Chapel, London.

Ecclef. xii. 7. 4° 1705. Fun. of Mrs. Lorrain.

SHUTTLEWOOD John

    Gen. ii. 22. 8° 1712. Wedding f. *Bod. Ch. Ch.* Oxon. *Pub. L.* Camb. *Sion.*

SHUTTLEWORTH John, R. of Oborn and Lillington, Dorfetf.

    Ephef. v. 19. 4° 1700. Open. an Organ. *St. John's.* Camb. *Sion.*

    * Rom. xv. 6. 8° 1718. A Vol. Perfuafive to Union.

SILL William, R. of St. Auftin, and St. Faith's, Arch-Deacon of Colchefter, and Preb. of Weftminfter.

    Heb. ii. 14, 15. 4° 1681. Palm S. Freedom from fear of Death, through the Death of Chrift. *All S.* Oxon. *Pub. L.* Camb.

SILVESTER Tipping, M. A. Fell. of Pemb. Coll. Oxon. V. of Shabbington, Bucks.

    Exod. xx. 5, 6. 4° 1732. *Oxon.* May 29. The doctrine of national Judgments and Bleflings confidered. *Worc.* Oxon.

    Deut. xxiii. 22. 4° 1732. *Oxon.* Nov. 5. Extraordinary and particular Vows confidered as not neceflary under the mofaic, or expedient under the chriftian Difpenfation.

    John xiii. 34. 4° 1734. Moral and Xn Benevolence. *Queen's.* C.

    Tit. iii. 10, 11. 8° 1735. Critical differtation on Herefy, and a Letter.

    John iii. 5. 4° 1738. Scripture Doctrine of Regeneration ftated and fhewn to concur with the baptifmal fervice of our Church.

    Phil. ii. 5. 4° 1744. Vif. Chriftian Magnanimity.

SIMMONS

    * Luke iv. 23. 8° 1724. Nov. 5.

SIMMONS John

    Pf. cxix. 37. 4° 1677. m. e. C. p. 423. How to get rid of fpiritual Sloth.

SIMMONS Thomas

    ‡ * Pf. xx. 6. 8° 1715. Th. for Acceffion.

SIMONS William, V. of Otterton, Devon.

    Exod. ii. 16. 8° 1734. Affize.

    Sermons in 8° 1743. *Exon.* on feveral Subjects.

SIMPSON Bolton, DD. of Queens Coll. Oxon. Minifter of Weft Cowes in the Ifle of Wight.

    Pf. xii. 26. 4° 1744. Affize. The fuperior Excellency of the righteous or moral Character. *Queen's.* Camb.

[SIMPSON David, M. A.] of Macclesfield, Chefhire.

    * Difc. in 8° 1774.

SIMPSON Jofeph, DD. late Fell. of Queen's Coll. Oxon. R. of Weyhill, Hants.

    * Prov. iii. 13. 8° 1761. *Oxon.* Act. Religion and Learning mutually affiftant. *Braz. N. Worc.* Oxon.

SIMP-

SIMPSON Will. DD. R. of St. George's in the East, Middlesex.
\Pf. xliv. 7. 4° 1732. May 29. b. Lord Mayor.
Matt. v. 6. 8° 1738. Ref. of Manners. The great Benefit of a good Example. *Queen's.* Camb.
SIMS Joseph, M. A. R. of St. John's, Westminster, and Preb. of St. Paul's,
Neh. ii. 19. 4° 1745. on Rebellion. *Brit. M.*
* 15 Serm. in 8° 1773. on various Subjects.
SINGLETON
* John xii. 28. 4° 1683. C. m. e. p. 905. God's Judgment.
SION Alexander
Mark vii. 37. 4° 1685. *Sion.*
SKEELER Thomas, M. A. Chapl. of All Soul's Coll. Oxon. V. of Lewknor, Oxon. and Chapl. to the Earl of Litchfield.
14 Serm. in 8° 1740. on several occasions &c. *Brit. M.*
* 14 Serm. in (Posth.) 8° 1772.
SKELTON Bernard, V. of Henton, Norfolk.
John xiv. 9. 4° 1692. on the Divinity of Christ. *Bod. Magd. Ox. St. John's.* Camb.
SKELTON Philip
* Disc. in 2 V. 8° 1754. Controversial and practical. *Braz. N. Ox.*
SKELTON William
‡ * 1 Thess. iv. 7. 17 *Brit. M.*
SKEPP John
* Serm. in 12° 1752. on the divine Energy.
SKERRET Ralph, DD. R. of St. Peter le poor, London, and V. of Greenwich, Kent.
- - - - - 1715. Th. Jan. 30. The great Duty and Happiness of waiting for God in the way of his Providence.
Pf. ix. 10. 4° 1715. Relig. trust in God, the best Security ag. the present Rebellion.
Rom. xiii. 1. 8° 1715. Jan. 30. b. Lord Mayor. The Subjects Duty to the higher Powers. *Ch. Ch* Oxon. *Sion. Eton.*
Gal. v. 1. 8° 1716. Assize. A sincere Zeal for the protestant Interest, and our happy Constitution in Church and State.
Ephes. iv. 25. 8° 1716. Assize.
Pf. cv. 45. 8° 1716. Th. for suppressing the Rebell. *Ch. Ch. Ox.*
Rom. xiv. 19. 8° 1716. Assize. *Eton.*
James iii. 17. 4° 1716. Elect. of Lord Mayor. True Wisdom explained and recommended. *Ch. Ch.* Oxon. *Eton.*
Rom. xiii. 4. 4° 1716. on swearing the Lord Mayor. A good Magistrate, a public Blessing. *Ch. Ch.* Oxon. *Eton.*
Pf. cxviii. 23, 24. 4° 1717. May 29. b. Lord Mayor.
Deut. xxxii. 29. 8° 1717. Assize. of Confideration. *Ch. Ch. Ox.*
Rom. xiv. 19. 4° 1720. Assize. Peace and Loyalty.
1 Cor. xiii. 5. 4° 1723. Spitt. W. Almsgiving without Charity unprofitable. *Eton.*
John iii 5. 8° 1739. Whitsunday. of Regeneration.

SKINGLE Richard, V. of Royden, Essex.
  Pf. cxxvi. 3. 4° 1698. Assize.
SKINNER William, M. A. Fell. of Pemb. Coll. Oxon. and Preb. of Hereford.
  * Luke vi. 36. 8° 1754. Sessions.
  * Matt. xxv. 36. 8° 1776. Infirmary.
SKYNNER John, M. A. Fell. of St. John's Coll. Camb. and Chapl. to the Countess of Gainsborough.
  Pf. xxxix. 8. 4° 1751. Fun. of the Earl of Gainsborough.
SLADE Joseph, M. A. Cur. of St. Mary's, and Lect. of St. Lawrence, Reading.
  Prov. xxix. 2. 8° 1713. Assize. The Character of a righteous Magistrate.
  Acts xviii. 14, 15. 4° 1721. Assize. (ag. Dr. Ibbot's serm.) The Magistrates duty with respect to Religion. *Eton.*
  Matt. xxiii. 23. 4° 1727. *Reading.* The order of Duties.
SLADEN *John*
  * 2 Thess. ii. 13. 8° 1732. 2 s. of particular Election. V. Limestreet s. Vol. I. p. 143.
  * Luke xiv. 34, 35. 8° 1733. Ministers and private Christians compared to Salt.
SLATER John, M. A. V. of Wotton, Bedfordf.
  Job xxvii. 6. 8° 1729. Assize.
SLATER *Samuel*, Minister of the Gospel at London.
  Heb. xiii. 7. 4° 1679. Fun. of Rev. *Thomas Vincent.*
  Pf. xcvii. 1, 2. 4° 1683. C. m. e. p. 385. *Bod. Pub. L.* Camb.
  Rom. xii. 3. 4° 1690. C. m. e p. 336. The Magistrates duty of suppressing Profaneness. *Bod. Pub. L.* Camb.
  Rom. xiii. 5. 4° 1690. *Bod.*
  Matt. vi. 6. 8° 1691. of Closet-prayer. *Bod.*
  * 2 Sam. i. 26. 8° 1693.
  Pf. xx. 5. 8° 1693. Th. Oct. 27. *Bod. Pub. L.* Camb.
  Josh. xxiv. 15. 8° 1694. 8 s. of Family-worship. *Bod. Pub. L. C.*
SLEECH John, M. A. Arch-Deacon of Cornwall.
  Luke x. 36, 37. 4° 1743. *Exon.* b. Gov. of *Devon* and *Exon* Hospitals. *Queen's.* Camb. *Eton.*
SLOCOCK Benjamin, DD. Chaplain of St. Saviour's, Southwark.
  Isai. lvii. 20, 21. 4° 1738.
SLOSS *James*, M. A.
  * Serm. in 8° 1736. Doctrine of the Trinity.
SMALBROKE Richard, Bp. of Litchfield and Coventry.
  John v. 28 29. 4° 1706. *Oxon.* Doctrine of an universal Judgment. *Bod. Ch. Ch. C. C. C. Univ. Magd. Jes.* Oxon. *Sion.*
  Pf. viii. 2. 8° 1715. on a new Charity-School. God's Praise perfected out of the mouths of Infants. *Eton.*
  2 Tim. i. 7. 8° 1715. Assize. of true Christian and Eng. Courage.
  Matt. iv. 10. 6° 1720. 2 s. Idolatry charged on Arianism. *Ch. Ch.* Oxon. *Eton. Queen's.* Camb.

Levit.

Levit. xix. 30. 8° 1722. The Reverence due to the houfe of God. *Queen's*. Camb.
Pf. cxxii. 6–9. 8° 1724. our Obligations to promote the public Intereft. *Eton*.
Matt. xxv. 34–36. 4° 1726. Spitt. W. Chriftian Charity a rational Duty. *Queen's*. Camb.
* 1 John xxxviii. 8° 17   Prop. of Gofpel.
Pf. cvi. 30, 31. 8° 1727. Ref. of Manners. Reformation neceffary to prevent our Ruin. *Ch. Ch.* Oxon. *Queen's*. Camb. *Brit. M.*
1 Sam. xxvi. 9. 4° 1728. Jan. 30. b. Lords. *Queen's*. Cam. *Eton*.
Pf. ii. 7, 8. 4° 1732. Prop. of Gofpel. *Queen's*. Camb.

SMALRIDGE George, Bp. of Briftol, and Dean of Ch. Ch. Oxon.
12 Serm. in 8° 1717. *Oxon*. on feveral occafions. *Bod. Ch. Ch. Univ. Bal. All S. St. John's. Or. Queen's. Trin. New C.* Oxon. *Pub. L. King's*. Camb. *Sion*.
60 Serm. in fo. 1724. *Oxon*. on feveral occafions. *Bod. Ch. Ch. Univ. Bal. All S. St. John's. Or. Queen's. Trin. New C.* Oxon. *Pub. L. King's*. Camb. *Sion*.

SMALRIDGE Philip, DD. Chancellor of the Diocefe of Worcefter.
* John xiii. 35. 4° 1749. *Worcefter*-Infirmary. Love of our Brethren, the diftinguifhing mark of Chrift's Difciples.

SMALWOOD George, M. A. R. of St. Margaret's new Fifh-ftreet, afterwards of St. Mary le bow, London.
Prov. xi. 18. 4° 1661. Fun. of Sir Abraham Richardfon. The wicked man's fad Difappointment—or the righteous man's fure Recompence.

SMALWOOD James,   Fell. of Trin. Coll. Camb. and Chaplain to the Earl of Romney.
Luke xxii. 36. 4° 1695. b. King William. on taking up Arms.
* Matt. xiii. 13. 4° 1696. on the difcovery of a Confpiracy ag. King William.
Pf. lxxx. 19. 4° 1699. Faft. b. Commons. *Sion*.
Deut. xvi. 16. 4° 1699. Chefhire-Feaft.
Deut. xx. 2–4. 4° 1705.

SMALWOOD Matthew, DD. Dean of Litchfield &c. and Chaplain in Ord.
Gen. v. 24. 8° 16
Matt. v. 34. 8° 1666.

SMEATON Samuel,   V. of Nether Wallop, Hants.
Gal. iv. 18. 4° 1704. Vif. Chriftian Zeal recommended. *St. John's*. Camb. *Sion*.

SMEDLEY Jonathan, M. A. R. of Ringcurrane, Dean of Killala, Ireland.
Gen. xii. 1–3. 8° 1714. Acceffion. *Queen's*. Camb. *Sion*.
Deut. xxx. 15. 4° 1715. Irifh Maffacre. The original Freedom of mankind. *Queen's*. Camb. *Eton*.
1 Sam. xii. 25. 8° 1716. Jan. 30. *Queen's*. Camb. *Brit. M.*
1 Pet. ii. 17. 4° 1716. Prince of Wales's birth-day. *Queen's*. Cam.
Serm. in 8° 1719. *Queen's*. Camb.

SMITH Benj.   V. of Great Waltham, R. of Boxworth, Camb.
 John ix. 4. 4° 1673. Fun.
 John xiv. 10. 4° 16
 Jude 3. 4° 1682. Affize.
SMITH Edward, Bp. of Down and Connor.
 Ifai. xxvi. 9. 4° 1689. *Dublin.* b. Levant Co.
 * 2 Sam. xxii 2, 3. 4° 1699 May 29.
 * Pf cxviii. 1–3. 4° 1703. Th. for Succefs.
 * Ifai. lxv. 25. 4° 1703. b. Houfe of Lords &c.
SMITH Elifha, M: A. Lect. of Wifbech, then R. of Tid St. Giles's in the Ifle of Ely and Caftle Rifing, Norfolk.
 John v. 14. 8° 1714. Th. on the Storm. *Pub. L. Queen's.* Camb.
 2 Chron. ix- 8. 8° 1714. Aug. 8.
 1 Theff. v. 12, 13. 8° 1714. Advent.
 1 Theff. v. 13. 8° 1715. Th. for Acceffion.
 1 Tim. ii. 1, 2. 8° 1715. Acceffion. Popular Difcontent felf-condemned.
 Luke ix. 55. 8° 1715. Nov. 5. *Queen's.* Camb.
 Luke xxi. 26. 8° 1717. on the phenomena of Light. *Brit. M.*
 1 Theff. v. 21. 8° 1719. Juftifying Sincerity.
 2 Cor. iv. 18. 8° 1721.
 Phil. ii. 4. 8° 1724. Affize. *Eton.*
 42 Serm. in 2 Vol. 8° 1740. on the moft important Concerns of a chriftian life.
SMITH Francis, E. A. P.
 Luke xix. 41–44. 4° 1691. Jerufalem's Sins, Jerufalem's Deftruction.
SMITH H.   M. A. V. of Stower, Bucks.
 - - - - - Th. The duty of Thankfgiving.
 Deut. v. 29. 4° 1711. The way to Happinefs and Profperity.
SMITH Haddon,   Curate of St. Matthew's Bethnal Green, and late Chapl. of his Majefty's Ship the Dreadnought.
 * 12 Serm. in 8° 1769. on the moft interefting Subjects.
 * 2 Cor. iv. 2. 8° 1770. Methodiftical Deceit. *Queen's.* Camb.
[SMITH Henry,]   Minifter of the Church of England.
 * Difc. in 4° 1660.
SMITH Henry,   of St. Clement's Danes, London.
 Serm. and Treatifes in 4° 1675. *Ch. Ch.* Oxon. *Sion.*
SMITH Henry, M. A. R. of Weybridge, Surrey, and Chaplain to the Earl of Lincoln.
 2 Sam. xviii. 28. 4° 1717. Th. for fuppreffing the Rebellion. *Ch. Ch.* Oxon.
 * 2 Pet. ii. 10. 4° 1720. Affize.
SMITH Humphrey, M. A. V. of Townftall, and St. Saviour's, Dartmouth, Devon.
 Pf. xxxix. 6. 4° 1690. Fun.   *Bod. AllS. Ch. Ch. Ox.*
 Ecclef. iv. 2. 4° 1690. Fun.   *Bod. AllS; Ox.*
 1 Pet. iii. 13. 4° 1698.
 John xx. 23. 4° 1708. *Exon.* Vif. The divine Authority and Ufefulnefs of ecclefiaftical Cenfures. *Ch. Ch.* Oxon.

SMITH James, M. A. V. of Lambourn, Berks, and Chapl. in Ord.
* Ecclef. vii. 1. 8° 1764. Fun. of Rev. Phocion Henley.
* Rev. ii. 10. 8° 1774. Fun. of Rev. Dr. Nichols.
* Ifai. i. 2, 3. 8° 1776. Faſt.
* 12 Diſc. in 8° 1777.

SMITH James, V. of Alkham, Kent.
* Heb. x. 24. 8° 1779. b. Free-maſons.

SMITH Jeremiah
* Ephef. iv. 11–13. 8° 1712. Ord. of Samuel Clark.
‡ * Jude 22, 23. 8° 1713. Ref. of Manners. Brit. M.
* Rom. xv. 19. 8° 1715. 4 f. The Happineſs of a ſucceſsful Miniſtry.
* 2 Cor. v. 6-8. 8° 1722. Fun. of Sir Thomas Abney.

SMITH John, late Fell. of Queen's Coll. Camb.
Select Diſc. in 4° 1673. in Divinity. Bod. All S. Univ. Cb. Cb. New C. Queen's. Bal. Oxon. Pub. L. Queen's. Camb.

SMITH John, M. D.
* Diſc. in 8° 1676.

SMITH John, R. of St. Mary's Colcheſter, Eſſex.
2 Cor. v. 1. 8° 1706. Fun.

SMITH John, DD. Preb. of Durham, and R. of Biſhop's Wexmouth,
1 Cor. xv. 1, 2. 4° 1709. an Apology to Chriſtians for the Gospel and its Miniſters. Cb. Cb. Pub. L. St. John's. Camb.
Exod. xx. 12. 4° 1712. b. the ſons of the Clergy at Newcaſtle. St. John's. Camb.
Matt. xxi 9. 8° 1712. Conſ. of a Chapel. Queen's. Camb. Eton.

SMITH John, M. A. Maſter of the Free Grammar School at Bottesdale, Suffolk.
* - - - - 8° 1755.
* 2 Tim. i. 10. 8° 1759. Viſ. God's Promiſes, the only foundation of future Hope.
* Gal. v. 13. 8° 1770. b. Free-Maſons.

SMITH John, B. A. R. of Nampwich, Cheſhire.
* 2 Chron. xiv. 11. 4° 1758. Faſt.
* Jer. iv. 19. 8° 1759. Faſt.
* Gal. iv. 16. 4° 1775. Freedom of paſtoral Advice.
* 1 Cor. xiii. 13. 8° 1780. b. Truſtees of a Work-houſe.
* Gen. ii. 24. 8° 1780. Polygamy indefenſible. Ag. Madan's Thelephora.

SMITH Joſeph, DD. Provoſt of Queen's Coll. Oxon.
Pſ. cxii. 6. 4° 1714. on the Death of Queen Ann. The Duty of the living to the Memory of the dead. Queen's. Worc. Linc. Ox.
1 Cor. iv. 2. 4° 1719. b. the Sons of the Clergy. The faithful Stewardſhip. Cb. Cb. Oxon.

SMITH Joſeph, Miniſter of Haworth, Yorkſ.
Rom. xii. 3. 17
* Matt xv. 6. 4° 1731. Tradition of the Clergy, not deſtructive to Religion. Ag. Bowman.

SMITH Joshua, M. A.
>   Pf. cxxvii 1. 4° 1706. *Oxon.* Affize. The divine Favour, the only Security of a people. *C.C.C.* Oxon.

SMITH Lawrence, LL. D. R. of South Warmborough, Hants.
>   2 Tim. i. 10.   } 4° 1701. 2 f. The Evidence of Things not
>   Luke xvi. 19-31. } feen.
>   Prov. xix. 2 4° 1702. School-Feaft. Knowledge and Virtue, the great Ornament of human Nature.

SMITH Matthew,   of Magd. Hall. Oxon. V. of Helyon Bumfted, Effex.
>   1 Cor. iv. 1, 2. 12° 1672. Vif.

SMITH Nicholas, M. A. V. of Braughing, Herts.
>   Heb. iv. 9. 4° 1675. of the Sabbath.

SMITH Roger, M. A. R. of Hufband's-borefworth, Leicefterf.
>   * 2 Cor. i. 12. 8° 1719. Teftimony of a good Confcience. *St. John's.* Camb.

SMITH Samuel, M. A. formerly of St. John's Coll. Oxon. and Ord. of Newgate, London.
>   1 Sam. xv. 35. 8° 1660. Samuel in Sackcloth.
>   Rev. xx. 11-15.   1665. Great Affize—or day of Jubilee. *Bod.*
>   Zech. xiv. 7. 4° 1680. b. Lord Mayor. Light out of Darknefs. *C.C.C.* Oxon.
>   Phil. i. 23. 4° 1685. Fun.

[SMITH Samuel]
>   1 Kings viii. 39.

SMITH Samuel, M. A.
>   Jer. xvii. x. 8° 1719. Affize. God alone is the Searcher of Heart.

SMITH Samuel
>   * Difc. in 12° 1726.

SMITH Samuel, LL. B. of Magd. Hall, Oxon. R. of All-Hallows on the Wall, and Lect. of St. Alban's, Woodftreet, Lond.
>   Ifai. xi. 9. 4° 1731. Col. of Georgia.
>   Matt ix. 13. 8° 1738. Ref. of Manners.
>   1 Pet. ii. 14. 8° 1743. Elect. Lord Mayor.
>   1 Theff. v. 21. 8° 1745. The Corruption of Popery.

SMITH Thomas, DD. and F. R. S. Fell. of Magd. Coll. Oxon.
>   1 Pet. iii. 19. 4° 1668. Levant Co. *Bod. Pub. L.* Camb.
>   2 Tim iii. 16. 4° 1675. The credibility of the Myfteries of the Chriftian Religion. *Bod. Ch. Ch. Magd. Bal. Queen's.* Oxon. *Queen's.* Camb. *Sion.*
>   Rom. xiv. 19. 4° 1675. (and 8° 1707.) Exer. Theol. De Caufis, Remediifque Diffidiorum &c. *Bod. Magd. Queen's.* Oxon.
>   1 Cor xi. 27. 4° 1679. of frequent Communion. *Bod. Ch. Ch. Magd.* Oxon. *Pub. L.* Camb.
>   Ephef. iv. 5. 4° 1682. The Doctrine, Unity and Profeffion of the chriftian Faith. *Bal. Magd. Queen's.* Oxon. *Pub. L. St. John's.* Camb.
>   1 John v. 7. 4° 1626. Ag. the Socinians.

SMITH Thomas, Lect. at St. Giles's, Cripplegate, Lond.
* Serm. in 8° 1758.
* Pf. xcvii. 1. 8° 1759. Th. after a Victory.
* Hofea x. 12. 8° 1762. Faft.
* Pf. cxix. 71. 8° 1763. 2 Difcourfes.

SMITH William, DD. R. of Cotton, V. of Mendlefham, Suffolk, and Preb. of Norwich.
1 Cor. vi. 9. 8° 1670. The unjuft man's Doom &c. *Bod.*
1 Pet. ii. 21. 8° 1674. } Affize. *Bod. C. C. C. Pub. L.* Camb.
1 John iv. 8. 8° 1674.
1 Theff. v. 17. 4° 1677. Wednef. in Rogation-week. *Pub. L. C.*
Pf. ii. 6. 4° 1677. May 29. *Pub. L.* Camb.
Luke xxii. 19 4° 1680. The great Sin and Danger of neglecting the holy Communion.
Pf. cvii. 8. 4° 1683. Th. Sep. 9. *Pub. L. Queen's. St. John's.* Ca.
Acts xvi. 30. 4° 1696. of the great Salvation in another world. *Sion.*

SMITH William, M. A. Preacher of St. Clement's Danes, London.
Prov. iv. 13. 4° 1708. Sch.-Feaft. The benefit of good Inftruction.

SMITH William, M. A. R. of Holy Trinity in Chefter, and Chapl. to the Earl of Derby.
Prov. xiv. 34. 4° 1741. Faft. *Worc.* Oxon.
John viii. 32. 8° 1746. Affize. The Gofpel an actual Friend to the Liberties of mankind.

SMITH William, M. A. Cur. of St. Martin's at Palace, Norwich.
Jam. ii. 18. 8° 1751. The abfurdity of an unworking Faith. *Queen's.* Camb.
* Rom. iii. 28. 8° 1752. of Juftification. *Queen's.* Camb.
* Gal. vi. 15. 8° 1753. 2 f. of the new Creature. *Queen's.* Cam.
* Matt. xxii. 29. 8° 1756. 2 f. The Chriftian's Encouragement to read the Scriptures.

SMITH Will. DD. Prov. of the Coll. and Academy at Philadelphia.
* Difc. in 8° 1759. on feveral public Occafions during the War in America.
* Serm. in 8° 1762. *Univ.* Oxon.
* 3 Difc. in 4° 1769.
* Jofh. xxii. 22. 8° 1775. The prefent Situation of American Affairs.

SMITH William, DD. Dean of Chefter.
1 * 9 Difc. in 8° 1782. on the Beatitudes.

SMITHIES William, jun. R. of St. Michael Mile-end in Colchefter, and Chapl. to the Earl of Sandwich.
* Lam. iii. 27. 8° 1684. Benefit of early Piety.
* Gal. vi. 1. 8° 1684. Spirit of Meeknefs.
Pf. xciv. 16. 8° 1706. Elect. of a Mayor in Colchefter.

SMITHSON Ifaac
* Pf. xx. 5-7. 8° 1756. on declaring War.

SMYTH Arthur, Abp. of Dublin.
* Ifai. xii. 1. 4° 1753.

SMYTH *George*, M. A. Min. of the Gospel at Hackney, Middlesex.
    1 Pet. v. 6. 8° 1720. Faſt. *Queen's*. Camb. *Brit. M.*
    Rom. xiv. 16. 8° 1727. Ref. of Manners. *Brit. M.*
    ‡ * Pſ. lxxxii. 6, 7. 8° 1726. Death of King George I.
    ‡ * Rom. x. c. 8° 1729. on Zeal.
    2 Cor. i. 24. 8° 1735. Jan. 30. V. Diſc. ag. Popery. Vol. I. *Braz. N.* Oxon. *Brit. M.*
    * Deut. xxiii. 9. 8° 1740. Faſt. The Lawfulneſs of War, and the Duty of a people entering into it.
    * 1 Sam. xvii. 29. 8° 1745. The Cauſe of British Proteſtants a good one. *Queen's.* Camb.

SMYTHIES William,   Cur. of St. Giles's, Cripplegate, Lond.
    Jude 12. 4° 1671. Norfolk-Feaſt.
    Gal. vi. 2. 4° 1684 Aug. 24. *All S. Ch. Ch. Queen's.* Ox. *Sion.*
    Prov. xxix 2. 4° 1692. Elect. of Ld Mayor. *Ch. Ch.* Ox. *Sion.*
    Pſ. xciv. 16. 4° 1692. Elect. of Lord Mayor.

SNAPE Andrew, DD. late Provoſt of King's Coll. Camb.
    45 Serm. in 3 Vol. 8° 1745. *New C.* Oxon.

SNASHALL *Samuel*
    * Job xii. 21. 8° 1739. Folly of depending on human Inſtruments in times of War and Danger.

SNAWSEL Robert
    * Prov. xi 29. ⎫
    * Prov. xii. 14. ⎬ V. Diſc. on conj. Duty. Vol. I. p. 163, 178.

SNELL Vyner, B. D. R. of Doddington, March, Wimblington, and Benwick in the Iſle of Ely.
    Gal. v. 17.   17
    Acts xxiv. 2, 3. 4° 1727.
    Pſ. cvii. 19. 4° 1728.
    Matt. xi. 28. 4° 1728.
    Acts xxvi. 18. 4° 1728.
    1 Cor. ii. 5. 4° 1728.
    2 Cor. vi. 3, 4. 4° 1728.
    1 Theſſ. ii. 3. 4° 1728.
    2 Tim. ii. 15. 4° 1728.
    2 Tim. iii. 14. 4° 1728.
    Tit. i. 5. 4° 1728.

SNOWDEN James, DD. late Fell. of Mert. Coll. Oxon. V. of Ponteland, Northumberland.
    * Dan. ix. 3. 8° 1757. Faſt. The Duty of faſting. *Worc.* Oxon.
    * Pſ. cxlv. 19. 8° 1758. Faſt. The genuine fear of God, the beſt foundation of private and national Happineſs. *Worc.* Oxon.

SNOWDEN Samuel,   R. of S   Norfolk.
    * Job vii. 21. 8° 1689. A Vol. Alexipharmacon ſpirituale.
    * Pſ. cxlvi. 3, 4. 4° 1694. Jan. 30.

SOLEY Joſeph, DD. R. of Alresford and Preb. of Wincheſter.
    Eccleſ. vii. 1. 4° 1719. Levant-Co. *Sion.*

SOME *David*
    * 1 Cor. xv. 10. 8° 1736. Fun. of Thomas Saunders. *Queen's.* Camb. *Brit. M.*

SOMERVILLE Thomas, V. D. M. at Jedburgh.
  * Prov. xvi. 10. 12° 1776. Heart-bitterness. V. Scotch Preacher.
    Vol. II. p. 87.
  * Matt. xxvii. 54. 12° 1779. Death of Christ. V. Scotch Pr.
    Vol. III. p. 77.
SOMERVILLE William, B. A.
  Luke xviii. 8. 8° 1715. on the Rebellion.
[SOMMERS John]
  * Jude 3. 8° 1731. Primitive Faith.
SOUTH Robert, DD. Canon of Ch. Ch. Oxon.
  12 Serm. 8° 1727. on several Occasions. Vol. I. II. III. IV. *Bod.
    Ch.Ch. All S. Magd. C.C.C. Univ. New C. Queen's. Pemb. Worc.
    Wadh.* Oxon. *Pub. L.* Camb. *Dr. W's. L.* London.
  12 Serm. and Disc. in 8° 1724. on sev. Subjects and Occasions.
    Vol. V. VI. *Bod. Ch. Ch. All S. Magd. C.C.C. Univ. New C.
    Queen's. Pemb. Worc. Wadh.* Ox. *Pub. L. C. Dr. W's. L.* Lond.
  2 Cor. v. 10. 8° 1717. (Posth. Works.) The Certainty of a Judg-
    ment after this life. *Bal.* Oxon. *Pub. L.* Camb.
  64 Serm. in (Posth.) 8° 1744. on several Occasions. Vol. VII.
    VIII. IX. X. XI.
  His Works. Or, *St. John's.* Oxon. *Pub. L.* Camb.
SOUTHALL Thomas, M A. V. of Harborne, Staffordshire.
  Eccles. vii. 10. 8° 1716. *Birmingham.* Assize.
SOUTHCOMB Lewis,   R. of Rose-Ash, Devon.
  Deut. xxxii. 29. 4° 1692. Fun. of Rev. Mr. Culme. *Bod.*
  2 Tim. ii. 19. 4° 1701. at the Baptism of one of riper Years.
  * Matt. vii. 12. 8° 1714. Rule of Charity and Justice.
  Tit. iii. 1. 8° 1735. Subjection to the higher Powers a Xn Duty.
  * John xiii. 34, 35. 4° 1752. Love the truest mark of a Xtian.
SOWDEN *Benjamin*
  ‡ * Ezek. xviii. 30. 8° 1747. Fast.
  * Prov. x. 7. 8° 1750. Death of the Prince of Orange.
  * John xiv. 28. 8° 1751. Fun. of Rev. Barth. Loftus.
  * - - - - 8° 1752. Ord.
  * - - - - 8° 1760. Death of King George II.
SOWDEN Choyce Benjamin,   Morning Preacher of All Hallows,
    London-Wall.
  * 1 Pet. iii. 8. 4° 1776. b. Gov. of *Westm.*-Gen. Dispensary.
  * Rom. xiv. 4. 8° 1780. Fast. Universal Toleration recommended.
SPADEMAN *John*, M. A.
  Prov. xxviii. 4. 8° 1698. Ref. of Manners. *Eton.*
  * John xi. 4. 8° 1699. Fun.   V. Shower's mourn.
    Companion.
  * 2 Tim. iii 14. 4° 1705. Fun.   *St. John's.* Camb.
  Judges v. 13. 8° 1706. Th. for a Victory. Deborah's Triumph
    over the mighty.
SPANHEIM Frederick
  Rev. iii. 20. 4° 1676. on the Inundation in Holland. *Bod.
    Pub. L.* Camb.

SPARK Tho. DD. R. of Ewhurſt in Surrey and Preb. of Litchfield.
  1 Cor. i. 10. 4° 1691. *Oxon*. Viſ. *All S. Jeſ.* Oxon. *Brit. M.*
SPARKE John,   Curate of Ch. Ch. Newgate-ſtreet, London.
  James i. 27. 8° 1745. The reſemblance between natural and moral Infection with its Malignity. *Brit. M.*
SPARKE Robert
  Gen. xxiii 2. 4° 1679. Fun. of Mrs. Fenn. *Bod.*
SPARKES Edward, DD.
  * Diſc. in 8° 1663. Primitive Devotions.
SPARKES Robert. DD.
  Pſ. xvi. 11. (or 12:) 8° 1660.
SPARROW Anthony, Bp. of Norwich.
  1 Theſſ. iii. 8. 4° 1669. Caution ag. falſe Doctrines. *Sion.*
  1 John i. 9. (preached 1637.) printed 4° 1704. Confeſſion of Sins, and the Power of Abſolution. *Sion.*
SPATEMAN Thomas, M.A. R. of St. Bartholomew the Great, V. of Chiſwick, and Preb. of St. Paul's, London.
  Heb. xiii. 7. 4° 1730. b. Sons of the Clergy. *Worc.* Oxon.
SPEKE Philip, M. A. Fell. of Wadh. Coll. Oxon.
  Matt. xii. 25.   1739. Jan. 30.
SPENCER John, DD. Preſident of C. C. C. Camb.
  Prov. xxix. 2. 4° 1660. *Cam.* Th. June 21. The righteous Ruler. *St. John's.* Camb. *Brit. M.*
  Deut. xxxiii. 8. 8° 1669. *Cam.* Diſſert. de Urim et Thummim. *Bod.*
SPILSBURY F.
  ‡ * 1 Chron. xvi. 22. 8° 1744. Acceſſion.
SPINCKES Nathaniel, M. A. R. of St. Martin's, Saliſbury, and Preb. of Sarum.
  1 Pet. iii. 14, 15. 8° 1714. of Truſt in God. *Bod. Sion.*
SPOONER *Thomas*,   Miniſter of the Goſpel at Cheſham, Bucks.
  * - - - - 8° 1756. Safety from God.
  * Decad of ſerm. in 8° 1771. (2d Edit.) preached at Cheſham, Bucks.
SPRAT Thomas, M. A. Arch-Deacon of Rocheſter.
  2 Pet. i. 7. 4° 1705. b. Sons of the Clergy. *Cb. Cb.* Ox. *Brit. M.*
  Col. i. 26. 4° 1702. b. Queen. Goodfriday. *Cb. Cb. Worc.* Ox. *Pub. L.* Camb. *Brit. M.*
SPRAT Thomas, Bp. of Rocheſter, and Dean of Weſtminſter.
  10 Serm. in 8° 1710. on ſeveral Occaſions. *Bod. All S. Cb. Cb. Magd. Or. St. John's. Worc.* Oxon *Pub. L. Queen's. St. John's. Cl. H.* Camb.
SPRINT *John*,   Miniſter of the Goſpel at Milborn Port, Somerſetſ.
  1 Theſſ. iv. 13. 4° 1692. Fun. of *Suſan Tyte.* The Chriſtian Mourner comforted. *Bod. Brit. M.*
  1 Pet. ii. 17.   1694. The Chriſtian Loyalty revived. *Bod.*
  1 Cor. iv. 24. 8° 1699. Wedd. ſ. The bride Woman's Counſellor. V. Diſc. on Conj. Duty. Vol. I. p. 80. *Univ.* Oxon.
  * Dan. xii. 3. 4° 1706. b. Diſſent. Clergy.
  * Zech. i. 5, 6. 8° 1706. Fun.

SPRY

SPRY John, DD. late Fell. of C.C.C. Ox. Arch-Deacon of Berks.
 1 Cor. ix. 14. 8° 1741. *Oxon.* Vif. The cafe of the Miniflerial Maintenance. ftated. *C.C.C. Worc.* Oxon. *Queen's.* Camb.
 2 Tim. iii. 14, 15. 8° 1744. *Oxon.* The Influence of Education juftified with regard to the Profeffion of Chriftianity. *C.C.C. Worc.* Oxon. *Eton. Brit. M.*
 Rom. i. 16. 8° 1745. *Oxon.* Rebel. The Duty of chriftian Confidence in times of Danger to the Church of Xt. *Worc.* Oxon.
 * John v. 44. 8° 1756. Conf. of 2 Bps. *Braz. N.* Oxon.
SPURSTOWE Will. DD. Minif. of the Gofpel at Hackney, Middlef.
 Rev. ii. 10. 4° 1662. Fun.
 * 2 Pet. i. 4. 16.
SQUIRE Fran. M. A. R. of Exford, and V. of Cutcombe, Somerfetf.
 Gal. vi. 10. 8° 1714. Univerfal Benevolence. *Queen's.* Camb.
 Gal. v. 1. 8° 1716. *Exon.* A brief exhortation to prot. Liberty.
 1 Sam. xii. 25. 8° 1718. Affize.
 Num. xxx. 2. 4° 1718. Affize.
SQUIRE Samuel, Bp. of St. David's.
 John xiii. 35. 4° 1745. Spitt. T. *Queen's.* Camb.
 Matt. vi. 19, 20. 4° 1749. An. meet. Char. Sch. *All S.* Ox. *Etcn.*
 Matt. xiii. 54. 4° 1749. Commencement. *Brit. M.*
 1 Pet. ii. 13. 4° 1751. Acceffion. b. Commons. *Brit. M.*
 * Rev. ii. 5. 4° 1756. Faft. b. Lords.
 * Pf. xli. 1. 4° 1760. b. Gov. of Small pox-Hofp. *Queen's.* Cam.
 * Pf. xviii. 3. 4° 1761. Faft. b. Commons.
 * 1 Cor. x. 11. 4° 1762. Jan. 30. b. Lords.
 * Luke x. 28. 4° 1765. b. Gov. of Lond-Hofp. *Wadh.* Oxon.
STACKHOUSE Thomas, M. A. V. of Beneham, Berks.
 ‡* Ecclef. xii. 12. 8° 17 Conc. continens verfus 1060 Hexamt.
 1 Cor. iv. 1. 8° 1726. Fun. of Dr. Brady. *Ch. Ch.* Oxon.
 1 Pet. iv. 17. 8° 1736. Jan. 30. *Worc.* Oxon. *Queen's.* Camb.
 Exod. xx. 3 &c. fo. 1743. on the Decalogue. V. Body of Divinity. p. 380. *St. John's. New C.* Oxon. *Queen's.* Camb. *Sion.*
STAFFORD John
 * 25 Practical Difc. (2d Edit.) in 12° 1774. on the 7th Chapter of Romans. The fcript. Doctrine of Sin and Grace confidered.
 * - - - - 8° 1774. Fun.
STAFFORD Richard, B. A. of Magd. Hall, Oxon.
 Pract. Difcourfes in 8° 1694. on fundry texts of Scripture. *Bod.*
  Pub. L. Camb.
 Ifai. xxxviii. 1. 8° 1696. 6 f. *Ch. Ch.* Oxon. *Sion.*
 Sermons &c. 8° 1696–7. *Bod.*
 Deut. viii. 2. 8° 1697. The nature of God's Kingdom.
 1 Chron. xxix. 18. 8° 1697. *Sion.*
 Matt. xiii. 20, 21. 12° 1697. *Sion.*
 Another Collection of his ferm. in 8° 1698. *Bod.*
 Pf. cxliii. 8. 8° 1698.
 Ifai. xxxviii. 2, 3. 8° 1699. 4 ferm.
 2 Cor. ii. 11. 12° 1699. of the Devil's Devices.

Phil. iv. 11. 8° 1699.
Phil. xi. 12. 12° 1699. 2 f.
Col. iii. 1. 12° 1699.
Heb. ii. 15. 8° 1699. Difc. The great Benefits of Chrift. *Bod*.
Pf. xxxix. 6. 8° 1700.
Pf. cii. 28. 8° 1701. Sev. Difc. Perfev. neceff. to Salvation. *Sion*.
Gal. ii. 20. 12° 1703.
Rev. iii. 2. 12° 1703.
Jer. vi. 4. 12° 17
Matt. xxv. 46. 12° 17
Mark viii. 56, 39. 12" 17
John ix. 31. 12° 17
Acts ii. 11. 12° 17
Acts vi. 4. 12° 17
Rom. ix. 6. 17   3 f.
Heb. x. 25. 12° 17

STAINFORTH William, DD. R. of Barnburgh, and St. Mary Bi-
fhophill, and Canon Refid. of York.
Prov. xxi. 3. 4° 1676. Affize. *Bod. Ch. Ch.* Oxon.
* Prov. i. 21.   1676. *Univ.* Oxon.
1 Tim. ii. 1, 2. 4° 1685. Affize. *St. John's.* Camb.
Prov. xxiv. 21. 4° 1686. Acceffion. *St. John's.* Camb.
2 Chron. xxxv. 24. 4° 1689. Jan. 30. *Bod. Univ.* Ox. *Cl. H.* Ca.
Pf. cxliv. 10. 4° 1706. Th.
Gal. vi. 15. 8° 1711. Ch. f.

STAINSBY Richard, M. A. Chaplain to the Bp. of Norwich, and
Lect. of St. Mary le Grand.
* Job xvi. 22. 8° 1762. Fun. of Bp. Hayter. *Queen's.* Camb.

STAMPER Francis
* Pf. lxxxix. 19. 8° 1694. May 3. *Bod*.

STAMPER Thomas, M. A. Lect. of St. Bennet Fink, London.
1 Sam. vii. 16. 8° 1721. Affize.
1 Cor. xiii. 13. 8° 1725.

STANDEN Jof.   Minifter at Coleford near Froome, Somerfetf.
* Ezek. xxxviii. 22. 4° 1707. Th. for Union. *Brit. M.*
* John xiv, 2. 8° 1710. Nov. 5.

STANDFAST Richard, M. A.
Matt. xxiv. 4. 8° 1660. A caveat ag. Seducers. *Sion.*
Num. xvi. 15. 4° 1676. Affize. *Bod.*

STANDISH John, DD. Mafter of Peterhoufe Camb. R. of Coning-
ton, Camb. and of Therfield, Herts, and Chapl. in Ord.
2 Cor. v. 20. 4° 1675. b. King. *Bod. Univ. Queen's.* Oxon. *St.
John's.* Camb.
Prov. xxiv. 21. 4° 1683. Affize. *Pub. L. St. John's.* Camb.
John x. 22. 4° 1683. at the Temple after its being repaired.
Univ. Oxon.
Deut. vi. 11. 12. 4° 1684. b. Lord Mayor. *St. John's.* Camb.

STANDISH Richard, M. A. R. of Ch. Ch. in Briftol.
* Luke ix. 30, 31. 8° 1680. Certain Queries concerning the receiving of the Sacrament.   STAN-

STANHOPE George, DD. Dean of Canterbury, R. of Lewisham and Deptford, Kent, and Chapl in Ord.
  Isai. xxvi. 4. 4° 1692. Th. Nov. 6. *Univ.* Oxon. *Cl. H.* Camb.
  Rom. viii. 17. 4° 1697. Fun. of Dr. Towerson. The christian's Inheritance. *Sion. St. John's.* Camb.
  Rev. xiv. 13. 4° 1698. Fun. of Mr. Castell. The Happiness of good men after Death.
  15 Serm. in 8° 1700. on several occasions. *Queen's.* Camb. Dr. *W's's. L.* London.
  Prov. xxiv. 23-25 4° 1701. Assize. The duty of Juries.
  Exod. xxiii. 1. 4° 1701. Assize. The duty of Witnesses. *Pub. L. C.*
  John xiii. 34. 4° 1701. County-Feast. Christian Charity.
  Luke xvi. 9. 4° 1702. Spittal W. The wisdom of Charity to the poor. *Pub L St. John's.* Camb.
  Levit. xix. 17. 4° 1703. b. Lord Mayor. Ref. of Manners. The duty of rebuking. *Ch. Ch.* Oxon. *Pub. L. St. John's. C. Eton.*
  Matt. iv. 1. 4" 1703. b. Queen. of Temptations. *Ch. Ch. Magd.* Oxon. *Pub. L.* Camb.
  16 Serm. at Boyle's Lect. 4° 1701, 1702. *Bod.* and fo. 1739. Vol. I. p. 631. &c. *Ch. Ch. New C. St. John's. Worc.* Ox. *Pub. L. C.*
  Matt. viii. 2, 3. 4° 1704. b. Queen.
  Pf. xciv. 20, 21. 4° 1705. Jan. 30. b. Com. *Magd. Worc.* Oxon.
  Luke xvi. 25. 4° 1705. An. meet. Char. School. *Bod. Univ.* Ox. *Queen's. Cl. H.* Camb. *Sion.*
  James iii. 17. 4° 1705. Conc. ad Synod. *Univ. Worc.* Ox. *Pub. L.* Camb. *Sion.*
  Matt. xviii. 35. 4° 1705. b. Queen. *Eton.*
  Deut. xxxiii. 29. 4° 1706. Th. b. Queen. June 27. *Bod. Magd. Worc. Hert.* Oxon. *Pub. L. Queen's.* Camb. *Sion.*
  Matt xi. 28. 4° 1706. b. Queen. Christianity the only true Comfort for troubled minds. *Bod. Magd.* Ox. *Queen's. C. Sion.*
  * Luke xxiv. 25. 8° 1709. Common Obstructions to Faith and good Life considered. *Queen's.* Camb.
  A Paraphrase and Comment upon the Epistles and Gospels in 4 Vol. 4° 1708. and 1715, 1716. *Ch. Ch. C. C. C. Univ. New C. St. John's.* Oxon.
  John xv. 5. 4° 1713. b. Queen. *Ch. Ch.* Oxon. *St. John's.* Cam.
  Isai. lx. 9. 4° 1714. Prop. of Gospel. The early conversion of Islanders, a wise expedient for propagating Christianity. *Ch. Ch.* Oxon. *Pub. L. Queen's.* Camb. *Sion.*
  Matt. v. 16. 4° 1715. b. Trinity-House.
  Pf cvii. 30, 31. 4° 1724. Fun. of Mr. Sare. Death just matter of Joy to good men. *Or.* Oxon.
  12 Serm. in 8° 1727. on several occasions. *Ch. Ch. Univ. Worc. St. John's.* Oxon.

STANHOPE Michael, DD. Preb. of St. Paul's, Canon of Windsor and R. of Leake, Nottinghamsf.
  Pf. xcviii. 1, 2. 8° 1708. Th. God, Author of Victory. *Magd.* Ox.
  Pf. xxx. 3, 4. 8° 1709. Recovery from Sickness.

John

John vi. 66–68. 8° 1710. The Sinfulness of Separation from the established Church of England. *Bod. Sion.*
Rom. x. 15. 4° 1717. The Church of England not guilty of the Schism charged upon them by Non-jurors. *Queen's. C. Eton.*
Eccles. viii. 14. 4° 1723. Jan. 30. b. Commons. The prosperity of the wicked, and the sufferings of the righteous, not inconsistent with the Goodness and Justice of Providence. *Worc. Ox.*
Matt. vii. 12. 8° 1724. *Nottingham.* Assize.

STANHOPE Thomas, M. A. V. of St. Margaret's, Leicester.
4 Occas. serm. in 8° 1670.

STANLEY Edward, DD. Preb. of Winchester.
Ps. xiv. 7. ⎫ Aug. 19.   1660.
Isai. xxvi. ⎬ Assize. Feb. 25.   1661. ⎱ *Bod.*
Lam. iv. 20. ⎭ Jan. 30. 8° 1662.

STANLEY William, DD. Clerk of the Closet, Dean of St. Asaph, and Canon Resid. of St. Paul's, London.
Col. ii. 5. 4° 1692. Cons. of Bp. Tenison. *Bod. Ch. Ch. C.C.C. Magd. Jes.* Oxon. *Pub. L.* Camb *Sion.*
Matt. ix. 37, 38. 8° 1708. Prop. of Gospel. *All S. Ox. Brit. M.*

STANNIFORTH William, M. A. Cur. of Hornsey, Middlesex.
Luke vii. 19. 8° 1734. Advent.

STANTON Thomas,   Minister at Colchester.
* 2 Cor. v. 17. 4° 1758. New Creature described.

[STANWIX Richard]
* 2 Cor. x. 4. 8° 1660. Christian Warfare.

STAPYLTON Miles, DD. Preb. of Worcester.
Rom. viii. 28. 8° 1736. *Worcester.* The Providence of God the Security of good men. p. 7.
Acts xx. 24. 8° 1736. *Worcester.* The great Importance of finishing our Course with Joy. p. 43.

STARKEY William, DD. R. of Pulham, Norfolk.
1 Pet. ii. 13. 4° 1668. *Camb.* Assize. The obligation of human Ordinances. *St. John's.* Camb. *Brit. M.*

STARKS Thomas, M. A. R. of Gravesend, Kent.
* Luke xxiv. 44. 8° 1755. Prophetic Character of David.

STAYNOE Thomas, B. D. R. of St. Ethleburgh, V. of Ch. Ch. &c. and Chaplain in Ord.
Ps. cxlv. 9. 4° 1685. b. Gov. of the City-Hospitals.
Rom. xiii. 5. 4° 1686. Accession. b. Lord Mayor. Subjection for Conscience sake. *Ch. Ch.* Oxon. *Pub. L.* Camb.
Acts xxvi. 8. 4° 1610. Easter. b. Queen. *Jes.* Oxon. *St. John's.* Camb. *Sion.*
* D. se. in 2 Vol. 8° 1700.
Prov. xxii. 6. 8° 1717. 7 Disc. Instructions for the education of Children.

STEAD William, M. A. V. of Reigate, Surrey.
* Prov. xvi. 33. 4° 1763. Th. May 5.

STEBBING Henry, DD. Chancellor of Sarum, and Chapl. in Ord.
Phil. iii. 7, 8. 8° 1721. The Excellency of the Knowledge of Christ Jesus. *Ch. Ch.* Oxon. *Sion.*   Acts

OF AUTHORS, &c. 319

Acts viii. 17. 8° 1729. *Camb.* Confirmation. *Queen's.* Camb.
Rom. viii. 3,4. 8° 1730. Of the ufe and advantages of the Gofpel-revelation. *Queen's. Cl. H.* Camb. *Eton. Sion.*
1 John iii. 17. 8° 1732. Ann. meeting Char. School. of Charity to the poor, and the relig. Education of poor children.
Deut. iv. 8, 9. 8° 1732. Hutch. Lect. The Excellency of the Church of England, as to the frequency of its Worfhip. *Worc.* Oxon. *Queen's.* Camb. *Brit. M.*
2 Cor. iii. 9. 4° 1733. b. the Sons of the Clergy. The Excllency ot the Chriftian Miniftration. *Queen's.* Camb.
Gal. vi. 15. 8° 1739. on the new Birth. Ag. religious Delufions. *All S. Linc.* Oxon. *Brit. M.*
Matt. xii. 37. 8° 1739. (and 12° 1741. p. 103.) on Speech and the Abufes of it.
Mark xvi. 20. 4° 1742. Prop. of Gofpel. *All S. Trin.* Oxon. *Queen's.* Camb.
Jerem. vi. 8. 4° 1745. on Rebellion. *Queen's.* Camb. *Brit. M.*
STEBBING Hen. DD. jun. Morning-Preacher at Gray's Inn, Lond.
* Luke xiii. 3–5. 8° 1756. Faft. Earthquake. *All S. Braz. N.* Oxon. *Queen's.* Camb.
* Serm. in 2 Vol. 8° 1759. on pract. Xnity. *Bod. Queen's.* Cam.
* Matt. vi. 9. 4° 1760. Hutch. Lect. on the Liturgy. *Braz. N.* Oxon. *Queen's.* Camb.
*Matt. xxv. 1. 8°1769. 2 f. Parable of the 10 Virgins. *Queen's. C.*
* James iv. 10. 4° 1777. Faft.
STEDMAN Thomas, R. of Wormington, Gloucefter.
* 2 Tim. ii. 6 12° 1776. The Country Clergyman's Advice to his Parifhoners.
STEEL *John,* Minifter of Stair.
* Serm. in 8° 1778.
STEEL *Richard,* M. A. Minifter of the Gofpel in London.
* 1 Cor. vii. 35. 8° 1667. Antidote ag. Diftractions.
12 Serm. in 8° 1670. The Chriftian Hufbandman's calling. *Bod. Magd.* Oxon. *Pub. L.* Camb.
Matt. xxvi. 27, 28. 4° 1675. m. e. P. The right of every Believer to the Cup in the Lord's fupper. p. 670.
Ephef. v. 33. 4° 1676. f. m. e. C. Duties of the married State. p. 362. *Bod.*
1 Cor. xv. 2. 4° 1683. C. m. e. Helps to a good Memory. p. 417.
Gal. v. 15. 4° 1690. C. m. e. Uncharitable Contentions. p. 45. *Bod. Pub. L.* Camb.
STEFFE *Thomas*
* 12 Difc. in 12° 1743. *Queen's.* Camb.
* Rom. xi. 22. 4° 1760. Faft.
STENNETT *Jofeph,* Minifter of the Gofpel in London.
Ecclef. xii. 1. 8° 1695. 3 f. Advice to the young. *Bod. Ch. Ch.* Ox.
* Judges v. 31. 4° 1704. Th. for Victory.
Deut. xxxiii. 29. 4° 1706. Th. *Sion. Eton.*
Judges v. 15. 4° 1707. Th. for Union. *Brit. M.*

Gen.

Gen. xiv. 18–20. 8° 1709. Th. for Victory. *Queen's*. Camb. *Brit. M.*
* Serm. in 5 Vol. 8° 1732. *Dr. W's. L.* London.
* Judges viii. 34, 35. 8° 1740. Nov. 5. *Queen's*. Camb.
* Isai. xxxii. 5. 8° 1741. Fun. of *S. Burch*.
  John xiv. 2. 8° 1742. Fun. of *Jos. Collett. Queen's*. Camb.
* Pf. cxliv. 9–11. 8° 1743. Th. f.
* 2 Kings xix. 27, 28. 8° 1745. Rebellion.
  2 Sam. xxiii. 2. 8° 1748. Fun. of Rev. *D. Rees. Queen's.* C.
* Pf. lxxxv. 8. 8° 1749. Th.

STENNETT *Samuel*, DD.
* Isai. liii. 1. 8° 1753. b. Diffenting Clergy. The Complaint of an unfuccefsful Miniftry. *Queen's.* Camb.
* 1 Chron. xxix. 27, 28. 8° 1760. Death of King George II.
* John iv. 41, 42. 8° 1764. b. Diffent. Clergy.
* Acts xx. 19. 12° 1767. Fun.
* - - - - - 8° 1769. Ord. of *S. Burford.*
* 17 Difc. in 2 Vol. 8° 1769. on perfonal Religion.
* Rom. xii. 2. 8° 1771. Folly and Danger of conforming to the World.
* 2 Tim. iv. 7, 8. 1771. Fun. of Dr. *J. Gill. Queen's.* Camb.
* 2 Cor. v. 8. 8° 1773. Fun. of Mrs. *Sufan. Britain.*
* Amos iii. 6. 8° 1781. Faft. National Calamity, the Effect of divine Difpleafure.

STEPHEN George, M. A.
* Matt. vi. 12. 8° 1770. at the King's Bench.
* Ezra ix. 13, 14. 8° 1774. Genuine Patriotifm.

STEPHENS George, M. A. Lect. of Guilford, R. of Weft Clandon, Surrey, and Preb. of Windfor.
Prov. xiv. 34. 8° 1728. Affize.
Rom. v. 7. 8° 1731. Fun. of Lady Onflow. The amiable Quality of Goodnefs as compared with Righteoufnefs.

STEPHENS Henry, M. A. Fell. of Mert. Coll. Oxon.
Prov. xvi. 7. 4° 1708. *Oxon.* Th. Aug. 19. *Bod. Univ. C. C. C. Pub. L.* Oxon. *Queen's.* Camb. *Sion.*
2 Cor. vi. 8. 8° 1719. Conf. of Bp. Boulter. *Ch. Ch.* Oxon.

STEPHENS Henry, M. A. V. of Malden, Surrey, and Chaplain to the Bp. of St. David's.
10 Difc. in 8° 1728. A true reprefentation of Popery. *Brit. M.*

STEPHENS Joseph, Lect. of St. Giles's Cripplegate, St. Margaret Lothbury, and St. Michael's, Woodftreet, London.
Luke xvi. 19–31. 12° 1697. 9 f. on the parable of Dives and Lazarus.
6 Serm. in 12° 1699. A pract. Expofition on the Lord's Prayer.
* Job xxvii. 5, 6. 12° 16
* Phil iii. 13, 14. 12° 16
* Prov. xiv. 32. 12° 16
* James iv. 17. 12° 16

STEPHENS Lewis, M.A. R. of Chilbolton, and Drekencfield Hants, and Arch-Deacon of Barnſtaple.
 Heb. xiii. 16. 4° 1721. Conſ. of Chapel. The great duty of Charity recommended. *Ch. Ch.* Oxon.
 Pſ. xxxvii. 11. 4° 1723. Fun. of Bp. Trimnell. *Cb. Ch.* Oxon.
 1 Tim. v. 17. 4° 1726. Conſ. of Bp.
 1 Tim. iv. 16. 4° 1726. Ord.   *Eton. Queen's.* Camb.
 Gen. xxviii. 16–18. 4° 1727. Conſ. of a Chapel.
STEPHENS Lewis,   Arch-Deacon of Cheſter and Canon of St. Peter's, Exon.
 2 Trin. i. 16–18. 4° 1735. *Exon.* on delivering a poor convert Jew out of priſon.
STEPHENS Richard,   R. of Stoke-Gallard, Dorſetſhire.
 Pſ. cxviii. 23. 4° 1704. Faſt. on the great Storm.
 Iſai. xlix. 23. 4° 1705. Acceſſion.
STEPHENS Thomas, M. A. Chapl. to Lord Cornwallis.
 3 Seaſonable ſerm. in 8° 1660. Ad Magiſtratum.
 3 (Aſſize) ſerm. in 8° 1661. *Camb. Ch. Ch.* Oxon. *Pub. L.* Cam.
STEPHENS Thomas, M. A. R. of Sherfield, Hants.
 2 Theſſ. ii. 3, 4. 12° 1745. on Rebellion.
STEPHENS William, B. D. R. of Sutton, Surrey.
 Lam. v. 16. 4° 1694. Jan. 30. b. Lord Mayor. *Bod. Pub. L.* Camb. *Sion.*
 Col iii. 15. 4° 1696. Th. b. Lord Mayor. April 16.
 Tit. iii. 1. 4° 1700. Jan. 30. b. Com. *Magd. Worc.* Oxon. *Sion.*
 Rom. xii. 10. 8° 1700.
 Rom. ix. 4, 5. 4° 1705. Nov. 5.
 John viii. 17. } 8° 1706. *Eton.*
 John viii. 32. }
 James iii. 17. 4° 1712. Commem. of Iriſh Maſſacre. *Bod. Worc.* Oxon. *Eton. Sion.*
 1 Tim. iv. 1, 2. 8° 1713. Commem. of Iriſh Maſſacre.
 1 Theſſ. v. 18. 8° 1714. A ſecond deliverance from Popery and Slavery.
 - - - - - 1717. Commem. of Iriſh Maſſacre.
STEPHENS William, M. A. V. of Lynton, Cambridgeſhire.
 1 Cor. xiv. 40. 4° 1705. Conſ. of Ch.
STEPHENS William, M. A. Fell. of Exeter Coll. Oxon. and V. of St. Andrew's Plymouth, Devon.
 Acts v. 3, 4. 8° 1717. The Perſonality and Divinity of the Holy Ghoſt. *Bod. New C. Linc. Worc.* Oxon. *Queen's.* Camb.
 John i. 14. 8° 1719. Viſ. The Union of the two Natures in the one Perſon of Jeſ. Xt. *Magd. New C. Worc. Linc.* Ox. *Queen's.* C.
 Heb. i. 6. 8° 1722. The divine Perſons, one God, by an Unity of Nature. *New C. Worc. Linc.* Oxon. *Queen's.* Camb.
 Col. ii. 8. 8° 1724. Viſ. The ſeveral heterodox Hypotheſes on the Trinity. *New C. Worc.* Oxon. *Queen's.* Camb.
 35 Serm. in 2 Vol. 8° 1737. *Oxon.* on ſeveral Subjects. *C. C. C. All S. Linc. Worc.* Oxon.

STERLING James, M. A. R. of St. Paul's Parish, Kent.
* Gal. iv. 18. 8° 1755. *Anapolis.* Zeal ag. the enemies of our Country pathetically recommended.
STERNE John, DD. Chapl. to the Lord High Cancellor &c.
* - - - - 4° 1691. *Dublin.* Nov. 5. King David's case applied to King James and King William.
* Pf. xc. 12. 4° 1695. *Dublin.* The Prayer of Moses.
* Job xxx. 24, 25. 4° 1699. *Dublin.* July 2.
STERNE John, Bp. of Clogher.
* - - - - 4° 1704. *Dublin.* Conc. ad Cler.
STERNE Lawrence, M. A. Preb of York.
* Serm. in 4 Vol. 12° 1760. and 1766. *Bod. Braz. N. Oxon. Pub. L. Queen's.* Camb.
* Serm. (Posth.) in 3 Vol. 12° 1769. *Pub. L. Queen's.* Camb.
[STEVANSON William]
‡* Job iii. 21, 22. 4° 1715. Fun. of Edw. Bulkeley. *Brit. M.*
STEVENS
* Serm. in   ag. Popery.
STEVENS John
* Rom. viii. 26, 27. 8° 1755. 2 f. Necessity of the Spirit's help in Prayer.
* 2 Cor. v. 21. 8° 1757. Christ made of God unto his people Wisdom &c.
* 1 Cor. i. 30. 8° 1758. Fun.
* Pf. cvii. 7. 8° 1758. Fun.
* 2 Theff. ii. 16, 17. 8° 1759.
* 2 Cor. v. 21. 8° 1760. on Conversion of R. Tilling.
* Pf. lxxxv. 1, 9. 8° 1763. Th.
* Pf. xvii. 15. 8° 1767. Fun. f.
STEVENS Samuel
* Luke v. 5. 8° 1762. b. Diffent. Min. The fpiritual Fisherman.
STEVENS Thomas,   Fell. of Trin. Coll. Camb.
* 1 Cor. xvi. 13, 14. 8° 1771. 2 f. Stedfastness in the Christian Faith, and Union of Charity with Zeal.
STEVENS T.   DD. V. of Beneham, Berks.
* Jer. xviii. 7, 8. 4° 1777. Fast.
STEVENSON B.   DD.
* 2 Cor. xi. 23. 8° 1747. Ord.   *All S.* Oxon.
STEVENSON William, M. A. Chapl. to the East India Company at Fort St. George.
John xvi. 2. 8° 1717. Nov. 5.
STEVENSON William, DD. R. of Colwall, Herefordshire, Preb. of Sarum.
Gal. iv. 18. 8° 1728. Vif. Zeal and Moderation reconciled. *Br. M.*
Pf. cxlvii. 1. 8° 1746. Th. after Rebellion. The true Patriot's Wishes.
STEUART Charles, M. A. Fell. of Pemb. Hall, Camb.
Rom. iii. 8. 4° 1742. Nov. 5.
* Mic. vi. 9. 4° 1743. Sept. 2.

STEWARD

STEWARD Thomas
* Serm. in 8° 1734. on practical Subjects.
STEWARD William, DD. Chapl. to Lancelot, Bp. of Exeter.
* 1 Cor. xv. 10. 8° 1717. Vif. of divine Grace. *St. John's*. Cam.
STEWART John, Minister of the Gospel at Tealing.
Luke xi. 35. 12° 1738. *Edinb*. b. Prov. Synod. *Brit. M*.
STILEMAN John, M. A. V. of Tunbridge, Kent.
Heb. xiii. 17. 4° 1663. Vif. of Church-government. *Or.* Oxon.
STILEMAN John, B. D. R. of East-Farndon, and Shepey Magna, Leicestershire.
Heb. xiii. 17. 8° 1707. Vif. Episcopal Authority, with the Duty both of Clergy and Laity. *Univ.* Oxon. *Pub. L.* Camb.
STILEMAN Timothy, B. D. R. of Hourne. Surrey.
Acts x. 38. 8° 1723. Fun.
Matt. xi. 30. 8° 1733. Eafinefs of a Christian's duty.
STILLINGFLEET Edward, Bp. of Worcester.
50 Serm. in fo. 1707. upon several occasions. *Bod. Bal. Ch. Ch. All S. Univ. Mert. New C. Queen's. Pemb.* Oxon. *Pub. L. Cl. H.* Camb. *Dr. W's. L.* London.
1 Tim. ii. 1, 2. 8° 1735. Miscell. Disc. p. 394. designed for. Th. 1694. *Bod. Ch. Ch.* Oxon. *Queen's.* Camb. *Brit. M.*
STILLINGFLEET James, M. A. late Fell. of Mert. Coll. Oxon, and Preb. of Worcester.
* 1 Cor. iv. 1, 2. 8° 1760. Xtian Ministry. *Braz. N. Worc.* Ox.
* Pf. cxxii. 6. 8° 1781. Faft. Unity of Faith, Righteoufnefs of life, and Obedience to the civil Power (the means of preferving the peace of our Jerufalem) recommended.
STINTON Benjamin
Jer. li. 15, 16. 8° 1714. Commem. of the Storm. *Ch. Ch.* Oxon.
STINTON George, DD. late Fell. of Ex. Coll. Oxon. Chancellor of Lincoln, F. R. S. and S. A.
* Tit. iii. 1. 4° 1768. Jan. 30. b. Commons.
* 1 Tim. iii. 1. 4° 1769. Conf. of Bp. Barrington. *Ex.* Oxon. *Queen's.* Camb.
* 1 Sam. ii. 7. 4° 1769. b. Gov. of *Linc.*-Infirmary. *Queen's.* Ca.
STITH John, M. A. R. of Henrico Parish,
Mark xii. 17. 4° 1746. b. Gen. Affembly at Williamburgh.
STOCK Thomas, M. A. Head Mafter of the Grammar School at Gloucester, and late Fell. of Pemb. Coll. Oxon.
‡ * Pf. cxxii. 6, 7. 12° 1782. May 29.
STOCKDALE Percival
* 3 Difc. in 4° 1773.
* 6 Difc. in 8° 1777.
STOCKWELL Joseph, B. D. late Fell. of Trin. Coll. Oxon. R. of Solyhull, Warwickshire.
Prov. xxx. 9. 8° 1717. *Oxon*. Opening Charity-School.
Mark iv. 28. 8° 1726. Rogation-Sund.
Pf. xciii. v. 8° 1727. opening an Organ at *Abingdon*. *Worc.* Ox. *Pub. L.* Camb.

AN HISTORICAL REGISTER

STOGDEN *Herbert*
 ‡ * 1 Theff. ii. 3-6. 8° 1718. Character of a primitive Preacher.
STOKES Charles,   R. of Knaptoft, Leicesterf. and Chaplain to the Duke of Rutland.
 Job xxix. 16. 4° 1750. Diligence and Courage now requisite in a Magistrate.
STOKES David, DD. Fell. of Eton Coll and Canon of Windsor.
 Job xxix. 15. 4° 1667. *Oxon.* Assize. Job in Honour and Wealth. *Bod.*
 1 Kings xvii. 15. 4° 1667. *Oxon.* Fast. for the Fire of London. The Widow of Sarepta in poverty. *Bod.*
STOKES Joseph, M. A.
 * Isai. xxvi. 9. 8° 1758. Fast.
 * 1 Cor. i. 23. 8° 1759. Effay. Preaching Christ crucified.
STONE Edward, M. A. late Fell. of Wadh. Coll. Oxon. R. of Horsendon, Bucks.
 Heb. xi. 17. 8° 1732. The cafe of Abraham.
 * Serm. in 8° 1771. *Oxon.*
 * 2 Additional ferm. in 8° 1777. *Oxon.*
STONE George, Primate of Ireland.
 Ecclef xi. 1. 4° 1742. *Dublin.* Eng. Prot. School. *Worc.* Oxon. *Queen's.* Camb.
 * Pf. xlvii. 7. 4° 1759. Th. b. Lords at *Dublin.*
STONE Robert,   R. of Clenchwarton, Norfolk.
 Rom ii 4. 8° 1744. Vif.
STONE Samuel, M. A.
 Prov. xiv 8. 4° 1662. b. Lord Mayor. Deceivers deceived.
STONEHOUSE George, M. A. V. of Iflington, Middlefex.
 2 Tim iv. 5. 12° 1739.
STONEHOUSE James, M. D. R. of great and little Cheverel, Wilts.
 * Acts xx 35. 8° 1771. b. Gov. of *Sarum*-Infirmary.
STONESTREET Henry, M. A. V. of Eyton Bray, Bedfordf. and Chaplain to the Earl of Manchester.
 1 Cor. ii. 5. 4° 1709. School-Feast.
STONESTREET William, M. A. R. of St. Stephen's, Walbrook, London.
 1 Cor. x. 31. 4° 1701. School-Feast. Education.
 Luke x. 16. 4° 1709. Conf. of Bp. Manningham.
STOOKE Francis, M. A.
 * Acts xviii. 7. 4° 1698. Easter. at *Boveytracy* Church, Devon.
STOPFORD James, Bp. of Cloyne.
 * 1 Tim. i. 5. 4° 1758. Prot. Ir. Sch.. *Braz.* N. Ox. *Queen's.* C.
STOPFORD Joshua, B. D. R. of All Saint's, York.
 Rev xviii. 23. 8° 1675. 2 f. The ways and methods of Rome's Advancement. *Bod.*
STORY Ferguson
 1 John iii. 1. 8° 1661.
STORY George Walter. DD. Dean of Limerick, Ireland.
 Jer. vii. 4-7. 8° 1714. Th. Oct. 23.

STORY T.   a Quaker.
* - - - - 1739. 2 f. *Leeds.* Salvation by Chrift. *Brit.M.*
* 4 Serm.   17
STOUGHTON William,   Preb. of St. Patrick's, Dublin.
   1 Sam. xii. 25, 25. 4° 1708. *Dublin.* Jan. 30. Or. Ox. *St. John's.* Camb. *Sion.*
   Pf. xiv. 5—7. 4° 1717. Irifh Maffacre.
STRADLING Geor. DD. Dean of Chichefter, and Chapl. in Ord.
   John xix 15. 4° 1675.   Jan. 30. b. King. *Bod. Univ. Ch. Ch. Queen's.* Oxon. *St. John's.* Camb.
   14 Sermons and Difc. in 8° 1692. upon feveral occafions. *Bod. Univ. All S. Ch. Ch. New C. Jef.* Oxon.
STRAIGHT John, M. A. of Queen's Coll. Camb. V. of Stourpaine, Dorfetf. and Chaplain to the Bp. of Sarum.
   Luke vi, 48. 4° 1670. Affize. *Bod.*
   Phil. iv. 4. 4° 1671. The Rule of rejoicing, or a direction for Mirth. *Bod.*
STRAIGHT John, B. D. Fell. of Magd. Coll. Oxon. V. of Finden, Suffex.
   Select Difc. in 2 Vol. 8° 1741. on moral and religious Subjects. *All S. Bal. Wadh.* Oxon.
STRATFORD Nicholas, Bp. of Chefter.
   Acts xxiv. 25. 4° 1681. Affize. *All S. Ch. Ch. Magd.* Oxon.
   Rom. viii. 3. 4° 1683. b. King. Chriftmas. *Bod. Univ.* Oxon. *Pub. L.* Camb.
   Rom. xii. 17. 8° 1684. A diffuafive from Revenge. *Bod. Univ.* Oxon. *Sion.*
   Col. iii. 16. 4° 1687. The Lay chriftian's obligation to read the Holy Scriptures. *Bod. Ch. Ch.* Oxon. *Sion.*
   Ecclef. v. 1. 4° 1694. b. King and Queen. Mar. 25. Of the reverence due to God in his public Worfhip. *Magd.* Oxon. *Sion.*
   1 John v. 5. 4° 1700. Faith which overcomes the World. *Ch. Ch.* Oxon. *Pub. C.* Camb.
STRENGFELLOW William, M. A. Lect. of St. Dunftan's in the Eaft, and of St. Andrew's Underfhaft, London.
   Matt. xx. 22. 4° 1693. Elect. of a Lord Mayor. *Bod. Sion.*
STRIPLING Thomas, M. A. Chapl. of New Coll. Oxon.
   2 Tim. ii. 12. 4° 1681. St. Andrew's-day. *Bod.*
STRODE William, DD. Canon of Ch. Ch. Oxon.
   Pf. lxxvi. 11. 4° 1661. Vif. *Queen's.* Oxon. *St. John's.* Camb.
STRONG James, M. A.
   Acts xvi. 14. 8° 1675. Sev. f. Lydia's heart opened. *Bod.*
   Pf. xxv. 11. 8° 1676. *Bod. Pub. L.* Camb.
STRONG James,   in the Diocefe of Armagh, Ireland.
   * Rev. xxii. 12. 8° 1738. Fun. of Rev. *Henry Grove. Queen's.* C.
   * 5 Serm. in 8° 1763.
STRONG Martin, M. A. Preb. of Wells, V. of Yeovil, Somerfetf.
   1 Cor. xi. 29. 8° 1708. Sacrament.
   Ephef. vi. 4. 8° 1708. Charity-School. The great Duty and Neceffity of a virtuous and religious Education of youth.

STRYPE John, M. A. V. of Low-Layton, Essex.
  1 Sam. xii. 7. 4° 1689. Assize. *Bod. Sion.*
  2 Sam. xii. 7. 4° 1689. Assize.
  Ps. cxix. 78. 4° 1695. Th. April 16. *Brit. M.*
  * 2 Serm. in 12° 1699. Lessons for youth and old age.
  Prov. xiv. 12. 4° 1707. Lessons proper for fallible men. *Pub. L.* Camb. *Sion. Eton.*
  Luke xvii. 16. 8° 1711. b. Lord Mayor. The thankful Samariton. *Eton.*
  Phil. iv. 8. 4° 1724. Farewel.
STUART Charles, M. A. Fell. of Pemb. Hall, Camb. and Chapl. to Lord Mayor.
  * Micah vi. 9. 4° 1743. Nov. 5.
STUART John, B. A. late Preb. of Chichester.
  * Rom. iii. 10, 11. 4° 1753. 2 s. The lamentable Growth of the wicked &c. *Bod.*
  * John x. 25–27. 4° 1753. 2 s. Necessity of hearing and practising the word of God. *Bod.*
  * 2 Cor. vi. 3, 4. 4° 1753. The duty of a Minister. *Bod.*
  * Lev. ii. 13. 4° 1753. Necessity of Faith in Prayer. *Bod.*
  * Gal. iii. 26. 4° 1753. Justification by Faith in Christ. *Bod.*
  * Heb x. 38. 4° 1753. Necessity of a life of Faith. *Bod.*
STUART Richard, DD. Dean of Westminster.
  Phil. iv. 17.   p. 1.
  Mark vi. 28.   p. 49.   12° 1661. Golden Remains.   *Pub. L. C.*
  Heb. x. 1, 2.   p. 109.
STUART William, DD. Chancellor of Exeter.
  1 Cor. xv. 10. 8° 1717. Vis. of divine Grace. *Ch. Ch.* Oxon. *St. John's.* Camb. *Sion.*
STUBBE Henry
  2 Thess. iii. 16. 8° 1675. Farewell *Bod. Pub. L.* Camb.
STUBBES John
  Heb. xiii. 17.
STUBBS Philip, B. D. Fell. of Wadh. Coll. Oxon. R. of St. James's Garlick Hyth, Chaplain at Greenwich, and Arch-Deacon of St. Albans.
  Matt. xxviii. 19. 4° 1693. b. Lord Mayor. of public Baptism. *Bod. Univ. C. C. C. Magd. Linc. Jes. Ox. Queen's. St. John's.* C.
  Heb. vi. ii. 4° 1693. of Confirmation. *Bod. Ch. Ch. Magd. Or. Worc. Linc.* Oxon. *Pub. L. St. John's.* Camb.
  Ps. xlix. 15. 4° 1701. Fun. The hopes of a Resurrection asserted and applied. *Ch. Ch.* Oxon. *Pub. L* Camb. *Sion.*
  Ps. cxxxv. 6. 4° 1701. of God's dominion over the seas, and the Seaman's Duty. *Bod. Ch. Ch Jes. Worc.* Oxon. *Pub. L.* Camb.
  Ps. cxviii 23. 4° 1702. Th. May 29. *Worc.* Oxon. *Pub. L. St. John's.* Camb.
  1 Kings xviii. 21. 4° 1702. for God or for Baal—or no neutrality in Religion. *Ch. Ch. Magd. Worc.* Ox. *Pub. L. Cl. H.* Cam.

1 Kings

1 Kings xviii. 21. 4° 1702. Of occasional Communion. *Ch. Ch. Magd. Worc.* Oxon. *Pub. L. Cl. H.* Camb.

Pf. cxxix. 1,2. 4° 1704. b. Lord Mayor. Th. Nov. 5. Of popish Conspiracies. The Church of England under God, the impregnable Bulwark ag. Popery. *Bod. Ch. Ch. Worc.* Oxon.

1 Pet. ii. 17. 4° 1704. Of relig. Charity and Loyalty. *Worc.* Ox.

Isai. lvii. 19. 4° 1706. Th. Peace on earth, the gift of God—and Goodwill to one another, the duty of Men. *Ch. Ch. Worc.* Oxon. *St. John's.* Camb.

Rev. xx. 13. 4° 1709. On the Death of the prince of Orange. The Sea Assize. *Ch. Ch. Worc.* Oxon.

Matt. xxviii. 19. 8° 1711. b. Lord Mayor. Prop. of Gospel. of the divine Mission of Gospel Ministers. *Bod. Sion.*

Matt. xxviii. 19. 4° 1712. Conc. ad Cler. Lond. De Missione evangelicâ. *Bod. Ch. Ch.* Oxon. *Pub. L.* Camb. *Sion.*

Acts xxiv. 21. 3° 1713. Of the hopes of a Resurrection, and the abuse of funeral sermons. *Worc.* Oxon.

Acts xxiv. 2, 3. 4° 1713. Thankfulness for Peace, the Subject's duty. *Worc.* Oxon. *St. John's.* Camb.

Matt. xxii. 21. 8° 1718. Accession. The divine right of Perogative royal. *Worc.* Oxon. *Eton.*

1 Sam. xxviii. 6, 7. 8° 1736.

STUKELEY William, M.D. R. of All Saint's in Stamford, Lincolnshire, now of St. George's Queensquare, Westminster.

Lam. ii. 6. 4° 1742. Jan. 30. b. Commons. National Judgments the consequence of a national profanation of the Sabbath. *Brit. M.*

* Matt. xi. 5. 4° 1750. b. Coll. of Physicians. The healing of Diseases, a Character of the Messiah. *Bod.*

* Pf. xviii. 7. 8° 1756. Faft. on Earthquakes.

* Gen. i. 11. 4° 1760–1763. 3 s. at Fairechild's Lecture.

[STURCH John]

* Luke ii. 10, 11. 8° 1751. Christ's appearance.

STURGES John, M.A. Preb. of Winchester, R. of Wonestone, Hants.

Jer. iii. 15. 4° 1721. Conf. of Bp. Green. *Queen's.* Camb.

STURGES John, M.A. Preb. of Winchester, and Chapl. in Ord.

* 1 Cor. xii. 5. 4° 1777. Conf. of Bp. Butler.

STURMY Daniel, M.A. of Catherine-Hall, and R of Easthatley, Camb.

Pf. cxlvi. 2. 8° 1708. on the Death of Prince George. Serious admonitions to great Persons.

* Heb. xi. 3. 8° 1711. A theological throng of a Plurality of worlds.

*Cant. vii. 11. 12° 1712. Sev. Disc. Advantages of a Country-life.

19 Disc. in 8° 1716. *Camb.* on several subjects, but principally on the separate State of Souls. *Ch. Ch. Wadh.* Oxon. *Sion.*

SUDBURY John, DD. Dean of Durham, and Chapl. in Ord.

1 Tim. iii. 1. 4° 1660. Conf. of 5 Bps. The office and dignity

Of a Biſhop. *Bod. Ch. Ch. Bal. Worc.* Oxon. *Pub. L. St. John's.* Camb.
Phil. iv. 22. 4° 1675. b. King. *Bod. Ch. Ch. C.C.C.* Oxon. *St. John's.* Camb. *Sion.*
1 Tim. iii. 15. 4° 1676. b. King. *Bod. Queen's. Or.* Oxon. *St. John's.* Camb. *Sion.*
Matt. xxviii. 20. 4° 1677. b. King. *Ch. Ch. All S. Queen's.* Oxon. *Pub. L.* Camb. *Sion.*

SUDELL Chriſtopher, M. A. R. of Trinity in Cheſter.
Deut. xxiii. 9. 8° 1716. In the Rebellion.

SUGER Zachariah, M. A. Chapl. to the Duke of Gordon.
2 Chron. xxxii. 7, 8. 8° 1745. *York.* Reb. The Preſervation of Judah from the Inſults and Invaſions of the idolatrous Aſſyrians.

SUMNER Robert, DD. late Fell. of King's Coll. Camb.
*Acts xvii. 21. 8° 1768. Con. Acad. pro Grad. Doct. *Queen's.* C.

[SUNDERLAND John]
* - - - - 8° 1779. Faſt. The neceſſity of making God our Friend at this alarming Criſis.

SUTTON Gibbon, M. A. Fell. of Trin. Coll. Camb. and Lect. of St. Benedict, Grace-church-ſtreet, London.
1 Cor. xiv. 40. 8° 1717. Decency and Order in the public worſhip of God. *Bod. Sion.*
12 Serm. in 8° 1718. Wherein the Miniſters of Chriſt and Salvation by him are defended. *Sion.*
Luke xxii. 44. 8° 1718. (Poſth.) Palm S.

SUTTON John
James v. 19, 20.

SUTTON Prideaux, M. A. R. of Bredon, Worceſterſhire.
Luke vii. 21. 8° 1730. of Miracles. Ag. Woolſton. *Bal.* Oxon.

SUTTON William, M. A. V. of Saxthorpe, Norfolk.
Phil. iii. 16. 8° 1714. Acceſſion.
Matt. vi. 19, 20. 8° 1722. Char. Education of poor children recommended. *All S.* Oxon.
Pſ. l. 15. 8° 1725. *Norwich.* Nov. 5.

SUTTON William, M. A. R. of St. Michael's Curhaies, Cornwal.
* 16 Serm. in 8° 1754. on various Subjects. *Bod. Sion.*

SWADLING Thomas, DD. R. of All Hallows in Stamford, Lincoln.
12 Anniv. ſerm. in 4° 1661. on the funeral of King Charles I.
* 1 Sam. i. 10. 8° 1661. Jan. 30.
Acts xiii. 28.

SWAFFIELD *Joſeph*
James iii. 2. 8° 1661.

SWANN Gilbert, DD. late Fell. of Magd. Coll. Oxon.
*Rom. iii. 1. 8° 1760. 2 ſ. on the Jewiſh Diſpenſation. *Worc.* Ox.

SWANNE John, E. A. P.
Pſ. xxv. 2. 4° 1697. Th. at *Cherbury,* Oxon.

SWIFT Jonathan, DD. Dean of St. Patrick's, Dublin.
3 Serm. in 4° 1744. *viz.*

1 Pet.

1 Pet. v. 5. p. 1. on mutual Subjection. ⎫
1 Cor. i. 12. p. 21. on Conscience. ⎬ *Worc.* Oxon. *Brit. M.*
1 John. v. 7. p. 41. on the Trinity. ⎭
2 Kings viii. 13. 4° 1745. Th. Difficulty of knowing one's self.
* Heb. xiii. 1. 8° 1754. Brotherly Love.

SWIFT Thomas, M. A. Chapl. to Sir William Temple, and R. of Puttenham, Surrey.
Isai. xi. 13, 14. 8° 1710. Th. Noah's Dove. *Bod. Worc. Linc.* Oxon. *St. John's.* Camb. *Sion.*

SWINDEN Tobias, M. A. R. of Cuxton, Kent.
Luke xi. 2. 8° 1713. The Usefulness of a general standing Liturgy &c.
2 Tim. iii. 16. 4° 1718. The divine original and authority of the Gospel.

SWINNEY Sidney, DD. F. R. S. and A. S.
* 1 Cor. i. 23, 24. 4° 1767 Commencement.
* Luke iii. 14. 4° 1769. Military Sermon.

SWINNOCK George, V. of Great Kimbel, Bucks, till the Ejection 1662.
* John iii. 5. 8° 1660.
Acts xx. 32. 4° 1662. Farewel.
1 Tim. iv. 7. 4° 1662.
* Ps. lxxiii. 26. 4° 1663.
Phil. i. 12. 4° 1663.

SWORDER Will. V. of Great Sampford and Hempsted, Essex.
* Matt. xxiii. 35. 8° 1706. Jan. 30. The Reasonableness of observing the 30 of Jan. Fast.
1 Kings xviii. 21. 8° 1714. 3 s. Ag. practical Atheism and occasional Conformity.
Phil. i. 21. 8° 1715. Fun.

SWYNFEN John, B. D. Chaplain to the Earl of Bradford, Lect. of St. Magnus, London-Bridge, Preacher at Whitehall, R. of Avening, Gloucestershire.
Ezek. xx. 44. 4° 1694. Th. Dec. 2. *Pub. L.* Camb.
James i. 27. 4° 1706. Ch. for Children.
Amos iii. 3. 8° 1712. Farewel.
Luke x. 42. 8° 1715. Assize.

SWYNFEN Robert
* Num. xxii. 21. 8° 1722.

SYDALL Elias, Bp. of Gloucester.
1 Cor. iv. 1. 4° 1706. Cons. of Bp. Tyler. *Ch. Ch.* Oxon. *Eton.*
Luke v. 34, 35. 4° 1713. on the Fast of Lent.
Eccles. iii. 1-4. 4° 1715. Accession.
2 Cor. iv. 5. 4° 1715. at *Tunbridge. Queen's.* Cam. *Eton. Brit. M.*
Acts xv. 10. 4° 1715. Nov. 5. The insupportable Yoke of Popery &c. *Queen's. Cl. H.* Camb.
2 Cor. iv. 5. 8° 1716. Vis. *Queen's.* Camb. *Brit. M.*

SYKES Arthur Afhley, DD. Dean of Burein, Preb. of Winchefter.
> John xviii. 36. 8° 1717. Vif. *Ch. Ch.* Ox. *Queen's.* Camb. *Eton.*
> Pf. xxxv. 20. 8° 1722. Nov. 5. The Confequences of the prefent Confpiracy to the Church and State confidered. *Queen's.* Cam. *Brit. M.*
> 1 Tim. i. 5, 6. 4° 1725. School-Feaft. *Queen's.* Camb. *Brit. M.*
> 1 Sam. ii. 25. 8° 1728. Affize. *Bod.*
> Matt xxii. 37-39. 8° 1728. Affize.
> Pf. cxvi. 7-9. 4° 1746. Th. after Rebell. *Queen's.* Cam. *Brit. M.*

SYKES Thomas, DD. Fell. of Trin. Coll. and Margaret-Profeffor of Divinity, Oxon.
> 1 Kings viii. 18. 4° 1694. *Oxon.* Conf. of Trin. Chapel. *Bod. C. C. C. Magd. Ch. Ch. Jef.* Oxon. *Sion.*

SYLVESTER *Matthew,* Minifter of the Gofpel in London.
> Prov. xxx. 6. 4° 1675. m. e. P. There are but 2 Sacraments under the new Teft. p. 701.
> Acts xx. 24. 4° 1676. f. m. e. C. How to overcome the love of Life, and the fear of Death. p. 733. *Bod.*
> 1 Theff. iv. 17. 8° 1688. *Bod. Pub. L.* Camb.
> Heb. x. 24, 25. 4° 1690. c. m. e. Lukewarmnefs. p. 321. *Bod. Pub. L.* Camb.
> Neh. ii. 20. 12° 1697. Ref. of Manners.
> * Luke xvi. 22. 8° 1702. Vol. II. p. 178. Chriftian's Race.

SYMONDS Edward, Minifter of Rayne, Effex.
> Phil. ii. 21. (1632.) reprinted 8° 1741. Ecclefiaftical felf feeking. *Wadh.* Oxon. *Queen's.* Camb. *Sion.*

SYMPSON Matthias, Minifter of Sterling,
> 1 Chron. xii. 32. 4° 1661. *Bod.*

SYMSON Matthias, M. A R. of Moorby, Lincoln, afterwards of Wenington, Effex, and Canon of Lincoln.
> Rom. x. 15. 4° 1708. Vif. The neceffity of a lawful Miniftry.
> 2 Sam. xix. 14. 8° 1729. May 29.
> * Luke xi. 2. 8° 1737. 3 f. on the Lord's prayer.

SYMSON Thomas, M. A. late Preacher of Tottenham High Crofs, Middlefex.
> Cant. v. 16. 8° 1662. A proteftant Picture of Jefus Chrift.

SYNGE Edward, Abp. of Tuam, Ireland,
> Job xxvii. 28. 4° 1704. The wifdom of being religious.
> 1 Tim. v. 17. 8° 1710. Conf. of Bp. Browne. The divine Authority of Church-government, and Epifcopacy &c. *Bod. Magd. Linc.* Oxon. *Pub. L.* Camb. *Sion.*
> * John xiii. 17. 8° 17
> Jer. xvi. 14, 15. 8° 1712. b. Commons in Ireland. Oct. 23. *Bod. Pub. L.* Camb. *Sion.*
> * - - - - 8° 1713. The Value of a good name.
> * Judges xvii. 6. 8° 17
> 1 Pet. iii. 15. 8° 1713. Religion tried by the teft of fober and impartial Reafon.

Matt.

Matt. xix. 16. 12° 1714. Eternal Salvation, the only end and design of Religion.
Gal. iv. 18. 8° 1716. b. Lords Justices. Xtian Zeal. *Ch.Ch.* Ox.
* Isai. i. 26. 8° 1716. May 29. Happiness of a Nation or People. *Ch. Ch.* Oxon.
Jam. v. 19, 20. 4° 1719. Charity-School.
* Luke ix. 55, 56. 4° 1721. Th.
Acts xxiv. 14. 8° 1721. St. Paul's Religion.
Tit. i. 7–9. 8° 1723. Conf. of Bp.
Pf. x. 4. 12° 1733. *Dublin.* The root and spring of true Virtue and Piety.
Gal. v. 1. 12° 1733. *Dublin.* A short Diff. on eating blood.
1 Theff. v. 21. 12° 1734. The way to eternal Salvation. *Brit. M.*
Luke xii. 57. 12° 1737.
2 Tim. ii. 23. 12° 1738. Vif. Essay on foolish Questions. *Brit. M.*
Jude 3. 12° 1738. Vif. Essay on contending for the Faith. *Br. M.*

SYNGE Edward, Bp. of Elphin, Ireland.
Pf. cxviii. 23, 24. 4° 1719. *Dublin.* Accession. b. Commons.
Luke xiv. 23. 8° 1725. Ann. of Ir. Rebell. The Case of Toleration considered with respect to Religion and civil Government. *Ch. Ch.* Oxon.
Gen. xlix. 5–7. 8° 1731. Ann. of Irish Rebellion.

SYNGE Richard, Preacher at the Savoy.
1 Sam. xii. 23, 24. 8° 1714. Accession.
Pf. xliii. 5. 8° 1714. on the Death of Queen Anne.
8 Serm. in 8° 1720.

SYNGE Samuel, DD. Dean of Kildare, and Prolocutor to the lower house of Convocation in Ireland.
Prov. xxiv. 21. 4° 1707. *Dublin.* Jan. 30.

T.   A.
* Luke iv. 6, 7.   } 8° 1660. Insolent Usurper and regal Intru-
* 1 Kings xxi. 19. } der. *Pub. L.* Camb.

T.   G.
1 Cor. iv. 1. 8° 1693. b. Diffent. Clergy. The Pastor's care and dignity, and the People's duty. *Bod.*

TALBOR John, DD. of Kalvedon, Essex.
Judges v. 7. 4° 1704. Accession.

TALBOT George, Hon. DD. late Minister of Temple Guiting, Gloucestershire.
* Pf. xli. 1. 4° 1755. Open. *Gloucester*-Infirmary.

TALBOT James,   R of   Salop.
* Difc. in 8° 1674. In speculum Mortis.

TALBOT James, DD. R. of Spofforth, Yorks. and Chaplain to the Duke of Somerset.
Matt. vii. 12. 12° 1706. Christian Equity. *Bal.* Oxon.
Matt. xviii. 17. 4° 1708. Vif. The judicial power of the Ch.

TALBOT Tho. DD. R. of Ullingswick and little Cowarn, Herefords.
* - - - - 1764. Frequenting public Worship, and proper Behaviour here.

TALBOT William, Bp. of Durham.
  Amos iv. 12. 4° 1691. Faft. Sep. 16. *Bod. Ch. Cb.* Ox. *Pub. L. C.*
  Luke xiii. 21. 4° 1695. Charity. The foolifh abufe, and the and the wife ufe of Riches. *St. John's.* Camb. *Brit. M.*
  Pf. cxxiv. 6, 7, 8. 4° 1696. Th. April 16. *Brit. M.*
  * Jonah iv. 4. 8° 17   *Ch. Ch.* Oxon.
  1 John iii. 8. } 8° 1702. Ref. of Manners. *Bod. Pub. L.* Ca. *Eton.*
                 { 4° 1702. Chriftmas. Chrift's Divinity afferted.
  * Prov. xxix. 2. 4° 1705. Acceffion. *Ch. Ch.* Ox. *St. John's.* Ca.
  John xiii. 34. 4° 1717. Ann. meeting Charity-Schools. *Ch. Ch. Wadh.* Oxon.
  Acts xvii. 30, 31. 4° 1722.
  12 Serm. in 8° 1731. (2d Edit.)
TANNER Thomas, M. A. R. of Brightftone, Hants.
  Cant. vi. 13. 4° 1674. A call to the Shulamite. *Bod. Magd.* Ox.
  Prov. viii. 12. 4° 1677. Affize. Wifdom and Prudence. *Bod.*
TAOALBOB
  * Acts xix. 34. 8° 1755. Nov. 5. Proteftant turned Papift. *Queen's.* Camb.
TASWELL William, DD. R. of St. Mary Newington, Surrey.
  Ephef. iv. 14. 4° 1712. Vif. The Artifices and Impoftures of falfe Teachers. *Linc.* Oxon. *St. John's.* Camb. *Sion.*
TASWELL William, M. A. V. of Wootton Underidge, Gloucefterf.
  1 Chron. xvi. 39, 40, 42. 8° 1742. The Propriety and Ufefulnefs of facred Mufick.
  * John iv. 23. 8° 1763. Vif. The Expedience and Neceffity of national Eftablifhments in Religion, with obfervations on that of the Church of England in particular.
TATE Faithful, DD.
  * Prov. xii. 5. 12° 1666. *Dublin.* The thoughts of the righteous are right.
TATHAM Edward, M. A. late of Queen's Coll. Fell. of Linc. Coll. Oxon.
  * 12 Difc. in 8° 1780. Introductory to the Study of Divinity.
TATNAL Robert, M A. Fell. of Trin. Coll. Camb.
  Heb. ii. 15. 4° 1665. an antidote ag. the fear of Death.
TAUBMAN Nathaniel, M. A. Minifter of the Factory at Leghorn.
  Ecclef. vii. 1. 4° 1717. Fun. of Dr. Bafil Kennet. *Ch. Ch.* Oxon. *Eton.*
TAYLER *Thomas*
  * Job xiv. 10. 8° 1778. Fun.
TAYLOR Abdias,   V of St. John's Bedwardine, near Worcefter.
  1 Theff. v. 31. 8° 1718. Affize. *Brit. M.*
TAYLOR *Abraham*
  ‡ * Dan. ii. xliv. 8° 1730. Nov. 5.
  * Rev. iii. 1–3. 8° 1732. Caufes of the decay of practical Religion. V. Lime-ftreet. f. Vol. II. p. 567.
  * 1 Cor. xi. 14. 8° 1732. Influence of natural Religion. V. Lime-ftreet. f. V. I. p. 37.
  * Rom. i. 22. 8° 1732. V. Lime-ftreet. f. Vol. I. p. 87.

* Rom. v. 20. to vi. 2. 8° 1732. Men's Salvation &c. V. Lime-
ſtreet. ſ. Vol. II. p. 485.

* - - - - - - 1733. Fun.

[TAYLOR Chriſtopher]
‡ * Pſ. xxxvii. 37. 4° 1704. Fun. of John Hind. *Brit. M.*

TAYLOR Duel, M. A. R. of Bath.
  * Deut. iv. 8. 8° 1754. Elect. of Mayor.

TAYLOR Jeremy, Bp. of Down and Connor, Ireland.
  1 Cor. xv. 10. 8° 1674. The worthy Communicant. *Bod. Ch. Ch. Mert. Queen's.* Oxon.
  Matt. xi. 30. 8° 1675. Xt's Yoke an eaſy Yoke. *Bod. Pub. L.* Cam.
  Luke xiii. 23, 24. 8° 1675. The way to Heaven a ſtrait Gate. *Bod. Pub. L.* Camb
  Serm. (ſince the Reſtoration) in fo. 1678. *Bal. Ch. Ch. St. John's, Or. Jeſ. Pemb. Queen's.* Oxon. *King's.* Camb.

TAYLOR John, M. A.
  Prov. xxiv. 21. 8° 1716. Jan. 30.
  * 1 Cor. iv. 1, 2. 8° 17   Viſ.

TAYLOR John, M. A. Arch-Deacon of Bedford.
  Phil. ii. 15, 16. 4° 1744. Conſ. of Bp. John Thomas.

TAYLOR John, M. A. R. of Broadway, Dorſetſ.
  * Gal. v. 13–15. 8° 1744. b. his Britannic Majeſty's Forces at Bruſſels.

TAYLOR John, LL. D. Arch-D. of Bucks, Chancellor of Lincoln.
  Num. xi. 29. 4° 1749. *Camb.* Sch. Feaſt. *Queen's.* Cam. *Brit. M.*
  * Judges xx. 23. 4° 1757. Faſt. b. Commons. *Queen's.* Camb.

TAYLOR John, DD. Miniſter of the Goſpel at Norwich.
  * Haggai ii. 8, 9. 8° 1756. *Norwich.* Opening meeting-Houſe.

TAYLOR John, M. A. Cur. of Farringdon, Berks.
  * Prov. xxvii. 1. 4° 1759. Fun. of   Pye, Eſq;

TAYLOR Nathaniel,   Miniſter of the Goſpel in London.
  Luke x. 21. 4° 1688. b. Lord Mayor. *Brit. M.*
  * Luke xii. 40. 4° 1691. Fun.
  ‡ * Job xxi. 26. 4° 1699. Fun. of Lady Lane. *Brit. M.*
  * Sermons in 8° 1703.

TAYLOR Nathaniel, M. A. Maſter of the Grammar School, at Brigg, Linc.
  Pſ. cxxii. 6. 4° 1691. Viſ. *Bod.*

TAYLOR Philip
  * Prov. x. 11. 8° 17   Virtuous Children, Joy of Parents. V. Dr. *Enfield's* Eng. Pr. Vol. IX. p. 289.

TAYLOR Richard
  * Sermons in 8° 1701.
  * Sermons in 3 Vol. 8° 1719.

TAYLOR Robert,   R. of Hadley, Middleſex.
  1 John iv. 21. 4° 1680. County-Feaſt.

TAYLOR Thomas,   Paſtor to a ſmall Congregation at Cambridge.
  Phil. ii. 9–11. 4° 1676. m. c. G. p. 232. Chriſt's Exaltation.
  Matt. xxi. 22. 8° 1692. The Neceſſity of Faith in Prayer. *Bod.*

TAYLOR

TAYLOR Thomas, M. A. V. of Burceſter, Glouceſter.
  Prov. xxi. 30, 31. 4° 1679. Th. for Peace.
TAYLOR Tho. M. A. V. of St. John's, Bedwardine, near Worceſter.
  Acts xvii. 6.   1683.
[TAYLOR Thomas,]   Preacher at Aldermanbury.
  * Luke i. 6. 12° 17.   V. Diſc. on Conj. Duty. V. II. p. 410.
TAYLOR Thomas
  * Pſ. cxii. 11. 12° 1776. Word of God, a hidden Treaſure.
  ‡ * Job xiv. 10. 8° 1778. Fun. of Rev. *Edward Pickard.*
TAYLOR Timothy
  *   - - - - 4° 1661. Coron.
  *   - - - - 4° 1661. b. Commons.
TAYLOR Zachary, M. A. V. of Ormſkirk, Lanc. one of the King's
    Preacher's in that County, and Cur. to the Bp. of Cheſter.
  Prov. xvii. 14. 4° 1683. *Eton.*
  * Numb. xxiii. 10. 4° 1695. Fun. of Lady Bradſhaigh. The
    Death of the righteous &c. *Queen's.* Camb.
TEASDALE John
  Tit. iii. 1, 2.   1706.
TEATE Joſeph, M. A. Dean of St. Canier, Kilkenny, Ireland.
  2 Tim. iii. 5. 4° 1670. *Dublin.*
TEMPLE A.   M. A. V. of Eaſtly, Yorkſhire.
  *   - - - - 1766.
  * Matt. x. 34. 8° 1772. Viſ. } The written word, the only rule
  * Acts viii. 30. 8° 1722. 2 f. } of chriſtian Faith and Manners
                                 } &c. *Queen's.* Camb.
  * Matt. xxvi. 26. }
  ‡ * 1 Cor. xi. 9. } 8° 1782. On the Lord's Supper.
TEMPLER John, DD. Fell. of Trin. Coll. Camb.
  Jude 3. 4° 1660. b. Lord Mayor. The Saints duty in con-
    tending for the Faith.
  Acts xv. 36. 4° 1676. *Camb.* Viſ. The reaſon of Epiſcopal In-
    ſpection. *Bod. Univ. All S. Ch. Ch. Magd.* Oxon. *St. John's.*
    Camb. *Sion.*
TENISON Thomas, Abp. of Canterbury.
  Pſ. cxii. 5. 4° 1681. Spitt W. Of Diſcretion in Almſgiving. *Bod.
    Jeſ.* Oxon. *Pub. L. Queen's.* Camb.
  2 Tim. iii. 1, 2. 4° 1689. b. Commons. Ag. Self-love. *Ch. Ch.
    Magd. Jeſ.* Oxon. *Pub. L. St. John's.* Camb. *Sion.*
  Pſ. lxxviii. 5, 6. 4° 1790. b. King and Queen. Of doing good
    to Poſterity. *All S. Ch. Ch. Magd. Worc. Linc.* Oxon. *Pub. L.
    Cl. H.* Camb. *Sion.*
  1 Cor. vii. 35. 4° 1690. of the wandering of the mind in God's
    ſervice. *Bod. Ch. Ch. Magd.* Oxon. *Pub. L.* Camb. *Sion.*
  Pſ. xiv. 1. 4° 1691. b. Queen. The Folly of Atheiſm. *Ch. Ch.
    Magd.* Oxon. *Sion.*
  1 Tim. v. 21. 4° 1691. b. the Sons of the Clergy. *Bod. Ch. Ch.
    Wadh. Pub. L.* Camb. *Sion.*

1 Cor. xv. 53. 4° 1694. Eafter. h. King and Queen. The celeftial body of a Chriftian. *Bod. Ch. Ch. Magd.* Oxon. *Pub. L. Camb. Sion.*

Pf. cxix. 106. 4° 1694. b. King. Of holy Refolution. *Ch. Ch. Bod. Magd. Linc.* Oxon. *Pub. L. Cl. H. St. John's.* Camb. *Sion.*

Ecclef. vii. 14. 4° 1695. Royal Fun. *Univ. All S. Ch. Ch. Bal.* Oxon. *Cl. H. St. John's.* Camb. *Sion.*

TENNENT Gilbert
 * Sermons in 8° 1742.
 * 3 Sermons in 8° 1743.

TENNISON Edward, Bp. of Offory, Ireland.
 1 Cor. x. 24. 4° 1711. School-Feaft. The Excellency and Ufefulnefs of a public Spirit. *Ch. Ch. Ox. Pub. L. Queen's.* Camb.
 Prov xxiv. 21. 4° 1733. *Dublin.* Th. Nov. 5. *Queen's. C. Sion.*

TENNISON Richard, Bp. of Meath, Ireland.
 2 Chron. xxviii. 9. 4° 1690. Th. b. Irifh Prot. *Pub. L. Ca. Sion.*
 Col. iii. 1–4. 4° 1690. Fun. of Bp. Hopkins.
 Rom. xii. 2. 4° 1695. Duty and Happinefs.

TERRICK Richard, Bp. of London.
 1 Tim. ii. 1, 2. 4° 1742. Acceffion. b. Commons. *Brit. M.*
 1 Sam. xii. 3, 4. 4° 1745. Faft. Dec. 18. b. Ld Mayor. *Worc.* Ox.
 * Jer. xviii. 7, 8. 4° 1756. Faft. b. Commons. *All S.* Oxon.
 * Pf. cxliv. 15. 4° 1758. Prop. of Gofpel. *All S. Braz. N.* Oxon.
 * James iv. 1. 4° 1758. Jan. 30. b. Lords. *All S.* Ox. *Queen's.* C.
 * Deut. xv. 11. 4° 1761. b. Gov. of *Lond.*-Hofp. *Braz. N. Worc. Wadh.* Oxon.
 * Ifai xi. 9. 4° 1764. Prop. of Gofp. *Braz. N.* Ox. *St. John's.* C.

TERRICK Samuel, M. A. Canon Refid. of York, R. of Waldrake, Yorkfhire.
 Pf. lxiv. 9, 10. 4° 1706. *York.* Th.

TERRY Ifaac, M. A. R. of St. Mary Bredman, and St. Andrew, in Canterbury.
 16 Serm. in 8° 1746. *Cant.* upon felect Subjects.

TEW Edm. DD. Fell. of Jef. Coll. Camb. R. of Boldon, Durham.
 Rom. xvi. 1, 2. 4° 1737. b. Sons of the Clergy at *Newcaftle.*
 2 Chron. ix. 8. 4° 1750. *Newcaftle.* Affize. The queen of Sheba's notions of Government confidered.
 * John vi. 12, 13. 4° 1756. b. Gov. of *Newcaftle*-Infirmary. Support of Charity.

THANE John, DD. Preb. of Chefter.
 * John xii. 26. 8° 1700. 2 f. Ag. Immorality and Profanenefs.
 * Gal. vi. 9, 10. 4° 1706. Ann. meet. of Clergy. *Queen's.* Cam.

THEED Richard, M. A. of Hertford Coll. Oxon.
 Luke xvi. 27, 28. 8° 1711. 2 f. On the ftory of Dives and Lazarus.
 Sev. Difc. in 8° 1712. Sacred Biography, or Scripture Characters illuftrated.

THEYER Charles, Lect. of Totteridge, Herts.
 Rom. xiii. 7. 4° 1707. Acceffion. *Pub. L.* Camb.

THOMAS

THOMAS H.　　M. A. Arch-Deacon of Nottingham, and Chapl. to his Grace the Abp. of York.
‡ * 1 Kings xii. 27.　4° 1750.　Conſ. of Bp. Frederick Cornwallis.
* Luke xix. 44.　8° 1761.　Faſt.

THOMAS Humphrey,　　of Blackheath.
* Luke xix. 44.　8° 1761.　Faſt.

THOMAS John, M. A. R. of St. Nicholas, Cardiff.
Ezek. xxi. 24–27.　4° 1679.　Ag. Popery. *Bod. All S.* Oxon.

THOMAS John
Iſai. lix. 1.　12° 1689.

THOMAS John,　　Miniſter of Yately, Hants.
Prov. xxiv. 21.　4° 1710.　Aſſize. Fear God and the King. *St. John's.* Camb.

THOMAS John, M. A. Cur. of Chorleton, and Miniſter of Ince, (Cheſhire.)
6 Pract. Diſc. in 12° 1728. on funeral occaſions.

THOMAS John, Bp. of Wincheſter.
2 Tim. ii. 22.　4° 1729.　Conſ. of Bp. Harris. *Bod. Worc.* Oxon. *Queen's.* Camb. *Eton.*
Matt. xviii. 14.　4° 1737.　Ann. meet. Charity-Schools. *Brit. M.*
1 Cor. x. 11, 12.　4° 1745.　Jan. 30. b. Commons.
Matt. xx. 3, 4.　4° 1747.　Iriſh Prot. Schools.
Jonah i. 7.　4° 1748.　Faſt. b. Lords. Feb. 17.
Job xxix. 11–13.　4° 1748.　Spitt. M.
John v. 6, 7.　8° 1748.　*Northampton*-Infirmary.
* Mark. xii. 42, 43.　4° 1750.　b. Gov. of *Middleſex*-Hoſp.
Rom. ii. 11.　4° 1751.　Prop. of Goſpel. *Brit. M.*
* Luke viii. 24.　4° 1758.　Faſt. b. Lords. *All S.* Ox. *Queen's.* C.
* Iſai. xxvi. 9.　4° 1756.　Faſt. b. Lords.

THOMAS John, Bp. of Lincoln.
Pſ. lxxvii. 9, 10　4° 1739.　May 29. b. Commons. *All S.* Ox. *Sion.*
Matt. xxv. 40.　4° 1740.　Ann. meeting Charity-Schools. *Sion.*
Tit. iii. 14.　4° 1743.　Iriſh Prot. Schools. *All S. Worc. Jeſ.* Oxon. *Queen's.* Camb. *Brit. M.*
2 Pet. ii. 19.　4° 1745.　Jan. 30. b. Lords. *All S.* Oxon.
Matt. vi. 10.　4° 1746.　Prop. of Goſpel. *All S.* Oxon. *Brit. M.*
Luke xix. 41.　4° 1749.　b. Gov. of *London*-Infirmary. *Wadh.* Ox.

THOMAS John, Bp. of Rocheſter.
Joel ii. 20.　4° 1745.　Rebell. The Principles and Practices of a popiſh Government deſtructive of civil and religious Liberty. *Queen's.* Camb.
Pſ. cxliv. 15.　4° 1749.　Th. for Peace.
Acts x. 4.　4° 1752.　b. Gov. of Lying-in Hoſp. *Brit. M.*
* Luke ix. 54–56.　4° 1773.　Nov. 5. b. Lords.
* Matt. vii. 24.　4° 1780.　Prop. of Goſpel.

THOMAS John, DD. R. of St. Peter's Cornhill, London.
* Rom. xii. 3.　4° 1758.　Jan. 30. b. Commons.

THOMAS Michael, R. of Stockton, Salop.
  Eccleſ. v. 1. 4° 1661. Aſſize. Church-reformation. *Bod.*
THOMAS William, Bp. of Worceſter.
  Luke xiii. 5. 4° 1678. Faſt. b. Lords. *Ch. Ch. Magd.* Oxon. *Brit. M.*
  Luke xvi. 9. 4° 1688. The mammon of Unrighteouſneſs detected and purified.
  Gal. iii. 24. 8° 1714.
TOHMAS William, Cur. of Roſſendale, Lancaſhire.
  Gal. iii. 24. 8° 1714.
THOMAS William, DD. R. of St. Nicholas, Worceſter.
  Pſ. xxxiv. 11. 8° 1728. Viſ. of a Free-School. The advantages of a good Education.
THOMPSON Richard, DD. Dean of Briſtol, and Chapl. in Ord.
  Tit. iii. 1. 4° 1685. June 21. *St. John's.* Camb.
THOMSON
  Iſai. lviii. 3.
THOMSON James, Miniſter of Hampton-Court, Middleſex.
  Prov. xxix. 2. 8° 1714. (b. Oliver Cromwell 1655.)
THOMSON Thomas, M. A. V. of Reculver, Kent.
  * Levit. xviii. 25. 8° 1757. On the Times.
THOMSON William, R. of Leigh in Eſſex.
  Deut. xxxiii. 18, 19. 4° 1683.
  Zech. xi. 2. 4° 1695. Royal Fun.
THORESBY Ralph, M. A. R. of Stoke-Newington.
  Gal. vi. 10. 4° 1748. Col. of Georgia. The Excellency and Advantage of doing good.
THORNBY John, Curate of Cheſhire.
  * Serm. in 8° 1742. Exhortations to Unity and Concord.
THORNE Edmund, M. A. Fell. of Oriel Coll. Oxon.
  Rev. xiv. 13. 4° 1684. Fun. of Col. Edw. Cook.
THORNS Joſeph, B. A. Cur. of Slarghwait, Yorkſhire.
  * James iv. 11. 8° 1732. The great Miſchiefs of Detraction and evil ſpeaking &c.
THORNTON Stephen, M. A. R. of Ludiſdown, Kent.
  Amos v. 15. 4° 1691. Aſſize. *St. John's.* Camb.
THOROLD William, M. A. R. of St. Martin's, Ludgate, London.
  James iii. 17. 4° 1731. Nov. 5. b. Lord Mayor.
THORP George, B. D. Fell. of Gonvil and Caius Coll. Camb. R. of St. Antholine's, and St. John Baptiſt's, London.
  Matt. vii. 12. 4° 1677. b. Lord Mayor. Sept. 9. Doing as we would be done by. *Bod. All S. Univ. Ox. Pub. L. St. John's.* C.
THORP Robert, M. A. V. of Chillingham, Northumberland.
  * Rom. xiii. 5. 4° 1769. Aſſize.
THORPE Henry, M. A. Fell. of New Coll. Oxon. V. of Preſhute, Wilts.
  Heb. xiii. 9. 8° 1716. Aſſize. Beauty of the proteſtant Religion to that of Popery.

THORPE Joseph
 Mic. vi. 8.
THORY John, M.A. R. of Hartley St. George, V. of Caxton, Camb.
 Pf. lxviii. 30. 8° 1711. Faft.
THURLIN Thomas, DD. Fell. of St. John's Coll. Camb. and R. of Gawood, Norfolk.
 Heb. xiii. 17. 4° 1686. *Camb.* Vif. The neceffity of Obedience to fpiritual Governors. *Bod. Bal.* Oxon. *St. John's.* Camb.
[THURLOE C.]
 John xi. 49, 50. 8° 1742.
THURLOW Thomas, Bp. of Lincoln.
 * 1 Pet. ii. 17. 4° 1780. Jan. 30. b. Lords.
TICHBOURN Robert
 1 Cor. xv. 55-57. 4° 1667.
TIDCOMBE Jerem.   Cur. of St. Peter's poor, Broadftreet, Lond.
 ‡ * Job xiv. 14. 8° 1732. Fun. of *Mary Motterfhead. Brit. M.*
 * Pf. cvii. 29-31. 8° 1734. Fun.
 * Serm. in 8° 1757.
TILLOTSON John, Abp. of Canterbury.
 Matt. vii. 12. 4° (1661.) 1677. m. e. C. Wherein lies that exact Righteoufnefs which is required between man and man. p. 183. *Bod. Worc.* Oxon. *Brit. M.*
 His works in 3 Vol. fo. 1735. *Bod. Univ. AllS. Ch. Ch. New C. Or. St. John's. Queen's. Mert. Magd. Worc. Wadh. Trin. Pemb. Hert.* Oxon. *Pub. L. Queen's. Cl. H.* Camb. *Sion.*
TILLY William, DD. Fell. of C.C.C. Oxon. R. of Albury, and Godington, Oxon.
 Prov. xxiv. 10-12. 4° 1705. *Oxon.* Affize. The Nature and Neceffity of religious Refolutions, and the Defence and Support of a good Caufe in times of Danger and Trial. *Bod. Univ. Ch. Ch. Magd. Jef.* Oxon. *Queen's.* Camb.
 2 Kings viii. 13. 8° 1709.
 * John iii. 19. 4° 1710. Men's vices and Sins the caufe of their Ignorance, and corrupt opinions in Religion. *Univ. Ch. Ch. Or. Worc.* Oxon.
 16 Serm. in 8° 1712. and 1737. *Bod. C.C.C. Or. Ox. St. John's Queen's.* Camb. *Sion.*
 1 Kings x. 9. 8° 1713. Acceffion. *C.C.C. Or. Linc.* Oxon.
 Phil. iii. 10. 8° 1718. *Oxon.* on Eafter-Tuefday. *Bod. C.C.C. Ox.*
 Ezra vi. 10. 4° 1727. Sunday after Inauguration. The religious King, and the People's Prayers for him. *Queen's. C. Sion Eton.*
 3 Serm. in 8° 1729. A prefervative ag. the growing Infidelity, and Apoftacy of the prefent Age.
TILLARD Richard M.A. R. of   Derbyf.
 * Gen. i. 26. 4° 1781. *York.*-Lunatic Afylum.
TISSER John, M.A. Fell. of Mert. Coll. Oxon. and Chapl. to the Factory at Smyrna.
 Matt. xvi. 26. 4° 1701. Levant Co. *C.C.C.* Oxon.
 Matt. xxvi. 6. 4° 1702. b. trading Co.

TODD

TODD Hugh, DD. V. of Penrith, and Canon of Carlisle.
  Ezek. xxxvii. 22. 4° 1707. Th. for Union.
  Pf. lxxxv. 1. 4° 1711. May 29. b. Commons. *Bod.*
TOLL Frederick, M. A. R. of Dogmersfield, Hants.
  John xx. 29 8° 1751. Vif.
TOLLER *Thomas*
  * 1 Cor. v. 7, 8. 12° 1769. 2 f. on the Lord's Supper.
  * Luke xii. 30. 12° 1772. At the Settlement of a Minister.
  * Prov. xxiii. 4. } 12° 1772. To Tradesmen.
  * Rom. xii. 11. }
  * - - - - 1773. Ch.
  * Matt. vi. 10. 8° 1779. b. Soc. for prop. Xtian Knowledge.
TOMBS   B. D
  ‡ * Mark xvi. 15, 16. 8° 17
TOMLINSON Matthew, M. A.
  Luke xii. 57. 8° 1743. Vif. The Protestant's birth-right, or the Christian's right of judging for himself in matters of Religion.
TOMLYNS *John*
  ‡ * Pf. cxvi. 12. 8° 1715. Th. for Accession.
TOMLYNS Samuel, M. A. of Trin. Coll. Camb. Minister of the Gospel at Malborough.
  Heb. xiii. 13. 8° 1682. The subject of sev. sermons.
  Jer. xxiii. 6. 8° 1696. Substance of sev. sermons.
  Pf. li. 9. 8° 1696. Faft.
TOMMAS *John*
  * 1 Cor. xvi. 14. 12° 1767. Ord.
  * 1 Tim. iv. 12. 8° 1774. Educat. Society.
TOMS *Isaac*
  * Pf. ix. 16. 12° 1776. Ann. Th. f. for Vict. at Culloden.
TONG *William*
  * 2 Kings ii. 9, 10. 4° 1704. Fun.
  * John xiii. 36. 8° 1704. Fun. of Rev. *Matt. Henry.*
  * Heb. xii. 3. 12° 1704. Ref. of Manners.
  * 2 Cor. iv. 7. 8° 1716. Fun.
TOOKIE Clement, M. A. Surmaster of St. Paul's School, London.
  Pf. (or Prov.) xxiii. 1. 4° 1717. School-Feaft.
TOPHAM Edward, M. A. Fell. of Trin. Coll. Camb.
  Pf. cxxxii. 18. 8° 1737. *York.* Charity.
TOPHAM George,   R. of Bolton, and Preb. of Lincoln.
  Pf. lix. 3. 4° 1679. Faft. April 11. Innocency no shield ag. Envy.
  Luke xii. 1. 4° 1690. Vif. *Brit. M.*
TOPLADY Auguftus, B. A. V. of Broad-Hembury, Devon.
  * Pf. viii. 4. 8° 1770. God's mindfulnefs of Man.
  * 1 Tim. i. 10. 8° 1770. 3 parts. Caveat ag. unfound Doctrine.
  * 1 Tim. iii. 16. 8° 1770. 3 Difc. On Jefus feen of Angels &c.
  * Matt. iv. 23. 8° 1772. Vif. Clerical Subfcription, no Grievance.
  * Pf. cxv. 1. 8° 1774. Free will and merit examined.
  * Pf. lxxxix. 15, 16. 8° 1774. Good news from Heaven.

* Luke xv. 7. 8° 1775. 2 Difc. Joy in Heaven over one re-
penting Sinner.
* James ii. 19. 8° 1775. Creed of Devils.
* Phil. iv. 5. 8° 1776. Faſt. Moral and political Moderation recommended.

TOPPING Henry, M.A. Lect. of St. Paul's Covent Garden, and
Chapl. to the Bp. of London.
John xiii. 35. 8° 1715. b. Lord Mayor. Chriſtian Love and
Charity. *Queen's*. Camb. *Sion*.
Pſ. xxii 28. 8° 1715. May 29. b. Lord Mayor. The certainty
of an overruling Providence.
Acts xvii. 6. 8° 1716. Ag. Popery, and the Rebellion.
1 Pet. ii. 17. 8°1716. b. Lord Mayor. Of our Duty to God and
the King.
Pſ. lv. 1. 8° 1719. Repairing a Church. Of the whole duty of
Prayer.
Matt. vi. 9. 8° 1719. *St. John's*. Camb. *Sion*.

TORRE Nicholas, M.A. Fell. of Trin. Coll. Camb.
* Iſai. lix. 14. 4° 1780. Aſſize at *York*.

TORRIANO Alexander, LL.D. R. of Holywell, Huntingdonſhire,
and Preb. of Lincoln.
1 Cor. xv. 58. 4° 1706. Viſ. *Ch. Ch.* Ox. *Pub. L. Queen's*. Cam.

TORRIANO Nathaniel, M.D. R. of Aldham, Suffolk.
* Serm. in 8° 1767. *Norwich*.

TOTTIE John, DD. Canon of Ch. Ch. Oxon. and Arch Deacon of
Worceſter.
Rom. vii. 23. 8° 1736. A view of Reaſon and Paſſion, as in their
original and preſent ſtate. *Worc*. Oxon. *Brit. M.*
Rom. xii. 15. 8° 1751. *Worceſter*-Infirmary. Sympathizing affec-
tion, a principle of nature, enforced by Reaſon and Religion.
Worc. Oxon. *Queen's*. Camb.
* 16 Serm. (Poſth.) in 8° 1775.

TOTTON William, Lect. of Hexham, Northumberland.
* Eccleſ. vii. 1. 4° 1754. Fun. of Mrs. Ann Dunſter.
* Eccl[us]. xxxvi. 26. 4° 1756. Faſt. Earthquake.
* 1 Pet. v. 6. 4° 1756. Faſt. Earthquake.
* Rom. xiii. 1, 2. 4° 1761. After an Inſurrection. Duty of Sub-
jects to civil Powers.

TOULMIN Joſhua, M.A. Min. of the Goſp. at Taunton, Somerſetſ.
* Serm. in 12° 1770. Principally addreſſed to Youth.
* Col. ii. 16. 8° 1770. Chriſtmas ſ.
* Jude 3. 8° 1771. Manner of contend. for the Faith. *Queen's*. C.
* Iſai. xlix. 4. 8° 1775. b Diſſenting Clergy.
* 1 Theſſ. v. 12, 13. 8° 1775. Ord.
* Jer. iv. 19. 8° 1776. American War lamented.
* Matt. v. 22. 8° 1780. Ord. of   Hell fire incurred
by denouncing it.
* Matt. ix 36–38. 8° 1780. Ord. of   Compaſſion
on the Multitude.
* 2 Cor. v. 1. 8° 1781. Fun. of Mr. *James Maynard*.

TOWERS John, Bp. of Peterborough.
  Rev. xiv. 13. 8° 1660. Fun. of Earl of Northampton. *Sion.*
  Matt. xix. 14. 8° 1660. At the Baptism of Earl of Northam. *Sien.*
  Matt. xxi. 13. 8° 1660. b. King. At Castle Ashby. *Sion.*
  John xiv. 2, 3. 8° 1660. b. King. Lent.
TOWERS John,   Minister at Bartholomew Close, London.
  * Matt. vi. 16. 8° 1778. Fast.
  * Rev. xvii. 5. 8° 1778. Accession.
TOWERS Johnstone, M. A. Usher of Tunbridge School, Kent.
  * 2 Tim. iv. 13. 4° 1754. *Tunbridge*-Sch. Feast.
TOWERS Joseph
  * Matt. v. 47. 8° 1777. Charity-School.
TOWERS Samuel, M. A. R. of Barnock, Northamptonshire, and of Uffington, Linc. and Preb. of Peterborough.
  Ps. xxi. 1. 4° 1660. Th. for Restoration. *Wrrc.* Oxon.
TOWERSON Gabriel, DD. R. of St. Andrew Undershaft, Lond. and of Welwyn, Herts.
  Ephes. v. 18, 19. 4° 1696. Whit. f. Open. an Organ. *Eton.*
  * Rom. viii. 17. 8° 16
TOWGOOD Micaiah
  * Eccles. vii. 14. 8° 1743. On a fire at Crediton, Devon.
  * 1 Tim. iv. 1. 8° 1746. Errors &c. of Popery.
  * Ps. cxviii. 27. 8° 1758. On taking of Cape Breton and St. John's. *Queen's.* Camb.
TOWGOOD Richard, B. D. Dean of Bristol.
  Acts vii. 8. 4° 1676. God's token of love to Abraham. *Bod.*
TOWGOOD S.
  ‡ * 1 Tim. iii. 1. 8° 1737. Ord.
TOWLE Thomas, B. D.   at Thaxted, Essex.
  * Phil. i 9–11. 8° 1770. Ord. of *N. Phene.*
TOWNLEY James, M. A. Lect. of St. Dunstan's in the East, R. of St. Bennet, Grace Church-street, London.
  Ps. l. 14. 4° 1741. May 29. b. Lord Mayor. *St. John's.* Oxon.
  Prov. xvi. 12. 4° 1741. Elect. of Lord Mayor. The duty of the Magistrate. *St. John's.* Oxon.
  2 Kings iv. 13. 4° 1752. b. the Sons of the Clergy. *St. John's. All S.* Oxon.
  * Ps. cxxii. 6. 4° 1759. Th. b. Lord Mayor.
  * 1 Cor. x. 24. 4° 1761. Ann. meeting Charity-Schools.
  * Zech. iv. 7. 4° 1769. On laying the first Stone in St. Giles's fields.
  * Prov. xviii. 14. 4° 1769. At the *Magd.*-Hospital.
TOWNSEND J.
  * 2 Cor. v. 17. 12° 1766. Treatise.
[TOWNSEND Meredith]
  * Isai. xxvii. 8. 8° 1746. Th. On the defeat of the Rebels.
  * Rev. ii. 10. 8° 1761. Coronation.
TOWNSEND Sampson
  1 Sam. xii. 14. 8° 1663.

TOWNSON Thomas, DD. late Fell. of Madg. Coll. Oxon. R. of Malpas, Cheshire.
* 8 Disc. in 4° 1778. On the 4 Gospels. To which is prefixed a Sermon on
* John xx. 30, 31. in 2 parts. p. 3–13. *Bod. Ch. Ch.* Oxon.
* Luke iv. 32. 4° 1778 Vis.
TRAIL Jacob, Bp. of Down and Connor.
* Dan. xii. 3. 4° 1779. b. the incorporated Society at Dublin.
TRAIL Robert
* Serm. in (2 Vol. 1705.) republished 12° 1778.
* 13 Disc. on Heb. iv 16. Throne of Grace.
* 16 Disc. on John xvii. 24. Lord's Prayer.
TRAPP Joseph, DD. R. of Harlington, Middlesex, V. of the united Parishes of Ch Ch. and St. Leonard, Foster Lane, London.
Prov. xxviii. 2. 4° 1706. Accession. The mischief of Changes in Government, and the Influence of religious Princes to hinder them. *Bod. Sion.*
* Ezek. xxxvii. 22. 8° 17   Th.
2 Sam. xii. 7. 4° 1708. Assize. *Univ.* Oxon. *St. John's.* Camb.
Isai. i. 26. 4° 1711. May 29. b. Lord Justices in Ireland. *Linc. Ch. Ch. Hert.* Oxon. *St. John's.* Camb.
Ps. cxx. 5–7. 4° 1711. Fast for Peace. *Bod. Linc. Hert.* Oxon. *St. John's.* Camb. *Sion.*
2 Chron. xix. 7. 4° 1713. Assize. The Nature and Influence of the fear of God. *Bal. Linc.* Oxon. *St. John's.* Camb. *Brit. M.*
John xviii. 36. 8° 1717. The real nature of the Church or Kingdom of Christ. *Linc. Worc.* Oxon.
Josh. xxiv. 15. 12° 1722. The duties of private, domestic, and public Devotion.
Perservative ag unsettled Notions &c. in 2 Vol. 8° 1722. *Magd. Bod. C.C.C.* Oxon. *St. John's.* Camb.
1 Kings ix. 3. 4° 1723. Opening a new Church. The honour and virtue of building, repairing, and adorning Churches, and the Sacredness of them, when built and consecrated.
Popery truly stated and briefly confuted. 8° 1726.
* Luke vi. 29. 8° 1726. Ministerial Virtue. *Worc.* Oxon.
Luke xxiii. 2P. 4° 1729. Jan. 30. b. Lord Mayor. *Bod. Worc.* Oxon. *Queen's.* Camb.
Prov. xiv. 34. 8° 1730. b. Gov. of *Lond.-Hosp. Queen's.* Camb.
James i. 21, 22. 4° 1730. Easter-Tuesday. Preaching, hearing, and practising the word of God. *Queen's.* Camb.
Lady Moyer's. Lect. 8° 1729, 1730, 1731.
Mark x. 14. 12° 1737. The case of Infant-baptism.
Gal. iv. 18. 8° 1732. Assize. Of religious Zeal. *Worc. Linc.* Ox.
Eccles. vii. 16. 8° 1739. 4 s. Ag. Methodists. The nature, folly, sin, and danger of being righteous overmuch. *Bal. Linc.* Ox.
Gal. vi. 2. 4° 1742. Ann. meet. Char. Sch. *All S.* Oxon.
Matt. x. 16. 4° 1743. Conc. ad Cler. Lond. *Queen's.* Cam. *Sion.*
3 Disc.

3 Disc. in 8° 1747. Explaining some illustrious Prophecies &c. prefixed to his Notes on the 4 Gospels. *Sion.*
28 Serm. in 2 Vol. 8° 1752. On moral and practical Subjects. *Magd. New C.* Oxon. *Queen's.* Camb.

TRAVERS Walter, V. of Wellington, Somersetf.
Pf. cxxvi. 4. 16

TREBECK Andr. DD. R. of St. George's, Hanover-Square, Lond.
13 Serm. in 8° 1730.
Prov. iii. 27. 8° 1733. Ch. for St. George's Hosp. *Ch. Ch.* Ox. *Queen's.* Camb. *Brit. M.*
Phil. iv. 6. 4° 1739. Char. in the hard Frost.
Gal. vi. 10. 4° 1744. b. the Sons of the Clergy. *Brit. M.*
2 Sam. i. 14. 4° 1746. Jan. 30 b. Commons.

TREBELL Joseph, M. A. V. of Tackbrook, Warwicksf.
* Serm. in 8° 1703.
* Pf. xxxvii. 16. 8° 1703. Assize.
* Isai. lv. 4, 5. 8° 1703. A Vol. Christ exalted.

TRELAWNEY Jonathan Sir, Bart. Bp. of Exeter.
Josh. xxiii. 8, 9. 4° 1702. Th. Nov. 12. b. Queen, Lords and Commons. *Ch. Ch. All S. Magd. Or.* Oxon. *Queen's. St. John's. Cl. H.* Camb. *Sion.*

TREN John
* 1 Thess. iv. 13, 14. 8° 1728. Fun. of *Daniel Gilson. Queen's.* C.
* Acts xxiv. 14. 8° 1734.

TRENCHARD John, M. A. R. of Whraxhall, Somersetf.
Pf. cxviii. 22–24. 4° 1694. May 29. b. Lord Mayor.

TREVANNION Hugh, V. of West Alvington, Devon.
* 2 Chron. xix. 7. 4° 1740. *Exon.* Assize.
* Jer. xxii. 15, 16. 4° 1740. *Exon.* Assize.

TREVEGAR Luke, M. A. R. of Herst Monceaux, and Preb. of Chichester.
* John xx. 22. 4° 1754. Conf. of Bp. Ashburnham.

TREVETHICK William
* Isai. xi. 25. 8° 1660. Fun.

TREVOR Richard, Hon. Bp. of Durham.
Isai. v. 20, 21. 4° 1745. Nov. 5. b. Lords. *All S. Worc.* Oxon. *Queen's.* Camb.
1 Cor. x. 11. 4° 1747. Jan. 30. b. Lords. *Worc.* Oxon.
Dan. xii. 3. 4° 1747. Ann. meet. Char. Sch. *All S. Worc.* Oxon.
Luke ii. 32. 4° 1750. Prop. of Gospel. *Worc.* Oxon. *Brit. M.*
Matt. xxvi. 11. 4° 1751. b. Gov. of *Lond.*-Infirmary. *Wadh.* Ox.

TREVOR William, Cur. of St. Alphage, Sion Coll. London.
Isai. lviii. 13, 14. 8° 1721. To a relig. Society of young men.
Hab. iii. 5. 8° 1722. The terror of God's judgments.

TRIBBEKO John, Chapl. to George Prince of Denmark.
2 Sam. iii. 31, 32, 38. 4° 1709. Fun. of that Prince.
* Deut. viii. 1–3. 8° 1710. Farew. s. The christian Traveller, preached to the Palatines before their leaving England.

TRIMNEL

TRIMNEL Charles, Bp. of Winchester.
 Matt. vii. 12. 4° 1697. County-Feast. The duty of a christian towards his Neighbour. *Queen's.* Camb.
 Pf. cxvi. 1, 2. 4° 1697. Th. Decr. 2. *Magd.* Ox. *St. John's.* Ca.
 Pf. cvi. 7, 8. 4° 1704. Th. for Successes under John Duke of Malborough. *Pub. L. Cl. H.* Camb.
 2 Kings iv. 1, 2. 4° 1707. b. the Sons of the Clergy. *Ch. Ch. Or. Wadh.* Oxon. *Queen's. St. John's.* Camb.
 Prov. xxi. 30, 31. 4° 1708. Fast. Jan. 14. b. Commons. *Ch. Ch. Bod. Univ. Or. Magd. Worc.* Oxon. *Cl. H. Queen's.* Camb.
 Rom. xii. 13. 8° 1708. *Norwich.* Charity-Sch. *Queen's.* Camb.
 Col. ii. 6, 7. 8° 1709. Farewel. Jan. 30. *Magd.* Oxon. *Queen's.* Camb. *Eton.*
 Pf. xx. 6. 4° 1709. Th. b. Lords. Feb. 17. *Ch. Ch. Magd. Worc.* Oxon. *Sion.*
 Matt. xi. 5. 4° 1709. Prop. of Gospel. *Ch. Ch. Magd.* Oxon. *Pub. L.* Camb. *Sion.*
 1 Cor. xii. 24, 25. 4° 1710. Spitt. M. *Bod. Ch. Ch. Magd. Linc.* Oxon. *Pub. L.* Camb. *Eton.*
 Rom. xv. 13. 4° 1711. Collection for the Minister at *Tunbridge. Ch. Ch.* Oxon. *Pub. L.* Camb. *Brit. M.*
 Prov. xvii. 14. 4° 1712. Jan. 30. b. Lords. *Magd. Worc.* Oxon. *Pub. L. Queen's.* Camb. *Sion.*
 Ephes. v. 11. 4° 1712. Ref. of Manners. *Ch. Ch. Oriel.* Oxon. *Brit. M.*
 Heb. x. 24. 4° 1715. Spitt. M. *Ch. Ch.* Oxon. *Queen's.* Camb.
 Col. iii. 15. 4° 1715. At *Tunbridge. Ch. Ch. Or.* Oxon. *Queen's.* Camb. *Brit. M.*

TRIMNEL David, M. A. R. of Stoke-Hammond, Bucks.
 Rom. xiii. 4. 8° 1714. Assize. End and Usefulness of Government. *Ch. Ch.* Oxon.

TRIMNELL William, DD. Dean of Winchester.
 Matt. x. 16. 4° 1727. Conc. ad Cler. Synod. *Queen's.* Camb.

TRIPP Robert, M. A. R. of Boneleigh, and Lushleigh, Devon, and Chapl. to the Earl of Egremont.
 * - - - - 178 . Fast.

TROTT Edmund, LL. D. Chapl. to the Earl of Hadington.
 2 Chron. xxxii. 7, 8. 8° 1746. On the Rebellion.

TROUGHEAR Thomas, M. A. Fell. of Queen's Coll. Oxon. V. of Carisbrook &c. in the Isle of Wight.
 2 Thess. iii. 10. 8° 1730. On Work-houses.
 1 Sam. ii 30. 8° 1733. *Oxon.* Elect. of a Mayor. *Linc.* Oxon.

TROUTBECK John, M. A. late of Queen's Coll. Oxon.
 2 Tim. ii. 19. 8° 1710. Assize. The good old Principles, the safest way to Salvation. *Worc. Linc.* Oxon.

TROUTBECK John,   Curate of Edenhall, and Lonwathby, Cumberland.
 * Prov. xxix. 15. 8° 1778. The pious Education, and timely Correction of Children recommended.

TRUSTLER

TRUSTLER John, DD.
* Prov. xi. 16. 8° 1759. On the Death of the Prince of Orange.

TUCKER Josiah, DD. Dean of Gloucester.
* Luke xiv. 12–14. } 8° 1749. Diff. *Queen's*. Camb.
* Rom. xiii. 1–4.
* Prov. xxii 6. 4° 1766. An. meet. char. Schools. *Wore*. Oxon.
* 6 Serm. in 12° 1773. On important Subjects.
* 17 Serm. in 8° 1776. On some of the most important Points on natural and revealed Religion, representing the Happiness both of the present and future life. *Queen's*. Camb.

TUCKER William, V. of Cobham, Surrey.
Lam. v. 16, 17. 4° 1702. Royal Fun.
Mal. iii. 8, 9. 4° 1704. Fast. (ag. Sacrilege.) The cause of God's Wrath. *St. John's*. Camb.

TUCKNEY Anthony, DD. successively Master of Eman. and St. John's Coll. and Regius Professor of Divinity in Camb.
Acts iv. 12. 8° 16.
1 Cor. xv. 55. 8° 16
40 Serm. in 4° 1676. Upon sev. occasions. *Bod. Pub. L. C. Sion*.

TULLIE George, M. A. Sub-Dean of York, Preacher of St. Nicholas at Newcastle upon Tyne, R. of Gateside, Northumberland.
Exod xx. 4, 5. 4° 1686. Of the worship of Images. *Bod. Ch. Ch. Magd. Sion*.
Phil. iv. 5. 4° 1689. b. Lord Mayor. Of Moderation. *Ch. Ch. Jes*. Oxon. *Pub. L*. Camb. *Sion*.
Prov. xxix. 2. 4° 1691. *York*. Th. Oct. 19. *Bod*.

TULLY Thomas, M. A. Chancellor of Carlisle.
Rev. xiv. 13. 8° 1688. Fun. of Bp. Rainbow. *Bod. Pub. L*. Cam.

TUNSTALL James, DD. R. of Rochdale, Lancashire.
Ps. cxxvi 3. 4° 1746 May 29. b. Commons. *Queen's*. C. Br. M.
* Academica or several Disc. on the Certainty, Distinction, and Connection of natural and revealed Religion, *viz.*
* Matt. xiii.   8° 1759. Conc. ad Cler. pro Grad. S. T. B.
* 1 Thess. v. 21. 8° 17 . 2 Disc.
* 1 Cor. iv. 2. 8° 17 . Vis. Character and duty of the Stewards of God's Mysteries.
* Lev. xviii. 4. 8° 17 . The similar Properties and Agreement of nat. and revealed Religion. *Braz. N. Worc. Ox. Queen's*. C.

TURNBULL George
* - - - - 1766. Fun.

TURNER Bryan, DD. Chaplain to the Earl of Carlisle, R. of Solderne, Oxon.
2 Tim. i. 7. 4° 1677. b. Lord Mayor. *Bod. Univ. C. C. C*. Oxon. *Pub. L. St. John's*. Camb. *Sion*.
Rev. xix. 10. 4° 1681. b. Lord Mayor. The Demonstration of the Spirit for the Confirmation of the Christian Faith. *C. C. C*. Oxon. *Pub L*. Camb.

TURNER D*a*niel, M. A. Minister of the Gospel at Abingdon, Berks.
* John xiv. 1. 8° 1761, Fun. of Mrs. *Tompkins.*
* 2 Tim. i. 12. 4° 1769. Fun. of Rev. Mr. *Joseph Stennett.*
* Meditat. in 12° 1771. *Abingdon.* On select Passages of Scripture.
* Amos ii. 11. 8° 1777. The christian Ministry considered.
* Col. iii.¹ 13. 8° 1780. b. Dissenting Clergy. On the Revival of a Dissenting Church at *Oxford.*

TURNER Daniel, M. A. of Woolwich, Kent.
* Expositions in 8° 1775. On select Passages of Scripture—to which is added 2 serm. on
* Rev. iii. 21.

TURNER Francis, Bp. of Ely.
    Lam. iv. 19–21. 4° 1681. Jan. 30. b. King. *Bod. Magd. Ch. Ch. Oxon. Pub. L. St. John's. Camb. Sion.*
    1 Tim. ii. 1, 2. 4° 1682. b. Lord Mayor. *C. C. C Oxon. St. John's. Camb. Sion.*
    Pf. cxliv. 9, 10. 5° 1683. b. King. Th. Sept. 9. *Ch. Ch. C. C. C. Queen's. Oxon. Pub. L. St. John's. Camb. Sion.*
    Hosea vi. 2, 3. 4° 1684. Easter. b. King. *C. C. C. Oxon. Pub. L. St. John's. Camb. Sion.*
    Luke xiv. 13, 14. 4° 1684. Spitt. M. b. Lord Mayor. *C. C. C. Ch. Ch.* Oxon. *Pub. L. St. John's.* Camb.
    Rom. iii. 8. 4° 1684. Nov. 5. b. King. *Ch. Ch. C. C. C. Queen's. Jes.* Oxon. *St. John's.* Camb.
    Gen. xviii. 19. 4° 1685. b. the Sons of the Clergy. *Ch. Ch. C. C. C. Wadh.* Oxon. *St. John's. Pub. L.* Camb.
    Acts v. 28. 4° 1685. Jan. 30. b. King. *Ch. Ch. Queen's. Magd.* Oxon. *St. John's.* Camb.
    1 Chron. xxix. 23. 4° 1685. Coron. *Bod. Ch. Ch. C. C. C. Magd. Or. All S. Worc. Queen's.* Oxon. *Pub. L. St. John's.* Camb.

TURNER Francis, M. A.
    Isai. xii. 2. 4° 1746. Th. after Rebellion.

TURNER *James*
* Jerem. xxxi. 33. 8° 1771. Fun.

TURNER John, M. A. Fell. of Christ's Coll. Camb. and Hospitaler of St. Thomas, Southwark.
    1 Cor. v. 7, 8. 4° 1679. b. Lord Mayor. Ag. Transubstantiation. *Pub. L.* Camb. *Sion.*
    Exod. iv. 21. 8° 1683. 2 s. The middle way betwixt Necessity and Freedom. *Bod. Pub. L.* Camb.
    Eccles. x. 20. 4° 1683. Th. Sept. 9. For the Discovery and Disappointment of the republican Plot. *Pub. L. St. John's.* Ca.
    Pf. cxxxix. 7–10. 4° 1683. Of the divine Omnipresence. *Sion.*
    1 Cor. xiv. 40. 8° 1683. b. Lord Mayor. *Ch. Ch. C. C. C.* Oxon.
    ——————— 20. 8° 1684. The true time of our Saviour's Passover. *Bod. Univ.* Oxon. *Sion.*
    Deut. xxv. 5. 8° 1685. Boaz and Ruth. *Bod. C. C. C.* Oxon.
    John iii. (or xiii.) 35. 4° 1686. Assize. Charity recommended. *Bod. Sion.*

OF AUTHORS, &c.

Matt. v. 3. 4° 1687. The praise of Humility. *Sion.*
Judges xvii. 6. 4° 1688. } Jan. 29. On her Majesty's Conception.
} June 17. On the Birth of the Prince.

TURNER John, DD. V. of Greenwich, Kent, and Chapl. to the Prince of Wales.
 Boyle's Lectures 8° 1708. or fo. 1739. V. II. *St. John's. Magd. Jef.* Oxon.
 Luke x. 16. 8° 1709. Vis. The sinfulness of despising christian Ministers. *Magd.* Oxon. *Queen's.* Camb. *Eton.*
 Pf. lxviii. 34, 35. 4° 1715. May 29. Public deliverances wrought by the power of God. *Ch. Ch.* Oxon.
 Matt. xxii. 21. 8° 1716. Accession. b. Lord Mayor. A national Establishment, the true foundation of Allegiance. *Ch. Ch.* Oxon. *Eton.*

TURNER *John*
 * Gen v. 24. 8° 1769. Fun.

TURNER Roger, M. A.
 2 Kings xi. 12. 4° 1661.

TURNER Seth, M. A. V. of Mendham, Suffolk.
 Job xix. 25–27. 8° 1713. Fun.   The good christian's support under Troubles, enforced from Job's firm belief of a Resurrection.

TURNER Tho. DD President of C. C. C. Ox. and Chapl. in Ord.
 Isai. i. 26. 4° 1685. May 29. b. King. *Bod. All S. Ch. Ch. C.C.C.* Oxon *Pub. L. St. John's.* Camb. *Sion.*

TURNER Thomas,   Cur. of Dorking.
 * Deut vi. 13. 4° 1754. Assize.

TURNER *William*
 * - - - - 8° 1776. Fast.
 * Tit ii. 1. 8° 1781. b. Dissent. Clergy. On St. Paul's sense of Soundness in Religion.

TURNOR Thomas, M. A. V. of Newcastle upon Tyne.
 James i 27. 8° 1731. b. Sons of Clergy at *Newcastle. Sion.*

TURTON Septimus, LL. B. R. of Sulham, Berks.
 1 Cor. xi. 19. 8° 1749. April 9.
 * Acts x 38. 4° 1752.

TUTTY William,   Fell. of Dulwich Coll. Surrey.
 Luke x. 37. 8° 1741. The duty of universal Benevolence.
 John iv. 10. 8° 1741. Divine love exemplified in the Redemption of mankind.

TUTTY William, M. A. Lect. of All Saints, Herts.
 1 Cor. xv. 33. 8° 1747. b. Criminals. The want of a religious Education, and keeping bad Company destructive to religious Principles.

TWELLS Leonard, DD. R. of St. Matthew's, Friday-street, Lond. Preb. of St. Paul's, Lect. of St. Dunstan's in the West.
 24 Serm. at Boyle's Lect. 8 at Lady Moyer's, and 3 occasional serm. in 2 Vol. 8° 1743. *Bod. All S. Bal. C. C. C. New C. Worc.* Oxon. *King's.* Camb.

TWENTYMAN T.　　　　　V. of Caſtle Sowerby, Cumberland.
　* Iſai. i. 19,20. 12° 1779. Faſt. A ſtrict conformity between
　　our Prayers and Actions earneſtly recommended.
[TWISSE Robert]
　* Lam. iv. 20. 4° 1665. Jan. 30. Dr. Wi's. L. London.
TYLER John, Bp. of Landaff, and Dean of Hereford.
　1 John iii. 3. 4° 1694. Lent. b. Queen. Bod. Pub. L. Camb.
　Eccleſ. viii. 14. 4° 1707. Jan. 30. b. Lords. Hert. Oxon. Sion.
TYREL Duke, M. A. R. of St. Paul's, Dublin.
　* Epheſ. iv. 11,12. 4° 1717. Conſ. of Bp. Lambert.
TYSON Thomas
　1 Cor. xv. 58. 8°
VANDER Eyken Sebaſtian,　Miniſter of the Church of England,
　　and Reader to the Dutch congregation at the royal Chapel
　　of St. James's.
　James i. 12. 4° 1706. Jan. 30.
　Pſ. cxxii. 6-9. 12° 1712. Faſt. Jan. 16.
VAUGHAN Thomas, M. A. Miniſter of Edengale, Staffordſhire,
　　and V. of Eccles, Lancaſhire.
　2 Cor. xiii. 11. 4° 1734. Elect. of Member of Parliament.
　2 Chron. xx. 12. 8° 1744. *Coventry*. Faſt. April 11.
　* Joel ii. 12. 8° 1747. Faſt.
VEAL Edward
　Pſ. lxii. 2. 4° 1675. m. e. P. Good works not meritorious of Sal-
　　vation. p. 401.
　Iſai. xxvii. 11. 4° 1676. ſ. m. e. C. Spiritual Knowledge. p.
　　108. *Bod.*
　Luke xxiii. 42. 4° 1690. c. m. e. Death-bed Repentance. p.
　　230. *Bod.*
　‡ * Neh. xiii. 14. 4° 1694. Fun. of *Jer. Butt.* Brit. M.
　* 5 Practical Diſc. in 12° 1703.
　* 2 Practical Diſc. in 12° 1705.
VENN H.　　M. A. V. of Huddersfield, Yorkſ.
　* James iii. 17. 4° 1758. Nov. 5. Popery a perfect Contraſt to
　　the Religion of Chriſt. *Queen's*. Camb.
　* Serm. in 8° 1759. On ſeveral Subjects.
　Matt. x. 35,36. 8° 1759. Real and nominal chriſtians compared.
　* Ezek. xx. 13. 8° 1760. Call to obſerve the Lord's-day.
　* Col. iv. 17. 8° 1760. Viſ. The duty of a Pariſh Prieſt &c.
　* Phil. i. 21. 8° 1763. Fun. of the Rev. Mr. Grimſhaw.
　* Zech. ix. 12. 8° 1769. Aſſize at *Kingſton*, Surrey. Man a con-
　　demned Sinner, and Chriſt a ſtrong Hold to ſave him.
　* Iſai. viii. 18. 8° 1770. *Bath.* On the Death of the Rev. Geor.
　　Whitfield. *Queen's* Camb.
　‡ * Ezra v. 1.&c. 1775. Eſſay on the Prophecy of Zacharias.
　* Pſ. cxix. 136. 8° 1778. Converſion of Sinners, the greateſt
　　Charity.
VENN Richard, M. A. R. of St. Antholine, London.
　Tracts and Serm. in 8° 1740. On ſev. occaſions. *Bod. Queen's.* C.

VENNING Ralph, M. A.
  Rom. vii. 13. 8° 1660. Sin the Plague of Plagues. *Bod.*
  * Heb. x. 23. 4° 1663. V. Coll. of Farew. f. *Magd.* Camb.
  * Ifai. xxxviii. 17. 8° 1675. 3 f. Sick-bed-Studies.
VERNEY Geo. DD. Lord Willoughby de Broke, Dean of Windfor.
  Job ii. 10. 4° 1705. b. Queen. Of Providence. *Ch. Ch.* Oxon.
  Acts xx 35. 4° 1712. Ann. meeting Char. Schools.
VERNON Edw. DD. R. of St. George's Bloomfbury-fquare, Lond.
  * Pf. cxix. 73. 4° 1753. (2d Edit.) b. Coll. of Phyficians.
VESEY John, Abp. of Tuam, Ireland.
  Pf. cxxii. 6. 4° 1683. *Dublin.* Affize. *Brit. M.*
  Pf. lxxxii. 6, 7. 4° 1684. b. King. 2d S. after Eafter. *Magd.* Ox.
  Pf. cii. 13. 4° 1689. Th. b. Prot. of Ireland. *Ch. Ch. Magd.*
    Oxon. *Sion.*
  Judges xvii. 6. 4° 1693. b. Lord Lieutenant. *Or. Ch. Ch.* Oxon.
VESEY William, M A. R. of the City of New York.
  Pf. xxxvii. 37. 4° 1709. *New York.* Fun. of Lord Lovelace. *Br. M.*
VICKERS William, M. A. (Author of the Companion to the Altar.)
  Pf. xciv. 19. 8° 1708. Sacrament. Chriftian Support under the
    Troubles of this world.
  Rom. xii. 18. 8° 1709. Sacrament.
VINCENT Nathaniel, M. A.
  * 1 Cor. xv. 55. 4° 1674. Fun.
  1 Cor. xiv. 55. 4° 1675. m. e. C. Prayer fhould be in a known
    Tongue. p. 295. *Bod.*
  * 1 Sam. xxv. 1. 4° 1677. Fun. of the Rev. *Thomas Cawton.* St.
    John's. Camb.
  2 Pet. iii. 18. 4683. c. m. e. How we may grow in the Know-
    ledge of Chrift. p. 304. *Bod.*
  1 Pet. ii. 21. 4° 1690. c. m. c. Xt our Example. p. 3114. *Bed.*
  * Difc. in 8° 1695.
VINCENT Nathaniel, DD. Fell. of Clare-Hall, Camb. and Chapl.
    in Ord.
  Pf. viii. 5. 4° 1684. b. King. The right notion of Honour.
    Queen's. Oxon. *Cl. H.* Camb. *Sion*
VINCENT Thomas, M. A. R. of St. Magdalen, Milk-ftreet, London,
    before the Ejection. 1662.
  Ifai. lvii. 1, 2. 8° 1667.
  1 Tim. iv. 1—3. 4° 1675. m. e. P. Popifh doctrine forbidding to
    marry is devilifh, and Wickednefs. p. 578.
  Pf. xxxii. 1. 4° 1676. f. m. e. Of Forgivenefs. p. 700. *Bod.*
VYNER Robert, DD.
  Luke ii. 1. 8° 1733. Againft the Excife.
VINES Richard
  * John vi. 44. 4° 1662.
  * Rom. ii. 28, 29. 4° 1662.
  * Serm. in 8° 1667. *Dr. Wi's. L.* London.

VINK Peter
   Luke vi. 22. 4° 1675. m. e. P. Proteſtants ſeparated for Chriſt's name. p. 492.
   Matt. xvi. 26. 4° 1683. c. m. e. How we may beſt know the Worth of the Soul. p. 913.
   * Rom. vi 6,7. 4° 1676. m. e. G. Orig. Sin in duelling. p. 106,

VIVIAN Thomas,   V. of Cornwood, Devon.
   John xxi. 17. 12° 1751. Viſ.

VYSE William, LL.D. R. of Lambeth.
   * Deut. xxiii. 9. 4° 1778. Faſt. b. Commons.

ULTYE (or UTYE) Emanuel, DD. V. of Chigwell, Eſſex, and Chaplain in Ord.
   1 Sam. xv. 22. fo. 1661.

UMFREVILLE Charles, LL. B. V. of Bradfield, Eſſex, and of Acton, Suffolk.
   Luke xi. 1, 2. 8° 1736.
   18 Serm. in 8° 1739.
   * 3 Diſc. in 8° 1759. On important Subjects, viz.
   * Acts iv. 12. Extent of natural and revealed Religion.
   * Deut xxix. 29. On the Trinity.
   * 1 John v. 7. On St. Athanaſius's Creed.

UNWIN Will. M. A. R. of Stock cum Ramſden-Belhouſe, Eſſex.
   * Rom. vii. 2. 12° 1773. The right Uſe of the Law.

USHER James, Abp. of Armagh.
   * 20 Serm. (Poſth.) in fo. 1678. Preached at *Oxford* before his Majeſty or elſwhere. Bod. Magd. *Queen's*. Oxon. Pub. L. Cam.

W.   I.
   Deut. xxxii. 29. 4° 1704. Fun. of Capt. George Pickering.

W.   J.   (author of the Clergyman's Companion in viſiting the ſick.)
   Rom. x. 15. 8° 1717.

W.   T.
   Tit. i. 16. 4° 1695.

WADDINGTON Edward, Bp. of Chicheſter.
   1 Cor. iv. 1. 8° 1718. Conſ. of Bp. Kennet. *Eton*.
   Luke xxii. 32. 8° 1721. Prop. of Goſpel. *Ch. Ch. Oriel*. Oxon. *Queen's*. Camb.
   Jer. xxvi 14, 15. 4° 1729. Jan. 30. b. Lords. *Queen's*. Ca. *Eton*.

WADE George. DD. V. of Gainſborough, and Preb. of Lincoln.
   James iii. 17. 8° 1720. Viſ.
   Rev. ix. (or xix.) 20. 8° 1722.
   Matt. xi. 2–5. 8° 1729. p. 1. Sund. b. Xtmas. } *Queen's*. Camb.
   1 Cor. xv. 20. 8° 1729. p. 25. Eaſter-day.   } *Eton*.

WADE John,   Miniſter of Hammerſmith, Middleſex.
   * Epheſ. v. 16. 12° 1692. On redeeming the time.
   1 John i. 9. 8° 1697. Confeſſion of Sins.

WADE Peter, M. A.
   * Deut. xiv. 11. 4° 1751. Aſſize.

WADS-

WADSWORTH Thomas, Minister of the Gospel in London.
    Heb. x. 12. 4° 1675. m. e. P. Christ crucified, the only proper Gospel Sacrafice. p. 784.
    1 Cor. xi. 24. 4° 1676. f. m. e. How it is every christian's duty to partake of the Lord's supper. p. 231.

WAGENER Peter, M. A. R of Sisted in Essex.
    Num. xxiii. 23. 8° 1716. Th.
    * Ecclef. vii. 1. 8° 1726. Fun. of Mr. S. Dubois, an eminent Painter.

WAGSTAFFE John, M. A. R. of little Wenlock, Salop.
    Josh. xxiv. 24–16. 4° 1684. The duty of household-Governors.

WAGSTAFFE Thomas, M. A. Cancellor of Litchfield, R. of St. Margaret Patton &c.
    Prov. i. 10–16. 4° 1683. Th. Sept. 9. For Victory over the Rebels. *Ch. Ch.* Oxon. *Eton.*
    1 Cor. viii. 12. 4° 1685. b. Lord Mayor. *All S. Ch. Ch. C. C. C. Magd.* Oxon. *St. John's.* Camb.
    1 Kings i. 5. 4° 1685. Th. July 26. *Bcd.*
    1 Pet. iii. 3–8. 4° 1688. County-F. *Bod. Ch. Ch.* Ox. *Pub. C.* Ca.

WAINHOUSE Richard, V. of Keevil, Wilts, and Chaplain to the Duke of St. Alban's.
    1 Tim. vi. 5. 8° 1745. On Rebellion.
    2 Tim. ii. 24. 8° 1745. On Rebellion.
    * 2 Tim. ii. 24. 4° 1757. *Bath.* Nov. 5. *Queen's.* Oxon.

WAITE Tho. M. A. Lect. of the Temple, and St. Vedast, London.
    Tit. i. 7. 4° 1728. Conf. of Bp. Sherlock.

WAKE Rob. M. A. Fell. of Trin. Coll. and V. of Fritwell, Oxon.
    A Rationale upon some texts of Scripture 8° 1701.
    Mal. iii. 8, 9. 4° 1703. On Tythe-stealing.

WAKE Robert, M. A. V. of Ogborn St. Andrew, Wilts.
    1 Tim. iv. 16. 4° 1704. Vif. *Pub. L.* Camb.
    1 Cor. xiii. 13. 8° 1712. Ch.
    1 Tim. iv. 8. 8° 1713.
    Tit. ii. 7, 8. 4° 1723. Vif.

WAKE William, Abp. of Canterbury.
    Joel ii. 15–17. 4° 1684. Jan. 30. at *Paris. All S.* Oxon. *Sion.*
    10 Serm. and 2 Disc. (2d Edit.) in 8° 1716. Vol. I. On several occasions. *Bod. Ch. Ch. Magd. Or.* Oxon. *Pub. L.* Camb. *Dr. Ws's. L.* London.
    8 Serm. and a pract. Disc. on swearing. Vol. II. in 8° 1702. *Bod. Ch. Ch. Magd. Or.* Ox. *Pub. L* Camb. *Sian. Dr. Ws's. L.* Lond.
    14 Serm. preached upon sev. occasions. V. III. in 8° 1722. *Bod. Ch. Ch. Magd. Or.* Oxon. *Pub. L.* Camb. *Dr Ws's. L.* Lond.

WAKEFIELD Thomas, B. A. Minister of Richmond.
    * Deut. xxix. 9. 4° 1780. Fast.

WAKEMAN Edw. R. of St. Matthew's, Friday-street, Lond.
    Acts xiii. 4, 5. 4° 1664. The pattern of ecclesiastical Ordination.

WAKER Nathaniel, R. of St. Catherine, Coleman, London.
    Job xiv. 1. 4° 1664. Fun.

[WAKES

[WAKES John]
    * Disc. in 12° 1747.
WALDER James
    * 2 Cor. xiii. 11. 8° 1779. b. Dissenting Clergy. The Perfection of the christian Character.
WALFORNE Joseph, M.A.
    * Num. xxv. 11. 4° 1701. Fast.
WALKER   Minister and Governor of London-Derry.
    ‡ * Judges xvii. 20. 4° 1689. b. Lords. Persecution stated on the Protestant Victory over the French and Irish Papists. *Br. M.*
WALKER Anthony, DD. of St. John's Coll. Oxon. R. of Fyfield, Essex, and Chapl. in Ord.
    2 Chron xxiii. 11. 4° 1660. May 30. On the King's Entry into London.
    Luke vii. 12, 13. 4° 1664. Fun. of Lord Rich. Planctus unigeniti, et spes resuscitandi.
    2 Sam. iii 38. 4° 1673. Fun. of the Earl of Warwick. *Bod.*
    Prov. xxxi. 29–31. 8° 1678. Fun. of the Countess of Warwick. The virtuous Woman found. *Bod. Sion.*
    2 Sam xiv. 12. 8° 1678. Assize. *Bod.*
    Eccles. x. 1. 4° 1682. Apoth.-Feast. *Sion.*
    Luke xii. 40. 12° 1682. Fun. of Nath. Duckfield.
    Several Disc in 12° 1682. On the great Evil of Procrastination.
    Rev. xiv. 7. 12° 1684. 2 s. At Tunbridge.
    Prov. xiv. 34. 4° 1691. The true Interest of nations impartially stated. *Bod.*
WALKER George,   Cur. of Twickenham Chapel, Middlesex.
    Eccles. xii. 1. 8° 1728. The necessity and Advantage of an early Piety.
WALKER George, M.A. V. of Rickmansworth, Herts.
    Luke xiv. 24. 8° 1730. Worldly Business no Excuse for not receiving the Sacrament.
WALKER George, M.A. Preb. of St. Paul's, London.
    Matt. vii. 12. 8° 1738. On the King's birth-day. Religion necessary both to constitute the Nature, and to inforce the Practice of moral Virtue.
WALKER George,   Minister of the Gospel at Nottingham.
    * Rom. i. 28. 8° 1776. Fast.
    ‡ * 1 Chron. xxii. 16. 8° 1778. Fast.
WALKER John, M.A. of Ch. Ch. Coll Oxon. Curate of Wood-Hay, Hants.
    Rom. xiii. 1. 8° 1684. Necessity of Subjection &c. *Eton.*
WALKER John, M.A. V. of Ledbury, Herefordshire.
    1 Kings xviii. 21. 8° 1710. Prophets Plea for Truth. *Linc.* Oxon.
    Ps. cxxiv. 6, 7. 8° 1710. Th. Nov. 5. *All S. Linc.* Oxon.
    * Acts xxiv. 16. 8° 1729. Sev Disc. Conscience displayed.
WALKER John, DD. Preb. of St. Peter's in Exeter.
    1 Cor. i. 20. 8° 1723. Assize. No contradiction in the received doctrine of the blessed Trinity. *Sion.*

WALKER Nathaniel
 * Prov. xiv. 1. 4° 1664.
WALKER *Robert,* one of the Ministers of the High Church at Edinburgh.
 * Matt. vi. 10. 12° 1748. b. the Society for propagating Xtian Knowledge.
 * Serm. in 8° 1765. 2 Vol. On practical Subjects. *Bod. Sion.*
WALKER Samuel, B. A. Curate of Truro, Cornwall.
 * Amos iv. 12. 8° 1756. 2 s. Fast. Earthquake.
 * 52 Serm. in 3 Vol. 8° 1763. On the baptismal Covenant, the Creed and ten Commandments.
 * 1 Sam. xx; 3. 8° 1753. Fun. of a person drowned.
WALKER Thomas, B. D. Fell. of Sidney Sussex Coll. Camb.
  Prov. xii. 26. 4° 1693. *Camb.* Assize. *Pub. L. St. John's.* Camb. *Brit. M.*
WALKER Thomas, Minister at North Chapel.
 * John iv. 23, 24. 8° 1753. Open. of a new Chapel. The christian Worship explained and recommended.
WALKER William, B. D. of Trin. Coll. Camb.
 * Matt xxviii. 19. 8° 1678. A Vol. Doctrine of Baptism.
WALKINGTON Edward, Chaplain to the House of Commons in Ireland.
  Isai. v. 9, 10. 4° 1692. *Dublin.*
WALL John, DD. Canon of Ch. Ch. Oxon. and Preb. of Sarum.
  Rom. v. 11. 8° 1660. Christian Reconcilement. *Bod.*
  Cant. iii. 9, 10. 8° 1660. Conc. ad Cler. Acad. *Bod.*
  Luke iii. 6. 8° 1662. *Oxon.* A divine Theatre, or a Stage for Christians. *Bod.*
WALLACE *Robert,* Minister of the Gospel at Moffat, Scotland.
  1 Thess. v. 20, 21. 8° 1731. b. Synod of Dumfries. The regard due to divine Revelation, and Pretences to it considered. *Bod.*
‡ * Ps. lxxiv. 20. 8° 1746. Rebellion. *Brit. M.*
 * James iii. 18. 8° 1746.
WALLER John, B. D. Fell. of C. C. C. Coll. Camb.
  Matt. xxii. 21. 4°. 1708. School-Feast. Religion and Loyalty.
  Luke xii. 48. 4° 1714. *Camb.* Commemor. *Queen's. St. John's.* Camb. *Brit. M.*
WALLIN Benjamin, Minister of the Gospel in London.
 * Luke xxiii. 34. 8° 1746. The compassion of the dying Saviour to his Crucifiers.
 * 2 Thess. v. 19. 8° 1748. b. young Men. Exhortation against quenching the Spirit.
 * Matt. xxii. 32. 8° 1754. Fun. of Mr. *Thomas Wildman.*
 * 1 Thess. v. 13. 8° 1755. Ord. of
 * 4 Serm. in 8° 1756. Occasioned by the late Earthquakes, and apprehensions of a French War.
 * Ps. cxviii. 27. 8° 1760. Th.
 * Sev. Disc. in 8° 1763.
 * - - - - 1763. Ord. of Mr. *Richard.*

 * 1 Cor. ix. 27. 8° 1764. 2 Difc. Chriftian's concern, that he may not be caſt-away.
 * 2 Sam. i. 27. 8° 1765. On the Death of Duke of Cumberland.
 * - - - - 8° 1766. Ord. of Mr. *Reynolds*.
 * 1 Theff. iv. 17. 8° 1767. Fun. of *Martha Keene*.
 * 1 Theff. iv. 14. 8° 17 Fun.
 * Heb. xi. 13. 8° 1769. Fun. of Mrs. *Rebecca Cox*.
 * 2 Cor. v. 1. 8° 1769. Fun. of Mr. *Thomas Cox*.
 * 1 Tim. ii. 8. 8° 1770. b. Diſſenting Clergy.
 * 1 Theff. v. 17. 8° 1771. On Prayer.
 * 2 Tim. iv. 7. 8° 1771. Fun. of Dr. *J. Gill*.
 * Gen. xviii. 19. 8° 1771. Importance of Family-religion.
 * 10 Difc. in 12° 1771. On the divine Filiation of Chriſt.
 * Pſ. xvi. 11. 8° 1773. Fun. of the Rev. Mr. *S. James*.
 * Rev. xxii. 17. 8° 1774. Fun.
 * Iſai. i. 26. 8° 1774. Choice of Reprefentatives.
 * Epheſ. ii. 22. 8° 1774. The Church, an Habitation of God through the Spirit.
 * Prov. xxv. 26. 12° 1775. A fallen Profeſſor.
 * 13 Difc. in 1776. On the Parable of the prodigal Son.
 * Job v. 26. 8° 1779. Fun. of Mrs. *Hannah Munn*.
 * Zech. iii. 2. 8° 1780. Fun. of the Rev. Mr. *Macgowan*.

WALLIN Edward
 * Iſai. liv. 5. 8° 1724. Fun.

WALLIS John, DD. Savilian Profeſſor of Geometry in Oxon. and Chaplain in Ord.
 1 Cor. xv. 20. 4° 1679. *Oxon*. Eaſter-day. The refurrection afferted. *Bod. All S. Or. Linc.* Oxon. *Pub. L.* Camb. *Eton*.
 John iii. 3. 4° 1682. 2 ſ. The neceſſity of Regeneration. *Bod. Pub. L.* Camb. *Sion*.
 * John xvii. 3. 4° 1691. 3 ſ. On the Trinity. *Bal. St. John'.* Oxon. *Brit. M.*
 Theolog. Difc. &c. ⎱ Pt. 1. 4° 1691. ⎱ *Bod. Bal. Magd. Or. St.* ⎰ Pt. 2. 4° 1692. ⎰ *John's.* Oxon. *Sion*.

WALLIS John, B. A. of Queen's Coll. Oxon.
 1 Cor. x. 32, 33 8° 1740. *Reading*. The duty of feeking all men's Salvation &c.
 * Serm. in 8°. 1748.

WALLIS William, Chapl. to Guy's Hofpital, London.
 James iii. 17. 4° 1730. Aſſize.

WALLS George, DD. Student of Ch. Ch. Oxon. Preb. of Worceſter, and R. of Holt, Norfolk.
 Neh. viii. 10. 4° 1681. County-Feaſt. *Ch. Ch.* Oxon. *Sion*.
 Jer. viii. 20. 4° 1704. Faſt. *Ch. Ch.* Oxon.
 Pſ. xxxix. 4. 4° 1706. Fun. of Mrs. Bromley. *Ch. Ch.* Oxon.
 Prov. xxiv. 29. 4° 1706. Aſſize. *Ch. Ch.* Oxon. *Brit. M.*
 1 Tim. 1–3. 8° 1715. Th. for Acceſſion.

[WALROND John]
 1 * Rom. xi. 13. 8° 1707. Dignity of the Miniſtry. *Brit. M.*
 John v. 35. 8° 1745. Fun.

WALSALL Francis, DD. R. of Sandy, Bedfordſ. Preb. of Weſt-
minſter, aud Chaplain in Ord.
2 Sam. xix. 14. 4° 1660. Th. *Bal.* Oxon.
Pſ. li. 17. 4° 1661. Cordiſragium, or the Sacrafice of a broken
Heart. *Bal.* Oxon.
WALSH Thomas
* 9 Serm. in 12° 1764.
WALTON W.   M. D. R. of Upton, Huntingdonſ.
* Heb. x. 23, 24. 4° 1766. *Camb.* Viſ. Religio Medici.
[WALWYN Robert]
* Serm. in 8° 1660. A general View of Fundamentals.
WALWYN William, B. D. Fell. of St. John's Oxon. V. of Eaſt-
Coker, Somerſetſ.
1 Sam. x. 24. 4° 1662. Th. *Univ. Or.* Oxon.
WANLEY Samuel, DD. R. of Elmly-Lovet, Worceſterſ.
* 1 Cor. xii. 25. 8° 1763. Infirmary. Affectionate concern for
one another recommended.
WAPLE Edward, B. D. Arch-Deacon of Taunton, V. of St. Se-
pulchre's, London.
30 Serm. Vol. I. in 8° (1714.) 1729. (2d Edit.) On ſeveral oc-
caſions. *St. John's. C. C. C.* Oxon.
20 Sermons Vol. II. in 8° 1718. On ſeveral Subjects. *St. John's.
C. C. C.* Oxon.
20 Serm. Vol. III. in 8° 1720. On ſeveral Subjects. *St. John's.
C. C. C.* Oxon.
WARBURTON W.   Miniſter of the Goſpel at Northampton.
‡ * Jer. xx. 29. 8° 1736. Diſcouragements of diſſent. Miniſters.
‡ * Jer. xxix. 7. 8° 1761.
WARBURTON William, Bp. of Glouceſter.
2 Pet. i. 5–7. 8° 1738. Viſ. for Confirmation. Faith working by
Charity to chriſtian Edification. Reprinted 1748. under the
Title of a "faithful Portrait of Popery." &c. *All S. Worc.* Ox.
Queen's. Camb. *Sion.*
Matt. v. 16. 8° 1742. Opening Infirmary at *Bath. Worc.* Oxon.
Queen's. Camb.
1 Pet. ii. 17. 8° 1745. At Mr. Allen's Chapel. *Worc.* Oxon.
Joel ii. 20. 8° 1745. Faſt for Rebellion. *Worc.* Oxon.
2 Cor. xiii. 17. 8° 1746. Th. after Rebellion. *All S. Worc.* Ox.
* Courſe of Sermons Vol. I. 8° 1753. Vol. II. 8° 1754. On the
principles of natural and revealed Religion. *Ch. Ch. Worc.* Ox.
* Pſ. xci. 1–3. 4° 1755. b. Gov. of *Lond.* -Small-pox. Hoſp.
* Rev. x. 11. 4° 1766. Prop. Goſpel. *Eraz. N.* Ox. *Queen's.* Ca.
* 1 Cor. xiii. 13. 4" 1767. b. Gov. of *Lond.* -Hoſp.
* Serm. in 8° Vol. III. 1767. On various ſubjects, and occaſions.
At the end is an Appendix containing 4 ſerm. 3 of which had
been publiſhed before.
WARD Abel, M. A. Arch-Deacon of Cheſter.
Rom. xiii. 7. 8° 1750. *Mancheſter.* Jan. 30. The duty of ren-
dering to all their Dues.

* - - - - 1756. Affize.
WARD Hamnett, M. D. V. of Stourminfter-Newton Caftle, Dorfet. and Preb. of Wells.
  Ephef. iii. 8. 4° 1674. Vif. *Bod. Ch. Ch.* Oxon. *Sion.*
WARD John, D. LL. F. R. R. P. G. C. and A. S. S. and T. B. M.
  ‡ * Differtations in 8° 1761. On feveral paffages of Scripture.
  * Serm. in 2 Vol. 8° 1775.

WARD John
  * 1 Cor. x. 33. 8° 1776. b. Diffenting Minifters.
WARD Jofeph, R. of Blakeney, Norfolk.
  * Rom. xii. 10. 12° 1726.
WARD Jofeph, M. A. V. of Preftbury, Chefhire.
  Pf. cvii. 2. 4° 1746. Th. after Rebellion.
  Col. iii. 14. 4° 1747. Affize.
  Pf. xxix. 11. 4° 1749. Affize.
  * John vii. 17. 4° 1760. Vif. The confiftent Proteftant.
WARD Richard
  Heb. xiii. 7. 8° 1718. Fun. of Dr. John Davis. *Brit. M.*
WARD Samuel, V. of Cotterfbrook, Northampton.
  * 2 Cor. xiii. 11. 8° 1774. Farew. f.
WARD Seth, Bp. of Salifbury.
  1 Cor. xv. 57. 4° 1670 Fun. of the Duke of Albermarle. The chriftian's Victory over Death. *Bod. All S. Univ. Ch. Ch. Magd.* Oxon. *Pub. L.* Camb. *Sion.*
  6 Serm. in 8° 1672. and 1674. *All S. Ch. Ch. C. C. C. Queen's. Magd.* Oxon. *Pub. L. Cl, H. Queen's.* Camb. *Sion.*
  Rom. i. 16. 4° 1673. An apology for the Mifferies of the Gofpel. *All S. C. C. C. Or. Jef.* Oxon. *St. John's.* Camb. *Sion.*
  2 Kings vi. 33. 4° 1674. Jan. 30. b. Lords. The cafe of Joram. *All S. Ch. Ch. C. C. C. Magd. Queen's.* Oxon. *Pub. L.* Camb.
WARD William, M. A. V. of Portfmouth, and Chapl. to the Earl of Warrington.
  James v. 19, 20. 4° 1700. Ref. of manners.
  Pf. xcvii. 1. 4° 1707. Th. Dec. 31. 1706.
  Pf. cl. 4-6. 1° 1718. Opening an Organ there.
WARHAM Francis
  * John xi. 11. 8° 1661. Fun.
WARING Robert, M. A. Student of Ch. Ch. Oxon.
  2 Sam. xii. 15. 4° 1672. Fun. of Mrs. Sufanna Gray. *Bod. Ch. Ch.* Oxon.
WARLY Jonas, DD. Arch-Deacon of Colchefter, V. of Witham, Effex, and Preb. of St. Paul's, London.
  Matt. xxiv. 3. 4° 1693. b. Lord Mayor. *Bod. Sion.*
WARNEFORD John, B. D. Camden-Profeffor of Hiftory in Oxon.
  * 20 Serm. in 2 Vol. 8° 1776. *Bod. St. John's.* Oxon.
WARNEFORD Richard, M. A. V. of St. Martin's Coney-ftreet, and fub Chantor of the Cathedral Church at York.
  * Serm. in 2 Vol. 8° 1757.

WARNER

WARNER Ferdinand, V. of Whitehaven, Hants.
  Matt. v. 14. 4° 1738. Vif. *Brit. M.*
WARNER Ferdinand, LL. D. R. of St. Michael, Queenhithe, and Holy Trinity, London.
  Ephef. v, 7. 4° 1748. Jan. 30. b. Lord Mayor.
  Jonah iii. 8. 4° 1749. Faft. Sept. 2. b. Lord Mayor.
WARNER James, a Proteftant.
  Job xxxiv. 12. 4° 1688. b. Lord Mayor. Sept. 30. The fureft way to the fafeft Peace in troublefome times.
WARNER Manifon, M. A. V. of St. Ives, Huntingd.
  ‡ * Joel ii. 13. 8° 1745. Faft.
  * Rom. xiii. 1, 2. 8° 1745. Rebellion.
  ‡ * 2 Chron. xiii. 18. 8° 1746. Th. after Rebellion.
WARRE Richard
  Rom. xiv. 19. 4° 1660. *C. C. C.* Oxon.
WARREN Erafmus, DD. R. of Worlington, Suffolk.
  1 Tim. i. 15. 4° 1684. End of Chrift's Advent.
  Prov. xxiv. 21. 4° 1685. Acceffion. Religious Loyalty—or old Allegiance to the new King.
  1 Tim. ii. 1, 2. 4° 1686. A defence of Liturgies.
  Ephef. iv. 3. 1° 1693. Divers rules for Xtian Unity. *Brit. M.*
WARREN John, DD. late Preb. of St. Peter's Exeter, formerly Fell. of Queen's Coll. Camb.
  ‡ * Heb. iii. 17. 8° 1716. Fun. of the Rev. J. Merrill.
  Serm. in 2 Vol. 8° 1739. Upon feveral Subjects. *Magd.* Oxon.
WARREN John, Bp. of St. David's.
  * Luke xiv. 18. 4° 1777. *Camb. Addenbrook*-Hofp.
  * James i. 14. 4° 1778. b. the Sons of the Clergy.
  * Joel i. 14. 4° 1780. Faft. b. Lords.
WARREN Langhorne, M. A. R. of Charlton, Kent.
  * Prov. xxiv. 21. 4° 1745.
WARREN Richard, DD. Arch-Deacon of Suffolk.
  1 Tim. iv. 16. 4° 1746. *Camb.* Vif. The mutual duty of Minifters and People.
WARREN Robert, DD. R. of St. Mary Stratford Bow, Middlefex.
  * Pf. iv. 4. 8° 1710. Duty of Self-examination.
  1 Tim. vi. 17–19. 4° 1711. Commem.
  Job ix. 23. 8° 1724. 2 f. On the Death of Sir William Dawes. The Death of a righteous man diftinctly confidered, both as a Judgment and a Mercy.
  Matt. xxii. 21. 4° 1725. Jan. 30. b. Lord Mayor.
  Rev. iii. 21. 4° 1731. Jan. 30. b. Lord Mayor. The glorious reward of chriftian Fortitude.
  1 Pet. ii. 12. 4° 1732. b. the Sons of the Clergy. The good Effects of public and exemplary Piety. *Brit. M.*
  1 Cor. vii. 20. 4° 1737. Col. of Georgia. Induftry and Diligence in our Calling. *All S.* Oxon. *Queen's.* Camb.
  52 Pract. Difc. in 3 V. 8° 1739. and 1748. On various Subjects.

WARRINDEN Thomas
  Acts xvii. 24. 8° 1736. Conf. of a Ch.
WARTER Thomas, M. A. R. of Cleobury North, Salop.
  * Pf. cxxxiii. 1. 8° 1767. The advantages and pleasures of Unity.
  * Prov. xvi. 6. 8° 1779. Salop Infirmary. The efficacy of Charity to purge Iniquity.
WARWELL James,   R. of Boxford in Suffolk.
  Pf. cxxvi. 1, 2. 4° 1660. Th. May 24 and June 28.
  Pf. cxlvi. 1, 2. 4° 1661. 2 f.
WASHBOURNE Thomas, DD. R of Dumbleton, Gloucester.
  Ifai. lviii. 12. 4° 1661. May 29. The repairer of the Breach.
WASHINGTON Henry, M. A. of Queen's Coll. Oxon. Curate of Greenwich, Kent.
  2 Cor xiii 11. 8° 1745. Farewel.
WATERHOUSE Thomas,   Fell. of Dulwich Coll.
  Pf. cxxiv. 1, 2. 8° 1746. Nov. 5. p. 3.
  Ifai. viii. 12, 13. 8° 1746. Faft. Dec. 18. p. 29.
  * 4 Serm. in 8° 1753.
WATERLAND Daniel, DD. Arch-Deacon of Middlesex, Master of Magd. Coll. Camb. and Chaplain in Ord.
  2 Sam. xx. 1, 2. 8° 1716. Camb. Th. for suppressing the Rebellion. Magd. Oxon. Trin. Queen's. Cl. H. Camb.
  8 Serm. in 8° 1720. At Lady Moyer's Lect. in defence of the Divinity of Christ. Bod. Univ. Ch Ch. Magd. Mert. Trin. Hert. New C. C. C. C. Pemb. Oxon. Trin. St. John's. Queen's. Camb.
  Matt. v. 16. 8° 1721. b. the Sons of the Clergy. Wore. Wadh. Oxon. Cl. H. Queen's. Camb. Sion.
  Eccles. vii. 14. 4° 1723. May 29. b. Lord Mayor. Sion.
  Prov. xxii. 6. 4° 1723. An. meet. Char. Sch. Trin. Camb. Sion.
  2 Cor. xiii. 14. 8° 1723. On the Trinity. Magd. Ox. Eton. Sion.
  Tit. iii. 4, 5, 6. 8° 1740. 2 l. Regeneration stated and explained. Braz. N. Linc. Oxon. Queen's. Camb.
  Serm. in 2 Vol. 8° 1742. On several important subjects of Religion and Morality. Bod. Magd. New C. Bal. Ox. Queen's. Cam.
WATERLAND Theodoric, DD. Fell. of Magd. Coll. Camb. R. of St. Benet Fink, London.
  Deut. iv. 7-9. 8° 1716. Camb. Accession. Cl. H. Camb.
WATERMAN Hugh, M. A. R. of St. Peter's, Bristol.
  Tit. ii. 14. 4° 1699. Bristol. Ch. f.
WATERS James,   Chapl. to Francis Baron Holles of Ifield.
  Heb. xiii 14. 4° 1682. Fun. of Lady Holles.
WATERS James
  * Col. iii. 3. 8° 1717. Fun. f.
WATKINS
  Ephes. ii. 3. 4° 1676. m. e. G. Misery of man's estate by Nature.
WATKINS Richard
  Rom. xv 5, 6. 8° 17
WATKINS Richard. M. A. R. of Clifton Campvile, Staffordshire.
  Pf. xcvii. 1. 8° 1745. God's government of the world, a ground of Joy to mankind.   1 Sam.

1 Sam. xii. 24, 25. 8° 1746. Th. after the Rebellion.
*Matt. xxiv. 7, 8. 8° 1756. Faſt. *Braz. N.* Oxon.
WATKINS Roger, M. A. late Fell. of Bal. Coll. Oxon. R. of Fillingham, Lincolnſhire.
 *1 Kings iii. 9. 4° 1778. Viſ.
WATKINSON Edward, M. D. R. of little   Kent.
 *Luke xiv. 28. ⎫
 *John xx. 7. ⎬ 12° 1763. Œconomy conſidered under Forecaſt, Order, and Prudence.
 *John vi. 12. ⎭
 *2 Kings iv. 13. 12° 1763. Eſſay. Gratitude as a ſacred Virtue.
 *Luke x. 21. 12° 1763. Eſſay. Gratitude as a religious Duty.
WATKINSON P.   R. of Edlington, Yorkſhire.
 Luke x. 42. 4° 1674. Fun. of Lady Mary Wharton. Mary's Choice. *Bod.*
WATSON Daniel
 *Iſai. xlix. 6. 8° 1763. Brief for American Colleges.
WATSON George, M. A. Fell. of Univ. Coll. Oxon.
 Pſ. xix. 4-6. 4° 1749. *Oxon.* Chriſt the Light of the world.
 *Jude 5. 4° 1755. A ſeaſonable admonition to the Church of England.
 *Gen. xviii. 42. 8° 1756. Doctrine of the Trinity.
 *Num. xvi. 47, 48. 8° 1756. Aaron's Interceſſion and Korah's Rebellion conſidered.
 *Tit. iii. 1. 8° 1763. Obedience to Government.
WATSON John, M. A. Fell. of Braz. N. Coll. Oxon. and Cur. of Hallifax, Yorkſhire.
 Phil. iv. 5. 8° 1751. *Mancheſter.* Moderation, or a candid Diſpoſition towards thoſe, that differ from us, recommended.
WATSON J. M. A.
 *Iſai. lx. 19. 8° 1769. Fun. of William King, DD.
WATSON John, M. A. Curate of Ripenden, Yorkſ.
 *Rom. xiii. 4. 8° 1754. Jan. 30.
WATSON Joſeph, DD. R. of St. Stephen Walbrook, London.
 John v. 14. 8° 1717. Sept. 2. b. Lord Mayor.
 Pſ. cxi. 4. 4° 1722. May 29. The reſtoration to be had in Remembrance.
 Luke vi. 35. 4° 1727. Spittal.
 Prov. iii. 28. 4° 1727. [Ann. meet. Charity-Schools. *All S.* Oxon. *Queen's.* Camb.
 Luke ix. 55, 56. 4° 1727. Nov. 5.
 Heb. x. 25. 4° 1728. Opening a Church. The duty of public Worſhip. *Brit. M.*
 Luke xi. 2. 8° 1731. Hutch. Lect. Forms of Prayer vindicated &c. *Queen's.* Camb.
 John xiii. 35. 4° 1735. Nov. 5. b. Lord Mayor.
WATSON Richard, Bp. of Landaff.
 *1 Cor. vi. 7. 4° 1769. Aſſize. Christianity conſiſtent with every ſocial Duty. *Queen's.* Camb.

*Rom.

* Rom. xiii. 3, 4. 4° 1776. May 29. The revolution vindicated.
* Isai. ii. 4. 4° 1780. Fast.

WATSON *Thomas*
* Disc. in 4° 1660.

WATSON *Thomas*, Pastor of St. Stephen, Walbrook, before the Ejection 1662.
* Ps. cxxxvii. to the end. 8° 1661.
Ps. xlvi. 5. 4° 1662.
2 Cor. vii. 1. 4° 1662. *Bod. Queen's.* Oxon.
Rev. ii. 10. 4° 1662.
Isai. ii. 10, 11. 4° 1663. V. Coll. Far. S.
Matt. xxvi. 26–28. 8° 1665.
Ps. xxxii. 6. 8° 1666.
Prov. xii. 26. 8° 1672. A plea for the godly. *Bod.*
Deut. xvii. 19. 4° 1676. s. m. e. C. How we may read the Scriptures with much spiritual Profit. p. 161.
* Acts xvii. 31. 4° 1676. m. e. G. The duty of Judgment. p. 442.
Luke ii. 49. 4° 1677. m. e. C. How must we make Religion our Business. p. 453.
* Ps. cxii. 4. 4° 1679. Deliverance unto the Church.
Num. xxi. 6–9.
1 John v. 3.   16

WATSON Thomas   16
‡* Heb. iv. 12. 4° 1749. Fast. b. Commons. *Brit. M.*

WATTS George, M. A. of Clare Hall Camb. Preacher of Lincoln's Inn, London.
Luke xii. 21. 4° 1733. b. Gov. of St. Bartholomew-Hospital, London, *Brit. M.*
Ps. cvii. 35–37. 4° 1736. Col. of Georgia. *All S. Worc.* Oxon. *Queen's.* Camb. *Brit. M.*
1 Sam. xii. 25. 4° 1742. Fast. Nov. 10. *Brit. M.*

WATTS *Isaac*, DD.
* His Works in 6 Vol. 4° 1753. *All S.* Oxon. The 1st and 2d V. contain his Discourses, *viz.*
* On various Subjects divine and moral.
* On the Joys or Sorrows of departed Souls at Death, and the Glory or Terror of the Resurrection.
* On some of the most principal Heads of the christian Religion.
* Evangelical Disc. on several Subjects.
* On the Holiness of Times, Places and People under the Jewish and Christian dispensations.
* On the love of God, and its Influence on all the Passions, with a Discovery of the right Use and abuse of them in matters of Religion &c. &c.

WATTS Robert, LL. B. Fell. of St. John's Coll. Oxon.
Matt. xxviii. 19, 20. 8° 1711. Trin. S. Prop. of Gospel. The duty and manner of prop. the Gospel. *Bod. Sion.*

WATTS Tho. M.A. V. of Orpington and St. Mary Cray, Kent.
   Pf. cxxiv. 1–3. 4° 1689. Th. for Deliverance from Popery &c. *Magd*. Oxon.
   Tit. i. 16. 4° 1695. Th. The English Cretes, and atheistical Christians.
   1 Cor. xiii. 13. 4° 1697. Affize. Universal christian Charity. *Pub. L.* Camb.
   - - - - - - - Vif. The christian indeed, and faithful Pastor &c.

WATTS Thomas, M.A.
   Mark vi. 4. 8° 1724. County-Feast.

WAUGH John, Bp. of Carlisle.
   Heb. xiii. 17. 4° 1705. Conf. of Bp. Bull. *Ch. Ch. Queen's.* Ox. *Pub. L. Queen's. St. John's.* Camb.
   Pf. xxvii. 10. 4° 1713. Ch. Duty of Apprentices and Servants. *Linc.* Oxon.
   Pf. lxxxiv. 10. 4° 1713. Open. a Ch. Public worship set forth and recommended. *Queen's.* Oxon. *St. John's.* Camb.
   Prov. xxiv. 25. 4° 1713. Ref. of Manners. *Ch. Ch. Linc.* Oxon. *Pub. L.* Camb. *Eton.*
   2 Cor ix. 6. 8° 1714. Spitt. W.
   Rom. xii 17. 8° 1715. Elect. of a Lord Mayor. *Sion.*
   Rom xii. 19. 4° 1717. Affize. Ag Revenge. *Ch.Ch.* Oxon.
   Neh. iv. 11. 4° 1717. Nov. 5. b. King. *Ch. Ch.* Oxon.
   Eccles. viii. 14. 4° 1719. Jan. 30. b. Commons. *Ch. Ch.* Oxon. *Cl. H.* Camb.
   1 Pet. iii. 19, 20. 4° 1722. Prop. of Gospel. *Ch. Ch.* Ox. *Pub. L. Queen's.* Camb. *Sion.*
   2 Chron. xxxv. 25. 4° 1724. Jan. 30. b. Lords. *Worc.* Oxon.

WAUGH John, LLD. Dean of Worcester.
   * Matt. iv. 23. 8° 1752. *Worcester*-Infirmary.

WAYMAN Lewis
   * John xvii 4. 8° 1753. Fun.

WEALES Thomas, DD. V. of St. Sepulchre's, London.
   * John viii. 7. 8° 1768. Ag. Slander.
   * John xii. 27, 28. 8° 1768. Good-friday.
   * - - - - 1777.

WEARE Thomas, M.A. late of Jes. Coll. Oxon.
   Pf. lx. 12. 8° 1741. Fast. Feb. 5.
   * Pf. lx. 11. 8° 1756. Fast.
   * Hosea iv 6. 8° 1763. Jan. 30. Necessity of relig. Knowledge.
   * Josh. xxiii. 11. 8° 1764. May 29. Gratitude to God for the Restoration.
   * Matt. vi. 11. 8° 1767. Trust in God in times of Scarcity. *Bod.*

WEARING Thomas,   V. of Bampton, Westmoreland.
   * Pf. cxxxvii. 1. 8° 1726. The last ferm. preached at St. Patrick's.

WEATHERBY John
   * Rev. iii. 2, 3. 8° 1750. Irreligion, the ground of God's Displeasure.

WEATE William, B. A. V. of Lupley, Staffordſ.
 * 1 Pet. i. 24,25. 8° 1754. On the Death of William Conelly, Eſq ; Member of Parliament in England and Ireland.
WEBB Francis
 * 18 Serm. in 2 Vol. 12° 1766.
 * 19 Serm. in 2 Vol. 12° 1772.
WEBB James
 * 1 Theſſ. v. 24. 8° 1781. Fun. of J. Conder, DD.
WEBB Jeſſop, M. A. R. of little Brandon, Norfolk.
 Rev. xiv. 13. 4° 1695. Fun. of Mrs. Coſtivel.
WEBB John, M. A. Curate of Shaw, Berks.
 Acts xx. 25. 8° 1720. Fun.
WEBBER Francis. DD. Rector of Ex. Coll. Oxon. and Dean of Hereford.
 Deut. xiv. 2. 8° 1738. *Oxon.* The jewiſh Diſpenſation vindicated ag. the moral Philoſopher. *All S. Linc. Worc.* Ox. *Cl. H.* Camb. *Brit. M.*
 Matt. vii. 28. 8° 1742. *Oxon.* Aſſize. The caſe of Authority conſidered, as it reſpects Religion, particularly the chriſtian. *All S. Worc.* Oxon.
 2 Tim. ii. 12. 8° 1750. *Oxon.* Conſ. of Bp. Conybeare. *Worc.* Oxon. *Eton.*
 * Prov. iv. 23. 4° 1758. *Oxon.* Government of the Heart. *Linc. Braz. N. Worc.* Oxon. *Queen's.* Camb. *Brit. M.*
 * John xiii. 34, 35. 8° 1739. b. Gov. of *Devon* and *Exon.*-Hoſp.
WEBSTER
 Eſth iv. 13, 14. 8° 1740. *Edinb.* The wicked Life; and fatal, but deſerved Death of Haman.
WEBSTER Alexander, Miniſter of Talbooth Church, Edinburgh.
 Eſth. viii. 17. 8° 1746. *Edinb.* Subſt. of 2 ſ. Th. after Rebellion. Heathen's profeſſing Judaiſm, when the fear of the Jews fell upon them.
 * Pſ. cxxxvii. 5,6. 12° 1776. 2 ſ. Zeal for civil and religious Intereſt of mankind. V. Scotch Pr. Vol. II. p. 328-34.
WEBSTER James, Miniſter at Edinburgh.
 Select. ſerm. in 12° 1723. *Edinb. Sion.*
WEBSTER R.
 * 1 Sam. xii. 25. 8° 17.
 Eph. iv. 32. 8° 1713. *Brit. M.*
WEBSTER William, DD. V. of Ware and Thundridge, Herts.
 Mark viii. 38. 8° 1737. Aſſize. The ſin of being aſhamed of our Religion. *Queen's.* Camb.
 Prov. xiv. 34. 8° 1738. Aſſize. *Queen's.* Camb.
 Tracts, Sermons, Diſc. Letters in 8° 1745. *All S. New C.* Oxon. *Trin. Queen's.* Camb
 * Pſ. cxviii. 23, 24. 8° 1742. May 29. b. Commons. *Queen's.* C.
 Rom. iii. 7, 8. 8° 1745. 2nd with Notes 1746. On Rebellion. A ſeaſonable Antidote ag Popery.

Luke

Luke xii. 20. 8° 1747. The folly and madness of Impenitency.
All S. Oxon.
Rom. xii. 18. 8° 1748. Of living peaceably,
2 Tim. iii. 1. 8° 1748. Of self-love and Benevolence.
Gen. ii. 2, 3. 8° 1751. 2 f. Upon the Sabbath. *Queen's.* Camb.
* Serm. in 2 Vol. 8° 1753.
* Matt. v. 6. 8° 1754. 2 f. Nature of Justice and moral Honesty.
* Phil. iv. 11. 8° 1754. Essay. New art of Contentment.
* Isai. xxvi. 9. 8° 1756. Fast.
V. Bellamy's Fam. Pr. (1st Edit.) V. II. p. 99. *Queen's.* Ca.
* Luke x. 42. 8° 1754. One thing needful. V. Bellamy's Fam.
Pr. Vol. II. p. 91. *All S.* Oxon.
* Heb. x. 25. 8° 1754. The duty of assembling ourselves. V.
Bellamy's Fam. Pr. Vol. II. p. 105. *All S.* Oxon.

WEDDERSPOON *Patrick*
* Occas. sermons in 8° 1733. *Brit. M.*
WEEDON James, DD. V. of Chalfont St. Peter's, Bucks.
* 10 (Posth.) serm. in 8° 1777.
WELCH *John*
* Disc. in 12° 1752.
WELCHMAN Edward, M. A. Fell. of Mert. Coll. Oxon. Arch-D.
of Cardigan, R. of Solyhul and Lapworth, Warwickshire.
A pract. Disc. in 8° 1704. On the parable of Dives and Lazarus.
Matt. xxviii. 19, 20. 4° 1706. The doctrine of Baptism. *Eton.*
Gal. vi. 9, 10. 8° 1717. Charity-School. The duty and reward
of Charity. *Magd.* Oxon.
WELD *Isaac*, DD.
* Heb. xiii. 7, 8. 8° 1766. Fun. of *T. Leland*, DD. *Queen's.* Cam.
WELD *Nathaniel*
* Jer. xviii. 20. 8° 1714. Fast.
WELLS *Edward*
Ephes. v. 18. 4° 1676. s. m. e. Psalmody. p. 174. *Bod.*
* Rom. v. 12. 4° 1676. m. e. G. The fall of Man. p. 95.
WELLS Edward, DD. R. of Cotesbatch, Leicesters.
Ps. cxix. 158. 8° 1710. Vis. The duty of being grieved at the
Sins of others. *Bod. Linc.* Oxon. *Sion. Eton.*
WELLS E. M. A.
* Acts xxvi. 22, 23. 8° 1735. Priority of Christ's Resurrection.
WELLS Zachary, M. A. Fell. of King's Coll. Camb. and Lect. of
St. Michael Basishaw, London.
Matt. xi. 22. 4° 1705. School-Feast. The advantages of a learned
and religious Education. *Ch. Ch.* Oxon.
WELSTEAD Henry, M. A. R. of Brettenham, Suffolk.
Levit. xxvi. 2. 4° 1714. Vis. Modern moderation, set in a
true light.
WELTON James, B. D. Master of the Free-Sch. at Norwich.
* 1 Chron. xxix. 11–13. 4° 1759. Th. s.
WELTON Richard, DD. R. of St. Mary, Whitechapel.
Ps. cvii. 8. 4° 1697. Th. for Peace.

Prov. xxii. 15. 4° 1705. Ch. The neceffity and advantage of an early Education.
Pf. cxlvi. iii. 5. 4° 1706. *Sion.*
1 Cor. xi. 25 8° 1708. Sacrament. The true Reformation.
Ezek. xxvii. 33 4° 1710. b. Corp. of Trinity-houfe. *Brit. M.*
Ecclef. viii. 2. 4° 1710 b. the Court of Lieutenancy. The wife man's Counfel upon the Teft. *Linc.* Ox. *Pub. L.* Camb. *Sion.*
18 Sermons in 8° 1724. The fubftance of chriftian Faith and Practice.

WENSLEY Robert, V. of Chefhunt, Herts.
2 Tim. i. 13. 8° 1679.
Prov. xi. 19. 4° 1682. b. Lord Mayor. The prefent Miferies and Mifchiefs of Sin. *Pub. L.* Camb. *Brit. M.*
Ezek. xxi. 25-27. 4° 1685. b. Lord Mayor. Ferguson's text explained and applied. *St. John's.* Camb.

WERGE Richard, M. A. R. of St. Mary's Church at Gatefhead, Durham.
Hofea v. 12. 4° 1683.
Heb. ix. 27. 4° 1683. Fun. of George Johnfon, Gent.
Ifai. lvii. 21. 4° 16
Matt. xvi. 26. 4° 16

WERNDLY J. C. V. of Wraifbury and Langley, Bucks.
Pf. cxii. 6. 4° 1704. Fun. of John Lee, Efq; The everlafting Remembrance of the righteous *Eton.*

WESLEY Charles, M. A. formerly Student of Ch. Ch. Oxon.
Ephef v. 14. 12° 1742. b. the Univerfity.
* Pf. xlvi. 8. 12° 1753. On Earthquake.

WESLEY John, M. A. formerly Fell. of Linc. Coll. Oxon. and Chapl. to the Countefs Dowager of Buchan.
Prov. iii. 17. 8° 1735. The pleafantnefs of a religious life.
Rom. viii. 32. 12° 1740. Free-Grace.
Serm. in 3 Vol. 12° 1746, 1748, 1750.
N. B. republifhed in 4 Vol. 12° 1771. *Briftol.*
* 2 Sam. xxiv. 17. 8° 1775. At Bethnal Green.
* Matt. xxv. 34. 12° 1777. At a collection for the Hum. Society.
* Num xxiii. 23. 8° 1777. On laying the foundation of the new Chapel near the City-road.

WESLEY Samuel, M. A. R. of Epworth, Lincoln.
Pf. xciv 16. 8° 1698. Ref. of Manners. *Eton.*

WEST *Edward*
1 Cor. xiii. 15. 4° 1675. m. e. P. Purgatory a groundlefs and and dangerous Doctrine. p. 813.
Ephef. iv. 29. 4° 1673. f. m. e. C. Government of the Tongue, p. 503. *Bod.*

WEST Rich. DD. R. of Shillingfton, Dorfetf. and Preb. of Wells.
1 Tim. iv. 7, 8. 4° 1670. Affize. Profitablenefs of Piety. *St. John's.* Camb. *Sion.*

WEST Richard, DD. Fell. of Magd. Coll. Oxon. Arch-Deacon of Berks, and Preb. of Winchefter.

Pf.

Pf. cxxii. 8, 9. 4° 1700. b. Sons of the Clergy. *Wore.* Ox. *Br. M*
Deut. xxxii. 35. 4° 1706. Th. June 27. *Ch. Ch.* Oxon.
Luke xii. 51. 4° 1707. Affize.
Pf. cxlvii. 20. 4° 1708. Affize.
Jer. xxxi. 29. 8° 1710. Jan. 30. b. Commons *All S. Magd. Or. Linc.* Oxon. *Trin. Queen's. St. John's.* Camb. *Sion.*
Pf. xli. 1–3. 4° 1711. Spitt. W. *Ch. Ch.* Oxon. *Pub. L.* Camb.
Pf. lx. 2. 4° 1716. On the public Breach. *Ch. Ch.* Ox. *Queen's.* Camb. *Brit. M.*

WEST *William*
* 7 Pract. Differtations in 8° 1759. On the Lord's Prayer.
* 16 Serm. in 8° 1762. On various important Subjects.

WESTCOTT *Samuel*
* Serm. in 2 Vol. 8° 1762.

WESTFIELD Thomas, Bp. of Briftol.
* Sev. ferm. in 12° 1660. The white Robe, or Surplice vindicated.

WESTON Edward, Right Honourable.
* 14 Family-Difc. in 8° 1768.

WESTON Phipps, B. D. R. of Whitney, Oxon. and Canon Refid. of Wells.
* Pf. v. 13. 4° 1779. Conf. of Bp. Thurlow.

WESTON Stephen, Bp. of Exeter.
Serm. moral and theological in 2 Vol. 8° 1747. On various Subjects. *King's.* Camb. *Eton.*
* Pf. xlvi. 8. 4° 1756. Faft. *Braz. N.* Oxon.

WESTON William, B. D. late Fell. of St. John's Coll. Camb. V. of Campden, Gloucefterf.
Phil. iii. 6. 8° 1739. 2 f. Some kinds of Superftition worfe than Atheifm. *Queen's.* Camb. *Brit. M.*
Gal. iv. 18. 8° 1746. *Camb.* The moral Impoffibility of conquering England. p. 1–23.
Deut. xxv. 11. 8° 1746. *Camb.* On Rebell. The Abfurdity of the difpenfing power of the Pope. p. 49.

WETENHALL Edward, Bp. of Kilmore.
1 Kings xviii. 21. 4° 1663. Vif. Ag. Neutrality. *Bod. Trin.* Ca.
Jerem. xv. 10. 4° 1668. Affize. Miferies of the Clergy and their Redrefs. *Trin.* Camb.
Hofea iv. 6. 4° 1672. Of deftructive and faving Knowledge.
2 Sam. xv. 11. 4° 1682. Th. *Bod. Magd.* Ox. *Trin.* Camb. *Sion.*
Heb. xii. 14. 4° 1682. Affize. The Proteftant Preacher exhorting to Unity. *Bod. Magd.* Oxon. *Trin.* Camb. *Sion.*
Ecclef. x 17. 12° 1686. On the King's birth-day.
Hexapla Jacobæa 12° 1686. 6 f. *Dublin. Trin.* Camb.
Pf. lxxvi. 10. 8° 1691. *Corke.* Lent.
2 Cor. i. 9, 10. 4° 1692. *Dublin.* Irifh Maffacre. The duty of Irifh Proteftants. *Bod. Pub L.* Camb. *Sion.*
* Rev. i. 10. 12° 1697. *Dublin.* On the Lord's-day. *Ch. Ch.* Ox.
* Heb. xii 23. 8° 1699. Fun. of James Bonnell, Efq; *St. John's.* Camb.

* - - - - 12° 1701. Of the Power of God's Grace in converting Sinners.

* - - - - 4° 1707. Of hum. coercive Power for reforming Sinners.

WHALEY Nathanael, M. A. R. of Broughton, Northamptonſ.
Diſc. in 8° 1695. and 12° 1704. On ſeveral Subjects. *C. C. C. All S. Magd. Pemb.* Oxon. *Pub. L.* Camb. *Dr. W's. L.* Lond.
2 Serm. and Diſc. in 8° 1698. and 12° 1704. *All S. Oriel.* Oxon. *Dr. W's. L.* London.
2 Cor. v. 4. 8° 1708. On Death. *Ma. d.* Oxon.

WHALEY Nathanael, M. A. Fell. of Wadh. Coll. Oxon.
2 Kings viii. 13. 8° 1710. *Oxon.* Jan. 30 b. Univ. The Gradation of Sin both in Principles and Practice. *Bod. Ch. Ch. Or. Linc.* Oxon. *Queen's.* Camb. *Sion.*

WHALLEY John, DD Maſter of Peterhouſe, Regius Profeſſor of Divinity, Camb. and Chaplain in Ord.
Heb. xi. 4. 4° 1740. Jan. 30. b. Commons. *Queen's. C. Brit. M.*

WHALLEY Peter, LL. B. V. of St. Sepulchre's, and upper Maſter of Chriſt-Hoſpital.
* Pſ. cxlix. 6. 8° 1758. Faſt.
* Matt. v. 16. 4° 1763. b. Gov. of Chriſt-Hoſp.
* 1 Cor. ix. 14. 4° 1770. b. the Sons of the Clergy.

WHARTON Henry, M. A. Chapl. to Abp. Sancroft, R. of Chartham, Kent.
14 Serm. in 8° 1728. Vol. I. } *Bod. Ch. Ch. Bal. St. John's. Pem.*
24 Serm. in 8° 1728. Vol. II. } Oxon. *Trin. Queen's.* Camb. *Dr. W's. L.* London. *Sion.*

WHATELEY Joſiah, M. A. of Trin. Coll. Camb.
1 Cor. vi. 19, 20. 8° 1715. *Sion.*
Phil. i. 27, 28. 8° 1715. *Sion.*

WHATLEY Robert, R. of Toft near Linc. and Preb. of York.
Acts xxvi. 28. 8° 1749. *Hull.* The Chriſtian. *Brit. M.*
Deut. xxxii. 29. 4° 1749. Viſ. The immortal—mortal. *Queen's.* Camb. *Brit. M.*

WHATLEY William, of Banbury. Oxon.
‡*Heb. xiii. 4. 12°17 Viſ. Diſc. on conj. Duty. V. II. p. 344.

WHEATLAND Tho. M. A. late Lect. of St. Stephen's Coleman-ſtreet, and St. Mary at Hill, and Cur of St. Magnus, Lond.
Iſai. liv. 17. 8° 1725. Nov. 5. b. Lord Mayor. The perpetual Security of the chriſtian Church.
26 Serm. in 8° 1739. On various Subjects. *Brit. M.*

WHEATLY Charles, M. A. V. of Furneaux Pelham, Herts.
The Nicene and Athanaſian Creeds explained, and confirmed by the Holy Scriptures. Lady Moyer's Lect. 8° 1738. *Bod.*
50 Serm. in 3 Vol. 8° 1746. On ſeveral ſubjects and occaſions. *New C.* Oxon.

WHEELER Jonathan
* - - - - 1765. Fun.

WHEELOCK Eleazer, DD.
* - - - - 8° 1767. Ord.

WHELDON John, M. A. R. of St. Ives, Huntingd. Preb. of Linc.
* 2 Serm. in 8° 1772.
* Rom. i. 16. 8° 1773. Affize. *Queen's*. Camb.
WHICHCOTE Benj. DD. Minister of St. Lawrence Jewry, Lond.
Select ferm. in 2 Parts. 8° 1698. *Ch. Ch. Magd. Or. Wadh.* Oxon. *Queen's.* Camb. Faft. *Dr. W's. L.* London.
Sev. Difc. Vol. I. II. 8° 1702. III. 8° 1703. IV. 8° 1707. *Ch. Ch. Magd. O, Wadh.* Oxon. *Queen's.* Camb.
WHINCOP Thomas, DD. R. of St. Mary Abchurch, and St. Lawrence Pountney, London.
Tit. iii. 8. 4° 1695. b. the Sons of the Clergy. *Wadh.* Oxon. *Queen's.* Camb. *Sion.*
1 John iii. 18. 4° 1701. Spitt. W. *Bod. Sion.*
Job v. 12. 4° 1702. Nov. 5. b. Commons. *St. John's.* Camb.
WHISTON Henry,   R. of Balcomb, Suffex.
Acts xvii. 11. 8° 1661. A Vol True Nobility.
WHISTON J.
* 3 Difc. in 12° 17
WHISTON Thomas, B. A. V. of Orby, Lincolnf.
Ifai. xxxvii. 33, 34. 4° 1744. On the intended Invafion.
WHISHAW H.   M. A. Canon of the Cathedral of Hereford, V. of Lugwardine &c.
* Prov. xxii. 6. 8° 1755. The great and important duty of training up Children.
‡ * Serm. (Pofth.) in 2 Vol. 8° 1782.
WHISTON Will. M. A. late Profeffor of the Mathematics, Camb.
Deut. vi. 10–12. 8° 1698. Dec. 17. At Clare-Hall. Memoirs. 8° 1749. p. 87.
2 Pet. i. 19. 8° 1708. 8 f. Boyle's Lect. or fo. 1739. Vol. II. p. 265 c&. Accomplishment of Scripture Prophecies. *Ch. Ch. St. John's. Magd.* Oxon. *Brit. M.*
WHITAKER Edward, B. A. R. of St. John's Clerkenwell, London.
* 1 Cor. xi. 31. 4° 1782. Faft.
WHITAKER John, M. A.
2 Pet. i. 19. 8° 1751. A furvey of the Doctrine and Argument of St. Peter's Epiftles &c.
WHITAKER Nathaniel, DD.
* - - - - 8° 1767. Ord.
* - - - - 8° 1768. 2 f. Doctrine of Reconciliation.
WHITAKER Thomas,   of Leeds.
Jer. xxxi. 17. 8° 1693. Fun. Difc. Comfort for Parents mourning over their hopeful Children that die young. *Bod. Pub. L.* Cam.
Serm. in 8° 1712. On fev. occafions &c. *Bod. Pub. L.* Ca. *Sion.*
WHITAKER William,   Minifter of St. Mary Magdalen, Bermondfey, Surrey
Col. iii. 11. 4° 1667. m. e. C. How are we to compleat in Chrift. p. 485.
* 1 Tim. ii. 5. 4° 1676. m. e. G. Mediator of the Covenant defcribed in his Perfon, Natures, and Offices.
* Difc. in 8° 1674.   WHITBY

WHITBY Daniel, DD. Chantor of the Church of Sarum.
    John vii. 47–49. 4° 1679. Ag. Popery. or in his Comment. fo. 1703. Vol. I. d. 569. *Bod. Ch. Ch.* Oxon.
    2 Tim. iii. 5. 4° 1685. *Sion.*
    Tit. iii. 1. 4° 1685. *Sion.*
    Rom xiii. 1 4° 1685. Elect. of a Mayor *Sion.*
    Matt. xvi. 24, 25. 4° 1703. Of Self-denial. *Sion.*
    33 Serm. in 2 Vol. 8° 1710. On the Attributes of God. *C.C.C. All S. Ch. Ch.* Oxon.
    Luke xii. 57. 8° 1714. Reason is to be our Guide in the Choice of our Religion &c.
    * Matt. xxiii. 7–13. 8° 1715. Nov. 5.
    * Matt. vi. 9. 8° 17 .
    Luke xxii. 19, 20. 8° 1716. Advent S.
    11 Serm. in 8° 1720. On several occasions. *Bod. Ch. Ch.* Oxon. *Pub. L.* Camb. *Queen's.* Camb.
    12 Serm. in 8° 1726. Preached at Sarum. *Queen's.* Cam. *Brit. M.*
    5 Disc. in 8° 1727 and 1728. (2d Edit.) in his last Thoughts. *Bal. Or. Jes.* Oxon. *Queen's.* Camb.

WHITCOMBE John, M. A. R. of Walesby, Lincoln, and Chaplain to the Right Hon. Lord Milford.
    * Mark xv. 16. 4° 1779. *Linc.* Prop. of Gospel.

WHITE
    Gen. xv. 11. 16
    Ps. cxviii. 22, 23. 4° 1660.
    Rom. xiii. 1. 16

WHITE
    * Rom. viii. 28. 4° 1676. m. e. G. Of effectual Calling. p. 264.
    James i. 6. 4° 1677. m. e. C. How must we pray in Faith. p. 280.

WHITE Abraham
    Heb. xiii. 21.

WHITE George, M. A. Minister of Colne and Marsden, Lancashire.
    * 1 Thess. v. 21. 4° 1741. The Englishmen's rational Proceedings in the choice of Religion. Ag. Popery and Presbyterianism.
    1 Cor. xiv. 33. 8° 1728. *Preston.* Ag. the Methodists.

WHITE Henry
    Matt. xxi. 42. 4° 1660.

WHITE Jeremiah
    1 Thess. iv. 14. 8° 1702. Fun.

WHITE John, B. D. Fell. of St. John's Coll. Camb. V. of Ospringe, Kent.
    Joel ii. 15–17. 8° 1745. Fast for Rebellion. *Brit. M.*

WHITE John, DD. late Fell. of All Soul's Coll. Oxon. and R. of Hampton, Gloucester.
    * Col. ii. 8. 8° 1764. Vis.

WHITE Joseph, B. D. Fell. of Wadh. Coll. Laudian Professor of Arabic, and one of his Majesty's Preachers at Whitehall.
    * Neh viii. 7, 8 4° 1778. Revival of the English Translation of the old Testament recommended. *All S. Wadh.* Oxon.

WHITE

OF AUTHORS, &c. 369

WHITE Nathan, at the old Jewry, London.
  * - - - - 1760. Nov. 5.
  * Job i. 21. 8° 1771 Fun.
WHITE Richard, B. D. V. of Kidderminster, Worcesterf.
  James i. 12. 4° 1693. Fun.
WHITE Richard, R. of Monêton Farleigh, Yorkf.
  Judges ix. 15. 8° 1716.
  Rom. xii. 18. 17 Aſſize.
  * Pſ. li. 12, 13. 8° 1738. Viſ.
WHITE Stephen, M. A. R. of Holton, Suffolk.
  Epheſ. iv. 28. 12° 1747. A Diſſuaſive from ſtealing.
WHITE Thomas, M. A. R. of Stepney, Preacher at Stratford le
  Bow, Middleſex, and Preb. of Litchfield.
  Pſ. lxxxii. (or lxxvii.) 5, 6. 4° 1695. County-Feaſt.
  Pſ. xcvii. 1. 4° 16
  Deut. v. 29. 4° 1706. Aſſize.
WHITE Thomas, M. A. Chaplain to Bp. Hoadly, R. of Ayſton,
  Rutland. and Nailſton, Leiceſterſhire.
  Deut. iv. 7–9. 8° 1717. Aſſize. The Happineſs and Duty of
    Subjects.
  Acts viii. 17. 8° 1723. Conſ. of Bp. Kennet.
WHITE Thomas, Preb. of the Cathedral of Litchfield.
  * Serm. in 8° 1757. On various Subjects.
  * Luke xii. 15. 8° 1771. 2 ſ. On Covetouſneſs.
WHITE William, V. of Blyton, Lincoln.
  * - - - - 1754. Elect. of Mayor.
WHITEAR William, M. A. Preb. of Chicheſter.
  1 Cor. iv. 13. 4° 1710. Viſ. An apology for the Church of
    England. *Bod. Pub. L.* Camb.
[WHITEFOOT John,] ſen. of Norwich.
  * 1 Pet. iv. 8. 8° 1694. On Charity.
WHITEHALL Rob. M. A. Vice Principal of St. Mary-Hall, Oxon.
  1 Cor. xiv. 26, 40. 4° 1694. *Oxon.* Concerning Faith and Edifi-
    cation. *Ch. Ch. Linc. Worc.* Oxon.
WHITEHEAD Edward
  2 Theſſ. ii. 10. 8° 1753. b: Soc. of Weavers.
WHITESIDE John, of Yarmouth, Norfolk.
  * James i. 21. 8° 1775. Ord. of Rev. Mr. *Barbauld,* &c.
WHITFELD Francis, V. of Godmerſham, Kent.
  ‡ * Prov. xix. 2. 4° 1782. School-Feaſt at *Aſhford.*
WHITFELD John, M. A. of Jeſ. Coll. Camb. R. of Bugbrook
    near Northampton.
  Jude 8. 4° 1682. b. Lord Mayor. *Pub. L.* Camb.
WHITFELD Will. DD. V. of St. Giles Cripplegate, and Chaplain
    in Ord.
  Pſ. l. 23. 4° 1698. The neceſſity of Revelation and an holy Life.
    All S. Oxon.
  1 John iv. 1. 4° 1698. Viſ. Of Enthuſiaſm. *All S. C. C. C.* Ox.
    St. John's. Camb.

Matt. v. 16. 4° 1698. Ref. of Manners. Of Example. *All S.* Oxon. *Pub. L.* Camb.
Gal. v. 1. 4° 1703. Aſſize. Of chriſtian Liberty. *Cb. Cb. St. John's.* Camb.
1 John iii. 20. 4° 1704. b. Lord Mayor. *St. John's.* Camb.
John xviii. 36. 4° 1708. Viſ. (Ag. the Rights of the chriſtian Church.) The Kingdom of Jeſ. Chriſt. *Univ. Or. Jeſ.* Oxon.
Pſ. cxii. 6. 4° 1713. Fun. of Bp. Compton. *Cb. Cb.* Oxon.
Pſ. cvii. 43. 4° 1714. Farewel. *Brit. M.*
Heb. xiii. 18. 4° 1714. Induction-ſermon. *Brit. M.*

WHITFIELD George, M. A. formerly of Pemb. Coll. Oxon.
10 Serm. in 8° 1739.
Serm. in 2 Vol. 12° 1739. On various Subjects.
John vii. 37-39. 8° 1739. Whitſunday.
John ii. 11. 8° 1739.
Acts xix. 5. 8° 1739. The marks of the new Birth.
Matt. xxv. 13. 8° 1740. The fooliſh and wiſe Virgins.
Matt. xxii. 42. 8° 1740. What think ye of Chriſt.
* 9 Serm. in 8° 1742.
Pſ. cv. 45. 8° 1746. Th. after the Rebellion. Britain's Mercy and Britain's Duty.
* Serm. in 8° 1771. *Bod. Pub. L.* Camb.

WHITFIELD Henry, M. A. R. of Caſtle Eaton, Wilts, V. of Bradwell, Oxon. and Chapl. to Lord Cadogan.
1 Cor. xv. 35-38. 8° 1751. *Oxon.* The Poſſibility of a Reſurrection illuſtrated by Analogy. *Worc.* Oxon.

WHITFIELD Henry, DD. V. of Britingſea, Eſſex.
* Job xxviii. 12. 4° 1769. *Oxon.* Act. *Worc.* Oxon.

WHITFIELD John, DD. Fell. of Trin. Coll. Camb. R. of Dickleburgh, Norfolk.
Zech. viii. 16, 17. 8° 1718. Camb. Aſſize. *Trin. Queen's.* Camb.
2 Tim. iii. 16, 17. 8° 1722. *Camb.* Viſ. *Trin. Queen's.* Camb.
Gal. v. 1. 8° 1724. *Camb.* Acceſſion. *Trin. Queen's.* Camb.

WHITFIELD John, M. A. R. of Biddeford, Devon.
* 2 Sam ii. 26. 8° 1763. Th. ſ.

WHITING Charles, DD. Fell. of Wadh. Coll. Oxon. R. of Roſs, and Canon Reſid. of Hereford.
Pſ. xxvi. 8.. 4° 1692. *Oxon.* Conſ. of a Ch. *Jeſ.* Oxon *Sion.*
Judges v. 1, 2. 4° 1703. Th. Dec. 3. 1702. *Bod. Cb. Cb. C.C.C. Jeſ.* Oxon. *St. John's.* Camb.

WHITING Charles, B. D. Fell. of Oriel Coll. Oxon.
John vii. 48. 8° 1748. *Oxon.* Conc. Acad. De Doctorum Auctoritate in rebus ſacris.

WHITLOCK John
Pſ. xviii. 23. 8° 16
Hoſea ii. 15. 8° 1698. Ref. of Manners.

WHITTELL John, R. of Foot's-cray in Kent.
Num. xiv. 14. 4° 1692. b. the King's forces. *Pub. L.* Camb.

Iſai.

Isai. xxxiii. 22. 4° 1706. Th. for Victory.
* Prov. xxiv. 21, 22. 4° 1715. Accession.
WHITTELL Matthias,　　Curate of Ludlow, Salop.
　Luke i. 74, 75. 4° 1683. Nov. 5.
WHITTLE Seth,　　R. of Balliachy, London-derry.
　Jer. i. 18, 19. 4° 1690. In the Extremity of the siege of London-derry. *Bod. Pub. L. Trin.* Camb. *Brit. M.*
WHITTY John,　　Minister of the Gospel at Lyme-Regis, Dorsetf.
* Serm. in 2 Vol. 8° 1766. and 1768.
* Disc. Vol. I. 8° 1772. On the Lord's Prayer, and other various Subjects.
* Disc. Vol. II. 8° 1772. Adapted to the Ordinance of the Lord's Supper.
WHYYLE Humphrey, M. A. V. of Welbourn, Warwickshire.
　Pf. cxii. 6. 4° 1694. Fun. of Lady Ann Burgoigne. *Trin.* Camb.
WHYNNEL John
　Pf. cxxvi. 3. 4° 1661.
WIBBERSLEY John, M. A.
* 1 Pet. ii. 13, 14. 8° 1752. Assize. Newcastle upon Tyne.
WICHART John, DD. Dean of Winchester, and Chapl. in Ord.
　Col. iii. 1. 4° 1690. b. King and Queen. *Magd. Oxon. Sion.*
　Prov. xi. 20. 3° 1710. b. Queen.
WIGAN William, M. A. V. of Kensington, and Chapl. in Ord.
　Matt. vi. 34. 4° 1694. b. King and Queen. *Bod. Magd. Oxon. St. John's.* Camb. *Linc.*
　Num. xxiii. 10. 4° 1697. Fun. of Lady Cutts. *Trin. Cl. H. Cam. Brit. M.*
WIGHT Robert, M. A. Preb. of the Cathedral Church of Exeter.
* 1 Cor. ix. 2. 4° 1765. b. Gov. of *Devon* and *Exon* Hosp.
WIGHT Thomas,　　Minister at Rumford, Essex.
* Acts viii. 2. 4° 1698. Fun. of Mr. *Jos. Brumley. St. John's.* C.
WILCOCKS Joseph, Bp. of Rochester and Dean of Westminster.
　1 Thess. iv. 1. 4° 1709. (at Lisbon.) Advice to Protestants residing in foreign parts. *Queen's.* Camb. *Brit. M.*
　Gen. xviii. 32. 4° 1720. b. Commons. Fast ag. the Plague. The Increase of Righteousness the best Perservative ag. national Judgments. *Ch. Ch. Linc. Worc.* Oxon. *Brit. M.*
　Pf. cxi. 4. 4° 1722. Nov. 5. b. Lords. *Or.* Oxon.
　1 Cor. xiv. 12. 4° 1723. Spitt. M.
　Prov. xxi. 11. 4° 1723. Ref. of Manners.
　John xiii. 34, 35. 4° 1724. School-Feast. The duty and measures of brotherly Love. *Or. Worc.* Oxon. *Sion.*
　Pf. lxvii. 5. 4° 1726. Prop. of Gospel. *Ch. Ch. Worc.* Oxon. *Pub. L.* Camb.
　Pf. xcvii. 1. 4° 1728. Accession. *Worc.* Oxon. *Eton.*
　1 Pet. iv. 10 4° 1731. Ann. meeting Char. Schools. The usefulness and excellency of Charity-Schools.
　Eccles. vii 10. 4° 1739. Irish Prot. Schools. *All S. Worc.* Oxon. *Queen's, Cl. H.* Camb. *Eton.*

WILCOX

WILCOX *Daniel*,   Preacher of the Gofpel in Monkfwell-ftreet, London.
    *65 Serm. in 3 Vol. 8° 1757.
WILDER John, M. A. R. of St. Aldates, and late Fell. of Pemb. Coll. Oxon.
    Exod. xv. 2. 4° 1706. *Oxon.* Th. for a Victory. *Bod.*
    15 Serm. in 8° 1720. Vol. I. *Oxon.* On feveral occafions. *Bod. Wore.* Oxon.
    1 John iv. 1. 8° 1739. *Oxon.* The trial of the Spirits—or a Caution againft Enthufiafm &c.
    15 Serm. in 8° 1741. Vol. II. *Oxon.* Preached before the Univ. of Oxon.
WILDING John
    ‡* Neh. v. 19. 8° 1780. Faft. Character of a true Patriot briefly delineated.
WILKINS David, DD. Arch-Deacon of Suffolk, and Preb. of Cant.
    Deut. xxxiii. 8. 4° 1722. Conf. of Bp. Bowers. *Oriel.* Oxon. *Queen's* Camb.
WILKINS John, Bp. of Chefter.
    Pf. iii. 4. 4° 1673. *Bod.*
    3 Serm. in 12° 1677. b. King, with a Difc. on the beauty of Providence. *Bod. Ch. Ch. Univ. Queen's. Pemb.* Oxon. *Trin. Magd.* Camb. *Sion.*
    15 Serm. in 8° 1682. Preached upon feveral occafions. *Ch. Ch. All S. Bal. Or. C.C.C. New C. Jef.* Ox. *Pub. L. Trin. Queen's. Cl. H.* Camb.
WILKINSON George,   of Ch. Ch. Oxon. and Chapl. to Lord Haverfham.
    Pf. cxii. 6. 8° 1736. Commem. of Founder at the Charterhoufe.
WILKINSON Henry, DD. Margaret Profeffor of Divinity, and Canon of Ch. Ch. Oxon.
    Luke xvii. 27, 28. 4° (1661.) 1677. m. e. C. Wherein we are endangered by lawful things. p. 444.
    2 Theff ii. 3–10. 4° 1675. m. e. P. Pope is Antichrift. p. 80. *Bod.*
    Col. iii. 17. 4° 1676. f. m. e. C. Of doing all in the name of Chrift. p. 390. *Bod.*
WILKINSON Henry, DD. Principal of Magd. Hall. Oxon.
    1 Cor. vii. 29. 4° 1660. *Oxon.* Conc. ad Baccalaureos. De brevitate opportuni Temporis. *Bod.*
    * 3 Decads of Sermons 4° 1660. *Bod. Sion. Dr. W's. L.* Lond.
    1 Tim. vi. 8. 8° 1671. Sev. Difc. The doctrine of Contentment. *Sion.*
    Sev. ferm. in 8° 1681.
WILKINSON John, M. A. Lect. of H. Trinity, Kingfton upon Hull, Yorkfhire.
    Deut. i. 18. 4° 1713. The inftitution and authority of fubordinate Magiftrates.
WILKINSON John, M. A.
    Heb. x. 23–25. 4° 1736. Ref. of Manners.

OF AUTHORS, &c. 373

WILKINSON Robert,   of Camb.
    Prov. xxxi. 14. 4° (1607) 1682. Wed. f. b. King. The Merchant royal. V. Difc. on Conj. Duty. Vol. I. p. 1. *Bod. Univ.* Oxon. *Sion.*

WILKS James
    James v. 19, 20.

WILLAN Edward, M. A. V. of Hoxne, Suffolk.
    Ecclef. x. 17. 4° 1661. Elect. of Burgeffes.
    Gal. ii. 20. 4° 1661. Concrucifixion. *Sion.*

WILLARD S.
    ‡ * Zech xiii. 1. 8° 1722. *Bofton.* Converfion of the Jews. *Br. M.*

WILLATTS Charles, M. A. R. of Pumtree, Nottinghamf.
    Rom. ii. 14, 15. 4° 1744. *York.* Affize The Religion of Nature, a mere Idol. *Queen's.* Camb. *Eton.*

WILLENSON Jacobus,   Minifter of Middleburgh, Zealand.
    * Zech. ix. 16. 8° 1747. On the Inveftment of the Prince of Orange as Stadholder.

WILLES John, DD. late Fell. of Trin. Coll. Oxon. R. of Bifhops Itchington, Warwickf. and Preb. of Litchfield.
    Amos iii. 6. 4° 1690. Affize. *All S. Ch. Ch. Jef.* Ox. *Trin.* Cam.

WILLES Samuel, M. A. Minifter of All Saints in Derby, and Preb. of Litchfield.
    Luke xx. 36. 4° 1679. Fun. of Lady Mary, Daughter of Ferdinando Earl of Huntingdon. *Pub. L.* Camb.
    * Pf. lxxxii. 1. 4° 1683. Affize. *Queen's.* Camb. *Brit. M.*

WILLET John, M. A. Fell. of Wadh. Coll. Oxon.
    Pf. lxxviii. 37. 4° 1708. *Oxon.* Affize. The nature and mifchiefs of Hypocrify. *Bod. Or.* Oxon. *Queen's. St. John':*. Camb.

WILLIAM George
    * Deut. xv. 11. 4° 1752. Ch. *Queen's.* Camb.

WILLIAMS   DD.
    1 Kings xix. 4.

WILLIAMS Benjamin
    * Difc. in 8° 1770. *Salisbury* On various fubjects and occafions.

WILLIAMS Charles, M. A. Lect. of Ifleworth, Middlefex &c.
    Lev. xix. 30. 4° 1707. Open. a Church. *Sion.*
    Ifai. xlix. 23. 4° 1707. On the Union. *Ch. Ch.* Oxon. *Sion.*

WILLIAMS Daniel, DD.
    1 Cor. iv. 30. 4° 1688. b. Lord Mayor. The Kingdom of God in power.
    Hof. x. 12. 4° 1690. c. m. e. Of repentance of national Sins. p. 42. *Bod. Pub. L.* Camb.
    * 2 Cor. i. 12. 12° 1707. Fun. of Rev. *T. Doolittle.*
    * 2 Cor. ii. 16. 12° 1709. Ord. of *B. Grofvenor,* DD.
    * Col. iv. 17. 12° 1709. Ord. of *S. Wright,* DD.
    ‡ * Mark x. 29, 30. 8° 1711. Duty of Diffenters.
    * Rom. xiv. 8. 8° 1714. Fun. of Rev. *Matt. Henry.*
    * Pract. Difc. in 5 Vol. 8° On feveral important Subjects &c. Vol. I. and II. in 8° 1738. Vol. III. IV. and V. in 8° 1750.

consisting

consisting chiefly of Tracts. *Brit. M. Dr. Ws's. L.* London.
* Isai. vii. 13–16. 8° 1767. Dissertation.

WILLIAMS David
 * Matt. v. 16. 12° 1775. V. Essays &c. *Queen's.* Camb.
 * Serm. in 2 Vol. 12° 1774. Chiefly upon relig. Hypocrisy.
 * Heb. x. 25. 8° 1776. On open. of a Chapel in Margaret-street Cavendish Square—with the Liturgy.

WILLIAMS Griffith, Bp. of Ossory.
 Tit. iii. 8, 9.   16
 2 Chron. xx. 17.   16
 Ps. cxxvii. 1.   16
 Acts vii. 32. fo. 1662. Jan. 30.
 Serm. in fo. 1662.
 Ps. cvi. 16. fo. 1663.
 Ps. lxxix. 9. 4° 1665.
 2 Cor. v. 1. 4° 1665.
 Serm. in 4° 1665. *Sion.*
 Amos v. 6. 4° 1666. *Oxon.* b. Commons at *Oxford. Bod.*
 * Jonah iv. 4. 1° 16   Th.
 Job viii. 3. 4° 1667.
 Matt. iv. 2. 4° 1667.
 Rev. xxii. 12. 4° 1667.

WILLIAMS John, Bp. of Chichester.
 Ps. lxxxiii. 3, 4. 4° 1678. Nov. 5. *Bod.*
 Ephes. iv. 16. 4° 1679. b. Lord Mayor. *Bod. All S. Oxon. Sion.*
 Luke xix. 8. 4° 1683.
 Ps. lxxxvii. 6. 4° 1683. County-Feast. *Bod.*
 Rom. iii. 7, 8. 4° 1685. Th. for Victory over the Rebels. *Sion.*
 Josh. xxii. 31. 4° 1695. Elect. of a Lord Mayor. *Ch. Ch. Oxon. Eton. Sion.*
 1 Sam. ii. 30. 4° 1695. Fast. b. Commons. Decr. 11. *Ch. Ch. Magd. Oxon. Queen's.* Camb. *Sion.*
 Matt. xxiii. 34–36. 4° 1696. Jan. 30. b. King. *Trin.* Camb.
 Heb. xiii. 20, 21. 4° 1697. Farewel. *Trin. St. John's.* Camb.
 Acts x. 40–42. 4° 1697. Spittal M. *Trin.* Camb.
 Heb. iv. 1. 4° 1698. Fun. of Dr. Tho. Jekyll. *Ch. Ch. Oxon.*
 Acts vii. 59, 60. 4° 1702. Jan. 30. b. Lords. The case of Martyrdom considered. *Sion.*
 Ps. cxlv. 4. 4° 1704. Accession. b. Lords. *Ch. Ch. Ox. Queen's. St. John's.* Camb.
 Acts xvi. 9. 4° 1706. Prop. of Gospel. *Ch. Ch. Jes. Ox. Queen's.* Camb. *Eton.*

 Heb. i. 1, 2.
 Gal. i. 8, 9.
 John v. 39.
 Acts xvii 11, 12.
 Luke xvi. 31.
 } 8° 1708. Boyle's Lect. or fo. 1739. Vol. I. {
 3 s. Of divine Revelation.
 The Perf. of evang. Revelation.
 Scripture, Rule of Faith.
 Of the Perspicuity of Scripture.
 Unreasonableness of Infidelity.
 Bod. Ch. Ch. C. C. C. St. John's. All S. New C. Jes. Linc. Ox. Pub. L. Trin. Queen's. St. John's. Ca.

Pf. lxxxix. 3.   17   Faft.
1 Theff. ii. 13. 8° 1708. Vif. Of Scripture being a Rule. p. 401. *Bod. Ch. Ch. Linc.* &c. &c,
Rom. v. 1. 8° 1708. b. Clergy. Of Juftification by Faith. p. 433. *Bod. Ch. Ch. Liuc.* &c. &c.
2 Cor. v. 21. 8° 1708. At the end of Boyle's Lect. b. King. Of a Propitiation. p. 465. *Bod. Ch. Ch. Linc.* &c. &c.
1 Pet. iii. 21. 8° 1714. The Cafe of Baptifm confidered. *Linc.* Oxon. *St. John's.* Camb. *Sion.*

WILLIAMS J.
 * Num. xvi. 24. 8° 1756. Faft. Earthquake.
 * 1 Sam. vii. 12. 8° 1759. The favors of Providence to Britain.

WILLIAMS J. LL. D.
 * - - - - 1771. Char. School.

[WILLIAMS John]
 * Jer. li. 15. 17

WILLIAMS Philip, DD. Pref. of St. John's, Camb. R. of Starfton, and Barrow in the Diocefe of Norwich.
Rom. xiii. 1. 4° 1738. *Camb.* Acceffion. The Love of our Conftitution in Church and State. *All S.* Ox. *Queen's.* Ca. *Brit. M.*
1 Sam. xii. 24, 25. 4° 1745. *Camb.* Faft for Rebellion.
 * John v. 14. 8° 1746. Th. *Queen's.* Camb.

WILLIAMS Richard, M. A. R. of Hawarden, Flintf.
 * Prov. xi. 11. 8° 1750. Affize. *Braz. N.* Oxon.

WILLIAMS Stephen
Phil. iv. 13.

WILLIAMS Thomas,   late Curate of Harwell, Berks.
 * John iv. 24. 8° 1778. The true Nature and Defign of Chriftian Worfhip.

WILLIAMS Walter,   R. of Llanddetti, Brecknockf.
Pf. xxxiii. 12. 4° 1731. b. Soc. of antient Britons.

WILLIAMS William, M. A. Minifter of St. Mary's, Haverfordweft, Pembrokefhire.
Luke xix. 8. 4° 1682. The neceffity and meafures of Reftitution.
Prov. xxiv. 21, 22. 4° 1685. Elect. of a Mayor. Religion expreffed by Loyalty.
Pf. lx. 12. 4° 1696. At the Eng. Camp near Ghent in Flanders.

WILLIAMS William, M. A. Preb. of Chichefter.
Luke xix. 9–12. 8° 1716. The prefent Schifm confidered.

WILLIAMS William, M. A.
 * Micah vi. 8. 4° 1752. b. Free-Mafons. Mafonry founded on Scripture.

WILLIAMSON James, M. A. Fell. of Hert. Coll. Oxon.
 * 1 Tim. ii. 1, 2. 8° 1779. *Oxon.* Acceffion.

WILLIAMSON Jofeph, M. A. V. of St. Dunftan's in the Weft, and Chaplain to Lord Mayor.
 * 1 Pet. iii. 8. 4° 1775. Elect. of Lord Mayor.

WILLINGTON G.
Pf. li. 17.   1670.

WILLIS Richard, Bp: of Winchester.
> Prov. xii. 20. 4° 1701. b. Lord Justices of England. July 20. St. John's. Camb.
> Phil. i. 27. 4° 1702. Prop. of Gospel. *Ch. Ch.* Oxon.
> Gal. vi. 10. 4° 1702. Spitt T. *Pub: L.* Camb.
> Acts xx. 28 4° 1702. Conc. ad Synod. *Ch. Ch. Worc.* Oxon. *Trin. Queen's. St. John's.* Camb.
> Acts x. 38. 12° 1704. Ref. of Manners. *Eton.*
> Gen. xviii 19. 4° 1704. Ann. meet. Char Schools *Bod Ch. Ch. C.C.C. Magd. Queen's.* Ox. *Trin. Queen's. St. John's.* Ca. *Sion.*
> Isai. xi. 13, 14. 4° 1705. Th. b. Queen. Oct. 23. *Ch. Ch. Univ. Magd. Worc.* Oxon. *Trin. Queen's.* Camb. *Sion.*
> Gen. xlix 7. 4° 1705. Nov. 5. b. Commons. *Ch. Ch. Worc.* Ox. *Pub. L.* Camb. *Sion.*
> 1 Cor. xiii. 4. 4° 1707. b. Queen. Ag. Envy. *Univ. Ch. Ch.* Oxon. *Pub. L. Trin. Queen's.* Camb. *Sion.*
> Pf. xc. 12. 8° 1709. b. Queen. On her Birth-day. *Ch. Ch. Univ. Worc.* Oxon. *Trin. Queen's.* Camb. *Brit. M.*
> Matt. xix. 23. 4° 1711. Spitt. T. *Bod. Ch. Ch. Linc.* Oxon.
> Isai. xxxiii. 6. 4° 1715. b. King. Th. Jan. 30. The way to quiet and stable Times. *Bod. Ch Ch. Magd.* Ox. *Trin.* C. *Sion.*
> Prov. xxiv. 21. 4° 1716. Jan. 30. b. Lords. *Bod. Ch. Ch.* Oxon. *Queen's.* Camb. *Sion.*
> 2 Cor. viii. 9. 8° 1717. Spitt. M.

WILLIS Thomas, DD. V. of Kingston upon Thames, and Chapl. in Ord.
> Prov. iv. 7-9. 4° 1676. Co. Feast. Excellency of Wisdom. *Bod.*

WILLIS Thomas, M. A. V. of St. Helen's, London.
> Pf. xviii. 47-49. 4° 1696. Th.

WILLISON John
> * Serm. in 12° 1761.

WILLOUGHBY Lord De Broke George
> * Acts xx. 35. 4° 1712. Ann. meet. Char. Schools. The blessedness of doing good. *Ch. Ch. C. C. C. Magd. Trin.* Ox. *Queen's.* C.

WILLOUGHBY Stephen, M A.
> Jon. iii. 4 4° 1685. Scourge to the rebellion. *Bod.*

WILLS Benjamin
> * Esther iv. 14. 8° 1711. Accession.
> * Pf. cxxiv. 6. 8° 1716. Nov. 5.
> Phil. i. 17. 8° 1720. Ministers set forth for the defence of the Gospel. *Bod.*
> * Ephes. iv. 11, 12. 8° 1732. Ord.   *Queen's.* Camb.

WILLS James, Chaplain to the Society of Artists, and Curate of Whitchurch, Middlesex.
> * Job xxxvii. 14. 4° 1767. b. the Society.

WILLS John, M. A. V. of Thorpe in Surrey, and Chaplain to the Bp. of Peterborough.
> Acts xvii. 11, 12. Cons. of Bps. Osbaldeston and Thomas.

OF AUTHORS, &c.

WILMOT George, M. A. Fell. of Bal. Coll. Oxon.
Pf. lxxxii. 1. 4° 1750. *Worcefter*. Affize. *Worc*. Oxon.
WILMOT William, M. A. V. of Margetting, Effex, Lect. of St. Ethelburgh, and Chaplain to the Bp. of Litchfield and Coventry.
Acts xxiv. 5. 4° 1751. Jan. 30. b. Lord Mayor.
WILSON Bernard, DD. V. of Newark upon Trent, and Preb. of Worcefter.
Heb. xi. (or vi.) 16. 8° 1723. On Oaths.
Joel ii. 18. 4° 1744. Faft. April 11.
* Matt. xxv. 4. 4° 1756. *Worcefter*-Infirmary.
* Eccl^{us}. iv. 1. 4° 1768. The Mifapplication of public Charities.
WILSON Ch.
Ifai. xlix. 23.
WILSON Chriftopher, M. A. Lect. of St. Margaret's, Weftminfter.
* Matt. v. 34. 4° 1700. Oct. 6. Ag. profane Swearing.
1 Cor. xi. 1. 4° 1700. Advent. b. Lord Mayor. The Pattern of an holy life
WILSON Chriftopher, DD. Canon Refid. of St. Paul's, and Chapl. in Ord.
* 1 Cor. xiii. 21. 4° 1754. Jan. 30. b. Commons.
WILSON Edward,   V. of Rye, Suffex.
Pf. cxxii. 6. 8° 1712. Jan. 30.
WILSON Edward, M. A. R. of Teverfall, Nottinghamf.
2 Cor. vi. 3, 4. 8° 1726. Vif.
WILSON J.
Pa. xc. 15. 8° 1716.
WILSON John
Pf. xxxix. 5. 8° 1676. State of Man, a ftate of Vanity. *Bod*.
Pf. lxxiii. 23-26. 8° 16   Man's Communion with God.
* Acts xxiv. 25. 8° 16
WILSON Samuel, DD. Minifter of the Gofpel in London.
* Phil. ii. 13. 8° 1732. 2 f. Doctrine of efficacious Grace. V. Lime-ftreet f. Vol. II. p. 211.
* Sev. ferm. in   1735. On various fubjects and occafions.
* Jerem. iii. 15. 8° 1736. 2 f. Ch. Induftry and Liberality recommended.
* Acts xx. 35. 8° 1739. Ch. For poor Widows &c. of diffenting Clergy.
* Job i. 20-22. 8° 1741. Fun.
* Ifai. v. 3-6. 8° 1741. Abufe of Mercy ftated and reproved.
*   -   -   -   1742. Faft.
* Pf. lxxiii. 25, 26. 8° 1744. Fun. of Mrs. *Rebekah Stennett*.
* 1 John iv. 10. 8° 1746. Chrift, the great Propitiation.
WILSON Thomas, M. A. R. of Arrow, Warwickf.
Pf. cxxiv. 1-8. 4° 1679. Nov. 5. Reflections on the Plot. *Bod*.
Rom. xiii. 1. 4° 1681. Jan. 30. With a Relation of fome rebellious Practices and Principles of Fanatics. *Sien*.

Vol. II.   B b b   WILSON

WILSON Thomas, M.A. Prefbyter of the Church of England.
Serm. in 8° 1701. On feveral Texts in Genefis, Exodus and Le-
viticus. *Pub. L.* Camb.
WILSON Thomas, Bp. of Sodor and Man.
John xiii. 38.   1734. Ch.
* Serm. (Pofth.) in 4° 1781. On the great practical Duties of
Chriftianity. V. Vol. II. of his Works. *Bod. Dr Wi's. L.* Lond.
WILSON Thomas, M.A. late Fell. of Bal. Coll. Oxon. Minifter of
Bungay, Suffolk, and of North Repps, Norfolk.
Prov. xxiv. 21. 8° 1745. Rebellion. *Worc.* Oxon.
WILSON Timothy, M.A. R. of Kingfnoth, Kent.
Jofh. v. 13. 4° 1690. Faft. June 18.
1 Pet. ii. 13, 14. 4° 1704.
WILSON William,   R. of St. Peter's in Norwich.
Pf. lxxxix. 3. 4° 16   Faft.
Micah vi. 8. 4° 1689. Affize. *Sion.*
Luke v. 26. 4° 1689. Th.
WILSON William,   Minifter of the Gofpel at Perth.
* Zech. xiv. 7. 8° 17   *Bod.*
‡ * Acts xiii. 36. 8° 1739. Fun. of Jofeph Aircy. *Brit. M.*
‡ * 1 Sam. xvii. 37. 8° 1747. Rebell. *Brit. M.*
WILTON Samuel, DD.
* Heb. vi. 12. 8° 1769. Fun. of Mr. *Jof. Longhurft.*
* Act. ix. 6. 8° 1770. Ch. School.
* Matt. xxv. 19. 8° 1775. Ch. School.
WILTON Thomas, DD.
Ecclef. viii. 2. 8° 17
WINCHESTER James, M.A. Minifter of the Gofpel at Jedburgh.
* 9 Sacramental ferm. in 12° 1771.
WIND J.   M.A. R. of Kirkby Knowle, and Curate of Thirk-
leby, Yorkf
Pf. cxxxvi. 1. 8° 1748. *York.* Diftemper of the Cattle.
WINER Robert, DD. R. of a noted Chapel, Weftminfter.
* Luke ii. 1. 4° 1733. Origin and Effence of a general Excife.
WINGFIELD Thomas, M.A. V. of Yelmefton, Devon, and Hof-
pitaler of St. Thomas, Southwark.
Gal. v. 1. 8° 1745. Rebell. The Reafonablenefs, and Neceffity
of ftanding faft in the Chriftian and Englifh Liberty.
2 Sam. xviii. 32. 8° 1746. Th. after Rebellion. The Lawfulnefs
of wifhing Deftruction to the King's Enemies.
Rom. xiii. 7. 4° 1749. Jan. 30. b. Lord Mayor. The Mifchiefs
of unreafonable Oppofition to Government.
Dan. ii. 4. 4° 1749. Acceffion. b. Lord Mayor. The Dignity
of the royal Character.
WINSTANLEY   R. of Llanwenarth, Monmouthf.
* 1 Cor. ix. 22. 8° 1753. On a Bill for naturalizing Jews. *Br. M.*
* Luke xiii. 4, 5. 8° 1756. Faft. Earthquake.
WINTELEY John
* 2 Tim. ii. 19. 4° 1701.

WINTER *Cornelius*
    * 2 Tim. iv. 7. 8° 1772. *Bath.* Fun.
WINTER John,   Minister of West-Acre, Norfolk.
    1 Pet. ii. 17. 4° 1662. Coron. *Univ.* Oxon. *Sion.*
    2 Chron. xxxv. 24. 4° 1662. Jan. 30. *Sion.*
    Gen. xviii. 25. 12° 1669. Assize. *Trin.* Camb.
    1 Sam. ii. 25. 12° 1669. Assize. *Trin.* Camb.
WINTER *Richard*
    * Jer. iv. 19. 8° 1756. On declaring War.
    * 2 Chron. xx. 27. 8° 1759. Th.
    * 2 Pet. i. 14. 8° 1759. Fun. of Rev. *Thomas Bradbury.*
    * Col. iv. 2. 8° 1759. Exhortation to Prayer and Thanksgiving.
    * Col. i. 18. 8° 1760. Ord.
    * Isai. lvii 2. 8° 1762. Fun. of Rev. *Thomas Hall.*
    ‡ * Dan. ix. 24–28. 8° 1777. 9 serm. On Daniel's 70 Weeks. Preached at the Merchant's Lect. at Pinner's-Hall.
    * - - - - 1776. Fun. of   *Winter.*
WISE *Lawrence*
    Prov. x. 17.   Fun.
WISE Thomas, DD. Fell. of Exeter Coll. Oxon. and Chapl. to the Prince of Wales.
    Prov. xxii. 6. 4° 1702. Roy. Fun. Of the Education of Youth.
    Pf. xcvii. 1. 4° 1703. Th.
    Pf. cvii. 21, 22. 4° 1706. Th. Dec. 31.
    Luke vi. 27, 28. 4° 1707. Farewel. *Ch. Ch.* Oxon. *Cl. H.* Camb. *Brit. M.*
    ‡ * 1 Cor. iv. 2. 8° 1710. Vis. *Brit. M.*
    Prov. xxiv. 21. 8° 1715. Access. Relig. and Loyalty. *Magd.* Ox.
    14 Discourses in 8° 1717. Preached in Canterbury Cathedral. *Ch. Ch.* Oxon.
    Luke xiii. 2, 3. 4° 1721. Fast.
WISHART *George,* M A. one of the Ministers at Edinburgh.
    ‡ * John vii. 13. 8° 1733. An honest mind, the best Security ag. Error in religious matters.
    Dan. xii. 10. 8° 1746. Rebell. Times of public Distress, times of Trial. V. Scotch Preacher. Vol. I. p. 32. *Brit. M.*
    Matt. xviii. 7. 8° 1752. *Edinburgh.* Ch. for promoting Christian Knowledge in Scotland. The case of Offences ag. Christianity. *Brit. M.*
WISHART *William,* DD.
    1 Tim. i. 5. 8° 1731. Ch. Universal Love, the Design of Christianity. *Bod. Sion.*
WISHART *William,* DD. Principal of the College of Edinburgh.
    * Serm. in 12° 1753. *Wadh.* Oxon.
WISHEART *William,* DD. Principal of the Coll. of Edinburgh.
    Disc. in 2 Vol. 8° 1716. *Edinb. Pub. L.* Camb. *Sion.*
    Pf. cxxxiii. 1–3. 4° 1719. *Edinb.* May 14. *Brit. M.*
WITHERS *George*
    * Matt. vi. 9–13. 8° 1665. Lord's Prayer.

WITHERS *John*
    Ezek. xvii. 15. 8° 1716. Th. f.
    * Micah. vi. 9. 8° 1722.
    * Acts xiii 2, 3. 8° 1728. Ord.
WITHERSPOON *John*, DD. Pref. of the Coll. New Jerfey.
    * Matt. vii. 20. 12° 1759. b. Synod.
    * Pract. Difc in 12° 1768. On the leading Truths of the Gofpel.
    * Serm. in 12° 17   On Regeneration.
    * Pf. lxxvi. 10. 8° 1775. Faft. The Dominion of Providence over the Paffions of men.
    * Ifai. li. 9. 8° 1778. Faft.
WOLCOMBE Robert, M. A. R. of Whitftone, Devon.
    James ii. 26. 8° 1712. *Exon* Affize. *St. John's.* Camb.
    James iii. 18. 8° 1712. *Exon.* Affize.
WOLLEY Edward, Bp. of Clonfert, Ireland.
    Gen. xxxv. 7. 4° 1673. *Dublin. Ch. Ch.* Oxon.
WOLSTENHOLME Henry, M. A.
    * Matt. xxv. 40. 8° 1722. *Liverpool.* Ch. Sch.
    Jude 3. 4° 1745. *Liverpool.* Rebellion.
WOMOCK Lawrence, Bp. of St. David's.
    Pf. cxxxii. 18. 4° 1660. On proclaiming the King. *Worc.* Oxon.
    1 Chron. xvi. 1. 4° 1663. A Difc. &c. *Sion.*
    1 Sam. xxiv. 5. } 4° 1675. 2 f. Mofes and Aaron—the King and
    Num. xvii. 10. } Prieft. *Bod.*
WOOD Andrew, Minifter of Darlington, Durham.
    * Gal. vi. 9. 8° 1755. b. the Sons of the Clergy at *Newcaftle.*
WOOD A. Edward, M. A. Fell. of Mert. Coll. Oxon.
    Serm. in 8° 1674. *Oxon.* Of the Knowledge of God and Xt. *Bod.*
WOOD Edward,   V. of Sandridge, Herts.
    * Matt. vi. 33. 4° 1698. The way to Riches.
WOOD *James*
    * Pf. xxxi. 5. 8° 1722. Fun. of
    ‡ * Matt. xxiv. 44. 8° 1724. Fun. of Mrs. *Kelley. Brit. M.*
    * 2 Tim. i. 12. 8° 1729. Fun. of   *Queen's.* Camb.
WOOD Thomas, Bp. of Litchfield.
    1 Kings i. 7. 4° 1661.
WOOD *William*,   Minifter at Leeds.
    * 1 Cor. xi. 1. 8° 1773. Duties of People and Minifters.
    * Serm. in 12° 1775. On focial Life. *Trin. Queen's.* Camb.
    ‡ * 2 Cor. iv. 7. 8° 1782. b. Diffenting Clergy. The Treafure of the Gofpel in earthern Veffels.
WOODCOCK *Francis*,   Lect. of St. Lawrence Jewry, London.
    * Matt. xxv. 34. 4° 1676. m. c. G. Of Heaven. p. 647. *Bod.*
    Nehem. viii. 6. 4° 1683. c. m. c. Of Amen. p. 999. *Bod.*
    Rom. xiv. 1. 4° 1690. c. m. c. Pract. Goodnefs. p. 241. *Bod.*
WOODCOCK *Jofiah*
    * 1 Chron. xxix. 11, 12. 8° 1708. Th. after Victory. *Ch. Ch. Linc.* Oxon.

WOOD-

WOODDESON Richard, M. A. of Magd. Coll. Oxon. Master of Kingston School upon Thames, Surrey.
  Matt. v. 4. 4° 1751. Fun. of Rev. Joseph Clarke, M. A.
  * Job xvi. 11. 4° 1758. Fun. of Rev. J. C. DD.
WOODFORD James
  James v. 19, 20.
WOODFORD Matthew, M. A. Sub-Dean of Chichester, and Chap. to the Duke of Richmond.
  Gen. ix. 6. 8° 1714. On the murder of Mr. Dobell *Bod. Linc. Oxon. Sion.*
WOODFORTH Thomas, LL. B. of Exeter Coll. Oxon. R. of All-Hallows, then of St. George's Botolph Lane, London.
  Heb. xii. 14. 8° 1735. Farewel.
WOODHOUSE John
  * Hagg. ii. 4. 8° 1617. Ref. of Manners.
  ‡ * Rev. xiv. 13. 8° 1698. Fun. of *Jane Papillon. Brit. M.*
WOODROFFE Benjamin, DD. Canon of Ch. Ch. and Principal of Gloucester-Hall, now Worcester Coll. Oxon.
  Pf. xi. 3. 4° 1679. b. Lord Mayor. *Ch. Ch. Ox. St. John's. Cam.*
  Jer. iii. 8. 4° 1685. Jan. 30.
  1 Tim. vi. 17–19. 4° 1700. *Oxon.* Ch.
  Dan. ix. 24–27. 4° 1702. Daniels 70 Weeks.
  Pf. lii. 1. 4° 1703. *Oxon.* Th. Dec. 3. 1702. *Bod. Ch. Ch. All S. C. C. C.* Oxon. *St. John's.* Camb.
  Pf. xviii. 50. 4° 1706. *Oxon.* Th. June 27. *Bod. Jef.* Oxon.
  1 Theff. iv. 13–18. 8° 17.
WOODS Lubbridge, V. of East Meon and Froxfield, Hants.
  * 5 Difc. in 8° 1747. More immediately relating to christian Practice.
WOODWARD Josiah, DD. Minister of Poplar, then of Maidstone, Kent.
  Zech. i. 5. 4° 1692. Fun. of Dr. Anthony Walker. *Bod.*
  Pf. cxxii. 8, 9. 4° 1693. Love and Faithfulness to our Country. *Bod.*
  Deut. ix. 26. 4° 1695. Faft.
  Lev. xix. 17. 8° 1696. Ref. of Manners. The duty of Compassion to the Souls of others.
  Luke xv. 18. 12° 1697. 6 f. To young persons.
  Ezek. xvi. 49. 4° 1697. b. Lord Mayor. Sodom's Vices destructive to other Cities and States. *Brit. M.*
  Prov. xxiii. 5. 4° 1698. Ch. A diffusive from World-mindedness, in order to the due Exercife of Charity.
  Prov. v. 23. 4° 1700. Ch. *Bod.*
  Acts viii. 8. 4° 1701. Elect. of Lord Mayor. The divine Joy of Religion.
  Pf. cvi. 30. 8° 1702. On the murder of John Cooper, Constable.
  2 Chron. xv. 2. 4° 1705. b. Lord Mayor. Faft. Aprii 4. *St. John's.* Camb.
  Heb. iv. 9. 4° 1705. Fun. of Mrs. Mary Watts.
  Hofea vi. 1. 4° 1706. b. Lord Mayor. Faft. Sep. 2.

Ifai.

Isai. xiv. 16, 17. 8° 1709. Th. *Trin.* Camb.
1 Pet. ii. 13, 14. 8°|1711. Elect. of a Mayor. The divine Right of civil Government.
* 8 Serm. at Boyle's Lect. p. 491. *Magd. St. John's. Jef.* &c. &c. Oxon. *Pub. L.* Camb.

WOODWARD Richard, Bp. of Cloyne, Ireland.
  * Prov. iii. 16. 4° 1764. *Dublin.* Irish Prot. Schools.
  * Luke xv. 10. 4° 1775. *Dublin.* Asylum for penitent Women.

WOODWARD William. M. A.
  Jer. xiii. 6. 12° 1696. Sev. S. The Lord our Righteousness.

WOOLLEY John, M. A. late Fell. of Trin Coll. Oxon. R. of St. Michael's Crooked Lane, London.
  Gen. xiii. 8. 4° 1675. Co. Feast. *Ch. Ch. Bal.* Oxon. *Pub. L.* Camb. *Sion.*

WOOLNOUGH Thomas, B. A. R. of St. Michael's, Gloucesters.
  Ecclef. xii 7. 4° 1669. Fun. of Tho. Lloyd, Esq; The dust returning to the Earth.

WOOLRICH T.
  * Micah vi. 8.

WOOLRIDGE Samuel
  Heb. xiii. 20, 21.

WOORDEN Thomas
  * John xi. 11. 12° 1688. Fun. of Susan Yeates. *Bod.*

WORSLEY Samuel
  * Isai. xxvi. 9. 8° 1777. Fast. Serious Reflections addressed to all parties on the present state of the American War.

WORTH John
  Exod. xvii. 15. 4° 1704. Th.

WORTHINGTON *Hugh*
  * - - - - 1752. Fast.
  ‡ * Phil. iv. 9. 8° 1757. Fun. of *J. Dawson.*
  * Prov. xxii. 1. 8° 1775. Good Character, better than a good Fortune.
  * 1 Cor. v. 6. } 8° 1778. Ch. School.
  * Gal. v. 9.
  * Matt. xi. 30. 8° 1778. Nov. 5.

WORTHINGTON John, DD. Preb. of Lincoln.
  Select Disc. in 8" 1725. *Pub. L.* Camb.
  * Matt. xxiv. 36. 8° 1725. Fun. of B. Bennett.
  * 3 Disc. in 8° 17

WORTHINGTON William, DD. Preb. of the Cathedral Church of York.
  * Num. xi. 29. 8° 1768. An. meet. Char. Schools. *Braz. N. Ox.*
  * Serm. in 2 Vol. 8° 1769. At Boyle's Lect. *Bod. Worc.* Oxon. *Pub. L.* Camb.

WORTON Israel
  * Jer. iv. 1. 8° 1711. Fast.

WOTTON James,   R. of St. Ann's at Annapolis Chapel.
  * Pf. cxxii. 1, 2. 4° 1704. Open. Ch. *Trin.* Camb.

WOTTON William, DD. Fell. of St. John's Coll. Camb.
  1 Tim. ii. 2. 4° 1706. Vif. The rights of the Christian Clergy afferted. *All S. Ch. Ch. Univ. Magd. Queen's. Jef.* Oxon. *Pub. L. Trin. Queen's. St. John's.* Camb. *Sion.*
  Mark xiii. 32. 8° 1720. The Omniscience of the Son of God, an undoubted Argument of his Divinity. *Trin.* Camb. *Sion.*
  Rom. xv. 5. 8° 1722. Welch-Featt. *Queen's.* Camb. *Brit. M.*

WRAY U. W. M. A. R. of Wrexham, Bucks.
  * 1 Cor. x. 31. 4° 1760. Commem. at Charter-House.
  * Num. xxiii. 10. 8° 1764. Fun. of Dean Bolton.

WRAY William, M. A. Chapl. to Lord Berkley of Stratton.
  Ezra iv. 15. 4° 1682. Faſt for the Fire of London. The rebellious City deſtroyed. *Pub. L. Trin. St. John's.* Camb. *Sion.*
  Gen. xlix. 6. 4° 1682. Nov. 5. Loyalty preteſting ag. Popery, and Fanaticiſm popiſhly aſſerted. *Bod. St. John's.* Camb.

WREN Matthew, Bp. of Ely.
  Pſ. xliv. 18. 4° 1662. On the Scotch Covenant. *Bod. All S. Magd.* Oxon. *Sion.*
  Prov. xxiv. 21. fo. 1750. Parentalia. p. 115.

WRENCH Jonathan, M. A. Fell. of Caius Coll. Camb. and V. of Ayleſham, Norfolk.
  Luke ix. 54, 55. 8° 1721. Nov. 5. The Spirit of Chriſtianity and Popery compared. *Cl. H.* Camb.

WRIGHT John, M. A.
  Heb. ix. 27. 4° 1691. Fun. of Ann Greſwold. *Bod. Magd.* Ox.

WRIGHT John, M. A. Canon Reſid. of Chicheſter.
  Acts xxiii. 14. 4° 1715. Nov. 5. b. Commons. St. Paul's Deliverance compared with that on Nov. 5. *Queen's.* Camb.
  Prov. xvi. 12. 8° 1716. Acceſſion.
  Matt. x. 16. 4° 1717. Ord. The rights of the chriſtian Prieſthood aſſerted. *Ch. Ch.* Oxon.

WRIGHT John, R. of Great Hampden, Bucks.
  1 Pet. ii. 17. 8° 1720. Aſſize.

WRIGHT Paul, DD. F. S. A. V. of Oakley, Eſſex.
  * Eccleſ. vii. 1. 8° 1773. Fun. of Iſaac Whillington, Eſq;
  * Lam. v. 3. 8° 1778. b. Gov. of *London*-Hoſpitals.

WRIGHT Robert, DD. R. of Hackney, Middleſex, and Chaplain to the Prince of Wales.
  John v. 14. 4° 1749. Th. for Peace.

WRIGHT Samuel, DD.
  * Pſ. xxxvii. 37. 8° 1707. Fun.
  2 John viii. 8° 1708. Farewel.
  Pſ. cxliv. 15. 8° 1709. Th. Nov. 22.
  * John xv. 12. 8° 1710. 2 ſ. Nov. 5. and Th. *Queen's.* Camb.
  James iv. 14. 8° 1711. Fun. of Dr. *Upton. Bod. Pub. L. Ca. Sion.*
  Pſ. xii. 1. 8° 1712. Faſt. *Bod. Pub. L.* Camb. *Sion.*
  Acts xxviii. 22. 8° 1712. 2 ſ. Character of Diſſenters.
  Pſ. cxix. 9. 8° 1712. To a Society of young Men.
  * Pſ. lxxii 1. 8° 1714.

Heb. x. 25. 8° 1714. To a Society of young Men. Of not forsaking the assembling of public Worship.
* 1 Pet. ii. 17. 8° 1715. Th.
1 Pet. iv. 4. 8° 1715. Ref. of Manners. *Brit. M.*
* 1 Sam. vii. 12. 8° 1716. Th. f.
‡ * Rev. xiv. 13. 8° 1716. Fun. of Rev. *J. Cunningham.*
* Exod. xxiii. 2. 8° 1716. Singular Piety.
‡ * Job xiv. 20. 8° 1717. Fun. of *J. Mills.*
* Gen. xl. 20–23. 8° 1718. King's birth-day. Conduct of Dissenters. *St. John's.* Camb.
* Pf. ix. 14. 8° 1719. Nov. 5. *St. John's.* Camb.
‡ * 2 Tim. i. 13. 8° 1720. Ord. f.
* 2 Tim. i. 13. 8° 1721. Ord.   *Bod. Pub. L.* Camb.
* James v. 12. 8° 1723. Ag. profane Swearing. *Queen's.* Camb.
* Lam. iii. 22. 8° 1723. Th.
* Dan. ii. 21. 8° 1724. Coronation.
* Rom. xiv. 9. 8° 1724. 2 f. Lordship of Christ.
‡ * Rev. xxi. 24. 8° 1727. Coronation.
* Job xiv. 10. 8° 1730. Fun. of Rev. Mr. *Cotton.*
‡ * 1 Cor. viii. 1. 8° 1731. Knowledge and Charity united.
* Luke xx. 34, 35. 8° 1734. Wedding f.
* Ephef. ii. 20. 8° 1735. Scripture and Tradition considered. V. Disc. Vol. I. Ag. Popery. *Braz. N.* Oxon. *Brit. M.*
* Isai. xxvi. 3. 8° 1736. Fun. of Mrs. *Eliz. Hughes.*
* Job i. 21. 8° 1736. Fun.
* Isai. xxxii. 8. 8° 1737. Ch. For Widows of Dissenting Clergy.
* 2 Tim. i. 10. 8° 1738. Fun.
‡ * Pf. xxxix. 9. 4° 1741. Fun.
* Occasional Preacher in 8° 1741. *Queen's.* Camb.

WRIGHT T.   M. A. Minister at Birmingham.
* Luke xvi. 27–31. 8° 1770. 2 f.

WRIGHT Thomas
* - - - - 8° 1763. Th.
* 1 Theff. v. 12, 13. 8° 1778. Ord. of Mr. *Isaac Smith.*

WRIGHT Timothy
Rom. ii. 7. 8° 1692. Fun. of Mrs. *S. Soame. Bod. Pub. L.* Camb.

WRIGHT William
* Matt. xvi. 26. 8° 1766. Ord.

WROE Christopher
* 2 Theff. iii. 10. 8° 1722.
Pf. cxxxiii. 1. 4° 1682. Open. of the Guild-merchant at Preston. The beauty of Unity. *Pub. L.* Camb. *Brit. M.*
Pf. cxii. 6. 4° 1684. Fun. of Sir Roger Bradshaigh. *Queen's. Trin.* Camb.
Heb. vii. 25. 4° 1691. Fun. of the Countess of Warrington. *Bod. Ch. Ch.* Oxon.
Eccles. xi. 3. 4° 1694. Fun. of the Earl of Warrington. *Ch. Ch.* Oxon. *Pub. L. St John's.* Camb. *Brit. M.*
Prov. xxix. 2. 4° 1704. Accession. *Ch. Ch.* Ox. *Queen's.* Camb.

WROUGHTON

WROUGHTON Charles, M. A. Preb. of Sarum, and R. of Codford St. Peter's, Wilts.
    Exod. xx. 8. 8° 1716. Sev. f. The duty of keeping holy the Christian Sabbath.
    * Serm. in 8° 1728.

WYATT Will. M. A. Student of Ch. Ch. Principal of St. Mary-Hall, and Public Orator in the University of Oxon.
    1 Cor. viii. 1. 4° 1679. School-Feast. *Bod. Bal. Ch. Ch. Magd. Worc.* Oxon. *Pub. L.* Camb.

WYCHE J.
    - - - - 1745. Rebell. At Salisbury.

WYKES Robert,   Lect. of St. Mildred's in the Poultry, London.
    Pf. cxxii. 6. 4° 1698.

WYLLYS J.   M. A.
    Matt. xxii. 21. 4° 1676. *Bod.*

WYNNE John, Bp. of Bath and Wells.
    Pf. cxlvii. 1. 4° 1715. May 29. b. Lords. *Ch. Ch.* Oxon.
    Matt. vi. 10. 4° 1724. Prop. Gospel. *Ch. Ch.* Ox. *Queen's.* Cam.
    Mark viii. 38. 4° 1726. Ref. of Manners. *Brit. M.*

WYNNE John, M. A. Fell. of Jes. Coll. Oxon. R. of Caery Druidion, Denbighshire.
    1 Thess. iv. 11. 8° 1724. b. University.
    1 Cor. i. 10. 8° 1726. Ordination. *Worc.* Oxon. *Queen's.* Cam.

WYNNE Robert, DD. Chancellor of St. Asaph.
    Ephes. iv. 3. 4° 1704. Jan. 30 b. Commons. Unity and Peace, the Support of Church and State. *Ch. Ch. Jef.* Oxon. *Trin. Queen's.* Camb.

WYNNE R.   M. A. R. of Ayot St. Lawrence, Herts, and Cur. of St. Vedast, London.
    * Pf. cxxiv. 2-5. 4° 1759.

WYNNE Thomas, M. A. R. of Llan Rwst, Denbyshire.
    Job v. 12. 8° 1732. Assize.

WYVILL Christopher, DD. Fell. of Trin. Coll. Camb. Dean of Rippon.
    1 Pet. ii. 17. 4° 1685. Accession. *Trin.* Camb.
    Judges xvii. 6. 4° 1686. Assize. *Bod.*
    Josh. xxiv. 15. 4° 1694. b Queen. The duty and Obligations of serving God.
    2 Sam. iii. 1. 4° 1695. Th.
    * 1 Cor. vi. 1-3. Assize. Christian Magistracy.

WYVILL Christopher, LL. B. R. of Black Notley, Essex.
    * Matt. xi. 3. 4° 1772. Vis.

WYVILL John, M. A. Chapl. to Bp. Robertson, Lord Privy Seal.
    Luke xxiv. 36. 8° 1713. Easter. On signing the Peace. *Queen's.* C.

YALDEN Thomas, DD. R. of Charlton and Clanfield, Hants, Preacher of Bridewell, and Preb. of Chumleigh, Devon.
    Dan. iv. 27. 4° 1721. b. Gov. of Bridewell and Bethlehem Hosp. The Prophets advice, or the best way to lengthen Tranquility.
    Isai. lviii. 10, 11. 4° 1728. Ann. meet. Ch. Sch.

YARDLEY Edward, B.D. Fell. of St. John's Coll. Camb. Arch-D. of Cardigan.
   1 Cor. xiv. 16, 17. 8° 1728. 4 f. The rational Communicant.
   Job xxxi. 16–18. 4° 1741. b. the Sons of the Clergy.
   Rev. ii. 4, 5. 8° 1746. Faſt. Dec. 18. 1745.
   2 Sam. xxii. 48–50. 8° 1746. Th. after Rebellion.
   Luke x. 37. 4° 1749. *Middleſex*-Hoſpital. The good Samaritan.
   Acts x. 40, 41. 4° 1749. Spitt. T. Chriſt's appearing to choſen Witneſſes, a ſufficient Evidence of his Reſurrection.
   Acts xx. 35. 4° 1750. Ann. meeting Charity-Schools. *Braz. N.* Oxon. *Queen's.* Camb.
   * Matt. xxviii. 19, 20. 12° 1763. 4 f.
   * 1 Cor. xiv. 16, 17. 12° 1763. The rational Communicant.
YATE John,   R. of Great Hampden, Bucks.
   1 Cor. xvi. 8, 9. 12° 1701. Ref. of Manners.
YONGE Philip, Bp. of Norwich.
   * 1 Theſſ. iv. 11. 4° 1756. Jan. 30. b. Commons. *Trin.* Camb.
   * Prov. iv. 23. 4° 1759. Jan. 30. b. Lords.
   * 1 John iii. 17. 4° 1760. b. Gov. of *London*-Hoſp. *Wadh.* Oxon.
   * Prov. xxi. 30, 31. 4° 1761. Faſt. b. Lords. *Braz. N.* Oxon. *Queen's.* Camb.
   * Joſh. xxiv. 13, 14. 4° 1763. Iriſh Prot. Schools.
   * Pſ. xli. 1. 4° 1764. b. Gov. Small pox-Hoſp.
   * Matt. xxviii. 18–20. 4° 1765. Prop. of Goſpel. *Braz. N.* Ox. *Queen's.* Camb.
   * John xiii. 35. 4° 1769. Ann. meet. Charity-Schools. *Braz. N. Worc.* Oxon.
   * Prov. xxii. 2. 4° 1772. b. Gov. of *Norfolk*-Hoſp.
YORKE James, Honourable, Bp. of Gloceſter.
   * Matt. x. 8. 4° 1771. b. Gov. of Small pox-Hoſp.
   * Rom. viii. 13. 4° 1775. b. Gov. of *Magd.*-Hoſp.
   * 1 Pet. iii. 8. 4° 1775. b. Antient Britons.
   * Pſ. cxxvii. 5, 6. 4° 1776. b. Gov. of Diſpenſary.
   * Matt. v. 9. 4° 1776. Jan. 30. b. Lords.
   * Mark xiv. 7. 4° 1777. *Lincoln*-Infirmary.
   * Mark xv. 16. 4° 1779. Prop. of Goſpel.
[YOUATT William]
   * Col. ii. 2. 8° 1776. b. Female-Society.
YOUNG Edward, LL.D. Fell. of Wincheſter, and Dean of Sarum.
   John xiii. 34, 35. 12° 1686. Conc. ad Cler. *Ch. Ch. Magd.* Ox.
   Serm. in 2 Vol. (2d Edit.) 8° 1706. On ſeveral occaſions. *Univ. Ch. Ch. C.C.C. Magd. New C. Or. Pemb.* Oxon. *Pub. L.* Cam.
YOUNG Edward, LL.D. Fell. of All Soul's Coll. Oxon. and R. of Welling, Herts.
   Col. iii. 2. 4° 1728. A Vindication of Providence, or a true Eſtimate of human life. *Worc.* Oxon. *Queen's.* Camb. *Sion.*
   1 Pet. ii. 17. 8° 1729. Jan. 30. b. Commons. An Apology for Princes, or the Reverence due to Government. *Worc.* Oxon. *Queen's.* Camb. *Sion.*

YOUNG Edward, Bp. of Ferns and Leighlin, Ireland.
* Matt. x. 34. 4° 1763. Anniv. of Irish Massacre.
* Prov. xix. 27. 4° 1766. Irish Prot. Schools.

YOUNG John, DD.
* Serm in 2 Vol. 8° 1764. On various Subjects.

YOUNG Toy William, B. A. Scholar of Pemb. Coll. Oxon. Curate of St. Martin's, Birmingham.
* Pf. xxxvii. 37. 4° 1778. On the Death of Rev. John Parsons, M. A.

[YOUNGE Hercules]
‡* Luke i. 3. } 8° 1770. 2 Crit. Dissertations.
‡* Jude 6.

ZAMBRANA De Barzia Joseph, DD.
*Eccl^{us}. x. 31. 4° 1685. Excellency of the Soul. *Magd*. Oxon.

ZINZANO Nicholas, M. A. R. of St. Martin Ouwich, London.
1 Thess. v. 21. 4° 1708. b. Lord Mayor and Judges.

ZINZENDORF Count, Bp. of the Antient Moravian Church.
* 16 Disc. in 12° 1740. On the Redemption of Man by the Death of Christ. Translated from the High Dutch. *Hert*. Ox.

[ZUBLY John,] DD.   Charles Town.
* James ii. 12. 8° 1775. Law of Liberty,
* - - - - 1781.

AN INDEX

OF

OCCASIONAL SERMONS, &c. &c.

Accession-Sermons.

Pag. 5, 10, 17, 19, 20, 24, 25, 27, 28, 31, 32, 34, 36, 37, 38, 43, 44, 45, 46, 48, 62, 66, 70, 73, 75, 78, 79, 80, 82, 83, 84, 88, 91, 94, 95, 97, 98, 100, 101, 107, 115, 118, 119, 120, 121, 125, 129, 142, 143, 158, 159, 213, 241, 308, 331, 334, 335, 336, 337, 378, 409, 410, 414, 415, 430, 431, 458, 459, 485.

Act-Sermons.

P. 17, 19, 24, 25, 30, 53, 73, 84, 103, 104, 105, 153, 160, 180, 191, 261, 300, 331, 339, 352, 354, 365, 367, 369, 373, 375, 400, 464.

Advent.

P. 66, 135, 150, 168, 171, 174, 199, 204, 211, 212, 218, 236, 255, 256, 262, 265, 268, 270, 295, 302, 308, 338, 340, 368, 376, 399, 438.

Before Antigallicans.

P. 19, 26, 95, 98, 111, 140, 172, 445, 460.

Before Apothecaries.

P. 37, 85, 99, 114, 125, 129, 319, 361.

Before Artillery Co.

P. 25, 32, 120, 234, 257, 305, 336, 362, 376, 391, 423.

Before Artists.

P. 55.

Ascension.

P. 63, 75, 202, 230, 259, 271, 282, 283, 286, 288, 289, 385, 398, 432, 434, 436, 438.

Ashwednesday.

P. 67, 83, 162, 175, 176, 189, 197, 208, 244, 379, 440, 481.

Assize-

INDEX OF

Assize-Sermons.

P. 5, 6, 8, 9, 11, 12, 13, 14, 16, 18, 19, 20, 21, 22, 24, 26, 27, 28, 29, 30, 31, 33, 35, 36, 37, 39, 40, 42, 44, 46, 47, 48, 49, 53, 54, 55, 59, 64, 65, 67, 73, 75, 76, 78, 79, 82, 84, 86, 87, 89, 94, 95, 96, 97, 98, 99, 101, 102, 107, 108, 109, 110, 111, 112, 113, 114, 115, 116, 118, 119, 121, 122, 125, 127, 132, 134, 136, 140, 143, 146, 147, 150, 151, 152, 156, 159, 161, 164, 165, 166, 169, 170, 172, 185, 193, 194, 195, 198, 200, 204, 209, 213, 214, 216, 222, 225, 226, 227, 240, 242, 255, 262, 265, 269, 270, 272, 273, 278, 279, 281, 285, 286, 287, 302, 304, 310, 311, 312, 314, 315, 316, 318, 319, 320, 322, 323, 324, 328, 332, 333, 334, 335, 336, 337, 338, 339, 340, 342, 346, 349, 350, 352, 361, 362, 363, 365, 368, 371, 377, 378, 386, 387, 394, 395, 399, 405, 407, 408, 410, 413, 414, 415, 416, 418, 420, 422, 425, 426, 429, 430, 431, 436, 438, 443, 444, 446, 448, 450, 451, 452, 453, 454, 456, 457, 458, 459, 460, 461, 466, 472, 476, 477, 478, 486.

Association or meeting of dissenting Clergy.

P. 36, 39, 59, 98, 143, 155, 158, 160, 169, 177, 192, 197, 198, 224, 234, 252, 269, 272, 281, 329, 338, 251, 370, 373, 394, 405, 406, 416, 419, 424, 436, 444, 477.

At the Asylum.

P. 100, 121, 161, 209, 219, 225, 235, 247, 250, 273, 313, 333, 387, 391.

At Bampton's Lecture.

P. 147, 223, 232, 234, 269, 278, 284, 330, 342, 375, 400, 435, 465, 468.

At Boyle's Lecture.

P. 4, 5, 7, 22, 24, 58, 59, 60, 69, 77, 136, 142, 144, 150, 152, 157, 159, 160, 171, 172, 173, 200, 206, 216, 223, 230, 251, 252, 255, 257, 260, 261, 267, 270, 271, 272, 281, 287, 310, 311, 319, 322, 325, 330, 331, 342, 344, 365, 410, 413, 418, 422, 428, 432, 433, 435, 416, 465, 467, 468, 474, 478, 482, 483.

Charity-Schools.

P. 6, 7, 10, 15, 17, 20, 21, 24, 26, 27, 40, 35, 53, 54, 57, 64, 66, 74, 75, 77, 90, 102, 103, 105, 109, 110, 114, 116, 117, 122, 124, 129, 131, 146, 149, 154, 160, 218, 219, 226, 233, 239, 244, 250, 251, 278, 288, 303, 303, 306, 308, 314, 317, 338, 339, 351, 380, 381, 390, 391, 413, 421, 426, 431, 440, 447, 455, 484.

Christmas.

P. 22, 38, 56, 58, 69, 75, 83, 136, 137, 134, 135, 141, 144, 147, 165, 173, 174, 182, 194, 202, 230, 231, 232, 233, 242, 260, 261, 264, 265, 280, 338, 342, 366, 376, 382, 395, 413, 414, 417, 422, 424, 430, 432, 433, 434, 460, 470, 471, 487.

Before Clergy, Sons of.

P. 50, 54, 65, 74, 95, 96, 113, 116, 129, 143, 153, 154, 155, 157, 161, 171, 177, 179, 181, 182, 199, 227, 228, 240, 255, 258, 263, 278, 286, 303, 318, 330, 339, 341, 342, 357, 371, 374, 375, 381, 391, 406, 409, 420, 428, 431, 437, 440, 446, 447, 450, 451, 457, 461, 464, 479.

Colony

OCCASIONAL SERMONS, &c.

Colony of Georgia.

P. 5, 23, 24, 87, 137, 371, 379, 380, 381, 394.

Commemoration, or Commencement.

P. 58, 71, 89, 94, 108, 140, 215, 249, 261, 271, 287, 307, 342, 348, 365, 371, 382, 410, 419, 421, 422, 426, 432, 447, 451, 460, 462, 473, 477.

Conciones Academicæ.

P. 33, 38, 39, 142, 180, 205, 252, 271, 274, 309, 344, 346, 378, 423, 464, 465, 477, 485.

Conciones ad Cleros.

P. 25, 40, 47, 107, 133, 150, 157, 199, 220, 225, 228, 239, 264, 285, 286, 303, 309, 310, 313, 319, 322, 327, 330, 331, 334, 340, 342, 343, 344, 349, 356, 357, 358, 360, 363, 364, 365, 370, 377, 380, 395, 396, 414, 419, 423, 424, 428, 429, 436, 446, 465, 477, 479.

Conciones ad Synodum.

P. 23, 72, 98, 133, 160, 280, 309, 313, 339, 341, 346, 352, 365, 384, 410, 419, 428, 452.

Consecration of Abps and Bps.

P. 24, 38, 51, 79, 98, 104, 135, 141, 151, 171, 197, 223, 224, 239, 234, 249, 269, 287, 288, 307, 310, 313, 335, 344, 345, 354, 357, 363, 365, 370, 386, 390, 402, 409, 416, 417, 419, 420, 421, 422, 424, 428, 430, 436, 440, 445, 447, 457, 461, 481.

Consecration &c. of a Church or Chapel.

P. 4, 7, 10, 14, 15, 16, 17, 19, 38, 43, 47, 56, 57, 62, 63, 70, 72, 79, 80, 82, 83, 94, 104, 125, 145, 147, 168, 212, 224, 227, 235, 236, 266, 272, 275, 310, 352, 358, 371, 384, 387, 430, 440, 447.

Coronation.

P. 29, 30, 36, 37, 38, 41, 42, 43, 44, 61, 62, 71, 75, 83, 84, 91, 97, 98, 107, 111, 133, 143, 158, 213, 414, 415, 430, 459, 480, 486.

Before Cutlers.

P. 125.

Before Debtors.

P. 165, 210, 244.

On Duelling.

P. 32, 184, 235, 334.

Easter-day.

P. 10, 11, 52, 60, 91, 157, 161, 213, 214, 222, 229, 252, 255, 258, 259, 263, 268, 271, 276, 286, 287, 288, 300, 301, 302, 306, 307, 311, 312, 315, 316, 318, 322, 324, 326, 327, 328, 339, 342, 346, 347, 359, 360, 361, 362, 384, 397, 403, 404, 422, 423, 436, 448, 455, 464, 467, 474, 475, 486.

Fairs opening of &c.

P. 117, 157, 165.

Fair-

INDEX OF

At Fairchild's Lecture.

P. 1, 58, 191.

Farewell-Sermons.

P. 7, 15, 21, 64, 67, 87, 88, 132, 156, 163, 186, 227, 235, 280, 300, 313, 327, 333, 334, 340, 341, 363, 365, 373, 376, 380, 392, 394, 396, 400, 401, 402, 407, 411, 412, 414, 439, 440, 444, 446, 448, 450, 464, 478, 479, 487.

Fast-Sermons.

P 6, 11, 15, 17, 18, 19, 21, 22, 23, 24, 25, 28, 29, 30, 31, 32, 34, 35, 36, 37, 38, 39, 41, 43, 44, 45, 46, 47, 48, 51, 56, 57, 58, 59, 60, 62, 63, 64, 65, 66, 69, 70, 71, 72, 73, 75, 77, 78, 79, 80, 82, 85, 88, 89, 92, 93, 94, 95, 96, 97, 98, 101, 102, 104, 108, 111, 112, 116, 118, 120, 121, 122, 126, 128, 129, 130, 134, 135, 136, 137, 138, 139, 140, 142, 143, 145, 146, 147, 149, 150, 151, 152, 153, 154, 155, 156, 157, 158, 161, 162, 163, 164, 165, 166, 167, 168, 169, 170, 171, 172, 175, 177, 183, 189, 191, 198, 199, 200, 202, 206, 213, 237, 238, 242, 244, 245, 251, 254, 255, 256, 267, 268, 301, 303, 304, 307, 319, 320, 329, 330, 335, 336, 344, 347, 350, 351, 371, 379, 389, 398, 399, 411, 419, 421, 425, 430, 431, 435, 442, 443, 453, 455, 458, 462, 463, 466, 467, 469, 479, 480, 481, 482, 485.

Feasts, Revels &c.

P. 5, 9, 27, 47, 72, 79, 80, 105, 109, 119, 120, 128, 140, 164, 193, 219, 222, 225, 231, 240, 278, 301, 303, 304, 313, 332, 339, 340, 346, 351, 357, 381, 400, 405, 407, 425, 458, 464, 471, 472, 473, 478.

Before Florists.

P. 1, 88, 101.

Before Free-Masons.

P. 38, 166, 197, 281, 326, 341, 378, 388, 434, 440, 485.

Funeral Sermons.

P. 3, 4, 5, 6, 7, 8, 9, 17, 18, 19, 24, 25, 26, 27, 29, 30, 32, 33, 34, 35, 36, 37, 39, 40, 41, 42, 43, 45, 46, 48, 49, 51, 52, 54, 56, 57, 58, 59, 60, 61, 63, 64, 65, 66, 67, 68, 69, 70, 71, 75, 76, 77, 78, 79, 80, 81, 82, 84, 85, 86, 87, 88, 89, 90, 91, 92, 93, 94, 100, 101, 104, 108, 109, 110, 111, 113, 114, 116, 122, 123, 124, 125, 126, 127, 128, 129, 130, 131, 132, 135, 137, 138, 139, 140, 141, 142, 144, 145, 146, 147, 150, 155, 156, 157, 158, 159, 160, 161, 164, 166, 168, 169, 170, 172, 178, 179, 197, 204, 208, 212, 214, 217, 218, 219, 220, 221, 229, 233, 236, 239, 240, 243, 245, 246, 247, 248, 253, 255, 257, 262, 263, 268, 274, 275, 276, 277, 278, 279, 280, 282, 284, 286, 303, 304, 305, 306, 307, 308, 313, 314, 315, 317, 320, 322, 323, 324, 325, 326, 327, 328, 335, 336, 339, 343, 344, 345, 346, 348, 349, 351, 359, 360, 361, 362, 363, 366, 367, 368, 371, 372, 382, 383, 389, 392, 393, 394, 397, 398, 403, 404, 406, 408, 411, 412, 414, 420, 421, 422, 423, 424, 426, 427, 428, 429, 434, 436, 437, 438, 439, 441, 442, 443, 444, 445, 446, 447, 449, 450, 455, 456, 459, 460, 462, 465, 467, 470, 480, 482, 483, 484, 485, 486, 487.

On Gaming.

P. 108, 167, 249, 331.

Gardi-

OCCASIONAL SERMONS, &c.

Before Gardiners.

P. 1, 2.

Good-friday.

P. 19, 144, 264, 286, 375, 402, 459, 461, 464.

Gospel, Propagation of.

P. 5, 23, 56, 74, 101, 129, 137, 143, 147, 159, 160, 171, 177, 188, 429, 483, 196, 197, 199, 204, 216, 222, 223, 229, 230, 233, 235, 246, 257, 275, 276, 281, 283, 303, 309, 311, 314, 317, 318, 320, 329, 330, 348, 372, 375, 378, 380, 394, 423, 426, 428, 429, 461, 471.

Before Gregorians.

P. 332.

Hospital or Infirmary, &c.

P. 3, 10, 22, 28, 29, 33, 41, 43, 54, 69, 64, 81, 82, 85, 86, 89, 95, 97, 104, 111, 112, 114, 115, 116, 121, 129, 143, 144, 146, 153, 267, 270, 272, 277, 278, 302, 306, 314, 326, 332, 338, 344, 349, 371, 377, 379, 380, 381, 387, 392, 406, 407, 421, 440, 445, 447, 455, 460, 462.

Before Humane Society.

P. 30, 85, 96, 338, 381.

At Hutchins's Lecture.

P. 20, 64, 78, 83, 126, 176, 187, 240, 241, 358, 428.

Inauguration.

P. 34, 42, 102, 105, 111, 121, 158, 337.

Induction.

P. 318, 364, 448.

Inoculation.

P. 49, 275, 321.

Invasion.

P. 37, 136, 137, 140.

January 30.

P. 3, 4, 6, 8, 9, 12, 15, 18, 22, 23, 25, 26, 27, 28, 29, 30, 31, 32, 33, 35, 36, 37, 38, 39, 40, 41, 45, 46, 47, 49, 54, 57, 58, 62, 63, 66, 67, 71, 72, 77, 78, 81, 82, 84, 88, 94, 98, 99, 100, 101, 106, 107, 111, 113, 114, 118, 119, 120, 122, 123, 126, 127, 128, 129, 137, 138, 139, 140, 144, 145, 146, 149, 151, 153, 154, 155, 158, 159, 161, 162, 163, 164, 169, 170, 172, 178, 180, 191, 193, 194, 202, 210, 212, 213, 216, 221, 224, 232, 238, 244, 252, 255, 267, 272, 274, 276, 282, 285, 301, 303, 304, 308, 309, 310, 314, 315, 316, 335, 336, 337, 350, 351, 355, 365, 372, 378, 385, 387, 388, 399, 408, 412, 414, 415, 418, 424, 425, 430, 431, 444, 449, 452, 453, 455, 457, 458, 459, 462, 466, 471, 473, 478, 480, 481.

Lecturer, Elect. of &c. Open. of a Lecture.

P. 289. Op. 315, 330.

D d d   Levant.

INDEX OF

Levant-Co.

P. 87, 92, 105, 127, 139, 140, 166, 208, 266, 360, 433, 461.

Marine Society.

P. 54, 115, 332.

Massacre Irish.

P. 59, 150, 185, 282, 363, 374, 402, 418.

Matrimony.

P. 2, 46, 48, 74, 87, 97, 143, 210, 248, 253, 262, 348, 390, 419, 445, 446.

May 29.

P. 12, 20, 21, 25, 26, 28, 31, 32, 35, 36, 41, 46, 47, 55, 56, 59, 60, 62, 63, 65, 70, 71, 74, 75, 76, 77, 79, 81, 83, 86, 87, 88, 89, 90, 91, 96, 97, 98, 102, 116, 118, 120, 127, 134, 139, 141, 142, 143, 146, 153, 157, 160, 161, 164, 169, 185, 212, 213, 223, 267, 289, 331, 335, 336, 337, 339, 350, 409, 410, 414, 415, 430, 457, 458, 466.

Mayor, Admission of &c.

P. 30, 36, 44, 47, 54, 82, 94, 95, 106, 113, 115, 119, 121, 128, 131, 134, 143, 149, 202, 211, 226, 239, 241, 245, 304, 312, 333, 335, 340, 345, 407, 415, 430, 456, 457, 460, 478.

Meeting-House, Opening of &c.

P. 303, 382.

Members of Parliament, Election of &c. &c.

P. 11, 25, 42, 79, 104, 129, 150, 308, 373.

Military Sermons.

P. 5, 17, 20, 22, 43, 44, 55, 61, 73, 77, 84, 148, 153, 234, 240, 242, 334, 354, 377, 378, 381, 389, 391, 396, 480.

Millenium.

P. 188, 196, 485.

At Moyer's Lecture.

P. 23, 50, 54, 136, 142, 176, 209, 228, 229, 250, 251, 259, 260, 261, 280, 303, 312, 329, 344, 348, 360, 395, 417, 431, 432, 461, 474, 475, 477, 481.

Music Meeting, &c.

P. 7, 30, 40, 42, 43, 70, 73, 74, 79, 80, 83, 84, 85, 87, 99, 102, 103, 124, 169, 188, 405, 407, 454, 485.

Naval [a] Sermons.

P. 32, 87, 167, 317.

New Year's day.

P. 9, 26, 81, 108, 124, 129, 131, 147, 152, 159, 245, 321, 389, 432.

Nov. 5.

P. 3, 9, 10, 11, 17, 19, 20, 24, 26, 27, 28, 30, 31, 35, 37, 42, 46, 47, 48, 49, 57, 58, 59, 62, 65, 66, 70, 71, 72, 73, 74, 75, 76, 77, 78, 79, 80, 86, 88, 90, 91, 94, 96, 97, 100, 101, 103, 104, 107, 109, 111, 117,

---

[a] V. Philips, Ramsey and Stockdale.

OCCASIONAL SERMONS, &c. 395

118, 119, 126, 129, 134, 135, 136, 137, 140, 143, 144, 153, 154, 158, 159, 163, 164, 165, 166, 169, 193, 194, 198, 202, 206, 216, 225, 231, 238, 239, 242, 246, 255, 262, 269, 273, 274, 278, 282, 285, 309, 310, 312, 314, 316, 318, 329, 335, 336, 337, 351, 356, 358, 363, 364, 370, 372, 376, 378, 411, 415, 420, 425, 426, 431, 440, 442, 452, 457, 458, 466, 472, 478, 483, 485, 486.

Ordination-Sermons.

P. 32, 112, 152, 155, 160, 170, 197, 198, 208, 224, 231, 272, 300, 313, 314, 330, 341, 342, 344, 345, 355, 358, 362, 363, 364, 365, 366, 367, 369, 378, 386, 392, 393, 396, 402, 406, 417, 419, 423, 426, 427, 428, 430, 432, 436, 448, 449, 462.

Organ, erecting of &c.

P. 52, 82, 94, 103, 390.

On Painting. [b]

P. 13.

Before Physicians.

P. 50, 85, 93, 100, 199.

Of Plays.

P. 388, 424.

Reformation of Manners.

P. 3, 6, 16, 25, 26, 27, 29, 30, 46, 47, 82, 92, 93, 94, 100, 107, 108, 111, 113, 115, 119, 120, 122, 128, 134, 135, 136, 143, 147, 149, 152, 160, 163, 168, 171, 181, 197, 216, 226, 227, 239, 247, 264, 306, 321, 336, 337, 339, 351, 377, 388, 423, 442, 454, 466, 400, 471, 480.

[b] V. Morer's Occ. S.

School-Feasts, &c.

P. 15, 35, 43, 53, 63, 68, 66, 65, 68, 75, 89, 103, 155, 271, 278, 304, 313, 314, 355, 381, 413, 426, 428, 458, 460, 462.

Schools, Irish Prot.

P. 26, 57, 75, 89, 95, 104, 108, 110, 115, 129, 137, 146, 147, 152, 154, 209, 211, 239, 247, 278, 380, 391, 406, 411, 412, 413, 418, 421, 431, 481.

Sessions.

P. 54, 58, 118, 235.

Society-Sermons.

Before Batchelors. 347. Char. 204. Educat. 364. Fem. 402. Friendly. 386, 445, 450. Grateful. 54. Loving. 146. Relig. 42, 93, 110, 118, 125, 147, 171, 226, 408 Virtuous 112. Young Women. 440, 477.

Spittal-Sermons.

P. 32, 48, 49, 54, 69, 88, 89, 95, 105, 109, 116, 126, 129, 140, 158, 177, 190, 210, 216, 218, 235, 239, 246, 248, 249, 251, 269, 278, 281, 286, 306, 307, 309, 313, 314, 333, 351, 355, 356, 357, 366, 368, 371, 380, 381, 388, 402, 403, 425, 440, 447, 455, 462, 471.

Style New.

P. 1, 394.

Suicide.

P. 13, 35, 69, 49, 51, 183.

Thanksgiving-Sermons.

P. 5, 9, 10, 11, 15, 18, 19, 20,

INDEX OF

21, 22, 23, 24, 25, 28, 29, 30, 31, 33, 34, 35, 36, 37, 38, 39, 41, 42, 43, 44, 45, 46, 47, 48, 55, 56, 57, 58, 60, 61, 62, 63, 64, 65, 66, 69, 70, 71, 72, 73, 74, 75, 76, 77, 79, 80, 82, 83, 84, 85, 86, 87, 88, 89, 90, 91, 94, 95, 96, 97, 100, 101, 103, 112, 113, 121, 129, 137, 138, 139, 141, 142, 143, 146, 147, 150, 153, 154, 156, 157, 158, 159, 164, 165, 167, 169, 179, 180, 196, 232, 234, 252, 254, 267, 268, 285, 315, 319, 325, 336, 339, 350, 363, 382, 390, 405, 406, 409, 110, 415, 425, 428, 430, 457, 459, 482, 485.

Trinity—and before Trin-House-Corporation.

P. 5, 23, 50, 85, 87, 142, 157, 176, 181, 222, 264, 267, 284, 344, 348, 350, 355, 356, 373, 383, 384, 404, 416, 417, 432, 436, 474, 475, 482.

Before Ubiquarians.

P. 41, 273, 304.

Visitation-Sermons.

P. 12, 22, 23, 24, 34, 38, 39, 47, 53, 55, 59, 75, 76, 84, 91, 94, 95, 96, 98, 99, 107, 108, 110, 118, 127, 142, 147, 157, 159, 160, 161, 170, 175, 171, 177, 180, 181, 187, 188, 195, 197, 198, 200, 204, 205, 209,

212, 213, 223, 224, 226, 229, 230, 234, 235, 241, 242, 244, 312, 355, 359, 370, 379, 381, 395, 399, 402, 406, 410, 429, 430, 431, 436, 439, 440, 445, 446, 447, 448, 452, 466, 467, 477, 481, 482.

At Warburton's Bp. Lecture.

P. 5, 137, 138, 142, 156, 158, 159, 160, 165, 167, 169, 204, 231, 244, 258, 278, 280, 285, 316, 411, 417, 479, 482, 485, 486.

Weaver's-Co.

P. 15, 117, 411.

Wedding-Sermons.

P. 2, 7, 29, 48, 97, 109, 114, 115, 123, 262, 348, 416.

Whitsunday.

P. 22, 41, 75, 143, 282, 283, 288, 289, 300, 301, 327, 343, 351, 354, 357, 365, 373, 390, 396, 432, 467, 468, 472, 481.

Workhouses.

P. 81, 219, 412.

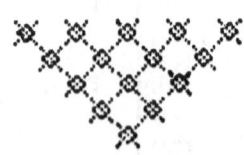

A LIST

OF THE

ARCHBISHOPS and BISHOPS of ENGLAND and WALES since the Restoration 1660 to the Year 1783.

*** O. and C. denote of which University the present were Members.

CANTERBURY, Archbp.

1660 *Sept.* William Juxon.
1663 *July* Gilbert Sheldon.
1677 *Jan.* William Sancroft, deprived Feb 1. 1690.
1691 *April* John Tillotson
1694 *Dec.* Thomas Tenison
1715 *Dec.* William Wake
1737 *Mar.* John Potter
1747 *Oct.* Thomas Herring
*1757 *April* Matthew Hutton
*1758 *April* Thomas Secker
*1768 *Sep.* Hon. F. Cornwallis. C.

ST. ASAPH.

1660 *Oct.* George Griffith

1667 *Oct.* Henry Glemham
1669 *Mar.* Isaac Barrow
1680 *Sept.* William Lloyd
1692 *Dec.* Edward Jones
1703 *Oct.* George Hooper.
1704 *July* William Beveridge
1708 *May* William Fleetwood
1714 *Nov.* John Wynne
1727 *Dec.* Francis Hare
1731 *Nov.* Thomas Tanner
1736 *May* Isaac Maddox
1743 *Nov.* John Thomas
1743 *Jan.* Samuel Lisle
1748 *Mar.* Hon. Rob. Drummond
*1761 *Aug.* Rich. Newcome
*1769 *Sep.* Jonathan Shipley. O.

BANGOR

BANGOR.

1637 died 1665. Will. Roberts
1666 *June* Robert Morgan
1673 *Oct.* Humphrey Lloyd
1689 *June* Humph. Humphreys
1701 *Jan.* John Evans
1715 *Dec.* Benjamin Hoadly
1721 *Nov.* Richard Reynolds
1723 *Aug.* William Baker
1727 *Feb.* Thomas Sherlock
1734 *Nov.* Charles Cecil
1737 *Jan.* Thomas Herring
1743 *Apr.* Matthew Hutton
1747 *Dec.* Zachary Pearce
*1766 *July* Hon. John Egerton
*1769 *Jan.* John Ewer
*1775 *Feb.* John Moore. O.

BATH and WELLS.

1632   William Pierce
1670 *May* Robert Creighton
1672 *Dec.* Peter Mew
1684 *Jan.* Thomas Kenn, *deprived* Feb. 1690.
1691   William Beveridge, *nominated* Apr. 23, *but refused it*.
1691 *June* Richard Kidder
1703 *Mar.* George Hooper
1727 *Sept.* John Wynne.
1743 *Aug.* Edward Willes
*1774 *June* Charles Moss. C.

BRISTOL.

1660 *Dec.* Gilbert Ironside
1671 *Dec.* Guy Carleton
1678 *Jan.* William Gulston
1684 *Aug.* John Lake
1685 *Nov.* Sir Jon. Trelawney
1689 *Oct.* Gilbert Ironside
1691 *Aug.* John Hall
1710 *Nov.* John Robinson
1713-4 *Mar.* George Smalridge.
1719 *Oct.* Hugh Boulter
1724 *Oct.* William Bradshaw
1732-3. *Jan.* Charles Cecil

1734 *Dec.* Thomas Secker
1737 *June* Sir Thomas Gooch
1738- *Dec.* Joseph Butler
1750 *Nov.* John Conybeare
*1756 *July* John Hume
*1758 *June* Philip Yonge
*1761 *Dec.* Thomas Newton
*1782 *Feb.* Hon. Lewis Bagott. O.

CHICHESTER.

1641   Henry King
1669 *Feb.* Peter Gunning
1675 *Mar.* Ralph Brideoke
1678 *Jan.* Guy Carleton
1685 *Oct.* John Lake
1689 *Oct.* Simon Patrick
1691 *Aug.* Robert Grove
1696 *Dec.* John Williams
1709 *Nov.* Thomas Manningham
1722 *Aug.* Thomas Bowers
1724 *Oct.* Edward Waddington
1731 *Oct.* Francis Hare
1740 *May* Matthias Mawson
*1754 Sir Will. Ashburnham. C.

Saint DAVID's.

1660 *Oct.* William Lucy
1677 *Nov.* William Thomas
1683 *Nov.* Laurence Womack
1686 *Oct.* John Lloyd
1687 *June* Thomas Watson, *deprived Aug.* 3. 1697. *See vacant* 5 *Years,* 8 *Months.*
1704-5 *Mar.* George Bull
1710 *Nov.* Philip Bisse
1712 *Feb.* Adam Ottley
1723 *Jan.* Richard Smalbroke
1730 *Jan.* Elias Sydall
1731 *Dec.* Nicholas Clagett
1742 *July* Edward Willes
1743 *Jan.* Hon. Rich. Trevor
*1752 *Oct.* Anthony Ellys
*1761 *May* Samuel Squire
*1766 *June* Robert Lowth
*1766 *Nov.* Charles Moss
*1774 *June* Hon. James Yorke
*1779 *July* John Warren. C.

ARCHBISHOPS and BISHOPS. 399

Ely.

1638   Matthew Wren
1667 *May* Benjamin Laney
1674 *Feb.* Peter Gunning
1684 *Aug.* Francis Turner, *deprived.* Feb. 1690.
1691 *Apr.* Simon Patrick
1707 *July* John Moore
1714 *Nov.* William Fleetwood
1723 *Sept.* Thomas Green
1738 *May* Robert Butts
1747 *Jan.* Sir Thomas Gooch
*1754 *Mar* Matthias Mawson
*1771 *Jan.* Edmund Keene
*1781 *July* Hon. James Yorke. C.

Exeter.

1660 *Nov.* John Gauden
1662 *July* Seth Ward
1667 *Oct.* Anthony Sparrow
1676 *Oct.* Thomas Lamplugh
1689 *Apr.* Sir Jon. Trelawney
1707 *Feb.* Offspring Blackall
1716 *Jan.* Lancelot Blackburn
1724 *Dec.* Stephen Weston
1742 *June* Nicolas Clagett
1746 *Dec.* George Lavington
*1761 *Nov.* Hon. Fred. Keppel
*1778 *Jan.* John Ross. C.

Glocester.

1660 *Nov.* William Nicholson
1672 *Oct.* J. Pritchet, *or* Pritchard
1681 *Mar.* Robert Frampton, *deprived* Feb. 1. 1690.
1691 *Apr.* Edward Fowler
1714 *Nov.* Richard Willis
1721 *Nov.* Joseph Wilcocks
1731 *Oct.* Elias Sydall
1734 *Dec.* Martin Benson
*1752 *Oct.* James Johnson
*1760 *Jan.* Will. Warburton
*1779 *July* Hon. James Yorke
*1781 *Sep.* Samuel Hallifax. C.

Hereford.

1660 *Dec.* Nicholas Monck
1661 *Jan.* Herbert Croft
1691 *May* Gilbert Ironside
1701 *Dec.* Humphrey Humphreys
1712 *Feb.* Philip Bisse
1721 *Sep.* Benjamin Hoadly
1723 *Jan.* Henry Egerton
1746 *Apr.* Lord J. Beauclerck. O.

Landaff.

1660 *Oct.* Hugh Lloyd
1667 *July* Francis Davies
1675 *Apr.* William Lloyd
1679 *June* William Beaw
1706 *June* John Tyler
1724 *Dec.* Robert Clavering
1729 *Apr.* John Harris
1738 *Dec.* Matthias Mawson
1740 *May* John Gilbert
1748 *Dec.* Edward Cresset
*1755 *Apr.* Richard Newcome
*1761 *Sept.* John Ewer
*1769 *Feb.* Jonathan Shipley
*1769 *Oct.* Hon. Shute Barrington
*1782 *Aug.* Richard Watson. C.

Litchfield *and* Coventry.

1643   Accepted Frewen
1661 *Dec.* John Hacket
1671 *June* Thomas Wood
1692 *Oct.* William Lloyd
1699 *Aug.* John Hough
1717 *Nov.* Edward Chandler
1730 *Dec.* Richard Smallbroke
1749 *Jan.* Hon. Fred. Cornwallis
*1768 *Nov.* Hon. John Egerton
*1771 *Sep.* Hon. Brownlow North
*1775 *Feb.* Richard Hurd
*1781 *July* Hon. J. Cornwallis O.

Lincoln.

1660 *Oct.* Robert Sanderson
1663

400 A LIST of the ENGLISH

1663 Mar. Benjamin Laney
1667 Sept. William Fuller
1675 May Thomas Barlowe
1691 Nov. Thomas Tenison
1694 Mar. James Gardiner
1705 July William Wake
1715-6 Jan. Edmund Gibson
1723 May Richard Reynolds
1743-4 Jan. John Thomas
*1761 Dec. John Green. C.

1674 Nov. Henry Compton
1675 Jan. John Fell
1686 Oct. Samuel Parker
1688 Oct. Timothy Hall
1690 May John Hough
1699 Sept. William Talbot
1715 Apr. John Potter
1737 Apr. Thomas Secker
*1758 May John Hume
*1766 Oct. Robert Lowth
*1777 May John Butler. O.

LONDON.

1633 William Juxon
1660 Oct. Gilbert Sheldon
1663 Sep. Humphrey Henchman
1675 Dec. Henry Compton
1713 Aug. John Robinson
1723 Apr. Edmund Gibson
1748 Oct. Thomas Sherlock
*1761 Oct. Thomas Hayter
*1762 Feb. Rich. Osbaldeston
*1764 June Richard Terrick
*1777 May Robert Lowth. O.

PETERBOROUGH.

1660 Nov. Benjamin Laney
1663 Apr. Joseph Henshaw
1679 Mar. William Lloyd
1685 Aug. Thomas White
1691 May Richard Cumberland
1718 Oct. White Kennet
1728-9 Feb. Robert Clavering
1747 Aug. John Thomas
*1757 June Richard Terrick
*1764 July Robert Lambe
*1769 Dec. John Hinchcliffe. C.

NORWICH.

1660 Nov. Edward Reynolds
1676 Aug. Anthony Sparrow
1685 June William Lloyd, deprived Feb. 1. 1690.
1691 Apr. John Moore
1707 Feb. Charles Trimnell
1721 Aug. Thomas Green
1723 Nov. John Leng
1727 Dec. William Baker
1732 3 Jan. Robert Butts
1738 Sept. Sir Thomas Gooch
1747-8 Feb. Samuel Lisle
1749 Oct. Thomas Hayter
*1761 Nov. Philip Yonge C.

ROCHESTER.

1637 John Warner
1666 Nov. John Dolben
1683 Nov. Francis Turner
1684 Nov. Thomas Sprat
1713 June Francis Atterbury, deprived June 1723.
1723 July Samuel Bradford
1731 June Joseph Wilcocks
*1756 Apr. Zachary Pearce
*1774 Nov. John Thomas. O.

SALISBURY.

1641 Bryan Duppa
1660 Oct. Humphry Henchman
1663 Sep. John Earle
1665 Dec. Alexander Hyde
1667 Sep. Seth Ward
1689 Mar. Gilbert Burnet
1715 Apr. William Talbot

OXFORD.

1640 Robert Skinner
1663 Nov. William Paul
1665 Nov. Walter Blanford
1671 June Nathaniel Crew

1721

ARCHBISHOPS and BISHOPS.

1721 Nov. Richard Willis
1723 Oct. Benjamin Hoadly
1734 Oct. Thomas Sherlock
1748 Nov. John Gilbert
*1757 June John Thomas
*1761 June Hon. R. Drummond
*1761 Nov. John Thomas
*1766 Sept John Hume
*1782 Sep. Hon. S. Barrington. O.

WINCHESTER.

1660 Sept. Bryan Duppa
1662 Apr. George Morley
1684 Nov. Peter Mew
1707 June Sir Jon. Trelawney
1721 July Charles Trimnell
1723 Sept. Richard Willis
1734 Aug. Benjamin Hoadly
*1761 May John Thomas
*1781 May Hon. Br. North. O.

WORCESTER.

1660 Oct. George Morley
1662 May John Gauden
1662 Nov. John Earle
1663 Oct. Robert Skinner
1671 June Walter Blandford
1675 July James Fleetwood
1683 Aug. William Thomas
1689 Oct. Edward Stillingfleet
1699 Jan. William Lloyd,
1717 Sept. John Hough
1743 May Isaac Maddox
*1759 Oct. James Johnson
*1774 Dec. Hon. Brownl. North
*1781 May Richard Hurd. C.

YORK, Archbishop.

1660 Sept. Accepted Frewen
1664 Apr. Richard Sterne
1683 July John Dolben
1688 Nov. Thomas Lamplugh
1691 July John Sharp
1713-4 Mar. Sir Will. Dawes

1724 Nov. Lancelot Blackburn
1743 Apr. Thomas Herring
1747 Nov. Matthew Hutton
*1757 May John Gilbert
*1761 Oct. Hon. R Drummond
*1777 Jan. Will. Markham. O.

CARLISLE.

1660 Dec. Richard Sterne
1664 July Edward Rainbow
1684 June Thomas Smith
1702 June William Nicolson
1718 Apr. Samuel Bradford
1723 June John Waugh
1734 Nov. Sir George Fleming
1747 July Richard Osbaldeston
*1762 Mar. Hon. Char. Lyttleton
*1769 Feb. Edmund Law. C.

CHESTER.

1619 John Bridgman
1660 Dec. Brian Walton
1662 Feb. Henry Ferne
1662 May George Hall
1668 Nov. John Wilkins
1672 Feb. John Pearson
1686 Oct. Thomas Cartwright
1689 Sep. Nicholas Stratford
1707 Feb. Sir William Dawes
1714 Apr. Francis Gastrell
1726 Apr. Samuel Peploe
1752 Mar. Edmund Keene
*1771 Feb. William Markham
*1777 Feb. Beilby Porteus. C.

DURHAM.

1660 Dec. John Cosin
1674 Oct. Nathaniel Crew
1721 Sept. Sir William Talbot
1730 Oct. Edward Chandler
1750 Aug. Joseph Butler
*1752 Oct. Hon. Rich Trevor
*1771 July Hon. J. Egerton. O.

A LIST

A LIST

OF THE

BISHOPS of SODOR and MAN.

The SEE from 1643 vacant till filled by
*1661 Samuel Rutter
*1663 Isaac Barrow
*1671 Henry Bridgman
*1682 John Lake
*1984 Baptist Levinz

*1697 Thomas Wilson

The SEE vacant for 5 years.

*1755 Mark Hildesley
*1773 Richard Richmond
*1780 George Mason

A LIST

OF THE

IRISH ARCHBISHOPS and BISHOPS, from the Year 1660 to the Year 1783.

ARMAGH, *Primate and Archbishop, vacant from* Usher's *Death in* 1655, *till filled by*

1660 *Jan.* 18. John Bramhall
1663 *Aug.* 29. James Margetson
1678 *Feb.* 27. Michael Boyle
1702 *Feb.* 18. Narcissus Marsh
1713 *June* 4. Thomas Lindsay
1724 *Aug.* 31. Hugh Boulter
1742 *Oct.* 21. John Hoadly
1746 *Mar.* 13. George Stone
*1762 *Jan.* 10. Rich. Robinson

MEATH, *vacant from Bishop* Martin's *Death in* 1650, *till filled by*

1660 *Jun.* 19. Henry Lesley
1661 *May* 25. Henry Jones
1681 *Jan.* 14. Anthony Dopping
1697 *June* 25. Richard Tennison
1705 *Sept.* 18. William Moreton
1715 *Jan.* 19. John Evans
1724 *April* 9. Henry Downes
1726 *Feb.* 10. Ralph Lambert
1731 *Mar.* 13. Welbore Ellis

1733

A LIST of the IRISH

1733 Feb. 2. Arthur Price
1744 May 24. Henry Maule
*1752 Jan. 11. John Ryder
*1758 June 3. Will. Carmichael
*1765 July 2. Rich. Pococke
*1765 Oct. 1. Arthur Smyth
*1766 Mar. 22. Hon. H. Maxwell

CLOGHER.[b]

1661 June 27. John Lesley
1671 Oct. 26. Robert Lesley.
1672 Sept. 29. Roger Boyle *died in 1687, and the See vacant, till King* William *filled it with*
1690 Feb. 28. Richard Tennison
1697 June 25. St. George Ash
1717 Mar. 30. John Sterne
1745 Aug. 26. Robert Clayton
*1758 April 1. John Garnett
*1782 April 6. John Hotham

DOWN and CONNOR.

1660 Feb. 19. Jeremy Taylor
1667 Sep. 11. Roger Boyle
1672 Sep. 20. Thomas Hacket
1694 Aug. 31. Samuel Foley
1695 Aug. 1. Edw. Walkington
1699 Feb. 21. Edward Smith
1720 Jan. 12. Francis Hutchinson
1739 Nov. 16. Carew Reynell
1743 Aug. 1. John Ryder
1751 Jan. 11. John Whetcombe
1752 Aug. 25. Robert Downes
*1753 Jan. 2. Arthur Smyth
*1765 Oct. 1. Jacob Trail

KILMORE and ARDAGH.[b]

1643 Robert Maxwell, *succeeded* Bedell *in* Kilmore, *and was advanced likewise*
1661 Feb. 21. To Ardagh.
1672 Jan. 10. Francis Marsh
1681 Feb. 15. William Sheridan

Upon *whose deprivation in* 1691. Ardagh *was separated from* Kilmore, *and given to*
1692 Apr. 7. Ulysses Burgh. Upon *whose death the same year, they were again reunited under*
1693 April 5. William Smith
1699 Apr. 18. Edward Wetenhall
1714 Jan. 16. Timothy Godwin
1727 July 27. Josiah Hort
1741 Jan. 27. Joseph Story
*1757 Oct. 18. John Cradock
*1772 Feb. 15. Den. Cumberland
*1774 Dec. 3. Geo. Lewis Jones

DROMORE.

1660 Jan. 19. Robert Lesley
1661 June 21. Jeremy Taylor
1667 Nov. 8. George Rust
1670 Feb. 6. Essex Digby
1683 Sept. 10. Capel Wiseman
1695 May 7. Tobias Pullen
1713 May 1. John Sterne
1717 Apr. 12. Ralph Lambert
1726 Feb. 16. Charles Cobb
1731 Mar. 20. Henry Maule
1744 May 30. Thomas Fletcher
1745 May 16. Jemmett Browne
1745 Aug. 30. George Marlay
*1763 Apr. 30. John Oswald
*1769 Aug. 2. Edward Young
*1765 Feb. 16. Hon. H. Maxwell
*1766 Mar. 22. Will. Newcome
*1775 Mar. 25. James Hawkins
*1780 Mar. 21. Will. Beresford
*1782 Apr. 20. Thomas Percy

RAPHOE.

1661 June 20. Robert Lesley
1671 Oct. 27. Ezekiel Hopkins
1681 Feb. 17. William Smith
1693 May 16. Alex. Cairncross
1701 July 4. Rob Huntington
1702 Sep. 12. John Pooley

[a] V. Bp. Berkley's life, p. 32. [b] V. Primate Boulter's Letters, V. 1. p. 118, 142.

404 ARCHBISHOPS and BISHOPS.

1713 Jan. 6. Thomas Lindsay
1714 Nov. 2. Edward Synge
1716 June 8 Nicholas Forster
1744 June 26. William Barnard
1746 Mar. 23. Philip Twisden
*1753 Jan. 2. Robert Downes
*1763 Aug. 2. John Oswald
*1780 Mar 21. James Hawkins

1678 Jan. 16. Anthony Dopping
1681 Feb. 13. William Moreton
1705 Sept 22. Welbore Ellis
1731 Mar. 16. Charles Cobb
1742 Mar. 19. George Stone
1745 May 14. Thomas Fletcher
*1761 Mar. 28. Rich. Robinson
*1765 Feb. 16. Charles Jackson

Derry.

1660 Jan. 22. George Wild
1666 Mar. 27. Robert Mossom
1679 Jan. 22. Michael Ward
1681 Nov. 11. Ezekiel Hopkins
1690 Jan. 9. William King
1702 Mar. 19. Charles Hickman
1713 Jan. 30. John Hartstonge
1716 Feb. 27. St. George Ash
1718 May 2. William Nicholson
1726 Feb 8. Henry Downes
1735 July 17. Thomas Rundle
1743 May 16. Carew Reynell
1745 May 11. George Stone
1746 Mar. 19. William Barnard
*1768 Jan. 30. Fred. Hervey [a]

Ossory.

1641   Griffith Williams
1672 Apr. 22. John Parry
1677 Jan. 24. Benjamin Parry
1678 Nov. 8. Michael Ward
1679 Feb. 7. Thomas Otway
1693 Apr. 8. John Hartstonge
1714 Apr. 28. Sir Thomas Vesey
1731 June 30. Edward Tennison
1735 Jan. 8. Charles Este
1741 July 9. Anthony Dopping
1742 Apr. 14. Michael Cox
*1754 Jan. 15. Edw. Maurice
*1756 Mar. 20. Richard Pococke
*1765 July 2. Charles Dodgson
*1775 Mar. 25. Will Newcome
*1779 Oct. 13. John Hotham
*1782 April 6. Will. Beresford.

Dublin, Primate and Archbishop.

1660 Jan. 25. James Margetson
1663 Nov. 27. Michael Boyle
1678 Feb. 28. John Parker
1681 Feb. 14. Francis Marsh
1694 May 24. Narcissus Marsh
1702 Mar. 11. William King
1729 Jan. 13. John Hoadly
1742 Mar. 4 Charles Cobb
*1765 June 1. Will. Carmichael
*1766 Mar. 22. Arthur Smyth
*1772 Feb. 15. John Cradock
*1778 Jan. 29. Robert Fowler

Ferns and Leighlin.

1660 Jan. 15. Robert Price
1666 June 7. Richard Boyle
1682 Feb. 27. Narcissus Marsh
1690 Feb 27. Barth. Vigors
1721 Feb. 10. Josiah Hort
1727 Aug. 4. John Hoadly
1730 May 26. Arthur Price
1733 Feb. 8. Edward Synge
1740 [Aug. 3.] George Stone
1742 Mar 24. William Cottercll
1744 Aug. 1. Robert Downes
1752 Aug. 25. John Garnett
*1758 Apr. 1. Will. Carmichael
*1758 June 3. Thomas Salmon
*1759 Apr. 10. Rich. Robinson
*1761 Mar. 28. Charles Jackson

Kildare.

1660 Mar. 6. Thomas Price
1667 June 1. Ambrose Jones

[a] Now Earl of Bristol.

*1765 Feb. 16. Edward Young
*1772 Sept. 3. Jof. Dean Bourke
*1782 July 30. Walter Cope

CASHELL, Archbiſhop.

1660 Feb. 1. Thomas Fulwar
1667. May 30. Thomas Price
1690 Feb. 26. Narciſſus Marſh
1694 June 26. William Palliſer
1726 Jan 28. William Nicholſon
1727 July 3. Timothy Godwin
1729 Jan. 6. Theophilus Bolton
1744 May 7. Arthur Price
1752 Aug. 25. John Whetcombe
*1754 Jan. 15. Michael Cox
*1779 Aug. 11. Charles Agar

LIMERICK, &c.

1660 Jan. 19. Edward Synge
1663 Mar. 16. William Fuller
1667 Oct. 28. Francis Marſh
1672 Jan. 11. John Veſey
1678 Mar. 19. Simon Digby
1691 Jan. 29. Nathaniel Wilſon
1695 Dec. 2. Thomas Smith
1725 June 15. Will. Burſcough
*1755 Oct. 4. James Leſlie
*1772 Feb. 15. William Gore

ARDFERT.

1660 Jan. 19. Edward Synge
1663 Mar. 16. William Fuller.
From whence it has been always united to Limerick.

WATERFORD and LISMORE.

1660 Jan. 19. George Baker
1665 Feb. 21. Hugh Gore
1691 July 13. Nathaniel Foy
1707 Mar. 11. Thomas Mills
1740 Oct. 4. Charles Eſte
1745 Jan. 15. Richard Chenevix
*1779 Oct. 13. Will. Newcome

CORK, CLOYNE, and ROSS.

1660 Jan. 22. Michael Boyle
1663 Dec. 21. Edward Synge

CORK and ROSS.

1678 Feb. 14. Edw. Wetenhall
1699 Apr. 18. Dive Downes
1709 Jan. 11. Peter Browne
1735 Dec. 19. Robert Clayton
1745 Aug. 27. Jemmett Browne
*1772 Feb. 15. Walter Cope.
*1772 Feb. 15. Iſaac Man

CLOYNE ſeparate from CORK and ROSS.

1679 Apr. 19. Patrick Sheridan
1682 Feb. 26. Edward Jones
1692 Feb. 14. William Palliſer
1694 Nov. 13. Tobias Pullen
1695 July 15. St. George Aſh
1697 Nov. 24. John Pooley
1702 Sept. 15. Charles Crow
1726 Sept. 6. Henry Maule
1731 Mar. 21. Edward Synge
1733 Mar. 5. George Berkeley
1753 Feb. James Stopford
*1759 Sept. 29. Robert Johnſon
*1767 Feb. 7. Fred. Hervey
*1768 Feb. 16. Charles Agar
*1780 Jan. 19. George Chinner
*1781 Jan. 20. Rich. Woodward

KILLALOE.

1660 Jan. 19. Edward Worth
1669 Aug. 19. Daniel Witter
1675 Apr. 19. John Roan
1693 June 5. Henry Rider
1695 Mar. 2. Sir Thomas Veſey
1714 Oct. 19. Nicholas Forſter
1716 June 9. Charles Carr
1739 Feb. 5. Joſeph Story
1741 Jan. 30. John Ryder.

ARCHBISHOPS and BISHOPS.

1743 Sept. 26. Jemmett Browne
1745 May 20. Richard Chenevix
1746 Jan. 22. Nicholas Synge
*1771 June 13. Robert Fowler
*1778 Dec. 29. George Chinnery
*1780 Jan. 19. Thomas Barnard

TUAM, *Archbishop*.

1660 Jan. 19. Samuel Pullen
1666 Aug. 9. John Parker
1678 Mar. 18. John Vesey
1716 June 8. Edward Synge
1741 Jan. 27. Josiah Hort
*1752 Jan. 11. John Ryder
*1775 Mar. 25. Jemmett Browne
*1782 July 30. Jos. Dean Bourke

KILFENORAGH, *united to* TUAM *in*

1660, *Under* Samuel Pullen, *but separated on the death of* Edward Synge, *and given in commendam to*
1741 Jan 30. John Whetcombe, *at which time* Ardagh *was united to* Tuam, *in the person of Archbishop* Hort.
1752 Jan. 11. Nicholas Synge

ELPHIN.

1660 Jan. 19. John Parker
1667 Aug. 10. John Hudson
1691 Jan. 12. Simon Digby
1720 June 13. Henry Downes
1724 Apr. 16. Theophilus Bolton
1729 Jan. 13. Robert Howard

1740 May 15. Edward Synge
*1762 Apr. 27. William Gore
*1772 Feb. 15. Jemmett Browne
*1775 Mar. 25. Charles Dodgson

CLONFERT.

1644   William Baily
1664 Mar. 10. Edward Wolley
1691 July 1. Will. Fitz-Gerald
1722 Sept. 12. Theophilus Bolton
1724 May 1. Arthur Price
1730 May 28 Edward Synge
1731 Mar 22. Mordecai Cary
1735 Dec. 23. John Whetcombe
1752 Jan. 11. Arthur Smyth
1753 Jan. 2. Will. Carmichael
*1758 Apr. 1. William Gore
*1762 Apr. 27. John Oswald
*1763 Apr 30. Den. Cumberland
*1772 Feb. 15. Walter Cope
*1782 July 30. John Law

KILLALA *and* ACHONRY.

1660 Jan. 19. Henry Hall
1663 Mar. 1. Thomas Baily
1670 Nov. 16. Thomas Otway
1679 Feb. 13. John Smith
1681 Feb. 18. Richard Tennison
1681 May 2. William Smith
1690 Feb. 28. William Lloyd
1716 Feb. 8. Henry Downes
1720 May 30. Charles Cobb
1726 Feb. 23. Robert Howard
1729 Jan. 23. Robert Clayton
1735 Dec. 20. Mordecai Cary
1751 Nov. 26. Richard Robinson
*1759 Apr. 10. Sam. Hutchinson
*1781 Jan. 20. Will. Cecil Pery

N. B. *The Bishoprick of Enaghdoen is united to Tuam, and that of Ardagh held in Commendam with it. The Deanry of Christ-Church, Dublin, is annexed to Kildare. The Bishoprick of Kilfenora is held in Commendam with Killaloe. Connor is united to Downe. The Bishopricks of Ardfert and Aghadoe are united to Limerick, as is Achonry to Killala, and Kilmacduagh to Clonfert:.*

APPENDIX TO THE FIRST VOLUME.

GENESIS.

Chap.	Ver.	Authors.	Edition.	Vol.	Title, Page, &c.		Occasion or Subject.
I.	1–3	Murray James	8° 1777	II	Lect.	287	Or. of Light.
	26	Tillard Richard	4° 1781		f f.		Lun. Asyl.
II.	15, 16	Murray James	8° 1777	I	Lect.	1	Ad. & Ev. Xr.
III.	1	Barrington Lord	8° 1770	III	Misc. sac.		Fall of Man.
		Murray James	8° 1777	I	Lect.	45	Civ. & rel. G.
	19	Horsemanden S.	8° 1766		f f.		On Labour.
IV.	16	Barrington Lord	8° 1770	III	Misc. sac.		G's presence
V.	24	Murray James	8° 1777	I	Lect.	75	Enoch's Tr.
VI.	6	Adam Thomas	8° 1781		Evang. D. 1		
VIII.	9 &c.	Murray James	8° 1777	I	Lect.	107	Deluge &c.
	15	Murray James	8° 1771	I	Lect.	75	Noah's Xter.
IX.	1	[Ward John, LLD]	8° 1761		Diss.	1	
X.	1	Murray James	8° 1777	I	Lect.	213	Peop. of W.
XI.	1–3	Murray James	8° 1777	I	Lect.	233	Babel &c.
	1 &c.	Ward John, LLD	8° 1761		Diss.	5	
XII.	10–12	Murray James	8° 1777	I	Lect.	250	Call Abrah.
XVI.	4 &c.	Murray James	8° 1777	I	Lect.	289	Marriage &c.
XVIII.	32	Harris Will, DD	8° 1740		f f.		F. f.
XIX.	1 &c.	Murray James	8° 1777	I	Lect.	298	Sodom &c.
XX.	1 &c.	Murray James	8° 1777	II	Lect.	1	Abrah. &c.
	5, 6	[Gell Rob. DD]	fo. 1676	I	Rem.	216	
		Taylor Jer. Bp	fo. 1679		27 f.		Curse cut off.
XXII.	1 &c.	Murray James	8° 1777	II	Lect.	25	Abrah. &c.
XXV.	1 &c.	Murray James	8° 1777	II	Lect.	73	Abr's Fam.
	19–21	Murray James	8° 1777	II	Lect.	132	Abr's Xrter.
XXVIII.	1 &c.	Murray James	8° 1777	II	Lect.	164	Jacob's Xrter
XXXVII.	3	Murray James	8° 1777	II	Lect.	229	Jos. Xrter.
XLII.	20–23	Wright S. DD	8° 1718		f f.		Cond. of Dis.
XLI. & XLVII.		Ward John, LLD	8° 1761	I	Diss.	9	
XLIX.	8 &c.	Murray James	8° 1777	II	Lect.	253	Jacob &c.

EXODUS.

Chap.	Ver.	Authors.	Edition.	Vol.	Title, Page, &c.		Occasion or Subject.
II.		Ward John,[a] LLD	8° 1761		Diff.	13	
VIII.	20	Harrison Rich.	8° 1781		f f.		F. f.
XX.	4, 5	Ward John, LLD	8° 1761		Diff.	30	
	7	Ramsey James	8° 1781		Sea. f.	117	Swearing.
	18	Adam Thomas	8° 1781		Evan.D.	343	
XXIII.	2	Dawes	8° 1773			19	
	29, 30	Reynolds Thomas	8° 1710		f f.		Th. f.
XXXIV.	24	Gregg J.	8° 1756		f f.		On Invasion.

NUMBERS.

XVI.	12	Ramsey James	8° 1781		Sea. f.	35	Mutiny.
XX.	1 &c.	Ward John, LLD	8° 1761		Diff.	23	
XXIII.	23	Cruso Timothy	4° 1689		f f.		Th. f.

DEUTERONOMY.

VI.	11, 12	Baker W. Bp	4° 1717		f f.		Aff. f.
X.	4	Ramsey James	8° 1781		Sea. f.	21	
XXI.	23	Ward John, LLD	8° 1761		Diff.	32	
XXII.	2	Goddard S. P. DD	8° 1781			233	Prea.& H.D.
	4	Hutchins R. DD	8° 1782			1	G's Justice.
XXXIII.	46	Read Henry	8° 1746		f f.		Th. f.

JOSHUA.

XXI.	43	Ward John. LLD	8° 1761		Diff.	35	

JUDGES.

III.	22	Murray James	8° 1772		7 f.		To Affes.
V.	12	Evans John, DD	4° 1704		f f.		Th. f.
	23	J. L.	4° 1680		f f.		
VIII.	34, 35	Brown Simon	8° 1717		f f.		Nov. 5.
IX.	14, 15	How Jasper	8° 1723		f f.		Trees & Bra.
XV.	11	Baxter Simeon	8° 1782		f f.		b. Loyalists.
XX.	26	Adkin Lancaster	8° 1782		f f.		F. f.

I. SAMUEL.

XIII.	37	Wilson William	8° 1747		f f.		Reb. f.

[a] And Acts 7.

II. SAMUEL.

Chap.	Ver.	Authors.	Edition.	Vol.	Title, Page, &c.	Occasion or Subject.
I.	26	Hughes Obad. DD	8° 1740		f f.	Fun. f.
II.	10	Burnet, Abp	8° 1710		f f.	Jan. 30.
VI.	7	Ward John, LLD	8° 1761		Diff. 39	
XXIV.	1 &c.	Ward John, LLD	8° 1761		Diff. 42	
	14	C. T.	4° 1704		f f.	F. f.
	18	Murray James	8° 1781		S. Min. St.	

I. KINGS.

Chap.	Ver.	Authors.	Edition.	Vol.	Title, Page, &c.	Occasion or Subject.
XII.	18	Murray James	8° 1781		S. Min. St.	

II. KINGS.

Chap.	Ver.	Authors.	Edition.	Vol.	Title, Page, &c.	Occasion or Subject.
V.	12	Hutchins R. DD	8° 1782		111	Pof. Inft. &c.

I. CHRONICLES.

Chap.	Ver.	Authors.	Edition.	Vol.	Title, Page, &c.	Occasion or Subject.
XIII.	10	Ward John, LLD	8° 1761		Diff. 39	
XXI.	1 &c.	Ward John, LLD	8° 1761		Diff. 42	
XXVIII.	9	Ramfey James	8° 1781		Sea. f. 151	

II. CHRONICLES.

Chap.	Ver.	Authors.	Edition.	Vol.	Title, Page, &c.	Occasion or Subject.
V.	13, 14	Bradfhaw Tho.	4° 1697		f f.	St. Cecil. day
XIV.	2	Murray James	8° 1781		S. Min. St.	
XV.	2	Gilbert R.	8° 1756		f f.	F. f.
XX.	4	Anonym.	8° 1781		f f.	
XXII.	7, 8	Egerton, Bp	4° 1757		f f.	F. f. b. L.

EZRA.

Chap.	Ver.	Authors.	Edition.	Vol.	Title, Page, &c.	Occasion or Subject.
V.	1 &c.	Venn Henry	1775		Effay.	Zach's Prop.

NEHEMIAH.

Chap.	Ver.	Authors.	Edition.	Vol.	Title, Page, &c.	Occasion or Subject.
V.	19	Wilding John	8° 1780		f f.	F. f.
VI.	11	Ramfey James	8° 1781		Sea. f. 53	Defertion.

JOB.

Chap.	Ver.	Authors.	Edition.	Vol.	Title, Page, &c.	Occasion or Subject.
V.	26	Howe Thomas	8° 1773		f f.	Fun f.

Chap.	Ver.	Authors.	Edition.	Vol	Title, Page, &c.	Occasion or Subject.
VII.	1	Barker John	8° 1738		f f.	Fun. f.
	16	Gerard Alex. DD	8° 1782			Long life &c.
XII.	23	Cooper Sam. DD	4° 1782		f f.	F. f.
XIV.	10	Taylor Thomas	8° 1778		f f.	Fun. f.
	20	Wright Sam. DD	8° 1717		f f.	
XXI.	26	Taylor Nathaniel	4° 1699		f f.	
XXII.	30	Barker John	8° 1721		f f.	Ref. M.
XXXI.	15	Nicolls John, DD	4° 1711		f f.	Ch. f.
XXXIV.	13	Anonym.	8° 1732		f f.	b. Soc. Linc.

PSALMS.

Chap.	Ver.	Authors.	Edition.	Vol	Title, Page, &c.	Occasion or Subject.
I.	1	Newman Thomas	8° 1738		f f.	Prog. Vice.
II.	11	Barker John	8° 1746		f f.	Th. f.
		Brown Simon	8° 1716		f f.	
III.	5	Amory Tho. DD	8° 1746		f f.	Daily Devot.
VIII.	5	Anonym.	8° 1731		f f.	
IX.	4	Wright Sam. DD	8° 1718		f f.	Nov. 5.
X.	4	Priestley Jos. DD	8° 1782		2 f.	Hab. Devot.
	14	Hartley John	8° 1716		f f.	Th. f.
XIV.	1	Anonym.	8° 1738		f f.	
XV.	2	Dawes	8° 1773		47	
XIX.	12, 13	Goddard S. P. DD	8° 1781		143	Sins inf. &pr.
XXX.	6, 7	Taylor Richard	8° 1704		f f.	Pref. in Prof.
XLII.	2	Newton, Bp	8° 1759	Diff.	12	Relig. Mel.
XLVI.	8	Jennings Dav. DD	8° 1721		f f.	Plague in Fr.
L.	15	Clarke Augustus	12° 1781		f f.	Ld Gord. rel.
	23	Masters Thomas	8° 1715		f f.	Th. f.
LXXVIII.	3, 4	Hodge John	8° 1751		f f.	Aug. 1.
	70, 72	Brown Simon	8° 1721		f f.	May 29.
LXXXII.	6, 7	Smyth George	8° 1727		f f.	Roy. Fun.
XCI.	1	Anonym.	8° 1738		f f.	
C.	3, 4	Manton Tho. DD	fo. 1688	pt. 2.	116	Cl. f.
CIII.	2	Dupree John	8° 1782		57	
CVI.	21–23	Reynolds Thomas	8° 1712		f f.	Nov. 5.
CVII.	23, 24	Barnett Christ.	8° 1712		f f.	Seam's call.
CXVIII.	24	Mayo Daniel	8° 1729		f f.	Acc. f.
CXIX.	68	Newton, Bp	8° 1759	Diff.	15	G's Goodn.
CXXII.	6, 7	Stock Thomas	12° 1782		f f.	May 29.
	6–9	[Roberts Samuel]	8° 1745		f f.	Reb. f.
	9	Howe Thomas	8° 1780		f f.	F. f.
CXXVI.	3	Gill Jeremiah	8° 1746		f f.	Th. f.
CXXXII.	18	Hughes Obad. DD	8° 1735		f f.	Coron. f.
CXXXVI	23	Bradbury Thomas	8° 1715		f f.	Acc. f.
CXXXIX.	7-10	Newton, Bp	8° 1759	Diff.	14	G's Omnipr.

APPENDIX.

PROVERBS.

Chap.	Ver.	Authors.	Edition.	Vol.	Title, Page, &c.	Occasion or Subject.
III.	6	Maulden J.	8° 1738		f. f.	Coll. poor M.
	9	Hutchins R. DD	8° 1782		129	Xn. Benefic.
	17	Dawes	8° 1773		1	
IV.	23	Newton, Bp	8° 1759	Diff.	18	Keep Heart.
X.	7	Earl Jabez, DD	8° 1725		f. f.	Co. King. W.
XII.	22	Brown Simon	8° 1716		f. f.	Nov. 5.
XIII.	11	Hutchins R. DD	8° 1782		199	
XIV.	34	Milner J. DD	8° 1747		f. f.	F. f.
XVIII.	14	Newton, Bp	8° 1759	Diff.	21	Chear.&w.S.
XXII.	6	Fancourt Sam.	8° 1746		f. f.	Ch. Sch.
		Jennings Dav. DD	8° 17		f. f.	
XXIV.	21	Brown Simon	8° 1716		f. f.	Jan. 30.
XXIX.	1	Mayo Daniel	8° 1700		f. f.	Ref. M.
XXX.	7-9	Newton, Bp	8° 1759	Diff.	24	Agur's wish.

ECCLESIASTES.

Chap.	Ver.	Authors.	Edition.	Vol.	Title, Page, &c.	Occasion or Subject.
II.	2	Goddard S. P. DD	8° 1781		43	Rid.no f.Tr.
VII.	30	Shepheard Rich.	8° 1776		f. f.	Conc. Lat.
X.	17	Brown Simon	8° 1715		f. f.	Acc. f.
	27	Anonym.	8° 1707		f. f.	
XII.	1	Hunt Jerem. DD	8° 1724		f. f.	Fun. f.
	5	Wright Sam. DD	8° 1727		f. f.	Roy. Fun.
	7	Anonym.	8° 1738		2 f.	

ISAIAH.

Chap.	Ver.	Authors.	Edition.	Vol.	Title, Page, &c.	Occasion or Subject.
I.	19,20	Twentyman T.	12° 1779		f. f.	F. f.
XXVI.	9	Clark Samuel	8° 1755		f. f.	——
XXXIII.	22	Atkinson B. And.	8° 1739		f. f.	Nov. 5.
XXXVIII.	1-3	Goddard S. P. DD	8° 1781		199	Hezek's beh.
XLVII.	7	Henley John	8° 1731		f. f.	Orig.of Evil.

JEREMIAH.

Chap.	Ver.	Authors.	Edition.	Vol.	Title, Page, &c.	Occasion or Subject.
VII.	10-12	Clifford Samuel	8° 1721		f. f.	F. f.
IX.	3	Gerard Alex. DD	8° 1782		3 f. 1	Ment. Indul.
XIV.	8	Maultby Joseph	8° 1714		f. f.	F. f.
XXIV.	16	Bradbury Thomas	8° 1710		f. f.	Th. f.
XXXII.	19	Hutchins R. DD	8° 1771		53	G's Knowl.

LAMENTATIONS.

Chap.	Ver.	Authors.	Edition.	Vol.	Title, Page, &c.	Occasion or Subject.
II.	22	Wright Sam. DD	8° 1723		f. f.	Th. f.

EZEKIEL.

Chap.	Ver.	Authors.	Edition.	Vol.	Title, Page, &c.	Occasion or Subject.
XVIII.	33	Sowden Benjamin	8° 1747		f f.	F. f.
	31, 32	Disney John, DD	8° 1782		f f.	—
XX.	25	Ward John, LLD	8° 1761		Diff. 46	

DANIEL.

II.	44	Taylor Abraham	8° 1730		f f.	Nov. 5.
IV.	37	Hoadly, Abp	4° 1708		f f.	Aff. f.
IX.	24–28	Winter Richard	8° 1777		9 f.	70 Weeks.

HOSEA.

| III. | 4 | Egerton, Bp | 4° 1761 | | f f. | Jan. 30. b. L. |

JOEL.

| II. | 12 | Barrow Isaac, DD | fo. 1687 | IV | 62 | Conc. ad Cl. |

St. MATTHEW.

II.	1 &c.	Ward John, LLD	8° 1761		Diff.	55	
IV.	10	Goddard S. P. DD	8° 1781			257	Conc. ad Cl.
V.	3	Smith Will. DD	8° 1782		Beatit.	1	
	4	Smith Will. DD	8° 1782			19	
	5	Smith Will. DD	8° 1782			39	
	6	Smith Will. DD	8° 1782			55	
	7	Smith Will. DD	8° 1782			71	
	8	Smith Will. DD	8° 1782			87	
	9	Smith Will. DD	8° 1782			103	
	10	Smith Will. DD	8° 1782			121	
	11	Smith Will. DD	8° 1782			139	
	13	Cardew Cornelius	8° 1782		f f.		V. f.
	20	[Burd J.]	8° 1759		f f.		Phar. Relig.

APPENDIX.   413

Chap.	Ver.	Authors.	Edition.	Vol.	Title, Page, &c.		Occasion or Subject.
V.	22	Newton, Bp	4° 1782		Diff.	493	Anger.
	28	Goddard S. P. DD	8° 1781			85	WomanCan.
	34	Newton, Bp	4° 1782		Diff.	113	Swearing.
VI.	9	Newton, Bp	4° 1782		Diff.	125	Ld's Prayer.
	11	Hunt Isaac	8° 1781		f f.		Ch. f.
VIII.	32	Ward John, LLD	8° 1761		Diff.	82	
XI.	2	Ward John, LLD	8° 1761		Diff.	62	
XII.	31, 32	Newton, Bp	4° 1782		Diff.	192	Blasph. &c.
XIII.	15–17	Westley John	12° 1771	IV		109	
	25	Newton, Bp	4° 1782		Diff.	203	
	33	Enfield Will. LLD	8° 1780		f f.		Rel. & Kno.
	43	Ball Jacob	8° 1727		f f.		Fun. f.
XVI.	18, 19	Mole Thomas	8° 1728		f f.		Nov. 5.
	19	Barrow Isaac, DD	fo. 1687	IV		46	Conc. Lat.
XVII.	27	Ward John, LLD	8° 1761		Diff.	99	
XVIII.	7	Newton, Bp	4° 1782		Diff.	213	Heresies &c.
XXII.	37–39	Milne Colin, DD	8° 1782		f f.		Ly. in Hosp.
	40	Newton, Bp	4° 1782		Diff.	223	G. Comm.
XXIII.	29, 30	Hutchinson M. DD	8° 1717		f f.		Count. Loy.
XXIV.	12	Jennings Dav. DD	8° 1737		f f.		Ref. M.
XXV.	14 &c.	Newton, Bp	4° 1782		Diff.	233	Of Talents.
	20, 21	Coleman Benj. DD	8° 1740		f f.		Fun. f.
	40	Mills Thomas	8° 1781		f f.		Suff. by Fire.
XXVII.	3, 4	Ward John,[a] LLD	8° 1716		Diff.	128	

ST. MARK.

V.	10	Gregory G.	8° 1782		f f.		Inoculation.
III.	4	Ward John, LLD	8° 1761		Diff.	99	
IX.	49, 50	Newton, Bp	4° 1782		Diff.	243	Explanation
X.	29, 30	Williams Dan. DD	8° 1712		f f.		Duty of Diff.
XIV.	7	Watkinson E. MD	8° 1746		f f.		Ch. f.
XVI	15	Murray James	8° 1781		S. Min. St.		

ST. LUKE.

II.	21	Newton, Bp	4° 1782		Diff.	70	Na. Jef. & Xt.
	46, 47	Newton, Bp	8° 1782		Diff.	296	Sav. Eloque.
	51, 52	Newton, Bp	8° 1782		Diff.	296	Sav. priv. life
	52	Knight Sam. DD	8° 17		f f.		
VI.	35	Ward John, LLD	8° 1761		Diff.	66	
VII.	2	Porteus, Bp	4° 1782		f f.		An. m. ch. fc.
	19	Ward John, LLD	8° 1761		Diff.	62	
VIII.	52	Bromley R. Anth.	8° 1782		f f.		Hum. Soc.
	33	Ward John, LLD	8° 1761		Diff.	82	
IX.	26	Goddard S. P. DD	8° 1781			143	Sinf. Compl.
X.	37	Newton, Bp	4° 17		f f.		Inf. f.
XV.	7	Roberts W. H. DD	4° 1782		f f.		Magd. Hosp.

[a] Or Acts i. 18.

Chap.	Ver.	Authors.	Edition.	Vol.	Title, Page, &c.	Occasion or Subject.
XV.	11	Newton, Bp	4° 1782		Diff. 254	Prod. Xrter.
	11 &c.	Wallin Benjamin	8° 1776		13 f.	Prod. Son.
XVI.	19	Newton, Bp	4° 1782		Diff. 265	Luxury.
XVII.	17,18	T. J.	8° 1715		f f.	Acc. f.
XIX.	41, 42	Goddard S. P. DD	8° 1781		125	D.o.G's wra.
XXIII.	42,43	Newman Thomas	8° 1751		f f.	Pen. Thief.

St. JOHN.

Chap.	Ver.	Authors.	Edition.	Vol.	Title, Page, &c.	Occasion or Subject.
I.	21	Ward John, LLD	8° 1761		Diff. 60	
II.	19	Ward John, LLD	8° 1761		Diff. 117	
IV.	7	Newton, Bp	4° 1782		Diff. 274	Savr's Difc.
VI.	68	Goddard S. P. DD	8° 1781		23	Eter. life &c.
VII.	13	Wishart George	8° 1733		f f.	Hon. mind.
	17	Baker Rich. DD	4° 1782		f f.	V. f.
VIII.	31, 32	Newton, Bp	4° 1782		Diff. 308	Xty trueLib.
X.	24, 25	Newton, Bp	4° 1782		Diff. 146	Xt's Miracles
XII.	20, 21	Ward John, LLD	8° 1761		Diff. 106	
XVI.	2	Brown Simon	8° 1718		f f.	Nov. 5.
XVIII.	16	Grove Henry	8° 1735		f f.	Xt's Kingd.
XXI.	22	Newton, Bp	4° 1782		Diff. 389	John's l. life.

ACTS.

Chap.	Ver.	Authors.	Edition.	Vol.	Title, Page, &c.	Occasion or Subject.
IV.	12	Lorimer William	8° 1713		f f.	Salv. thr. Xt.
VI.	1	Ward John, LLD	8° 1761		Diff. 155	
VII.	1 &c.	Ward John, LLD	8° 1761		Diff. 162	
IX.	6	Cappe Newcome	8° 1770		f f.	Fun. f.
X.	40, 41	Foster James, DD	8° 1720		f f.	Xt's Refurr.
XI.	28	Pierce Tho. DD	4° 1661		f f.	Conc. ad Sy.
XIII.	9	Ward John, LLD	8° 1761		Diff. 171	
	36	Wilson William	8° 1739		f f.	Fun. f.
	40	Roscwell Samuel	8° 1715		f f.	Riots.
XV.	1 &c.	Ward John, LLD	8° 1761		Diff. 174	
XVII.	21	Newton, Bp	4° 1782		Diff. 441	Love of Nov.
XIX.	25	Anonym.	8° 1735		f f.	Nov. 5.
XXIV.	10 &c.	Newton, Bp	4° 1782		Diff. 413	St. P. b. Felix.
XXVIII.	1	Newton, Bp	4° 1782		Diff. 422	St. P. at Mcli.
	22	Wright Sam. DD	4° 1712		f f.	Xrter of Diff.

ROMANS.

Chap.	Ver.	Authors.	Edition.	Vol.	Title, Page, &c.	Occasion or Subject.
I.	11	Ward John, LLD	8° 1761		Diff. 181	Diff. 187
	16	Westley John	12° 1746	I	187	
	21	Ward John, LLD	8° 1761		Diff. 177	
II.	14	Sterne Lawrence	12° 1769	V	Posth. 147	Conscience.
	14, 15	Shepheard Rich.	8° 1776		f f.	

Chap.	Ver.	Authors.	Edition.	Vol.	Title, Page, &c.	Occasion or Subject.
III.	31	Taylor Richard	8° 1704		f f.	Law eſt.b.G.
VI.	22	Mayne Zechariah	4° 1693		f f.	
VIII.	12	Weſtley John	12° 1750	III	77	
	34	Howe Thomas	8° 1770		f f.	Fun. f.
X.	2	Brown Simon	8° 1715		f f.	Nov. 5.
XI.	12	Steffe J.	8° 1760		f f.	F. f.
	13	Walrond John	8° 1707		f f.	Dig. of Min.
XII.	20	Ward John, LLD	8° 1761		184	
XIII.	8	Newton, Bp	4° 1782		449	Run.in debt.
XIV.	15	Bradbury Thomas	8° 1715		f f.	Unanimity.

I. CORINTHIANS.

Chap.	Ver.	Authors.	Edition.	Vol.	Title, Page, &c.	Occasion or Subject.
I.	3	Peirce James	8° 1719		f f.	Diviſions.
II.	2	Jennings John	8° 1722		f f.	Preach. Xt.
II.	27	Oakes A. LLD	8° 1739		f f.	Sacr. worth.
III.	2	Peirce James	8° 1720		f f.	
IV.	1	Maullby Joseph	8° 1715		f f.	Ord. f.
VII.	8	Snape Andr. DD	8° 1745	I	193	Epiphany.
VIII.	1	Wright Sam. DD	8° 1732		f f.	Kn.& Ch.un.
X.	2	Ward John, LLD	8° 1761		Diff. 185	
	11	Harris Will. DD	8° 1740		f f.	F. f.
	15	Anonym.	8° 1721		f f.	Right.pr.Ju.
		Pillok Thomas	8° 1734		f f.	Immor.Soul.
XI.	9	Temple A.	8° 1782		f f.	Sacra.
	29	P. C.	12° 1693		f f.	
	31	Whitaker W. E.	4° 1782		f f.	F. f.
XIII.	1 &c.	Newton, Bp	4° 1782		Diff.	St.P'sde.Xy.
	1–3	Devis James	8° 1756		f f.	Nov. 5.
	14	Anonym.	8° 1771		f f.	At Quak. m.
XIV.	1	Dawes	8° 1773		33	
	40	Boughen Edw.	4° 1738		f f.	
XV.	1 &c.	Ward John, LLD	8° 1761		Diff. 195	
	29	Ward John, LLD	8° 1761		Diſſ. 189	
	32	Ward John, LLD	8° 1761		Diff. 198	
XV.	56,57	Hunt Jer. DD	8° 1731		f f.	Fun. f.
	57	Burroughs Joseph	8° 1752		f f.	

II. CORINTHIANS.

Chap.	Ver.	Authors.	Edition.	Vol.	Title, Page, &c.	Occasion or Subject.
I.	24	Amory Tho. DD	8° 1751		f f.	Ord. f.
IV.	5	Latham Eben. MD	8° 1722		f f.	
	7	Wood William	8° 1782		f f.	Aſſoc. f.
V.	4	Calamy Edm. DD	8° 1729		f f.	Fun. f.
	5	Row Benjamin	8° 1704		f f.	
	7	Anonym.	8° 1739		f f.	Regenerat.
VI.	11–13	Howe Thomas	8° 1767		f f.	Fun. f.
XIII.	5	Newton, Bp	4° 1782		Diff. 473	Kno.ourſelv.
	11	Mole Thomas	8° 1728		f f.	Far. f.

GALATIANS.

Chap.	Ver.	Authors.	Edition.	Vol.	Title, Page, &c.	Occasion or Subject.
II.	1 &c.	Ward John, LLD	8° 1761		Diff. 201	
VI.	11	Ward John, LLD	8° 1761		Diff. 205	

PHILIPPIANS.

I.	21	Barker John	8° 1728		ſ ſ.	Fun. ſ.
	27	Manton Tho. DD	8° 1726		ſ ſ.	Far. ſ.
II.	4	[Cumming John]	8° 1738		ſ ſ.	Pub. Spirit.
	20	Jollie Timothy	8° 1704		ſ ſ.	Fun. ſ.
	21	Gill John, DD	8° 1758		ſ ſ.	
IV.	5	Ibbot Benj. DD	8° 1720		ſ ſ.	Aſſ. ſ.
	9	Worthington Hugh	8° 1757		ſ ſ.	Fun. ſ.

COLOSSIANS.

IV.	6	Newton, Bp	4° 1782		Diff. 509	Conversat.

I. THESALONIANS.

II.	3-6	Stagden Herbert	8° 1718		ſ ſ.	Prim. Preac.
V.	22	Newton, Bp	4° 1782		Diff. 519	Abſtain &c.
	25	Evans John, DD	8° 1723		ſ ſ.	Min. pray. ſ.

I. TIMOTHY,

II.	15	Ward John, LLD	8° 1761		Diff. 210	
III.	1	Towgood S.	8° 1737		ſ ſ.	Ord. ſ.
IV.	10	[Bayes Joſeph]	8° 1722		ſ ſ.	Ref. M.
	15	Nicholls Bouch. R.	8° 1782		ſ ſ.	V. ſ.
	16	Gordon James	8° 1735		ſ ſ.	Ord ſ.

II. TIMOTHY.

I.	12, 14	Ward John, LLD	8° 1761		Diff. 213	Ord. ſ.
	13	Wright Sam. DD	8° 1721		ſ ſ.	Bible ſoc.
III.	15	Robinſon Robert	8° 1782		ſ ſ.	Div. of Scrip.
	16	Pindar Thomas	8° 1728		ſ ſ.	Inſpiration.
		Shepheard Rich.	8° 1776		ſ ſ.	Fun. ſ.
IV.	7, 8	Simmons Thomas	8° 1709		ſ ſ.	

APPENDIX.

TITUS.

Chap.	Ver.	Authors.	Edition.	Vol.	Title, Page, &c.	Occasion or Subject.
II.	1	Gerard Alex. DD	8° 1782			

PHILEMON.

| | 9 | Ward John, LLD | 8° 1761 | | Diff. 215 | |

HEBREWS.

III.	12	Newton, Bp	4° 1782		Diff. 568	Infid. of age.
	17	Warren John, DD	8° 1716		f f.	Fun. f.
IV.	12	Watson Thomas	4° 1749		f f.	F. f. b. C.
V.	7	Ward John, LLD	8° 1761		Diff. 217	
XI.	33, 34	Newton, Bp	4° 1782		Diff. 589	Rec. of Rew.
XII.	1	Newton, Bp	4° 1782		Diff. 599	The Sin &c.
XIII.	4	Whatley Will. [a]	12°17		f f.	Wed. f.
		Owen Char. DD	8° 1758		f f.	Marriage.
	16	Miles Henry	8° 1738		f f.	Ch. f.

JAMES.

I.	27	Chandler Samuel	4° 1736		f f.	Ch. f.
		Lowthian S.	8° 1761		f f.	———
		Read Henry	8° 1728		f f.	Hear. insuff.

I. PETER.

I.	8	Lorimer William	8° 1722		f f.	Far. f.
	24, 25	Bayes Joshua	8° 1728		f f.	Fun. f.
		Read J.	8° 1730		f f.	Op. meet. H.
II.	24	Ward John, LLD	8° 1761		Diff. 223	
III.	15	Dodson Joseph	8° 1722		f f.	Assoc. f.
	16	Newton, Bp	4° 1782		Diff. 630	Diff. of Scrip.
IV.	14–16	Atkinson B. A.	8° 1726		f f.	Ref. M.

II. PETER.

| I. | 12–14 | Hunt Jer. DD | 8° 1731 | | f f. | Fun. f. |
| | 15 | [Jenkyn Will. | 4° 1675 | | f f. | ——— |

[a] V. Disc. on Conj. Duty. v. 2. p. 344.

I. JOHN.

Chap.	Ver.	Authors.	Edition.	Vol.	Title, Page, &c.	Occasion or Subject.
II.	18	Anonym.	8° 1715		f f.	Priestcra.&c.
IV.	16	Carpenter Jos.	8° 1742		f f.	Ch. f.

II. JOHN.

V.	10	Ward John, LLD	8° 1761		Diff. 225	

JUDE.

	3	Burroughs Joseph	8° 1733		f f.	b. Society.
	6	[Younge Hercules]	8° 1770		Diff.	
	22, 23	Smith Jeremiah	8° 1713		f f.	Ref. M.

REVELATION.

II.	17	Ward John, LLD	8° 1761		Diff. 229	
III.	2	Some David	8° 1730		f f.	Rev. of Rel.
	15, 16	Harris Will. DD	8° 1732		f f.	Lukewarmn.
XIV.	13	Wright Sam. DD	8° 1716		f f.	Fun. f.
XVII.	6	Lorimer Will. DD	8° 1713		f f.	Nov. 5.
XIX.	16	Ward John, LLD	8° 1761		Diff. 233	

APPENDIX
TO THE
SECOND VOLUME.

❌❌❌❌❌❌❌❌❌❌❌❌❌❌❌❌❌❌❌❌❌❌

p. 9. **AMORY** Tho. DD.
   Pſ. iii. 5. 8° 1746. Daily Devotion.
   2 Cor. i. 24. 8° 1751. Ord. ſ.

p. 13. ANONYM.
   Pſ xxxiv. 19. 4° 1692. Fun. of Eliz. Gibſon. *Brit. M.*
   Job xxxiv. 13. 8° 1732. b. a Society at Lincoln's Inn, by a Layman.

p. 16. Acts xix. 25. 8° 1735. Nov. 5.

p. 17. 1 Cor. xiii. 14. 8° 1771. At a Quaker's meeting.
   1 Cor. x. 15. 8° 1721. Right of private Judgment.

p. 18. 1 John ii. 18. 8° 1715. Prieſtcraft diſtinguiſhed from Chriſtianity.

p. 21. *ATKINSON* B. *Andrew*, &c.
   1 Pet. iv. 14–16. 8° 1726. Ref. of Manners.
   Iſai. xxxiii. 22. 8° 1739. Nov. 5.

p. 24. *BALL Jacob*
   Eccleſ. xi. 9. 8° 1725. Fun. of *John Fryer. Brit. M.*
   Matt. xiii. 43. 8° 1727. Fun. of *W. Drew.*
   BAKER William, Bp.
   Deut. vi. 11, 12. 8° 1717. Aſſize.
   1 Tim. ii. 1, 2. 8° 1723. Jan. 30. b. Lords.

p. 26. *BARKER John*
   Phil. i. 21. 8° 1728. Fun. of *J. Gledhill.*
   Pſ. ii. 11. 8° 1746. Th. ſ.

p. 28. [BARNETT Chriſtopher]
   Pſ cvii. 23, 24. 8° 1711. The Seaman's Calling.

p. 31. [BAXTER Simeon,] a Licentiate in Divinity.
   Judg. xv. 11. 8° 1782. Tyranicide proved lawful. Delivered to the Loyaliſts at Symſbury in the Colony of Connecticut.
   BAYES Joſhua
   1 Pet. i. 24, 25. 8° 1728. Fun. of *J. Cornish.*

p. 33. BELBIN Peter, &c.
Rev. xiv. 13. 8° 17. Fun. of &c.

p. 39. *BILLINGSLEY John*
Luke i. 74, 75. 8° 1710. Nov. 5.

p. 46. [BOUGHEN Edward]
1 Cor. xiv. 40. 4° 1738.

p. 48. *BRADBURY Thomas*
Ifai. xxiv. 16. 8° 1710. Th. f.
Pf. cxxxvi. 2. 8° 1715. Acceffion.
Rom. xiv. 15. 8° 1715. Unanimity.
Jonah iii. 5. 8° 1721. Faft.

p. 50. BRADSHAW Tho.   R. of Painfwick, Gloucefterf.
Pf. xcviii. 1. 4° 1781. Th. for Admiral Rodney's Victory.

p. 52. BREKELL J.
Acts xxvii. 4. 8° 1744. Dangers of the Sea.

p. 56. BROWN *Simon*
Ecclef. x. 17. 8° 1715. Acceffion.
Rom. x. 2. 8° 1715. Nov. 5.
Prov. xii. 22. 8° 1716. Nov. 5.
Prov. xxiv. 21. 8° 1716. Jan. 30.
Judges viii. 34, 35. 8° 1717. Nov. 5.
John xvi. 2. 8° 1718. Nov. 5.
Ecclef. x. 17. 8° 1715. Acceffion.

p. 59. [BURD J.   ]
Matt. v. 20. 8° 1759. Religion of the Pharifees.

p. 62. BURNET Gibbert, Abp. of York.
2 Sam. ii. 10. 8° 1710. Jan. 30.

p. 63. BURROUGHS *Jofeph*
Jude 3. 8° 1733, b. Society of Saltburgers. *Brit. M.*

p. 68. CALAMY *Edmund*, DD. &c.
Pf. ix. 10. 8° 1726. Fun. of Rev. *J. Bennet.*
2 Cor. v. 4. 8° 1729. Fun. of

p. 70. CAPPE *Newcome*
Acts xix. 16. 8° 1770. Fun. of Rev. *E. Sandercock.*
CARDEW Cornelius, &c.
Matt. v. 13. 4° 1782. Vif. f.

p. 71. [CARPENTER Jofeph]
1 John iv. 16. 8° 1742. On Charity.

p. 75. CHANDLER *Samuel*, DD. &c.
James i. 27. 8° 1736. Ch. f.

p. 81. [CLIFFORD Samuel]
Jer. vii. 10–12. 8° 1721. Faft.

p. 86. COLMAN *Benjamin*, DD.
Matt. xxv. 20, 21. 8° 1740. Fun. of *S. Holden.*

p. 96. [CUMMING John]
Phil. ii. 4. 8° 1738. On public Spirit.

p. 103. DEVIS *James*
1 Cor. xiii. 1–3 8° 1758. Nov. 5. Ag. Popery.

p. 104.

APPENDIX. 421

p. 104. DISNEY John, DD. &c.
Ezek. xviii. 41, 32. 8° 1782. Faſt.

p. 106. DODSON Joſeph, M.A.
1 Pet. iii. 15. 8° 1722. b. Diſſent. Clergy.

p. 112. EARL Jabez, DD. &c.
Luke xv. 7. 8° 1704. Ref. of Manners.
Prov. x. 7. 8° 1725. In memory of King William

p. 116. ENFIELD William, LL. D. &c.
Matt. xiii. 33. 8° 1780. Progreſs &c.

p. 118. EVANS John, DD. &c.
Judges v. 12. 4° 1704. Th. &c.
1 Theſſ. v. 25. 8° 1723. Miniſters &c.
1 Pet. ii. 5. 8° 1730. On. Open. a Meeting-Houſe.

p. 120. FANCOURT Samuel
Prov. xxii. 6. 8° 1746. Ch. ſ.

p. 125. FLEXMAN R. DD.
Gen. xviii. 19. 8° 1752. Char. Sch. Abraham's Character.
FORD John
Prov. xxvii. 23. 8° 1733. Diligence in Buſineſs.
Prov. xxiv. 10–13. 8° 1734. Aſſize.

p. 128. Foſter James, DD. &c.
Acts x. 40, 41. 8° 1720. The Reſurrection of Chriſt.
GERARD Alexander, DD.
Serm. (Vol. II.) in 8° 1782.

p. 139. GILBERT R.
2 Chron. xv. 2. 8° 1756. Faſt.
Jer. xviii. 7, 8. 8° 1757. Faſt.
GILL Jeremiah
Pſ. cxvi. 3. 8° 1746. Th. ſ.

p. 143. GORDON James, M.A.
1 Tim. iv. 16. 8° 1735. Ord.

p. 145. GREGG J.
Exod. xxxiv. 24. 8° 1756. On the threatened Invaſion.

p. 147. GREGORY G. Cur. of St. Nicholas, Liverpool, Cheſhire.
Mark iii. 4. 8° 1782. Inoculation defended.

p. 148. GROSVENOR Benjamin, DD. &c.
John vi. 2, 3. 8° 1725. Nov. 5.

p. 149. GROVE Henry, &c.
John xviii. 16. 8° 1735. On Chriſt's Kingdom.

p. 157. HARRIS William, DD. &c.
Rev. iii. 15, 16. 8° 1732. On Lukewarmneſs in Religion.
Gen. xviii. 32. 8° 1740. Faſt.
1 Cor. x. 11. 8° 1740. Faſt.

p. 159. HARTLEY John
Pſ. x. 14. 8° 1716. Th. after Rebellion.

p. 163. HENLEY John, (orator) &c.
Iſai. xlvii. 7. 8° 1731. On the origin of Evil.

p. 168. HILL Joſeph
Dan. iv. 17. 8° 1726. Acceſſion.

p. 172.

p. 177. HORSEMANDEN Samuel, &c.
Gen. iii. 19. 8° 1766. On Labour.

p. 180. HOWE *Jasper*
Judges ix. 14, 15. 8° 1723. The Trees and Bramble.
HOWE Thomas, &c.
Rom. viii. 34. 8° 1770. Fun. of *Persis Eldridge.*
2 Cor. vi. 11–13. 8° 1767. Far. s.
Job v. 26. 8° 1773. Fun. of Mr. *Eldridge.*
Pf. cxxii. 9. 8° 1780. Fast &c.

p. 182. HUGHES *Obad.* DD.
Pf. cxxxii. 18. 8° 1735. Coronation.
2 Sam. i. 26. 8° 1749. Fun. of *A. Walburgh,* Esq;

p. 183. HUNT *Jeremiah,* DD. &c.
Ecclef. xii. 1. 8° 1724. Fun. of Mrs. *Hollis.*
1 Cor. xv. 56, 57. 8° 1731. Fun. of Mr. *T. Hollis.*
2 Pet. i. 12–14. 8° 1731. Fun. of Dr. *Kinch.*

p. 185. HUTCHINSON M. DD. &c.
Matt. xxiii. 29, 30. 8° 1717. Counterfeit Loyalty displayed.

p. 188. IBBOT Benjamin, DD. &c.
Phil. iv. 5. 8° 1720. Assize.

p. 190. JENNINGS *David,* DD.
Pf. xlvi. 8. 8° 1721. Plague in France.
Matt. xxvii. 12. 8° 1737. Ref. of Manners.
JENNINGJ John, M. A. &c.
1 Cor. ii. 2. 8° 1723. Preaching Christ.

p. 193. JOLLIE *Timothy*
Phil. ii 20. 8° 1704. Fun. of *J. Jollie.*

p. 199. KENNICOTT Benjamin, DD. &c.
1 Sam. vi. 19. 8° 1768. *Oxon.* Observations.

p. 200. KIPPIS *Andrew,* DD.
Rom. i. 16. 8° 1782. Ord. of *Hugh Worthington* and *R. Jacomb.*

p. 207. LATHAM *Eben.* M. D. &c.
2 Cor. iv. 5. 8° 1722. Ord. of

p. 216. LORIMER *William*
Acts iv. 12. 8° 1713. Salvation through Christ.
Rev. xvii. 6. 8° 1713. Nov. 5.
1 Pet. i. 8. 8° 1722. Farewel.

p. 217. LOWTHIAN S.
Acts ii. 29. 8° 1758. Ord. s. Ministers ought to speak freely.
James i. 27. 1° 1764. On Charity.

p. 228. MASTERS Thomas
Pf. l. 23. 8° 1715. Th. for the Accession.

p. 229. MAULTBY *Joseph*
Jerem. xiv. 8. 8° 1714. Fast.
1 Cor. iv. 8. 8° 1715. Ord. s.

p. 230. MAYO *Richard*
Prov. xxix. 1. 8° 1700. Ref. of Manners.

[OWEN

APPENDIX.

[OWEN J.   DD.] of Rochdale.
2 Sam. xviii. 18. 8° 1746. Th. f.

p. 254. PALEY William, M. A. Arch-Deacon of Carlifle.
Ephef. iv. 11, 12. 4° 1782. Conf. of Bp. Law. A diftinction of Orders in the Church defended upon principles of public Utility.
PALMER John
- - - - 1757.

p. 257. [PARNTHER T.   ]
- - - - 1756.

p. 263. PEERS Richard
- - - - 1737. Pub. Worfhip.

p. 272. PORTEUS, Bp. of Chefter.
Luke vii. 22. 4° 1782. An. meet. Ch. Schools.

p. 285. ROBERTS W. H. DD. Provoft of Eton Coll. and Chaplain in Ord.
Luke xv. 17. 4° 1782. b. the Gov. of the Magd-Hofp.

p. 286. *ROBINSON Robert*
2 Tim. iii. 15. 8° 1782. b. the Bible-Society.
ROLLS Sam. DD.
1 Sam. xxv. 5. 8° 1678. 2 f. Confcience and Jan. 30.

p. 297. *SCOTT Thomas*
- - - - 1757.

p. 330. T.   J.
Luke xvii. 17, 18. 8° 1715. Acceffion.
TAYLER J.
- - - - 1765. Ch. Sch.

p. 359. WATKINSON Edward, M. D. &c.
Mark xiv. 7. 8° 1746. Charity.

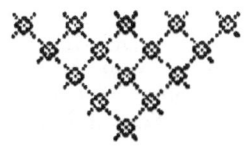

Addenda to the *first* Volume.

Pag. 6. Knaggs Thomas *insert* F. f.
 50. Cornwallis J. *insert* Bp. — and elsewhere.
 51. Milner John, DD *insert* Fun. f.
 129. Guyse J. DD *insert* New Year's day.
 135. Watson Richard *insert* Bp. — and elsewhere.
 143. Henry Matt. *insert* Nov. 5.
 190. Hole Matt. *insert* 15 Sun. Trin.
 206. Calamy Ed. DD. *insert* Glory of Church.
 255. Lowman Moses *insert* Ref. M.
 317. Franklin Thomas *insert* Shipwrecks.
 325. [Unwin Will.] *insert* Right Use of Law.
 329. Smith George *insert* Zeal.
 372. Baxter Richard *insert* Fun. f.
 423. Wright S. DD. *insert* Ord. f.
 451. Milbourne Luke *insert* Debt. and Cred.

Addenda to the *second* Volume.

Pag. 4. Jer. 5. 15. *insert* Conf. of Bp. Fleetwood.
 John 21. 17 *insert* Conf. of Bps. Robinson and Bisse.
 13. Job 34. 30. *insert* Jan. 30.
 Prov. 31. 4. *insert* Royal Merchant.
 14. Dan. 11. 31. *insert* Popish Success.
 16. Acts 13. 2, 3. *insert* Ord.
 21. 1 Cor. 10. 15. *insert* Private Judgment.
 2 Tim. 3. 15. *insert* Scriptures, a perfect Rule.
 23. Bagshaw H. *insert* Fun. of Sir J. Fanshaw at Madrid. Br. M.
 35. Job 14. 10. *insert* Fun. of J. Parry.
 39. 1 Kings 10. 9. *insert* Acc. of K. George I.
 Isai. 42. 3. *insert* Fun. of H. Stagden. Brit. M.
 68. Isai. 56. 19. *insert* The Glory of the Church.
 Rom. 10. 15. *insert* Dissent. Ministry vindicated
 75. Rom. 6. 23. *insert* Fun. of T. Hadfield, M. D.
 1 Pet. 5. 4. *insert* Fun. of Rev. Moses Lowman.
 1 Cor. 1. 21. *insert* Ord. of Rev. T. Wright.
 105. John ii. 35. *insert* Fun. of Dr. Clark.
 150. Prov. 11. 24. *insert* Charity.
 172. Hole Matthew *insert* Disc. in $12°$ 1701 &c.
 182. Isai. 57. 2. *insert* Fun. of Dr. J. Oldfield.
 195. Isaac John *insert* Fun. of Mrs Neville.
 204. Rev. 14. 13. *insert* Fun. of Lady Russel.
 207. Ps. 23. 4. *insert* Fun. of Mrs Wood.
 217. Matt. 9. 37, 38. *insert* Fun. of J. Wilkinson.
 211. Luke 14. *insert* Nov. 5. Ag. Persecution.
 222. Mann Isaac *insert* Bp. of Cork and Ross.
 248. John 4. $8°$ 1718. *insert* Sincerity in worship.
 253. 2 Sam. 18. 20. *insert* Th. after Rebellion.
 287. Rogers Thomas *insert* Fun. of Rob. Linager.

(425)

Errata in the *first* Volume.

Pag. 9. Murray James *lege* in Italics — and elsewhere.
17. Henry Matthew *lege* in Italics.
25. Cruso Timothy } The dates transposed.
    Allen Richard }
34. [Martyn] *dele* the whole line — and elsewhere.
47. Sylvester Matt. *lege* in Italics.
53. Freke Tho. *lege* in Italics — and elsewhere.
71. Scott Jos. Nicol *lege* in Italics.
89. *Evans John*, DD. *dele* whole line.
118. Gilbert, Bp. *lege* Abp.
137. Whitaker Will. *lege* in Italics.
146. Erskine G. *lege* in Italics.
152. Weld Nath. *lege* in Italics.
171. *Wake Robert lege* in Roman.
182. Mauduit Isaac *lege* in Italics.
204. *Jelinger Christ. lege* in Roman.
215. Seagrave *lege* in Italics — and elsewhere.
228. Romaine William *dele* whole line.
270. Nalton James *lege* in Italics.
278. Chandler Sam. *lege* in Italics, and DD.
319. Walker George *lege* in Italics.
329. Smith George *lege* in Italics.
344. Green John, DD. *lege* Bp.
351. Hibbert Hen. DD. *lege* in Italics.
361. Ford William *lege* in Italics.
381. Parsons John *lege* Jonathan.
403. Shepherd Tho. *lege* in Italics.
406. Mickleburgh *insert* it in 2 Thess. 3. 10.
413. Skelton P. *dele* whole line.
427. Pigott John *legè* in Italics.
434. *Price Sam. dele* whole line.
435. Wilson Tho. DD. *lege* Bp.
442. Rogers Tim. *lege* in Italics.
454. Eaton Sam. DD. *lege* in Italics.
480. *Clarke S*, DD. *lege* in Roman.
484. Cooke Thomas *lege* 4° 1709.
476. Evans Caleb *lege* 8° 1773. Ord. s.

Errata in the *second* Volume.

17. Resurrection *lege* regeneration.
71. Carte S. *lege* St. Martin's.
96. Crownfield *lege* in p. 95.
154. 1 Kings 8, 66. *lege* 1715.
305. Skelton Will. *dele* whole line.
325. *lege* 329 &c.
377. *lege* 385 &c.

FINIS.

www.ingramcontent.com/pod-product-compliance
Lightning Source LLC
Chambersburg PA
CBHW030542300426
44111CB00009B/832